KRLA ARCHIVES

KRLA
*Chronological Archives
Volume 3*
November 13, 1965 to February 12, 1966

KRLA ARCHIVES

Bby November 1965, the KRLA Beat was on a regular publishing schedule. And although just threeyears later the entire publication would be just a memory, there was no sign of that ever happening in late 1965 and early 1966, the issues featured in this third volume.

The publication stayed on a weekly schedule, and featured articles on many of the bands of the day, in addition to the standard columns supposedly geared toward the teen-age, radio listening crowd.

The Beatles, of course, continued to command a strong presence, as did the Rolling Stones. Gary Lewis and his Playboys, Sonny and Cher, the Grass Roots, The Walker Brothers, Dusty Springfield all were featured, as were the Byrds, The Yardbirds, Simon & Garfunkle, Bob Dylan, The Everyly Brothers...the list goes on and on.

The Adventures of Robin Boyd, originally conceived as a short series of articles, continued to make a presence in most issues, as did a movie feature. Everything you could want on a weekly basis.

In presenting these original issues, we've moved a few of the pages around to ensure that the spreads still lined up. Not a big deal to most people unless you are severly OCD and have access to the original issues.

Copyright © 2016 White Lightning Publishing

KRLA BEAT

Los Angeles, California — November 13, 1965

A BEAT EDITORIAL
Save Shindig

Surely ABC Television is not real. It's all a big put-on, right? Can they really be serious about yanking Shindig off the air—*both* weekly shows—and replacing them with a comic book character who calls himself Batman and runs around trying to fly like a bird?

Quick, call the guy with the net! Better yet, let's get our own net. Or maybe a rope.

With whatever sanity remains in a world rocked by such cock-eyed events, let's try to reconstruct this crime which has been perpetrated against the viewing public:

The show which is now fizzling out blasted off like a rocket in September, 1964. It was born with a small budget but a bag-full of brilliant ideas.

A Good Start

The guiding genius behind it was a cockey little Englishman in a derby hat, Jack Good. No one was ever better named. Shindig *was* Good.

Ratings soared. While viewers blinked in amazement, Good gave them the fastest-paced, best-produced talent show ever seen on television. The show was so successful that imitators knocked themselves out in their frenzy to get other shows like it on the air. So successful that the network moguls in New York forgot that they had reprimanded Good for producing a show with such "low-class" entertainment and quickly convinced themselves that Shindig was all *their* creation. To them it was now good, but not *Good*.

Reasoning that if 30 minutes was successful one twice as long would be twice as successful, they extended it to an hour. And they interferred to the point that the independent little Englishman became fed up and told them to stick it in their ear. Good returned to England to produce shows without their kind of help.

Twice Weekly

At the end of the season the network geniuses—still working under their theory that twice as much would be twice as successful—broke up Shindig and scheduled it twice weekly. But many of
(Turn to Page 5)

Groups, Duos Only In New Pop Poll

The first Annual *BEAT* International Pop Music Awards Poll rolls into its fourth week with a triple treat. This week you get a chance to vote for the Best Female Vocal Group, Best Duo and Best Instrumental Group of 1965.

That leaves us with only the Best Vocal Record, Best Instrumental Record, Best Vocal Album and Best Instrumental Album to go.

As you probably know by now, all ballots will be counted and the finalists in each category will be placed in one issue of *The BEAT* for the final do-or-die voting.

Then after all the ballots are in the results will be tabulated and the winners will be presented with International Pop Music Awards at formal presentation ceremonies.

Your Choice

We have felt for quite awhile that you, the people who buy the records, should be able to vote on who you consider to be the most outstanding performers in their field. So, *The BEAT* is giving you the opportunity to do just that. The winners will be the ones whom *you* have chosen. So be sure and get your ballot in right away. Only in this way can you be certain that the best and most deserving performers win.

And please use the official *BEAT* entry blanks because only these ballots can be counted by the judges.

Dusty Says Newspapers Chased Beau

Dusty Springfield has some peculiar dislikes—among them Sunday newspapers, wigs and her nose.

She doesn't really dislike all Sunday newspapers but one did upset her a bit recently.

"There was a man in my life recently," she explained, "but not any more. A Sunday newspaper printed an article about it and frightened him off.

"I told the writer that if I got engaged at all I would like it to be this man. They didn't print his name. But it was enough. And it embarrassed both of us."

Wears Wig

About wigs she said, "Yes, I do wear a wig sometimes, but not very often. I don't really like it because it's not a very good one. I use a piece of hair called a switch instead. I stick it on top of my head to make it all big and lovely."

And her nose? Well, some people have said that she has a beautiful nose and it has been rumored that she has had a nose-bobbing operation.

She denies this but adds "I'm definitely going to have it done one day. I just do not like it as it is."

But she's not too upset over her cute little nose for she adds, "Meanwhile, folks, I'm just going to have to learn to live with it."

Inside the BEAT

Tom Says Goodbye	3
Donovan A TV Star	6
Magic Of Motown	7
Mick's Christmas Plans	8
Orbison To Make Movie	11
Roosters Like Beatles?	11
British Top Ten	13
Stones Win Gold Album	13
Yardbirds Set New Trend	14
Adventures of Robin Boyd	15

The BEAT is published weekly for KRLA listeners by BEAT Publications, Inc., 6290 Sunset Blvd., Suite 504, Hollywood, California 90028. U.S. bureaus in Hollywood, San Francisco, New York, Chicago and Nashville; overseas correspondents in London, Liverpool and Manchester, England. Sale price, 15 cents. Subscription price: U.S. and possessions, $3 per year; Canada and foreign rates, $9 per year. Application to mail at second-class postage rates is pending at Los Angeles, California.

THE TWO CHERS are captured by BEAT Photographer Chuck Boyd. At left, she sings her solemn "Where Do You Go?" At right, she smiles for her snappy new record with husband Sonny, "But You're Mine."

FRIENDS NOTICE CHANGES
Is Dylan Now Too Personal?

People used to spend their time contemplating how long the Beatles were going to last but now that the Beatles have shown that they're going to be here a while, a new topic of discussion has entered the scene.

The big thing now is to try to explain Bob Dylan. Latest to add their opinions as to who or what Dylan is, are folk singers Peter, Paul and Mary.

All three of them met Dylan and are very well acquainted with him and his music but Mary says she doesn't care for a lot of the things he's doing lately.

Personal Revolt

"He has really become more introspective. Not that that is wrong in itself—Bobby has the right to develop in whatever direction he wants—but the thing that I am worried about is that I feel there are signs of kind of personal anarchy in some of the things he is doing."

Peter feels that Dylan is changing but will definitely last. "Bobby's songs were initially simply direct expressions of an attitude toward the world. Since he has changed and started writing songs of a more inward-looking kind. He has become described as a poet; but he is Bobby Dylan first, and a poet or singer second.

Will Endure

"He is a human being who has said things that many people feel very deeply, in a very articulate fashion. He will endure: either as a poet or a folk singer—but he will endure."

Paul tried to explain how Dylan is changing. "There are two ways an artist can grow—further inside into himself in search of the true meaning of his art or outwardly in a bid to solve the problems outside him. And Bobby initially concerned himself with the world around him.

"Now I am sure he has stopped concerning himself with it and he's trying to solve the riddle of himself."

BEAT Pop Music Awards Poll
CATEGORY IV: FEMALE GROUPS, DUOS AND INSTRUMENTAL GROUPS

FEMALE VOCAL GROUPS (Please Check 5)
- ☐ BLOSSOMS
- ☐ BONNIE & THE TREASURES
- ☐ DIXIE CUPS
- ☐ IKETTES
- ☐ MARTHA & THE VANDELLAS
- ☐ ROYALETTES
- ☐ SHANGRALAS
- ☐ SUPREMES
- ☐ TOYS
- ☐ WRITE IN: _____

DUOS (Please Check 5)
- ☐ APRIL & NINO
- ☐ CHAD & JEREMY
- ☐ DICK & DEE DEE
- ☐ EVERLY BROTHERS
- ☐ IKE & TINA TURNER
- ☐ JACKIE & GAYLE
- ☐ JAN & DEAN
- ☐ JOE & EDDIE
- ☐ PETER & GORDON
- ☐ RIGHTEOUS BROTHERS
- ☐ SAM & BILL
- ☐ SONNY & CHER
- ☐ WRITE IN: _____

INSTRUMENTAL GROUPS (Please Check 3)
- ☐ HERB ALPERT & THE TIJUANA BRASS
- ☐ HOLLYWOOD PERSUADERS
- ☐ RAMSEY LEWIS TRIO
- ☐ SOUNDS, INCORPORATED
- ☐ SOUNDS ORCHESTRAL
- ☐ THEE MIDNITERS

MAIL TO: Pop Music Poll, KRLA BEAT, 6290 Sunset, Suite 504, Hollywood, Calif. 90028

Win $1,110 in KRLA Football Sweepstakes—p. 10

KRLA ARCHIVES

THIS WAS QUITE A SESSION! Bob Dylan turned up unexpectedly at a Hollywood nightclub where the Byrds were playing and joined them in several numbers.

Yeah, Well Bob...
Message Clear As Mud

By Tammy Hitchcock

Well, look who's on our "Yeah, Well" hot seat this week None other than the folk singer to end all folk singers—Bob Dylan.

When asked Dylan what he thought of those people who reject a folk singer the minute the wail of an electric guitar is heard on one of his records, Dylan replied: "I don't really know. I don't know any of the people who do those things. I don't hang out with people who would do that. You know, I like everybody."

Yeah, well then how come you don't like *me*, Bob?

Great Message

You know, although people repeatedly credit Bob with some sort of message he always has denied that he has any message. But now the secret's out—he *does* have a message: "Keep a good head and always carry a light bulb." Yeah, well I understand just exactly what you're saying Bob—only thing is I can't *explain* it.

Someone asked Dylan what he writes about and he came up with a classic: "I don't write about anything." Yeah, well now we know why you mumble on your records.

Bob says: "A lot of people who are teaching other people in the United States—they're teaching, but they don't want people to know more than they know, really."

Yeah, well that makes a lot of sense, Bob. You know, that's why I don't teach—it's impossible to know any less than I do!

Phonies?

Of course, everyone knows that "Gates of Eden" was on the flip side of "Like A Rolling Stone." Bob says: "I can't see a phony audience being forced to accept a song like "Gates of Eden."

A lot of pure folk addicts have condemned Dylan for using electric guitar but Dylan really couldn't care less. "Oh man, somebody's got to be a little bit whacky to say: 'I don't like electrified guitar.' What's wrong with electrified guitar?"

Yeah, well nothing's wrong with electrified guitar, Bob. As long as you don't get shocked, that is.

Titles Key

Masses of Dylan listeners have criticized him for writing songs which defy understanding. So Bob has given us a small clue: "They are scattered between different things and the lead for the listener will lie in the title of the song."

Yeah, well listen, Bob, we really do appreciate your leads but do you think you could make them a little bit bigger maybe?

Bob used to worry cause his songs weren't perfect but not now: "There's nothing perfect anywhere, so I shouldn't expect myself to be perfect."

Yeah, well maybe *you're* not perfect but I guess you've never met *me*.

Understands Himself

Even if other people don't understand Bob *he* understands him. Here he explains the meaning of "The Times They Are A 'Changing":

"That's one thing I wanted to get in the song. Well, I don't know if the song is true but the feeling's

...BOB DYLAN

true. Oh yeah, it's no good saying there's no answer to things—it's freedom of expression I want. And it's nothing to do with a political party or religion. It's in yourself."

Yeah, well that's why I like you so much, Bob—you're really explicit and you explain things *so* well.

Dylan's friend and folk cohort, Joan Baez, had this to say about Bob: "There's a lot about Bobby I don't understand."

Yeah, well why don't you just ask him—he'll explain it to you just like he did to us and then you'll really be confused!

FAIRY TALE COMES TRUE

Once upon a time there was a girl named Pauline Behan who wanted to run a fan club for this group that she thought was great.

So she got to know the group's leader, Gerry Marsden better, and as the group, known as Gerry and the Pacemakers, became more and more successful she got better and better acquainted with Gerry.

So well acquainted that he asked her to marry him and they lived happily ever after.

Luckily, this fairy tale is true and *The BEAT* wishes the new Mr. and Mrs. Gerry Marsden all the best in the world.

Among the lucky few who attended the wedding were the group's manager, Brian Epstein, and record producer, George Martin, both of whom also work for the Beatles, and both the bride and groom's mothers.

...TOM JONES

Tom Jones Glad To Say Goodbye

America is a nice place to visit but "I wouldn't want to live there," said Tom Jones on his return to his home in Wales.

Jones didn't seem to think an awful lot about America in general.

"I'm glad to be back. When I'm in Britain I feel I'm in the middle of the pop business. You get the feeling it's all happening here. In America it's so big you never feel you are the center of things."

"I didn't like the places I played on my tour. There were baseball parks where the P.A. systems were bad and there was no atmosphere, and the dressing rooms were worse than they are here."

Liked Elvis

Tom did have a few good memories of his American tour. He definitely was impressed over getting to meet Elvis.

"He was a great fella," Tom said.

Tom met him on the set of an Elvis movie and Elvis told him that "With These Hands" was his favorite record and even sang a few bars of it for him.

Tom did say that he got to meet most of the people he wanted to in America including Ben E. King, Solomon Burke and Little Richard.

And he reports that his next single will be from the James Bond Movie "Thunderball" for which he is doing the title song.

KRLA ARCHIVES

GREETINGS TO HERMAN'S HERMITS from the BEAT. Since we couldn't all make it over to MGM to visit Herman on the set of "Hold On" Herman was nice enough to personally autograph a picture for us. He's moving so fast nowadays that it's a real wonder he even had time to sit down and write at all! Besides the movie and numerous TV shows, Herman has sent yet another hit soaring up the charts, "Just A Little Bit Better." And it looks as if everyday IS just a little bit better for Herman too — which ain't bad.

On the BEAT
By Louise Criscione

Belated congratulations to Chris Dreja of the Yardbirds and his American bride, Pat. They announced their wedding last week but have actually been secretly married since August.

And speaking of the Yardbirds, it's just possible that they will be spending their Christmas in New York. They've been asked to come over for six weeks beginning December 15 but their manager, Giorgio Gomelsky, has yet to confirm the proposal so I guess we'll just have to wait and see.

Expecting Baby

Since she's expecting her first baby, Marianne Faithfull has been relatively inactive on the pop scene. But last week she journeyed to a recording studio to cut "Yesterday" — yes, the same "Yesterday" which Paul McCartney has made into such a fantastic hit here in America.

In England, however, the Beatles have not seen the song released as a single, though it is on their "Help" album. At Marianne's invitation, Paul attended her session which was reported to have had a 100-voice choir backing.

Matt Monroe of "Walk Away" fame has already cut the record and has succeeded in getting it onto the British hit lists so it will be interesting to see if Marianne can catch up and knock Monro's disc right off the charts.

... MARIANNE FAITHFUL

The Beatles have really cut their personal appearances down to the absolute minimum. They have decided to forget their annual Christmas show in London and their "huge" winter tour of Britain has been slashed to only nine dates which will include among others — London, Liverpool and Manchester.

Minus Mindbenders

Well, the Wayne Fontana — Mindbenders controversy has finally been resolved... *I think*. Wayne is undertaking the Herman's Hermits' tour of England minus the Mindbenders. He's got himself a new backing group but he's really playing this solo bit to the hilt and so his new group will remain unnamed.

QUICK ONES: The Everly Brothers — Cilla Black tour of England playing to packed houses everywhere and everybody including show's promoter, Brian Epstein, extremely pleased... Hoping to visit Stateside — Dave Berry, Lulu and Dusty Springfield... Speaking of the redhaired Lulu, she and Herman recently threw a joint party to celebrate their birthdays... Brian Jones wrote a song for the Checkmates to record... Ringo's fans have renamed his house "Zak's Shack"... English pop paper, "Music Echo," repeatedly states that the Stones are seriously considering moving to America but the Stones just as repeatedly deny it — Keith declaring it "rubbish, absolute nonsense"... Congrats to Gerry Marsden and his brand new bride, Pauline... Putting in an appearance at the Leaves' party — a shorter-haired, better looking Mike Clarke of the Byrds.

Nice quote from George Harrison when some reporter asked him if he didn't think the fact that two of the Beatles were married would hurt their popularity: "Maybe it would hurt the image — but I'm more worried about personal happiness than about world happiness."

Mick On Marriage

Jagger on marriage: "I just don't reckon the idea of marriage. I don't fancy being responsible for anybody. I wouldn't mind my life, but I'd never be there to bring the children up." Okay, but I wonder where that leaves Chrissie?

I don't really dig all these protest songs and it looks as if I've found a partner in the person of Don Everly.

Don says: "They irritate me. This anti-war attitude is really unsurping the authority of the U.S. Government. Boys are dying in Vietnam and someone's got to do the fighting. If they must sing anti-war songs they should sing them to the enemy." Enough said!

... GEORGE HARRISON

Guess who I just rode up in the elevator with? Billy Joe Royal — and is he a doll!!

KRLA ARCHIVES

Quips 'N Quotes
By Eden

Joey Paige fell by *The BEAT* offices the other day just to say hello and chat for a little while. So, while Joey chatted, I scribbled-et voila!-Instant Interview!

On Dylan and the protest songs:

"I think he's a great writer and I think he has a great mind.

"I believe in people who express their thoughts if it's in the best interests of our country. But much of this protest music isn't.

"My next record is going to be a message song — but people call them "protest" songs, and that's wrong.

"I like to sing all types of songs — from ballads to R 'n' B — and I like to sing what the audiences like."

On clothes:

"I like anything that's unusual — within reason! I think that a person should have enough sense to know that if you're going to a nice restaurant, or to a party, to dress properly. I don't think dressing weird gives you any right to act differently or weird."

On his proposed TV show:

"I'm excited now about my new TV show — "*Way Out*." We've just finished taping the pilot — in color — and we're all very excited about it."

* * *

Alexander Graham Bell finally made himself useful the other eve, 'cause he made it possible for me to speak to Mr. Chad Stuart. And if you have never spoken — on the telly-phone — to Chad Stuart, you are missing out on one of life's greater experiences!

Therefore, I'll share our conversation with you.

Wouldn't Cut Hair

Chad informs us that his beautiful wife, Jill, had been awarded the continuing part of the airline hostess on the upcoming series "Woody" which stars Will Hutchins of "Sugarfoot" fame. Jilly was signed for a five year contract with the Mirisch Co., and the series would have brought in around $200,000 — BUT . . . they wanted her to cut her hair (*dastardly* thought!), so she promptly informed them that the deal was off! "We think she's pretty enough to get another series anyway," reflects Chad.

Chad also confesses to having indulged himself once again in his pet extravagance — guitars. "I've just bought a thousand dollars worth of guitar. It's a double-necked Gibson and it looks like a monster — it costs about as much too! Anyways, it does everything a six-string and a twelve-string ordinarily do, all on one guitar. So when I'm on stage I won't have to keep saying, 'Excuse me,' while I change guitars. Jeremy and I are also having matching golden guitars made up."

On November 7 Chad and Jill left for England and Chad said that while they were over there, "Jill and I are having waistcoats — matching vests — made out of a Union Jack."

Jeremy Again

Speaking of his upcoming English trip, Chad assured me that he and Jeremy will definitely get together and record two or three albums. Then he thought for a moment, and laughed as he wondered aloud: "Sometimes I wonder if Jeremy is *real!* Oh well, I do have a cardboard replica of him standing here in my living room!"

Chad also spoke briefly about the two little kittens which he and Jill had adopted. "Their names are Oliver and Hattie and they are very cute. One of them thinks it's a squirrel 'cause it keeps running up the curtains in the living room! And the other one looks like a cow!!"

Chad closed our little conversation by assuring me that he was going to bring me a gift from England when he returns. What kind of gift? "I'm going to bring you a receptacle of fog! I'll also bring you Jeremy and Paul McCartney's autograph!!"

Thanks *heaps*, Chad old bean!

Leslie Gore Limits Her Appearances

Lesley Gore, although often rated as the top female teenage singer in America, is not neglecting her education in the face of a busy career.

In fact she seems to be neglecting her career for her education. She has restricted her appearances in order to keep up her grades at Sarah Lawrence, one of the top Eastern ivy league schools, where she is a sophomore.

She was seen in one of her rare appearances Oct. 28 on *Hullabaloo* singing her latest release "My Town, My Guy and Me."

Miss Gore is proof of the fact that an education is important and it is possible to continue higher education even in the midst of a soaring career.

'Baby' Annette Becomes Mother

Any of you ex-Mouseketeers remember a cute little girl with short black hair named Annette who went on to become a star in her own right?

Well, that little girl now has a little girl of her own.

Congratulations and best wishes from *The BEAT* to Annette Funicello and hubby Jack Gilardi, a talent agent, on the birth of their first child.

Annette gave birth to a six-pound, 12-ounce girl recently and they have named her Gina.

Makes you ex-Mouseketeers feel a little older maybe.

SAVE SHINDIG
(Continued from page 2)

the television stations refused to go along with this arrangement and ran only one of the shows weekly. From the outset, the ratings began taking a nose-dive.

The telephone lines between New York and Hollywood quickly became even busier with the first signs of panic. Without Good, working under the increased pressure of producing two shows weekly on a budget which had shrunk even smaller, the Shindig staff was ineffectual in its frantic attempts to shore up the ratings. The network boys destroyed any remaining hope with a desperation attempt to imitate Hullabaloo (which had begun as a poor imitation of Shindig but later improved remarkably and achieved ratings success after the loosely-padded hour program was trimmed down to 30 minutes). Thus, the remaining Shindig viewers were treated to a conglomeration which included Hullabaloo-type guest hosts and spectacles such as Zsa Zsa Gabor trying to act the part of a hip emcee.

Final Blunder

Now the final stupendous blunder. Both Shindig and Hullabaloo enjoyed their greatest success as weekly half-hour programs. But instead of cutting Shindig back to one show per week and beefing up the budget to secure top stars, top production and fresh new ideas, they are jerking the entire package off the air.

Shindig deserves a better fate. And so does the viewing public, which has proven that it enjoys this type of show if it is a *good* show administered in proper doses.

At this stage only two things could save Shindig: (1) a dramatic climb in ratings, which appears highly unlikely; (2) an avalanche of letters from an angry public, demanding that one weekly Shindig show be kept on the air and given a second chance. If you want this, start writing. Have your friends write. Tell ABC you think it's a dirty deal.

Send your protests to: Shindig, 4151 Prospect Ave., Hollywood 27, Calif. It might also be helpful to write the local ABC-TV outlet.

Shindig has deserted the public, but you can show ABC that the public has not deserted Shindig.

SONNY AND CHER walk down the steps of their "old" home for the final time. The world-famous stars are pictured here moving to their beautiful new $80,000 home outside Los Angeles. (When Sonny decided to buy it he reached into his pocket and produced the down payment — $15,000 cash.) Watch for pictures of it soon in the BEAT.

KRLA ARCHIVES

MAIL BOX

Dear Editor:
There has been much ill feeling about the methods of choosing Oscar and Emmy award winners. We are proud that *The BEAT* is letting us make our own choices in the pop music field.

In return we voters should co-operate and must realize how difficult it is to set up a poll like this — this is fair to the artists and acceptable to their fans.

When you think of a male singer, you think of "voice" and "talent." In Hawaii, Elvis reigns. In England, Roy Orbison has repeatedly won the Battle of the Giants. Gene Pitney, also big in England, names Roy as his own favorite singer. In the U.S., Roy and Dean Martin were the only male vocalists to earn a gold disk by the end of '64.

You may find it disappointing that you cannot vote in a Beatle as outstanding singer. Paul, for example, with his versatility in singing everything from slow ballads to the "colored" sound, his part of the group harmony, and his superb phrasing in "Yesterday." But note the other categories you can squeeze him into: Best Vocal Group, Best Vocal Record, Best Vocal Album.

If anything is lacking, it is a spot to vote for outstanding R & B singers. Like Eric Burdon and Paul Jones — to reach them I'd have to vote the Animals or Manfred Mann as my favorite group. And with me, as with the majority (I am sure) it's Beatles and Hermits forever.
Elinore

Dear *BEAT*:
I hear a lot of people say that they don't understand Bob Dylan's songs. I listen to the words and I understand all his songs that I've heard.

I just got his album "Highway 61 Revisited" and I understand all the songs on it. His songs are just as easy to understand as all others that come out. I honestly think Bob Dylan is a genius and what's the matter with that. He thinks, he writes and he says what he feels.

I hope *The BEAT* will print more stories on Bob Dylan.
Nancy Smith

Dear *BEAT*,
A young lady recently wrote a latter on England in which she wrote all the benefits of seeing England. I have just returned and *my* purpose for going was only to see the Beatles' homeland.

To my surprise, most of the teens there were dying to visit America — they thought of it as the same "Home of the Stars" as *I* thought of England.

It seemed very unusual to me, but I think I now understand. "The grass is always greener . . ." (where the Beatles tread!)
Barbara C.

Dear *BEAT* Editor:
I'd like to say I got to meet my favorites (to put it mildly) Sonny & Cher, backstage at their concert appearance in San Jose. They are the most natural and friendly people, devoid of any conceit. They were very nice to everyone. They haven't lost any of their glitter for me. If anything, they've gained a lot of it. I'd just like to pass this along to anyone that is dying to meet their fave but afraid they might become disenchanted afterwards with them. Thank you for your great newspaper and keep up all those fab pics and info on Sonny and Cher.
Karen Enz

Dear *BEAT*:
I am writing to tell all *BEAT* readers about the latest English group to hit the pop scene, they are "Scrooge and the Misers". The line-up is Pete Harper (lead singer and tambourine), Les Harris (drums), Geoff Warren (lead guitar), and Brian Youngs (rhythm guitar).

Scrooge and the Misers came in first out of eighty-eight in an Essex beat competition, so you know they're gear! If anyone wants more information on this fab English group, contact me. Write to 3976 Alzada Rd., Altadena, California.
Nora Titus

Donovan In TV Feature

Donovan has joined the list of popular singers who have gone into movies.

But his movie won't be of the fast moving, colorful variety with girls in bikinis and weird settings for songs.

Donovan is the star of a documentary made by Rediffusion TV, tracing his career from a wandering nobody to a successful folk and rock singer.

Most of the film was shot in a studio in London and in St. Ives in Cornwall where he lived for some time. But it also has some scenes of him singing in a concert in Croydon.

There has been no word yet as to where and when the film will be released or if it will ever be shown in America.

...DONOVAN

PAUL McCARTNEY IS CREDITED with starting a musical revolution. The success of his "Yesterday" has prompted a frantic search through other centuries-old material for similar sounds. Matt Monroe and Marianne Faithfull are the latest to record "Yesterday." Strangely enough, despite its huge success in the U.S., Paul's version of the song has not been released as a single in England — only on album.

Dear Susan

By Susan Frisch

Is it true that Dennis Wilson of the Beach Boys is married and has two children?
Vickie Kubota

Dear Vickie,
This is just another one of those silly rumors. Don't worry.

When will the Byrds new LP be out? And where did Jim McQuinn get the crazy glasses that he wears? Also how's Lucy Hesky?
Judi Weinberger

Dear Judi,
The relase date for their new album has not been set as yet, but it should be out quite shortly. Jim got his glasses at an army surplus store in Hollywood. Who's Lucy Hesky, ha, ha????!!!!

Can you tell me anything about the next Beatle film?
Billie Washington

Dear Billie,
All I know about their next movie is that it will be filmed in Spain (it's cheaper over there) and that it will have the flavor of a cowboy western.

Did Herman's Hermits enjoy working on their new movie?
Sally Howler

Dear Sally,
All of the boys had a complete ball filming. They just loved every minute of shooting — well, maybe not getting up early in the morning.

What kind of gum does Bill Wyman prefer, and what kind of candy do the Stones like?
Marcy Hernandez

Dear Marcy,
Once I saw Bill chewing Doublement, again I saw him chomp Juicy Fruit. I don't and really couldn't say if these brands are his favorites. I don't know about all the Stones, but Brian loves red and chocolate licorice.

Do you know what Jonathan Winters is trying to get across in "Everyone's Gone to the Moon"?
Connie Stephens

Dear Connie,
Ever hear the expression, "Beauty is in the eyes of the beholder?" I suppose whatever you want it to mean, but it is kind of obvious.

What was Cher's and Cynthia's maiden names?
Tom Smith

Dear Tom,
Cher's maiden name was La-Pierre. Cyn's maiden name was Powell.

When is "Having A Wild Weekend," The Dave Clark Five's movie, coming out to California?
Mae Blaha

Dear Mae,
This is something that you will have to check at your local nearby theatres.

Is Bobby Sherman going to be in a movie called "Shindig"?
Jan Patterson

Dear Jan,
Bobby has said nothing about a movie. Sorry.

KRLA ARCHIVES

Motown's Magic — 4 More Hits

... MARVIN GAYE

... THE SUPREMES

... THE FOUR TOPS

... THE TEMPTATIONS

CHECK THE RECORD SALES CHARTS and You'll Always Find the Motown Label of Detroit With Several Listings. These Four Acts Are Largely Responsible

KRLA ARCHIVES

For Girls Only
George Still Rules

By Shirley Poston

Challo and all that! (Boys, that doesn't mean you.)

Guess what I discovered today! You know how I'm always talking about thinking I've lost a marble or two (dropped one, that is) along the way? Well, I never really *meant* it until right now.

A few moments ago I was sitting here dreamily, writing myself little notes about all the things I could talk about in my column, providing I didn't get off and running about myself, or orange popsicles, or something equally fascinating (har).

Well, when I looked at the notes, I discovered that I had spelled girl like this—*gril*. I laughed and corrected my mistake. By spelling it *girll*.

If you happen to see a man racing by, carrying a large net, three guesses where he's headed.

Before I start raving about George (I do that sometimes) (sometimes?), I've heard about two more things to do to windows (huh?) if you're trying to redecorate your room on 29c.

Paste On Panes

One is to cut out squares of colored construction paper and paste them on the panes. The other is to paint the panes (hey, I think I'll say that to the next person who gives me a rough time—you know, "Oh go paint a pane." Sorry about that interruption. I can't think about one subject very long. My mind (what's left of it) has a tendency to skip (it also plays a great game of hop scotch).

Anyway, you paint the window glass very light colors. It isn't transparent at night, but the sunlight filters through in the daytime—in the color of your choice; yet.

Oh, enough of this sensible stuff. Let's talk about George (rant, pant). I got the nicest letter about my Harrison ravings (and about a jillion that raved right along with me) that asked me to please put in a good word for Paul now and then.

Well, George, I hope you'll forgive me (you forgave me for making up that day dream about meeting John in a blizzard, didn't you?) (however, Cynthia did not), but I must admit Paul is about the cutest boy I have ever seen with my own two eyes.

WOW! I just thought of the wildest thing! Here is the kookiest do-it-yourself-dream I've dreamed up yet! And it just came to me in a blinding flash!

Tonight when I go to my trundle bed, I'm going to lie awake and make up a dream about George lying awake making up a dream about me!

Sick, Sick, Sick

Boy, I may not be much to look at, but I sure am sick!!

Now, what was I saying previous to that most recent tangent? Oh, yes, about Paul being so cute. Isn't he though? I just love the way he bounces.

Prepare yourselves. I'm about to tell you something I shouldn't. I write to a boy who knows the Beatles quite well, and when I told him that John is my second favorite Beatle, and told him *why*, he laughed and laughed. Then he told *John* what I said (that wretch) (my pen pal, not John). Then *John* laughed!

I guess I might as well tell you the *why* so you can laugh, too. Here's what I said in my letter... "John is so... well... he's just... you know, it's the way he stands there and... no matter what Beatle or what star you like best, John still flips you... there's just something about him... or something."

I don't think it's so funny, do you? I'll bet a lot of you feel the same way about him, right?

Fiendish Idea

Hmmmm. I just had another fiendish idea. Since my friend (when he stopped laughing) said all this was news to John, why

Stones Say Yule Shows Are 'Drags'

Why aren't the Rolling Stones going to do a Christmas show this year?

"We don't *want* to do a Christmas show," says Mick Jagger. "It'd be too much of a drag. All the mums and dads trotting in to see us after having a few sherries... no thanks! We won't go all show business and branch out as 'entertainers' over the Christmas period."

Mick explained why it would be dull: "Staying in one place all the time is a drag. You report at the theater at the same time every day, do the show and go home at the same time. It becomes like a boring office job."

If the Stones extend their upcoming American tour, they may be in the United States for Christmas. England's loss is our gain!

Supremes Deny Break-up Rumor

The rumor machines are grinding again and this time about the Supremes.

Lead singer Diana Ross still says she has "no comment" about her going solo.

"I've just never thought about it. We're too busy, working and traveling. Anyway it would be stupid to break up, because we're so successful. I don't think it'll happen for some time.

"I guess if the group got very low, and one of us wanted to get married or something, then we might possibly split," she added.

don't we sort of let him in on the secret. (Yeah, yeah, yeah!)

If anyone reading this shares my feeling (which I explained very well, I think) (at least it was true to form—totally confusing), why don't you write it down, send it off to me c/o *The BEAT* and I'll then send all the letters off to my friend. Who, if I know my friend, will show them to John! Who will utterly *flip*!

And George, please don't think I'm being fickle. After all, you already *know* we're all absolutely loony over *you*, and since John doesn't seem to realize how whatever-it-is he is, it's too kooky an idea to pass up! Don't worry, I'll never forget that GEORGE HARRISON RULES.

One of these days I'm going to come to my senses, but I have a feeling it may be a while yet.

Oh, remember that goofy thing I said a few thousand paragraphs back? (I know, I know, *which* goofy thing.) I mean the one about "go paint a pane." Well, I just thought of another one. If you know someone who acts really witchy, tell them to "go cackle around a cauldron!"

I Need Help

Back to something sensible for a short (I promise) moment. I have a problem and I need help (which is hardly any secret). I have two friends who LOVE to talk on the telephone, and they always call me at the wrong moment. One of them is the kind of friend I can practically hang up on if I have to, although sometimes that doesn't even stop her. You know, I mean she understands me. But the other one! Whew! She just goes right on talking no matter what! And it really hurts her feelings if I try to end the conversation.

What do you do with someone like that? She's such a good friend in every other way, but this is driving me nuts! (Nutsier, that is.) I just *can't* have a heart to heart talk with her. She'd just feel *horrible*!

If any of you can think of a way out of this plight, please let me know. Quick, before my ear falls off.

If I don't stop all this blabbing and typing, my *fingers* are going to fall off!

Before I say farewell, mustn't forget to tell you that the "Hard Day's Night" album I found in my closet went to Janet Milner of Covina, Calif. Her letter was the first one I received.

And guess what! I've just inherited another Beatle album that's a duplicate of one I have! Stay tuned next week and I'll tell you the boring... er... fascinating story of how that happened and how you can inherit the album from me! I'd tell you right now, but I'm using up else's room already.

Bye for now and I'll see you next *BEAT*!

THE MOJO MEN—Quality sound, danceable rhythms are their goals.

Mojo Men Seek New Gold Rush

By Carol Deck

They came from New York and Florida like pioneers heading West and now they are seeking their place in the scene.

The Mojo Men have just released their newest called "Dance With Me" and this may be the start of a gold rush for them.

The Mojo Men are Jimmy Alaimo, Paul Curcio, Don Metchick and Dennis De Carr and they share a common goal of providing quality sound and danceable rhythms for their fans.

Their tastes run from the Beatles to Sophia Loren yet they have a lot in common.

All four say that their favorite composers are John Lennon and Paul McCartney and that the Beatles are their favorite group.

Hates Phonies

Jimmy is the shortest, 5'8", and oldest of the group. He's 24 and says he likes Joan Baez, Ray Charles, Sophia Loren and eating in good restaurants. His only dislike is one shared by many entertainers—phony people.

Dennis is the tallest, (6 Ft.), and has the unbeatable combination of blue eyes and black hair. He says he likes Italian food, expensive continental suits, the Kinks, and staying up all night. He also adores Pepsi but hates it when it's warm.

Don plays the organ, piano, tambourine and bass and writes songs. His likes range from Nancy Wilson to Bobby Bland to Kirk Douglas. He digs large restaurants but hates large parties and he and Jimmy own a Siamese cat named Ghee.

Likes Jazz, R & B

Paul likes jazz and rhythm and blues type music and says his favorite entertainers are Nancy Wilson, Andy Williams, Ray Charles, Mel Torme, Paul Newman and Audrey Hepburn. He owns a dog he calls Tiki and says his pet peeve is loud people.

All four of the boys have been to college—Jimmy attended the University of Miami, Hastings Law School and the University of California at Berkeley. Dennis went to the University of Florida, and Don and Paul both attended the University of Miami.

They all make their home in the San Francisco area now where they are constantly searching for greater sophistication in music trends. These boys just may come up with an entirely new, sophisticated sound any day now.

Watch for them and their latest record, "Dance With Me".

KRLA ARCHIVES

Tokyo Karate Federation

Introduces to Southern California
'THE ART OF KARATE'

 is an *art form* and should be taught in the tradition of *Great Art*.

 is considered to be one of the finest forms of *physical fitness* available to the human body—it is currently the fastest growing *new sport* in America—and unquestionably the most practical and complete form of *self defense* available!

 can be *learned* by both *men and women* of all ages!

If you desire to learn Karate or would like to see it demonstrated, call or visit:

Hollywood: Tokyo Karate Federation - 6170½ Santa Monica Blvd. - HO 3-9807
Culver City: Tokyo Karate Federation - 4208 Overland Ave. - 837-3117

KRLA ARCHIVES

Dick Moreland Has Two Jobs— Both Factors in KRLA Success

Dick Moreland spends less time "on the air" than any other KRLA disc jockey . . . and yet he is a major factor in the KRLA success story.

Since most of his work is done behind-the-scene, Dick misses out on much of the publicity and most KRLA listeners are not as familiar with him as they should be. So when he invited us to hop aboard the D.M. Line and have a look around, we decided to do just that.

Virginian

According to the man himself, Dick was born (he *swears* that he was!) in Parkersburg, Virginia, in 1933, and attended schools in Virginia, Texas, Arkansas, and West Virginia.

"I graduated from high school and joined the Navy and spent two-and-a-half years in Korea and Japan. Following that, I went into radio in Mineral Wells, Texas; I decided I was a *terrible* radio announcer and came to California and went to Don Martin's school for radio announcers. I attended two years of classes and ended up teaching there."

Being a disc jockey was certainly not a mere accident for Dick:

"I decided when I was fourteen years old that I was going to be a radio announcer, so most of my high school training was spent in speech and dramatics classes.

Early Start

"I actually started in radio when I was still in high school, and I was really a general *flunkie* to a DJ by the name of John Trotter, and I kind of credit John for the beginnings of my style in radio. After that, I worked for a station in Mineral Wells, Texas—in the middle of the Cow Pouch!! It was a 250-watt "teapot" which broadcast for about five miles in every direction! From there I went to school at Don Martin's and then

on to a station in Oxnard, California, where I was program director. We set up an interesting format and developed some pretty good talents—those of Bob Eubanks, Jim Steck, and Bill Keffury—and all of us kind of drifted into KRLA, each helping the other get here!"

Long Hours

Looking at the D.M. Line, we find that Dick spends the major part of his waking hours working in the field of pop music, and yet he has retained a fine appreciation of all music forms.

"My taste in music varies in all different directions—jazz, pop music, country and western, and classical selections. I'm a *nut* for music—I've got three stereo sets in my house: one in my bedroom, one in the den, and one in the living area. I have every record ever recorded by Hank Williams and Buck Owens; a full collection of Beatles and Rolling Stones records; a full collection of Bob Dylan—and every once in a while, I like to put on a few of Dylan's records, turn off the lights, and get into some other world!"

Music Director

Far beyond his chores as a disc jockey on KRLA, Dick is deeply involved in many related activities for the station.

"As music director, it's my responsibility to see that the stores are surveyed in the area, and that we look at national listings from national sales reports to determine what records we play. For the most part, that is how we make up our play-list of about forty-seven tunes each week. The other criterion, of course, is major artists with major records. *Nobody* would be foolish enough to wait for a Beatle record to start selling before they played it! Outside of that, I handle a great deal of production, which is doing the silly little things and the contests that we have on the air. I'm the general idea man.

Public Service

"I also do a lot in the public service area if it deals with music: charity shows, such as our yearly benefit for the March of Dimes, and that type of thing. I have the responsibility of putting those together."

As we near the end of our little excursion down the D.M. Line, it becomes more and more evident that Dick Moreland is one very good reason for the overwhelming success of KRLA.

Oh, by the way, Dick—thanks for the ride!!

GREAT WESTERN EXHIBIT CENTER
"Battle of the Bands"
NOV. 17-20
FOR INFO: RA 3-3678

NO ADMISSION
NO AGE LIMIT
PANDORA'S BOX
8118 SUNSET STRIP

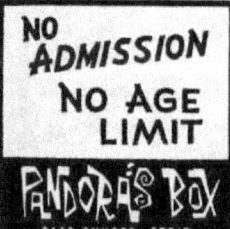

NEW!! NEW!! NEW!!
AT THE "HOLE IN THE WALL"
BIRD SUN GLASSES
COMES IN TWO COLORS: GOLD OR SILVER, WITH CASE
$7.95 PAIR

WE WILL MAIL TO YOU PREPAID
SEND MONEY ORDER OR CHECK
NAME:
ADDRESS:
CITY: STATE:
CHECK COLOR WANTED: GOLD ☐ SILVER ☐

432 N. La Cienega
Los Angeles 48, Calif.
HOLE IN THE WALL

KRLA $11-10 Football Sweepstakes

The KRLA BEAT will award $1,110.00 to everyone accurately predicting the scores of 10 of the 11 games listed below (games to be played Friday, Nov. 12). This contest will be repeated each week for the remainder of the high school football season.

ENTRY BLANK

1. WILSON_____ GARFIELD_____
2. ROOSEVELT_____ SOUTH GATE_____
3. SAN PEDRO_____ NARBONNE_____
4. BANNING_____ GARDENA_____
5. JORDON_____ CARSON_____
6. MARSHALL_____ BELMONT_____
7. LINCOLN_____ VERDUGO HILLS_____
8. LOS ANGELES_____ JEFFERSON_____
9. MANUAL ARTS_____ DORSEY_____
10. FREMONT_____ WASHINGTON_____
11. FAIRFAX_____ PALISADES_____

Weekly Contest No. 4
Name_____ Telephone_____
Address_____
City_____ State_____ Zip_____

$11-10 CONTEST RULES

1. Scores for all 11 games must be filled in. Everyone correctly guessing the scores of any 10 of these varsity games will win the jackpot of $1,110.00.
2. Entries should be addressed to: KRLA BEAT 11-10 Contest, 1401 S. Oak Knoll, Pasadena, Calif.
3. Entries for this week's contest must be postmarked no later than 12 p.m. Wednesday, Nov. 10, 1965.
4. Enter as many times as you like. Each entry must be made on a *BEAT* official contest blank or on a hand-drawn facsimile.
5. Employees of KRLA and *The BEAT*, and members of the families of employees, are not eligible to compete.

Hear the scores of all varsity football games every week on the KRLA-Herald Examiner Sports Line. Listen for Danny Baxter's Weekly Predictions on KRLA—"The Station That Knows The Score!"

KRLA BEAT SUBSCRIPTION

you will SAVE 60% of the regular price!
AN INTRODUCTORY SPECIAL . . . if you subscribe now . . .

☐ 1 YEAR—52 Issues—$3.00   ☐ 2 YEARS—$5.00

Enclosed is $_____
Send to:_____ Age:_____
Address:_____
City:_____ State:_____ Zip:_____

MAIL YOUR ORDER TO: **KRLA BEAT**
1401 South Oak Knoll Avenue
Pasadena, California 91106

Outside U.S.: $9.00—52 Issues

The Shindigger

Howdy hi, Shindiggers — ready to go exploring with me? Great! 'Cause this week we're gonna do a little snooping backstage at the hallowed halls of SHINDIG!

Oh — here's someone we've visited with before: it's Billy Joe Royal. Hi Billy, how was your tour of England?

"It was a short one, but it was great."

Did you find any differences between the audiences of the two countries?

"Not that much — a little bit — but not that much."

Y'know, Billy, fashions are very important now — did you notice anything unusual while you were across the Big Pond?

Hipsters Big

"Hipsters are really the thing over there. But I like casual-looking clothes for myself; rugged-looking jackets and corduroy pants."

By the way, Billy, last time you were here you were telling us that you had plans of recording "Down in the Boondocks" in other languages. Have you done that as yet?

"Yes, we went in and recorded it in German and in Italian on October 28, and we'll be doing a tour in Australia this coming January."

... BILLY JOE ROYAL

That's great; looking forward to hearing the Italian version. Thank you, Billy.

Concerning one Mr. Delaney Bramlett — he is twenty-four years old, and was born July 1, 1941, in Mississippi.

He has been in show business since he was eight years old and he plays guitar, bass, and drums — and all very well!

He says, "I sing everything from jazz to country."

Philosophy of life, Mr. Bramlett? At your service!

"I think everybody should always do exactly what they want — within reason, of course — or else they are going to be unhappy. I don't think anybody should have to feel backwards or embarrassed."

Onward and upward we go now to blond, be-Beatled Joey Cooper. Joseph was born March 21, 1943 in Tennessee, and he plays guitar, bass, drums, and piano.

Musical preferences?

"I like any kind of music — any kind at all."

Thank you, Mr. C. Now, would you philosophize briefly, for us, in fifteen words or less?

"I want to be good and make a lot of money!!"

Thank you again Joey.

Here's an interesting note that I bet you didn't know about: David Mallet — who is the assistant producer on SHINDIG and also somewhat English — has his hair cut by Chuck Blackwell — who is the drummer for the Shindogs and is also very American. David swears that he has never in his life had his hair cut by a barber, and also informs us that Chuck handles all the "clipping" honors for the other Shindogs, as well.

Now that we've got that out of the way, let's wander down this hallway of dressing rooms and — well look at what we've found. It's George Patterson of the Wellingtons. Howdy, George. I hear that you and Eddie and Kirby have moved into a new home. Will you tell us about it?

"Sure. It's up in the hills, just like our old house, and we have a swimming pool; everybody is invited to come swimming — if they can FIND the house!!"

Oh dear, I guess we've used up all of our time again, but I hope you'll be watching the show this week.

Till then, Shindiggers — maintain your soul, and remember: no matter what *anybody* says — ROCK ON!!!!

THE SHINDOGS — DELANEY BRAMLETT, JOEY COOPER, CHUCK BLACKWELL, JAMES BURTON.

THE RED ROOSTERS — (from left) Randy Wolfe, Jay Ferguson, Ed Cassidy, Mike Fondelier and Mark Andes.

ROOSTERS LIKE BEATLES?
Red Roosters Not Chicken

By Louise Criscione

They're called the Red Roosters but they don't look much like chickens. They look like just any other five guys except for one thing — they're a group, and a talented group at that.

And there's nothing "chicken" about their ambition. They aim big. "One of our main aims is to mean the same to America as the Beatles do to England," they state matter-of-factly.

Inspired by Song

The first thing which strikes you about the group is their unusual name. By now everyone has heard the record "Little Red Rooster" so I asked the boys if the record had anything to do with their name.

"No, not the record but the song did. The song's been around for a long time," Jay answered.

The group consists of Mark Andes, 17, Mike Fondelier, 17, Jay Ferguson, 18, Randy Wolfe, 15, and Ed Cassidy who wouldn't tell me his age! Anyway, the point is that they belong to different age groups so I wondered how they all got together.

"Jay and I were playing in a blue-grass group and Jay was acquainted with Randy so we gave him a buzz and asked if he wanted to join the group," Mike explained.

"I played with some other groups and we got to know Randy and then I joined," Mark continued.

So, four of the Red Roosters were together and the hunt was on to find a drummer with Ed finally winning the job.

"I played with all kinds of different groups. I used to play opera and jazz, ballet and background music for television series," Ed explained.

They're Different

But the Red Roosters don't fit into any of those bags. They're up-beat blues and folk-rock and Jay thinks this is the reason the group will eventually make it big and "hit at the heart of America."

Probably the Rooster who stands out the most is the drummer, Ed. You notice him immediately because his head is absolutely bald!

"It grows on the inside," Ed grinned. "No, really, I shave it."

Ed also wears shades continually. Why, I wanted to know. "Because the light on stage comes down in my eyes," Ed answered. I had the feeling I was being put-on but decided we had delved deeply enough into that subject anyway. So we immediately switched topics — like to the music the Roosters play.

Do Everything

The Roosters do all their own arranging and most of their own writing with each member of the group contributing.

"It's hard to pattern ourselves after anybody because we have our own sound," Mark commented.

"The thing is we are the Red Roosters because we arrange our songs. The arrangements have some sort of pattern and I think it's the arrangements which make us sound like us," Jay added.

On stage the group remains anything but stationary. They change instruments, they take turns singing lead and sometimes they all sing together. One of their big ambitions in life is to reproduce their on-stage sound on their records.

"We don't want 100 musicians backing us on record," Randy said. "We want to do it all ourselves."

"We want continuity all the way through," Ed said. "You know, when you hear the Rolling Stones in person and then you hear them on record, it's the same sound. Well, that's how we want to be, we don't want any phoniness on our records," Ed finished.

Orbison To Make Movie

Roy Orbison is going into movies and will star in "The Fastest Guitar in the West."

The movie appearance is just one of the provisions in the 20-year contract Roy signed this summer with MGM.

He will have the romantic lead in the movie which will be produced next year by Sam Katzman.

He'll sing six or seven songs while portraying a Union cavalry officer who is trying to return some gold to the Sacramento mint without anyone knowing it.

KRLA ARCHIVES

Tips to Teens

Q: I have very curly hair and have finally found jumbo rollers that leave my hair semi-straight. But my bangs still curl. I tape them down, but they flip upward at the ends. I am trying to grow them out and wear them to the side, but what can I do while I'm growing them? I can't go without bangs because then I'd look even worse (and that's getting pretty bad).
(Sandy L.)

A: First of all, trim just a smidge off your bangs every two weeks or so. Curly hair has a tendency to become extra-curly at the ends. Also try taping your bangs to your forehead (make sure all the ends are covered with tape) every night in an effort to train them. If all else fails, roll them forward on one of the jumbo rollers. They probably won't reach all the way around the roller, so tape the ends securely. This method will straighten more than curl.

Q: I've heard about a jillion answers to this question, so now I'm going to ask The BEAT's opinion. Is it okay for a girl to call a boy? There's a boy in school whom I have no possible way of meeting other than just coming right out and making the first move. Please help me.
(Cynthia G.)

A: The reason you've heard so many answers to his question is because there really isn't one answer. There never is when something is really just a matter of opinion. Many people think it's perfectly okay for a girl to call a boy, if she has a good reason, of course. In your case, you'd need to do something like ask him to a girl-invite-boy party to keep the call from sounding too forward. But other people disagree. Hopefully, the boy you have your eye on won't fall into the latter category. And there's only way to find out.

Q: I have very oily skin. I use a medicated product, but it looks like makeup and I don't like makeup. What can I use?
(Kim H.)

A: Try one of the medicated soaps designed to remove excess oil. Also, wear the product you spoke of during the night instead of the day.

Q: Please give me some advice on how to stay on a diet. I can have 1,200 calories a day, the doctor said. Please don't tell me to get lots of exercise. I already do that, even though it makes me all the hungrier.
(Tammy K.)

A: With a 1,200 calorie limit, you don't have to go hungry. Just try your best to learn to like foods that won't go over the limit. The best way to stay on a diet is to keep busy. Food provides energy, but it also relaxes you. That's why the evenings probably seem so much longer now that you haven't been calmed down by a sumptuous din-din. Do something with that time. Within the next five minutes you can probably think of fifty things you've been "meaning to get to" for ages. So get to them. If you run out of things to do before you run out of pounds to lose, nag your friends into going for long walks, etc. Anything to keep active and keep your mind off the hollow, nervous feeling you experience so much of the time during the first few weeks of dieting. Incidentally, letter writing is a great way to get your mind off your stomach. If you run out of pen pals, start down the list of your favorite stars.

Q: I am fourteen years old and people are forever asking if I'm eleven. I'm only 4'8" tall and I hope you'll be able to give me some hints on how to look my age.
(Mary N.)

A: Experiment with hairstyles until you find one that looks more fourteen than eleven. The latest styles are so popular because of their youthful effect, but in your case, you may have to choose between being fourteen and being fashionable. Try something upswept and away from your face. This will add height, and so would shoes with an inch or so of heel.

HINT OF THE WEEK

As long as I can remember, I've had the problem of nail-biting. I always meant to stop but never did until a friend of mine told me to wear a rubber band around one of my fingers. I tried it and every time I felt like biting my nails, I fidgeted with the rubber band. Try it! Wear it to school and everywhere. After you get embarrassed enough or feel you're cured, take it off. It worked for me, and it might for you, too. Don't get too embarrassed though. You might think you look silly wearing a rubber band, but you look a lot sillier sitting around with your hand in your mouth.
(Vicky K.)

If you have a question you'd like answered or a hint you've discovered, drop a line to Tips To Teens care of The BEAT.

Stones Win Gold Album

The Rolling Stones have added another gold one to their collection.

They have been awarded a gold record for their album, "Out of Our Heads" on the London label.

The album has been the fastest selling album in the history of the company, according to Herb Goldfarb, national sales manager.

BEAT Photo: Chuck Boyd

THE TOYS PERFORMING "LOVER'S CONCERTO." The trio (l. to r. Judy, Barbara and Barbara) hails from New York and all of the girls were once lead singers with different groups. However, none of them made it big until they got together and dug up Bach's "Lover's Concerto." Now they're threatening to unseat the Supremes as top female group.

PORTMAN'S PLATTERPOOP
By Julian Portman

HOLLYWOOD – Have you noticed a possible new trend in pop music? Two prime examples of it are "Yesterday" by *Beatle Paul* and that Gregorian chant the *Yardbirds* have revived from the middle ages, "Still I'm Sad." Both come from the same bag, and it'll be interesting to see how it develops.

Congratulations to the *Yardbirds*, incidentally. Three records, three hits ... *Sonny & Cher* have signed to star in a Capitol Records motion picture starting Jan. 10. As we mentioned last week, Capitol is going into the film business too ... *Gary Lewis* and the *Playboys* are putting on makeup for their cameo appearance in Universal's "Out of Sight" motion picture.

Wonderful *Petula Clark* goes onto the Hollywood Palace boards Jan. 22 ... Sat in recently and watched RCA Victor's Liverpool 5 slice their next album. They're a great group! "Honey," *Tony Harris'* first effort for Dee Gee Records, is becoming the talk of Chicago. It'll be a monster in that town, so take five minutes to hear a hit ... *Chad Stuart* will probably do the producing of his wife *Jill's* initial effort for Columbia Records ... *Hullabaloo* looks like it's going back to a one-hour program. Hooray!

Do Yourself a Favor Dept: Write *ABC-TV*, 4151 Prospect, Los Angeles, California 90027 and tell them how unhappy you are about them taking *Shindig* off the air. Ask them to keep at least 30 minutes on the air. Write today... don't delay!

New teen pactees: Dot Records inked pretty 15-year-old *Yolanda White*, a young gal with a great big voice ... Dee Gee Records long-termed 10-year-old moppet star *Denise Regan*. Her first record will be "A Hole in the Stocking" and "A Date With Santa Claus," both Christmas-type songs that should have lasting power!

Capitol's *Beach Boys*, besides doing a film for their parent company, go the Disney route in "Monkey Go Home" ... Era Records' *Jimmy Lewis* was former lead with *The Drifters* ... Hanna-Barbera inked *Louis Prima* and crew to a contract. Whatever Louis does is always good ... *Barry McGuire* and *Barbara McNair* have co-billing on Nov. 22 *Hullabaloo* offering ... *George Maharis* trying for a record comeback with "World Without Sunshine" ... Lovely *Melody Patterson* introduced her Warner Bros. offering, "You're the One," on Shindig.

Frankie Randall, getting the big build-up from RCA Victor, has been talked about as the summer replacement for *Dean Martin*. They're hoping to retain high ratings during the dull summer season by catering to the teens.

The *Lettermen* must be aging. They gave up sweaters for tuxes... *Sonny & Cher* have a line of clothes featuring their names heading for the clothing markets. Can't wait till I see Shindig's *Dick Howard* wearing Sonny-type boots and jacket. He might be asked to join the Tarzan trek.

It's Happening... By Eden

Funny story being told 'bout Illya's scene-stealing Mama-in-law.

Just recently, when David's mother-in-law winged into the City of the Angels, our favorite Super Spy was on hand to greet her at the L.A. International Airport. Also around for some *Dodger*-type greetings were some 5,000 zealous baseball-type fans.

Quipped the clever mama with a wink of her eye: "It was so sweet of you David – but you didn't have to go to all this trouble."

★ ★ ★

Sonny and Cher have ambitions for someday owning a chain of fashion boutiques featuring clothing of their own design. First step in that direction has been taken, and their brand new line of threads will be unraveled for the public by Yuletide this year.

★ ★ ★

A little back-patting is in order for the Rolling Stones, for receiving a gold record award for their "Out of Our Heads" LP on London Records less than *four months* after it's initial release.

The hit-disc has been the fastest-selling record in the history of London Records, and has already chalked up one million dollars in sales. Yep – these boys are gathering lots of "moss" – green colored money!

★ ★ ★

The Animals will launch an eight-day "attack" on Turkey beginning November 3, then they will embark upon a tour of Poland – being he first rock 'n' roll group to perform behind the iron curtain.

★ ★ ★

Granada television in Britain is preparing an exciting special to be screened on New Year's Eve. Invitations have been extended to all the top pop composers, including Mssrs. John Lennon, Paul McCartney, Bob Dylan, Burt Bacharach, Sonny Bono, and many others. Each composer will introduce the artist or group who recorded his hit composition during the year.

There are many here in the Colonies hoping that we'll also get to view this fab film, but negotiations are still up in the air. Don't hold your breath, kiddies, but you might try crossing your fingers for a while.

KRLA ARCHIVES

Person to Person

To Jim (Organist) of the Castaways:
I luv ya and thanks for the hair. I hope to meet you again when I'm famous (or before). Hope you have another hit record.
    Sioux

To Janet Amass of Hertfordshire, England:
Hi! I'm sorry I didn't send *The BEAT* to you sooner, but to make up for it, I had your name printed in it. How do you like it? Great, huh? Paul McCartney rules! (As if you didn't know).
    Donna

To Robin:
I can't imagine any other guy looking like Mr. McCartney, but if Dave does, you've got a good thing going.
    "O"

To Viv:
Wouldn't it be groovy if we really did meet "you know who" when we get to England? Till then, keep hoping, and keep reading *The BEAT*.
    Barb

To George McVey, Ayrshire, Scotland:
Isn't it dead great having your name in the fantabulous *BEAT*? The Stones and Joey Paige Rule — Right? Best wishes. See ya in Scotland soon.
    Cheryl

To Brian S. and Charlie G:
Thanks a lot for returning my pictures autographed. Sonny and Cher Rule!
    Stephi M.

To Jean Hamblin of Wakefield, Yorkshire and her "mates" of Loughborough Training College in England:
Ye "old" England may have Liverpool but the U. S. has fab California and the groovy *BEAT*.
    Paulette Lucania and the Sunny Hills Gang of Fullerton

Jackie:
Thanks loads for Cher's album and the cards. They're the greatest, and so are you.
    Jeannie

To Wilma Watson in England:
How does it feel to have your name in the greatest newspaper in the entire world?
    John

To Gregg:
I really miss your letter, couldn't you please write again?
    Dyann

To Marilyn Wright of Hull, Yorkshire, England:
In one year I'll be there and we can dream about John and George together.
    Suzi

To Paul and Kathy:
The best of everything to both of you. We've really had some fab times. Just hope there's a lot of the same in the future.
    Goerge & Pam

To Sue of Warwickshire:
Hope you had a blast on your birthday. I'll be waiting to hear from you.
    "Pedwin"

Dear Richard of the D.C.:
We are very sorry you got hurt and we apologize for it. You'll have to try to understand the over-anxious fans.
    All D.C. 5 Fan Club Members

To P.L.B.W.:
People say that in the teen years friends go their ways and find other friends. I hope it will never be that way with us. I suppose it will but if we do go our own ways who am I going to go to England with?
    M.J.T.L.

...GARY LEWIS

Jerry Lewis No Help In Son Gary's Career

Gary Lewis doesn't seem to know the meaning of the word rest. He keeps ploughing ahead, making records and movies at breakneck speed.

He has just signed for his fourth film role in "Birds Do It" with Soupy Sales and he and the Playboys will also be seen in cameo roles in "Out of Sight," a Universal picture produced by Bart Patton and directed by Lennie Weinrib.

Gary's first film was with his father, Jerry Lewis. After that he and the Playboys were seen in "A Swingin' Summer" and "The Family Jewels."

Five movies in your first year of show business is a pretty good start for anybody, but Gary adds to this several top selling records and numerous personal appearances.

Unknown Group

Just one short year ago Gary and the boys were an unknown musical group auditioning at Disneyland for the teenage dances held in the park during the summer.

Out of that audition the group got a full summer's job. The entertainment director of the park didn't find out until the end of the season that the lead singer of this group that packed the house every night was the son of Jerry Lewis.

News of their success spread and Snuff Garrett, a producer for Liberty Records, contacted Gary's mother, who was managing the group at that time, and arranged for the boys to cut a demonstration record. The Liberty executives liked it and signed Gary and the Playboys to a contract.

Great Sales

Their first release, "This Diamond Ring" topped the country in less than two months with sales of over a half million copies and the boys were on their way to a very busy year.

Liberty quickly followed their first record with an album of the same title and two subsequent singles, "Count Me In" and "Save Your Heart For Me."

With their success in records came television appearances including *Ed Sullivan, Hullabaloo, Shindig, Shivaree, Hollywood A Go Go* and *The Sam Riddle Show*.

On top of all this they also made a European tour with television appearances in Amsterdam, Berlin, Stockholm and Paris in conjunction with their latest release, "Everybody Loves a Clown."

One Nighters

After returning from this they jumped right into a tour of one night concerts in 20 cities across the country which will take them through November.

If hard work is what it takes to be a star, these guys must be superstars by now.

Yet Gary doesn't seem to think he has enough to do. He also finds time to serve with Patty Duke as National Youth Chairman for his father's favorite charity, Muscular Dystrophy.

What *does* he use for time and energy?

British Scene Wacky

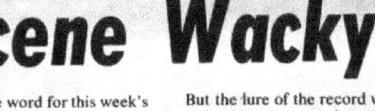

Unbelievable! That's the word for this week's British charts. As you can see, funny man Ken Dodd is *still* number one and, in fact, the first five chart places remain the same. But the second five undergo radical changes.

Chris Andrews, only on the charts for three weeks, has jumped into the top ten this week way up there at number six. Chris is the man who writes and produces Sandie Shaw's records and in this way has made quite a stack of money.

But the lure of the record world was just too great and so Chris not only wrote but also recorded "Yesterday Man," thus making himself a hit singer as well as a hit writer — and doubling his royalties in the process!

Another Hit

Following Chris at number seven is Sandie Shaw with "Message Understood" — a record which Chris wrote as well as produced. Looks like he's got the top ten sewed up.

In at eight are the Hedgehoppers Anonymous and their "Good News Week." The boys are having their share of troubles despite their chart success. Three members of the group are in the RAF, and although they've put in for discharges they haven't had any word yet so they're sitting pretty nervous right about now.

Fortunes Back

The Fortunes, just off their smash "You've Got Your Troubles," are back on the charts and riding high with their new one, "Here It Comes Again."

Last week *The BEAT* predicted that the Yardbirds' new British single was going to soar up the charts and for once we were right! "Evil Hearted You" landed in the Magic Circle this week, hanging in at number ten. And the other side of the record, "Still I'm Sad", is in hot pursuit at number 14.

British Top 10

1. TEARS — Ken Dodd
2. ALMOST THERE — Andy Williams
3. IF YOU GOTTA GO, GO NOW — Manfred Mann
4. HANG ON SLOOPY — The McCoys
5. EVE OF DESTRUCTION — Barry McGuire
6. YESTERDAY MAN — Chris Andrews
7. MESSAGE UNDERSTOOD — Sandie Shaw
8. IT'S GOOD NEWS WEEK — Hedgehoppers Anonymous
9. HERE IT COMES AGAIN — The Fortunes
10. EVIL HEARTED YOU — The Yardbirds

EDDIE HODGES' NEW IMAGE. Eddie's had several records released but none of them have really gone as far as he would have liked them to. So now he's changed his image, he's changed his sound and he's gotten himself a great big hit with the Dylan-penned "Love Minus Zero."

KRLA ARCHIVES

Looking At The World Thru Carole's Glasses

... CAROLE IS GLAMOUR

Through the magic looking-glass lightly, and past the enchanted horn-rimmed glasses—come with us now as we visit the far-off world of Carole Shelyne, Shindig dancer supreme.

Carole was born in Brooklyn, New York, on July 20, 1945. She has attended one year of junior college, and spent a year and a half at UCLA as a dance major.

"I didn't really start studying dancing till I was around seventeen, and most of my dance education came from the American School of Dance under scholarship. I have studied acting for two years at the Actor's Studio and I have just started studying voice about one year ago."

Back ... back ... back through time and space now, to the far-distant days of Carole's childhood. Was she an ambitious little girl?

Not Many Ambitions

"I didn't have many childhood ambitions; the only ones I remember were like most kids—either they want to be school teachers or movie stars. I never really wanted much because when I was younger I did an awful lot of modeling and photographic things, and I did a couple of movies."

As all little girls are wont to do, little Carole grew up; and soon she entered a brand-new world—the world of entertainment.

"My professional career started with dancing in stock and I had a chance, while I was working in stock, to do some acting and singing. In stock, you've got a great chance to watch the *real* people. Most of the kids would sit in back and play cards or run around and carry on backstage; but I'd go out front and sit there when I wasn't on or changing and I'd watch these people. And like a vulture—pick things up that I could use and learn from.

"The choreographer there told me: 'You're not an ingenue and you might as well get used to it right now. You don't have the face or the voice or the carriage for it. You're going to be a very good comedienne. Something else I want you to remember—first of all, you're only as good as you are today, so don't let things depress you because you only have to get better if you *want* to. Second of all—you can get *any*thing if you want it badly enough.'

"And I really started thinking

Something New

One bright, sun-filled day—something new came into Carole's life; something *Shindig*. As Carole describes it:

"The choreographer saw me in class one day—he had substituted for a regular teacher—and he walked over and said, 'We're holding auditions for *Shindig* next week and I think you'd be very right for the show!

"I went to the audition and made that one as well as a second audition, and then I did the pilot. Then a couple of weeks later I did the first show.

"The glasses bit? Well, the producer—Jack Good—came over to me on the rehearsal for the second show, and he said that he'd seen me on the first show, and had heard from a lot of people that I was a very good actress, and he wanted me to wear the glasses. I couldn't figure out why—I thought he was putting me on at first! It was a big joke then—I hated those glasses in the beginning! But I sort of like 'em now.

"We start working on Sunday—six hours on Sunday, six hours on Monday, around seven hours on Tuesday—and these are just the rehearsals. Then we start camera-blocking on Wednesday and we start about 7:30 in the morning and finish late Wednesday night. And on Thursday, it's usually the same. We *do* do a lot of rehearsing because there are so many numbers that we're always rehearsing."

Although she lives in a lofty Wonderland which is the envy of millions of girls across the country, Carole is a modern-day Alice with her feet planted firmly on the ground.

To Be Happy

"I want what most people want —I want to be happy.

"In the long run, I want to go into musical comedy and I want, more than anything else, to do my own Broadway show someday, which is kind of wild and far-fetched, but I think it's good to have far-fetched goals because then you never sell yourself short. It's better to want something that you can't really attain, than to get something that's *too* easily attainable.

"I think if I eventually attain my own goals in the fields I want to, I'd like to branch out and try directing. I watch directors and there's such a *creative feeling*."

Having worked on Shindig for over a year now, Carole has had an excellent opportunity to observe at first hand the pop scene and many of its artists at close range. Speaking of the British sound and influence of the past year, Carole reflects:

"It's kind of trite to say, but it's been a big influence; it's a *new* sound (which is also very trite!) I don't know that much about it except that at the beginning I liked it, but now I really *dig* it. I think it's great because it has more than an immediate value. I can see this music being *remembered* in about fifty years from now—this music is going to last—like all *good* popular music does."

Is Never-Never Land *really* all they say it is, and is Carole really happy with this dream-like sort of life she is living now?

The Problems

"I've got so much of what I want right now, but my problems are the same problems of someone who has *nothing*; problems of communicating with people, and making sure you're loved and wanted and needed. This is more important than getting ahead and being the biggest movie star in the world and the biggest musical comedy star—and I'm just starting to realize this. You're never too big for anybody. Never look down on people—you can always be friendly."

And so we must return to our own world of reality now—back through the magic looking-glass, and past the enchanted horn-rimmed glasses—back to the world of here and now.

Funny—somehow things seem just a little brighter and more cheerful over here now ... looking through Carole-colored glasses!

Barry McGuire Becomes Actor

Busy Barry McGuire, in the midst of a European tour, has announced that he's adding a movie to his already crowded schedule.

The movie will be filmed in January for Paramount and Barry says "I will be playing one of two men in the life of Ann Margaret, and this will give a great start to my acting career."

With the way his singing career got off to a big start with "Eve of Destruction" where can he go but up?

IS THIS A TREND?

Yardbirds' Locks To Be Sheared Shorter

The Yardbirds are getting their hair cut! Or so they say, anyway.

"We are going to have radical haircuts," Keith revealed. "Long hair is so unmanageable," Jeff commented with a shake of his long locks.

After seeing the group with long hair for so long it seems almost sacreligious to get it cropped short but apparently the boys have made up their minds on the subject.

They've also come to the decision that they need more publicity —not for themselves personally, but for the kind of music they play. Perhaps the boys don't realize just how difficult it is to write about their music since it almost defies description.

"Something very drastic is going to happen. The present mood of the group is frustration," Keith said pensively. "But it's a calculated period of frustration," he added without bothering to explain what a "calculated period of frustration" is.

It's hard to see what the Yardbirds have to be depressed about. Their latest record is literally flying up the charts and looks as if it will be their biggest hit to date. They're headlining a giant tour of Britain and they will soon appear at the Paris Olympia.

But the Yardbirds continue to wail "Still, I'm Sad"—and so they are.

Upbeat of the Week
By Eden

Climbing higher and higher on the charts is Petula Clark's new platter "Round Every Corner." Isn't that three-in-a-row for pert Miss Pet?

The Beatles claim she is their favorite female singer, so Mary Wells shows her gratitude with her latest LP "Mary Wells Sings Love Songs to The Beatles."

* * *

Sorry to be the one to say this, but Bobby Rydell's recent waxing of "When I See That Girl of Mine," just isn't up to his usual Number One Warbling. Bobby has recently changed labels, and this reporter, for one, hopes that this won't mean a change in style for the young singer. The new disc has a good sound and Bobby is in fine voice, but the platter still comes off sounding like an Oldie-But-Goodie.

* * *

One of the nicest and most talented young men in town is Jerry Naylor. And Mr. Blue Eyes has written and recorded a song called "I'll Walk Away." It's a beautiful song and both the disc and it's singer deserve a berth right at the top of the charts.

* * *

This reporter wishing Much Mazel to Mr. P.F. Sloan with his latest 45 RPM'er "Halloween Mary." I'm not scared if *you're* not, Flipper!!

* * *

Complimentations going out: To the Walker Brothers for their fab lyricising of Jerry Butler's old disc, "Make It Easy On Yourself" ...

To the Yardbirds for having the courage to chant "Still I'm Sad" Gregorian-style on their new record ...

To Jay and the Americans for "Some Enchanted Evening." Almost *too* beautiful to play on the air, huh Mr. D.J.??!!! ...

To the Silkie (Brian Epstein's new folk group) for a fine performance and a valiant effort with the Lennon-McCartney composition, "You've Got to Hide Your Love Away." Guess John-John just beat you to the punch, kids.

And to Joey Paige—just for being such a luv!!

KRLA ARCHIVES

The Adventures of Robin Boyd...

By Shirley Poston

Editor's Note: If you're a regular reader of The BEAT, you already know about Shirley Poston. She has a weekly column called "For Girls Only," and she also has a problem.

She's nuts! Well, not really nuts. Just kooky. In other words, she has the wildest imagination in captivity!

The story you're about to read proves it. It's the first installment of a series about a very unusual bird named Robin, who will be getting into more scrapes and meeting more famous people than Agent 007 himself!

CHAPTER ONE

Robin Boyd was a 16-year-old bird. And a rare one she was. She wasn't just the Beatles' bird, or the Stones' bird. She was *everone's* bird! Because she was crazy.

Not the talk-to-yourself-then-answer type of crazy (Robin rarely answered). *Star* crazy! Absolutely blithery-wild-nuts over every singer and actor in the universe!

Had any of these stars known Robin was alive, the admiration society would have been mutual. This bird wasn't the flighty sort. She never screamed or fainted. (She did gasp a lot at concerts, but no one is perfect.) And she was a real worker, always busy running fan clubs, circulating petitions, sneaking to the airport in the dead of night to welcome arriving favorites. That kind of thing.

Robin was also a very pretty bird with long red hair. And blue eyes that peeped up at you (if her bangs didn't need cutting).

But, alas and alack, Robin's love was unrequited. In spite of her many plots and plans, and her repeated attempts to convince various security guards that she was the owner of *The Saturday Evening Post* (again, no one is perfect), her efforts were always in vain.

A Lot of Gasping

The closest she had ever come to a real live star was a front row box seat at the Hollywood Bowl Beatle concert. (Boy, did she ever do a lot of gasping *that* night!)

At first, all this one-sidedness didn't bother Robin. She went right on running fan clubs, circulating petitions and sneaking to the airport.

But, one day, she finally put her foot down. (Fortunately, her sister's toe was under it at the time, so the motion served a dual purpose.)

"I've had it," she announced, not even smiling as her sister hopped away, bellowing. "This bird is turning in her feathers!"

At that very moment, her mother entered the room to discuss a certain toe, now turning a rather attractive shade of purple. However, hearing this last remark, Mrs. Boyd instead went to the telephone book and began searching frantically for the number of the men in the white coats.

For the next couple of weeks, Robin's life was dreadful but dull. No fan clubs, petitions and/or airports. Things even progressed to the dreary point where she was thinking of dismantling the Lennon shrine in her room. (Although Robin was not a partial bird, should she ever *have* to make a choice, John's chances were excellent.)

Then it happened...

One day when Robin was dragging wearily home from school, she spied an object glittering atop an ash can. Looking cautiously about, she removed her glasses from her purse and put them on. (Robin was blind as six bats without her specs, but never wore them in public for vanity was among the few flaws in her character.)

After peering more closely at the glittering object, and thinking the matter over at great length (eight seconds), she stole it. Whoops... *rescued* it.

A Tea Pot

When Robin walked into the house moments later, carrying a tea pot, her mother raced for the telephone book.

"I stole it... whoops rescued it," Robin offered. Her mother paged faster.

"It was made in England," she further explained. (Although she was not a partial bird, should she ever *have* to make a choice, England's chances were excellent.)

Robin then placed the tea pot on her dresser and stared at it morosely, longing for the good old days when she would have been getting ready to sneak off to the airport.

But never again! Why should she risk getting pneumonia (not to mention grounded for the next eleven years) for some star who didn't even know she was *alive!*

"There's a place for people who sit around staring at pots," she muttered grimly after much vacant gazing. "Next I'll be thinking there's a magic genie in it."

Then she sighed thankfully. At least it would be a while before she was *that* far gone.

It was exactly twenty-three minutes (well, that's a while, isn't it?) before she leaped for the tea pot and began polishing it with her sweater.

"Mirror, mirror on the wall," she crooned, rubbing with vigor. She stopped. No, no, stupid. That's not what you said to awaken genies. Besides, they lived in lamps, not *pots*.

"*Abra-ca-dabra?*" she tried hopefully and got nowhere.

After uttering a few more phrases including "Open Sesame" and "Shazam" she gave the pot one final rub. "Ratzafratz," she exclaimed impatiently, this being her favorite expression. Well, it's better than *golly-whizzers*.)

Placing the tea pot back on her dresser with a thump, Robin glowered at herself in the mirror. "You're sick," she decided aloud.

"No I'm not," said the reflection of a young man with longish dark hair. The one who was standing directly behind her, his accent crowded with distinct Liverpudlian overtones. "I'm George!"

Robin gasped, which was quite an innovation because she only did that at concerts. She was seeing things! And *hearing* things, too! But she whirled around, expecting the mirage to fade.

But it didn't. George went right on standing there, grinning at her!

So Robin did the only thing that seemed to make any sense in such a moment.

She fainted.

(To Be Continued)

(Could this possibly be the George? And, if not, what George could it possibly be? And why is he standing in the middle of Robin's room, whoever he is? And how on earth did he get there? And what about Robin flying to England next week, without a plane?? We'll never tell. But Chapter Two will, so stay tuned to The BEAT!)

KRLA ARCHIVES

HEADLINERS' HAIR BEAT

After the Fall...

By Robert Esserman and Frank De Sanctis

There are very few changes predicted for this winter as far as new hairstyles, clothing and make-up approaches are concerned. Most of the radical styling patterns have already been set.

The Headliners "Guy Cut" does, however, have a new variation, the nape area still remaining very short but with all hair one length. This eliminates the lacquered look in the back giving a more attractive over-all effect.

Pierced ears are going to be bigger than ever this winter, with big loops and small rope gold loops predominating. Reason behind the earring trend is the wish to add an additional touch of femininity to the more severe short cuts.

Wow! Bad news for the hairdresser. Guess what's coming back again this year... Yes, it's the up-do's with curls... this Fall finding the curls placed on top of the crown rather than the previous style with curls loosely falling down the neckline. Now each curl is individual and distinct requiring hairdressers to consume a large portion of their time creating the individual up-do.

Long straight hair is still holding on strong carrying a large majority of hairstyle preference.

"Frosting Can Look Natural"

Frosting or two-toning long hair has become a very big thing to do. However, up until quite recently most girls who had long hair couldn't frost their hair because it wouldn't fit through the frosting cap.

The Headliners have now devised a new method of frosting that uses tin foil and two hairdressers working on the customer resulting in a beautifully natural looking frosting job. The price ranges from $35-$40.00... insuring no touch-ups necessary for from six to eight months.

"What to Wear to Fit Your Hair"

Headliner's recommend a casual wardrobe of poor boy shirts... bell bottom pants or boss cords as the "in" things to be seen in. Bright color tops in contrast with white bell bottoms can really attract that certain boy's eye.

School dress should include colored sweaters... in deep golds, royal blues and olive greens... with your favorite matching skirts and tennies or flats in either black or white.

"Oops... Here Comes Another Star"

Beverly Washburn had an audition for "The Patty Duke Show" recently and gave us a rush call to dream up something for her "hair-wise." We asked one of our operators — Fred Lytle — to see what he could do with the former 1965 Debutante. (Beverly has previously starred with Bing Crosby, Bob Hope, and Lon Chaney, as well as having appeared on Wagon Train, Four Star Playhouse, The Loretta Young Show and many others.)

Here is the styling selected by Fred for Beverly's audition hair-do. Possibly you could see yourself in this particular hair-do. This coif is one that could be worn for evening or casual wear.

HERE IS THE NEW LESLIE GORE. Hair fashionably done in the latest Guy Cut, the pretty hitmaker has forsaken the long locks that identified her previously. Will the new Leslie sing any better with shorter tresses?

HERE WE SEE ROBERT working on one of the new up-do styles with the curls which make girls look pretty and hairdressers work hard.

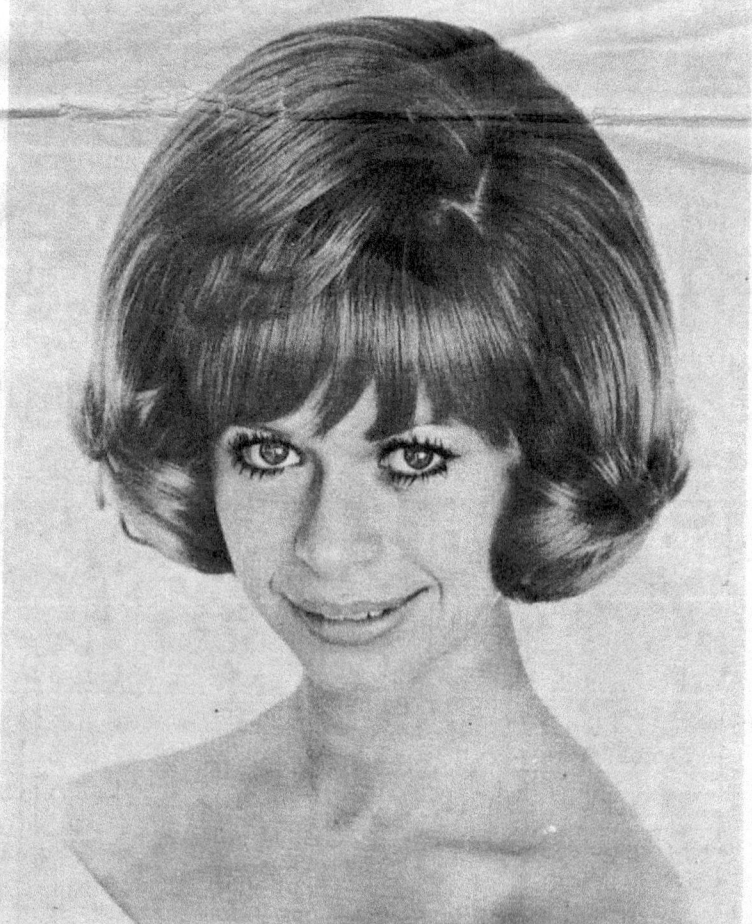

BEVERLY WASHBURN SHOWS US HER NEW HAIR STYLE. Being an actress means that Beverly's hair must always look not only good but also "in" hair-wise. So, Beverly regularly rushes into the Headliners to see if they can dream up a hair style which is just right for her — and she hasn't been disappointed yet.

KRLA ARCHIVES

KRLA Tunedex

EMPEROR HUDSON

CHARLIE O'DONNELL

CASEY KASEM

JOHNNY HAYES

BOB EUBANKS

DAVE HULL

DICK BIONDI

BILL SLATER

KRLA BEAT
6290 Sunset, No. 504
Hollywood, Cal. 90028

This Week	Last Week	Title	Artist
1	2	GET OFF OF MY CLOUD	The Rolling Stones
2	1	YESTERDAY/ACT NATURALLY	The Beatles
3	3	A LOVER'S CONCERTO	The Toys
4	5	YOU'RE THE ONE	The Vogues
5	13	ONE-TWO-THREE	Len Barry
6	7	MAKE ME YOUR BABY	Barbara Lewis
7	4	KEEP ON DANCING	The Gentrys
8	22	TURN, TURN, TURN	The Byrds
9	9	EVERYBODY LOVES A CLOWN	Gary Lewis & The Playboys
10	8	HANG ON SLOOPY	The McCoys
11	6	HELP!/I'M DOWN	The Beatles
12	23	TASTE OF HONEY/3rd MAN THEME	Herb Alpert—Tijuana Brass
13	25	RESCUE ME	Fontella Bass
14	12	LIAR, LIAR	The Castaways
15	14	I LIVE FOR THE SUN	The Sunrays
16	11	JUST A LITTLE BIT BETTER	Herman's Hermits
17	15	BUT YOU'RE MINE	Sonny & Cher
18	30	MAKE IT EASY ON YOURSELF	The Walker Brothers
19	26	I KNEW YOU WHEN	Billy Joe Royal
20	17	RESPECT	Otis Redding
21	24	ROUND EVERY CORNER	Petula Clark
22	41	I HEAR A SYMPHONY	The Supremes
23	29	WHERE DO YOU GO	Cher
24	31	MY GIRL HAS GONE	The Temptations
25	—	I'M A MAN	The Yardbirds
26	32	STEPPIN' OUT	Paul Revere & The Raiders
27	—	MYSTIC EYES	Them
28	35	MY HEART SINGS	Mel Carter
29	—	AIN'T THAT PECULIAR	Marvin Gaye
30	38	STILL I'M SAD	The Yardbirds
31	35	LET'S HANG ON	The Four Seasons
32	34	PIED PIPER	The Changing Times
33	36	I LOVE HOW YOU LOVE ME	Nino Tempo & April Stevens
34	—	I MISS YOU SO	Little Anthony & The Imperials
35	—	MY BABY	The Temptations
36	—	DON'T TALK TO STRANGERS	The Beau Brummels
37	—	I GO CRAZY	Bocky & The Visions
38	—	MY TOWN, MY GUY AND ME	Lesley Gore
39	40	UPON A PAINTED OCEAN	Barry McGuire
40	39	YOU'VE GOT TO HIDE YOUR LOVE AWAY	The Silkie

KRLA ARCHIVES

KRLA *Edition* BEAT

Volume 1, Number 36 LOS ANGELES, CALIFORNIA 15 Cents November 20, 1965

It's As Easy As 1-2-3 For Len Barry – p. 6

Pick the Best Records of 1965 - p. 15

KRLA BEAT

Los Angeles, California — November 20, 1965

Why Shindig Died— Stars Give Views

Even before Shindig breathes its final gasp, entertainers and viewers alike are debating the cause of its death.

Among the scores of entertainers contacted by The BEAT this week, almost all seem to regard Shindig's cancellation with genuine concern and regret. But each has a different theory as to what caused it.

Even the Beatles, who certainly don't need the exposure, seem troubled by the failure (some call it "destruction") of what had previously been America's most successful pop music television show.

George Harrison—speaking for all the Beatles—told The BEAT in London: "We hope they replace it with another pop show."

George declined to place the blame on any *one* particular thing or individual—but other performers did not hesitate at all.

Bosses' Fault?

Jim McGuinn of the Byrds believes that the blame rests entirely with the television executives. "We're all very sad about Shindig because it was a show that really tried to do things the right way.

"It's just proof of the wretchedness which dominates American television and allows people who have no discernment to remove good programs from the air," Jim told us.

Leon Mirrell, executive producer of Shindig, disagrees slightly with Jim. "Evidently, Shindig twice a week, did not draw a strong enough rating to survive the battle of television. The network officials were only doing their job," Mirrell explained.

Too Much Pop

Other performers blame the large amount of pop shows which quickly followed in Shindig's footsteps, causing our TV screens to become literally saturated with rock 'n' roll shows.

Bobby Hatfield, who with his Righteous Brother, Bill Medley, was once a semi-regular on Shindig, agrees with this viewpoint.

"There are too many rock 'n' roll shows and the competition was just too much," Bobby commented.

Agreeing with Bobby is Roy Head: "I think it's terrible that

(Turn to Page 7)

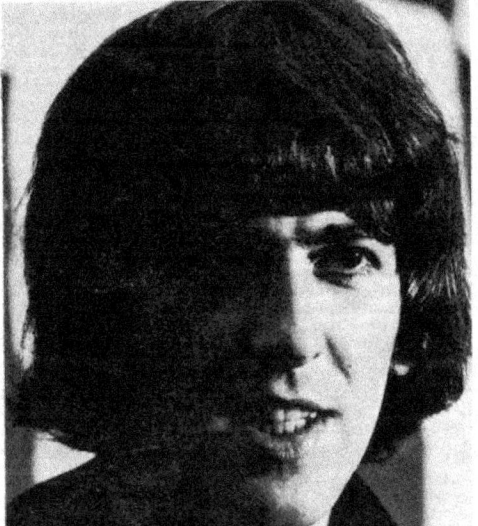

GEORGE — "We hope they replace Shindig with another pop show."

JIM McGUINN — "It's just proof."

Beatles Skip Queen's Show

By Louise Criscione

The Beatles have finally done it—said no to royalty!

The four were invited to appear before the Queen and Duke of Edinburgh at the Royal Variety Show but after discussing it with Brian Epstein the Beatles turned thumbs down on the show with Paul declaring it "not our audience."

Paul went on to say that the Beatles *will* do something for charity (which is where the proceeds from the show go): "We're making our contribution with a show of our own soon."

The Beatles have appeared on the Royal Variety Show before and at that time they were only too pleased and honored to accept. So, why the big change of heart now?

Apparently, the Beatles are a bit afraid and uncertain of their present popularity status in England. Now, don't you all start writing nasty letters to The BEAT telling us how absolutely horrible we are for saying that just *perhaps* the Beatles' British popularity is on the decline. Read on and see what Paul had to say and then make up your own mind.

"If we went on and those people didn't like us everyone would say 'ha ha, the Beatles failed, they're on the slide.'"

Those were Pauls' exact words when announcing to the press the Beatles' decision not to accept the Royal invitation.

When the Beatles made public their decision the Dave Clark Five were quickly chosen to take place. The DC5 probably didn't enjoy being second choice but for such an honor (and it really is an honor) they just as quickly hid their pride and accepted.

So, the Royal Variety Show will go on without the Beatles but with an assured packed house anyway. After all, the Queen will be there.

1ST ROUND VOTING TO END THIS WEEK IN POP MUSIC POLL

We're down to the final ballot in The BEAT's first annual Pop Music Awards Poll.

The subject this week is records —the best vocals and instrumentals of 1965, both singles and albums. You'll find this week's ballot on page 15. Please fill it out and mail it as quickly as possible.

Next week, if the tabulations are completed in time, we will run the final ballot—a list of the finalists in each category. From that ballot you will elect your favorites for the first International Pop Music Awards.

Also next week, The BEAT will announce the details as to when and where the awards will be presented.

CHANGED THEIR MINDS

50-Million Frenchmen Not Wrong—Beatles Prove It!

Vive la France!

If you're wondering what that burst of enthusiasm is all about, here's what.

Several BEATS ago, we published an article lamenting the fact that although John, Paul, George and Ringo were hitting the international charts with every new release, they had yet to crack the almost impregnable record market in France.

We went on to chide this country-sans-Beatlemania by saying their lack of interest perhaps proved that fifty million Frenchmen could be wrong after all.

Well, if this was the case, they've changed back to being right. The Beatles have now scored not one but two Left Bank blockbusters. "Yesterday" holds down the number 7 slot on the French charts, with "Help" following on its heels at number 8.

International Charts

Elsewhere in the world, the roar of Beatlemania continues. Last week, "Help" was 3 in Argentina, 6 in Australia, 5 in Belgium, 3 in Holland, 5 in Malaysia, 2 in Norway and 10 in South Africa.

Other Beatle discs on the international charts at the moment are "Yesterday (1 in Hong Kong) and "The Night Before" (2 in Hong Kong and 6 in Malaysia).

As fifty million Frenchmen are putting it (and it's about time), Vive le Beatles!

BARRY McGUIRE, just back from a successful cultural and promotional visit to the British Empire, reacts with typical reserve upon learning that he has received three write-in votes for the Atlanta Rotary Club's monthly Americanism award.

Inside the BEAT

Elvis Hates Wigs	3
Adventures of Robin Boyd	5
Fortune Smiles on Len Barry	6
For Girls Only	7
Beatles Find New Sound	8
Royalty Calls Sonny & Cher	11
Paul Buys Lovenest	13
Herman Meets Mr. Ed	14
Pop Music Poll	15
Movies—"Redline 7,000"	16

The BEAT is published weekly for KRLA listeners by BEAT Publications, Inc., 6290 Sunset Blvd., Suite 504, Hollywood, California 90028. U.S. bureaus in Hollywood, San Francisco, New York, Chicago and Nashville; overseas correspondents in London, Liverpool and Manchester, England. Sale price, 15 cents. Subscription price: U.S. and possessions, $3 per year; Canada and foreign rates, $9 per year. Application to mail at second-class postage rates is pending at Los Angeles, California.

Johnny Tillotson Has No Need for Watches

By Louise Criscione

He strolled into the office the other day looking very much like he had been this route a thousand times before. And so he had. He's Johnny Tillotson and he's been in show business since he was very young—about nine years old to be exact.

"I was the smallest kid in my class at nine. I was 47 pounds, I think," Johnny recalled.

So, while the other little boys were playing football Johnny was singing. He wasn't so certain of himself that he didn't need a little shove to get into the business. And he got it in the person of his grandmother.

Grandma's Shove

"My grandmother suggested to me that since I liked to sing, I ought to go down to the juvenile show they had on the radio at the time and sing for them," Johnny said.

"I did, and I realized that I really enjoyed singing. That's very important to me. I'm in a business now where I never look at my watch—I really enjoy it."

Most performers, whether they admit it or not, go into the business for money, Johnny did and he's honest about it: "I wanted to make some money. My late father was a gas station attendant in a station which he owned but he made very little money.

"I would listen to Hank Williams sing on the weekends and think, 'If I could just make people happy like that it would be great.' Then once I read in a book that Hank Williams made close to a quarter of a million dollars in one year and I told my father about it. He said that Hank Williams was just a hillbilly and that I should forget it."

Dual Motives

But Johnny didn't forget it. He had a dual reason for going into show business—he enjoyed it and there was plenty of money to be had in a singing career. So he plowed ahead.

It was rather slow going for awhile. Johnny, determined to learn all about music, enrolled in a music class at school. "Everyone else was reading music, etc. but I was too ashamed to tell the teacher that I just didn't understand. But my practical work was good and I sang in the choir so she passed me anyway!"

And Now Movies

Johnny has now turned to the movies, a facet of the entertainment industry which many singers eventually find themselves involved in.

"I recently did a movie that was a lot of fun, 'The Fat Spy,' in which I played a character named Dodo. In the picture I fall in love with a mermaid by the name of Naiomi," Johnny enthused. Sounds lovely, Johnny.

Johnny's records have been anything but protest songs, so I wondered how he felt about this wave of protest which is currently pounding our musical shores.

"I think when it's good—it's good. When it's written just to be protesty—it's a drag. I like it when it's clever but I hate it when everyone give titles to people and songs in the business, like 'folk-rock,' etc." Johnny answered.

Johnny once had an amusing experience with the king of folk, Bob Dylan. "I tried to sell Bob Dylan some bookshelves once. I was riding in a cab and I saw him get out of a car and walk into a furniture store.

"So, I stopped the cab and went in and told him who I was and that I had recorded one of his songs. I talked to him for a while and he seemed like a very warm individual—but he didn't want to buy the bookshelves!"

Oh, well you can't win 'em all, Johnny. And anyway I should think you make enough money from records and personal appearances. You don't really need to peddle bookshelves to Bob Dylan!

...JOHNNY TILLOTSON

Elvis Hates Wigs; Has Film Fright

Girls, the King doesn't like wigs!

Elvis has revealed that he hates wigs. But don't worry, girls, it's not your wigs that he hates, but his.

He not only hates to have to wear a wig, but when he does he gets a terrible case of stage fright.

"I love what I'm doing," he says, "except in 'Kissing Cousins' when they gave me a dual role and I had to wear a blond wig."

"When I put on the wig I looked so stupid in it I didn't dare come out on stage. I stayed in my dressing room for almost two hours, sulking. I was embarrassed. How I hated that wig."

The King also revealed that he really works himself into a state when he's working on a movie.

"I'm always nervous and worried about a new picture. By the time I've wrapped up a picture, I've lost as much as 15 pounds."

Strange that Elvis should ever worry. Every one of his movies has been a huge financial success and well-received by the public.

Donovan's Wish

Singing stars sometimes lead rather hectic lives with little or no order and their goals in life may be rather vague but at least one British star has a very definite rule to his life.

Donovan says his golden rule is "to live until I die and fill in the space in between."

Donovan Wearing Sonny and Cher Clothing Styles

Sonny and Cher have a new fan but for a different reason.

Donovan now has a new shirt made by Sonny and Cher's seamstresses, the two California girls who design all the outfits worn by the duo.

Donovan's shirt is bloused with full sleeves similar to those worn by P.J. Proby and is in a startling brilliant floral design.

The quiet British singer seems to be going for wilder clothes lately. He's also added to his wardrobe a white shirt with half-inch orange polka dots on it and some black bell bottom trousers which he wears with gaucho type boots.

Sandie Can't Be Herself

What effect does stardom have on a beautiful, bare-foot young girl?

Nothing, says Sandie Shaw, "Except that I just feel 50 instead of 18.

"Well, sometimes I do anyway. But really the only difference is that I have to be more careful who I say 'drop dead' to.

"That's about the only thing I don't like—having to be nice to people I can't stand. Catty people—like the old pros who complain I've only been in the business five minutes. I get that all the time. But people won't take cheek or sauce from you when you're only 18—and a girl as well," she added.

Last Week For Dodd?

Well, suppose by now you've guessed that Ken Dodd is still crying and his "Tears" is topping the British charts for the *sixth* straight week in a row!

But this may very well be Dodd's last week as the chart-topper. The Rolling Stones released their "Get Off My Cloud" on a Friday and the following Tuesday when our survey was compiled, they had succeeded in climbing all the way up to number three! Not bad for only three days of record sales.

British Top 10

1.	TEARS	Ken Dodd
2.	YESTERDAY MAN	Chris Andrews
3.	GET OFF MY CLOUD	Rolling Stones
4.	GOOD NEWS WEEK	Hedgehoppers
5.	ALMOST THERE	Andy Williams
6.	HERE IT COMES AGAIN	The Fortunes
7.	YESTERDAY	Matt Monro
8.	IF YOU GOTTA GO, GO NOW	Manfred Mann
9.	EVE OF DESTRUCTION	Barry McGuire
10.	HANG ON SLOOPY	The McCoys

If the Stones topple Dodd it will be about the most ironic situation ever. For, you see, just six weeks ago it was Dodd who knocked the Stones and their "Satisfaction" from that number one spot. And it looks very much like the Stones will be repaying Dodd next week. Which is only fair, after all.

Another record which zoomed from practically nowhere into the top ten this week is the Matt Monro version of Paul McCartney's "Yesterday."

Yet another high debuter this week and it belongs to the Animals. Their "It's My Life" came in at number 14. The Animals seem to enjoy much more popularity in Britain than they do here in America. So far, each of their records have reached the echelons of the British charts and apparently "It's My Life" will prove no exception.

Right behind the Animals flys Bob Dylan with his "Positively 4th Street." Bob's "Like A Rolling Stone" dropped off the chart this week but "4th Street" came in at number 18 to take it's place.

November 20, 1965 THE BEAT Page 4

The Shindigger

Howdy Hi, Shindiggers. You'd better savor that greeting, kids, 'cause it's gonna be one of our last "Howdy Hi's." Guess you've heard the news by now—Shindig has been cancelled and within a short period of time, it will be no more.

After spending the entire day at the show's rehearsals, stayed on through the taping last night. It has been an unusually wild and wonderful show, and yet there is still a sadness about the whole thing. We've all had a lot of fun together here at Shindig and it's awfully hard to think of saying good-bye.

But, while we are still together, let's be happy. And besides—George Patterson has dropped by to tell us a rather amusing tale, so everybody gather 'round and listen.

No More "Hangover"

"I finally got a new king-size bed—it's seven feet long—because I'm six-foot-two and I always find my feet hanging over the regular beds.

"But after all this time, when they finally got the bed up to the new house we just bought—it wouldn't fit!! The only way we can get it inside is to take the windows off the second story bedroom, so I'm gonna have to take it back!"

Gee George—that really is a shame! Well, there's always the nice, long floor!!

Turtle Tour

Hey everybody—here comes Howard Kaylan of the Turtles. Hi Howard—I hear you're all going on tour soon.

"Yes, we leave Nov. 2 and we'll be touring the East and the Mid-West, and then we'll wind up in New York some time around Christmas. I'm very excited about my first White Christmas too! Then after we finish this tour, we're going to be appearing at the Fremont Hotel in Las Vegas."

Well, it looks as though you're going to have a busy schedule ahead of you.

I've got an idea, Shindiggers—let's take a walk around "Shindig" since it may be about the last chance we'll have to do so.

Onstage right now Kirby is doing one of his funny little dances, and Roy Head is rehearsing his new record, "Apple of My Eye," for the show.

Rick Nelson

If you will look to your left, you will see Rick Nelson sitting in the front row in the audience section with his guitar and his manager. Seems like Ricky's deep in conversation about something.

And here's a surprise for you—right down in front next to the stage, the pretty red-headed girl with the little blond baby boy is Karen Medley; yep—she's Bill "Righteous" Medley's wife, and the baby is his brand new son.

The Shindig dancers are all in the far right-hand side of the stage going over some of the dance routines which they will use on this evening's show. The are probably some of the hardest working people in town.

Donna Loren has just walked out on stage in one of the beautiful dresses which she will wear on tonight's show. The song she is going to rehearse now is "Where Have All The Flowers Gone," and she really does it proud.

Dinner Break

The day is growing late now and the cast and crew of Shindig are about to take their dinner break—one of the last dinner breaks they will ever take on Shindig—and then they will come back and begin the taping of tonight's show.

We'll be back here in our usual spot next week for another visit to Shindig. It will be our last visit so we will probably have a lot of old friends stopping by to chat for a few minutes. Hope you will stop by too, and in the meantime—don't forget to tune in this week when the guest stars on "Shindig" will include Rick Nelson, Roy Head, the Turtles, the Gentry's, the Righteous Brothers, Barbara Lewis, David Jones, Donna Loren, and all the Shindig regulars.

Till then, Shindiggers—maintain your soul, and remember: no matter what *anybody* says—ROCK ON!!!

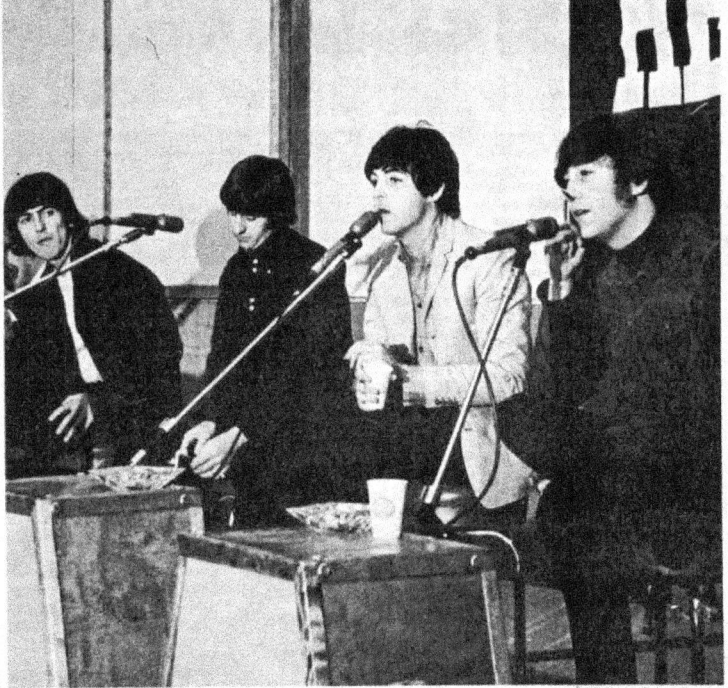

... THE BEATLES
BEAT Photo: Robert Young

... HOWARD KAYLAN

... DONNA LOREN

Yeah, Well Beatles... Chance Of A Lifetime

By Tammy Hitchcock

This week we really scored and managed to cram all four of the Beatles onto the Yeah, Well Hot Seat.

You know, everytime one of the Beatles has a birthday the post office must be notified so that they can assign extra men to the Beatle beat.

Yeah, well I have that same problem. Everytime I get a letter they have to put an extra man on my beat. Not because I get so many letters but because I get so *few* they've taken *my* mailman away!

The Young Paul

Paul's father was recently reminiscing about his son's childhood. One thing about the young Paul which particularly stands out in his mind was Paul's amazing ability to do two things at the same time and do them both well.

Yeah, well Paul has certainly progressed a lot. Now he can do *three* things at once. He can sing, play the guitar and still manage to keep both eyes glued to those girls!

Of course, everyone knows that the Summit Meeting took place between Elvis and the Beatles when the Beatles visited L.A. last August. They all sat around and talked and played guitars and all that. Yeah, well I'm hurt. How come you guys didn't invite me?

The Boss and I

Actually, they *did* invite me. Well, the boss and I that is. I blush everytime I think of it. Are you ready for this? All of the Beatles were waiting for us in their living room. It was like a chance of a lifetime and the boss and I blew it! We got *lost* on the way over!

You should have seen us. We were two hours late when we finally found the right street. So the boss really let her Stingray go and by the time we reached the Beatles' place we had the police sirens chasing us, the Beatle fans chasing us—and J. P. G. & R were *gone!* They had left without us. Yeah, well.

When a reporter asked John if the Beatles were primarily entertainers or musicians, Lennon quipped: "We're money makers first—then we're entertainers."

Yeah, well I'll say you're money makers and MBE'ers too. Some people just have to hog it all!

Blow Their Cool

Lots of performers really blow their cool when a fan comes up to them in a restaurant and asks them for their autograph right when they've got their mouth full of spaghetti. But not George.

"I sign the autograph and thank them profusely for coming over and offer them a piece of my chop."

Yeah, well then I just want to know one thing, George, how come you offered me your napkin?

A reporter asked Ringo if he thought there would be another world war soon and he grinned: "I hope not. Not just after we've got our money through the taxes."

Yeah, well with all the money you guys have it probably takes two years to get it through the taxes! You had better spend it fast before the Queen gets it. And if you have any trouble figuring out just how to spend it—there's always me!

Tams Are Tops In Headwear

What's at the top of the list of today's above-the-eyebrow fashions? Tams are what am (if you'll pardon the most ungrammatical sentence in the history of the continental United States.)

Ringo may or may not have prompted the teen world's sudden fascination for tam-type head-gear by wearing same in the recording-on-the-moor scene from "Help." But whatever started the rush to the knit-wit section of your favorite department store, it is definitely on.

At this stage of the game, plaids seem to be taking a front seat to the solid color variety. One of the most popular tams is the blue-and-green "Black Watch," imported from England and decorated with a crested sable pin.

Do-it-yourself knit-wits will be happy to hear that tams are the world's easiest items to knit (with the possible exception of Barbie Doll blankets.)

All you need is yarn, needles, patience, a few choice locks snipped from your grandfather's favorite shaving brush, and you'll soon be shantering about in your very own tam creation.

The Adventures of Robin Boyd...

By Shirley Poston

CHAPTER TWO

Robin Boyd yawned, slowly awakening, smiling to herself. Wow! What a dream *she'd* had! Before going to bed, she'd rubbed that old English tea pot she'd stolen . . . whoops . . . rescued from someone's ash can, and that had *really* started her off. Next thing she knew, she was talking to a handsome young Britisher named George!

Robin's smile turned to a chortle as she snuggled closer into her pillow, but the chortle froze solid. Her pillow wasn't there! Come to think of it, neither was her bed!

She stretched out a frantic hand and let out a gasp (something she usually saved up for rock and roll concerts). All she could feel for miles was *rug*!

Good grief, she thought. Rubbing tea pots was bad enough. Sleeping on the floor was going *too* far!

This is what I get for running all those fan clubs and being everybody's bird, she contemplated sadly. A nervous breakdown.

Suddenly, she stopped *thinking* she was having a nervous breakdown and *had* one. Her hand, still wandering restlessly about on the carpet, ran smack into a shoe.

"It's only you, George?" she bellowed, leaping to her feet. "What am I saying?" Then she lurched dizzily against the mirage. George's feet might be alive and kicking, but her's had passed away.

"I've gone off my head," she murmured, allowing the mirage to guide her to the chair in front of her dressing table.

"You've only fainted," he explained, settling angularly into a chair across the room. "You'll be all right in a moment."

Robin curled her lip in an unladylike but effective manner. "Sure I will," she snapped, her courage returning. "In a moment I'll be so far gone I won't even *mind* talking to people who aren't really there." She tossed her long red hair angrily.

"You look just like George Harrison!" she quaked. And he did! Although he was several feet away and she was blind as six bats without her glasses, he *did* look like the famous Beatle! *"Are you George Harrison?"* she shrieked quietly.

George shook his head. "No, I'm just George. I just make people's wishes come true."

Robin brightened. Going crazy was fun!!

"How did you get to be a genie?" she inquired, hoping he wasn't going around thinking she was disappointed about him not being George Harrison. (Heaven only knew what happened to people who offended people who weren't really there.)

"All that's a secret. If I told you, I'd lose me magic powers."

Robin got to her feet and walked over to get a closer look at him (she wasn't *about* to put on her glasses in front of a total stranger, even if he *wasn't* really there—she might have lost her marbles, but she still had her price.) No, he wasn't George Harrison, she decided. But he would certainly do nicely.

One Wish

"I'm here to grant a wish for *you*," George said, smiling up at her.

Robin sat back down in her chair, missing it by about two feet.

"What did you say?" she breathed, getting up from the floor (gracefully, she hoped). (That floor and her were getting to know each other better all the time. If this kept up, they might one day become engaged.)

"I said," George answered rather dramatically (no one is perfect), "your wish is my command. One to a customer," he added.

she decided. What the heck? Tomorrow her mother would start paging through that phone book again, looking for the number of a nearby doctor, only this time she'd *find* one. This was her last night of freedom, so she might as well enjoy it.

"George," she said at last. "I do have a wish. It's incredibly silly, but it has to do with my being a bird these past two years." (She fully expected George to take his turn on the carpet at that last sentence.)

Loyal Bird

But George didn't pass out cold. He nodded. "And a very loyal bird at that. That's why I'm here to reward you!"

Robin tingled, wondering why people weren't standing in *line* to go off their rockers. "Really and truly?"

"Both. Please continue."

"Well, it's a crazy idea, but now that *I* am crazy, it sounds like even *more* fun! I used to wish I were a real bird, with feathers and stuff, so I could fly to England and everywhere and see all my faves, and perch in dark corners and find out what's happening . . . you know, all that . . ." Robin's voice came to a standstill. George wasn't even laughing. He was just sitting there.

"It's *too* crazy, isn't it," she finished, crestfallen.

George looked away. "Nothing sounds *too* crazy to someone who lives in a *tea pot*."

Robin started to say something comforting, but the words just wouldn't come. For some incredible reason, they were lost in the sudden and overwhelming desire for a midnight snack.

A nice big bowl of birdseed.

(To Be Continued Next Week)

MORE ADVENTURES OF THE EMPEROR by Mike McGuckin!

...THIS WEEK FEATURING... CAVENDISH

THIS WEEK WE FIND CAVENDISH SEARCHING HIS REFRIGERATOR FOR A "MIDNIGHT SNACK"...

LET'S SEE...DO I HAVE EVERYTHING...PICKLES...FISH...ICE CREAM (TUTTI FRUTTI)...AVACADOS...MY CHOCOLATE COVERED CELERY...AND WHAT'S THIS?...

A CAN OF BEANS? I DON'T NEED THAT...

AND SOON... UM-M-M YUM-YUM SLURP!

IN A FEW MINUTES... NOW THAT'S WHAT I CALL A (URP?) SANDWICH!

...I THINK I'LL GET A LITTLE SHUT-EYE. YAWN

ZZZZZ

BUT...WHAT IS THIS??

CAVENDISH SHOULDN'T HAVE HAD THAT "MIDNIGHT SNACK"—IT LOOKS LIKE HE'S GOING TO HAVE A BAD DREAM... ITS A BEAN STALK! THOSE BEANS I THREW OUT MUST HAVE BEEN MAGIC!

I'LL JUST CLIMB UP AND SEE WHAT'S AT THE TOP!

(GULP) I'M GETTING KIND OF HIGH...EVEN THAT BIRD HAS A NOSE BLEED!

GEE...I WONDER WHERE I AM NOW

AND SUDDENLY... FEE·FIE·FOE·FUM YIPE

DON'T MISS NEXT WEEK'S EPISODE WHEN CAVENDISH MEETS THE FEARSOME GIANT!

KRLA ARCHIVES

WRITER TURNS SINGER
Fortune Smiles On Len Barry

"It's as easy as one, two, three"... Len Barry is heading straight for Hitsville.

His face is familiar, 'cause you've seen him as lead singer for the Dovells; his sound is great, and his record is headed toward the top; his future is the brightest, 'cause he's got a lot of talent. With that as an introduction, then, let's take a look at dynamic Len Barry: past, present, and future.

Past: He was born June 12, 1943 in Philadelphia, Pa., where he was graduated from high school and went on to attend one year at Temple University on an athletic scholarship.

Good Faker
His formal musical training has consisted of "the Musical College of Hard Knocks out here on the road," although Len claims that "I *fake* very well! I fake drums, guitar, sax, a little bit of bass, and some mouth organ." That's some kinda faking, Mr. Barry!

Len has been writing music for about three or four years now, and says, "I think that writing is much tougher than performing, because sometimes you don't get the self-gratification out of it — because you don't get the same acclaim as the artist that recorded your song, even if it is a hit. It's a lot tougher to be successful as a writer than an artist."

Sound Background
In the *present,* Len has a great sound going for him, but it isn't something which was simply delivered to him for Christmas; he has been developing it for quite some time:

"As far as a distinctive, or an individual sound goes — I don't know if I have one yet, but I hope to acquire one. Now, I think it's more or less of an R 'n' B sound with Negro overtones that I've gotten from performing for four or five years on the road with mostly Negro tours."

Len has a great deal of interest in everything that is going on about him in the present, and he has some very definite ideas about such present people as one Mr. Bob Dylan:

"Real Genius"
"I think that as a writer he is brilliant; I think he has a genius — I mean actual, flagrant genius that you can touch. As far as these protest records are concerned — predominantly the Barry McGuire record and the Dylan things — I think that in reality, they are speaking the truth and these problems *do* exist and they're not saying anything against the grain of what's actually happening. But I don't personally believe that it should be said 20 times a day on the radio."

Len is a man of firm conviction, and he eagerly told *The BEAT* of his own personal favorites in the field of entertainment:

Favorites
"My personal favorites — I have very few, but I'm firm on them — include Sammy Davis Jr. I think he's great, and I enjoy him; he's an entertainer's entertainer. But I think if it hadn't been God's will, in a few years Sam Cooke would have been the greatest entertainer that ever lived. I also enjoy the Miracles, Mary Wells — the entire Motown label."

What does the *future* hold for Mr. Barry? Len is very thoughtful and concerned about this, and he shared some of his ideas with *BEAT* readers:

"Every man that *is* a man, has personal ambitions; and I'm glad to say that I'm no different. I'm very common where that's concerened. I love people and they don't frighten me. When I was a little boy, my mother once told me — 'Don't be afraid of people because they're only here to help you; and if you give them a chance they will.' — and I've found this to be true.

Future
I would like to be an established entertainer and while I'm having my hit records, the world is very, very rosy — but I know that someday it's gonna be a lot tougher to get them, probably, and I'd like to establish myself as an act. I'd just like to help people forget their troubles for a couple of hours, and establish myself in that way."

For that all-important *future,* there is an album — already released — appropriately entitled, "One, Two, Three," and possibly Len's next single will come from this LP.

Len Barry is a talented, outgoing, sensitive young man who is searching for his star, and his philosophy-of-the-road is one well-worth repeating:

Return Favors
"I don't want to sound like a ham or anything, but everybody needs help in this world in order to make it, and I've gotten *more* than my share of help — not once, but *twice!* And it's very difficult to explain just how thankful and how grateful I am because I'm not really prepared to do anything else in life; and it's a very wonderful thing when you can make a living doing what you like to do. I would just like to thank the people — instead of protesting *against* them — Thank you very much for giving me a chance to live a good life!"

The pleasure is all ours, Len!

Gold Rush On Again

The gold rush is on again and the Beatles and Beach Boys are coming out ahead.

Both groups record for Capitol and both just received more gold records for sales over a million.

The Beach Boys just received their third and fourth straight gold disks for albums "Beach Boys Today" and "Summer Days and Summer Nights."

The Beatles added another one to their collection with the million sales of "Eight Days a Week."

... LEN BARRY

Liverpuddles
By Rob McGrae
Manager, The Cavern

American recording artist Ben E. King recently appeared at the "home" of the Beatles — The Cavern Club.

Interest in his appearance had been building up as his scheduled appearance drew near, but no one expected the scenes that we witnessed the night he played.

The Cavern is notorious as the place where the audience doesn't scream at any star, no matter how big he is. However, this night proved to be the exception.

A huge crowd was already forming at the club when Ben arrived. Some of the girls recognized him as he entered and it took six men to get him out of the midst of the girls and into the club.

Ben Impressed
Ben was very impressed with the Cavern when he first saw it and was enthusiastically looking forward to performing on the stage. After introductions between Ben, Ray McFall (owner of the Cavern), Bob Wooler (the discoverer of the Beatles) and myself, we decided to show Ben around Liverpool.

We left by a side door to avoid his fans and took him to see the Liverpool sights. By the time we returned the club was filled with expectant fans.

Taken Off Stage
The girls went mad when he got on stage and no one could hear what he was singing. The girls almost succeeded in breaking through the cordon of men protecting the stage and Ben had to be taken off the stage after only one number. The audience was warned that they would have to calm down or he would not come back.

After ten minutes he came back on stage and was able to complete four numbers before he had to be taken off again.

Ben was visibly overcome by the reception and asked if he could go on again after the audience was warned once more to calm down. He was finally able to do 35 minutes on stage including his hit songs "Amor," "Spanish Harlem" and "Ecstasy." He rounded off the chaotic show with a terrific version of "Twist and Shout."

Ben told me after the show that it had been the best reception he had received outside of America and that he would always remember his performance at the Cavern.

Visited Another Club
We then went to another club in town called the Blue Angel where a group called the Delmonts were performing. The Delmonts asked Ben and his guitarist, Jimmy Brown, if they would like to perform a number and they gladly agreed. The night turned into one of the best jam sessions ever seen in Liverpool.

Ben summed up his feelings at the end of the evening by saying that he would never forget his visit to Liverpool and intended to come back as soon as possible. I know that everyone here hopes that he does come back soon.

Another Record
And yet another record was set by a Liverpool group recently when the Merseybeats appeared at the Cavern to try to set a world record for playing beat music. They performed a record 9½ straight hours of beat music before their drummer John Banks collapsed. They had hoped to play for 12 hours solid.

Even more impressive was the fact that they had just appeared on another show and had motored through thick fog to arrive at the Cavern at 5 a.m., when they immediately went on stage. The boys went on for the first 3½ hours without even having to repeat a song and it was a first class show right up to the end.

Well, I'll be seeing you in this column next week so don't forget to be around.

KRLA ARCHIVES

Disc Stars Give Views On Collapse of Shindig

(Continued from Page 2)

the other shows have overdone it to the point that Shindig is going off. After all, they started it all."

Good Cause

Still others believe that when Jack Good left the show it simply died a natural death.

"It was at its peak when Jack Good was producing it and since he left it seemed to lose its old magic," answered Chad Stuart when *The BEAT* questioned him.

We wondered what Dick Clark as producer of two pop shows (American Bandstand and Where The Action Is) thought of Shindig going off the air.

"They buried it when they made it into an hour show. The able producer, Jack Good, left when he saw the big hole in the ship. Shindig's format was worn out too fast. They stretched it too far and they've killed it," Dick said.

A Trend?

Did the fact that Shindig was going off the air because of low ratings indicate to Dick a possible trend *away* from pop shows?

"No, our shows are pretty healthy. Of course, it could happen to anybody. What *does* worry me is that in a last-ditch effort they're copying everyone.

"You know, they're even going to Hawaii to tape shows. Around here we call it 'Where The Shindig Is,'" laughed Dick.

Some haven't decided just where the blame belongs. They only know that Shindig should not be taken off the air.

'Crying Shame'

Howard Kalan, lead singer for the Turltes, says: "I think it's a crying shame. Shindig was one of the most well-produced and well-run programs for popular talent."

But *is* Shindig's removal a possible trend? Will the other pop shows follow it off as quickly as they trailed it on?

Joey Paige thinks so: "I think it's the beginning of the end. So many people are going to take advantage of its going off the air to knock rock 'n' roll."

Thus, the disagreements and uncertainties remain, even as Shindig passes. And also the regrets. May it rest in peace.

BOBBY HATFIELD — "Too Many"

ROY HEAD — "Overdone It"

Person to Person

To Pam and George:
Isn't little Zak a doll! Sorry you had to miss the party. It was a blast!
— Paul & Kathy

To BEAT Readers:
I am a devoted Beatle Fan who wants Beatle Pen Pals. My girl friend and I thought of a "Pen Pal Beatles Fan Club". For information write to Claire Misaki, 1453 70th Avenue, Oakland, Calif. You must be at least 13 years old and be a devoted Beatle fan. You'll have lots of fun.
— Claire Misaki

To Randy (of the fab Challengers):
How are your watermelon plants coming along? Thanks for everything.
— Susie W.

To Ian Whitcomb:
I recently read that you are planning to move to either Seattle or New York after you get your degree. Please move to Seattle. After all, you said yourself that Seattle is your "home-town" because you were discovered here. And, it was Seattle that made "You Turn Me On" a giant national hit. Say "hi" to Robin for us.
— S., L., C. and T.

Males only:
I would like to write to an 18 or 19 year old male whose favorites include The Beach Boys, Herman's Hermits, Richmond High, drive-ins, etc. My address is 1737 Gaynor Ave., Richmond, Calif.
— Miriam Gould

For Girls Only

'It' Returns

By Shirley Poston

Boys, stick around for a moment. You just have to hear my first amusing (oh, sure) anecdote of the week.

You may have noticed that I've been in a very good mood of late. Well, I've sobered up. *It* is back. It being my 16-year-old brother.

He hasn't actually been away (although he could use a nice long rest), but he's been busy with school and all that and hasn't been driving me nuts for a while.

You'll be glad to hear that things are back to normal in our household. So far this week he has spray-painted his bicycle (kids will be kids) right under my bedroom window, "accidentally" turned the hose on me full blast and flattened an enormous bug with a book I was reading.

Wild Shirt

But the best is yet to come. Yesterday he came racing home with this weird looking shirt he'd bought on sale at a drug store of all places.

When he unpinned it and started trying it on, our whole family cracked up (now we're a matched set). It wasn't a shirt at all! It was a floor length granny gown! That kids needs medical attention, and if he ever comes out of his room again (he's in there blushing), I'm going to suggest a good psychiatrist.

My thanks to the *BEAT* reader who has my brother pegged. Her letter said: "You talk about your brother a lot, and you've also mentioned that you have a sort of famous relative. Personally, I think they're one and the same and your brother is Dennis The Menace."

Hear, hear! I'm inclined to agree with said reader.

Now, boys go away so we can tell all your secrets. And a few of our own.

Odd Feet

Has This One Ever Happened To You Department: Have you ever gone into a store to try on shoes and left knowing that the clerk would be wondering about you for days? Not only because you tried on eleven thousand different styles and ended up buying a set of laces for your sneakers. Because there was something slightly odd about your feet.

Like maybe you had on one red sock and one blue, or had your toenails painted black, or you had eighty-four runs or some such?

Well, a classic example of clerk-frightening has just happened to me. I went to try on boots and I'd forgotten what nylon I was wearing until I saw the salesman staring open-mouthed at my foot.

You see, I have this nylon that I can't seem to wear out. When I don't have dry nylons in the morning, I sometimes bake them dry in the oven (no wonder my mother's cakes have been tasting strange of late). I did this to that *certain* nylon, only the oven got carried away and burned a huge hole right in the toe.

Conservative soul that I am, I immediately dipped the toe in nail polish and sewed it up with black thread. It worked, but it does look a bit riduculous to say the least.

When I noticed the clerk gaping at it, I said "Sorry about that nylon, I over-baked it."

And instead of accepting that logical explanation as the gospel truth, he giggled and ran for the back room. When he returned, having re-gained his composure, I soon noticed that other clerks were dropping by to chat with him for a moment and then *they* were giggling and running for the back room.

Well, I fixed him but good. Just as I was leaving, I leaned over and said, very confidentially, "You're going to have to do something about those speckles."

Obviously, he'd never seen a certain commercial on the telly, because he just sort of snarled. And you know what? He didn't even offer me a balloon!

Rational?

Well, I guess I don't have to tell you what's happening. Here I'd promised myself that I'd write something rational in this column for a change, instead of spending all my room raving about George. And what am I raving about instead? *Feet!*

And it's not the first time either! In one column not long ago, I rattled on indefinitely as to whether it was barefoot or barefooted. Incidentaly, I never did find out the answer to that one. Incidentally, I have also never found out how to spell incidently.

Oh, that reminds me. I have a question to answer. Several of you have written and asked what I consider proper garb for a rock and roll concert.

Although several parents will probably be waiting for me with large boards soon, I think a concert is the kind of event where it's okay to let your fashion imagination wander, even if your choice of styles makes everyone else *wonder*. So, get out your velour granny gowns and your alligator hip boots and live it up! And tell your folks not to hit me too hard. I bruise easily.

Just a note about a terrific time-waster discovered by another *BEAT* reader. Thanks to Kathy Jenson of Los Angeles for suggesting a way of staying awake in study hall (although you probably need the sleep.) What you do is pretend you're going to change your name and also pretend you only have one hour to decide what your new moniker is going to be.

It sure wouldn't take me any hour to make up my mind! It would take me about three seconds to decide on Mrs. George Harrison.

Another fun thing to do is make a list of all the "pet names" people have for you and try to remember where and how the tags originated. When I heard about this time waster, I wasted about three hours trying to recall why my older brother (seldom mentioned here because he's away at college) (whew) has called me "Edgar" ever since I can remember.

It finally dawned on me that this all started because I wanted to be a great poet when I was younger. (You know, Edgar Allen Poe.) Fortunately, I outgrew that dream. Now I want to be something sensible. A fireman.

Before I run out of room, here's the news I promised about the new album I'm going to give away. I have a friend who manages a record store, and he likes to have lots of clever little signs around the place. So, I made him a deal. If he'd give me an album every now and then, to give away in my column, I'd write some of those clever (hah!) little signs for him. (I've been up till all hours every night since we arrived at this "bargain" and I can't think up one sign. Me and my brilliant ideas.)

Album Prize

Anyway, I managed to talk him out of a copy of "Help" (by the Beatles, whom else?) for a starter. And I'm going to give it to one of you, providing, of course, that you're a George Harrison fan (isn't everyone?)?

If you don't have a copy of this gear album, send me a letter c/o *The BEAT*. Don't forget to put the initials G.P.H. (which stand for George (Pant) Harrison in the lower left hand corner of the envelope.

Then I'll put all your letters in a giant John Lennon hat (or some such) and draw out the winner!

Down, girl. You've over-blabbed again.

Get those letters in the mail and I'll see you next *BEAT!*

Stones Go From Earth To Clouds

One drove a truck, one was a student and one drew pictures. Now they are members of one of the top popular singing groups in the world.

Who are they? The Rolling Stones.

Before they became the Stones, Mick Jagger was a student at the London School of Economics, Brian Jones drove a coal lorry, Bill Wyman was a maintenance engineer, Keith Richards worked in a post office and Charlie Watts was a commercial artist.

But luckily for us they all gave up their jobs to become one of the top selling acts in the entertainment industry. They now top the U.S. charts with their latest release, "Get Off My Cloud."

KRLA ARCHIVES

THE SILKIE — Kev, Mike, Ivor and Silvie

BEATLES PITCH IN, HELP SILKIE FIND HIT SOUND

They have talent, an unusual name, a mastermind manager and the personal help of John Lennon, Paul McCartney and George Harrison.

With all that — the Silkie just couldn't lose. And they didn't either.

Of course, as it most always is, the Silkie's road to record success was long and rather bumpy. They attended Hull University and there in the summer of 1963 three of the Silkie — Silvie, Mike and Ivor — began the first of what was to be many long hours of practice. In October of the same year, the last member of the group, Kev, joined their arduous rehearsals.

Friday, The 13th

But it was not until Friday, August 13, 1965 that the group's big break finally rolled their way. It was on this traditionally unlucky day that three of the Beatles showed up at the Silkie's recording session to oversee the birth of the Silkie's version of the Beatle song, "You've Got To Hide Your Love Away."

Kev Silkie tells us about that historical day: "It all began as a routining session really. We'd no intention of making a record at the time. After working out a basic arrangement with Paul, we asked John to come and help us prepare the number for recording.

"He happened to bring George with him. At first, we were not getting it at all. Too many people making suggestions at once. Then Paul started to play rhythm guitar. It's what you now hear at the start of our record. John shouted: 'That's good — let's use that.' So we all joined in and the instrumental backing was worked out," Kev continued.

Something Extra

"Then we found one of the recording studios was empty and decided to hear what the whole thing sounded like on tape. When we heard our playback, George decided it needed something extra and added the tapping on the back of the guitar.

"Finally we put on the vocal, with George playing tambourine. Four takes and we finished the record as you hear it," Kev explained.

And as we hear it — it sounds pretty good! A hit for the Silkie, the Beatles and, of course, yet another feather in the overloaded cap of the groups' manager, Brian Epstein.

Upbeat of the Week
By Eden

The Yardbirds are on the Upbeat this week with a double-sided smash. I like the "I'm A Man" side better, but they seem to be bringing Gregorian chanting back into vogue with the flip side — "Still I'm Sad."

* * *

If you're a girl under the age of 25, and you think you're in the "in" crowd — drop an ear lobe on P.F. Sloan's hit-disc, "Halloween Mary" — it may just be auto-biographical for you, luvs!!

* * *

The Animals are getting restless again and it's a pretty safe bet that they're gonna cause some kinda commotion in this waxen jungle of pop. Their new single — "It's My Life" — shows every sign of continuing their current winning streak.

* * *

The Weird Wax of the Week has just got to be "May The Bird of Paradise Fly Up Your Nose," by Jimmy Dickens.

Anything you say, babe, but I could have sworn that a "wet bird never flies at night!!"

* * *

There were many self-styled prophets who predicted a complete musical revolution in the field of pop after Beatle Paul released his beautiful ballad, "Yesterday."

Sorry, but no such luck yet, Beethoven lovers. I'm afraid that it is left to the Beatles to be not only trend-setters, but unique as well. And "Yesterday" is a perfect example of their successful solitude.

Steve Douglas has produced an instrumental version, in two parts, of "Yesterday" for his latest effort on the Capitol label. In Merrie Olde across the Pond, everyone seems to be recording this tune, notably Matt Munro and Marianne Faithfull, who is rumored to have had a 100-piece orchestra backing her.

Brief complimentations extended to:

The Zombies, for their new single "Just Out of Reach";

The McCoys, for a smash follow-up to their "Sloopy" sizzler with their new 45 RPMer — "Fever." This one is a revival of a Golden Oldie, but it looks like they're gonna strike it rich all over again.

The Wellingtons, with their long-awaited disc, "Go Ahead And Cry." Good things are always worth waiting for, and this one's a beauty.

Who Is Buying Ken Dodd's Tears

Ken Dodd's recording of "Tears" is the number one single in England but no one knows who's buying it.

The record overtook the Beatles' "Help" and has almost reached the million mark but no one can figure out who the buyers are.

The song was originally recorded in 1929 by Rudy Vallee and the experts say that it just couldn't possibly be selling to teenagers. But adults have never yet bought a single with enough enthusiasm to make it a million seller. So who's buying it?

Someone discovered that the largest sales have been in Northern England which includes Liverpool, which is where Dodd lives. But he couldn't have bought that many records himself, could he?

No matter who is buying it over there, the record is now being released in the United States on the Liberty label. Do those mysterious people who bought it in England also exist in America? Watch the charts and see.

Pebbles New Star

A new star is about to be born. Her first release will soon be heard on several nationwide television shows.

She is Pebbles of Hanna-Barbera's television cartoon "The Flintstones" and she has just cut her first recording, a single called "Open Up Your Heart."

A film strip showing Pebbles singing her first song has been requested by no less than *Shindig, Hullabaloo, Hollywood A Go Go, The Jimmy Dean Show* and numerous local television stations.

Pebbles is assisted on her first release by Bamm Bamm (Bamm Who?)

...CHAD STUART

Chad To Air For Columbia

Chad Stuart, still denying rumors that he and Jeremy have split up, has just signed an independent producers contract with Columbia Records.

The arrangement is independent from the contract Chad and Jeremy have with the same label and has provisions for Chad to record with his wife, Jill.

The new contract runs for four-and-a-half years, which also happens to be when Chad & Jeremy's contract expires.

The duo will record three albums during November in London. Names have not been announced for the albums but one is reported to be Chad and Jeremy hits, another favorite songs and the third mood music for teen parties.

Jeremy took a leave of absence from the duo last June and is appearing in the play, "Passion Flower Hotel," in London. Chad and his wife have been touring the United States.

KRLA ARCHIVES

LOOKS REAL, DOESN'T IT? Dick Biondi built this realistic model of the KRL"A", photographed at Manhattan Beach. Dick's creation features working headlights and tail lights, but he's not eligible for any of the 200 prizes in the model contest, of course. Entries will be accepted until Nov. 30. Pick up entry blanks and contest rules at model shops throughout the Southern California area.

Sonny, Cher Re-Schedule Europe Trip

The ever-busy Bonos, Sonny and Cher, are off again.

This time for Europe and a two week tour set for December. They have been offered an appearance in the Palladium in England but may not be able to take it because of billing problems.

Their British manager, Larry Page, reports: "There is only a fifty-fifty chance of me allowing them to do it unless they get top billing."

The duo was originally scheduled to make a three-day visit to England in October but could not make it due to the shortage of time arrangements.

As well as having three records in the top 100 in America, Sonny and Cher also have five records on the top 100 in England including their latest release there, "The Letter."

THE SPOKESMEN STATE THEIR CASE during a visit to **KRLA** to celebrate the success of their new album, titled naturally, "The Dawn of Correction." From left, Ray Gilmore, Program Director Mel Hall, Dave White, John Madara and **KRLA**'s Dick Moreland.

UNDER THE WATCHFUL EYES OF KRLA'S Dave Hull and Casey Kasem, five "Miss Teenage America" candidates (Miss Teenage Salt Lake City, San Francisco, Portland, Los Angeles), climb the stairway to success. In case you're confused, Dave is second from the left and has short hair.

KRLA BEAT SUBSCRIPTION
you will SAVE 60% of the regular price!
AN INTRODUCTORY SPECIAL... if you subscribe now...

☐ 1 YEAR — 52 Issues — $3.00   ☐ 2 YEARS — $5.00

Enclosed is $....................

Send to:..Age:...............

Address:...

City:...State:................Zip:............

MAIL YOUR ORDER TO: KRLA BEAT
1401 South Oak Knoll Avenue
Pasadena, California 91106

Outside U.S.: $9.00 — 52 Issues

BEAT BACK ISSUES

YOU DON'T HAVE TO MISS OUT...
on any great pictures, fab interviews or newsy items appearing in any of the following KRLA *BEATS* which you might have missed. For a limited time only, these *BEATS* are still available.

ISSUES AVAILABLE
- 4/14 — INTERVIEW WITH JOHN LENNON
- 4/21 — INTERVIEW WITH PAUL McCARTNEY
- 5/5 — HERMANIA SPREADS
- 6/9 — BEATLES
- 6/30 — PROBY FIRED
- 8/7 — DYLAN
- 8/14 — HERMAN
- 8/21 — STONES TESTIFY
- 8/28 — KRLA PRESENTS THE BEATLES
- 9/4 — BEATLES... IN PERSON NOW!
- 9/11 — THE THREE FACES OF BOB DYLAN
- 9/18 — PROTESTOR BARRY McGUIRE
- 9/25 — SONNY — HE & CHER HAVE 5 HITS
- 10/2 — WAS YARDBIRDS' ORDEAL IN VAIN?
- 10/9 — PAUL & RINGO — NOW SOLOING
- 10/16 — ELVIS — KING OF POP?
- 10/23 — BEVERLY BIVINS — WEE ONE OF WE FIVE
- 10/30 — RIGHTEOUS BROTHERS — NEW IMAGE
- 11/6 — DAVID McCALLUM — 'UNCLE' HERO
- 11/13 — MICK JAGGER — CHRISTMASES RUINED

To order a back issue, send 25¢ (15¢ plus 10¢ postage and handling charge) to: KRLA BEAT, Suite 504, 6290 Sunset Blvd., Hollywood, Calif. 90028. IT IS NO LONGER NECESSARY TO SEND STAMPS OR SELF-ADDRESSED ENVELOPES

KRLA ARCHIVES

The World of Bob Eubanks

When was the last time you met the perfect example of a clean-cut, good-looking, all-American boy—and *liked* him?!

Well, I did yesterday when I met KRLA's own "Boy Millionaire," Bob Eubanks. He's tall, blue-eyed, and *very* cute; and after all that—he's still a real nice guy!

Bob was born January 8, 1938, in Flint, Michigan, at precisely 7:05 in the morning.

After graduating from Pasadena high school, Bob attended two years of classes at Pierce College and one year at San Fernando Valley State College, and then spent 17 months at Don Martin's Radio School.

Ambitions

Was he an ambitious child? Well, Bob says, "I wanted to be a pilot—until I was old enough to realize that I didn't want to be a pilot! Then when I was in my sophomore year of high school, I wanted to be a radio announcer."

Bob's professional career in radio had its beginnings at station KACY in Oxnard, California, on September 1, 1958. Bob says he worked as a part-time announcer for two years—most of the time working eight-hour shifts, selling radio time, being a newsman, and a disc jockey all at the same time. Only an ambidexterous person could perform these feats simultaneously.

"Then I walked into KRLA one day—the hick from the street!—and I asked them if they had any jobs open and that night their all-night man had a sore back, and they needed somebody desperately—so they used me."

Bob is probably one of the most active young men in Hollywood today and his many activities carry him far beyond the boundaries of the radio dial:

"I use radio as the center of a wheel and I try to extend my activities from that center using radio as a home base all of the time. I'm interested in television production—I'm currently doing a show called 'Hit or Miss,' and I and my partner, Michael Brown, are the producers of that show; we're also interested in concert promotions in which Eubanks and Brown Productions presented the Beatles two years in a row, the Rolling Stones two years in a row, and Bob Dylan. And we're going to be the producers of a rodeo in May at the Rose Bowl."

Bob literally lives in a world of music, but when he is not on the air, he indulges himself in his own personal musical preferences:

Western Fan

"It all depends on my mood—when I'm getting ready to go to work, I like to listen to country and western music; when I'm coming home from work, I normally listen to the conversational stations. There are times, however, when I like to listen to jazz, and there are times when I like to listen to the Tony Bennett stuff. Mostly country and western, though, and rarely rock 'n' roll at home, outside of the Rolling Stones sometimes. I really like blues a lot."

For the last year and a half, the air waves have been pervaded by a sound which is distinctly British. In regard to the musical invasion from across the Big Pond, Bob says: "I think it's been a boon to the record industry; it has certainly been a boon to radio and it has helped everybody—regardless of what nationality they are—if they're in show business at all. It's been a great thing for R 'n' R—and I use that term in quotes, because I have no real definition of R 'n' R, nor do I think *anybody* has a definition for it. My feeling is that good music is music that is enjoyed, so what may be good music for you, perhaps is not good music for me."

Likes Beatles

And then there were four—*Beatles*, that is; and Bob has had the rare opportunity of personally meeting our favorite mop-tops two years in a row. Your impressions, Mr. Eubanks?

"Of all the British groups that I've met, the Beatles are the classiest. They are certainly by far the cleanest personally, and Paul and George are certainly the most personable.

"First of all, John is the boss of the group—period! Ringo is very moody, and says very little. George, the first year, was very nice, however Paul both years has been the nicest. In fact, when you walk into a room—if Paul has met you before—Paul will *get up* and *walk over to you* and say hi to you. He's certainly the most congenial."

The "in" thing to do this week is to "sing a song of protest;" but Bob goes one step farther as he protests against the *protests*!

Hates Protests

"I have very harsh feelings about the protest movement. I believe that everybody has the right to write a song that has protest in it, but I also believe that people have the right to either play it or not play it, and the way it's set up now—we do not have that right. I do not believe in it. I think politics does not belong in music, I think singers are not politicians, and I think they should keep their opinions to themselves and try to entertain rather than educate."

Hmmmm—well, guess we'll be seeing you on the trail, Robert!

AT HOME ON THE RANGE, where he is an accomplished rider and calf-roper, Bob is sometimes mistaken for the famous "Granny Goose."

TWO HITS AND A GORGEOUS MISS—In addition to his own show on Channel 5, "Hit or Miss," KRLA Deejay Bob Eubanks has often appeared as a guest on other programs. Here Ricky Nelson looks on as Bob discusses 17th century music with Mamie Van Doren during rehearsals for Ozzie and Harriet Show.

NO ADMISSION NO AGE LIMIT
PANDORA'S BOX
8118 SUNSET STRIP

WANTED!!
Ex-KRLA Staffer Seeking Qualified SONGWRITERS — SINGERS — GROUPS (Rock and Folk Rock ONLY) For Record Production Co.
CONTACT: BOB RAUCHER
AX 1-3967

NEW!! NEW!! NEW!!
AT THE "HOLE IN THE WALL"
BIRD SUN GLASSES
COMES IN TWO COLORS: GOLD OR SILVER, WITH CASE
$7.95 PAIR

WE WILL MAIL TO YOU PREPAID
SEND MONEY ORDER OR CHECK
NAME:
ADDRESS:
CITY: STATE:
CHECK COLOR WANTED: GOLD ☐ SILVER ☐
433 N. La Cienega, Los Angeles 48, Calif.
HOLE IN THE WALL

FREDDIE AND THE DREAMERS—another tour and more mischief.

Freddie Doing American Tour

Freddie's back! The man, the dance, the laugh, the group—they're all back Stateside again.

Freddie and his Dreamers kicked off their second tour of America in royal style by appearing on the Danny Kaye Show where the two funny men—Freddie and Danny—got a chance to clown around. An art both have mastered expertly.

Laffs and Dances

The last time the boys paid us a visit they caused quite a sensation with their ad lib humor and their now-famous legs and arms in the air dance.

They stopped off at Hullabaloo long enough to teach the entire cast and crew how to to "The Freddie." Don't suppose we'll ever torget the sight of the Hullabaloo cameramen and technicians doing "The Freddie!"

This time around the boys will visit Hullabaloo again—maybe they'll even have the audience dancing in the aisles! It's a thought, anyway. And with Freddie nothing's improbable or even impossible.

What A Tour!

The group began their personal appearance tour on October 31 in Phoenix, Arizona and will wind it up November 29 in Macon, Georgia hitting practically all the big cities in between.

All *The BEAT* can say is—happy dancing, Freddie!

Record Quiz

If you're in the mood for answering eight great mindbenders about the record world, dis must be the place. If not, that means you have something better to do! So why are you reading this when you could be out doing it?

1. One of Sonny and Cher's recent hits was released a year ago! Can you name it?
2. Jay and the Americans' "Some Enchanted Evening" is one of America's best-loved songs, from the score of one of our best-loved musical comedies. In what Broadway play did the song originate?
3. "Like A Rolling Stone" by Bob Dylan was this year's longest hit record. What was last year's?
4. A certain group which made its debut in "The Tami Show" now has a heading-for-a-hit-disc called "Are You A Boy Or Are You A Girl"? Name that certain group.
5. The Tijuana Brass is in the same boat with "A Taste Of Honey". What famous foursome also made a hit with this number?
6. P. F. Sloane, who wrote "Eve of Destruction" has now taken up recording. What's the title of his debut disc?
7. What two singers each have a version of "Universal Soldier" on the national charts?
8. Patty Duke's "Don't Just Stand There" didn't! Her second record is on its way up, too. Can you name it?

RECORD QUIZ ANSWERS (WHICH YOU HAD BETTER STOP READING UPSIDE DOWN THIS INSTANT!): 1—"Baby Don't Go", 2—"South Pacific", 3—"You've Lost That Lovin' Feelin'" by the Righteous Brothers, 4—The Barbarians, 5—The Beatles, 6—"The Sins Of A Family", 7—Donovan and Glen Campbell, 8—"Funny Little Butterflies".

Dear Susan

By Susan Frisch

Can you tell me when the new Beatle movie will be released in America? Eva Szymkiewicz.
As of now no date has been set.

Where can I get the British Beatle albums here? Jan Benepe.
The best way is to go to your nearest record store and ask them to order it for you. It will be quite expensive, but I'm sure they'll be able to do it.

Where can I write to Gerry and the Pacemakers and be sure of them getting it? Susan Flemming
Second Floor, Service House, 13 Monmouth Street, London W.C. 2, England.

Where can I write to Tommy Quickly? Georgia Delson.
c/o Jeanie Anderson, P.O. Box 966, Glendale, California.

Can The BEAT possibly print any of John Lennon's real paintings? Not the ones from his books. C.L.S.
So far John has not sold or granted any reproduction rights to his actual paintings or drawings. When and if he does, *The BEAT* will have them for you!

Will the Beatles be coming back to California next year? Ruth Merrick.
Yes.

Can you please give me Rich's, of the Sunrays, home address? Mary Thomas.
Sorry, we don't give out any home addresses unless they have already been published. The BEAT thinks too much of the artists' privacy to intrude in such a manner.

Can you please tell me where I can write to Donovan. Not a fan club, please. Dawn Oven.
8 Denmark Street, London W. 1, England.

Where can I write Sonny and Cher a fan letter? And is it true that Cher is going to have a baby? Kathy Shea
7715 Sunset Blvd., Hollywood, Calif. NO, she's not expecting!

Is it true that Cher is slowly dying of T.B.? Cheryl Harrison.
I don't know where these ridiculous rumors get started. Last week she was supposedly dying of leukemia. NO. NO. To both.

Can you please tell me what movies the Beatles saw while in California? A Beatle Fan.
From what I could find out the fab four didn't see any movies.

Where can I write to the Walker Brothers? Cindy E.
29 Upper Addison Gardens, London W., 14, England.

Where can I write to Kink Ray Davies, and be sure he'll get my letter? Monica Starr.
25 Denmark Street, London W. C. 2, England.

Can Elvis play any other instruments than guitar? June Hardy.
Elvis can also play the drums.

Where can I write to the Yardbirds? Mary Lester.
18 Carlisle Street, London W. 1, in care of Mr. Ray Lipton.

How old is Dino, of Dino, Desi and Billy? Steve Milican.
13 years old.

Sonny & Cher To Entertain Meg & Tony

Sonny and Cher can do no wrong.

First they flew to New York to appear at a posh party at the request of the guest of honor, Jackie Kennedy.

Now they have British royalty coming to see *them*.

Princess Margaret and the Earl of Snowdon will arrive in the United States Nov. 7 for their first trip to America.

The royal three week tour of the country will include the annual WAIF Ball Nov. 8 at the Hollywood Palladium. Bob Hope will host the event and starring in the entertainment for the royal couple will be our own Sonny and Cher along with Frank Sinatra and Polly Bergen.

Where can they go from here—to Buckingham Palace?

Although some say they are just good friends, and others say they are engaged, they are certainly not married.

What is Donovan's favorite food and color? Charky Dunn.
Donovan's favorite color is tangerine. His favorite food is scampi, mushrooms and chips.

Can you please tell me Petula Clark's real name? Steve Rothmin.
Petula Sally Olwen Clark.

Can you please give me Hilton Valentin's (of the Animals) address? Susan Patterson.
56 Church St., North Shields, England.

How long have Sonny and Cher been married? Betsy McCormick.
2 years.

Is Bob Dylan married? Rose Stisen.
No.

When will the Beatles officially be knighted with their MBE medals? Correen Cosbey.
The big date was October 26, 1965.

Under what record label do the Sunrays record? Marcia Schecter.
Capitol Records.

What kind of cigarettes does Herman smoke? Hilda Farrel.
Herman has his cigarettes specially blended at Clarke of London.

What is Herman's favorite color? Janet Felt.
It seems our Herman has changed mind. A few months ago his favorite color was blue, but now it is RED, RED, RED!!!

How old is Sonny Bono? Harriet Townsend.
24 years old, HE says.

Is it true that Mick Jagger and Chris Shrimpton are married? Kay Corner.

Will you please give me Peter Noone's home and office address? Cathy Stanley
His office address is, 20 Manchester Sq., London, England. His home address is, 9 Chestnut Lane, Roby, Liverpool, England.

Does Bobby Sherman have an album out, and are he and Donna Loren dating? Connie Welsh
Bobby doesn't have an album out yet, but plans are being made for one. He and Donna are just friends, nothing more.

Would you please tell us something about the fab Liverpool Five? Jane, Rosemary, Lora, Dora, Evelyn.
This fab fivesome hail from England. They have been together for about two years.

Could you please tell me what Clare Asher, Peter and Jane's sister, looks like? Cynthia J.
Clare is 16 years old, has red hair, and blue eyes. She looks very much like Jane, only a younger version.

KRLA ARCHIVES

On the BEAT
By Louise Criscione

Well, they made the Beatles into cartoon characters. So, why not the Beau Brummels? The television bosses decided that there was no reason why not, so if you keep one eye glued to The Flintstones you'll soon see the Beau Brummels.

'Course, you might not recognize the Brummels in their cartoon form but you'll be sure to recognize their voices 'cause they'll narrate the episode themselves.

It's a one-shot deal but if the response is big enough—who knows, you just may be seeing the Brummels each week on The Flintstones!

I only have one question—what will they think of next?

That doll, Brenda Holloway, figures she's not busy enough so she is planning on enrolling in some courses at USC in the fall. Also, she is busily preparing an act for her up-coming tour of England.

Of course, you know Brenda was the lucky girl who toured with the Beatles on their last visit Stateside. So, Brenda is hoping to hitch onto the Beatles annual tour of Britain. But at the rate the Beatles' personal appearances are disappearing Brenda had better get over there *but fast!*

Lennon Murals

You'll never guess what John Lennon did on his last vacation—stayed home and painted murals in his new house. John says they're all abstracts and if he let that Lennon humor show through (which I'm sure he did) they ought to be the wildest bunch of murals you've *ever* seen.

... SAL VALENTINO

Yet another cat is out of the bag and yet another Yardbird is married. Jeff Beck, lead guitarist and newest member of the group, has been married since he joined the Yardbirds. So says a British pop paper—and so it probably is.

QUICK ONES: The Leaves sound a good deal like the Byrds, don't they? However, they really are a great group, seem like nice guys and with a little bit of luck just might make it big... Marianne Faithfull and husband, John, now have a maid and butler... Eric Burdon seen roaming Hollywood long after the other Animals had departed... A nice honor for Herman—being named the first group leader to host Hullabaloo.

Wonder who The Wonder Who are? Well, so do we! The boys sent us a picture of themselves but we can't tell much from that as all four of the boys are invisible. Honest! Lots of clever publicists in this business, huh?

Busy Supremes

Those Supremes have a schedule which just won't stop. On their agenda—a return trip to New York's Copa, the club where the girls triumphed not too many months ago. Diana, Mary and Florence will make their Las Vegas debut at the Flamingo Hotel next September and will also appear at the Fairmont Hotel in San Francisco and the Deauville Hotel in Miami Beach.

James Brown has decided to do that which he has never done before—appear at a night club for ten straight days. The Trip on Sunset Strip will host Brown starting March 11 for ten consecutive days.

BYRD NOTES: When the Byrds visited the Beatles they played a game called "Try And Spot The Commando." The object? To guess how many fans would scale the brush-infested hills surrounding the Beatles' Benedict Canyon "hideaway"... Interesting to note that since Jim McGuinn started wearing those "Byrd Glasses" their price has soared from *one* dollar to *eight* dollars... Did Mike Clarke really get his hair cut? I thought so until I saw him at a party the other night—now I'm not sure... But I will tell you one thing for sure—Gene Clark *didn't* get his cut... What's with David and that cape?... I've been watching Chris Hillman and although he's gotten a lot cuter—he ain't smiled yet!

Donovan has an interesting aim in life: "To live until I die and fill in the space in between."

... CHRIS HILLMAN

UNDERGROUND VIEW OF THE GRASS ROOTS: From left, Denny Ellis, Dave Stensen, Joe Larson, Bill Fulton.

The Grass Roots Have A Language Of Their Own

The Grass Roots are four in number and much of their growth was accomplished in the San Francisco area.

The boys individually are Bill Fulton, Joe Larson, Denny Ellis, and Dave Stensen; collectively they are all nuts! Not really—but they *are* a lively group and when they're all together, they joke and kid about incessantly in a language all their own.

They most enjoy playing folk-rock and James Brown music, but occasionally they write their own material.

As we turn on our handy-dandy, all-purpose *BEAT* microphone, Denny Ellis explains:

Part-Time Songwriters

"We've written a few songs—some of them are kinda protesty—but they're not really too commercial. Bill and I write—mostly Bill, though. Maybe we'll come up with something soon."

At this point, Bill commandeered the *BEAT* mike and added: "P.S.—Denny and I don't think that we should play any of our songs until they're really something worth playing. As long as we're writing them, we don't want to play them until they are as good as we think they should be."

Speaking on the unique sound of the GrassRoots, Dave Stensen explained:

"The whole sound of our group is a lot of different sounds together with what we can put into it—just the way we play in our own style. Each person has his own particular style and when you put those together—it's the Grass Roots."

Styling

Joe agreed with Dave here, but added: "Intonation is absolutely important—you must have it to have any good sound of any kind. Intonation and good tuning, and balance are the main things. We try to mix the instruments so that one thing is not too loud. We always try to get the best possible sound."

Four very talented young men, are the Grass Roots, and versatility is just one of their many attributes. For example, their division of labor in the instrument department:

Bill: "I play lead and rhythm guitar, a little bass, a little drums, I play very little organ, and I play a little kazoo—ad lib in C!—and a little cathedral music!!!"

Dave: "I play bass, a little rhythm guitar—a C progression and about five chords!—and I play a little ad lib in L minor diminished thirteen; I play a little drums—tap my foot!—and I play tambourine, kazoo, maraca, woodblock, triangle, and hawaiian guitar."

Denny: "I play rhythm and lead guitar, a little bit of organ, piano and harpsichord, I *try* to play bass every once in a while—just for laughs!—and I took cello lessons for one day!"

On Dylan:

Bill took this opportunity to seize *The BEAT* microphone in order to render a few timely opinions on the man of the hour—Bob Dylan:

"I think that Dylan doesn't really care too much about playing music or singing as much as he does about saying what he has to say; and music is the best way to get it across to the largest number of people—especially the younger generation now. He could put it down in poetry—which some of it was before he put it to music and which a lot of it is—but it wouldn't get across to as many people. A lot of people say, 'Well look—he's going commercial, he's going rock, he wants to make more dough'—well, I don't think that's the reason.

Larger Audiences

I think that he's just doing that because this way he gets a lot larger audiences of the age he's mostly trying to tell something to."

The Grass Roots are more than just four musicians—they are four talented individuals who have combined their talents to produce a truly great sound.

One thing is very certain about this group—the Grass Roots are *growing!*

London Whirl Is Prize For Revlon Winner

What girl doesn't dream of meeting and even going out with her favorite male singer?

One lucky young lady recently did just that and her entire adventure will be the subject of an article in the November issue of Seventeen Magazine.

The lucky girl is 16-year-old Kathy Sheron, the winner of Revlon's Natural Wonder "Swingstakes contest. She won a weekend whirl through London with the Dave Clark Five.

Kathy's dream-of-a-lifetime weekend included a visit to the Ad Lib Club, where both the Beatles and Rolling Stones have been known to visit, and a rehearsal of "Ready, Steady, Go!".

Accompanying Kathy and the DC5 were her mother and a London disc jockey.

In addition to Kathy's wonderful weekend, over 9,000 other prizes were awarded in the nationwide contest including Dave Clark Five albums, portable television sets, record players, transistor radios and electric hairdryers.

San Francisco For Donovan

Donovan's schedule of appearances during his American tour in November has been announced.

The tour, lasting from Nov. 1 through 28, will include New York, Boston, Philadelphia and Santa Monica and San Francisco, California.

He will also tape appearances on *Hullabaloo*, *The Steve Lawrance Show* and *Grand Ol' Opry*.

Donovan's latest album release is "Fairy Tale" and his latest single features two songs he wrote himself, "Turquoise" and "Hey Gyp."

KRLA ARCHIVES

THE WALKER BROTHERS — Scott, Gary and John — proudly display "Brightest Hope of 1965" award given them by a British publication. Their newest record is "Make It Easy On Yourself."

Walker Brothers Make It Easy

By Louise Criscione

Well, they finally did it, didn't they? The Walker Brothers have made a name here in America by simply making it easy on themselves.

By now I'm sure everyone knows their story. They met by literally bumping into each other. Scott and John were already playing together as the Walker Brothers and one day they had a car accident. The other car involved? You guessed it — Gary Leeds. And so now there were three Walker Brothers.

The Local Walkers

The boys played the local Hollywood clubs. They appeared on local pop shows, released a record (which didn't do much) and even made it on "Shindig."

But nothing. They made no huge impact on anybody and being clever as well as realistic — they knew it. What to do? At that time the British were invading the American record scene from all sides. To be "in" you almost had to be English and the Walker Brothers weren't.

Turn Tables

But they did want to be big-time. So they decided to turn the tables on the British and invade *them*. It was a kind of do-or-die, last-ditch effort. If the Walkers didn't make it in England, that would be that.

If they bombed out in England they'd come back to America and content themselves with something else. But they didn't have to come back — their trick worked.

The British took to the Walker Brothers so fast and so completely that the whole thing looked like a press agent's dream.

Only the Walkers had no press agent. "We had no publicity machine working for us, we had nothing but determination," said Gary.

Still, the whole thing seemed almost unbelievable. Too good to be true, really. The mobbing, sobbing, screaming masses of Walker fans became so wild and frenzied that the Walkers were continually being dragged from the stage and placed entirely at the mercy of their fans.

The Walker Brothers caused such a commotion everywhere they appeared that the British press began giving them a phenomenal amount of space every week. And it was not long before word of their success drifted back across the Pond.

Vague Memories

American teens thought back and vague memories of the Walker Brothers came to mind. Hollywood teens remembered the three Texas boys slaving away on Gazzari's stark stage to a minimum of audience reaction.

Teens across the nation remembered the Walkers on "Shindig" and recalled their opinion of the group at the time — a nothing sort of group.

We all winced as we discovered our mistake. We tried to make it up to them by pushing their latest record, "Make It Easy On Yourself," up the nation's charts.

Too Late?

Is it too late — will the Walker Brothers come back to America? Apparently not, for Scott says: "We weren't accepted over there (America) at first. They didn't want us — but England did. So, it's England for us, this is THE place!"

Of course, the boys are probably still pretty bitter about the rejection they encountered here. I wouldn't take Scott's word too seriously. When the bitterness and hurt fades away, I wouldn't be at all surprised to find the three Walker Brothers winging their way back home.

British to See Beatles In U.S.

The British are going to get to see part of the Beatles' last tour of America.

The Fab Four's concert in New York's Shea Stadium last summer was filmed and will be shown on British television this Christmas.

This may be in place of the Christmas show that the Beatles have said they aren't doing this year.

Manager Brian Epstein flew to America recently to make final arrangements for the film.

It's Happening...
By Eden

Hot flash off the BEAT-line: looks like it's for real this time, Beatlemaniacs — Paul and Jane are gonna get married.

According to BEAT sources in London Town, Paul has recently purchased the home in which he and his Jannie will live after their upcoming marriage.

The house is a large, eight-bedroom affair located on fashionable Cavendish Avenue right in London.

Unlike a certain Mr. Starkey and spouse, Paul and Jane have received no adverse comment as yet from their new neighbors-to-be about their planned residence in the exclusive neighborhood. In fact, they seem only too happy to have a family of Beatles, M.B.E. on the old block.

Until the renovations on the property are completed, Paul will reside in the home of Dr. Richard Asher on Wimpole Street in London — the good Doctor just happens to be Jennie's father, and the Asher family has welcomed their future member with open arms.

Oh well — tearful though we may be, Paul — The BEAT wishes you both all the very best. (Sob!!!)

* * *

The day before the awards ceremony, the boys each received a "light trim" on their famous mop-tops, and when asked if they planned to wear the optional, but traditional top hats, John Lennon replied: "Are you kidding? We couldn't get *our* mops under those toppers!!"

That's all right, John-John — we love you anyway!

* * *

Shorts across the board: Shelley Fabares has been signed to do a pilot and five flicks for MGM. Isn't that the lot where heart-throb David McCallum does his spying?

P.F. Sloan and Barry McGuire have returned from an overwhelmingly successful tour of England where they seem to have befriended just about everyone. P.F. has a hit-bound with his "Halloween Mary," and Barry has just put the wraps on a brand new album. Welcome home boys.

For the information of all those sour lemons in the audience who have been hoping otherwise recently — Sonny and Cher definitely *did* become *Mr. and Mrs.* Bono on September 7, 1963, in the quaint little pueblo of Tijuana. So *THERE!*

* * *

British-born, Scottish-named, Irish-schooled student of American history — Ian Whitcomb — has been signed by Lester Wood to star in Surrey Production's "It's Fab." (Where have we heard that before?!)

The flick will start shooting in England in January and will have pretty Cilla Black dropping in as co-star.

* * *

Congratulations and other Royal things of the sort go out to our boys, the Beatles, who were officially presented their M.B.E. ships (well, *you* know what I mean!) by the Queen on October 26 last.

HERB ALPERT AND THE TIJUANA BRASS continue their long string of hits with two of the big instrumental singles of the year — "A Taste of Honey" and "The Third Man Theme."

KRLA ARCHIVES

Herman, Hermits Meet Mr. Ed

LET ME TELL YOU ABOUT THIS HORSE I MET . . .

Take the world's only talking horse. Add four Hermits. Throw in a Herman just 'cause he's cute. And what do you have?

An episode of Mr. Ed's television show with Herman and the Hermits as guest stars.

After spending over a month in California to film their movie, Herman and the boys decided they liked sunshine and didn't want to leave.

Mr. Ed, being the world's most clever horse and the world's only talking horse, knew a good thing and asked the boys if they'd like to be on his television show.

Everyone knows that hermits are great animal lovers so how could they turn down a chance to spend a few more days goofing around in the sun with good ol' Mr. Ed.

Herman also took advantage of the chance and asked the world's cleverist horse to help him find a title for the movie the Hermits had just finished. It seems the studio big-wigs are having a bad time making up their minds.

Herman likes "There's No Place Like Space" but Ed suggested that "Hold On!" might be better, or maybe a combination of the two—"Hold On! There's No Place Like Space."

We'll have to wait for the final decision to see if they take Ed's suggestion.

Joining Ed and the Hermits were the co-stars of the show, Alan Young and Connie Hines. The episode is scheduled to be shown sometime before Christmas.

Herman and the Hermits finally ran out of excuses for not going home and left for England, but they leave behind another loyal fan, Mr. Ed.

HEY ED, TELL HIM THE ONE ABOUT . . .

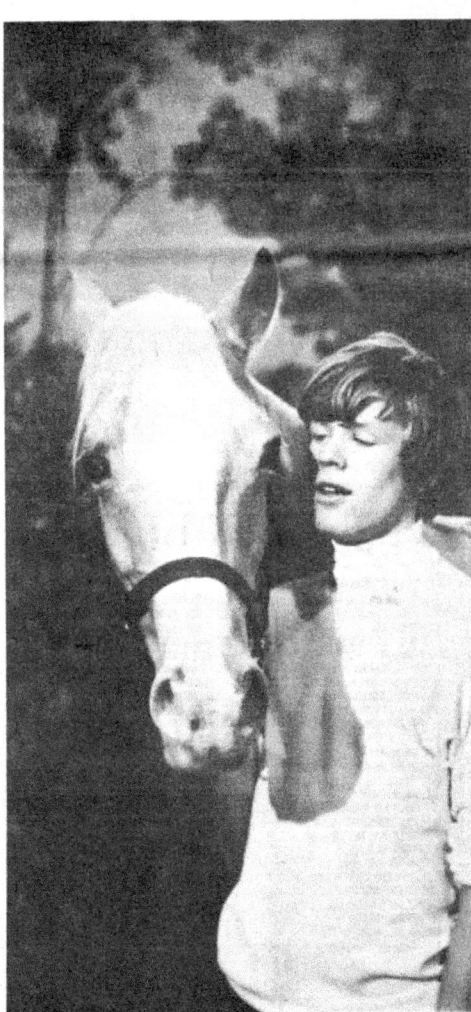

HOW DO YOU SPELL THAT LAST ONE, ED?

MY FRIEND THE HORSE—Look Ed, you and I are friends, right? I mean I let you come watch me make my movie and you let me come be on your show and we all had a lot of fun didn't we? And I didn't say anything about you being able to talk, right? So how about being a true pal, **and getting off of my foot!**

KRLA ARCHIVES

Tips to Teens

Q: I have been going steady since last April. I don't have any problems with my boyfriend, but I do have one with his parents. They simply don't like me. They're nice to me, but I can tell they don't really mean it. This makes me terribly uncomfortable. What can I do to make them change their opinion?
(Sharon G.)

A: Just give them a chance. If this is the first time your boyfriend has gone steady, his parents probably resent you a little because in a way you're "taking him away" from them. They'll come around. Every parent has to adjust when teenagers develop more and more interests outside the home, and this isn't an easy process. As long as they're already "nice to you," you've won the first part of your battle, and the next victory can't be far away.

Q: I'm just starting to wear makeup, and I can't decide on what shade to buy. Can you give me some pointers on how to decide?
(Yvonne L.)

A: Rub just a touch of several shades into the back of your hand. Choose the shade that doesn't turn pinkish or change the color of your skin in any way.

Q: This may seem like a crazy question, but I don't know who else to ask. I am trying to learn how to play the harmonica, and am getting nowhere fast. To make things worse, I get dizzy every time I practice. What am I doing wrong?
(Gary K.)

A: This happens to many harmonica beginners. Some notes are played by exhaling, others by inhaling. When you're playing the latter, stop swallowing all that hot air! (And don't be insulted by that answer—we didn't mean it personally. There's just no other way of putting it.)

Q: Before I invest money in shoe dye, I would like to know if this works on all kinds of shoes. Can you help me?
(Francis E.)

A: The new dyes work best on leather shoes. They have a tendency to streak on imitation leathers, so you'd better experiment on an old pair you were planning to throw away anyway.

Q: I spent my whole month's allowance on a pullover with matching socks, and when I got home I discovered that the socks are too short. They come just above the knee (my legs are as long as a giraffe's) and when I took them back, I was told they couldn't be returned because the set was on sale. Can you think of a way I can salvage this outfit?
(Arlene S.)

A: Fold the top part of the stockings into cuffs and wear them as knee socks! No one will know the difference. Since you do have long legs, always remember to try stockings, slacks, etc. on before making the purchase.

HINT OF THE WEEK

I have the kind of long hair that looks terrible when it's completely straight. I can't stand to sleep in rollers, so I've been putting big pin curls in the ends of my hair. They come out fine, but the sharp ends of the bobby pins keep me awake half the night. I finally solved this problem by setting the ends of my hair with giant paper clips. They stay in fine and I'm getting some sleep for a change. Try it!
(Karen C.)

If you have a question that needs answering, or a helpful hint you'd like to share, drop a line to Tips To Teens, c/o The BEAT.

Times Are Changing And How!

"The Times They Are A 'Changing." So says Bob Dylan, much of today's youth and The Changing Times.

The Times, known to the inside world as Artie Kornfield and Steve Duboff, freely admit that their name was inspired by the Bob Dylan composition, "The Times They Are A'Changing." The name was chosen partly because Artie and Steve liked the sound of it and partly because they really feel that the times are indeed changing.

Although "The Pied Piper" is the boys first release, they are not new to show business. Between the two of them they have written hits for such people as Dusty Springfield, Jan & Dean, Freddy Cannon, Jay & The Americans, The Shirelles, Betty Everett and Jerry Butler. Quite an impressive list of credits Artie and Steve have compiled, isn't it?

If they were such successful songwriters (and they were) why then did they turn to singing? "Writing is a groove but there isn't a songwriter I've ever met who wouldn't fall down to be a hit recording artist," Steve answered.

Seeger Praises Protest Songs

Protest songs have come under a lot of criticism lately but at least one folk singer thinks that protests are an improvement over the past.

Folk singer and writer Pete Seeger says, "Protest is a word like love, democracy or liberty which can mean very many different things to different people. Many of the hymns people sing in church are in fact protest hymns.

"The unrequited lover sings a protest about his girl turning him down. But I suppose these songs about war and peace are a step forward—thirty years ago the charts were all moon and June."

THE CHANGIN' TIMES—Artie Kornfield and Steve Duboff keep pace.

Movies Grab Beach Boys Sonny & Cher, Others

Chad and Jeremy have joined the growing list of singing groups going into movies.

The British duo, currently soloing with Chad and his wife Jill touring America and Jeremy in a play in London, have been signed by Columbia for a teen feature film of the beach and surf variety.

This follows Capitol's signing of the Beach Boys for both the group and the recording company's first film.

Capitol also snatched up Sonny and Cher for a film after five different companies had been after America's most popular married couple for a movie contract.

Both the Beach Boys and Sonny and Cher movies will be produced by Steve Broidy, former president of Allied Artists.

Another company going into the teen movie field is Universal International, which has signed two young producers, Len Weinreb and Bart Patton, to a two-year contract which calls for 14 rocking films.

With the diminishing of teen-type television shows, including the upcoming death of Shindig, these kind of movies may become the big thing for both singers and fans.

England has already gotten a head start on teen films with the first two Beatle movies, "Hard Day's Night" and "Help," and the just-released Dave Clark Five film "Having a Wild Weekend."

Weinreb, one of UI's new producers, says the entire field of teenage movies has been elevated to a new high.

"When you read that Steve Broidy has been signed to make films for the Beach Boys and Sonny and Cher, you realize that it's becoming fashionable for executives to get into this field. The field's being elevated. It's one thing when young guys like us are doing it. But when the big money companies get involved, you have to realize that something's happening," he said.

Something's happening in the field all right. Television may lose some of it's appeal to teens as more and more pop singers go into movies. After all, a television screen is only up to about 21 inches, but a movie screen is bigger than size and who wants a 21 inch Paul McCartney when he can have the larger than life variety.

Peter And Gordon Expect A Flop

Peter and Gordon think their next record may flop.

"Since we've had two biggies," says Gordon, "It's about time for another baddy."

"Look at someone like Dusty Springfield," adds Peter, "She has made failure records, but she is great and people still rate her. Everybody makes failure records sometimes except the Stones and Beatles."

BEAT Pop Music Awards Poll
CATEGORY V: OUTSTANDING RECORDS OF 1965

VOCALS—45 r.p.m.
(Please Check 10)

- ALL I REALLY WANT TO DO
- BABY DON'T GO
- CRYING IN THE CHAPEL
- DOWNTOWN
- DO YOU BELIEVE IN MAGIC
- EIGHT DAYS A WEEK
- EVE OF DESTRUCTION
- FERRY ACROSS THE MERSEY
- GET OFF MY CLOUD
- GO NOW
- HANG ON SLOOPY
- HEART FULL OF SOUL
- HELP
- HELP ME RHONDA
- HERE COMES THE NIGHT
- HOLD ME, THRILL ME, KISS ME
- I'M A FOOL
- I'M HENRY VIII I AM
- I'M TELLING YOU NOW
- IN CROWD, THE
- IT AIN'T ME BABE
- IT'S NOT UNUSUAL
- I'VE GOT YOU BABE
- KING OF THE ROAD
- LAST TIME, THE
- LAUGH AT ME
- LAUGH, LAUGH
- LIAR, LIAR
- LIKE A ROLLING STONE
- LOVER'S CONCERTO
- MAKE IT EASY ON YOURSELF
- MOHAIR SAM
- MR. TAMBOURINE MAN
- MRS. BROWN
- MY GIRL
- NAME GAME, THE
- ONE, TWO, THREE
- PAPA'S GOT A BRAND NEW BAG
- RED ROSES FOR A BLUE LADY
- RESCUE ME
- RIDE AWAY
- SATISFACTION
- STOP IN THE NAME OF LOVE
- THIS DIAMOND RING
- TICKET TO RIDE
- TREAT HER RIGHT
- TURN, TURN, TURN
- UNIVERSAL SOLDIER
- WE GOT TO GET OUT OF THIS PLACE
- WHAT THE WORLD NEEDS NOW IS LOVE
- WHAT'S NEW PUSSYCAT
- WOOLY BULLY
- YESTERDAY
- YOU TURN ME ON
- YOU WERE ON MY MIND
- YOU'VE GOT TO HIDE YOUR LOVE AWAY
- YOU'VE LOST THAT LOVIN' FEELING
- WRITE IN: _____
- WRITE IN: _____

INSTRUMENTALS—45's
(Please Check 5)

- IN CROWD, THE
- TASTE OF HONEY
- WHITTIER BLVD.
- COTTON CANDY
- WALK IN THE BLACK FOREST
- DRUMS A-GO-GO
- HOME OF THE MOUNTAIN KING
- CAST YOUR FATE TO THE WIND
- WRITE IN: _____
- WRITE IN: _____
- WRITE IN: _____
- WRITE IN: _____

ALBUMS — PLEASE WRITE IN YOUR CHOICES:

VOCALS
1. _____
2. _____
3. _____
4. _____
5. _____

INSTRUMENTALS
1. _____
2. _____
3. _____
4. _____
5. _____

CLIP AND MAIL TO ADDRESS ON BACK COVER

KRLA ARCHIVES

THE BEAT GOES TO THE MOVIES—AGAIN

RED LINE 7000

By Jim Hamblin

One-time racing driver Howard Hawks has been making movies for a long time. He is credited with such "finds" as Lauren Bacall, Rita Hayworth, Joan Collins, and Jane Russell.

Hawks may have done it again. RED LINE uses only unknowns in its cast list, and the result, far from being what you might expect, is a power-packed bundle of exciting entertainment.

Like a lot of "overnight" discoveries, Laura Devon has been working for years for a big break in films. Hopefully, this is it. She's got the nicest new approach to acting of any starlet, and her scenes in RED LINE are impressive.

Laura is not the only one to watch. John Robert Crawford, who plays her romantic lead in the picture, carries off his part very well.

RED LINE 7000 is a racing picture, filled with some of the best action footage taken. They don't switch to some grainy old newsreel footage for the pile-ups—it's all there, with fast-paced action.

SCENE TO WATCH FOR: Early in the picture, Laura Devon and John Robert Crawford act out an intimate scene non-stop in front of the color camera for several minutes. The dialogue, the actions by the two is as real as anything ever put on the screen. And a scene that long is hard to do!

There are, of course, all kinds of sub-plots and problems, but for creditable performances by newcomers (including not-so-new-comer singer Carol Connors) and lots of action, this wide-screen Paramount release fills the bill.

CRASH SCENES FROM FILM are realistically done. Actual race footage was made by designing cameras to fit on stock cars. Many of the cars, even though they had to stop frequently for film re-loads, actually finished in the Top 10 in many real races. The result is excitement on the screen in Paramount release.

NEWCOMER TO FILMS, JOHN ROBERT CRAWFORD has been on Broadway, is now under contract to Howard Hawks, Paramount.

FILM SCENES are usually shot in little chunks and then spliced together for continuity. In this unusual sequence, players LAURA DEVON and JOHN ROBERT CRAWFORD talk together for several minutes non-stop. The acting of both is outstanding.

RACE DRIVER decides to take the high road out of town...

THE WATUSI COMES TO WARNER BROS.! As part of the trouble that Sinatra has, DAVEY DAVISON dances into his life. Notice how all those girls above look alike?

MARRIAGE ON THE ROCKS

By Jim Hamblin

Here comes another one of those Dean Martin and Frank Sinatra home movies, with glittering color, glib dialogue and about the smallest contribution to the art of cinema it's possible to make.

Except for one thing. MARRIAGE ON THE ROCKS is an entertaining film. That, we contend, is the highest ideal of any motion picture.

So the story involves that modern day fad: Wife-swapping. Only Dean Martin's got no wife to swap. Sinatra, married with two children, is considered Dullsville by wife Deborah Kerr. Her lawyer prescribes a second honeymoon.

One thing leads to another, and soon the family is in Mexico for a vacation. But thanks to fast-talking marriage and divorce specialist Cesar Romero, they wind up *divorced* after all.

The story wheezes through several more problems, including another marriage and divorce again, but finally we all get straightened out and everybody lives happily ever after.

The picture, produced by Warner Bros., follows on the heels of one of Sinatra's best flicks, VON RYAN'S EXPRESS.

Daughter NANCY SINATRA plays his movie daughter fresh from her divorce from Tommy Sands. Watch for special performance by Watusi dancer DAVISON. She's enough to put *any* marriage on the rocks!

SIGRID VALDIS gets some close instruction on how to be a good secretary. Technicolor comedy features DINO as a happy bachelor living in a beach pad, while family man SINATRA has domestic problems. Until things get switched around. There's one thing special we noticed about SIGRID... aren't those lovely earrings?

SOMEHOW THIS PICTURE, rarest shot we know, shows the Thin One with a glass of MILK! Role is latest in series of non-singing appearances for SINATRA.

KRLA ARCHIVES

KRLA Tunedex

EMPEROR HUDSON

CHARLIE O'DONNELL

CASEY KASEM

JOHNNY HAYES

BOB EUBANKS

DAVE HULL

DICK BIONDI

BILL SLATER

KRLA BEAT
6290 Sunset, No. 504
Hollywood, Cal. 90028

This Week	Last Week	Title	Artist
1	5	1-2-3	Len Barry
2	1	GET OFF MY CLOUD	The Rolling Stones
3	8	TURN, TURN, TURN	The Byrds
4	4	YOU'RE THE ONE	The Vogues
5	2	YESTERDAY	The Beatles
6	3	A LOVER'S CONCERTO	The Toys
7	7	KEEP ON DANCING	The Gentrys
8	12	TASTE OF HONEY	Tijuana Brass
9	6	MAKE ME YOUR BABY	Barbara Lewis
10	18	MAKE IT EASY ON YOURSELF	The Walker Brothers
11	30/25	STILL I'M SAD/I'M A MAN	The Yardbirds
12	10	HANG ON SLOOPY	The McCoys
13	9	EVERYBODY LOVES A CLOWN	Gary Lewis & The Playboys
14	22	I HEAR A SYMPHONY	The Supremes
15	19	I KNEW YOU WHEN	Billy Joe Royal
16	13	RESCUE ME	Fontella Bass
17	26	STEPPIN' OUT	Paul Revere & The Raiders
18	15	I LIVE FOR THE SUN	The Sunrays
19	17	BUT YOU'RE MINE	Sonny & Cher
20	21	ROUND EVERY CORNER	Petula Clark
21	20	RESPECT	Otis Redding
22	23	WHERE DO YOU GO	Cher
23	27	MYSTIC EYES	Them
24	11	HELP	The Beatles
25	16	JUST A LITTLE BIT BETTER	Herman's Hermits
26	24	MY GIRL HAS GONE	The Miracles
27	29	AIN'T THAT PECULIAR	Marvin Gaye
28	32	PIED PIPER	The Changing Times
29	31	LET'S HANG ON	The 4 Seasons
30	28	MY HEART SINGS	Mel Carter
31	--	LET ME BE	The Turtles
32	39	YOU'VE GOT TO HIDE YOUR LOVE AWAY	The Silkie
33	36	DON'T TALK TO STRANGERS	Beau Brummels
34	--	YOU'RE ABSOLUTELY RIGHT	The Apollos
35	--	HALLOWEEN MARY	P. J. Sloan
36	--	HEARTBEAT	Gloria Jones
37	--	DON'T THINK TWICE	The Wonder Who?
38	--	RISING SUN	The Deep Six
39	--	I FOUGHT THE LAW	The Bobby Fuller Four
40	--	THE LAST THING ON MY MIND	The Dillards

KRLA BEAT
KRLA Edition

Volume 1, Number 37   LOS ANGELES, CALIFORNIA   15 Cents   November 27, 1965

The Rolling Stones - Bound for California

Dylan, Sonny, Cher Lead Pop Music Poll

KRLA BEAT

Los Angeles, California — November 27, 1965

DYLAN, SONNY, CHER LEAD POP MUSIC POLL

Highlighted by threatened sweeps by Sonny and Cher and Bob Dylan, first-round voting has been completed in *The BEAT's* first annual Pop Music Awards Poll.

Finalists have been selected in each category. You'll find them all listed in the final ballot printed below. From this ballot you, the public, will select the winners to be awarded 1965 International Pop Music Awards. Vote now for your top choice in each division and mail as quickly as possible.

IAN WHITCOMB — GENE PITNEY — DONOVAN — BARRY McGUIRE — BOB DYLAN

ROGER MILLER — JAMES BROWN — BILLY JOE ROYAL — SONNY BONO — ELVIS

Excitement is mounting with the approach of Dec. 8, when winners will be announced and awards presented at a glittering awards dinner, to be attended by top stars from throughout the recording and entertainment industry.

Many famous Hollywood film stars have already indicated they will attend—some of them taking part in the ceremonies—to make this first International Pop Music Awards presentation an outstanding success.

Recognition

The BEAT is originating the Pop Music Awards to provide recognition to those who have contributed most to the recording industry during 1965—as selected by the public.

More than 50,000 votes were received in the primary balloting to select the finalists. The photos to the left include all the finalists in one category—Outstanding Male Vocalist of 1965.

Sonny and Cher demonstrated their popularity by sweeping to the finals in every category in which they were entered—both individually and as a duo. This included Outstanding Male Vocalist, Outstanding *New* Male Vocalist, Outstanding Female Vocalist, Outstanding *New* Female Vocalist and Outstanding Duo. Their records made the finals in both the 45 r.p.m. singles and albums competition and in addition Sonny was recognized as one of the year's outstanding composers.

Their overall showing was matched only by Bob Dylan, who also rode an avalanche of votes to the finals in every category for which he was eligible. This included Outstanding Male Vocalist, Outstanding *New* Male Vocalist (Dylan has been world-famous as a singer for years, but became a sensation in the pop field only this year) and Outstanding Composer. Three of the top ten singles of 1965 were penned by Dylan, and his own vocal offerings were among the top ten records in both the singles and albums competition.

With voters indicating their top ten preferences, both Dylan and *(Turn to page 13)*

Stones' Concerts Packed

The Rolling Stones are rolling through their most successful American tour to date, drawing huge mobs of fans and capacity concert crowds from New England to California.

The tour began Oct. 29 in Montreal and will wind up in early December with a concert in Oakland Dec. 4, an afternoon show in San Deigo Dec. 5 and a night performance in Los Angeles later that evening.

A typical performance occurred in Rochester, N.Y., where two persons were injured and police finally moved through the screaming crowd to halt the show after the Stones had finished seven of their 11 scheduled numbers.

A police detail of more than 30 uniformed officers and plain-clothes detectives teamed with 30 uniformed guards and ushers to quell the disturbance.

With 16 concerts already concluded, here is the remainder of their schedule:

Stones' Schedule
- Nov. 25 — Pittsburgh, Pa.
- Nov. 26 — Detroit, Mich.
- Nov. 27 — Dayton, Ohio (1) Cincinatti, Ohio (2)
- Nov. 28 — Chicago (2 shows)
- Nov. 29 — Denver, Colo.
- Nov. 30 — Scottsdale, Ariz.
- Dec. 1 — Vancouver, B.C.
- Dec. 2 — Seattle, Wash.
- Dec. 3 — Sacramento
- Dec. 4 — Oakland
- Dec. 5 — San Diego (afternoon) Los Angeles (evening)

BEAT Pop Music Awards Poll
CATEGORY V: OUTSTANDING RECORDS OF 1965

MALE VOCALIST
- ☐ SONNY BONO
- ☐ JAMES BROWN
- ☐ DONOVAN
- ☐ BOB DYLAN
- ☐ BARRY MC GUIRE
- ☐ ROGER MILLER
- ☐ GENE PITNEY
- ☐ ELVIS PRESLEY
- ☐ BILLY JOE ROYAL
- ☐ IAN WHITCOMB

NEW MALE VOCALIST
- ☐ SONNY BONO
- ☐ DONOVAN
- ☐ BOB DYLAN
- ☐ BARRY MC GUIRE
- ☐ IAN WHITCOMB

FEMALE VOCALIST
- ☐ JOAN BAEZ
- ☐ CILLA BLACK
- ☐ CHER
- ☐ PETULA CLARK
- ☐ MARIANNE FAITHFULL
- ☐ LESLIE GORE
- ☐ BRENDA HOLLOWAY
- ☐ DUSTY SPRINGFIELD
- ☐ CONNIE STEVENS
- ☐ TINA TURNER

NEW FEMALE VOCALIST
- ☐ JOAN BAEZ
- ☐ CHER
- ☐ PETULA CLARK
- ☐ MARIANNE FAITHFULL
- ☐ BARBARA LEWIS

VOCAL GROUP
- ☐ ANIMALS
- ☐ BEACH BOYS
- ☐ BEATLES
- ☐ BEAU BRUMMELS
- ☐ BYRDS
- ☐ DINO, DESI & BILLY
- ☐ HERMAN'S HERMITS
- ☐ THE LOVIN' SPOONFUL
- ☐ ROLLING STONES
- ☐ YARDBIRDS

NEW VOCAL GROUP
- ☐ BEAU BRUMMELS
- ☐ BYRDS
- ☐ DINO, DESI & BILLY
- ☐ GARY LEWIS & THE PLAYBOYS
- ☐ LOVIN' SPOONFUL

FEMALE VOCAL GROUP
- ☐ BLOSSOMS
- ☐ MARTHA & THE VANDELLAS
- ☐ SHANGRALAS
- ☐ SUPREMES
- ☐ TOYS

INSTRUMENTAL GROUP
- ☐ HERB ALPERT & TIJUANA BRASS
- ☐ RAMSEY LEWIS TRIO
- ☐ THEE MIDNITERS
- ☐ SOUNDS INCORPORATED
- ☐ SOUNDS ORCHESTRAL

DUO
- ☐ CHAD & JEREMY
- ☐ JAN & DEAN
- ☐ DICK & DEEDEE
- ☐ RIGHTEOUS BROTHERS
- ☐ SONNY & CHER

COMPOSER
- ☐ SONNY BONO
- ☐ DONOVAN
- ☐ BOB DYLAN
- ☐ MICK JAGGER/KEITH RICHARD
- ☐ JOHN LENNON/PAUL MC CARTNEY
- ☐ P. F. SLOAN
- ☐ BRIAN WILSON

RECORD PRODUCER
- ☐ HERB ALPERT
- ☐ JIMMY BOWEN
- ☐ BARRY GORDY
- ☐ GREENE & STONE
- ☐ TONY HATCH
- ☐ GEORGE MARTIN
- ☐ TERRY MELCHER
- ☐ ANDREW OLDHAM
- ☐ PHIL SPECTOR
- ☐ BRIAN WILSON

RECORD COMPANY
- ☐ A&M
- ☐ ATLANTIC/ATCO
- ☐ AUTUMN
- ☐ CAPITOL
- ☐ COLUMBIA
- ☐ LIBERTY
- ☐ LONDON
- ☐ SMASH
- ☐ TAMLA/MOTOWN
- ☐ WARNER BROS./REPRISE

VOCAL RECORD — 45's
- ☐ BABY DON'T GO
- ☐ CRYING IN THE CHAPEL
- ☐ EVE OF DESTRUCTION
- ☐ HELP
- ☐ KING OF THE ROAD
- ☐ LIKE A ROLLING STONE
- ☐ MR. TAMBOURINE MAN
- ☐ MRS. BROWN
- ☐ SATISFACTION
- ☐ YESTERDAY
- ☐ YOU'VE LOST THAT LOVIN' FEELING

INSTRUMENTAL — 45's
- ☐ THE IN CROWD
- ☐ TASTE OF HONEY
- ☐ WHITTIER BLVD.
- ☐ COTTON CANDY
- ☐ CAST YOUR FATE TO THE WIND

VOCAL ALBUM
- ☐ BEACH BOYS TODAY
- ☐ BRINGING IT ALL BACK HOME — DYLAN
- ☐ HELP — BEATLES
- ☐ INTRODUCING HERMAN'S HERMITS
- ☐ LOOK AT US — SONNY & CHER
- ☐ MR. TAMBOURINE MAN — BYRDS
- ☐ OUT OF OUR HEADS — STONES
- ☐ ROLLING STONES NOW
- ☐ WHERE DID OUR LOVE GO — SUPREMES
- ☐ YOU'VE LOST THAT LOVIN' FEELING — RIGHTEOUS BROTHERS

INSTRUMENTAL ALBUM
- ☐ BEATLE SONG BOOK — HOLLYRIDGE STRINGS
- ☐ GOLDFINGER — SOUND TRACK
- ☐ THE IN CROWD — RAMSEY LEWIS
- ☐ MORE GENIUS OF JANKOWSKI
- ☐ WHIPPED CREAM & OTHER DELIGHTS — HERB ALPERT

MAIL TO: Pop Music Poll, KRLA BEAT, 6290 Sunset, Suite 504, Hollywood, Calif. 90028

Inside the BEAT
- "Real" Teen Revolt — Byrds 3
- Tea Bags and Sweatshirts 4
- Fortunes Got Their Troubles 5
- English Top Ten 5
- Shindigger Sings Off 6
- Adventures of Robin Boyd 8
- Get Off My Cloud 12
- Stones Manager Back with Marianne 13
- It's In The Bag 13
- Beau Brummels Black Balled? ... 15

The BEAT is published weekly for KRLA listeners by BEAT Publications, Inc., 6290 Sunset Blvd., Suite 504, Hollywood, California 90028. U.S. bureaus in Hollywood, San Francisco, New York, Chicago and Nashville, overseas correspondents in London, Liverpool and Manchester, England. Sale price, 15 cents. Subscription price: U.S. and possessions, $3 per year; Canada and foreign rates, $9 per year. Application to mail at second-class postage rates is pending at Los Angeles, California.

KRLA ARCHIVES

THE BYRDS — Dave, Gene, Mike, Jim and Chris sing "Turn, Turn, Turn" for our photographer, Robert Custer.

"Real" Teen Revolt–Byrds

By Bob Feigel

The Byrds' sound is uniquely beautiful and their success is evident not only in the sale of their records but also in the rapidity with which their "sound" is being copied.

And, although the Byrds dislike the label "folk-rock," they are considered by many in the music field to be the founders of the folk-rock trend and one of contemporary music's most important influences.

There have been countless articles written about the Byrds, so many in fact that the average fan could probably tell you more about them than they could themselves. Yet, an air of mystery surrounds these five young musicians.

In keeping with The BEAT's policy to bring it's readers fact rather than fiction and real life situations rather than make-believe, we asked the Byrds to answer some of our questions and give us their concept of the so-called "Teenage Revolution." A subject in which we are all very interested and, in some way, involved.

Q: What is your concept of the "Teenage Revolution?"
JIM McGUINN: "I think the natural evolution of man has stages, like each generation does a thing — a growing thing.

"A generation will span into consciousness — another level — everybody will catch up to it. And then another generation will emerge and one generation gets on top and then another comes from underneath and goes ahead of the last. And the last generation resents it.

"I think the label 'Teenage Revolution' is given by people who resent the fact that another generation is here."

Q: Do you think teenagers understand these "message" songs?
JIM: "If they listen to a song that has a message they're bound to pick up what the words are saying because they're hip to what words say in songs. They know.

Q: Do you think the teenagers are actually interested in the problems these songs talk about?
JIM: "I don't know what the whole feeling about that is. But I think the kids today are hip to it. They're sensitive, alert human beings, intelligent and well-educated. And, as a mass, they have a feeling that everything should be harmonious."

Q: What is your concept of the Teenage Revolution?

DAVID CROSBY: "It definitely is a revolution and it definitely involves the teenagers and a great many more people than the teenagers.

"Over half of the people in the country are under 25. The country isn't being run as they know and feel it should be. The discrepancies are too obvious. The wrongness and the corruption disturbs and upsets them.

"And the uncertainty of the nuclear thing, which is something we've lived with since we were born. They definitely want to change this and a lot of other things."

Q: And what are they interested in changing?
DAVID: "They're interested, as far as I've been able to discern, in the possibility of love as opposed to war. They're interested in trying to learn, trying to grow and they're resentful of the situation they've been handed as their lot."

Q: Do you think that the vast majority of young people know what the problems are?
DAVID: "I think that, naturally, only a small percentage of them are intellectually aware of that. However, they are emotionally disturbed with the feeling of the times."

Q: Do you think that message songs help to make them more aware?
DAVID: "Message songs imply an area which I doubt adds very much. I think people get a great deal of truth out of Dylan's word cologes but I doubt if they get much truth at all out of the 'surface' or very shallow copies of Dylan and Dylan's work."

Q: Chris, what do you think about the "Teenage Revolution?"

CHRIS: "It's really happening. We run across a lot of very bright kids these days. For example, not as many kids watch TV anymore — that's good."

Q: When does this start?

CHRIS: "As young as 11 or 10. They're asking more questions. They're much sharper."

Q: And is music the main source of communication?

CHRIS: "Well, not just music but everything that goes on around them. Their eyes are much more open to things."

Q: Do you think the "protest" songs are an important factor?

CHRIS: "I don't know if it would take a song to do it. There are some good protest songs and there are some which are not very subtle. They come right out and say, 'this is bad' without saying 'how' or 'why.'"

Q: Are there too many "protest" songs?

CHRIS: "Yes, there are. It's becoming very commercial. They're just writing songs to attack something without any reasons."

Q: With the variety in popular music, do you think people are becoming more sensitive to sound?

GENE CLARK: "Yes, I think so — I really do. I think that people are becoming much more sensitive to music because music in the pop field is much more sensitive."

Q: With this increased sensitivity do you think the Teenage Revolution is an extention of this?

GENE: "It's a reality instead of a fad. It's real and it counts."

Q: And when do they find this out?

GENE: "Whenever they are capable of comprehending what it could possibly mean."

Q: What do you think about Herman's statement that "the Byrds are second hand Rolling Stones?"

MIKE CLARKE: "I don't know any Herman. Who's he?"

On the BEAT
By Louise Criscione

Well, they're back! The Rolling Stones arrived Stateside for a six week tour to a fervor of adulation which has probably never been equalled.

When they landed in New York they were greeted by a 100 ft. illuminated picture of themselves high atop Times Square! All of their concerts have been sold-out for months and extra security and first-aid stations have been set up to protect the Stones and care for their fainting fans wherever they appear.

This time around the Stones have hired their own plane and for their New York stay they booked two entire floors of the Warwick Hotel. A far cry from their first tour where they played to half-filled auditoriums and smart-mouth emcees, isn't it?

Herman's Third

Plans are now in the works for Herman to begin his third film early in 1966. If his managers approve, Herman will star in "Mrs. Brown, You've Got A Lovely Daughter" for MGM. The plot will be based on the song which will leave the scriptwriters with plenty of lee-way to come up with some wild ideas.

Anyway, if all goes well the movie will be shot both in England and Hollywood. Herman's turning into quite an actor, isn't he? And he didn't do half-bad as the host of "Hullabaloo" either. I guess there's just no stopping Herman now.

... HERMAN

The Yardbirds sure go all out to be different. You know, like recording Gregorian chants and things like that. Well, now they're trying to top even themselves by appearing in a pop satirical revue!

Huge Risk

They realize that they're taking a big chance because the audience will be coming to see a pop show and not a show full of sketches and skits as well as songs. But knowing the Yardbirds, they'll no doubt be hilarious and win over the entire audience.

QUICK ONES: An English pop paper has come up with a picture of Mick Jagger on stage which looks exactly like Herman – honest! ... Dusty Springfield told me her favorite dance is The Jerk but "the kids in England can't do it" ... Are you ready for this? Bob Dylan just may appear in a movie with Marlon Brando. It ought to be a too much picture – the way the two of them mumble we won't be able to understand a word of the script ... Speaking of Dylan, Joan Baez says she is temporarily off him because: "I'm fed up with his antics." Probably vice-versa too ... Although the Beatles and Herman have long since vacated that Benedict Canyon house the girls continue to stream past it ... Dave Clark's next movie set to roll in January ... Mick Jagger, Keith Richard and Andrew Oldham have formed an independent production company, We Three Productions.

Paul Doesn't Mind

Paul McCartney says it doesn't bother him at all when another artist cuts one of the Beatle songs. "I'm always pleased when somebody has a hit with one of our songs – it's almost as good as us doing it."

ON THE BEAT reported a few columns back that Paul disliked protest songs. Well, now he has gone so far as to predict what will replace them. "We think that comedy numbers are the next thing after protest songs." And so accordingly Paul and John have written several "funny songs."

All I can say is that if "May The Bird Of Paradise Fly Up Your Nose" is any indication of things to come, Paul's prediction will be coming true in the not too distant future.

The Beatles have just completed taping a 50 minute show which included 89 other performers, which must be some kind of record. The Beatles even got Peter Sellers to appear on the show and sing "A Hard Day's Night" which has got to be the funniest thing ever!

Snooped around and found out who The Wonder Who are. You guessed it – they're really the Four Seasons. Nice trick boys, you now have two records in the charts instead of one.

... PAUL

KRLA ARCHIVES

BEAT PHOTOGRAPHER, Robert W. Young, captures the Rolling Stones as they wait patiently (?) for their plane to carry them on to the next stop on their American tour. Mick Jagger, Keith Richard, Brian Jones and Bill Wyman are all present and accounted for — but what happened to Charlie Watts?

Yeah, Well Rolling Stones...
Tea Bags And Sweatshirts

By Tammy Hitchcock

Yeah, well we're Stoned again this week. Oops, that didn't come out sounding just right, did it? What I meant to say is that we have the Stones all anchored onto our Yeah, Well Hot Seat this week.

Quite a few of his fans have been wondering why Keith never makes any on-stage announcements. He assures us that it's not because he's lazy or has perpetual laryngitis or anything as disasterous as that.

It's just that "I have to change guitars, alter volume and tone controls, plug into fuzz-boxes and all sorts of things."

Yeah, well I have your whole problem solved for you, Keith. From now on *I* will accompany you on all of your personal appearances and while *you* introduce I'll plug your tone control into your fuzz-box for you!

The End

Bill has now gone into the talent discovery bag. One of his latest discoveries is a group called The End. Yeah, well Bill, I have a real hot tip for you.

There's this girl who has the most fantastic voice and the way she looks is unbelievable. I mean, everyone just *stares* and then when I start singing they all race for the exits.

Fact is, half of them don't even wait for me to sing — they practically kill themselves getting *out* the minute I come *in*. I really can't understand why. There's nothing wrong with an orange and red shirt, green and white checked skirt, textured hose and black knee-boots — is there, Bill?

The Stones owe an American disc jockey $5 'cause they bet him "Satisfaction" wouldn't reach number one in the nation. Yeah, well that jock shouldn't feel too bad.

Stones' Debts

The Stones owe me one flo-through tea bag which prematurely flowed through, a rubber band which once held my hair up but which now holds Bill's sock up, a half a stick of bubble gum, a "Rolling Stones, Now" album which Mick sat on, a picture of Keith which Charlie tastefully decorated with googles, go-tee, blacked-out teeth and warts, one fountain pen which George Harrison touched, and one slightly used Kleenex.

'Course, I'm not about to ask for all those valuables back. Mainly because I owe them one roll of undeveloped film which I dropped into a sink full of soap suds, one copy of their British "Out Of Our Heads" album which I sat myself on, one guitar strap which I broke, and an apple which possessed one healthy and hungry worm in it.

I owe to Charlie one half-finished painting on which I spilled my liquid eye-liner and then tried unsuccessfully to wipe off with some old striped rag. And to Brian I owe — one striped shirt.

The last time the Stones were in town Charlie was lugging around this black hat. I asked him if he was going to wear it and he said: "No, I'm going to sit on it." Yeah, well you don't have to do that, Charlie — I've already done the honors!

Like A Date, Brian

Brian is forever wearing sweatshirts which people give him. Like he wears this one which says "Radio Syd" and other one which has "Rudolf Rosmussen Sport" on the front.

Yeah, well I can hardly wait until I see you again, Brian. I've had a sweatshirt made for you too. It says "Tammy Hitchcock Wants A Date."

You all know that the Stones like to record at the RCA Studios. And Mick tells us why: "Mainly because of a bloke called Dave Hassanger. He's the Sound Engineer there and he knows exactly what we're trying to do, he doesn't mess about getting exact settings on the dials."

Mick — It's Me

Yeah, well listen, Mick, it's not really Dave at all — it's me. You know why "Get Off My Cloud" came out so well? It's 'cause *I* helped Dave! I put my purse down right on top of the dials. That way he *couldn't* mess with the dials — he couldn't even move 'em!

Keith was talking about the difference between a European audience and an American or English audience. "Here they are mostly girls — which is just fine with me."

Yeah, well it's not just fine with me! All you girls had better stop chasing Keith. You should all be thoroughly ashamed of yourselves. I mean, how utterly UNLADYLIKE!

And besides, I'M chasing Keith myself and all you girls keep getting in my way!

ANOTHER BEAT PHOTOGRAPHER, Chuck Boyd, discovered Charlie — pounding his beloved drums.

KRLA ARCHIVES

BARRY McGUIRE ISN'T PROTESTING over these momentos of success. Clutched between his knees is his gold record of "Eve of Destruction." Sandwiched between record charts listing his hit as number one in the nation are earlier copies of **The BEAT** praising his talents.

PORTMAN'S PLATTERPOOP

Hugo Montenegro, RCA Victor's talented master musician, was a wee miffed at *The BEAT* when we failed to give his album "The Man From U.N.C.L.E." some mention. It's selling as fast as *The BEAT* with *David McCallum* on the cover . . . *Johnny Tillotson*, the boy wonder of MGM records, singed to tour the U.S. bases in the Pacific this Christmas . . . *Andy Williams*, the man with sagging TV-ratings, immediately inked *The Beach Boys* to give his show a teen-age injection . . . Dot records *Barry Young*, the *Dean Martin* sound-alike, is insuring record sales with his new release. It's called "9th Street West."

It had to happen. *The Batman* comes to television and Superman goes on Broadway . . . *Tony Harris*, Dee Gee records fair-haired youth, has written and recorded a gassy-tune titled "Superman." If the B'way producer doesn't hurry, he may have to change the name of his show.

Bill Cosby, the talented actor-comedian who has sold many comedy albums for Warner Bros., tries a new bag called singing. His first release is a Christmas ditty "Little Fir Tree" . . . Not that Cosby isn't a good vocalist, but *Denise Regan*, the 10 year old vocalist with Dee Gee records has one of the finest recordings of a Christmas type tune ready to hit the market. *The Platterpoop* predicts it'll be one of this year's biggest releases. It's titled "Hole in the Stocking."

Free Offer: *The Platterpoop* has made arrangements with Dee Gee records so that the first 100 readers who write to *The Platterpoop* c/o Dee Gee records, 1953 Pontius, Los Angeles, California 90025 will receive Denise's record. Hurry, offer is limited to first 100 letters!

For the Old Timers (mothers and dads who read their offsprings' newspaper): *Al (Jealous Heart) Morgan* has a bright new tune, "Love Is A Place" b/w "I'll Take Care of Your Cares" that's become a huge seller in Chicago. It should be a must for your record collections. Young, talented *Keith Green*, ASCAP's youngest writer (he's written over 100 tunes) has penned "How to be Your Guy" and recorded same for Decca records. The flip side is a *Brian Wilson (Beach Boys)* tune, "Girl Don't Tell Me" . . . A faithful fan of my column is *Linda Mino*. She always has something good to say!

Roy Orbison, filming the "Fastest Guitar in the West," goes the promo route with a cameo on the TV series "Man Called Shenandoah" . . . *Sonny & Cher* have just about captured the English charts. Couldn't happen to two nicer people . . . *Charles Boyer*, the old movie lover and TV millionaire, has released an ablum on Valiant (he owns a large portion of this label) titled "Where Does Love Go." If Charles don't know, who does? . . . Big cheers for the *New Christy Minstrels* for planning to spend their Christmas cheering-up the G.I.'s in Viet-Nam.

Piccola Pupa departed Reprise records for Capitol. Mama Pupa is tired of the U.S., and would like to return to Italy for a breather. It's been two years since she tasted home cooking . . . *Jack Jones* is joining the *Bob Hope* Christmas tour this year. He's the most requested male vocalist amid the G.I.'s. Are you listening, *Mr. Sinatra?* . . .

Dick Howard, Shindig's "Man of the Hour," called to ask if I remembered the late and great *Mario Lanza?* "Certainly," I replied, "who doesn't?" Dick informed me that the oldest offspring of Mario's, lovely 16 year old Colleen, is ready to follow in her father's footsteps by signing a contract with Dee Gee records. Her first release will be a rock-folk tune!

Stones Reign Supreme

The Rolling Stones have done it – knocked Ken Dodds' "Tears" from that number one spot! Dodd reigned for six straight weeks, gaining the chart-topping position by knocking off the Stones' "Satisfaction."

So, now the Stones have repayed Dodd by capturing top spot with "Get Off My Cloud," dropping "Tears" down to number three.

The Fortunes and "Here It Comes Again" moved up one place this week falling in at number five. And Matt Monro's "Yesterday" did likewise coming in at number 6.

The Animals took another big jump – all the way up from number 14 to number 7 with "It's My Life." Looks like their chart life is pretty good right about now!

The Yardbirds find themselves this week in a rather unique but certainly enjoyable position. Both sides of their record are in the top ten – "Still I'm Sad" is up from 12 to 8 while the flip, "Evil Hearted You," plopped down in the number 10 spot.

The Australian Seekers are literally flying up the British charts with their new one, "The Carnival Is Over." The record debuted last week at number 27 and this week is all the way up to number 11.

Another flyer this week is Len Barry and "1-2-3." Len also debuted last week and this week moved himself from 28 to number 16. A double country hit for Len who is wisely paying our cousins across the ocean a visit to further bolster his chart status.

This week's highest debuters are The Who, the guys who play up the pop art craze to the hilt. Their "My Generation" came in this week at number 18 – a nice debuting position for any record.

British Top 10

1. GET OFF MY CLOUD — Rolling Stones
2. YESTERDAY MAN — Chris Andrews
3. TEARS — Ken Dodd
4. GOOD NEWS WEEK — Hedgehoppers
5. HERE IT COMES AGAIN — The Fortunes
6. YESTERDAY — Matt Monro
7. IT'S MY LIFE — The Animals
8. STILL I'M SAD — The Yardbirds
9. ALMOST THERE — Andy Williams
10. EVIL HEARTED YOU — The Yardbirds

Fortunes Got Their Trouble

The Fortunes, who's first hit in America was "You've Got Your Troubles," have got *their* troubles. They need an image. It seems most of their fans can't tell them apart and they have no definite distinguishing mark.

"We don't expect a wild image," said Barry Pritchard," I suppose if we started doing all beat numbers and leaping about we'd get an image. But, we wouldn't sacrifice a good stage act to get an image."

What kind of image do they want? "Any image that makes money," quipped Barry.

KRLA ARCHIVES

The Shindigger Signs Off

Howdy hi, Shindiggers. Welcome to our very last get together here at "Shindig."

I'm sitting here alone in the audience section of the set, thinking about all of the good times we have had together here at Shindig.

The stage is dark now, and the dancers have all gone home. The "Shindig" band has put their instruments away, and all that can be heard now is the lonely sound of silence.

If these darkened walls have any memories at all, I know that the ghosts of the good times past are here with us tonight. In fact, I can almost hear the echoing voices now.

I can hear the Beatles as they were presented by "Shindig" in "Around the Beatles." I can still feel the excitement I felt the night the Rolling Stones introduced "Satisfaction" for the first time on "Shindig," and I hear the wild screams of the girls the night that Gerry and the Pacemakers were here. In fact, two of those little girls were so excited that they had to be taken to a hospital.

Last TV Appearance

I remember the night that Sam Cooke was on the show; it was one of the last television shows he appeared on before his untimely death.

I can still hear the thunderous applause the night that Ray Charles was here. I remember the excitement of the opening medley as all of the guests sang one of Ray's songs, and then there were trumpets and a drum roll and then Ray himself sang "Georgia." He was the only performer ever to get a standing ovation—from both the audience and the "Shindig" cast and crew—on "Shindig."

I can hear Sonny and Cher singing the night that "Shindig" first became a network show, telecast all across the country, and I remember the fun we had when the Dave Clark Five were guests on the show.

I can hear all of the laughter ringing out around me from all of the practical jokes we have all played on one another. Kirby with his wild sense of humor, and Bobby Sherman with his even *wilder* sense of humor. I remember the Halloween show when Bobby Sherman broke up all the rehearsals as he came bounding out in a long, red-haired wig yelling 'Sonny . . . Sonny where are you??!!!

I think of all the people who have gotten their start right here on "Shindig," and all of the other shows which got their start *because of* "Shindig!" I think most of all of that jolly, good-natured, and brilliant man who *started* it all—Jack Good. Without Jack, there would have been no "Shindig" and television—and a lot of people—would have missed out on a great deal of fine entertainment and a great deal of happiness. We all owe a debt of gratitude to Jack.

I can still hear Glen Campbell and Jerry Naylor as they sang a duet for me backstage during the taping of one of the shows, and I remember the day that Dick and Dee Dee were on the show, and had the entire cast and crew in absolute stitches all through rehearsals!

I remember the great fun we all had at the parties that the Wellingtons threw for everyone at "Shindig," and the fun that everyone had on the "Shindig" tours that traveled cross country.

I can still hear the Righteous Brothers singing one of their great, soulful numbers and just breaking up the show with excitement. And I can't forget all of the hard work—the "blood, sweat and tears"—of all the people in the cast and crew of "Shindig" for the last year and a half. They've all been just the greatest.

The Other Side

And you. I can't stop thinking about you, the people at home on the *other* side of the television set. We all hope that you have had as much fun and enjoyment *watching* the show, as we have all had presenting it to you.

"Shindig" is going off the air now and what used to be will be no more. But we would still like to hear any opinions you may want to express. If you have anything you would like to say about "Shindig," please write to me—The Shindigger—in care of *The BEAT*, or address your cards and letters to ABC TV, 4151 Prospect Ave., Los Angeles, Calif. 90027.

For myself and for everyone on "Shindig," I would like to thank you for your support and appreciation of "Shindig" and for the last time ever ask you to maintain your soul, Shindiggers; and remember: no matter what *anybody* says—ROCK ON!!!!!

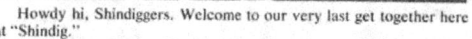

KRLA ARCHIVES

VISITOR FINDS LANGUAGE BARRIER
British Speak English, Not American

Dear *BEAT*:

Regarding your recent articles on what one may expect when traveling in Britain, I think it is only fair to warn readers that one major problem they will have to face is that of the language barrier. My own first trip to England was nearly a disaster because of this, and the second trip was only slightly better.

As Art Buchwald once said, "English is a vast, beautiful but improbable language that resembles American about as closely as Spanish resembles Italian. Just enough to throw you off." He's right, too.

Everyone knows that jam sandwiches are jam butties, and a cuppa refers to a cup of tea, but how many know that a coat belongs in the front cupboard (closet)? Everybody knows that one takes the lift to get to the fourth floor flat but how many people know what the "closet" (water closet or w.c.) is.

One spends a rainy afternoon at the cinema or seeing a film—or even "at the flicks." That may sound very very "antique," but then you must remember that in many English towns, you ring up the operator on the phone and she will connect you with the number you want. (Remember the old "Lassie" T.V. show—same type of phone system, only they still have it in many places.)

Foods don't vary too too much. Cookie is biscuit, a steak is a sirloin roast, crackers are (ugh) digestives, bacon is gammon or streaky. What we call Canadian bacon is what they call bacon, corn is maize and hamburger is mince meat (their most well-known type of what we call hamburgers are called "wimpeys", and believe me—that's exactly what they are.

When shopping, or referring to things around the house, a wall plug is a multiple outlet adaptor, a sink is a basin, a clothes pin is a clothes peg, not much difficulty there. Remember also, that a limousine is a saloon, cheesecloth is butter muslin (or mutton cloth) a van, suspenders (for slacks, etc.) and braces, braces (for your teeth) are bands.

One does not stand in line, one stands in a queue, and one "queues up." A model is a mannequin, a magazine stand is a kiosk, gasoline is petrol, one wears plaits, not braids and one gets a ladder, not a run in her nylons.

This is just spoken English. The written language is even "crazier." Color is *colour*, realize is *realise*, defense is *defence*, jail is *gaol*, curb is *kerb*, traveled is *travelled*, skillful is *skilful*, maneuver is *manoeuvre*, anesthesia is *anaesthesia*, plow is *plough*, draft is *draught*, stories (on a building) are *storeys*, program is *programme* etc., etc., etc.

As for pronunciation—well, that varies in every county and has to be learned from experience. Most words with "ew" are pronounced as in "you"—that's universal. But words like grass differ from grass to grahss to grawss.

As Art Buchwald concluded his article—"there'll always be an England."

Name withheld by request

Beatle Voices Now On TV

Did you know that the Beatles are on television here every Saturday morning?

Well, the voices of two of them at least.

King Features has a new television show on now called "The Beatles' Series." It's a cartoon feature produced in London using the voices of the real George Harrison and Ringo Starr as well as authentic Beatle recordings.

The show features the Beatles in short cartoon features in wild escapades all over the world. Even their fans are in the show. The fab four have been seen being chased by adoring fans everywhere from Africa to Arizona. And each cartoon includes at least one Beatle song.

HOWARD HAWKS PRESENTS **RED LINE 7000**
WHERE ENGINES MELT AND YOUNG BLOOD BOILS!
...where girls can go only for men who think fast, love fast, ...The Speed Breed!

TECHNICOLOR® Co-starring JAMES CAAN · LAURA DEVON · GAIL HIRE · CHARLENE HOLT · JOHN ROBERT CRAWFORD · MARIANNA HILL · JAMES WARD · NORMAN ALDEN
Directed and Produced by HOWARD HAWKS Screenplay by GEORGE KIRGO Music Scored and Conducted by NELSON RIDDLE A Paramount Picture

OPENING WED., (NOV. 24) AT THEATRES AND DRIVE-INS ALL OVER TOWN

KRLA ARCHIVES

Life + Laughs = Dusty Springfield

By Louise Criscione

Dusty Springfield's voice came over the house phone: "Why don't you come on up to my manager's room? I'll be up in a few minutes. You see, I sent my clothes out to be cleaned and they're only coming back in dribbles and drabbles! So, as soon as I get a proper outfit I'll be up."

I had no sooner settled down to a cup of coffee when footsteps were heard running down the hall and Dusty burst into the room apologizing for being late. She was wearing a bright green print dress, a most proper outfit, and one which looked great with her blonde hair.

"I've been having so much trouble with my clothes. You see, in England we don't have color television so all my clothes are light colors which doesn't look well on color TV. It comes out looking all white and it drives the television people mad," Dusty bubbled.

It was then that our BEAT photographer suggested that we all go poolside to take some pictures. Dusty wrinkled her nose, gave the photographer a funny look and then said: "Okay, I'll be back in a second." And with that she raced out of the room and down the hall again.

She *was* back in a second, this time dressed in white capris and a black and white striped top—looking very, very American.

Once poolside we began the interview. Of course, Dusty has had several huge hits here in America but lately she has encountered her share of trouble in getting onto the charts.

"I don't know why. It's just one of those things," Dusty said. "It's completely the opposite in England but here I don't know what went wrong." She thought on it for a while and then added: "It might be that I'm not here enough."

"Soul" Sound

Whenever people write about Dusty's music they invariably use the word "soul" to define her sound. But what is it—this illusive quality they call soul?

"Soul is something that can't be defined—you just know it when you hear it. It's such an overworked word that I feel ill-equipped to try to define it," Dusty answered.

"It's nice of people to say I'm a soul singer. I *am* influenced by R&B but I'm certainly not an R&B singer," Dusty grinned.

Dusty Springfield is not her real name. In fact, her real name is Mary O'Brien but "Dusty" was tagged onto her during her childhood years when she was somewhat of a tomboy.

"I don't know where I got it but I've been trying to get rid of it ever since," laughed Dusty.

Tea Cup Hurtling

A lot has been written about Dusty's habit of throwing tea cups. "Well, I haven't thrown any here yet! And I only do it under extreme stress and only in my own place and I *always* clean up the mess," Dusty assured me.

Which rather relieved me as I didn't particularly fancy the idea of having a tea cup thrown at me—even if it *was* thrown by Dusty Springfield.

Dusty and her group of London-based friends have quite a time playing practical jokes on each other. There was the time Dusty had cans and cans of "petrol" sent to a friend's house and the time she opened her purse to find it filled with soap powder just wet enough to make a huge mess and total ruin!

"And whenever I put on weight," said the slim-figured Dusty, "they send me dresses which are about this big," continued Dusty indicating about a size 24 dress.

No one is immune from Dusty's jokes and the Shangri-las found that out when they went to put on their boots one morning only to find them filled with anchovies!

The Performer

Enough jokes—now back to Dusty the performer. As you probably know, Dusty once sang with her brother's group, the Springfields. At the time they broke up they were the top group in England.

"People said we were crazy. And at first it was awfully hard. I was used to having two boys with me and suddenly there was so much space I didn't know what to do with my hands!" Dusty exclaimed.

Most performers suffer from nerves before a show and Dusty is no exception. "If I'm doing a week somewhere I'm nervous the first night. But when it's some big occasion, then I'm nervous the whole time."

The biggest occasion for a British entertainer is coming up soon. It's the Royal Variety Show and Dusty has been invited to appear on the show in front of the Queen.

"I'm very excited about it. I've been on one before with the Springfields and I met the Queen then," Dusty enthused.

"I'm flying back next week to work out the arrangements. I'm not nervous yet but I will be," predicted Dusty.

Loves Singing

Dusty is completely enthusiastic about most things and especially so about her career. "I enjoy it. I love singing. I like doing tours but I also like clubs because they give you the chance to progress.

"There is more opportunity to progress here than in England. Because in each big city there is at least one big club in a hotel or something but it's not like that in England," Dusty explained.

Besides her singing, Dusty is probably best known for the amazing amount of eye make-up which she wears. "It's a trade mark," Dusty said. "I take a lot of it off for television. I look anemic without it."

I don't know. I can't see Dusty Springfield ever looking anemic—she's too full of life and fun for that.

WHAT'S SO FUNNY? Only BEAT reporter, Louise Criscione, and Dusty Springfield know and neither one of them will let us in on the joke. But from the looks of Louise, it sure must have been funny!

"LIKE THIS" says Dusty—helping BEAT photographer, Robert Custer, focus his picture of darling Dusty.

By Susan Frisch

Can you please give me the birthdays of Sonny and Cher.
—Carol Benovidez

Their birthdays are: Sonny, February 16. Cher, May 20.

Where can I write to the Byrds and be sure of them getting my letter? Not a fan club please.
—Fran Brunel

Write to the Byrds at, 9000 Sunset Blvd., #407, Hollywood, Calif.

Are Peter Asher and Millie Small engaged? Do any of Bob Dylan's albums have Mr. Tambourine Man, It Ain't Me Babe, and Love Minus Zero on them?
—Mickey Smith

First of all, NO!, Peter and Millie aren't dating. Quite a few of Dylan's albums have those recordings on them.

Has Bob Dylan been in town lately? Why hasn't he been on Shindig, Hullabaloo, etc?
—Gail Dash

Bob Dylan has not been in town since the beginning of September.

What kind of makeup does Jane Asher use, and was it true that she was in a car accident with another girl friend?
—Jane Asher

The "real" Jane Asher uses Max Factor makeup base and M.F. cake eyeliner. No, she wasn't in any car accident.

Where did Sony and Cher meet?
—Peggy Clifford

Sonny and Cher met while at a recording session. They were background singers.

Can you give me an address where Cher will get a personal letter? This is very important, and I must be sure she gets it.
—Carolyn Nelson

Write to Cher, and label it PERSONAL, at, 7715 Sunset Blvd., Hollywood, Calif.

KRLA ARCHIVES

"FASTEST GUMS IN THE WEST" — That's the title awarded KRLA's Dick Biondi in this groovy sketch sent in by talented Debbie Wilson.

HELP!

I desperately need a story or essay for use as the basis for a motion picture. Please write to: Don, Imperial Pictures, 5250 Wood Avenue, South Gate, Calif. 90281.

HELP!

I would like to trade the L.P. "Introducing Herman's Hermits" for the Beatle L.P., "Something New." Also, I would like to trade the album, "Beach Boys Today" for Ian Whitcomb's first album (or the Marianne Faithfull or "Glad All Over" by the DC 5. Anyone interested contact me. All L.P.'s are in good condition. Fernie Habush, 6220 Bluebell Ave., No. Hollywood, Calif.

HELP!

Anyone interested in helping start a Robert Vaughn Fan Club write Glenna Hawley, 6351 West 79th St., Los Angeles, Calif. 90025 or Marilyn Warne, 7507 Westlawn Ave., Los Angeles, Calif. 90045.

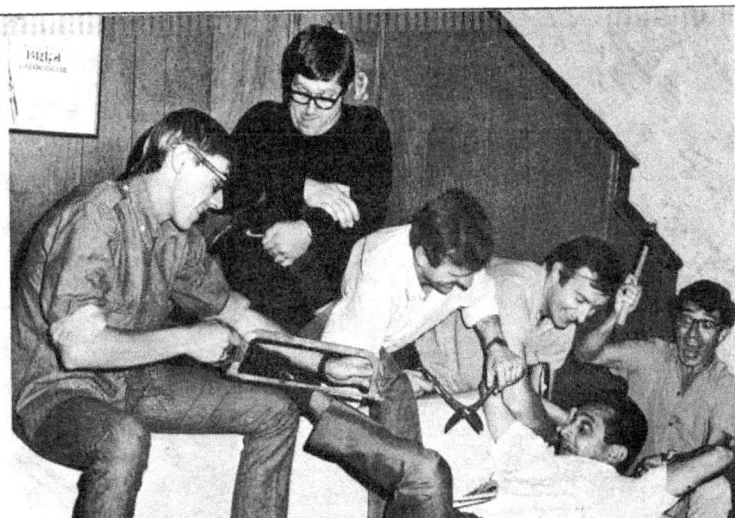

PITY THE POOR HULLABALOOER! Dave Hull was taking a peaceful nap between records when he was pounced upon by a bloodthirsty gang of terrorists — known by many as Freddie and the Dreamers. Fortunately for Dave, he was able to convince them the guy they really wanted was Dick Biondi.

HOLE IN THE WALL
422 N. La Cienega
Phone: 652 7562
Fab Clothes
Groovy Accessories
For the 'IN' Crowd

Out of Sight!!! real "BYRD" style SUNGLASSES

Simulated gold frames, including SMASHING solid metal case to protect the lens.

$7.95 PAIR
PLUS 25c MAILING CHARGE

By Tropic, Calif.

WE WILL MAIL TO YOU PREPAID
SEND MONEY ORDER OR CHECK

NAME: _____
ADDRESS: _____
CITY: _____ STATE: _____
CHECK FINISH WANTED: GOLD ☐ SILVER ☐

422 N. La Cienega
Los Angeles 48, Calif.
HOLE IN THE WALL

AFTER THE BIG BATTLE, Freddie and his mob are completely BEAT!

Stop Worrying!

Here's an Easy Way to Solve Your Christmas Shopping Chores.

A subscription to *The BEAT* makes an ideal gift. Think of all your friends who like to read YOUR copy of *The BEAT* every week! They'll remember you all year long. Just send in the form below — and then forget about fighting the crowds to do your Christmas shopping. We'll send them a special gift card with your name attached. If you want to send more than one, simply fill in the additional names and addresses on a plain sheet of paper, enclosing $3 for each subscription. (P.S. If you're not already a subscriber, how about sending one to yourself?)

GIFT SUBSCRIPTION

To: (Name) _____ Age: _____
Address: _____
City: _____ State: _____ Zip: _____
Enclosed is $ _____

MAIL TO: KRLA BEAT, 1401 S. Oak Knoll, Pasadena, Calif.

KRLA ARCHIVES

LOOK FAMILIAR? Of course *The BEAT* looks familiar, but so does the chap who's reading it. Ian Whitcomb, one of the first *BEAT* subscribers, dropped by for a chat during his recent tour of the West Coast area.

Person to Person

To Dwarf and King:
I'll feel a whole lot better when you're gone.
A Byrd

To Donna:
I hope you had a nice visit here in Martin's Ferry. Say "hi" to Lynn and Penny for me. (Robin and Gert too).
Marsha and Snookie

To McCumiskey, Oldell, Hadnutt, and the other two:
I love you cause you're you. You're great... I love you!!
Who else but ME?!

To Mike Smith of the D.C. 5:
You're the nicest, sweetest, cutest, most talented boy I know. I hope I'll get to talk to you again when you return.
Billie Jo

To Gidget:
Where did you find Dennis? How did he look? Where did you go? Just heard about it! Call soon.
Cyn

Dear BEAT:
The other day I heard the group called The Marbles and I think they were so great! If they have a fan club would you please ask the readers to send it to *The BEAT*.
A Devoted Reader

KRLA's Johnny Hayes Is Versatile Personality

He is tall, handsome, and young. He is the boy next door and the son away at college. He is a little bit of everyone you have ever known and a lot of everyone you've never met. He is Johnny Hayes.

Johnny was born 26 years ago on March 10 in Macon, Georgia. After completing his high school training, he spent some time in the Air Force and then went on to his first job in radio as a disc jockey in another city in Georgia.

Johnny's interest in radio had been stimulated by his first visit to a radio station with a friend. He found himself fascinated by the equipment and the whole idea of radio broadcasting, and it didn't take him very long to decide that this was his chosen profession.

Problem

But there was one problem which he had to face: having been born in the South, Johnny had in his possession a distinct Southern drawl which *definitely* had to go if he was to be successful as a radio announcer.

So, he undertook to rid himself of his native "you all's"—all by himself. It wasn't easy, but Johnny listened to every radio announcer on every radio program which was broadcast in Georgia, and within a few years, he succeeded in completely losing his drawl and even managed to lower the range of his voice by several octaves.

Johnny has now been a member of the winning team of disc jockeys on KRLA for eight months. And speaking of his beginning with the station, Johnny says: "I only want to work for a winner—I don't want to work for losers—and of course that eliminated every other station in town. I'm not just saying that, becuase I *have* to believe in any station I go to work for—that's very important—I *have* to believe in them, and I believe in KRLA. It's a winner!"

Swing Shift

Johnny is the man upon whom all of the other disc jockeys at KRLA must rely at one time or another. Aside from his regular weekly chores on the Saturday Top Thirty Tunedex show, Johnny is the man who steps in and saves the day for everyone whenever one of his fellow disc jockeys is taken ill or making personal appearances. This is probably one of the most difficult tasks in radio—to successfully take over someone else's program for a short period of time—and Johnny is one of the few men who can do this, and do it *well!!!*

Johnny's preferences in music generally depend on his particular mood of the moment. "Whatever I want to hear at the moment; like

songs that say something to me. One day it might be classical and the next day it might be pop."

His personal favorites in performers follow pretty much the same pattern, but he does have a special interest in Dylan's work. Just what does he think of Dylan?

"I like him, that's all. He is interpreting life as he sees it, as he lives it, as it really is. You know, I just came to a realization not long ago. It's so obvious that it almost seems ridiculous to mention it, but people who write of love and of pain and of hate have usually lived through it and experienced it themselves."

Not Sure

As far as the protest movement in music is concerned, Johnny sums up his feelings on the matter by saying: "I'm not sure just what they're protesting. I don't know if they are really protest songs at all."

There are many people who have tried to foretell the future of pop music, though few seem to have been successful. Johnny makes no great presumptuous predictions here, but simply says: "I can't look into the future. There are many trends, and trends are always changing. I don't really know what is coming."

Optimism

Although Johnny won't make any claims at being a gypsy or a fortune teller, he did leave us with one very optimistic note looking into the future. Speaking about the current younger generation, he enthusiastically says:

"I think they're great. Look—they are the promise of the future; *our* future! Come good or bad, they are going to see a lot of things, and have a lot of experiences, and the future depends on them. *My* future is in their hands!"

Regardless of *who* is holding the strings on Johnny's future, it is undoubtedly going to be a bright one.

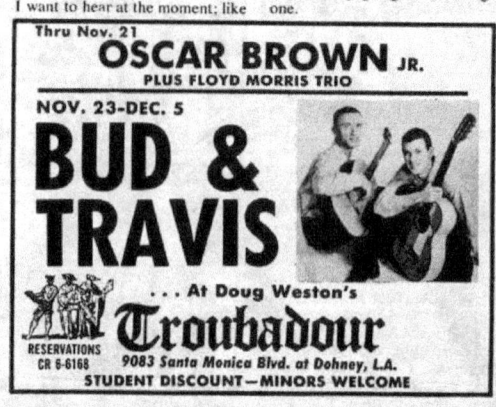

Thru Nov. 21
OSCAR BROWN JR.
PLUS FLOYD MORRIS TRIO

NOV. 23–DEC. 5
BUD & TRAVIS

...At Doug Weston's
Troubadour
RESERVATIONS CR 6-6168
9083 Santa Monica Blvd. at Dohney, L.A.
STUDENT DISCOUNT — MINORS WELCOME

STATEMENT OF OWNERSHIP, MANAGEMENT AND CIRCULATION

1. DATE OF FILING: October 25, 1965
2. TITLE OF PUBLICATION: THE BEAT — WEEKLY
4. LOCATION OF KNOWN OFFICE OF PUBLICATION: 6290 Sunset Blvd., Los Angeles, Calif. 90028, Los Angeles County
5. LOCATION OF HEADQUARTERS: 6290 Sunset Blvd., Los Angeles, California 90028
6. PUBLISHER: Cecil Tuck, 145 Hurlbut, Pasadena, California
   EDITOR: Cecil Tuck, 145 Hurlbut, Pasadena, California
   MANAGING EDITOR: Gayle Tuck, 145 Hurlbut, Pasadena, California

7. OWNER:

NAME	ADDRESS
Cecil Tuck	145 Hurlbut, Pasadena, California
Michael Brown	5900 Highridge Road, Calabasas, California

8. KNOWN BONDHOLDERS, MORTGAGEES, AND OTHER SECURITY HOLDERS: None

	AVERAGE NO. COPIES EACH ISSUE DURING PRECEDING 12 MONTHS	SINGLE ISSUE NEAREST TO FILING DATE
A. TOTAL NO. COPIES PRINTED (Net Press Run)	49,000	55,635
B. PAID CIRCULATION 1. SALES THROUGH DEALERS AND CARRIERS, STREET VENDORS AND COUNTER SALES	40,000	46,000
2. MAIL SUBSCRIPTIONS	6,500	6,575
C. TOTAL PAID CIRCULATION	46,500	52,575
D. FREE DISTRIBUTION BY MAIL, CARRIER OR OTHER MEANS	800	1,400
E. TOTAL DISTRIBUTION (Sum of C and D)	47,300	53,915
F. OFFICE USE, LEFT-OVER, UNACCOUNTED, SPOILED AFTER PRINTING	1,700	1,720
G. TOTAL (Sum of E & F—should equal net press run shown in A)	49,000	55,635

KRLA ARCHIVES

Adventures of Robin Boyd

By Shirley Poston

CHAPTER THREE

"Hey, what's going on here," Robin Boyd chirped in amazement, directing this question to George the Genie (of tea pot fame) who was still seated on the other side of the room.

George grinned handsomely, looking even more like George Harrison than usual. "You said you wanted to be a *real* bird so you could fly to England and all, didn't you?"

Robin giggled. "It must be the power of suggestion. All of a sudden I have the *strangest* craving for *birdseed*!"

George ambled to her side and picked her up with one hand. Then he held her in front of the mirror and she stopped giggling in one large hurry.

"George," she choked, looking at the odd object crouched in George's palm. An odd object that oddly resembled a *bird*.

"Is that *me*?" she further choked.

George drew himself up proudly (he was given to moments of melodrama) (even Genies are not totally perfect) (however, they are close).

Robin

"That it is!" he bragged. "And you're a *robin*, just like your name!"

Robin flapped her wings in disbelief. "Can I fly?" she quaked, flapping some more.

"You can learn," said George. "Right now," he added devilishly, tossing her high into the air.

"*George!*" shrieked Robin, flapping furiously around the room.

George made no move to rescue her. "You'll get the hang of it," he offered.

"George," purred Robin a moment later as she got the hang of it and soared about in graceful swoops. "This is fab!"

Back To Earth

George held out his hand. "Come back to earth now."

Peering near-sightedly at the outstretched "runway," Robin zoomed in for her first happy landing.

It wasn't very. She missed the field completely.

After picking her up gently, George placed her atop the tea pot (of George the Genie fame) on her dresser.

"Now," he said in a schoolteacherish tone, "I am going to give you bird lessons."

Robin twittered. *Bird lessons*.

"This is a serious matter," frowned George, drawing a small book from the pocket of his jacket (which wasn't easy because his jacket had no pockets).

"Now listen carefully," he ordered, opening the book. "Lesson number one. You now possess the powers to change yourself into a bird, as requested when you were asked to relate your fondest wish to the Genie at hand. You are a *robin*," he re-bragged. "When you wish to become a bird, you will say the word 'Liverpool'. That's me hometown," he added.

Robin nodded excitedly, which caused her to teeter dangerously on the tea pot. (Also to wonder about her sanity for she had never figured she would live to see the day when she'd be teetering on a tea pot.)

"*Two*," continued George at masterful volume. "When you wish to change back into the *real* Robin (he paused to smile confidently) (the luvable ham), you must say the word 'Worchestershire'."

"Can I fly anywhere I want?" Robin interrupted. "And can I fly as fast as I want?"

5,000 M.P.H.

George silenced her with an impatient glare. "*Three*. You may fly anywhere you please, at the sensible speed of no more than 5,000 miles per hour."

Robin teetered off the tea pot in ecstasy. But George snarled so she hopped right back up.

"It is important that you do not exceed this speed limit," he read on. "If you do, you will be apprehended by the Bird Patrol."

"Quiet!" thundered George. "*Four*. You will be oblivious to the elements during any given flight or perch."

Robin stared poignantly.

Any Questions?

"You won't get cold, hot, wet, or blown away in a typhoon," he translated. "Are there any questions?"

Robin raised her hand (well, she tried) and George nodded, giving her the floor (well, the tea pot).

"When I fly places, how will I explain my absence when I return?" she asked, an intelligent question if she did say so herself (and, she did).

George searched through the book for a brief moment.

"That," he said, snapping it shut and putting it back in the pocket that wasn't there, "is your problem."

Robin shrugged. One couldn't have everything.

"Are my bird lessons finished?" she asked, praying no one was listening outside the door.

"Almost," replied George. "There's just one more thing. You are going to wear your glasses from now on."

"*No!*" pleaded Robin.

"*Yes*," George said firmly. "You are blind as six bats without them."

Robin bristled. "How many times have you seen a *bird* wearing *glasses*?" she wailed.

George laughed hysterically. "Only once," he pointed.

Robin flew over to the mirror. Then *she* laughed hysterically. Perched on her nose (er . . . beak) were the world's tiniest pair of bird (er . . . Byrd) glasses. Dark ones with square, wire-framed lens.

Turn Me Back

"George," she cried, flying over to him. "Turn me back into me so I can hug you!"

In an instant, she was herself again, but George was not. Anywhere to be seen, that is.

She searched the room frantically, suddenly afraid she'd dreamed it all.

"George?" she whispered hopefully, raising the lid of the tea pot as a last resort.

Then she let out a large whoosh of relief. George wasn't in the tea pot. But something was.

And as the tiny glasses sparkled and winked at her from their hiding place, Robin winked back. *(To Be Continued Next Week)*

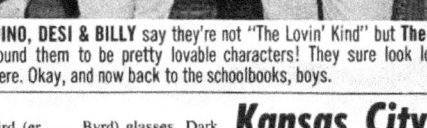

DINO, DESI & BILLY say they're not "The Lovin' Kind" but The BEAT found them to be pretty lovable characters! They sure look lovable here. Okay, and now back to the schoolbooks, boys.

Kansas City Not For Sale

If you bought a copy of the Beatles' "Boys" and "Kansas" single in the last couple of weeks you now own a collector's item.

Capitol Records released the single in the United States recently and then took it off the market almost immediately.

They discovered a clause in a contract that says they can't lift songs from past albums and release them while new releases are on the market.

Both "Boys" and "Kansas City" are on past Beatle albums and the Beatles currently have "Yesterday" and "Act Naturally" on the charts.

So if you bought one of the few copies of the single that got out, hang on to it. There aren't many like it.

England Calls Ballads Slush

People in England have been calling this the summer season of slush because of records by Matt, Andy Williams and Ken Dodd.

"They call ballads square and slushy," Matt complains.

"But who cares if they think it's slush, and what does square mean anyway? If a ballad is a good song, okay, it's a good song. That doesn't mean it's square.

"You don't need a great beat bashng away all the time, do you? Even the groups don't need a beat all the time. Paul doesn't have a beat on 'Yesterday,' does he?

"I like the Beatles very much, of course. But I don't like beat in general. I do like Eric Burton with the Animals though. He's a good singer – he swings."

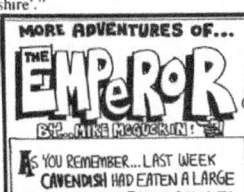

KRLA ARCHIVES

Tips to Teens

Q: I don't know if boys are supposed to write in to this column, but I have a problem so I'm going to. I'm letting my hair grow a little longer and I don't want it to part on the side (like it always has been). How can I train my hair?
(Brian W.)

A: Don't hit us for what we're about to suggest, okay? If your mother or girlfriend or sister has a hair dryer, borrow it (in the dead of night). Then wash your hair and dry it. Relax, you don't have to wear the "hood" or anything. Just direct the hot air at your hair, paying special attention to where the part used to be. After a few of these midnight sessions, it should be gone forever (the part, not your hair).

Q: I have the same problem every year and here I go again. Whenever I eat lunch, I get so sleepy it's all I can do to drag myself to my next class. Fourth period is my most difficult subject, and I just sit there like a lump. If I skip lunch, I feel fine, or would if my mother didn't start raving about malnutrition. Which is pretty funny, because I'm about six or seven pounds overweight. Help!
(Catherine M.)

A: Try packing a can of diet drink in your pocket and substituting that for lunch. It won't give you that lumpy feeling, it'll keep your mother happy, and it will probably help you shake those extra pounds.

Q: What do you do when you find out that some of your "friends" have been saying "unpleasant" things about you behind your back, send them nasty notes?
(Kay R.)

A: Not unless you want to add some more fuel to their nasty little furnace. When people say things behind your back, the best thing to do is confront them, privately of course, with what "someone said that you said that I said, etc." They'll probably deny all, but will think twice about making any more remarks now that they know they've been telling secrets to someone they can't trust (for a change).

Q: This will probably be the first time you've received a letter from a parent, but I think you will be able to help me. My 14-year-old daughter is a pretty girl, but I think she files her nails with a hacksaw. She ends up with claw-like points and I know this is not the latest style. I don't want to hurt her feelings by mentioning this outright. Can you suggest some less obvious way of letting her know this detracts from her appearance?
(Mrs. K.D.)

A: First of all, thanks for realizing how easily feelings can be hurt (too many parents forget this). Second, treat her to a manicure and hairstyle at a nearby salon for her birthday or a special occasion. She is probably totally unaware of her nail problem, and won't think you're trying to tell her something. Even if she does catch on, she won't be able to keep from appreciating the fact that you chose to make your point at your expense instead of hers.

Q: I just saw that article in an old BEAT about the electric air comb. I think this is wonderful for girls who wear their hair straight and long. Could you please tell me if this item is for sale and where I can get one?
(Cynthia E.)

A: While you're going through old BEATS, you'll probably also find where we've answered this question before. But, in case you missed that issue, you can buy an electric air comb in most beauty supply houses.

HINT OF THE WEEK

This isn't a beauty hint, but students at my school have found a great new pastime, called B.C.'s. That stands for Birthday Clubs, and we use the initials because the other sounds kind of square, which it isn't. What many of us did was write our birthdays on a big long list. Then birthdates were picked at random and separated into groups of twelve, with one birthday falling in each month.

Each group became a B.C., and all twelve get together once a month to celebrate one of the member's birthdays. Each member of a B.C. can bring a guest, and honestly, these parties are more fun than anything that's happened in our shcool's history.

The best part of the fun is getting to know new kids, not that there's anything wrong with the ones you pal around with all the time.

Anyway, it's just a ball, and I heartily recommend that everyone give it a try!
(Elaine R.)

If you have a question you'd like answered, or a hint you'd like to share, drop a line to Tips To Teens, c/o The BEAT.

Beach Boys Good Judges of Talent

The Beach Boys are not only talented performers in their own right, they are also good judges of talent.

Carl Wilson met three guys at the Hollywood Professional School and was impressed by their sound. He introduced them to his father, Murray Wilson, who manages the Beach Boys.

His father was also impressed. He arranged for the three guys and two others in their group to cut their first record which is reported to have gone "absolutely nowhere."

But they didn't give up and now the Sunrays, discovered by the Beach Boys, have a best seller in their second release, "I Live For the Sun."

Rolling Stones Riled By Fan's Criticism

If you're having trouble understanding the words to the Rolling Stones' "Get Off Of My Cloud" don't tell the Stones.

An Englishman by the name of David Jacobs criticized the song on England's "Juke Box Jury" because he said he couldn't hear the lyrics.

This was the reply from the Stones: "Perhaps he's a bit deaf," suggested Keith. "The first impression you get of our records is an exciting sound. We've never brought any vocal out much more than on 'Cloud.' It's a case of hunt the words. But you can hear them if you concentrate. Jacobs should stick to records like 'Tears.'"

Bill Wyman added that to suggest that you can't hear the lyrics because the recording company was at fault is nonsense.

"We do all our own recording," he said. "This was recorded in Los Angeles. I don't know all the words myself, but it makes no difference to the overall sound."

...Judge for Yourself
GET OFF OF MY CLOUD
By Mick Jagger & Keith Richard

I live in an apartment on the ninety-ninth floor of my block,
And I sit at home looking out the window, imagining the world has stopped.
Then in comes a man all dressed up like a Union Jack
And says I've won five pounds if I have his kind of detergent pack.

*Chorus

The telephone is ringing, I say "Hi, it's me, who is it on the line?"
A voice says "Hi, hello, how are you?" Well, I guess I'm doing fine.
He says "It's three a.m., there's too much noise, don't you people ever go to bed?
Just 'cause you feel so good, do you have to drive me out of my head?"

*Chorus

I was sick and tired, fed up with this, and decided to take a drive downtown,
It was so very quiet and peaceful, there was nobody not a soul around.
I laid myself out, I was so tired and I started to dream.
In the morning the parking tickets were just like a flag stuck on my wind-screen.

*Chorus

I says, Hey! You! Get off of my cloud.
Hey! You! Get off of my cloud.
Don't hang around 'cause two's a crowd.
On my cloud, baby.
Hey! You! Get off of my cloud.
Don't hang around 'cause two's a crowd.
On my cloud, baby.

HERB ALPERT AND THE TIJUANA BRASS are still riding high on the charts these days as well as premiering in New York City's Basin Street East. Above, Bill Dana congratulates Alpert after introducing the group in their first New York appearance.

KRLA ARCHIVES

For Girls Only
Column for Boys?
By Shirley Poston

Special message to all boys who are reading this whether I like it or not (and I don't)—I think I've finally dreamed up a way to get you to mind your own biswax. What you need is a special corner of *The BEAT*, like we have (or *would* have if you'd start minding the aforementioned biswax), where you can rave on about boy stuff to your heart's content.

That way we could rave on about you to ours (whatever that means)!

I'm really serious. Just to prove it, I hereby announce that I'm taking applications from prospective For Boys Only authors! If enough of you will write me and let me know you'd like to compose a weekly brilliant column (which would be just the opposite of mine), maybe I can talk *The BEAT* into letting you do just that.

Well, why are you sitting there still reading *my* column? Why aren't you busy writing your own?

Dream Of The Week

Onward to something interesting (for a change). Mucho thanks for your response to my "You Tell Me Your Dream And I'll Tell You Mine" (by the way, it *is* a song). The next sound you hear will be our very first Dream Of The Week, courtesy of *BEAT* reader Sandra Carl of San Francisco.

"My favorite dream (one I make up myself, I mean) concerns Paul McCartney. Here's what happens.

"I'm in London and I'm in one of those weird phone booths, and it looks like I'm there to stay because I can't get the door open to get out!

"Well, I'm pounding on the door and shrieking for help when who should walk by but Paul! He immediately sees that I'm in trouble and doll that he is, decides to help me out.

"When he can't open the door from the outside either, he makes this terrific lunge at the door and knocks it open. But he ends up inside the phone booth with me and the door slams shut again.

"Now neither of us can get out! (What a *shame*.) So all that Paul and I can do while we're standing all over each other's feet (tut, tut) is relax and get acquainted until someone lets us out!

"I'm beginning to think no one is ever going to. We've been in that phone booth since May 19, 1964."

Bravo To Sandra

Bravo to Sandra for a real original. Reminds me of the time I daydreamed that George (slurp) Harrison and I were locked in the Cow Palace all by ourselves.

Next time I'll try a phone booth. It's so much cozier.

I hope you aren't getting tired of my ridiculous stories about my ridiculous antics. Why? Because I'm about to tell you another one.

If you ever have the misfortune to set one foot in my room (neatness is not one of my many virtues), you would soon ask "what's that in the corner?"

I would say "It is a pumpkin."

You would reply, "Oh, is that what you turn into at midnight."

Then I would never speak to you again, so it's just as well if you *don't* ever have the aforementioned misfortune.

But, back to what I was saying. It really is a pumpkin. Two years ago I decided to make a Jack-o-Lantern (I'm not well), so I did. And I named it George (I name everything George) and put it in the corner of my room to keep.

Well, I naturally forgot about it two seconds later (because two seconds later it was hidden from view by a new pile of things I was going to hang up any day now).

About a year later, I saw this funny lump sitting in the corner. "What's that?" I said out loud. "That's George!" I answered, rushing to his side.

But the funny-lump-sitting-in-the corner wouldn't budge because it was now made of *concrete* instead of pumpkin! And it was firmly stuck to the rug and still is!

I ask you. Do I not lead a fascinating life? Never answer that question.

Oh, here's another of those things I'm not supposed to tell anyone but am going to (are going to?) anyway.

Beatles On Skates

Are you ready for this? Guess what the Beatles did at a New York hotel when they were there this summer! They went roller-skating at 4 o'clock in the morning. In a hotel banquet room on about the 34th floor! Isn't that wild?

Sometimes I get such a kick out of thinking about all the kooky things the Beatles do. Other times I get myself into a big grump, because I wish I could be there doing those kooky things with them!

Speaking of the Beatles (I do that sometimes as you may have noticed), I nearly flipped when I discovered that "Kansas City" had been released as a single. Several months ago, my girlfriend was trying to tell me how she about blew her mind every time the group yelled "Hey, hey, hey, hey" in that song.

Now I see what she means. Wow!!

I'm curious about something... How do all of you feel about long hair. On boys, I mean. Maybe I'm some kind of a nut (the chances are good), but I like it. Not floor length or anything. But I do think longer hair makes most boys look better, or anyone look better for that matter. (If you don't agree, walk over to the mirror and imagine yourself in a crew cut.)

I really don't see what all the fuss is about, except in rare cases where some boys could hire themselves out as part-time floor-mops.

How about writing and letting me know your views on this subject.

Now if I don't quit letting you know my views on every subject in the entire world, *The BEAT* is sure to take away my typewriter ribbon.

Bye for now and I'll see you next *BEAT*.

THE LATEST THING for record collectors is the Disc-Card, a novel container for both 45 r.p.m. records and albums, designed by artist Jan Green, a syndicated cartoonist. She has created a set of very cute as well as serviceable greeting card envelopes (such as the one above) which are ideal for gift records. No other gift-wrapping or card is necessary, and they also protect the records for storage. Already available at leading record shops throughout the West Coast.

It's In The Bag
By Eden

Are you looking for a Happening? Well look no further, 'cause it's *Happened*! It's all "In The Bag," now!!

Gorgeous George Chakiris has been signed to do the hosting honors on the "Wide World of Entertainment" which has already begun taping in Europe. This could just be the new series which will be filling in for the recently departed "Shindig." It's nice to see George back again.

★ ★ ★ ★ ★

The upcoming Sonny and Cher film we've been telling you about has finally gotten itself a title. The flick will be tagged "I Got You Babe" after the couple's hit-disc. Sounds to me like Sonny and Cher have got *us*, Babe!!

★ ★ ★ ★ ★

Who's "In The Bag" this week? A young man named Bob Dylan definitely is and so are some of his many ideas.

About Donovan, Dylan says: "I especially liked his record of 'Catch The Wind.'" It was a good song and he sang it well. But he's still very young and people might try to make him into something that he isn't. He'll have to watch that!"

There has been so much controversy lately over the idea that Bob Dylan has been going "commercial" that we decided to go right to the man himself for the final answer to this question. Is there any possibility that there is an attempt being made to turn you into a pop idol of sorts?

"They can't turn me into anything. I just write my songs and that's that! Nobody can change me and by the same token, they can't change my songs. Of course I vary things once in a while, like with the different backing I had on "Subterranean Homesick Blues." But that was entirely my own doing. Nobody talked me into it. Just so happens that we had a lot of swinging cats on that track, real hip musicians.

"Certainly my work as a writer has changed over the last couple of years. The big difference is that the songs I was writing last year were what I call one-dimensional songs. But I'm trying to make my new songs more three-dimensional. There's more symbolism, and they're written on more than one level. And I guess that's affected my work as an artist, too."

Are you really speaking for everyone of your own generation?

"I don't know, really. I mean, someone who's 17? I can't be anyone else's voice. If they care to identify themselves with me, that's okay—but I can't give a voice to people who have no voice, can I?"

Finally, Dylan has been labeled the "father of protest," the originator of the current trend of "protest" or "message" songs. Just how does Mr. Dylan feel about this movement? Are there just too many of these so-called "protest songs" out now?

"Yes. Half of 'em don't understand what they're trying to say. I'm all for protest songs if they're sincere. But how many of them are?!"

★ ★ ★ ★ ★

Funny story about Halloween comes from a rising group of Liverpudlians called the Liverpool Five. The quintet has been residing Stateside for some months now, however they hadn't yet been initiated in the custom of Halloween when all of a sudden it snuck up on them!

In recounting the details of that eventful night to *The BEAT*, Jimmy said: "I just opened the door and saw these two black eyes—they'd rather *fight* than switch!—and some skeletons and witches and they looked at me and said something that sounded like 'Tick or Tack.' Finally the lady in the apartment next to us opened her door and handed the two little girls something and told me to give them some sweets as well, so I did."

Yeah—I guess it would be kind of upsetting to open your door and find a couple of skeletons standing there and demanding some goodies! Oh well—Happy Halloween, boys!

★ ★ ★ ★ ★

Keep your ears wide open for a brand new album by Barry McGuire, soon to be released. I had the pleasure of sitting in on the recording session for this new LP and it's gonna be something else!!

Stones' Manager Back Again With Marianne Faithful

Andrew Oldham, manager of the Rolling Stones, has once again taken over the management of Marianne Faithfull's career.

Marianne's business manager, Allen Klein, announced that Oldham now has executive control of all of her future recordings on the British Decca label in the United States and the London label in England.

Oldham, currently in the United States for the Rolling Stone tour, is working on negotiations for a film for Marianne. She has not been recording in recent months due to the upcoming birth of her first child.

She has a single due for release immediately entitled "Go Away From My World." The song was performed by her at the Brighton Song Festival, was the title track of a top selling album in England and will be the title song of an upcoming American album.

Sonny & Cher On Most Ballots

(Continued from page 2)

Sonny and Cher were included on most ballots. It will be very interesting to see who wins the honors for top vocalist, top composer and top records when voters must choose between them.

However, a number of others were right up there with them in the primary voting, so there is no certainty that either will win in any given category.

Another highly competitive battle will occur in the voting for Outstanding Group, pitting the Beatles and Rolling Stones against a field which also includes such popular favorites as the Byrds, Herman's Hermits, Animals, Beach Boys, Beau Brummels, Dino, Desi and Billy, the Lovin' Spoonfull and Yardbirds.

With everyone eagerly awaiting the outcome, the decision is yours.

KRLA ARCHIVES

...THE KNICKERBOCKERS

Performers Go Wild For Knickerbockers

It isn't often that the world of entertainment becomes genuinely excited and enthusiastic about any of its own inhabitants, but it has done just that with a talented group of young men known as The Knickerbockers.

The capacity crowds which they have been drawing nightly at a Hollywood night club have included Tom Jones, Tommy Sands, and Roy Head; the Righteous Brothers found their way to the club every night recently when they were in town, and Glen Campbell thinks that they are the greatest recording group in the world.

The cause of all the commotion is four, good-natured, talented young men who hail from the New York area and have decided to take California—and the world—by storm.

Individually they are Buddy Rendell—the unofficial leader and spokesman for the group—who was born on November 2, 1942.

"I've been playing saxophone since I was seven years old; I took two years of lessons then started playing professionally, and at that time I was on the Paul Whiteman show. I also sing and play a smattering of piano—very *smatteringly*—in the key of C!"

Accompanied Roy Head

What Buddy neglected to mention here was that recently he played a sax accompaniment for Roy Head during a number which he performed at the club. This particular number called for a two-saxophone accompaniment in one part, and when he came to it—Buddy surprised Roy and everyone else within earshot as he put *two* saxophones in his mouth and proceeded to play them both *simultaneously!*

All skin-pounding for the group is ably handled by Mr. Jimmy Walker, who was born in 1941—"I'm an old man—what're you gonna do?!"—in the Bronx in New York City. Jimmy claims:

"I started playing drums because everyone else in my crowd decided to play drums and I happened to come out the best. I liked it and I stuck with it, 'cause they were all terrible—and I was just a *little less* terrible!!!"

Good-looking Beau Charles is the lead guitarist and one half of the Knickerbocker's own personal brother act. Of his beginnings in this world, Beau explains:

"I was born in New York City on October 31, 1944—that's Halloween, and if you *saw* me, you'd know why!! I started playing the guitar at the age of fourteen and got very interested in rock 'n' roll. I studied with various teachers for a while and took some music courses in high school."

"Soul Banjo"

Beau also plays bass, organ, piano, drums, and as pal Buddy puts it—"soul banjo."

The other half of the Charles Brothers is a young man named Johnny. He was born in New York on July 3, 1943 and is the bass player for the group.

Buddy interjects another of his many witicisms here as he informs us that: "Johnny plays several notes on sax—but we haven't utilized it in our act yet because he plays pretty badly! He also does the high falsetto part in the four-way, Beachboy-type numbers we do."

It is common practice nowadays to label artists with a certain 'sound', or 'bag', but Jimmy doesn't believe in this, as he explains:

"Our group just plays whatever the material calls for, yet it will always come out sounding like The Knickerbockers, because *we're* doing it.

"Our material consists of almost everything that you hear on the radio—from the English sound to the blues sound, 'soul' sound. We enjoy playing *every* type of music that we hear on the radio, because we usually wind up working at it very hard, and it comes out pretty well; and anything you do well—you're gonna like. We always feel that people love to go to a night club or a show and hear a group that can imitate, or come close to, the sound that they hear on the radio every day, because this way they can judge how good or bad you are."

Feels Dylan Sound

Johnny has some feelings of his own about a certain type of sound—the one produced by a fellow named Dylan:

"When I first heard him, I just about flipped over his new ideas with the folk-rock; I think it opens our eyes to a lot of things that are happening and it almost gives you an education while listening to a 'happening'-type song. I think it's great. Our new record "The Coming Generation" is something like that and I guess that's why we chose it, because we really do like the folk-rock."

The Knickerbockers have made a great impact on the entertainment business and their future looms big and bright ahead. They have already recorded an album called "Sing-Along" with Lloyd Thaxton, as well as recording commercials for the Diet-Rite and the Suzuki people, and there is a possibility that they will be doing a movie for Universal-International with the Lovin' Spoonful, Gary Lewis and the Playboys, Freddie and the Dreamers, the Turtles, and many others.

In a rare serious moment, Buddy sincerely says: "We really get a tremendous enjoyment out of working for a younger audience, because they're such an enthusiastic group of people to work for, and they really enjoy what you're doing. We're just sold on working for kids—we love 'em, they're a gas!"

This is one group of boys that *everyone* can enjoy—the young and the young-at-heart. They are talented, enthusiastic, and full of fun—and they have the support of everyone who has heard and seen them perform. They were discovered in Albany, New York by Jerry Fuller, who is now their manager, and Jerry is just one of many professional people who is predicting bigger and better things for these boys.

You know something—*The BEAT* thinks that they are all right about The Knickerbockers!!

Freddie In TV

While everyone else seems to be going into movies, Freddie and the Dreamers are going into television.

They have been signed by King Features Syndicate to appear in the pilot of a situation comedy about a musical group.

The pilot is to be shot in dreamy color on various European locations with production centered in London.

New Manfred Group to Tour With Yardbirds

Manfred Mann is expanding. Manfred, a group of five at present, is looking for three more to add to the group.

Mike Vickers, lead guitarist, is taking a three month leave of absence to write the music for a film called "The Sandwich Man" but will return and is expected to switch to playing alto sax.

Meanwhile the group is searching for a tenor sax player, a bass guitarist to take over for Tom McGuiness who's going to lead guitar, and a trumpeter.

Wants Jazz Group

The real Manfred explained what they are trying to do. "We want a really good modern jazz group within the group, and if we can get someone who doubles on drums then Mike Hugg can play vibes. We want someone like Ray Warleigh on alto, who can play jazz and doesn't mind playing pop."

Tour With Yardbirds

If they can find the extra musicians in time, the new line-up will be seen on the upcoming Manfred Mann-Yardbirds tour in England.

"The enlargement is primarily for the Yardbirds tour," Manfred said.

The group has an album due to be released in England in December called "No Living Without Loving," but no word has been released on any upcoming American releases.

Mick Doesn't Know Where He's Headed

Where does a group go when it reaches the top?

Mick Jagger of the Rolling Stones says the Stones don't plan their next moves, they just let things happen.

"We just don't know the direction we are moving in," he said frankly. "I don't think anyone knows. In fact, who can ever say how they are progressing? We've evolved a sort of policy of letting things happen to us.

"We don't plan the future or try to mould the group into patterns. We just sit back and let things happen the way they will.

"Musically, we've never had a set policy either. We just do the things we like. Nowadays, we like a lot of new things, but we still do the old stuff as well.

"We always try to progress and improve, of course. That's natural. But it's never a planned campaign," he added.

Now in the midst of their American tour, the Stones just keep climbing higher and higher in their unplanned campaign, letting things happen to them, like letting fans make their records number one in the nation.

KRLA ARCHIVES

Upbeat of the Week
By EDEN

The Knickerbockers! Remember that name, 'cause you're going to be hearing more – and *more* – about them as the weeks go by.

This is a great new group who have been causing waves of excitement everywhere they go, and now they have released their first single record called "Lies," which has to take our weekly award for being totally Out Of Sight!!

The boys seem to sound a little bit like the early Beatles with the harmony on this one, and the instrumentation is somewhat like that of the Kinks; but all together, it comes out totally Knickerbockers – and completely *great!!*

Watch for this one to be a giant.

* * *

Alright Mr. Bono – don't you think that's just about enough, now? I mean, we had a protest about your hair and the dead ranger you wear 'round your shoulders and the people who protest people, but now you're protesting the people who protest the protest songs!!

Come off it, Sonny babe. This is not only a horrible waste of wax, but we honestly never thought you'd be cutting your 941st record without Cher!! I'm afraid your "Revolution Kind" isn't even going to start a small riot in this world of pop!!!

* * *

Another big disappointment this week has been the new 45 RPMer by Peter and Gordon – "Don't Pity Me." These boys are capable of much better than this, and this new single certainly doesn't live up to their past list of hits.

That's alright boys, we'll forgive you. After all – we're all entitled to *one* mistake, aren't we??

* * *

Gene Pitney, who has been one of America's best international ambassadors of good will the last few years has another chart topper in the running with "Princess in Rags."

As usual, Gene has come up with a strong lyric and a powerful vocal on this new single and it looks like another addition to his already very lengthy string of hits.

* * *

Unbelievable! The new Capitol Beach Boy album is *unbelievable!* Entitled "Beach Boy's Party," the album cover has pictures of the boys at a party all over it, but the album also includes fifteen color, wallet-sized snap out pictures of the boys! Clincher for this is the promo campaign for the album: one million tiny potato chip bags with a reproduction of the album cover on it to stand on the record counters across the country.

Whew! Getting a little salty here, aren't we boys??

* * *

We are all anxiously awaiting the Beatles single which, theoretically should appear some time towards the close of this month. But then, who knows? The boys are also preparing a brand new LP for Christmas release, so it looks like Beatlemaniacs everywhere can plan on a Kool Yule this year.

... BEAU BRUMMELS (l. to r.) Sal Valentino, John Peterson, Ron Elliot, Ron Meagher.

Beau Brummels Blackballed?

By Louise Criscione

The Beau Brummels' press agent says that they "penetrate". And so they did – they penetrated right into *The BEAT* offices the other night. They had driven over directly from a television show and so the remains of make-up still lingered on the faces of Sal Valentino and Ron Meagher.

The Brummels dropped into chairs thankful for the chance to sit still for awhile. Only they didn't – sit still, that is. Instead they smoked, sipped cokes, laughed and read *BEAT*. And talked – about everything and anything.

Like their unusual name. "Well, we wanted something with beau in it and the name, Beau Brummel, came up," explained Ron Elliot (prolific song writer in the extreme). "So, I did a little bit of research into it and it just seemed to fit."

Brummel Image

The Beau Brummels then had a name and a distinctive sound. All that was lacking was an image. And, of course, that's what a press agent is for. So, without the boys' approval and probably without their liking it much, the Beau Brummels found themselves being tagged "the most English sounding American group."

"That's what we were told we were," Ron Meagher offered, "but we didn't have anything to do with it."

The group feels that the English tag neither helped nor hindered them. "The fans who accept us just accept us," said John Peterson, the group's able drummer.

Another way to acquire an image is through the way you dress. The Brummels' dress is distinctive but not too far-out. They say they try to dress differently without being sloppy.

"We have been dressing alike on stage but in the future we won't," said Sal Valentino, the Brummels' vocal sound. "There were too many hassles. So, we'll wear what we want to but still looking sharp."

Blackballed?

Many artists have encountered the problem of getting a record high in the national charts while certain cities refuse to play the record. Not because of the lyrics or anything like that – but just because.

What about the Beau Brummels? "That happens a lot," said John. "Some cities will only play the top 30, others play the top 40. It just all depends on the play list," added Ron Meagher.

You all are aware, I'm sure, that there were once five Beau Brummels while now there are only four. The Irish member of the group has fled the scene. There were lots of reasons for his departure – he wanted to go back to Ireland, he wanted to get married. "But there was no fight," assures Sal.

Whenever a group member leaves there is always the possibility that the group as well as the solo man will suffer. The Brummels disagree among themselves as to whether their sound has been hurt.

Ron Meagher thinks it has: "Sure it has because we lost a guitar." But Sal disagrees: "No, it hasn't hurt. We've gotten better – we seem to get better all the time."

Toe-Guitarist

The Beau Brummels are branching out into the cartoon field where they will appear on a segment of The Flintstones. The boys play themselves but actually the sound of the Brummels which you will hear on The Flintstones was all taken off a record. Still, I wondered what the boys thought of being made into cartoons.

"It's going to be groovy," enthused John. Ron Meagher thinks so too: "I like it because I get to play the guitar with my toes!"

The Beau Brummels were formed while the boys were still attending college. Did taking music in school help the boys professionally?

"I learned a lot of theory," explained Ron Elliot. "It was all math. But I look at music as a feeling and not a bunch of numbers," Ron continued.

How the public categorizes a group's sound and how that group categorizes their sound are often two very different things. In the case of the Beau Brummels, the public has fit them neatly into the folk-rock bag, Beau Brummel folk-rock maybe, but folk-rock just the same.

A Combination

The Brummels themselves hesitate to categorize their music at all. They prefer to call it a "combination of a lot of things." "We don't play anything really difficult – we play melodically and rhythmically," said Ron Elliot.

"I think that's why the Stones have made it. They don't do anything really fantastic but they have good taste and good taste is more important than speed," continued Ron.

"We're a lot of things. It's well-programmed and we try to keep the people interested," Ron said.

The Beau Brummels are glad that the British groups hit our scene with such impact because it forced our American groups to stay on their toes and come up with better sounds in order to keep a toe-hold on our own charts.

Different Bag

"Before it was different, the whole bag was different," said Sal, and the artists are a lot closer because they identify with the groups. You know, they even dress like the artists now."

"Artists before commanded a lot of respect," said Sal, hastening to add that "anyway, it's better now."

And so it is – because now we have the Beau Brummels.

KRLA ARCHIVES

KRLA Tunedex

EMPEROR HUDSON

CHARLIE O'DONNELL

CASEY KASEM

JOHNNY HAYES

BOB EUBANKS

DAVE HULL

DICK BIONDI

BILL SLATER

KRLA BEAT
6290 Sunset, No. 504
Hollywood, Cal. 90028

This Week	Last Week	Title	Artist
1	1	1-2-3	Len Barry
2	3	TURN, TURN, TURN	The Byrds
3	2	GET OFF MY CLOUD	Rolling Stones
4	11	STILL I'M SAD/I'M A MAN	The Yardbirds
5	4	YOU'RE THE ONE	The Vogues
6	14	I HEAR A SYMPHONY	The Supremes
7	5	YESTERDAY	The Beatles
8	6	A LOVER'S CONCERTO	The Toys
9	8	A TASTE OF HONEY	Tijuana Brass
10	10	MAKE IT EASY ON YOURSELF	The Walker Brothers
11	29	LET'S HANG ON	The Four Seasons
12	7	KEEP ON DANCING	The Gentrys
13	9	MAKE ME YOUR BABY	Barbara Lewis
14	13	EVERYBODY LOVES A CLOWN	Gary Lewis & The Playboys
15	16	RESCUE ME	Fontella Bass
16	12	HANG ON SLOOPY	The McCoys
17	17	STEPPIN' OUT	Paul Revere & The Raiders
18	15	I KNEW YOU WHEN	Billy Joe Royal
19	28	PIED PIPER	The Changing Times
20	23	MYSTIC EYES	Them
21	31	LET ME BE	The Turtles
22	27	AIN'T THAT PECULIAR	Marvin Gaye
23	26	MY GIRL HAS GONE	The Miracles
24	30	MY HEART SINGS	Mel Carter
25	32	YOU'VE GOT TO HIDE YOUR LOVE AWAY	The Silkie
26	38	RISING SUN	The Deep Six
27	36	HEARTBEAT	Gloria Jones
28	--	SOMETHING ABOUT YOU	The 4 Tops
29	33	DON'T TALK TO STRANGERS	Beau Brummels
30	34	YOU'RE ABSOLUTELY RIGHT	The Apollos
31	--	RUN BABY RUN	The Newbeats
32	--	OVER AND OVER	Dave Clark Five
33	--	HANG ON SLOOPY	Ramsey Lewis Trio
34	35	HALLOWEEN MARY	P.F. Sloan
35	--	I CAN NEVER GO HOME ANYMORE	Shangri-Las
36	--	ENGLAND SWINGS	Roger Miller
37	39	I FOUGHT THE LAW	Bobby Fuller Four
38	--	HERE IT COMES AGAIN	The Fortunes
39	--	REVOLUTION KIND	Sonny
40	40	THE LAST THING ON MY MIND	The Dillards

KRLA ARCHIVES

America's Largest Teen NEWSpaper

KRLA *Edition* BEAT

Volume 1, Number 38 LOS ANGELES, CALIFORNIA 15 Cents December 4, 1965

The Byrds 'Turn, Turn, Turn' on Again

KRLA ARCHIVES

KRLA BEAT

VOTE NOW

Los Angeles, California — December 4, 1965

BEAT Pop Music Awards Poll
Final Ballot – Please Check One in Each Category

MALE VOCALIST
- SONNY BONO
- JAMES BROWN
- DONOVAN
- BOB DYLAN
- BARRY MC GUIRE
- ROGER MILLER
- GENE PITNEY
- ELVIS PRESLEY
- BILLY JOE ROYAL
- IAN WHITCOMB

NEW MALE VOCALIST
- SONNY BONO
- DONOVAN
- BOB DYLAN
- BARRY MC GUIRE
- IAN WHITCOMB

FEMALE VOCALIST
- JOAN BAEZ
- CILLA BLACK
- CHER
- PETULA CLARK
- MARIANNE FAITHFULL
- LESLIE GORE
- BRENDA HOLLOWAY
- DUSTY SPRINGFIELD
- CONNIE STEVENS
- TINA TURNER

NEW FEMALE VOCALIST
- JOAN BAEZ
- CHER
- PETULA CLARK
- MARIANNE FAITHFULL
- BARBARA LEWIS

VOCAL GROUP
- ANIMALS
- BEACH BOYS
- BEATLES
- BEAU BRUMMELS
- BYRDS
- DINO, DESI & BILLY
- HERMAN'S HERMITS
- THE LOVIN' SPOONFUL
- ROLLING STONES
- YARDBIRDS

NEW VOCAL GROUP
- BEAU BRUMMELS
- BYRDS
- DINO, DESI & BILLY
- GARY LEWIS & THE PLAYBOYS
- LOVIN' SPOONFUL

FEMALE VOCAL GROUP
- BLOSSOMS
- MARTHA & THE VANDELLAS
- SHANGRALAS
- SUPREMES
- TOYS

INSTRUMENTAL GROUP
- HERB ALPERT & TIJUANA BRASS
- RAMSEY LEWIS TRIO
- THEE MIDNITERS
- SOUNDS INCORPORATED
- SOUNDS ORCHESTRAL

DUO
- CHAD & JEREMY
- JAN & DEAN
- DICK & DEEDEE
- RIGHTEOUS BROTHERS
- SONNY & CHER

COMPOSER
- SONNY BONO
- DONOVAN
- BOB DYLAN
- MICK JAGGER/KEITH RICHARD
- JOHN LENNON/PAUL MC CARTNEY
- P. F. SLOAN
- BRIAN WILSON

RECORD PRODUCER
- HERB ALPERT
- JIMMY BOWEN
- BARRY GORDY
- GREENE & STONE
- TONY HATCH
- GEORGE MARTIN
- TERRY MELCHER
- ANDREW OLDHAM
- PHIL SPECTOR
- BRIAN WILSON

RECORD COMPANY
- A&M
- ATLANTIC/ATCO
- AUTUMN
- CAPITOL
- COLUMBIA
- LIBERTY
- LONDON
- SMASH
- TAMLA/MOTOWN
- WARNER BROS./REPRISE

VOCAL RECORD – 45's
- BABY DON'T GO
- CRYING IN THE CHAPEL
- EVE OF DESTRUCTION
- HELP
- KING OF THE ROAD
- LIKE A ROLLING STONE
- MR. TAMBOURINE MAN
- MRS. BROWN
- SATISFACTION
- YESTERDAY
- YOU'VE LOST THAT LOVIN' FEELING

INSTRUMENTAL – 45's
- THE IN CROWD
- TASTE OF HONEY
- WHITTIER BLVD.
- COTTON CANDY
- CAST YOUR FATE TO THE WIND

VOCAL ALBUM
- BEACH BOYS TODAY
- BRINGING IT ALL BACK HOME – DYLAN
- HELP – BEATLES
- INTRODUCING HERMAN'S HERMITS
- LOOK AT US – SONNY & CHER
- MR. TAMBOURINE MAN – BYRDS
- OUT OF OUR HEADS – STONES
- ROLLING STONES NOW
- WHERE DID OUR LOVE GO – SUPREMES
- YOU'VE LOST THAT LOVIN' FEELING – RIGHTEOUS BROTHERS

INSTRUMENTAL ALBUM
- BEATLE SONG BOOK – HOLLYRIDGE STRINGS
- GOLDFINGER – SOUND TRACK
- THE IN CROWD – RAMSEY LEWIS
- MORE GENIUS OF JANKOWSKI
- WHIPPED CREAM & OTHER DELIGHTS – HERB ALPERT

MAIL TO: Pop Music Poll, KRLA BEAT, 6290 Sunset, Suite 504, Hollywood, Calif. 90028

KRLA'S DAVE HULL looks over his new teen nightclub with Gary Bookasta (left), executive vice president of the "Hullabalooer." The new club, which will be the scene of **The BEAT** Pop Music Awards Dinner Dec. 8, will stage it's grand opening Dec. 9. It was formerly the Moulin Rouge, famed as the world's most lavish and glamorous nightclub. You'll find more details inside on pages 9 and 10.
BEAT Photo: Robert Custer

Finalists - Outstanding Female Vocalists of 1965

BRENDA HOLLOWAY

GINA BLACK

DUSTY SPRINGFIELD

JOAN BAEZ

CHER

PETULA CLARK

MARIANNE FAITHFULL

CONNIE STEVENS

TINA TURNER

LESLIE GORE

SEND BEAT GIFT SUBSCRIPTIONS TO YOUR FRIENDS FOR CHRISTMAS

Inside the BEAT
Young John and George	3
Gary Lewis Dreams of Girls	3
Is Recording Easy?	4
Adventures Of Robin Boyd	5
Rising Sons—Up In West	6
For Jeremy—What Now?	8
Agent 007—Coffin Polisher	8
Letter To Beatle Fans	11
Bonos Can't Win 'Em All	11
For Girls Only	12
A Dylan Fan Speaks	12
Stones Still Rolling	15
Up-Do's And Curls	16

The BEAT is published weekly for KRLA listeners by BEAT Publications, Inc., 6290 Sunset Blvd., Suite 504, Hollywood, California 90028. U.S. bureaus in Hollywood, San Francisco, New York, Chicago and Nashville; overseas correspondents in London, Liverpool and Manchester, England. Sale price, 15 cents. Subscription price: U.S. and possessions, $3 per year; Canada and foreign rates, $9 per year. Application to mail at second-class postage rates is pending at Los Angeles, California.

KRLA ARCHIVES

...GARY LEWIS

Gary Lewis Dreams Of Girls And Chaos

By Carol Deck

He lounged in the luscious living room of his home and described his ideal girl for this *BEAT* reporter.

He is Gary Lewis. His ideal girl is 5'10" (he's 6'), a brunette with brown eyes who can "take orders instead of give them" as well as "get up in the morning and be beautiful."

Thinking he hadn't already asked for a major miracle he went on to describe what styles he likes to see on girls. "I love a good skirt on a girl 'cause I like to look at a girl's legs. I like bell bottoms too, they're OK but the girls are getting to look too much like guys."

His taste in girls' hair styles runs to extremes too. He likes long (brunette) hair worn like Cher's or short (brunette) hair worn like Barbra Streisand's.

Digs Cool Pants

For himself, he says, "I dig cool pants and boots." And *was he ever wearing* cool pants and boots! Sprawled across a chair in his living room, Gary was a shocking contrast to the staid room in his bright orange velour shirt and green corduroy pants with black boots.

Gary just plain likes girls, particularly the fan type. His idea of the perfect audience is "some place like the Cow Palace packed with girls and pure medlem."

He likes medlem so much that he says the Playboy's all time greatest concert was one that was pure unadulterated madness.

"We were playing this stadium in New Haven, Conn.," he recalled with relish. "The stadium held 6,000 and was packed. There were 15 acts and we all shared this one huge dressing room that was 200 yards from the stage. We had to run through the crowd to get to the stage.

"We were the second to last act and we watched the others come back all torn and beat up. We were scared--scared to death."

15 Police Officers

With the help of 15 police officers Gary and the Playboys managed to get on stage and do the show, but getting off stage was something else.

"We got killed, literally killed," Gary exclaimed, looking strangely very alive. "All 6,000 of those girls must have been right on top of us. We had to get all new uniforms after that one."

Gary's idea of heaven may be a chaotic audience but he does have one complaint about such audiences.

"I don't dig it when they leave their seats," he explained. "If they'd just stay right there and do whatever they have to and *don't throw things!*"

Gary's had everything from scissors to combs to poems thrown at him during concerts. Carl Radle, the group's bass player, has even been hit by a can opener. They love their fans just as long as they don't throw unidentified flying objects at them.

Let His Hair Grow

Gary is one of the few male performers topping the charts today that hasn't let his hair grow into a British style, but he admits that he did try it once. He let it grow during a tour because he said, "I just had to what it was like, and I dug it." But after the tour was over, his long hair kick was over, too, and he cut it back to its present length.

The Playboys have had a few personnel changes, but now the group is permanent, Gary says. The Playboys are Tommy Tripplehorn, 21, head guitar; Carl Radle, 23, bass; Jim Keltner, 23, drums; John West, 26, cordovox, and Gary, 20, lead singer. Gary used to play drums for the groups but has switched to singing and playing guitar.

A cordovox, by the way, is an amplified accordian. Gary says he can't understand why everyone insists on calling it an accordian when it's a cordovox. What does it look like? "An accordian," he said.

Gary, who has been playing drums since he was two ("I was beating on pans with spoons"), finds many good drummers on the popular scene today. He says that Dennis Wilson of the Beach Boys is one of the greats and that Ringo, well "he's got class."

Trying to explain the style of the group, Gary finally just said, "Well, our records have made the top ten on Billboard Magazine's easy listening list. I guess it's just easy listening.

"I can't believe it when I'll be standing in an airport somewhere and a 90 year old lady will say 'your music is so easy to listen to.'"

But watch out for the next release from Gary and the Playboys due any day now. It's called "Just My Style" and Gary says it's just the style of the Beach Boys. The group felt they were ready for a change. "The same thing over and over again, no matter how good it is, will soon be nothing," Gary explained.

Asked about goals for the future, Gary replied, "I'm satisfied with what I'm doing. So is Sheriff John and he's been on the air 20 years."

A Peek At Young John And George

By Jamie McCluskey III

If you are a loyal Beatlemaniac, you have undoubtedly wondered, at some time in your life, just exactly what our Fab Four were like as children. Anyways, I know *I* have, so I have begun a *BEAT* scrapbook of "Beatle Snapshots;" little flashbacks into the childhood adventures of the Mersey Mop-Tops. I'd like to share some of them with you, so if you're ready--

Let's begin with John. John was raised by his aunt, Mimi Smith, from the age of five, and her recollections of him provide a very clear picture for our *BEAT* scrapbook.

"He was a loveable rebel; he hated any kind of conformity and those who wanted to make him conform, especially his school masters. He was always the leader of his little gang, and insisted on being the Indian and never the Cowboy. His word was law; if he said, 'You're dead,' than his friend had better accept the fact that he was dead!"

John is now world famous for his off-beat writing and Aunt Mimi tells us of the early beginnings of some of John's literary endeavors.

"He had this little house built in a tree, in our back garden. From the spring onwards it was impossible to see through the leaves, and he used to hide in there for hours. He called it his 'den' and used to sit there drawing and making up rhymes, just like those in his books. I used to get annoyed because he kept stealing all my clothes lines to make alterations to his tree-house."

Now that we've seen a little of John's childhood, let's turn the page and glance briefly at some snaps of George.

George's mother tells of George's early interest in performing for people: "He has always been fond of entertaining other people. When he was ten years old, his Dad gave him some hand-puppets for Christmas. From then on, whenever we had visitors, he always insisted on giving a little show kneeling behind the settee. The first time he ever got a big urge to play the guitar was when he was 13 years old. His brother Peter bought one and George promptly tried to learn to play it. Eventually, he formed a small group with some friends and they went along for an audition at the Speke British Legion Hall. The main act did not turn up, so George's group played instead. They only knew two songs and once they had done both of them, they started again with the first and went on playing the same two over and over again!"

Even as a child, George was concerned about the clothes he wore. Today he designs much of his own clothing and then has them made up for him. But a few years ago, George had to take matters into his own hands. His father explains that he and his wife used to emcee some of the local old-time dances, and George used to get quite a big chuckle out of the wide-bottomed trousers that most of the dancers were wearing. "He decided to do something about his own because he said he did not want to be old-fashioned, so one day, when I bought him a new pair of flannels for school, he sat up till late at night and altered them on his mother's sewing machine until they were narrowed to his satisfaction."

These are just a few of the many little Beatle snapshots which are in our *BEAT* scrapbook, but it's time to put the book away for now.

If you will join us again next week, we'll re-open our scrapbook and take a look back into the childhood of one Mr. Paul Beatle, MBE as well as his three long-haired companions.

See ya then, luvs. Cheerio!

'Hold On!' For Herman

Hold on, it looks like they have finally made up their minds.

Yep, executives at MGM have decided on the final title for the movie that Herman's Hermits just completed.

It's to be called "Hold On!" and not "There's No Place Like Space."

The title comes from one of the 10 new songs that the boys recorded for the movie which is produced by Sam Katzman.

KRLA ARCHIVES

JOEY PAIGE AND MARSHALL LIEB — sure look serious as they go over the sheet music for Joey's session.

Is Recording Easy?

You can't possibly appreciate records until you actually witness the blood, sweat and toil which goes into making them.

The whole thing seems so easy, doesn't it? The singer goes into a recording studio and sings the song through once — maybe twice. The A&R man keeps one eye on the lead sheet and the other eye on the performer. The engineer twists the buttons and pushes the levers in the control room until both he and the A&R man are completely satisfied.

It's as simple as that, right? Wrong! It's not anywhere near as simple as that. Take for instance Joey Paige's session last night. The BEAT arrived on the scene at about 7 o'clock. Tiny Studio C was already crammed with Joey's fans and well-wishers.

Alas, there were no seats left and the mighty BEAT had to stand! It wasn't really so bad though, because we stood in the back with the "executives." At least, that's what Marshall Lieb tried to tell us they were.

Fidgety Marshall

Marshall A&R'd the session. He's such a kick to watch — the man never sits still. Never. He's either tapping his finger or his foot in time to the music or else he's jumping around giving signals to the musicians.

Marshall's a top a&r man — one who settles for nothing short of perfection. If he hears a wrong chord he stops the whole thing and the musicians go through it again. And again. Until it's just right.

Of course, this makes for a lot of takes but it also makes for a fantastic sounding record in the end. If the end ever comes, that is.

On Joey's session Marshall decided to do the tracks first and then Joey's vocal. They only had two songs to cut. The total playing time of both sides completed will probably be no more than six minutes.

You'd think it wouldn't take them much more than an hour or two to complete the whole show. Well, if you think that — you're dead wrong. The clock kept spinning around. 7 o'clock - 8 o'clock - 9 o'clock. More takes. More wrong notes.

Studio In Stitches

To keep the session musicians from becoming discouraged, Marshall kept up a steady flow of ad lib remarks which threw the entire control room into stitches. It also eased the tension which had been building up inside the recording studio.

While Marshall kept talking and musicians kept playing, the clock continued its endless cycle. 10 o'clock - 11 o'clock. Success! Both tracks were finally completed to everyone's delight and a break was called.

It was at this point that one of the company big wigs came through the door and Marshall yelled: "Quiet everyone, money's here!"

"Money" laughed along with everyone else, inquired if there was by chance a party going on and was he supposed to bring the beer. Told that, of course, he was supposed to bring some goodies, he grinned: "Well, then you should've called me sooner."

You've no doubt been wondering where Joey was all this time. After all, it *was* his session. Well, Joey made good use of his time by sitting in the control booth going over the lyrics about a million times. Then when he tired of sitting he would walk around the studio chatting with his fan club members of friends of his who had dropped by.

Joey wasn't really feeling too well. He had a cold which he couldn't seem to shake so he spent the entire night downing hot tea, cough medicine and throat discs.

The break over and the instrumental tracks completed, they decided to do the vocal backing next. And another hour flew by.

When the clock reached midnight The BEAT staff decided we were just that — beat. We'd waited hours to hear Joey sing and Joey had waited hours to hear Joey sing too! But Marshall said no — not with that cold.

All those hours and only two tracks finished. Recording is not the easy business you thought it was, now is it?

Henry Older Than Herman

Herman's Hermits may be a group of very young men but their song "I'm Henry VIII" sure isn't.

In fact, the song is almost four times as old as Herman. It was written in 1911 by Fred Murray and first sung by a singing comedian named Harry Champion.

It was revived once by Joe Brown and his Bruvvers and now has had another rebirth with the Hermits, who made it number one in America.

On the BEAT
By Louise Criscione

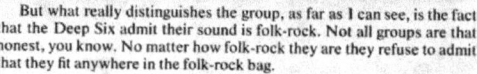

It seems that Eric Burden always has something in the works. He is constantly on the go, continually speaking his mind and repeatedly getting himself in the news.

He is currently writing a book, sweating out a court appearance for Customs evasion and declaring that the Animals' latest British chart success, "It's My Life," is not one of his favorites.

Instead, Eric reveals that: "Personally, I don't like the disc." But from the way the record is bounding up the English charts, it looks as if Eric is definitely in the minority. Which is not too unusual for Mr. Burden.

Poor Sandie Shaw has met her first defeat in the hard world of entertainment. It was nothing short of complete disaster when Sandie attempted to open at the packed Savoy Hotel. Reports from our sources in London say she looked darling in a pink dress with her dark hair shining.

Voice Trouble

It was her voice that caused all the trouble — it refused to do anything she wanted it to. So the teaming Savoy was treated to a gallant effort but one which ended in failure. Sandie just wasn't ready to tackle the club scene.

Finally caught the Deep Six, the group which is making noise with "The Rising Sun." The five man, one girl group is out of San Diego. They all dress alike (except the girl, of course) and all have short hair, except for Tony Scott whose hair defies description — it's neither long nor short!

... ERIC BURDEN

But what really distinguishes the group, as far as I can see, is the fact that the Deep Six admit their sound is folk-rock. Not all groups are that honest, you know. No matter how folk-rock they are they refuse to admit that they fit anywhere in the folk-rock bag.

Byrds Say No

Even the Byrds, who many consider to be the founders of folk-rock, cringe at the mere suggestion that they are folk-rock with Jim McGuinn announcing: "We don't like that label."

QUICK ONES: Interesting note in the English papers saying that Lulu's friendship with Herman is "blossoming." I don't know. It wasn't too long ago that they were heralding the Herman-Twinkle "romance." But Herman told The BEAT that the "romance" never took place anywhere except in some press agent's imagination ... Rolling Stones now are second to only the Beatles in world-wide record sales ... Donovan has managed to get Rediffusion to pitch in about $30,000 for his television documentary. Ought to be some show, hope we get to see it Stateside ... Belated Happy Birthday to Herman — now an old man of 18 ... Is Dave Clark really going to get himself a new nose? His old one looks all right to me ... A little bird told me that Capitol withdrew the Beatles' single, "Kansas City/Boys," because it wasn't selling ... What have The Who got against The Yardbirds ... The next Beatle album, due out in time for Christmas presents, will feature only Beatle compositions. Or so they say now ... Plans for "The Assassination Of Mick Jagger" now scrapped. That was the movie Mick was set to make with friend, David Bailey.

Mick Jagger has come out with a prediction — England will have a good R&B scene before long. "People coming on now are different from the earlier ones in that they acknowledge they have a lot to learn and they *are* learning fast."

The Stones have been hoping R&B would hit it big in their homeland ever since they began way back at the Crawdaddy. Guess they have done a lot to further their cause by proving that R&B does sell.

... MICK JAGGER

KRLA ARCHIVES

Adventures of Robin Boyd

By Shirley Poston

CHAPTER FOUR

The next morning, Robin awakened happy as a lark.

It was Saturday, there was no school, and it was also the day she was going to try her wings for the first time.

Where was she going to fly off to? England, where else? And she already knew exactly how she was going to explain her absence over the weekend. She'd stayed awake for hours the night before, after George the genie had rushed off, figuring out her plan.

Less than an hour later, Robin walked into the kitchen carrying a small suitcase.

"Good morning, mom," she cried jovially.

Her mother looked up from the stove and gave Robin a wary glance. She had been fearing for her daughter's sanity of late, especially since she'd come home dragging a *tea pot*. In fact, she'd sat up half of last night, going through the yellow pages in hopes of finding a nearby doctor.

"Good morning dear," she replied, trying to hide her fears. Which doubled when she noticed Robin's suitcase. "Where are you off to?"

Robin crossed her toes (fearing her mother would have noticed had she crossed her fingers). "I'm going over to Catalina to visit Aunt Zelda for the weekend."

Robin's mother dropped a plate noisely as her fears tripled.

"Aunt Zelda?" she echoed. "The one you always refer to as 'that creep who lives out in the middle of nowhere on an island and doesn't even have a telephone'?"

"Mother," Robin said patiently, pausing for effect (she was fast becoming a chip off the old Genie). "I'm a grown woman now. I realize the importance of respecting my elders."

With this, she dashed out the back door before her mother tried to stop her (or became ill).

"You're only sixteen," her mother murmured, watching her daughter's retreating figure from the window. "And you're nuts."

Then she walked sadly toward the yellow pages.

When Robin was certain that her mother was no longer watching, she doubled back and slipped into the garage.

For a moment she considered the possibility of taking her suitcase with her, but she decided against it. She and George hadn't discussed the subject of baggage. And besides, a bird carrying a valise might attract too much attention. (A bird wearing *glasses* was going to attract *quite enough*, thank you.)

With trembling hands, she hid the suitcase on a dusty shelf.

With trembling-er hands, she removed the tiny glasses from her jacket pocket (which wasn't difficult because there was a pocket in her jacket). Byrd glasses, she thought, smiling to herself. It wasn't as bad as she'd figured. George making her wear them so she wouldn't go falling out of trees and stuff.

Then Robin cleared her throat, shaking like a leaf. She'd always dreamed of flying to England. But she had planned to do so on a plane. Then she took a deep breath and said the magic word that would turn her into a *real* robin.

"Liverpool!!"

Three seconds later, she flew out of the garage.

Four seconds later, she flew back in and perched disgustedly on an old bicycle seat.

"Ratzafratz!" she said, furious. How could she fly to England when she didn't even know where England was? And couldn't very well go to the nearest gas station and ask!

Then she brightened. England was East! Of course, silly!

Flapping her wings, she prepared for her glorious take off. Then her feathers dropped again.

So England was East, was it, silly. Well, which way was East?

Five seconds later, she flew out of the garage again. She still did not know for sure which way was East. She simply no longer cared. Being hopelessly lost had certain advantages over perching on old bicycle seats.

So, rare bird that she was, Robin chose a direction at random and stepped on the gas.

Not too hard, of course, being careful not to exceed the speed limit George had set. She wasn't *about* to go over 5,000 miles per hour and be stopped by the Bird Patrol! So she kept it down to a sensible 4,999.

This being her first trip aloft, it seemed like no time until she was passing over what appeared to be a never-ending city. In fact, she was so busy watching life go on as usual on the ground, she nearly ran smack into a huge building!

"The Eiffel Tower," she breathed excitedly as she screeched to a halt about two inches from the Empire State Building. She flew backwards for a better look at the famous landmark and immediately blushed. *Eiffel Tower. Now, really.*

But at least she was doing *something* right. Since this was obviously New York, she was headed in the right direction. And moments later she was happily winging further Eastward across the choppy Atlantic.

Half an hour later, surprised that her wings weren't even tired, Robin came to rest on a coil of rope at the end of a cluttered pier.

"London?" she breathed hopefully, noticing clouds of fog hugging the shoreline. And, for a change, she was right.

Why had she chosen London as the first stop on her weekend flight? So who chose? She had only aimed as best she could and here she was!

And what was she going to do about it?

One need hardly ask, need one? Hardly.

After resting for a moment and drinking a bit of rain water out of an old shoe (which tasted rather good, all things considered), Robin straightened her glasses and flew off to find the Beatles.

(To Be Continued Next Week)

Person to Person

VAN:
I love your natural hair. I think I'll go to that store after Sunday School. Ha. Please wear your Jim-glasses.
Martha, Judi & Katy

V.H.:
Did you know the sun never sets on British soil? Well, it was once like that. Shall we demonstrate for the LP-5 Protest Australia or start digging.
K. K. of W. C.

CHRIS:
The Junior Court is better than the Senior Court.
Kathy

DANNY DE'LACY:
I'm still waiting for you to come back to The Rose Garden.
Linda

BERYL BOOTH:
Happy Anniversary. What better way to announce four months of happy correspondence than thru the fab *BEAT*?
Paulette

GEORGE:
Please send me a lock of your hair and some pictures. It's your turn to write.
Brenda

FAITH:
I want my false eyelashes back.
G.R.

LINDA NOBLE, SURREY:
Thought you might like to see your name in *The BEAT*. If you're roaming around "Jollie Olde London Town" and pop into Mick or Brian, say "hi" for me.
Tina

LYNNIE JAY, EL PASO:
Merry Christmas early. Can't think of a nicer present than *The BEAT* for a whole year.
Patty

JIM McGUINN:
Hope you found my note on the floor of your car. Next time, don't leave your checkbook on the front seat. The show was fabulous!
Sharon

REBECCA SCHNIEDER, Seattle:
Reb, this is the greatest newspaper in the world. How do you like your name in it?
Senya

CHRIS S., Orange:
I know how much you love Peter A. so I won't make fun of him any more. O.K.?
Mary

CAVES AND CHIPPE:
Thanks bunches for the gear party you threw for me on my birthday. I'm still picking confetti out of my hair.
Johnee

JOHN LENNON:
Sorry we took your shirts. Please forgive us.
C. & F.

MASTER CONTROL:
Congratulate the Flying Ace for me. Say "hi" to U-2.
Deuce

KRLA ARCHIVES

EARL PRESTON'S REALMS taking part in a recording session at Cavern Sound Studio.

Liverpuddles
By Rob McGrae
Manager, The Cavern

An interesting thing about the Cavern is that it is not only a club but also a recording studio. The studio was opened in October 1964 by Peter Hepworth and Nigel Greenberg.

Peter and Nigel had wanted for a long time to open an independent recording studio to record and distribute records by Liverpool groups. They considered this essential to keep Liverpool music at the top of the charts.

Before they opened their studio there was no independent recording studio in the city and if a Liverpool group wanted to cut a demonstration record, they had to travel down to London and that entailed a lot of expense.

The actual venture turned out to be rather expensive. The studio, located in the cellar next to the Cavern, cost over $30 thousand. But these two 24 year old engineers threw themselves into opening it.

Now it's a very busy studio indeed. Over half of the studio time goes to making commercial radio programs for such English companies as Radio Caroline and Radio London. They have already recorded one series of live programs in the Cavern and sold it to an American sponsor for a weekly half hour series which will run for six months. They are very interested in producing Liverpool flavored programs for America and would like to hear from any one in America who's interested.

Country and Western

Two of the records they have cut are available now to Americans. One is a single by the Ranchers called "An American Sailor at the Cavern" with "Sidetracked" on the flip side. The Ranchers are Liverpool's number one country and western group and will soon be featured on an album called "Liverpool goes Country" to be released in America on Decca.

"Sidetracked" was written by Bob Wooler and first released in March of this year. All of the proceeds from this record go to mentally handicapped children.

The other Cavern record which you can purchase is an extended single called "Pantomania" featuring the Roadrunners and several Liverpool University students. It was produced for the students' annual money raising project for charities. It topped the Liverpool charts for five weeks.

If you wish to buy either of these records, you may send $2 for "Sidetracked" or $3 for "Pantomania" to me at Cavern Sound Limited, 8/12 Mathew Street, Liverpool 2. You'll also be helping some charities.

Rising Sons Up In West

The Rising Sons are coming up in the West.

After performing at night spots around California for the last seven months, the group has signed an exclusive recording contract with Columbia Records and cut their first single, which should be released soon.

The Rising Sons are Taj Mahal, Jesse Lee Kincaid, Gary Marker, Ry Cooder, and Devin Kelley. Terry Melcher, who has had great success producing records for the Byrds and Paul Revere and the Raiders, will produce all the group's recordings.

Lead guitarist of the group, Ry is 21 years old and plays five different instruments. He's a native of California.

Jesse Lee Kincaid, 21, rhythm guitarist, is from Detroit but was raised in California. He met Taj Mahal in Boston and they formed a folk and blues duo. They came west early this year and formed the Rising Sons.

Taj Mahal is the oldest member of the group, 23, and the leader. He was raised in New England and is the group's lead vocalist. He also plays harmonica, tambourine and several string instruments.

Native Californians

Bass player of the group is Gary Marker, 22, another native Californian. He took up the clarinet at the age of nine and has since learned to play the alto saxophone, drums, cello and double bass.

The group's drummer, Devin Kelley, 22, is another native Californian. He started playing drums at the age of 11, switched to guitar at 16, and back to drum after a three year hitch in the Marines. Devin also plays saxophone, piano and bass. He is a cousin of bass player Chris Hillman of the Byrds.

With as many instruments as these five have they should be able to come up with a really new sound. Watch for the Rising Sons coming up in the West.

CROWD SHOT — Sam the Sham and the Pharaohs must have someone important on the other end of the telephone as they crowd into booth at MGM studios during filming of "When the Boys Meet the Girls."

Q: I am fifteen years old and my folks keep trying to make me go to bed at ten o'clock on school nights. They seldom succeed, but we get into arguments about the subject far too often (it makes me feel awful because we're very close in other ways). How can I convince them that I don't need more than eight hours of sleep? I get up at 7:30 and so do they. If I go to bed earlier than 11:30 or twelve, I'm awake at 6 a.m. I tell them that, but they won't listen. What can I do?
(Sandie C.)

A: Since you and your folks are close, they probably wouldn't mind a bit of ribbing. The next time you wake up at six a.m., after having been hurried off to bed at ten, make sure they're awake by cooking breakfast. In large, noisy kettles. Get the picture? So will they.

Q: I'm rather average looking, which doesn't bother me much, but I do have this problem. Moles. I have about six of them on my neck and it's just horrible. Is there anything I can do except go to a doctor? If not, will any doctor do this and could you tell me the price? I'm desperate!
(Becky M.)

A: No, no, no, there isn't anything you can do except go to a doctor, if you want them removed! Any other method would be unbelievably dangerous, possibly even fatal. Go to your family doctor. If he can't help you, he'll send you to someone who can, and will be able to tell you how much it will cost (it shouldn't be too much because the "operation" is performed right at the doctor's office.)

Q: This is a dumb question but here goes. My girlfriend asks me over to her house nearly every Saturday afternoon, and I like to go over there. I think I'd ask her to go steady if it weren't for this dog of hers. It lays around all over the furniture, and when I come home from an afternoon at her house, I look like a St. Bernard. It's a white dog with long hair. Should I just say something about this? Do you think it'll tee her off?
(Bill M.)

A: Why don't you just ask her to bring out a whiskbroom and brush you off just before you leave her house? That should get the point across without your having to come right out and say it. Doubt if she'll totally give you the brush if you handle the matter this way.

Q: I bought a pair of wool knee socks and they're very cute. There's only one problem. They make me itch like I can't believe. I'm embarrassed to wear them because about five minutes after I put them on, I look like I belong in a zoo. I can't afford to get another pair so what can I do?
(Andrea P.)

A: Do like many girls do. Wear a pair of nylons under the knee socks! Clever, no?

HINT OF THE WEEK
I've found a great way to make extra money, by going into "business" with my girlfriend. I can draw and she can write crazy things, so we make cards for people. They tell us what they want, you know, something they can't find in a store, or something really nutty, and we make the card by hand, and the envelope! We made $10 last month which might not sound like much, but it sure came in handy!
(Sharon T.)

If you have a question you'd like answered, or a hint you'd like to share, drop a line to Tips To Teens, c/o The BEAT.

KRLA ARCHIVES

Dear Susan

By Susan Frisch

I would like to know where I can write to Elvis and be sure of his getting my letter.
Carol Henderson

You can write to Elvis in care of R.C.A. Victor, 6363 Sunset Blvd., Hollywood, California.

Can you please give me the address of the Leaves, other than a Fan club?
Leanne

You can write to the Leaves in care of Penthouse Recordings, 9025 Wilshire Blvd., Beverly Hills, California.

Can you please tell me if Glenn Campbell is married?
Linda Katuna

Yes, Glenn is married.

Will the Beatles be back next year, and can you also print my address so I may have Beatle pen pals from all over.
"Beatle-Nut"

First of all, yes. The Beatles will be coming back next year. Here is your address so people may write you: 1453 - 70th Ave., Oakland, California.

Are you absolutely sure that it was Jane Asher who appeared in "Help" for about 15 seconds?
Wendy Mills

Yes.

When did John Lennon start wearing his contact lenses?
Diane May

John began using them about 6 months ago.

Can you please give me the address where I can write to the Supremes, other than a fan club?
Mike Vlanis

Motown Records, 6290 Sunset Blvd., Hollywood, California.

Can you give me the address where I can write to Sonny and Cher concerning some business?
George J. Ziblay

Write to Sonny and Cher in care of Greene/Stone Publications, 7715 Sunset Blvd., Hollywood, California

What is Robert Vaughn's address?

MGM Studios, 10202 Washington Blvd., Culver City, Calif.

At what address can I write to Peter Noone and be sure of him getting it personally?
Lori Joseph

Write to Peter at 9 Chestnut Lane, Roby, Liverpool, England.

Has Bob Dylan written a book?
Henrietta Calderon

No, Bob hasn't written a book as yet, but we're hoping for one.

Is Dave Clark married?
Karen Springer

No, Dave isn't married . . . yet!

How tall is Marianne Faithfull?
Phil

Marianne is 5 feet 5 inches tall.

Are the Silkies the group that recorded "You've Got To Hide Your Love Away," an American or English group?
Puzzled One

The Silkies are all English.

Can you tell me who recorded the song, "Nobody I Know?" And do you think there is any hope for me and Bobby Sherman?
Deanne Wilson

Peter and Gordon recorded that song. If you don't mind competition then sure there is hope!

How can I get the British version of "Help?"
Jerry Albert

The best thing for you to do, is ask your local record stores to order it for you.

Can you please tell me what kind of cars the Beatles have?
Ruth Montag

John has a green V.W., a blue Ferrari 350 G.T., a white Mini, and a black Rolls Royce. Ringo has a Facel Vega, which is maroon, John's old Rolls Royce and a maroon Mini. Paul has a blue Aston Martin D.B. 5 and a white Mini. George has a white Aston Martin D.B. 5, and a green Mini.

Where can I write to Donovan?
Steffi Berkowitz

Write to Donovan in care of Panton House, 25 Haymarket, London, S.W. 1, England.

Can you please tell me Sam the Sham's real name, and of what nationality he is?
Hope Gimmel

His real name is Domingo Samudio. He is Mexican-American.

Does Sally Fields, Gidget, date Bobby Sherman?
Larry White

No, she doesn't.

"BUT FELLAS, I DON'T HAVE ANY MONEY EITHER," says Eric Burdon of the Animals as Charles Chandler, right, tries to nail him for the ciggies and cokes consumed by the boys during a Hollywood recording session.

Eric The Loser

Eric Burton of the Animals had to spend an extra day in America on their last tour because of a lost passport.

"I lost my passport—a fan took it. I thought my road manager was looking for it and he thought I was. So there was a mixup. I wanted to meet Ray Charles and I was going out to see him, but I had to go to the Embassy instead.

But Eric used the rest of his time in America to work on the book he is writing.

"I spent a lot of time in New York collecting material for my book. This was the last trip planned for collecting material and when I have finished I will transcribe my notes onto a tape recorder. I'm taking my time with the book, I don't want to rush into it.

"It deals with race relation and music, which are directly involved with each other, people I have met and things I've seen," he explained.

Tom Jones' Sound Alike

There's a new face and a new sound going 'round the pop circles these days, and both of them belong to a young man by the name of Denny Provisor.

He was born in Los Angeles on November 9, 1943, and he attended three years of college, as well as studying piano for four years.

"My father wanted me to be a lawyer and I was going to, until music completely took me over. I started playing piano for people at their houses and at parties, then I started playing professionally in clubs and auditioning for people."

Denny is currently a member of a group called The Originals, but his ambition is to be recognized as a singer and a performer in his own right. In describing his sound on his first Valiant record, "It really tears me up," he says:

"It's like Tom Jones, in a way—it's in between a colored and a white sound; between a funky rock and a funky folk. I like singing songs in which there's a lot of room to improvise. I like to sing 'soul music' and this record is a folk sound."

Best For Beatles

The Beatles are the best and they demand the best to go with them.

For their upcoming December special on BBC they have signed two of the top entertainers in the world. And they don't stick strickly to English entertainers either.

For this special they have signed an American, Henry Mancini, and an Englishman, Peter Sellers.

You always know that you're getting the best if it's a Beatle production.

DOES CHER DIG NINO TEMPO? If so, Sonny doesn't seem jealous as he and April Stevens (Nino's sister and singing partner) become better acquainted at a party by Atco Records for their two top duos.

KRLA ARCHIVES

Dishy 007 Once Was A Dreary Coffin Polisher

Down this darkened alley, and just around that corner, and... WATCH OUT!!! It's agent 007—licensed to break every female heart in sight!

Yep, we're talking about none other than our favorite spy-guy, Sean Connery.

Sean is currently in Hollywood putting the wraps on his latest film for Warner Bros., "A Fine Madness," which co-stars Joanne Woodward, and Jean Seberg. No fancy spy-tacular this one, instead Sean plays an average, everyday, violently impulsive poet from Greenwich Village. Well, at least it *is* a change of pace for our fast-moving friend.

Sean was born on August 25 in Edinburgh, Scotland (yes, his name *is* Irish!!), and though his father drove a lorry in order to support his family, Sean can trace his ancestors back to the Scottish Highland Kings, not to mention a bit o' the Celtic blood in his family tree!

Hard though it may be to believe, Sean has not always spent his leisure moments dashing from bullet to boudoir. Quite on the contrary—Sean put in his share of time as a milk man, a cement mixer, a bricklayer, a steel bender, a printer's assistant, a lifeguard, and a *coffin polisher*! Mr. Connery also served for three years as a seaman in the British Navy as a trainee with a gunnery outfit and as a member of an anti-aircraft carrier squadron.

Sean's first introduction to the world of show business was really accidental, when he happened to run into a friend while he was on a holiday in London. His friend was then in the musical "South Pacific," and suggested that Sean try to fill a vacancy which had occurred in the show. Then, lo and behold! Much to the surprise of nearly everyone—including Sean! —he was hired, and spent the succeeding eighteen months as a chorus boy in the show.

After "South Pacific," Sean appeared in a small repertory company, and then went on to do his first work in films. His first movie was a low-budget item entitled "No Road Back." Sean subsequently appeared in several Hollywood-produced movies, including "Hell Divers," "Another Time, Another Place," "The Frightened City," and several others. He returned to London and succeeded in gaining a good deal of critical praise for his co-starring performance with Claire Bloom in the BBC's television adaptation of "Anna Karenina."

Bond Role

And then it happened. The readers of the *London Express* chose Sean as their ideal actor to portray the part of one Mr. James Bond in "Dr. No." Yes, they created a giant. There has seldom been a series of pictures which have received such general popularity from the public, and never have pictures in a series chalked up the phenomenal grosses which now stand behind all of the James Bond pictures. And every time that they are re-released, they are even *more* successful!

Now? Well, girls—I'm afraid that all we can do now is just wait for December to roll around again. Why? Well, that's when the next "Bond" picture—"Thunderball"—will be released. Can you think of a nicer way to "kill" a Christmas vacation?

I can't!!! Merry Christmas, James!

Rock Show For Adults?

All you Flintstones fans are going to have to miss your favorite program one time. It's being pre-empted on Jan. 28 to make way for a rock and roll video special called "Swing-Ding at T.J.'s."

ABC-TV and sponsors Procter & Gamble are going to try to put on a rock program that will appeal to the older generation, but you teenagers will be allowed to watch too.

The show will be in a 17th century London setting and will feature the Dave Clark Five. Emcees for the special will be Sal Mineo and Phil Spector.

AGENT 007, otherwise known as Sean Connery, took time out from his James Bond adventures to film another movie, "A Fine Madness."

JEREMY, sans Chad, sits on top of his London flat and ponders what will happen to him, to Chad and to Jill when his play folds.

What Happen's To Jeremy Now?

By Louise Criscione

A press party is one of the best places to see people and pick up on all the latest happenings and Pat Boone's party for the Leaves was no exception.

One of the nicest couples at the party was Chad Stuart and his pretty wife, Jill. Since Chad and Jill now live here permanently it seems that I am forever running into them, which isn't bad, is it?

He had hardly said "Hi" when he started in a mile a minute to tell me all about his brand new '66 Mustang GT which he considers to be the most fantastic thing ever made and I guess his is!

Fab Car

It's green with black upholstery and wood paneling. The only fault Chad can find with the car is that it has horses (Mustangs, of course) firmly implanted on the backseat upholstery and Chad pronounces them "a bit childish" so he's having them taken off.

When I found out that Chad was going to England for 21 days I heroically offered to take care of his new Mustang for him to make sure that the battery didn't run down. I thought it was very generous of me but Chad declined with the flimsy excuse that while he is away the horses are being removed and a stereo is being installed.

Well, all of that is fine and dandy —but what about Jeremy? Controversy has waged on ever since Jeremy left to do "Passion Flower Hotel" in London. The first reports were that the duo was breaking up. This they both denied emphatically.

The "will they, or won't they?" died down for some time and then Chad began making appearances on stage with Jill and the question then became "Will the old Chad & Jeremy become the new Chad & Jill?"

Jeremy Calls

In London, Jeremy received word of this new development and immediately phoned Chad. What was going on? Even Jeremy didn't know. Several heated phone conversations later Jeremy was apparently satisfied that all was well and that Jill was merely filling in for him while he was doing the play.

It probably all boils down to too many people trying to stick their fingers in too many pies. Jeremy wants to be a singer and an actor. Chad would rather be a singer and record producer. Jill wants to be an actress but she also likes singing. Kind of like the eternal triangle, isn't it?

The whole mess will shortly be resolved though. Jeremy's "Passion Flower Hotel" is folding up and when it does he will be free. Logically then, he and Chad will once again be a team. But what happens to Jill?

Personally, I hope Chad & Jeremy get back together again. Jill is certainly a doll but she and Chad singing together looked like an English version of Sonny & Cher. Not that that's bad—but Chad & Jeremy were much better.

KRLA ARCHIVES

Hollywood's Moulin Rouge *Rocks In!*
GRAND OPENING DEC. 9
The Showplace of the World Becomes The Rock & Roll Showplace of the World

THE PALACE GUARD ENTER HOLLYWOOD'S FINEST NEW CLUB (left). DAVE HULL IS CAUGHT TRYING TO "BORROW" A UNIFORM.

DAVE HULL'S
HULLABALOO

6230 Sunset
Across from Palladium

Featuring
The Palace Guard
Plus
The World's Top Recording Stars

(Follow The BEAT for details on scheduled Guest Appearances)

Plus
- ★ Continuous entertainment—on three stages—Including one of the world's great revolving center stages!
- ★ Continuous dancing—Good Food—All the Glamor and Showmanship of Hollywood's Finest.
- ★ Home of the Rock & Roll Hall of Fame—Footprints, Handprints and Momentos of the great rock stars.

ROCK WITH DAVE HULL AT THE HULLABALOO
AGES 15-21 — NO MINIMUM — NO COVER — ALL FOR $1.50 ADMISSION

Special Premiere Dec. 8
Hosting The BEAT's 1st Annual Pop Music Awards Dinner

KRLA ARCHIVES

Charlie-O: Sense of Humor Behind the Innocent Look

"I was born August 12, 1932, in Philadelphia, Pennsylvania—which makes me 21 years old now!"

So begins Charlie's story about —Charlie!! Please continue, Mr. O'Donnell.

"I graduated high school at 16, with a scholarship to Theatre Arts Institute, and later went to Catholic University in Washington, where I was an English major. I left there after a short time and went back to radio, but one of these days I'm gonna finish—really!"

Child Star

Charlie is somewhat of a veteran actor in radio, going all the way back to the days of The Lone Ranger.

"I've mentioned several times that Casey Kasem's career and mine sort of parallel each other. We were both child actors. Casey was on all the big shows—he got all the money!—because he was doing "Lone Ranger" and "Green Hornet." I played Hiawatha and just about every child part in some of the great children's stories."

Now, you may all well wonder how a big-time, professional disc jockey—such as Charlie—begins his career in radio. Well..."When I was in high school, I used to do a disc jockey show—on the PA system!!

Prior to the morning assembly, I'd give weather reports, and who was late to class that morning, and sort of inner-school chat and gossip. You know: 'The basketball team lost *again* last night,' just like the KRLApes always do!"

Charlie got his first professional job in radio at the age of 17, and followed it with several other successful jobs in the Pennsylvania area, finally winding up at station WHAT in Philadelphia in 1952. in 1952.

The station was one of the first to ever play rock 'n' roll and r 'n' b, and Charlie remained there for eight years, building a fine reputation for himself. "At 21, I was one of the youngest program directors in the country.

By the time I was 23, I'd worked my way up to station manager, and spent about five years in management, getting a pretty solid background in radio."

Somewhat later, he entered the field of television as somewhat of a pioneer, and had one of the first all-night TV shows. It was six hours long, six nights a week, and it was filmed in a studio with an electric camera—which means that Charlie performed *all* alone from one o'clock to six o'clock in the morning every single night.

"I guess I had one of the highest ratings of any TV personality in the US because no other station was on the air at that time!!"

Life With Dick

In the early 1950's, Charlie first became associated with Dick Clark as his announcer—and his life hasn't been the same since! Although Dick has become one of Charlie's closest friends, he has also been his greatest source of "practical jokery."

"For nine years now, every time I do an announcement—all you see on camera is my face. Dick is usually giving me a hot foot, or rolling down my sock, or pulling up my pant leg, or untying my shoe laces, or tying them together, or whatnot.

"I finally got a chance to get even when we did the special for KRLA a year ago. I handed Dick the microphone and said, 'Go ahead, Dick—say whatever you want,' and in front of millions of people I finally got a chance to pull *his* pant leg up. But *I* was blamed! He said, 'Oh Charlie's always a joker!!"

Charlie has already appeared in two motion pictures, including the soon-to-be-released Rock Hudson flick, "Blindfold." But this is not the end of Charlie's aspirations in show biz.

"I want to do everything! I would like to continue acting, but my secret ambition is musical comedy, because it's the combination of everything I have tried to develop—talent-wise—in myself.

He also enjoys dabbling in painting—which he is currently studying three hours a week—and occasionally indulges himself in a little writing. Now, if you will turn your radio dial to 1110 every morning about 9:00, you can indulge yourself in the delightful experience of listening to Charlie "dabbling" in a very fun-type radio show. We'll see you then, Charlie.

...KRLA'S CHARLIE O'DONNELL

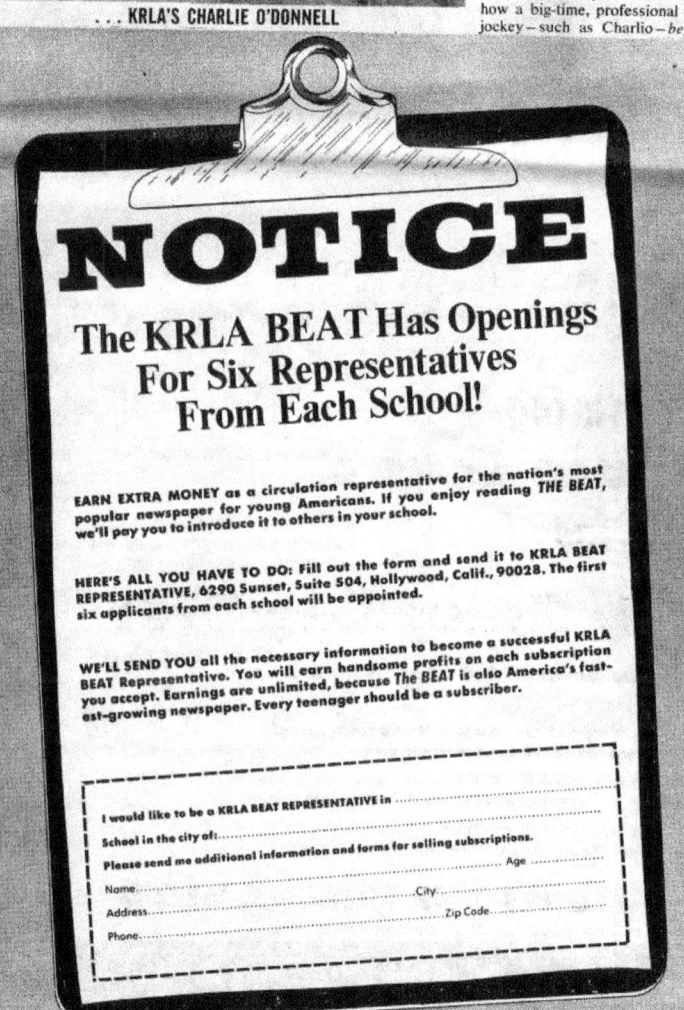

NOTICE

The KRLA BEAT Has Openings For Six Representatives From Each School!

EARN EXTRA MONEY as a circulation representative for the nation's most popular newspaper for young Americans. If you enjoy reading THE BEAT, we'll pay you to introduce it to others in your school.

HERE'S ALL YOU HAVE TO DO: Fill out the form and send it to KRLA BEAT REPRESENTATIVE, 6290 Sunset, Suite 504, Hollywood, Calif., 90028. The first six applicants from each school will be appointed.

WE'LL SEND YOU all the necessary information to become a successful KRLA BEAT Representative. You will earn handsome profits on each subscription you accept. Earnings are unlimited, because The BEAT is also America's fastest-growing newspaper. Every teenager should be a subscriber.

I would like to be a KRLA BEAT REPRESENTATIVE in ....
School in the city of: ....
Please send me additional information and forms for selling subscriptions.
Name...Age.......
Address...................................City..................
Phone...Zip Code..........

Thru Dec. 5
Bud & Travis

Dec. 7-Dec. 19
Hoyt Axton

...At Doug Weston's
Troubadour
9083 Santa Monica Blvd. at Dohney, L.A.
RESERVATIONS CR 6-6168
STUDENT DISCOUNT — MINORS WELCOME

KRLA BEAT Subscription
SPECIAL OFFER—Subscribe Now
SAVE 60% Of Regular Price
☐ 1 YEAR—52 ISSUES—$3.00
Enclosed is $3.00   ☐ CASH   ☐ CHECK
Send to:.................................Age..........
Address:.................................
City...................State.......Zip................
MAIL YOUR ORDER TO: The BEAT
1401 So. Oak Knoll
Pasadena, Calif.
Foreign Rate: $14.00—52 Issues

KRLA ARCHIVES

Open Letter To Beatle Fans

Hello there, fellow idiots!

Now that we're all together we can talk about some things we wouldn't DARE talk about among Herman's Hermits fans (even though you probably are one—I am.)

We've got to admit it. We Beatle fans ARE letting our thoughts wander from just George, John, Ringo and Paul. Think back. Haven't you during the past week, thought about how yummy Herman is? Maybe it isn't Herman—perhaps it was Donovan (or Dave Clark, or Mick Jagger). Oh sure, you're probably saying, "Yeah, well, sure, but George is my very favorite."

Now think back a few months. When you went to the Beatles' concert. How did you act? Were you just sitting there listening to them? Why? Because you could see no reason to scream. Or were you one of the few who ran up to the stage? Why? Because you wanted to be able to go up to your friends and say "Hey, guess what I did that I bet you didn't." Well, I'll admit that I just sat and listened to them. I didn't scream either. Well, once when George went to pick up his guitar. Now that you've been honest with yourself do it again. How did you act a year ago. Weren't you more than a bit more hysterical? You were! What happened between you and the Beatles? Was it Peter Noone, Keith Richard or the boy across from you in Spanish? Whoever it was, he did something to change the feeling you had for Paul or John or Ringo or George. But aren't you happier now?

Maybe it was that Ringo got married. Sure you always loved George but it made you wonder how long it would be till George went to the altar, too.

All right all you Beatle fans, I see that a lot of you are wearing doubtful looks. You're not so sure you ARE Beatle fans. You are, but you have some other interests, that's all. We've all grown up a bit, too. But all the same, deep down inside we'll always be Beatle fans even if right now we're beginning to wonder (and wander.)

Just remember, BEATLES 4 EVER!

Karen Call
Millbrae, California

PAUL McCARTNEY—Have your thoughts strayed from him?

Bonos Blow One—Oh Well, Can't Win 'Em All

In the language of show biz, Sonny and Cher have finally "blown one."

The trade industry newspapers came right out and said flatly that the couple who wowed Jacqueline Kennedy laid a royal egg before the visiting princess and her husband.

At the specific request of Princess Margaret, Sonny and Cher joined Bob Hope, Polly Bergen and the Freddy Martin Orchestra in entertaining at the WAIF charity ball.

But the critics called their segment the low point of the evening, criticizing them for their far-out dress during the highly formal affair and for performing too long. There were loud hisses and catcalls from the audience before they finally gave way to Bob Hope, who immediately got the entertainment back on the right track.

With America going all-out to entertain the royal couple it was considered a high honor to be asked to perform. But Sonny and Cher—despite their great popularity among teenagers and young adults—apparently found out the hard way that it's dangerous for an entertainer to step out of his element.

For Girls Only
Rhyming Problem

By Shirley Poston

I have a problem (which is hardly news to anyone who's read this column before). And you'll be happy to hear (*sure* you will) that I'm going to tell you all about it. It's George.

You see, about two hours ago I decided to write a cute little poem for my weekly ravings. And since George is what (whom?) I do most of that raving about, I thought I'd make him the subject of my terse little verse.

Well, I ask you. Have you ever tried to rhyme something with *Harrison*? All I can say is lotsa luck.

I'm almost embarrassed (but not quite) (you know me) to tell you what I managed to come up with after spending all that time, but here it is.

George
Is gorge-
Ons.

Okay, you can stop that laughing right this minute. So I'm no poet. George loves me anyway (don't I wish).

Say, have you ever heard of a Bear Scare?

I hope not, because I'm wondering about you if you have. No, seriously, there is such a thing (would I lie to you about something this important?). And it's not something you scare bears with (fortunately). It's a magic charm!

Yes, yes, I know, I've lost my mind (still going through that English phase, I am). I *realize* there is no such thing as a magic charm, but that doesn't mean I *believe* there is no such thing as a magic charm. (Let's face it, I am a true simp.)

Anyway, a Bear Scare is a piece of rawhide about the size of a shoestring (foot type, not potato) that's tied in three knots around your wrist.

Well, isn't *that* easy to understand. Let's take that one from the top again. A Bear Scare is just long enough to go around your wrist after it's been tied in three knots, one for each wish you make when putting the Bear Scare on.

Oh, forget the whole thing.

Mid-Western Fad

Anyway, it's a big fad all over the mid-Western portions of the country. After the wishes are made, you can't take the "bracelet" off for one solid year. Which, of course, makes all three wishes come true!

Like I always say, (I always say that) there is no such thing as a magic charm, maybe. So what does it hurt to give it a try?

Oh, I have a feeling one of my best friends is going to have me drawn and quartered. Because I'm about to do it again.

Every time she gets her weekly copy of *The BEAT*, she gives me a series of the world's dirtiest looks. Why, you ask (providing that you haven't drifted off to sleep mid-column)? Because she thinks I am a thief.

Simply because I mention her now and again and say a few (thousand) words about something she's done, she thinks she ought to get paid or something.

Light-Fingered

Well! Do I have news for her. And I think she'll also have news for me when this week's *BEAT* comes out. Light-fingered Poston Rides Again.

Here's what I've stolen...er... chosen to reveal about her this week. Remember when I was just raving about magic charms? Well, my girlfriend agrees that there is no such thing as same.

But does that stop her from getting up in the middle of the night, making a wish, lighting a black candle and burning it in the *midnight wind*? Hardly. And I am *serious*! The poor kid—I mean the wonderful person actually thinks her wish is going to come true.

Don't go telling it around, but I think I'll try it myself. All I have is a red candle (a Christmas reject from last year), but I hope that won't mess up the magic charm. You know, the one there is no such thing as.

Hmmmm. I had something in mind (using the term loosely) that I was going to be sure and tell you and now it's gone with the wind. Oh, now I remember.

You know all of those secrets we've been blabbing to each other? About lying awake nights making up dreams about stars (George Rules!) and all? Well, here's another one for you.

Do you ever, right in the middle of school or something, stop and suddenly wonder what your special someone is doing right that minute? And when (and if) you do this, doesn't it give you the *creepiest* feeling when you realize that he *is* doing something and that he does actually *exist*?

I hope you know what I mean. Our favorites are so far away from us, most of the time they don't seem completely real. But every once in awhile, you can just picture them brushing their teeth or something like that, and they seem so much closer.

Whenever that happens to me, I just stand there with my mouth hanging open, thinking incredulously, "somewhere he's *breathing*."

Have you ever had the feeling that someone was coming for you with a very large net? Well, join the crowd.

If the man in white doesn't see me first, I'll see you next *BEAT*. And please don't forget to write me!

A Dylan Fan Speaks, The BEAT Listens

At twenty-four years of age, Bob Dylan is the voice of a generation—and he has a whole generation listening intently to every word he sings and writes.

His influence has inspired reams of words to be written, sung, and spoken, including a poem submitted to *The BEAT* by one of our readers — Beverly Boynton.

Beverly has followed Dylan's efforts and the following poem is her own personal expression of the feelings she experiences while hearing his songs and reading his poetry.

mr. dylan

this strange young man
of whom i speak
i never have
nor will ever meet
with eloquent mind
perceptive and grand
he plays reality
right into his hand
manner is modest
face is kind
his type of person
you rarely find
we love his work
applaud his fame
he writes of dream-places
where people are tame
hate is absent
and people's faces
are lined with laughter
free of disgraces
like a robin
on the highest tree
where his heart lives
i'd love to be
he'll put you down
if you criticize
and looks at life
through x-ray eyes
when you hear his laugh
you too will smile
when he's serious
you think awhile
phony people
he's exposed like dogs
and crawly bugs
under logs
if you're a phony
he's first to know it
can't hide facts
from this young poet
don't waste time wondering
what's inside his head
there's much to learn
listen instead
and come morning
when sun climbs up
i'll drink wine
from my coffee cup
and dream of eden
so far away
where fountains wash
hatred away
while he speaks of life
and we listen
gazing out the window
raindrops glisten
someday soon
i hope we find
this utopia
if the blind
open their eyes
so they can see
mr. dylan's message
to you and me

Meet the Leaves—Not Falling but Soaring

JIM PONS — JOHN BECK
BOB REINER — TOM "AMBROSE" RAY — BILL RINEHART

KRLA ARCHIVES

The World Of Protest

Teenagers of today are an active, alert, inquisitive lot. They ask questions and they demand answers.

They want to know about everything. They want to know why adults don't understand them, why protest songs are written and why they sell, why a musician can sue the Beatles, and if one of the Beatles is secretly married.

They pose these questions to themselves, to teachers, to friends and relatives, and to The BEAT.

We can't answer them all but we can pass them on to others. We can let other people know that teens do care and do ask questions.

Destruction?

Dear *BEAT:*

I agree with Mary Andrews' letter on "Eve of Destruction." The attitude of the whole crowd of protestors seems to be "let's show everyone how good we are by pointing out the bad in everyone else, or the "save the world by pretending it's not worth saving."

I am thoroughly disgusted with all these characters. They've certainly a right to be heard but you'll not catch *me* listening to their putrescence! In evaluating the world situation, as in everything, he who ignores the good is just as blind and stupid as he who ignores the bad—and a good deal more *trying*, too.

There are many kids (I'm 20 now but am speaking about former thoughts and experiences) who care deeply about what's going on in the world today but who have the sense to know that the world's wrongs can't be corrected by nasal-voiced draft-dodgers, which is what many of these "demonstrators" are.

Jeri P.

To *The BEAT:*

I really see no point in Barry McGuire's "Eve of Destruction." The eve of destruction is no new thing to this world of ours. We've been on the verge of possible destruction since the beginning of time.

The world didn't go when the proverbial apple was eaten long ago and probably won't go for quite a while.

If the song was to be written, it should have happened long ago. And now it's too late—or is it? It really depends on our generation.

Milfie Howell

Shindig Cast Off to Hawaii

Cast and crew of *Shindig* have gone to Waikiki to tape two shows.

Guest stars for the two episodes are Tommy Sands, Ian Whitcomb and Len Barry.

Shindig regulars making the trip include host Jimmy O'Neill, Bobby Sherman, Donna Loren, Glen Campbell, the Shindogs, Billy Preston, the Blossoms, the Wellingtons and the *Shindig* dancers.

Paul and Jane

Dear *BEAT,*

I am writing this letter in connection with some of the statements Jane Asher has been making about Paul McCartney and her relationship with him.

Recently, she stated in a magazine, written exclusively about the Beatles, that not only was Paul very selfish, but that he was also blind to the fact that her "adulation" for him, as she called it, was real and that ours (his fans) was not. Not only this, but when asked, she firmly states that she and Paul have definite plans to marry. On the other hand, Paul states that he is not engaged to anyone, and no date has been set. Yet, Jane openly contradicts him, in public no less, by making statements which practically call Paul a liar.

Why does she insist on saying such things? Doesn't she know she is endangering not only Paul, but herself as well, by discussing what should not be said in the first place? It seems to me that Paul stopped seeing Jill Haworth for exactly the same reason. Perhaps the fact of the matter is she isn't really concerned with anyone's happiness but her own.

In my opinion, the only thing Paul is blind to is the fact that Jane Asher is a fake; she is the worst kind of phony.

Pam Francis

Dear Staff,

There's two sides to every story or so it goes. Right now I am torn between these two sides. It's the age-old question—are they or aren't they?

By they I am referring to Paul McCartney M.B.E. and Jane Asher. Everyone say yes, but they say no. I can and do believe them.

But there are times when everything seems to point in the opposite direction. Why, oh why, can't "trash" magazines stop all the lies and start printing the truth? Is that so hard? It's magazines like these that can change a Beatle fan's mind about her fave. And the same applies for any group—Stones, Animals, Byrds and the like.

Sure, they say "Don't believe anything you read." And what are we supposed to do—hibernate for the rest of our lives? We can't help but hear, and doubt, only because we're human and they are too.

Maybe I'm feeling sorry for myself, and I'm not alone. Maybe I'm just plain selfish.

Or maybe I'm feeling sorry for them—the people who conjure up and publish the trash. I'm feeling sorry for them because they have nothing better to do.

If they only knew that with a little bit more trouble, they could come up with the *truth*—that's the only word I can use, because it makes a lot more sense than any other word in the dictionary. And because the truth would also save us heartbreaks, the worry, tension and sleepless nights, and them a mal-adjusted printing press.

If they only knew...

A *BEAT* Representative

Teens vs Adults

Dear Editor:

Regarding your editorial "Maybe It's Time to Protest":

I was pleased to find these opinions so authoritatively offered, and to find that at least somewhere there is a spokesman for the intelligent teenager of today. You have voiced an argument with which the great majority will agree. Unfortunately, the "great majority" will include very few parents and adults.

Incidentally, I am proud to say, I am not included in the latter class. I am a teenager.

The difference between "my" generation and the previous one is only as wide as the gap between honesty and hypocrisy. We teenagers will either accept or abandon an opinion, belief or custom; we will not wear a mustache and order others to shave.

For some reason, almost inexplicably, it seems the present generation has grown up without prejudice, while members of the previous generation are still enslaved by this vice and do their best to pass it on to us.

We can forestall the "Eve of Destruction" if we teenagers show ourselves in our true colors. We are free of prejudices, we love life and all mankind, and though many will doubt it, we seem to have been born with a type of native wisdom. Without being taught, we realize what was taught 1930 years ago; the same teachings adults pretend to believe and pay lip-service to.

There's still hope.

G. John Edwards

Dear Editor:

From one parent who "listened" to your editorial protest ("Teen Side of Story—Maybe It's Time to Protest"), may I have equal time?

I have read and re-read your message and I've been thinking of the many points you mentioned. You speak of teenagers as a responsible group. I agree. They are responsible to the adult world! Someday they, too, will be adults. They are in a transition state of their lives. They are growing and learning. It is only after you are grown up that you realize how little of the world you really understand and begin to try, as hard as you can, to learn what, where, when and how you can contribute.

In your plan to substitute the ugliness in the world with beauty, keep in mind the need of man to be free, first, last and always! Keep in mind that the world and country you live in now is a lot better place than in any other time in history. Keep in mind that evil is an ever present threat to man. Now, spell it backwards—it spells "live." You cannot dig up all the weeds in the world. You cannot get rid of all evil and still live. But you can be realistic, face life with a strong heart and hand. Try to do right and bring good to your fellow man. The balance of the future is in everyone's hands. Not just teenagers, adults or any "group." But unless we remain free to choose our own destiny, (and some will succeed and some will fail) no plan, society or human desire will be worth the trouble it takes to breathe in and out!

Mrs. Betty M. Swope

Best and the Beatles

Dear *BEAT* Editors:

An article which appeared in the October 16th issue of *The BEAT* moved me to write this letter. The following is in reference to the article about Pete Best's law suit against Beatle Ringo Starr, Brian Epstein and others.

I suppose before I go much further I should explain that I am an enormous admirer of the Beatles and I'll have to admit partiality to Ringo.

When I first read your article I found it hard to believe that Pete Best could possibly sue them for such a large sum. I realize the Beatles are a long way from the poorhouse but $45 million isn't exactly a few shillings in any man's wallet!

True, I have to agree that he has a perfect right to demand his "fair share" of the profits and recognition from those records made in Germany. *He* did the playing of drums *not* Ringo and it's only just that his name appear somewhere along the line. Personally, I can't see how Epstein could afford to let an oversight like this escape him.

I have never been much of a Pete Best fan from the beginning and even if I had, I fear, after this he would have lost my support.

There is not much to be said for his originality when it comes to the name of his new group—"The Best of the Beatles." The thought of him borrowing (I should like to say 'steal,' but I'm not one to stick my neck out) the name, reputation and fame of the Beatles is both misleading and deceiving. If he can't find work or get started with his own name I dare say he can't be very good. In effect, he's actually *using* the popularity of the Beatles to gain his revenge. I'll have to give him credit for his cunningness. He knows how to get publicity.

Then, to add insult to injury, he has to use the Beatles now well-earned title, to sell *his* new single.

I don't know much about legalities, nor do I pretend to, but you won't find me adding any of my precious pennies to Pete's "fund." As a matter of fact, I'm quite curious to know just how many Pete Best fans there are who will! Or, how many Pete Best fans there are?

Laurie Platin

KRLA ARCHIVES

"THE GANG FROM SHEBANG" — Steve Bates, Ron Rameriz, Bud Schwimmer, Bob Rollo, Casey Kasem, Mike Loyet and Famous Hooks.

Inside KRLA

Hi gang. What's new out there in the land of "the station that's won the West?" Oh yeah? Well, there's a whole lot going on *Inside* KRLA as well, so c'mon in for a while, won't you?

I suppose you recognize the funny-looking horn over there. Well, as *everybody* knows — it belongs to Dave Hull, and the Hullabalooer has some pretty exciting news to blow on it for us this week. Hi'ya Dave, what's up? I hear you have some pretty exciting news about a brand new night club?

"Yes, it's going to be called "Dave Hull's Hullabaloo," and it's the old Moulin Rouge. We have redecorated it and it's gonna be the largest and most glamorous nightclub for young adults in the world. The first opening night will be the night of *The BEAT's* Pop Music Awards ceremony, and we're all very excited about it.

"It's going to have the largest room with the finest meals for teenagers — with the lowest prices! — in the world. I want this to be a Mecca for teens — we will have the very *biggest* acts there, really great entertainment, and there will be two bands playing all the time.

"We will be able to accomodate a *total* capacity crowd of 4,000 in the club at once — 2,000 in the dining area alone, at one time. Also, we can have crowds of up to 250 people dancing at one time, because we can roll out as much floor for dancing as we need.

"Also, it is just possible that the club will become the downtown headquarters for all of the KRLA DJ's, and it's for certain that *I* will be there, so I will be looking forward to seeing everyone down there."

Most of you are probably supposed to be asleep when Bill Slater comes on the air every night at midnight — but since what you're *supposed* to do usually doesn't mean too much! — you will probabaly be interested in what Bill has been doing lately.

He has been accepting calls from all the kids in the audience to be taped and sent to our boys in Viet Nam. Pretty great, huh? Well, most of the people here at KRLA *are* pretty great, so it sort of figures. If you have someone in Viet Nam you would like to send a message to, or if you would just like to speak to *all* of the wonderful guys over there, why don't you give Bill a ring tonight?

Those Lovable Losers — the KRLApes — are still trying to win a game, but so far they are upholding their outstanding record of an unbelievably large number of losses!!

Stop Worrying!
Here's an Easy Way to Solve Your Christmas Shopping Chores.

A subscription to *The BEAT* makes an ideal gift. Think of all your friends who like to read YOUR copy of *The BEAT* every week! They'll remember you all year long. Just send in the form below — and then forget about fighting the crowds to do your Christmas shopping. We'll send them a special gift card with your name attached. If you want to send more than one, simply fill in the additional names and addresses on a plain sheet of paper, enclosing $3 for each subscription. (P.S. If you're not already a subscriber, how about sending one to yourself?)

```
GIFT SUBSCRIPTION
To: (Name) _____ Age: _____
Address: _____
City: _____ State: _____ Zip: _____
Enclosed is $ _____ From: _____
   MAIL TO: The BEAT, Suite 504, 6290 Sunset Blvd., Hollywood, Calif.
```

KRLA ARCHIVES

"YOU DON'T HAVE TO BE SO NICE" chant the Lovin' Spoonful. But they sure posed nicely for our BEAT photographer, Chuck Boyd. Well, **they** thought it was nice, anyway!!

The BEAT Pauses To Remember

Every now and then *The BEAT* takes time out from reporting what's happening to report something that isn't part of the latest scene. This is one of those times.

Columbia Records has a new album out that is the sort of thing you may want. It's not by the Beatles or the Rolling Stones and there isn't an electric guitar on it.

It is "John Fitzgerald Kennedy ... As We Remember Him." It is part of the Columbia Records Legacy Collection and includes a set of two long playing records and a 242-page book with over 200 photographs.

The records trace JFK's life from childhood to the White House through the voices of people who knew him, including Adlai E. Stevenson, his mother, his brother, roommates at school and wartime shipmates.

The book includes pictures, official documents, over 70 reproductions of letters by and to Kennedy and a foreword by President Lyndon B. Johnson.

The tastefully designed Collection edition has just been released and all royalties from the sale of the records and the book will be donated to the John F. Kennedy Memorial Library.

Stones Still Rolling

The Stones have maintained their chart-topping position again this week, making it two weeks in a row for "Get Off Of My Cloud."

It should be interesting to see if the Stones can hold on for another week because they certainly have some strong challengers coming right up there behind them.

British Top 10

1.	GET OFF OF MY CLOUD	Rolling Stones
2.	YESTERDAY MAN	Chris Andrews
3.	1-2-3	Len Barry
4.	MY GENERATION	The Who
5.	IT'S MY LIFE	The Animals
6.	HERE IT COMES AGAIN	The Fortunes
7.	TEARS	Ken Dodd
8.	THE CARNIVAL IS OVER	The Seekers
9.	YESTERDAY	Matt Monro
10.	A LOVER'S CONCERTO	The Toys

Len Barry has moved his "1-2-3" all the way up to number three this week. He has only been on the British charts for three weeks and this week he jumped up from number 16. Maybe next week he will unseat the Stones?

Another record which is threatening the Stones is "My Generation" by The Who. These boys debuted last week at number 18 and this week have succeeded in moving all the way up to number four.

The Toys and their "Lover's Concerto" are doing all right in England too. They debuted last week at number 20 and this week finds the three girls in at number ten.

Those perennial favorites, the Everly Brothers and Elvis Presley, are practically back-to-back on the British charts. The Everlys debuted this week at number 17 with "Love Is Strange."

The other top English favorite, Elvis Presley, is in this week at number 20. It's a funny situation. In the U.S. the old King has certainly had his share of trouble hit-wise. But in England he finds himself continually in the charts. This time around he's inside with "Tell Me Why."

KRLA ARCHIVES

HEADLINERS HAIR BEAT
Tips on Combing Your Hair

By Robert Esserman and Frank DeSanctis

All accessories are just right, your dress fits perfectly, your makeup is on perfectly, yet something is wrong. You try combing your hair every which way but to no avail. You leave for your party feeling very low. The problems most girls have with their hair is not being able to set it properly.

Hairdressers know how difficult it is for girls to set and comb out their own hair. This is why the Headliners Hair Beat will give you a few inside tips of the trade.

First, be sure to have all your hair combed straight down—no tangles.

Second, when putting your rollers in, be sure to first comb the section of hair in the direction you want to comb it after the set.

Third, when putting in your rollers, be sure the section of hair is combed straight up, then proceed to roll rollers in a downward motion but keep the section of hair straight and uniform.

Fourth, always be sure to have your hair dry before combing it out. Brush out all the elasticity.

Let us remind you gals once again that home color and permanents can be very harmful to you. Always let a professional advise you first what to use, and how to do it.

Girls are coming by the droves, asking the Headliners for up do's with curls. It seems curls are back to stay until next summer. Short do'ers are also asking for whispy curls.

The Headliners Headache Section

If a girl is heavy in the legs, do you think she should wear bell bottoms?

No—be sure you never accent what is not flattering to you.

I have a round face and I like to wear my hair very low and casual. Should I?

Heavens NO. Be very careful you maintain an oval effect to your face. Wear your hair just a little higher than you've been wearing it.

How may I make an appointment with your shop? I live in Arizona and am coming to California for Christmas.

Drop us a card with your name and the date you desire the appointment. We'll take care of the rest.

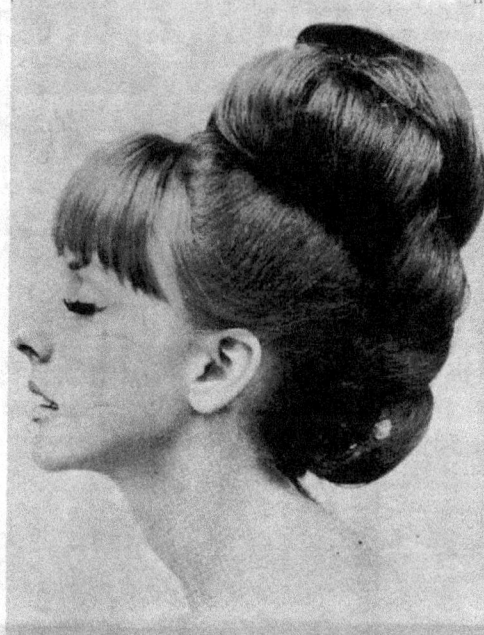

TV STARLET BRENDA SCOTT models one of the Headliner up-do's.

It's In The Bag
By Eden

Messrs. John Lennon and Richard Burton will be sharing byline honors this Yule in a National Mag in this country. Merry Christmas, boys.

* * *

A long time ago, when we were all in our Bobbysox and Blue Suede Shoes, Frankie Avalon used to share a date or two with a pretty little pair of Mouske*tears* named Annette. Now she shares the role of parenthood with Annette and hubby Jack Gilardi as he becomes the godfather to their new little girl, Gina Luree Gilardi.

My, my how time does fly!

* * *

Whaddaya know about that? Remember a show called "Shindig?" (Oh *of course* you do!!) Well, it was produced by Selmur Productions. Now Selmur has a new little goody for all of us called the "Wide World of Entertainment." Originally this was scheduled to be a one-shot special, taped all over the world, and aired some time in December.

Well, there have been some changes made, and now the show is set to roll sometime around the first week or so in December as a continuing series. Scheduled host for the new package—George Chakiris. It's nice to know that George will be going steady with the telly-tube for awhile now, 'cause he has been depriving all his female fans of his presence too much since "West Side Story."

* * *

Well, your favorite manager and mine—Brian Epstein—is currently dickering with "certain officials" for a British screening of the film which was made of the overwhelmingly successful Beatles' concert at New York's Shea Stadium last August.

Now I'm not making promises or anything, but we might just receive this package all gift-wrapped in time for Christmas over here in the Colonies.

* * *

Tom Jones was so pleased with the success of his waxing of flick-theme, "What's New Pussycat?" that he has gone out and purred still another one. This time it's the theme for "Thunderball." Looks like everybody's favorite spy-type will be serenaded in style.

* * *

Rumors from Across the Pond dept:

Ex-drummer for the Beatles—Pete Best—isn't suing Brian Epstein after all. Well, who then? Santa Claus??!!!

A certain producer is trying to sign a certain Cynthia Lennon for an appearance on his British telly-show. Sorry luv, but a certain Mr. John Lennon has already signed her to a long-term, exclusive contract.

A FORMAL UP-DO designed for premiere of "Agony and the Ecstacy."

DISCussion
By Barrie

Instrumentals seem to be on the *Upbeat* this week, and "instrumental" among them are "Hang On Sloopy," by the Ramsey Lewis Trio—a good sing-along type thing for their second Top Ten'er in a row—and a revival of the old Ben E. King smash—"Stand By Me"—by the talented Earl Grant.

★ ★ ★ ★

The Lovin' Spoonful are also going the follow-up route this week with their brand new wax, "You Didn't Have To Be So Nice." Well, it *is* a nice record, but another bit of "Magic" it's not.

★ ★ ★ ★

Sorry to hear Roy Head's new Wax Waste—"Apple of My Eye." This one was recorded some time ago, and as far as this reporter is concerned—they should have left it right there in the Dark Ages!

★ ★ ★ ★

Roger Miller: you've done it again, luv. Your new single, "England Swings," does just that—it swings! Don't quite know how you keep right on being quietly great, but you do. Keep up the good work, Mr. M.

★ ★ ★ ★

Gene Pitney is an American singer who has become one of our biggest international stars (especially in Great Britain) and one of our best ambassadors of good will. He also just happens to be one of the most talented young men around today—in *any* country!

His new 45er—"Princess in Rags"—looks like another addition to his long line of hits, and the new elpee just released—Gene Pitney "Looking Through The Eyes of Love"—has got to be a winner.

★ ★ ★ ★

Speaking of records Elpee style (yes, were were!), the Stones have Rolled themselves right into another fantastic album smash. This one, entitled "December's Children (And Everybody's)" has been released on the London label and is available now.

★ ★ ★ ★

I don't believe that the Dave Clark Five are going to cause any great tidal waves in this sea of pop music with their latest vessel, "Over and Over." That's just the point, boys—we have heard this song *and* this sound, OVER AND OVER!!

★ ★ ★ ★

Did'ja know that Mr. P.F. Sloan penned four of the tunes—including the title song—for the Herman's Hermits upcoming flick, "Hold On?" He did and they are something else. But then, so are the Hermits and their latest flick.

★ ★ ★ ★

I think we all can say a few words of gratitude to Paul Beatle, MBE for his service to mankind when he released his beautiful "Yesterday." Of course, there are a few others who could thank Paul as well—such as Marianne Faithfull and Matt Munro—who have also recorded the tune in England. Now there is a new name to be added to the list. Are you ready? That of Barry McGuire. Nope, I'm not putting you on. Barry has recorded "Yesterday" for his latest album, and this one is just simply *more* than out of sight. Barry babe—you did good!!

KRLA ARCHIVES

KRLA Tunedex

EMPEROR HUDSON — CHARLIE O'DONNELL — CASEY KASEM — JOHNNY HAYES

BOB EUBANKS — DAVE HULL

DICK BIONDI — BILL SLATER

KRLA BEAT
6290 Sunset, No. 504
Hollywood, Cal. 90028

This Week	Last Week	Title	Artist
1	4	STILL I'M SAD/I'M A MAN	The Yardbirds
2	1	1-2-3	Len Barry
3	11	LET'S HANG ON	Four Seasons
4	2	TURN, TURN, TURN	The Byrds
5	6	I HEAR A SYMPHONY	The Supremes
6	5	YOU'RE THE ONE	The Vogues
7	3	GET OFF MY CLOUD	Rolling Stones
8	8	YESTERDAY	The Beatles
9	7	A LOVER'S CONCERTO	The Toys
10	10	MAKE IT EASY ON YOURSELF	The Walker Brothers
11	9	A TASTE OF HONEY	Tijuana Brass
12	20	MYSTIC EYES	Them
13	15	RESCUE ME	Fontella Bass
14	19	PIED PIPER	The Changing Times
15	14	I GOT YOU (I FEEL GOOD)	James Brown
16	17	STEPPIN' OUT	Paul Revere & The Raiders
17	26	RISING SUN	The Deep Six
18	25	YOU'VE GOT TO HIDE YOUR LOVE AWAY	The Silkie
19	21	LET ME BE	The Turtles
20	22	AIN'T THAT PECULIAR	Marvin Gaye
21	33	HANG ON SLOOPY	Ramsey Lewis Trio
22	23	MY GIRL HAS GONE	The Miracles
23	24	MY HEART SINGS	Mel Carter
24	—	LIES, LIES	The Knickerbockers
25	35	I CAN NEVER GO HOME ANYMORE	Shangri-Las
26	—	IT'S MY LIFE	Animals
27	28	SOMETHING ABOUT YOU	The Four Tops
28	29	REVOLUTION KIND	Sonny Bono
29	29	DON'T TALK TO STRANGERS	Beau Brummels
30	32	OVER AND OVER	Dave Clark Five
31	27	HEARTBEAT	Gloria Jones
32	31	RUN BABY RUN	The Newbeats
33	36	ENGLAND SWINGS	Roger Miller
34	38	HERE IT COMES AGAIN	The Fortunes
35	—	YOU DON'T HAVE TO BE SO NICE	The Lovin' Spoonful
36	37	I FOUGHT THE LAW	Bobby Fuller Four
37	—	FLOWERS ON THE WALL	Statler Brothers
38	—	DON'T THINK TWICE	Wonder Who
39	—	SOUNDS OF SILENCE	Simon & Garfunkle
40	—	APPLE OF MY EYE	Roy Head

KRLA ARCHIVES

America's Largest Teen NEWSpaper

KRLA Edition BEAT

Volume 1, Number 39   LOS ANGELES, CALIFORNIA   15 Cents   December 11, 1965

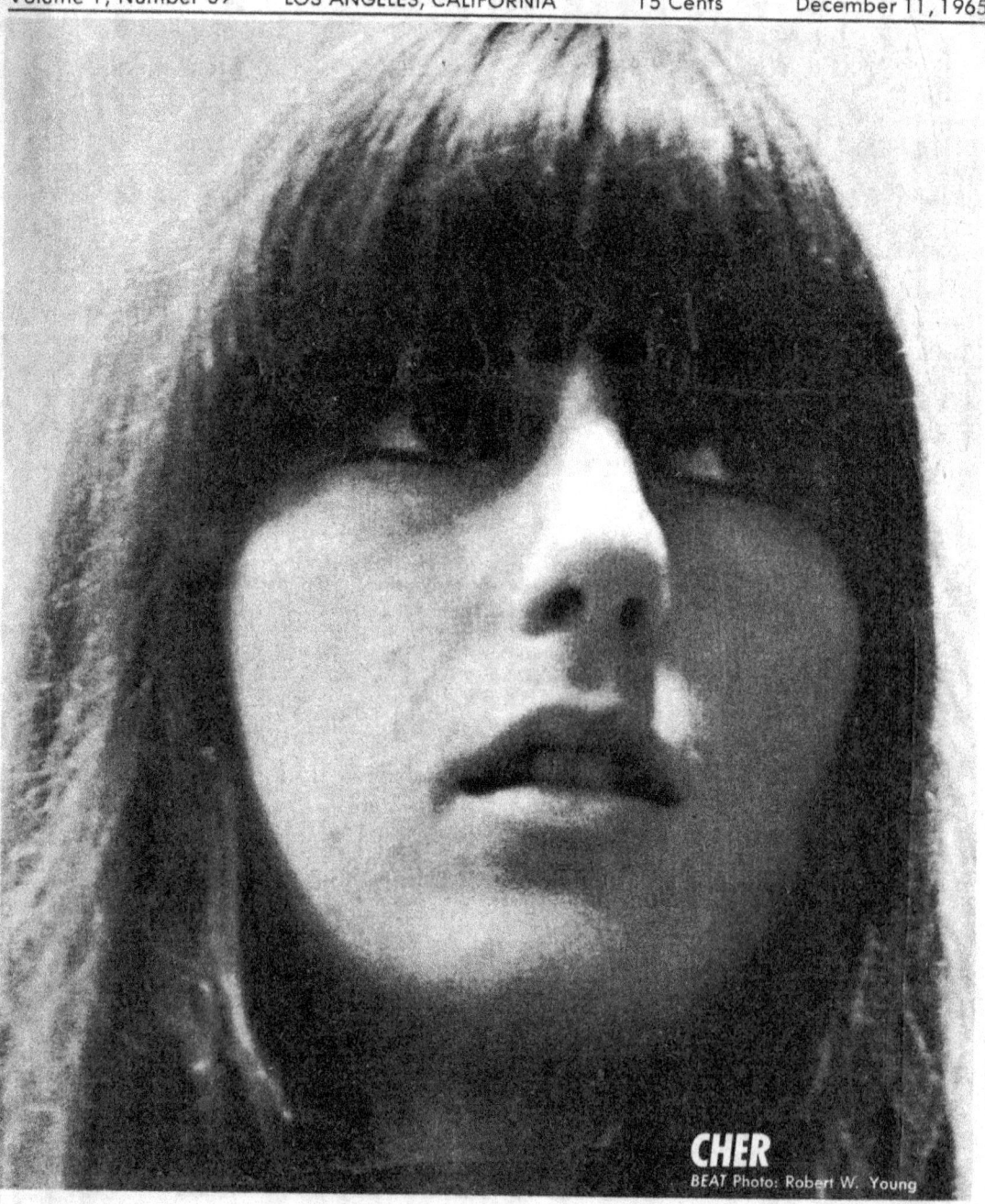

CHER
BEAT Photo: Robert W. Young

KRLA ARCHIVES

KRLA BEAT

Los Angeles, California — December 11, 1965

FRIENDLY COMPETITORS — SONNY AND CHER, RIGHTEOUS BROTHERS AMONG TOP DUOS OF 1965

CHAD AND JEREMY — ONLY BRITISHERS AMONG TOP DUOS

DICK AND DEEDEE — STILL ONE OF THE WORLD'S FAVORITE DUOS

SURF KINGS JAN AND DEAN

SEND BEAT GIFT SUBSCRIPTIONS TO YOUR FRIENDS FOR CHRISTMAS

Inside the BEAT

- Miracles Have Soul 4
- No Gimmicks For Mel 4
- British Top 10 5
- It's In The Bag 5
- The Young Paul 6
- Righteous Bros. Sue 7
- Chuck Berry Show 8
- Orbison Eyes Movies 12
- April & Nino — A New Bag 12
- Small-Fry 'Beatles' 13
- For Girls Only 14
- Bonos Have A Problem 15
- Maharis Faces Life 16

The BEAT is published weekly for KRLA listeners by BEAT Publications, Inc., 6290 Sunset Blvd., Suite 504, Hollywood, California 90028. U.S. bureaus in Hollywood, San Francisco, New York, Chicago and Nashville; overseas correspondents in London, Liverpool and Manchester, England. Sale price, 15 cents. Subscription price U.S. and possessions, $3 per year. Canada and foreign rates, $9 per year. Application to mail at second-class postage rates is pending at Los Angeles, California.

BEAT Pop Music Awards Poll
Final Ballot - Please Check One in Each Category

MALE VOCALIST
- SONNY BONO
- JAMES BROWN
- DONOVAN
- BOB DYLAN
- BARRY MC GUIRE
- ROGER MILLER
- GENE PITNEY
- ELVIS PRESLEY
- BILLY JOE ROYAL
- IAN WHITCOMB

NEW MALE VOCALIST
- SONNY BONO
- DONOVAN
- BOB DYLAN
- BARRY MC GUIRE
- IAN WHITCOMB

FEMALE VOCALIST
- JOAN BAEZ
- CILLA BLACK
- CHER
- PETULA CLARK
- MARIANNE FAITHFULL
- LESLIE GORE
- BRENDA HOLLOWAY
- DUSTY SPRINGFIELD
- CONNIE STEVENS
- TINA TURNER

NEW FEMALE VOCALIST
- JOAN BAEZ
- CHER
- PETULA CLARK
- MARIANNE FAITHFULL
- BARBARA LEWIS

VOCAL GROUP
- ANIMALS
- BEACH BOYS
- BEATLES
- BEAU BRUMMELS
- BYRDS
- DINO, DESI & BILLY
- HERMAN'S HERMITS
- THE LOVIN' SPOONFUL
- ROLLING STONES
- YARDBIRDS

NEW VOCAL GROUP
- BEAU BRUMMELS
- BYRDS
- DINO, DESI & BILLY
- GARY LEWIS & THE PLAYBOYS
- LOVIN' SPOONFUL

FEMALE VOCAL GROUP
- BLOSSOMS
- MARTHA & THE VANDELLAS
- SHANGRALAS
- SUPREMES
- TOYS

INSTRUMENTAL GROUP
- HERB ALPERT & TIJUANA BRASS
- RAMSEY LEWIS TRIO
- THEE MIDNITERS
- SOUNDS INCORPORATED
- SOUNDS ORCHESTRAL

DUO
- CHAD & JEREMY
- JAN & DEAN
- DICK & DEEDEE
- RIGHTEOUS BROTHERS
- SONNY & CHER

COMPOSER
- SONNY BONO
- DONOVAN
- BOB DYLAN
- MICK JAGGER/KEITH RICHARD
- JOHN LENNON/PAUL MC CARTNEY
- P. F. SLOAN
- BRIAN WILSON

RECORD PRODUCER
- HERB ALPERT
- SONNY BONO
- JIMMY BOWEN
- BARRY GORDY
- GREENE & STONE
- TONY HATCH
- GEORGE MARTIN
- TERRY MELCHER
- ANDREW OLDHAM
- PHIL SPECTOR
- BRIAN WILSON

RECORD COMPANY
- A&M
- ATLANTIC/ATCO
- AUTUMN
- CAPITOL
- COLUMBIA
- LIBERTY
- LONDON
- SMASH
- TAMLA/MOTOWN
- WARNER BROS./REPRISE

VOCAL RECORD — 45's
- BABY DON'T GO
- CRYING IN THE CHAPEL
- EVE OF DESTRUCTION
- HELP
- KING OF THE ROAD
- LIKE A ROLLING STONE
- MR. TAMBOURINE MAN
- MRS. BROWN
- SATISFACTION
- YESTERDAY
- YOU'VE LOST THAT LOVIN' FEELING

INSTRUMENTAL — 45's
- THE IN CROWD
- TASTE OF HONEY
- WHITTIER BLVD.
- COTTON CANDY
- CAST YOUR FATE TO THE WIND

VOCAL ALBUM
- BEACH BOYS TODAY
- BRINGING IT ALL BACK HOME — DYLAN
- HELP — BEATLES
- INTRODUCING HERMAN'S HERMITS
- LOOK AT US — SONNY & CHER
- MR. TAMBOURINE MAN — BYRDS
- OUT OF OUR HEADS — STONES
- ROLLING STONES NOW
- WHERE DID OUR LOVE GO — SUPREMES
- YOU'VE LOST THAT LOVIN' FEELING — RIGHTEOUS BROTHERS

INSTRUMENTAL ALBUM
- BEATLE SONG BOOK — HOLLYRIDGE STRINGS
- GOLDFINGER — SOUND TRACK
- THE IN CROWD — RAMSEY LEWIS
- MORE GENIUS OF JANKOWSKI
- WHIPPED CREAM & OTHER DELIGHTS — HERB ALPERT

MAIL TO: Pop Music Poll, The BEAT, 6290 Sunset, Suite 504, Hollywood, Calif. 90028

Pictured Above – Top 5 Duos in BEAT Pop Music Poll Finals

KRLA ARCHIVES

Dick & Deedee Volunteer for Viet Nam Duty

Dick and Deedee, accustomed to the bedlam of teen concerts, will soon be performing on a tour where such sounds have a new and deadly significance.

They're going to Viet Nam to sing to the U.S. troops.

In announcing their plans they make it a point to emphasize that they are volunteering their services without fee. They also, apparently, take a verbal poke at other young American artists for not going to Viet Nam.

Says Dick: "For years troupers like Bob Hope and Ethel Merman have been good enough to give up what little spare time they have to entertain American servicemen in far-off places.

"For one reason or another, too few of the younger artists have, apparently, been prepared to go. We believe it is up to young people to do what they can because the troops themselves are there doing the best *they* can."

In making the announcement he gave no date or other details of the tour, which presumably will be in *South* Viet Nam.

THE DAVE CLARK FIVE, completing a successful tour of the U.S., hit a new high on popularity. They have a new hit, "Over and Over."

YEAH! FUNNY ENVELOPES "disc-cards" FOR RECORDS

A FUNNY CARD AND GIFT WRAP IN ONE! THE GEAR WAY TO GIVE A RECORD — THAT'S IN!

FUNNY CARTOONS — WITH FUNNY CAPTIONS — IN FUNNY COLORS — LIKE
- GOLD DIGGER
- PINK-PONG
- HULLA-BLUE
- HOME-ON-ORANGE

FUNNY! SEND FOR SOME!

L.P.	45	
		L.P. SIZE .... 3 FOR $1.00
		45 SIZE .... 3 FOR .50
		'I finally bought YOU this record FOR ME! since all the time you kept borrowing MINE!
		Did you really want this record — or do you just need a new wheel for your TRICYCLE?
		Open me first! It won't play in the envelope!
		Music to A-Go-Go Listen to it someplace else!
		Merry Christmas — Merry Christmas — Merry Christmas — This is a recording!
		Me girl! You boy? — Me boy! You girl? For lovers of long hair!

PLEASE SEND ME _____ 'DISC-CARDS' ___ L.P. ___ 45.
I HAVE CHECKED THE ONES I WANT.
I'M ENCLOSING _____ ☐ CASH ☐ CHECK
NAME _____
ADDRESS _____
CITY _____ STATE _____ ZIP: _____

MAIL COUPON TO: "DISC-CARDS"
2350 LAKEVIEW AVENUE
LOS ANGELES, CALIFORNIA 90039

KRLA ARCHIVES

Mel Carter–Singing Since He Was Four

Mel Carter got his recording career with Imperial Records off to a good beginning. He started as "The Richest Man Alive."

But "Richest Man Alive," his first record on that lable, wasn't really the beginning. It was more like the turning point in a singing career that started when he was just four years old.

He probably doesn't remember when he first started singing, but he clearly remembers his first record, cut at the age of four. His grandmother held him up to the microphone in one of those 25c recording booths in a penny arcade and he belted out a Negro spiritual with all his little heart could muster.

Local Radio Show

This one amateur waxing told his parents enough to keep him singing for the next couple of years at church socials and on local radio shows in Cincinnati until, at the age of nine, he won an amateur contest at the Regal Theater in Cincinnati and was awarded a spot on the Lionel Hampton Show.

But even this big honor for such a young kid wasn't enough to keep him busy and so he joined the Air Corps when he was 16 and became a member of the Robert Anderson Gospel Singers. While he was in the service he also managed to win a scholarship to the Cincinnati Conservatory of Music.

He took music very seriously and became leading vocalist and assistant director of the Greater Cincinnati Youth and Young Adult Choral Union. In 1957 the National Convention of Gospel Choirs and Choruses of America named him top American tenor in the gospel field.

After forming his own group and touring the West Coast, Imperial finally caught him and he's been putting out top sounding and selling records since.

After "Richest Man Alive" he did "When a Boy Falls in Love," which sold well in England as well as America, and "Hold Me, Thrill Me," his biggest single to date.

Now he's climbing the charts again with "My Heart Sings." There's no gimmick to this man. He just uses talent and a good voice to constantly come through with great sounds.

Keep it up Mel.

Dome Opens For Supremes

The Supremes have added another first to their soaring career.

They've just been signed to co-star with Judy Garland at the first entertainment booking in the Houston Astrodome Dec. 17.

The Astrodome, which seats 50,000, has previously been used mainly for sports events.

The Motown recording trio, Diana Ross, Mary Wilson and Florence Ballard, just completed a tour of one nighters and a week's engagement in Pittsburgh.

The Beatles Don't Forget

The Beatles haven't forgotten the people that have helped make them what they are today.

The Beatles aren't doing a Christmas special this year but the television special honoring John and Paul's writing will be shown in England around Christmas time.

Paul says they are doing the show to repay someone who helped them earlier.

"One of the reasons we're doing this show is as a favor to Johnny Hamp, who risked his job by including us on an early TV show when we were unknown," he explained.

John added, during the taping of the show, that there aren't many other performers who really get a lot out of his and Paul's writings.

"There are only about 100 people in the world who really understand what our music is all about," he said, and that 100 includes George and Ringo.

Class and Soul Spell Success For Miracles

By Carol Deck

When the Miracles are performing in a club you don't eat. You don't drink. You don't even think. You just feel.

You feel the pure unadulterated *soul* or their words and their actions. You can't really call the Miracles an act. They're a happening.

Bill (Smoky) Robinson, lead singer and writer for the group, can stand perfectly still and pull soul out of the excited atmosphere of where ever he's playing. But he doesn't call it soul. He calls it "luckin' up."

Smoky is backed up in his "luckin' about" by Bobby Rogers, Ronnie White and Warren "Pete" Moore. All four are native Detroiters and Smoky, Ronnie and Bobby have been married for several years. Pete will tie the knot this month. And these guys have some pretty talented wives, too.

Talented Wives

Smoky's wife, Claudette, sings on most of the Miracles' records but doesn't perform live with them, and Bobby's wife is the leader of the Marvelettes.

Like all the groups on the Tamla-Motown label, these guys have class. They dress well and sing fantastically. And they put the finishing touch on their performance by having some of the smoothest choreography around.

Most of their choreography is done by Bobby, Ronnie and Pete but they get a lot of help from a guy named Charlie Atkins who does choreography for all of the Motown groups including the Supremes.

The group's been together since 1954, but they joined Motown in 1960. In fact, they are probably more responsible than any other single group for getting the label started. Their first hit, "Shop Around," sold over a million copies and established Tamla-Motown as a winner.

Respect Too

The Miracles have nothing in common with today's young singers who cause mass hysteria at every concert. The Miracles' fans love them, but they *respect* them too. Bobby feels that if a performer gets mobbed during a performance that he asked for it.

"An audience can tell whether or not they can come on stage," he explains. "It all depends on how you carry yourself on stage. We project a thing, like well, we want to entertain." And that's what they do, entertain.

Nobody ever asks 'how long do you think they'll last?' It's understood from the first time you see or hear them that they'll last. There's nothing that can stop their combination of class and soul.

New Release

And with their latest release, "My Girl Has Gone," they continue to live up to their name, a name which they drew out of a hat.

Bobby swears that they just threw five of six names in a hat and Miracles was the one they drew. It was mere luck that made them the Miracles and not the Clouds or the Lyrics, or any of the other names in that hat.

SMOKEY ROBINSON

... PETE MOORE, BOBBY ROGERS AND RONNIE WHITE

KRLA ARCHIVES

It's In The Bag
By Eden

Hey—this is a put-on, right? What's Ed Sullivan trying to pull by having the Dave Clark Five appear with fresh, neat hair-*cuts*? You remember those—they are affected with comb, scissors, and a goodly amount of screaming.

Gee, I'm beginning to get a little bit worried now. I mean, what is our youth coming to? Pretty soon the whole world is going to be corrupted by these few tainted individuals.

Hmmmm—you don't suppose that short hair is coming back, do you? Oh shun the hideous thought!

* * *

Speaking of haircuts, Hullabaloo pulled a silly. When Barry McGuire appeared as host on a recent segment they forced him to cut his hair. But then they had it coiffed a la Phil Spector.

* * *

"Animal tracks"—did'ja know that negotiations are currently in progress for the Animals to make a satirical war flick early next year? Other artists are expected to put in appearances on the Silver Screen with the boys, including one Mr. Donovan. While they await further news of the film, Eric is keeping himself occupied with the writing of his first book—"Going Out Of My Head."

* * *

Well, what do you know! It's "Ay, ay, ay—a go-go" down in Mexico City these days!! Suddenly, the Mexican TV is being flooded with a musical inundation of Watusi. If you set your sombrero in the right direction and tune in at prime time now, you can watch any one of four hard-rock shows on the Mexican telly-tube and frug to the stirring strains of such R 'n' R combos as Los Hooligans, Los Crickets, Los Rocking Devils, Los Loud Jets, and Los Crazy Birds.

The Spanish artists jerk, twist, and pluck their electronic guitars in time to the music as they lip-sync the English-language lyrics. Well fans—that's La Musica! Si, si, si!!!

* * *

Of all the young artists in this business who have enjoyed the pleasures of success in the past few years, one of the nicest is a young fellow named Gene Pitney.

Gene is an extremely talented chap who composes and arranges the songs he sings. He has built up a large following all around the globe, and especially in the Mother Country across the Pond.

Just recently Gene took a good look around him in this nutty world of pop, then turned around and said: "I consider myself to be a freak."

Uh, just a minute now, Mr. Pitney. Are you *sure* about that?? "Yeah. For the last two or three years I've been touring around with guys wearing long hair and crazy clothes—just about all of them with some gimmick going for them. But me, I just have an ordinary hair-cut and clothes and I step out on the stage and *sing*. So straight that, in constrast to the others, *I'm* the oddball!"

* * *

Oho—they're putting us on, again!! Are you ready for this, fellow Beatlemaniacs? Nonesuch Records (with a Company name like that, *already* you know it's good for a laugh!) has released "The Baroque Beatles Book"—an album of Lennon-McCartney compositions, each and every one rendered in 18th century baroque style.

Selections offered include "Epstein Variations," by Murray the Klavierkitzler; "Hold Me Tight," by the same Mr. K; and one grand orchestral suite which is entitled "The Royale Beatleworks Musike," and performed by the Baroque Ensemble of the Merseyside Kammermusikgesellschaft.

Aw c'mon now fellas—you *are* putting us on, *aren't* you?? Oh the beautifulness of itself!!!

"I WILL?" Even Dean Martin appears surprised by the success of his easy-listening ballads among teenagers. He's even keeping up with son, Dino. Pappa Dean remains a top favorite of record-buyers of all ages.

'It's My Life' Surprised Eric

The Animals's "It's My Life" is doing as well in England as it is here, and no one is as surprised as Eric Burdon.

In fact, Eric didn't even think it was going to be released in England.

"None of us wanted it released here," he said. "It was meant as a follow-up to 'We Gotta Get Out of This Place' in America."

"I was shocked when I learned it was going to be released here (England.) I really find it a strain reaching some of the notes."

Stones On Top Again

With all the strong competition coming their way, the Rolling Stones still managed to hold down that number one spot with "Get Off Of My Cloud."

The Stones' strongest contender seems to be Len Barry and his smash, "1-2-3." It has taken Len exactly one month to reach the number two position and just perhaps next week will find him firmly entrenched as the chart-topper.

British Top 10

#	Title	Artist
1.	GET OFF OF MY CLOUD	Rolling Stones
2.	1-2-3	Len Barry
3.	THE CARNIVAL IS OVER	The Seekers
4.	MY GENERATION	The Who
5.	YESTERDAY MAN	Chris Andrews
6.	IT'S MY LIFE	The Animals
7.	TEARS	Ken Dodd
8.	HERE IT COMES AGAIN	The Fortunes
9.	YESTERDAY	Matt Monro
10.	A LOVER'S CONCERTO	The Toys

Of course, with the British charts it is never safe to make predictions. So, it is entirely possible that the Stones will remain number one for the next four months!

The Seekers are hot on Len's heels with their "The Carnival Is Over." They took a nice little jump this week within the top ten —from number eight to number three.

The Animals and "It's My Life" took a one place drop, from number five to number six. Still, this record has been one of their fastest risers and certainly a big hit.

The highest debuter this week belongs to one of England's very favorite entertainers (and one of ours too)—Gene Pitney. Gene has enjoyed more success in England than he has in his own native America—though, of course, he is extremely popular Stateside as well.

Anyway, Gene has just released a new record, "Princess In Rags," and this week finds it entering the charts at a mighty number 14. So if he keeps jumping it is quite feasible that Gene will capture the top spot next week.

KRLA ARCHIVES

BEATLE SNAPSHOTS
Paul's Father Recalls Brothers Inseparable

By Jamie McCluskey III

'ello, la – 'ow yer doin' this week? It's time once again to open up our *BEAT* scrapbook, and this week as we peer inside we find none other than Mr. Paul Beatle staring back at us. Hello Pauly! Paul's father James McCartney, provides some of our first glimpses of Paul as a child with these poignant snapshots:

"Michael (Paul's brother) and Paul did everything together, especially anything that they were told specifically *not* to do!

"As children, they were inseparable. Wherever one went – so did the other. I remember that amongst their friends they were known as the 'Nurk Twins,' but I never did find out why. I believe that John and Paul used the same name for one of their first playing dates.

"Paul was 18 months older than Michael so naturally, he was the leader. I remember that he always seemed to know exactly what he wanted and usually knew how to get it. He didn't moan or nag in any way, but persuaded us in the nicest possible manner. I think he was a born diplomat!"

Did'ja ever wonder how Paul was able to get up on stage with his three long-haired cohorts, and sing, play guitar, and *still* have time to flirt with *every* girl in the audience all at the same time? Well, it seems that Pauly has *always* been somewhat "ambi-dexterous!"

"He also had the fascinating ability of being able to do two things at once. In the evenings, he would sit at the table doing his homework and watching television at the same time. How he managed it, I don't know, but the extraordinary thing was, that afterwards, he usually knew more about the program than I did. And he got his homework correct as well!

"He seemed to have the sort of mind that could easily-grasp things that used to take a lot of concentration from other boys."

While Paul's father is only too happy to show us these little snaps of Paul – complete with halo over his Beatled head – he also has a few candid shots of Paul being *not* so angelic.

"Although Paul was a typical tearaway, ragamuffin, he was very close to Mike. I always remember one incident when they were caught stealing apples, Paul, Mike and another boy went scrumping from a farm in Speke. They were only 12 and 10 at the time, and they called the place Chinese Farm, although I didn't know why.

"Apparently, they were just about to climb the trees when the farmer appeared. They all ran away, but Paul got stuck and Mike went back to help. The first I knew about it was when the farmer rang me up and told me that my two sons were locked up in his barn.

"I went along to the farm to see him and he was very reasonable about it, so we decided to scare the boys a bit before we let them off. We stood outside the barn door and said things like: 'Do you think they will get a long sentence', or 'Shall we just spank them now and not tell the police?' When we thought they had enough, we opened the barn door to let them out only to find we'd been completely wasting our time.

"The two boys trotted out and greeted me with 'Hello Dad, about time you got here.' I was really amazed that both of them seemed so completely unconcerned by the whole proceedings.

"When I talked to them afterwards, I found that because they didn't actually steal any apples, they considered that they had done nothing wrong and therefore were not worried. I did the usual thing and sent them straight to bed without any supper, although at the time I didn't think it would do the slightest good. I believe that a few years later, they did realize that they had done wrong."

There are many more snapshots of Paul which Mr. McCartney has brought along to share with *The BEAT* scrapbook, but I'm afraid that they are going to have to wait for next week.

See ya then? Ta for now, luvs.

Liverpuddles
By Rob McGrae
Manager, The Cavern

Lots of you have asked me to tell you about the Escorts, a local Liverpool group. This I am glad to do because these lads certainly deserve to be popular and judging from the letters which I have received they already seem to be quite popular in the U.S.

The Escorts are four in number – John is lead guitarist, Mike is bass player and vocalist, Terry is rhythm guitarist and vocalist, and on drums is Pete.

Pete has just rejoined the Escorts after having a spell with two other groups. Pete left the Escorts in the first place in order to pursue bigger things in the record industry. He really is a terrific drummer and if he had his own way Pete would be playing in a modern jazz quartet.

However, now that Pete is back with the group I am convinced that big things are in store for the Escorts. They have a new record coming out which was written by their friends, the Hollies.

Visit U.S.

One of the Escorts biggest aims is to visit America. If it is at all possible, the boys would like to visit the U.S. as a top group. So, they are most interested in making fans in America and would very much like to hear from any of you *BEAT* readers.

... THE ESCORTS

Great news from the Cavern this week is that Wilson Pickett, currently riding high in the British charts with his "Midnight Hour," will be playing the Cavern on December 21. A nice idea would be for Wilson's fans in California to send him their best wishes on his opening at the Cavern.

If anyone would like to win one of the posters which will be used to advertise Wilson's appearance at the Cavern just send me a request for Wilson to perform on stage. I will then award a poster to the most original request.

I will also send a giant Escorts poster (5 ft. by 4 ft.) to the person who sends me the most original reason why they like the Escorts.

Send your answers to me at 17 Heydean Road, Allerton, Liverpool 18, England.

MARTHA AND THE VANDELLAS appear to have another nationwide hit, "Love Makes Me Do Foolish Things."

KRLA ARCHIVES

Adventures of Robin Boyd...

By Shirley Poston

CHAPTER FIVE

It's quite possible that a few observant citizens of London will never be the same.

How could they be after viewing a small but mysterious object streaking through the city skies at impossible speeds?

"Is it a bird?" some wondered. "Is it a plane?" other pondered.

"Blimey!" chorused the less conservative. "It's superman!"

They were right the first time. It *was* a bird, in both senses of the word. A rare one by the name of Robin Boyd.

After being such a good and helpful bird of the fan variety, sixteen-year-old Robin was rewarded for her untiring efforts. She was gifted with the knack of secretly turning herself into a *real* robin (with feathers yet) so that she could fly all over the world in search of her favorites.

And how did Robin come by this slightly (slightly?) unusual capability? She simply made a wish, and George (the Liverpudlian genie who lives in a tea pot on her dresser) granted it. (George, by the way, looks so much like that other George—Harrison, who else?—it's almost unbelievable.) (Gasp.) (But, he isn't that other George.) (Darn.)

Although Robin had faithfully promised George that she wouldn't exceed the 5000 mph speed limit, her first trans-Atlantic flight had somewhat lessened her fear of the Bird Patrol. And after arriving in London, she soon found herself flying at a rousing (but drafty) 5100 mph. Unfortunately, in circles around Big Ben.

"Nuts," Robin muttered at last, dizzily coming to rest near the hour hand. The newspaper back home in California had clearly stated that the Beatles would be in London for a show this very day, but she had completely forgotten where their performance was to be held.

Ordinarily a friendly sort, Robin curled her lip (which is difficult for a *real* robin) at several pigeons who were staring openly at her.

So what if they'd never seen a bird wearing glasses before? No one was perfect.

Blast that George anyway, making her wear glasses (which she was blind as six bats without). Oh well, at least they were byrd glasses, which helped soothe her ruffled feathers somewhat.

Suddenly Robin uncurled her lip and smiled with great warmth (which was also difficult). Pigeons got around, you know. Maybe they knew the whereabouts of John, Paul, George and Ringo!

Then she stopped smiling and frowned darkly. Exactly how did one go about conversing with *pigeons?* Did one chirp, or talk, or what? And, come to think of it, *could* one talk when one was a bird in both senses of the word?

Robin cleared her throat experimentally and one of the pigeons fell startled from his (or her) perch. But the others looked at her curiously.

"I say," she ventured forth, trying to sound teddibly British failing. "Do you know where I can find the Beatles?"

One pigeon turned to her (or his) companion. "A yank," she (or he) said snobbishly, trying to sound teddibly British and succeeding. But another of the group returned Robin's smile (which wasn't exactly on the easy side either). "They're at the London Palladium for a show, he (or she) replied in a thick brogue.

The snob turned to her (or his) companion again. "A mick," she (or he) snapped.

"Don't you talk that way about my favorite Rolling Stone" retorted said companion, preparing to kick her (or his) fine feathered friend directly in the shins.

Fortunately, Big Ben chose this moment to chime the time, and *all* the birds fell startled from their perchs. Including Robin, who then recovered from the shock and took wing in search of the London Palladium. Whatever that was.

Nearly an hour later, after much zooming about, she found it. The famous theatre where the marquee proudly announced that evening's Beatle concert.

Shivering with delight, Robin then began searching for a way into said famous theater.

Moments later she was angrily circling the building at a speed of 6000 mph. (Bird Patrol, Schmird Patrol.)

A person—er—bird would think that *someone* inside the edifice would at least like a breath of fresh air and for Pete's sake lift a window. But no. The English obviously didn't believe in oxygen because the Palladium was locked up tighter than Ringo's drum.

The only other way in was through the door, and her attempts to open same were pointless (where some things are next to impossible, others are completely).

Then it happened. In the midst of her supersonic circling, Robin saw him. *John Lennon!* And he was, of all things, *lifting a window!*

Robin gasped so hard, she suffered a sudden loss of altitude. (She was not a partial bird, but should she ever be *forced* to make a choice, John's chances were excellent.)

Through a bit of rather wild flapping, Robin managed to keep from crash-landing on the sidewalk. Then she hovered out of sight near the window until John (gasp) disappeared from view.

When he did, she fluttered stealthily to the window sill. She then gasped again (inwardly, of course, not being as dumb as she undoubtedly looked), for there, sitting in a chair, reading a copy of his latest book, was the leader himself!

Robin was right in the middle of praying that John wouldn't look up and notice her when John looked up and noticed her.

Not unlike several pigeons of Robin's acquaintance, John stared openly. Then he spoke.

"Ringo," he called in the direction of the next room. "I see a bird at the window."

"Anyone we know?" came Ringo's complacent retort.

"I mean a *real* bird," John said nervously.

"There's nothing odd about seeing a real bird at the window," Ringo soothed, fearing for his leader's sanity.

John put his book down with trembling hands. "There is when it's wearing *glasses*."

(To Be Continued Next Week)

Seekers To Tour America

The Seekers are seeking a chance to show their stuff in America.

The English group has just finished arrangements for a three week tour of America and Australia to take place some time next February.

FONTELLA BASS wails "Rescue Me," her first smash since leaving the singing company of Bobby McClure.

...THE RIGHTEOUS BROTHERS
BEAT Photo: R. R. Custer

Righteous Bros. Wronged? They Sue Record Co.

The Righteous Brothers are back in the news this week, and they are also back in the calendar—the Los Angeles Superior Court calendar, that is.

Bobby Hatfield and Bill Medley have filed suit against Philles Records and Moonglow Records, and they have accused Moonglow of wrongful accounting.

They had originally been signed to Moonglow records, and then they were leased by Moonglow to Philles, which is the record company owned by boy-millionaire Phil Spector.

Want Release

They are asking release from both companies, but if they are granted a release from Moonglow, they will automatically be relieved of any obligation to Philles Records.

Although the duo with dual cool have not recorded since this suit was filed, there was an album and a single record—both of which had previously been scheduled for release—which have now been, at least temporarily, canned.

"Look What Santa's Bringing This Year!"

A subscription to The BEAT makes an ideal gift. Think of all your friends that like to read YOUR copy of The BEAT every week! They'll remember you all year long. Just send in the form on Page 10 and then forget about fighting the crowds to do your Christmas shopping. We'll send them a special gift card with your name attached. If you want to send more than one, simply fill in the additional names and addresses on a plain sheet of paper, enclosing $3 for each subscription. (P.S. If you're not already a subscriber, how about sending one to yourself?)

KRLA ARCHIVES

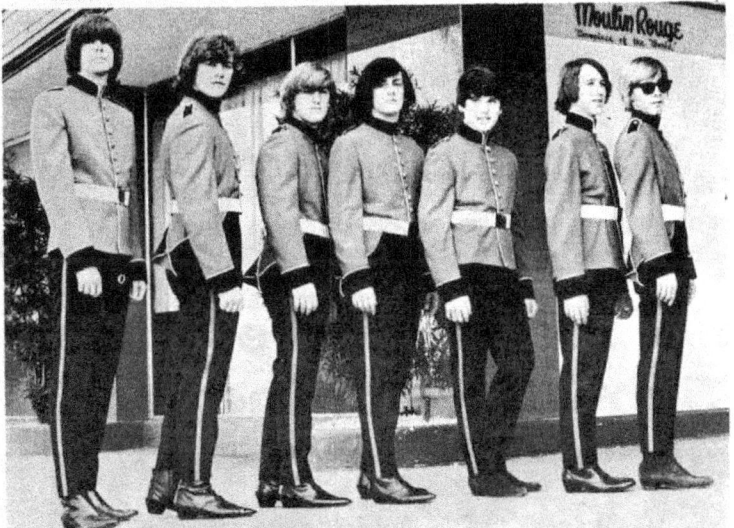

THE PALACE GUARD (l. to r. — Chuck, Don, John, Dave, Emitt, Rick and Mike) prepare to march on the old Moulin Rouge and turn it into a brand new, swinging teen club, The Hullabalooer.

Salute The Palace Guard

By Tammy Hitchcock

Once upon a time a little boy lay in a hospital bed. Think I'm lying, don't you? Well, I'm not. His name was John Beaudion and during his hospital stay Queen Elizabeth and Prince Philip came to visit. Not just him, of course. They came to see everyone in the hospital.

When the Queen got around to John she told him that one day he would grow up to be a Palace Guard. And you know that a loyal subject is always supposed to obey his Queen. So naturally when John grew up he did become a Palace Guard. Only it was not exactly the kind of Palace Guard which the Queen had in mind.

John became the kind of Guard which sings and plays instruments and in general has all of the characteristics of a beat group.

And when *The BEAT* holds its First Annual Pop Music Awards ceremony the Palace Guard will be providing the entertainment for the star-studded audience.

Unusual Guard

The Guard is an unusual group for a number of reasons. First off, just the amount of members who make up the Guards set them apart from other groups. For there are *seven* Palace Guards.

And instead of just getting up on stage and singing the boys intend to do all kinds of things in their act. Unlike many other groups, the Palace Guard intend to become a visual act as well as a sound act.

Three of the Palace Guard are brothers and hail from Canada. Don, John and Dave all arrived in the U.S. not knowing how to play any instruments. In fact, not knowing anything except that they wanted to form a group.

So they added Rick Moser (bass guitar), Chuck McClung (lead guitar), Emitt Rhodes (drums) and Mike Conley (singer) and became the Palace Guard.

Life was tough for the budding musicians because none of them really knew how to perform. "It took us a whole week sometimes just to learn one song," Don revealed.

But learn they did. They say they owe all of their success to St. Jude. Because it was to this Saint that the boys made a pledge. If he would help them become successful they would in turn build a ranch for under-privileged children. They feel that St. Jude has kept his part of the deal, so they fully intend to keep theirs.

Still another thing which differentiates the Palace Guard from some other groups is the fact that they imitate no one.

"Whatever we know we learned ourselves," said Don. "We've studied other groups but we've never copied them."

On stage the group presents a varied program. Probably because all seven members have different tastes. So to keep everyone happy they are forced to do a variety of songs.

Guard Choices

John and Chuck would do Rolling Stone songs if they had their choice, Don would choose the Beatles and Dave would pick the Animals.

Speaking of animals, Chuck must have the wildest hobby yet. He collects all kinds of animals and actually keeps them in his apartment.

Some of his collection includes an alligator, snakes, poison frogs, fish, and a snapping turtle. I voiced the opinion that all of his neighbors must hate him madly. I know I would. Just imagine coming home to a jungle like that!

However, Chuck pronounces his menagerie groovy because "it sounds just like Disneyland at night." Oh, groovy.

The Guard all sport long hair and they confidently predict that it will not go out of style. "It's in such a groove. It's not like a fad. It's something which is going to last for a long time," said John.

I don't know about the long hair, but I do know that if the Palace Guard continue to grow and improve *they'll* be around for a long time to come.

Chuck Berry Stays Alive

It takes constant changing to keep up with the times and stay alive in the record industry.

One excellent example of how much a performer changes as he grows older is Chuck Berry, singer and composer of many hit songs sung by groups like the Beatles.

Chuck really showed the diversity in his writing at a recent concert in the Village Theater in New York. The show was divided into four parts, each depicting a phase in Chuck's sky rocketing career.

The first part was a low down blues segment opening with "Back Home." The second part featured some of Chuck's songs about automobiles and gadgets that fascinate him so much.

Instrumental tunes made up the third and the fourth and final part was devoted to the rhythm and blues greats that he's best known for including "Memphis" and "Roll Over Beethoven."

That's what it takes to stay in this business.

On the BEAT

By Louise Criscione

Every artist should be so lucky. Len Barry was all set to fly off to England for a series of promotional shots to help push his "1-2-3" even higher up the charts.

Len wasn't exceptionally well-known or extremely popular here in the U.S. before his "1-2-3" became such a hit. So, no one really cared if Len took off for England or Iceland or anywhere else.

But now things have definitely changed and the U.S. promoters who once couldn't care less are now exercising their options on Len. Which means that his Stateside commitments will keep Len here for quite a while.

Donovan decided that he was spending money for a personal manager when his own father could better use the money. So, he promptly hired his dad to act as his personal manager. Good for Donovan. There's nothing nicer than keeping it in the family.

Beatles in Hollywood?

Don't go getting all jazzed just yet — but it is possible that the Beatles will sign a movie contract which will keep them moviemaking right here in the good old U.S.A.

It would really be to the Beatles' advantage to clench the deal 'cause it calls for $500,000 for each movie PLUS 50% of the profits. Which ain't bad at all.

... LEN BARRY

Them has changed members so often that it is practically impossible to write about the group because you never know who's in it! I do know one member who is no longer a Them. Billy Harrison, former lead guitarist, is out on his own now and has started a new group.

The name of Billy's new group? *Some of Them*, of course!

Another old Them, John McAuley, will play organ for Some of Them. I'm still not sure what members of the original Them are still left, but whoever they are they sure sound good on "Mystic Eyes."

Speaking of "Eyes" you do realize that the record is not a new one, don't you? The record was originally released during the very first part of the summer. But it went nowhere fast. Then months later someone somewhere started playing it and there you have it — an instant hit months later.

Animals in Movies

And now it's the Animals who have turned movie-makers. They're about to do a 30 minute short, tentatively entitled "Animal Life In Poland."

Subject of the film will be the Animals' life on tour, on tour in Poland naturally. Anyway, the Animals are doing the movie themselves and the whole thing is to be spontaneous.

The Stones have taken care of any more concerts in West Berlin. After their concert there a few months back the officials have now banned all future pop concerts in West Berlin. Oh, well.

John Lennon was going on about how much the Beatles dislike protest songs when Paul butted in: "I'm writing a protest song — about John!"

Scrambled Egg

Did you know that "Yesterday" was for a long time dubbed "Scrambled Egg?" The Yardbirds let *The BEAT* in on the secret months ago but John has just now gotten around to confirming it.

"We called it 'Scrambled Egg' and it became a joke between us. We almost had it finished, we had made up our minds that only a one word title would suit and, believe me, we just couldn't find the right one.

"Then one morning Paul woke up and the song and title were both there — completed. I was sorry in a way. We had so many laughs about it."

John's probably not so sorry about it now — not with all the money that record has dragged in!

Leave it to Keith Richard. He caused complete panic aboard the Stones' private plane as it was winging its way toward Montreal for a concert. All of a sudden he decided he couldn't find his passport!

Bill says they had to smuggle Keith into Canada and then call like crazy to try and locate the lost passport. And now all is well. Until Keith loses it again, that is.

... KEITH RICHARD

KRLA ARCHIVES

Hollywood's **Moulin Rouge** *Rocks In!*

GRAND OPENING DEC. 9

The Showplace of the World Becomes The Rock & Roll Showplace of the World

THE PALACE GUARD ENTER HOLLYWOOD'S FINEST NEW CLUB (left). DAVE HULL IS CAUGHT TRYING TO "BORROW" A UNIFORM.

DAVE HULL'S
HULLABALOO

6230 Sunset
Across from Palladium

Featuring
The Palace Guard
Plus

The World's Top Recording Stars

(Follow The BEAT for details on scheduled Guest Appearances)

★ Continuous entertainment — on three stages — Including one of the world's great revolving center stages!

Plus ★ Continuous dancing — Good Food — All the Glamor and Showmanship of Hollywood's Finest.

★ Home of the Rock & Roll Hall of Fame — Footprints, Handprints and Momentos of the great rock stars.

ROCK WITH DAVE HULL AT THE HULLABALOO
NO MINIMUM — NO COVER — ALL FOR $1.50 ADMISSION

Special Premiere Dec. 8 Hosting The BEAT's 1st Annual Pop Music Awards Dinner

KRLA ARCHIVES

KRLA Tunedex

DAVE HULL

BOB EUBANKS

DICK BIONDI

JOHNNY HAYES

This Week	Last Week	Title	Artist
1	3	LET'S HANG ON	Four Seasons
2	1	STILL I'M SAD/I'M A MAN	The Yardbirds
3	5	I HEAR A SYMPHONY	The Supremes
4	2	1-2-3	Len Barry
5	4	TURN, TURN, TURN	The Byrds
6	11	TASTE OF HONEY/3RD MAN THEME	Herb Alpert
7	7	GET OFF OF MY CLOUD	Rolling Stones
8	15	I GOT YOU	James Brown
9	24	LIES, LIES	The Knickerbockers
10	6	YOU'RE THE ONE	The Vogues
11	17	RISING SUN	The Deep Six
12	19	LET ME BE	The Turtles
13	25	I CAN NEVER GO HOME ANYMORE	The Shangri-Las
14	8	YESTERDAY	The Beatles
15	13	RESCUE ME	Fontella Bass
16	21	HANG ON SLOOPY	Ramsey Lewis Trio
17	26	IT'S MY LIFE	The Animals
18	24	PIED PIPER	The Changin' Times
19	30	OVER AND OVER	Dave Clark Five
20	12	MYSTIC EYES	Them
21	10	MAKE IT EASY ON YOURSELF	Walker Brothers
22	18	YOU'VE GOT TO HIDE YOUR LOVE AWAY	The Silkie
23	22	MY GIRL HAS GONE	The Miracles
24	--	EBB TIDE	Righteous Brothers
25	20	AIN'T THAT PECULIAR	Marvin Gaye
26	32	RUN, BABY, RUN	The Newbeats
27	27	SOMETHING ABOUT YOU	The Four Tops
28	23	MY HEART SINGS	Mel Carter
29	29	DON'T TALK TO STRANGERS	Beau Brummels
30	35	YOU DIDN'T HAVE TO BE SO NICE	Lovin' Spoonful
31	37	FLOWERS ON THE WALL	Statler Brothers
32	--	THE LITTLE GIRL I ONCE KNEW	Beach Boys
33	33	ENGLAND SWINGS	Roger Miller
34	34	HERE IT COMES AGAIN	The Fortunes
35	36	I FOUGHT THE LAW	Bobby Fuller Four
36	40	APPLE OF MY EYE	Roy Head & Traits
37	--	ALL OR NOTHING	Patti LaBelle
38	--	THUNDERBALL/KEY TO MY HEART	Tom Jones
39	--	THE DUCK	Jackie Lee
40	39	THE SOUNDS OF SILENCE	Simon & Garfunkel

EMPEROR HUDSON

CASEY KASEM

CHARLIE O'DONNELL

BILL SLATER

Inside KRLA

"Friday night, November 12, saw a first in the annals of broadcast history as, once again displaying the extreme versatility of radio as a media of mass communications—KRLA demonstrated its wide acceptance and sincere ability to serve as only KRLA has in the past.

For the first time in the entire world, the entire student body of a Southern California high school was led in its school cheers—*over the radio*—while seated in the grand stands of their home stadium, watching their team perform.

"KRLA DJ, Dave Hull, who was denied permission to lead a yell at the school stadium, told the students on his show that afternoon, to take with them to the game their transistor radios, and then he announced that he would return to the air later that evening, sitting in for Bob Eubanks.

Long Distance Yell

"Then as the students listened to him on the radio at the game, he promised that he would lead them in a yell from the confines of his announce-booth many miles away in Pasadena.

"At the last minute a special telephone-equipped car was pulled onto the field in front of the stands, and the response of the kids in the stands was heard back at KRLA, and at the same time was re-broadcast to 14,000,000 Southern California ears—all tuned to KRLA.

"Needless to say, the noise was deafening—the project, hilarious and confusing. But the Scuzzy, Dum Dum Head Hullabalooer struck again! Another first for KRLA!!!!

... DAVE HULL

"What might be further noted here that, KRLA—not wishing to slight the opposing team—was represented on the *other* side of the field by the amazing gesticulations of Dick Biondi, who was admitted to the opposing side of the field so that he could lead their side in the cheering. It was a night to remember!"

Jazz Jockey

Did'ja know that Dick Moreland used to be a jazz disc jockey? Yep, he was and what's more—he used to conduct jazz sessions at a place called the Tiffany Club in Hollywood, which has since become the world-famous Shelley's Manne-Hole.

During one of those sessions, a young jazz singer by the name of Gene McDaniels drifted in and wanted to sing, and it was then and there that he was discovered by our own "DM" and sent on his way to fame and fortune.

Were you listening recently when a couple of our own KRLA nuts started playing jokes on one another again? The one and only "ugliest and skinniest" DJ in the world—Dick Biondi—came into the one and only Hullabalooer's show and raised all kinds of havoc.

... DICK MORELAND

It was one of the few times that Dave has ever really been broken up on the air, and it was a pretty funny scene. Well, leave it to the Hullabalooer to get his due revenge, which is just exactly what he did! Later that evening, he snuck back into the studio during Dick's show, armed with all his horns. Needless to say, it was complete bedlam!

The Apes will be at Northview High in Covina on the 10th of December, and at Mark Keppel High on the 15th, so go out and cheer them on to victory—they need *all* the help they can get!

Thru Dec. 5

Bud & Travis

Dec. 7-Dec. 19

Hoyt Axton

... At Doug Weston's

Troubadour

9083 Santa Monica Blvd. at Dohney, L.A.
RESERVATIONS CR 6-6168
STUDENT DISCOUNT — MINORS WELCOME

NOW! thru Dec. 12
The Big Sound Of
THE ASSOCIATION
with their hit song
"One Too Many Mornings"
At
The ICE HOUSE GLENDALE
folk music in concert
Reservations: 245-5043
Thursday thru Sundays. 50c Discount on admission with this ad on Thursdays **and** Sundays (Only).

DEADLINE NEAR...
You have until Jan. 1 to take advantage of the introductory subscription offer of $3 for 52 issues.
SUBSCRIBE NOW — SAVE 60%

KRLA BEAT Subscription

SPECIAL OFFER — Subscribe Now
SAVE 60% Of Regular Price
☐ 1 YEAR — 52 ISSUES — $3.00
Enclosed is $3.00   ☐ CASH   ☐ CHECK
Send to:................................Age..........
Address:..
City..................State..........Zip..........
MAIL YOUR ORDER TO:
KRLA BEAT
6290 Sunset, Suite 504
Hollywood, Calif. 90028
Foreign Rate: $14.00 — 52 Issues

GIFT SUBSCRIPTION

Please send a one-year gift subscription to:
_____
Who lives at: _____
City: _____ State _____ Zip _____
Send a card saying it is from: _____
Enclose $3 for each subscription. Mail to:
KRLA BEAT, Suite 504, 6290 Sunset, Hollywood, Calif 90028

KRLA ARCHIVES

THE ANIMALS are celebrating another big year. "We Gotta Get Out of This Place" re-established them as one of the world's top vocal groups. Their latest is "It's My Life."

KRLA ARCHIVES

New Bag For April & Nino

By Carol Deck

They say every successful actor wants to be a singer and every successful singer wants to be an actor and Nino Tempo, of Nino and April, is no exception.

And, by the way, it is Nino and April and not the other way around. They started as April and Nino but changed to Nino and April with their smash hit, "Deep Purple." But April says she doesn't know how much longer she's going to let Nino get away with that.

And now Nino's aspiring to be an actor. He says he doesn't think he's exactly the current leading man type but would rather play "today's guy – not necessarily 6' 2" with blue eyes."

There's going to be a few other changes in the act too, probably a lot quicker than the start of Nino's acting career. Both members of the brother and sister singing duo are going to be doing more solo work starting in January.

Solo Artists

They both started as solo artists. April had two successful records by herself, before she joined her brother. And Nino says he had many unsuccessful releases. He also played back-up music on sax and clarinet for many artists including Bobby Darin.

The two finally decided to try singing together about three years ago and have had several top sellers. After 'Deep Perplizing' the country a while back, they hit us again with "I Love How You Love Me" complete with bag pipes which Nino himself learned to play just for that one record.

One song written by Nino that he considers a "smash flop" was the flip side of "Deep Purple." Nino likes it because it has the longest title imaginable – "I've Been Carrying a Torch For You So Long That I've Burned a Great Big Hole in My Heart!"

Another innovation in their act will also be released in January. It's a jazz album with no voices, featuring Nino on tenor sax and the Eddie Cano Quartet.

But right now they are hitting us with another single. This one is "Hey Baby," a song written and made famous by Bruce Chanel. It's produced, as are most of their songs, by Nino and Ahmet Ertegun, Turkish vice president of Atlantic Records.

Nino says "Hey Baby" was actually what inspired him to do "Deep Purple" before, and now they're doing "Hey Baby."

SEND BEAT GIFT SUBSCRIPTIONS TO YOUR FRIENDS FOR CHRISTMAS

Person to Person

DAVE:
I got you Babe, too. Don't worry about the miles you can always "borrow" a horse if your thumb gets tired.
Clever One

P.F.C.:
I wish you hadn't been on a case when I was at 2850. Missed you terribly.
Commander

LIMEY AND THE YANKS:
We want to say how great you are. Don't ever change. Your supporters...
Alana & Linda

RINGO RIGGS:
The Meek are on their way. They're getting bigger every day.
A Meeker

MIKE:
To the most wonderful nut in Hull, England; Happy Harf Birday or even Byrday.
Judi

RAY OF THE CASTAWAYS:
Thank you very much for letting me have the strap to your guitar.
Kustin

ANN BENFIELD, Cheshire:
You privileged character! Are you completely happy now? Long live the Beatles, Byrds and MFQ. Right? Be prepared. The MFQ you save may be your own.
Kathy

JEFF:
So you have a "Heart of Stone." Who cares.
Geri

HERMAN:
And WE'VE got five million groups as good as Herman's Hermits.
Debbie & Jill

FREDDIE & THE DREAMERS:
Remember the chicken noodle soup with worms? Remember the coo-coo razor blades, the telly phone call that didn't come through? Remember the five girls at CBS studios? We do!
Carol, Cher, Gale, Linda & Nora

Beatles Go For Baroque

You've heard Beatle songs done by everyone from Marianne Faithfull to the Boston Pops Orchestra. But are you ready for the "Baroque Beatles Song Book?"

It's a newly released album by Lennon-McCartney admirer and classical composer Joshua Rifkin with the blessings of the Beatles.

Rifkin has arranged the songs in an authentic baroque way and conducted a group of New York musicians, called the Merseyside Kammermusikgesellschaft for this album, in a rather unusual recording of some great hits.

The album includes "I Want To Hold Your Hand," "I'll Cry Instead," "Things We Said Today," "You've Got To Hide Your Love Away," "Ticket To Ride," "Please Please Me," "Hard Day's Night," "She Loves You," "Eight Days a Wekk" and "Help."

This adds another feather to the Beatles' cap. It isn't everyone who can write smash rock and roll hits that can be arranged in baroque fashion.

...ROY ORBISON takes a look into the future.

EXPANDING PERSONALITY

Roy Eyes Movies

"I just wanted to be a fellow who sold a few records. I think I was afraid to be really big. But now I look into the future and hope for other things. I'd like to write a movie score and maybe produce a picture. Honestly, I'd like to be more and more of an all-around showbusiness personality."

These are the words of one of the most talented and successful young artists in the entertainment industry. His name – Roy Orbison.

Roy grew up in the oil town of Wink, Texas, and has spent the last decade making hit records which have enjoyed international success.

Roy first began playing the guitar when he was just six years old, and by the time he reached his teen years he was the leader of a group called the Wink Westerners, as well as doing his own radio show in Vernon, Texas.

Famous Friend

Roy spent some time at North Texas College as a geology major where he became acquainted with another talented student – one Pat Boone. It was through Pat that Roy finally realized his true interest in music.

In 1956, Roy celebrated his first hit record – "Ooby-Dooby" – and two years later in 1958 he wrote, recorded, and had a hit with a song called "Claudette," after his wife

Roy's talents extend into many different fields, and besides being a fine singer and an accomplished musician, he is also a very talented writer and composer. Roy has penned hit tunes for such artists as the Everly Brothers, Jerry Lee Lewis, Buddy Knox, and the late Buddy Holly.

Of his writing efforts, Roy explains: "When it's time to make a record, we quickly get some ideas together, rush into a studio and usually finish writing the songs on the spot. It was that way with both 'It's Over' and 'Pretty Woman'."

Roy has enjoyed a great deal of success in his own native country as well as countries all over the world. However, he has been exceedingly popular in Great Britain the last few years.

In regard to his friends across "The Pond," Roy sincerely says: "I felt especially close to the British people in general. Things started happening for me over there just about when the Beatles started getting bigger and bigger.

"I was on tour with the Beatles when it really started for me, and I can even remember them attending my birthday party."

Currently Roy has a great new single – "Crawling Back" – riding the charts with its sights set right on the very top notch. This is a record to watch and to listen to, and the same holds true for its talented singer. He is a young man to watch, to listen to, and to enjoy.

...APRIL AND NINO

KRLA ARCHIVES

SIMON AND GARFUNKLE, New York City folk singers, have added a strange title to the hit charts, "Sounds of Silence." They've been singing together since high school days with Paul (right) doing all their composing. Paul and Art have also recorded an album, "Wednesday Morning, 3 a.m.," and are due here soon.

Small-Fry Bantams Will Capture Everyone's Heart

By June Cross

Well, it's happened. They have finally come up with an answer to the Beatles for the lollipop-set of America. Just yesterday they came, they saw, and they captured our hearts—and the offices of *The BEAT* may never be the same again!

Yesterday afternoon, we were visited by three small boys—aged 9, 10, and 12—called The Bantams. Complete with blonde Beatle haircuts, black corduroy velours with red turtle-neck sweaters, and at least a million freckles.

Jeff, Mike and Fritz (I *swear* it; his name *is* Fritz!) set up their instruments and began to perform. Result? The complete destruction of all cool possessed by anyone who happened to be present.

These three small boys are miraculous. Mike, who is the oldest and the "leader" of the group, plays guitar, while brother Fritz rattles up a storm on his maraccas and the youngest brother—Jeff—plays a mighty mean set of bongos.

Mike has the voice and manners of a very miniature John Lennon while Fritz is definitely the Paul McCartney, junior-grade, of the younger set. Jeff—well, he's definitely the Ben Casey of the Ringo Starr brigade.

Movie Star

Jeff, who is nine years old, was chosen to play the title role in the upcoming motion picture, "Methuselah Jones," for World-Cine Associates. The story is about a nine-year old ordained, singing Arkansas minister, and this is the first acting experience the boys have ever had. In fact, the boys have never had *any* professional training of any kind.

About one year ago, they saw the Beatles on the "Ed Sullivan Show" for the first time—and it was love-at-first-scream. The boys promptly appeared in front of their mother with pleas for instruments which she very wisely granted.

Under the leadership of Chief Bantam Mike—"who is all business and will stand for no foolishness at all!"—the boys formed their own little rock 'n' roll trio and taught themselves to play every Beatle number which they had heard.

They have also recently completed their first album which was finished in record time—just six hours in the studio, and they had 14 songs "in the can."

Active Lives

Right now the boys are leading very active lives, running between movie sets, class rooms, skateboards, and pillow fights. Mike is a straight-A student and helps his two younger brothers when it comes time to learn their lines for the next day's shooting.

He hopes that someday he will be writing songs for his little group, but of his attempts in that direction to date he simply sighs and says: "It's kinda easy to get the music, but it's awfully hard to get the words!"

The boys come from a family of eight children, and they have a younger sister—aged seven—who has waist-length blonde hair and is "an expert Watusi dancer!" She has accompanied them on some of their engagements already and the four of them make a wild quartet!

They tear it up on wild numbers like "Twist and Shout," "Sheila," "She Loves You," and finally they musically question their audience "Do You Love Me?" Well boys, with your talent, looks, determination—and freckles!—the world is just bound to fall in love with you!!

Yeah, yeah, yeah!!!

Q: *Help! I'm a senior this year and I'm already worrying about graduation. The principal always has a swimming party in his private pool for the graduates, and whenever my hair gets wet it frizzes all over the place. I love to swim and don't want to stay out of the water. What can I do?*
(Stephanie B.)

A: With all the glamorous bathing caps on the market, you shouldn't have any trouble finding one that will solve this problem and keep you looking your best.

Q: *My lips are naturally red. What color lipstick could I use to get them a brown beige?*
(Lisa B.)

A: Your question is difficult for us to answer because we'd almost have to see your natural color before we could recommend the right lipstick shade. We suggest you go to the cosmetic department in a large store (where they have a qualified person to help with make-up problems) and discuss the matter in person.

Q: *I wear a very good brand of eye makeup, but it always smears on the top of my eyelids and looks terrible. I've tried making the line thinner, but it still smears. Can you suggest a remedy?*
(Cindy C.)

A: You didn't say whether you wear liner pencil or liquid, but if you do use pencil, that's what is causing your problem. Pencil has a tendency to smear on even a non-oily complexion. Why don't you try the brush-and-cake method?

Q: *A girlfriend of mine told me that you can make a boy jealous by wearing a boy's ring for a few days. Then, after you have taken the ring off, the boy you're after will ask you to go steady. The boy I like is very cute and popular. What do you think of my girlfriends advice?*
(Jade H)

A: We have mixed emotions about your pal's plan. If a boy "sort of likes" a girl, he often starts liking her a lot more if he thinks she belongs to someone else. But there's no guarantee that the above crafty scheme would bring about the desired results. Pretended romances can often get out of hand. If you start wearing a boy's ring, others are going to want to know who it belongs to and you may have to invent an imaginary steady. And we don't have to go into detail about how easily you could get in over your head with no way out. Why don't you just make an effort to be as "cute and popular" as he is, so that he'll notice you. This plan is less dangerous and could be just as effective.

Q: *My collection of hair rollers is something just short of enormous. I have so many I don't have anything to keep them in. I have small curler caddies, but they don't help. Can you suggest something large but attractive that I could keep them in?*
(Elizabeth O.)

A: Try buying a large basket (with a handle for easy toting) and painting it (use spray paint, it's easier) to match the decor of your room. Then heap it with curlers. You'll find it will be both decorative and useful. If you have no place to put such a basket, buy a big, inexpensive straw purse that you can hang out of sight in a closet.

HINT OF THE WEEK

I've found an unusual but wonderful home remedy for skin trouble. I have always had problems with my complexion because of oil and breakouts. Then I tried Epsom Salts (honest). It's very cheap; you can buy a large box for only 39c. What you do is put 2 tablespoons of salts in a cup and add just a little bit of boiling water. Then mix it until it dissolves and set it aside to cool. After you wash your face (very clean), pat on the solution before going to bed. Do this for three nights, then stop for one night. Next day, start the process all over again. This has really worked wonders for me and I know it will help you, too.
(Anita R.)

If you have a question you'd like answered or a hint you'd like to share, drop a line to Tips To Teens, c/o *The BEAT*.

THESE ARE THE BANTAMS. They may become the answer to the Beatles for America's lollypop set.

KRLA ARCHIVES

For Girls Only
New Contest

By Shirley Poston

Before I start this week's ravings, I think I'd better warn you. I'm kind of on my soap box today. And here's what about.

You know how all of us have swapped star dreams and stories via this column, and rattled on about favorites.

Well, this has been a lot of fun for me, and judging from your letters, most of you feel the same way. It's really a blast to have someone special because it makes life so much more interesting and full. You know what I mean, it just sort of adds something to you and makes you happier.

But *all* of you don't feel this way, I've discovered. Because I received a letter today that still has me in an uproar. From someone whose life has gone downhill instead of uphill because of that special someone.

The following is an excerpt from that letter...

"Two years ago I really fell for Paul McCartney and it sort of ruined my life. I was sixteen then. I was dating, but I lost interest in all boys except Paul. In fact, I lost interest in *everything* except Paul.

"I used to stay in my room and do nothing but sit in the dark for hours and cry every night. I got so depressed thinking about how I'd never get to meet Paul that I tried to kill myself four times. But somebody always stuck their nose in my business and stopped me.

"I'd be better off dead now. Here I am, eighteen years old, a freshman at college. In high school, I was a National Honor Student and in all sorts of activities. Now I'm failing all my subjects and I'm nothing but a walking corpse.

"I just don't care what happens to me if I can't even meet Paul. I really don't want to live anymore. I never date now—I'm just not interested. The only time I ever go out of the house is to see "Help."

"I have no idea what is going to happen to me. I don't really care either. Can you imagine caring about someone else so much that you don't care about yourself?

"I'm serious about what I'm going to say next. I would sell an arm or a leg or even my parents just to meet Paul. So the next time you think you've got a problem, just have a look at mine."

I've had a good long look at it, because I've thought of nothing else since I opened that letter.

I don't know how all of you feel about this, but I personally think the writer of this letter isn't even trying not to let this thing get the best of her.

Every single one of us who cares deeply about someone we know will probably have moments of desperate sadness. I should know. I've spent a lot of time day-dreaming about George, but I've also spent some blithering. I was lucky enough to finally meet him, just momentarily, and although that made me wildly happy, remembering it makes me kind of miserable sometimes. Because I care so much, a hello and a handshake just wasn't enough, particularly when it probably will never happen again.

But I don't get that way very often, because right at the beginning of my big Harrison passion, I took a good look at the situation and came to a decision. I sort of weighed the good against the bad.

What I mean is I sat down and figured out whether my love for George made me miserable more times than it made me happy. I soon discovered that I was in the clouds more than I was in the doldrums. And I don't think that the measure of sadness is too high a price to pay for all the fun and excitement of caring for someone.

Every person's life is full of incidents and situations that could ruin the present *and* the future, *if you let them*.

I don't advise the girl who wrote the letter to try to forget about Paul. Instead I hope she will start remembering herself, too. All of us have to do bloody battle with ourselves at one time or another, but the fight is worth it.

I don't know. I may be saying all this wrong. When I really feel deeply about something, it's so hard to put it into just the right words.

In case I am going about this in a way that could do more harm than good, I wish you'd come to my rescue and also to hers.

Many of you have probably had this same problem and have found a way to either solve it or live with it. If so, please, please, please send a letter to this girl in care of me. I won't open them or anything. I'll just send them on to her.

She needs help and no one can give it better than those who have had a similar difficulty.

Just address your letters to For Girls Only, in care of *The BEAT*, and write the word *Bev* in the left hand corner of the envelope. I'll forward your mail to her right away. And please hurry before things get any worse for her.

Gosh, I'm sorry to have raved on so long about all this, but it really has me upset.

On to something a little less upsetting. Remember our little contest where I promised to give away the "Help" album? Well, it was won by Mary Ann Francis of Anaheim, California. Congratulations, Mary Ann. I'll get the album mailed off to you very soon.

Now get set for a brand new "Contest." I've now inherited the "Out Of Our Heads" album by the five-and-only Rolling Stones. And here's how you can inherit it from me.

Just put your name and address on the front of a postcard, and Mick Jagger's middle name on the back. Then send it to me in care of *The BEAT*. I'll put all the cards with the correct answer into a big vat or something and then close my eyes and draw out the winner!

I'm about to run out of room again, but before I go, I want to bring you up to date on my newest passion. I'm fast becoming a real knit-wit. I used to think that knitting was something little old ladies from Pasadena did while swaying gently in rocking chairs. Then I tried it myself (without the rocking chair) and I've gone off my rocker about knitting! Really, you can add the greatest things to your wardrobe, and knitting is a good past-time and calmer-downer when something is needling you (pardon pun) (I couldn't resist).

At present I'm taking knitting lessons (so help me) at a yarn shop, which is really a ball (there I go again).

Oh, I forgot to tell you something that was in the "Help" winner's letter. Mary Ann's typewriter has a small problem and she closed her letter with this P.S.

"If you think your eyes are bad because the typing is going downhill, never fear. I am proud to say I am the only person alive who can type a crooked line."

Funny, huh? Gotta go now. Keep your letters coming and I'll see you next *BEAT*.

ERNIE AND THE EMPERORS pose at the corner so that you won't miss their new record, titled strangely enough "Meet Me At The Corner." The Emperors are a local Santa Barbara group who wear dog collars and long hair. The boys say that they are not going to let their hair grow any longer 'cause then they might have to wear dog tags!

Bud and Travis Back Together

The folk world has a reputation of being peopled by rather far out wandering minstrels who dress any old way and make folk music their world.

One very refreshing exception to this image is Bud and Travis, a very talented folk duo who's interest include a wide variety of things outside the folk world. And neither one is the sort who just lives in a hole in the wall some where and comes out only to sing.

Bud is an athletic Parisian who enjoys reading Japanese haiku poetry and is a graduate of the Art Center School in Los Angeles.

He's an excellent guitarist who caught the folk bug while he was a boy in New York. He used to sit in on the legendary get-togethers of the folk greats including Huddie Ledbetter, Josh White, Woody Guthry and Pete Seeger.

Speaks Several Languages

His ability to sing very well in several languages may come from the fact that his native language is French and he learned Italian before he ever spoke English.

His life on a Virginian farm and his experiences in the Korean War add great sincerity to his blue grass songs and compositions about war, like "Shiloh."

Travis is about as different from robust out-going Bud as possible. He is always labeled a serious young man even though he can be a bit wild at times. He was raised in a border town in the Arizona desert and is a late rising chain smoker.

Travis sang with many duos and groups before he met Bud. He sang with Roger Smith, who went on to fame on the television show "77 Sunset Strip," for a while. Then while appearing as a single artist at San Francisco's Purple Onion he met and joined up with Limelighter Lou Gottlieb.

He and Lou joined a couple of others to form the Gateway Singers. While appearing with the Gateways at Hollywood's Ciros, Travis got together with Bud whom he'd met earlier and the duo was formed.

Very Successful

The combination of the two proved to be very successful, particularly with numbers like "Raspberries and Strawberries" and their own compositions of "Bon Soir Dame" and "Truly Do."

But in 1960 they fell into a groove that many groups find. They just plain got tired of the road and each other. "We didn't really break up," says Travis, "We broke *down*." They tried going their own ways and forming other groups. Travis even worked for a year as a writer on a Broadway Show, but people always asked for more Bud and Travis stuff.

So now, they are back together again and sounding even greater. A good folk act like Bud and Travis just doesn't die.

... BUD And TRAVIS

KRLA ARCHIVES

Dear Susan

By Susan Frisch

Are Chad and Jeremy really breaking up?
Vicki Kirsch

Don't worry, this is just a rumor.

How can I get John Lennon's newest book, and how much is it?
Jill McCartney

Check around with your local bookstores for the catalogue on newly-released books. I'm sure they can help you.

Where can I get a John Lennon hat? I've tried all the stores but this has failed.
Susan Cox

If the stores were not able to help you, then I'm afraid I can't.

Can you please tell me how old Sally Fields is and her home address?
Bill G.

Sally is 19 years old. Sorry, but we can't give out home addresses.

Can you please tell me if "I've Just Seen A Face," one of the numbers on the British version of "Help," will be released in America?
Sally Smitkin

This is something that is left up to the record company. I don't know whether or not they have decided to release it yet.

What would be the best address reach Roy Orbison personally?
Jackie Guerette

Write Roy in care of 1540 Broadway, New York, N. Y. 10036.

Is Mike Clarke married, engaged, or going steady?
Kim Vorgas

Good news! Mike is none of the three!

Do the Beatles use nylon or steele strings on their guitars?
Jan Wilson

For their electric guitars they use steele, always. For their regular guitars they use the nylon-type string.

Is it true that Paul has blue eyes?
Georgia McLenster

No. Paul has brown eyes.

What is the address of United Artists Studios?
D. May

4041 N. Fermosa Ave., Hollywood, Calif.

Is it true that Mick Jagger has been secretly married to Chris Shrimpton for two months and is thinking of going solo?
Jay Ling

This is just one of the many millions of rumors that has been spread, said, and thought up by fans, adults, *and* newspapers!

When Jane and Paul get married, will Jane quit her career as an actress?
Sandy Passmore

When, or should I say IF, they get married Jane will then decide. Until now she hasn't made any statement.

Where can I write to Bobby Sherman?
Lynn Crowther

Write to him in care of ABC-TV, 4151 Prospect, Hollywood, Calif.

Can you give me some information on Tommy Quickly?
Patty Mayard

Tommy was born in Norris, Green, Liverpool, on July 7, 1945. He is 5 ft.-9 inches and weighs 146 lbs. He has dark brown hair and blue eyes. His favorites in music include Ray Charles, Ketty Lester, Chuck Berry, and Dave Brubeck. He likes fishing, taking long walks, girls with dark hair, and his dog, Floss. He dislikes untidy people, noisy girls, and having his hair cut.

What is the name of the drummer in the Castaways, and how old is he?
Joan Kadi

Drummer Denny Craswell, who is the youngest member of the group and still goes to high school, just turned 18.

Is the version "Sealed With A Kiss," by Herman's Hermits, just a British release?
Cher C.

Yes, as of now. We hope that it'll be released over here.

Do the Beatles believe in charity?

Taking into consideration that charity begins at home, I would definitely say YES!

Sonny and Cher Having Problems

Sonny and Cher are one of the top selling acts in the industry right now but they've got legal problems.

Gene Pitney is sueing them for over 180,000 pounds (approximately $.5 million) for alleged breach of contract.

Pitney is sueing over the recent tour through the Eastern states which he headlined.

He says he invited Sonny and Cher to join the package deal some time earlier in the year, just before they made their big break in the record charts.

Sonny Collapsed

The tour was all set to open in Chattanooga when Gene got a message from California that Sonny wouldn't be able to make it because he had just collapsed. And Cher said she wouldn't consider appearing without him.

So the entire tour went on without Sonny and Cher.

But Pitney feels there was a breach of contract and has filed suit in New York. No date has yet been set for a trial.

The only comment from Sonny and Cher at the time of the cancellation of tour was from their British representative Larry Page, who said, "All I know is that Sonny was taken ill with a throat infection and attended by a specialist. I talked to him and Cher over the transatlantic phone and he could hardly speak."

THE YARDBIRDS have a world-wide hit with "I'm A Man." But they've really started something with the flip side, "Still I'm Sad." It apparently has now inspired the arranging of the Beatle hits into Baroque ballads.

KRLA ARCHIVES

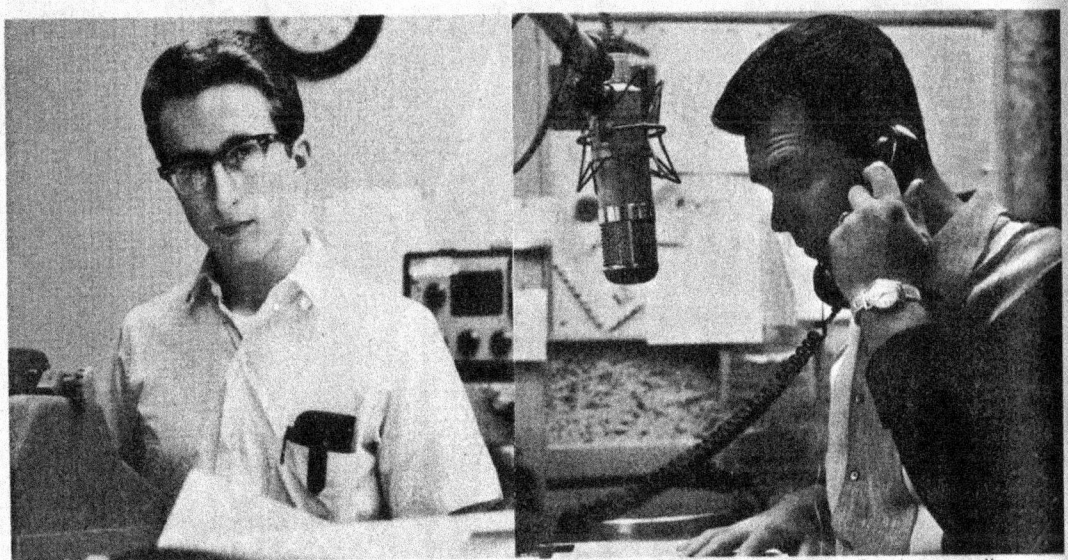

VAUGHN FILKINS tabulates the weekly survey...   **BOB EUBANKS** takes a nightly Teentopper call.
BEAT Photos: Dennis Dewenter

KRLA Teentoppers Provide Accurate Survey of Campuses

The KRLA Teen Topper program is in full swing again this year, providing Southern California's most accurate survey of musical preferences in the junior and senior high schools.

More than 300 area schools are represented weekly in the survey, sending in their list of the top tunes on the campus.

Almost everyone has heard the Teen Toppers spotlighted on Bob Eubank's show from 5:45-8:45 p.m. nightly. Here's how it works:

Each junior and senior high school has a Teen Topper correspondent—some have two or three—who send in a weekly list of the top records. Four nights per week—Monday through Thursday—Bob selects the survey from an individual school and plays all the songs on the list in a one-hour salute.

Every Friday night Bob plays a composite list from all the surveys, as tabulated by KRLA's Director of Teen Affairs, Vaughn Filkins, who coordinates the Teen Topper program.

Here's a schedule of the schools to be spotlighted in coming weeks, along with the Teen Topper correspondent from each:

Date	School	Correspondent
Dec. 2	NORTH HOLLYWOOD HIGH	Janet Vickman / Arlene Dibben
Dec. 6	PORTOLA JR. HIGH	Sharon Lidz
Dec. 7	WILLIAM H. TAFT HIGH	Theresa Leff
Dec. 8	ROBERT E. PEARY JR. HIGH	Sally Oylear
Dec. 9	LA HABRA HIGH	Diana Klass
Dec. 13	FAIRFAX HIGH	Sharon Weisz
Dec. 14	PALOS VERDES HIGH	Diane Gourley / Lorraine Lyon
Dec. 15	MILLIKAN HIGH	Judy Caro
Dec. 16	SOUTH HILLS HIGH	Merri Phillips
Dec. 20	EDGEWOOD HIGH	Carla Pettigrew
Dec. 21	BLAIR HIGH	Pat Woolford
Dec. 22	DANIEL WEBSTER JR. HIGH	Janet Marks

Little Women
Casual to Cotillion

GASSY GARB FOR GROOVY GIRLS
Pre-teen Sizes   6-14
Jr. Petite Sizes   3-13
Junior Sizes   3-15

Open every nite till Xmas, Mon.-Fri.
Starting Monday, December 6

136 SOUTH BEVERLY DRIVE
BEVERLY HILLS, CALIFORNIA

Validated Parking in Crest & Triangle Lots

KRLA ARCHIVES

America's Largest Teen NEWSpaper

KRLA Edition BEAT
MFP

Volume 1, Number 40   LOS ANGELES, CALIFORNIA   15 Cents   December 18, 1965

KRLA ARCHIVES

KRLA BEAT

Los Angeles, California — December 18, 1965

Send Us a Listing Of Favorite Oldies

Among all the thousands and thousands of records released in previous years, a few are so outstanding and steeped in memories that it brings a lump to the throat or quickens the heart whenever you hear them.

And KRLA wants you to be able to hear them. That's why we're providing the request form below, so that we'll know the one you want us to play.

Please do KRLA a favor — and yourself a favor as a listener — by sending us a list of your ten all-time favorites among the oldie records which were release more than six months ago.

If you wish, you may list more than ten by adding the others on a separate sheet of paper. It will help if you can remember the artist who performed each number, but it isn't necessary.

Return your request form quickly, for the sooner we recieve it the sooner we can begin playing the ones on your list.

Mail to: KRLA Klassics, 1401 S. Oak Knoll, Pasadena, Calif.

Please play the following records — my favorites among all the oldies from previous years.

RECORD TITLE	ARTIST
1.	
2.	
3.	
4.	
5.	
6.	
7.	
8.	
9.	
10.	

MY NAME _____ AGE ___ SCHOOL _____
HOME ADDRESS _____ CITY ___ STATE ___

REJECT MOVIE SCRIPT

Beatles Quiet

By Louise Criscione

The Beatles have a new single out. Another number one I'm sure. But what have they been up to since they tore across the U.S. last August? They've kept pretty quiet, haven't they?

Of course, they did cause quite an uproar when they appeared before the Queen to receive their MBE's. And they also evoked a murmur of controversy when they refused to appear in the Royal Variety Show several weeks ago.

But besides the record, the MBEs and the Royal Show the Beatles have kept well out of the public's eye. They were originally scheduled to begin their third movie, "A Talent For Loving," immediately upon their return from America.

However, the film was postponed for several reasons. The official explanation given was that the weather in Spain (where "Talent" was to be filmed) was highly unreliable during that time of year.

Beatles Unhappy

But conflicting reports leaked out of London. The weather was not the real reason at all. The Beatles were, and apparently still are, a bit dissatisfied with the script as it stands.

If you've read the book, you'll know why. The plot just isn't enough to base a successful Beatle movie on. With a little rewriting, though, it is fairly certain that the Beatles will go ahead and film "A Talent For Loving" as their third movie venture.

The Beatles didn't shed any tears over the postponement. It meant some unexpected free time

(Turn to Page 16)

Inside the BEAT

Rolling Stone Tour	3
Agents of G.R.O.O.V.E.	5
Everlys On Tour	6
Eric's Kind Of Life	7
Another Liverpool?	8
British Top 10	11
'In Crowd' Upset	12
For Girls Only	13
Praise & Protest	14
Dear Susan	15
Hollywood Report	16

The BEAT is published weekly by BEAT Publications, Inc., editorial and advertising offices at 6290 Sunset Blvd., Suite 504, Hollywood, California 90028. U.S. bureaus in Hollywood, San Francisco, New York, Chicago and Nashville; overseas correspondents in London, Liverpool and Manchester, England. Sale price, 15 cents. Subscription price: U.S. and possessions, $3 per year; Canada and foreign rates, $9 per year. Application to mail at second class postage rates is pending at Los Angeles, California.

COVER-UP JOB — Dave Hull, known far and wide for his modesty, throws a protective jacket over the famous bronze statue in the lobby of the Moulin Rouge which is re-opening as Dave Hull's Hullabaloo. The new teen night club, known as the "rock and roll showplace of the world," marks its Dec. 8 grand opening by hosting the First Annual Pop Music Awards.

BEAT Photo: Robert Custer

'Who' Not Splitting Up; 'Rubbish,' Says Manager

Why is it that when a group makes it big someone always starts rumors that they are splitting up?

This time the rumors are aimed at the Who, who have finally got a hit with their release of "My Generation." The rumors are flying around London and Wales that 20-year-old singer Roger Daltrey is leaving the group.

Chris Stamp, co-manager of the English group, has repeatedly denied the rumors.

"Quite seriously I've never heard such a lot of rubbish. Does anybody in their right mind think the Who would split at a time like this?

"Everybody knows there is a conflict within the group, and there have been some hefty rows lately, but this doesn't mean that the group will bust up.

"They just argue about their sound and talk about all the things they want to achieve soundwise. They each have different ideas. If any of them went through with it we'd probably see a 20-piece orchestra backing the Who, with seven drummers and nine guitarists or something.

"The Who, once and for all, are not breaking up."

Big Response Indicated For Pop Awards

Heavy response from performers, executives and others within the record industry indicated solid support and a heavy turnout for the First Annual Pop Music Awards Poll Dec. 8, sponsored by KRLA and *The BEAT*.

Ballot-counting continued right up to the last minute as extra postal deliveries brought in tens of thousands of additional votes for the outstanding pop musical contributions of 1965.

The event, which brought star performers and record industry representatives pouring into Hollywood from throughout the world, was also designated as grand opening for Dave Hull's Hullaballoo, which served as host for the awards dinner.

The Hullabaloo, located at 6230 Sunset, was previously known as the Moulin Rouge — one of the largest and plushest night clubs in the world and a perfect setting for the pop awards banquet.

Next week *The BEAT* will have a complete report on the Pop Music Awards, including an announcement on the winners in each category as selected by you, the readers.

DEADLINE'S HERE FOR SENDING MAIL BEFORE CHRISTMAS

If you're planning to remember your favorite star at Christmas, now is the hour to start doing something about your plans.

The mail slows down to a snail's pace during the holiday season, and if you intend to send anything larger than a card, better rob that piggy bank and get your morsel on its way.

If you don't know the address of his record company or movie studio, send your cards in care of *The BEAT* and we'll forward them for you.

THE KNICKERBOCKERS IN ACTION are like no other group. Besides wailing "Lies, Lies" the boys also manage to do take-offs on other performers and come up sounding more like the Beach Boys than the Beach Boys do! Besides sending "Lies, Lies" bounding up the nation's charts, the Knickerbockers have also recorded an album which will be titled after their hit and which should be out in time for Christmas.

BEAT Photo: Chuck Boyd

KRLA ARCHIVES

Rolling Stone Tour Contin

By Louise Criscione

And so the Rolling Stone tour rolls on, facing capacity crowds every night at every stop. What a feather in the cap for the five boys who once toured America to sparsely filled auditoriums and criticism everywhere they went.

I caught up with the Stones in New York several days after they had arrived. They were ecstatic and they had a right to be. They had just heard the news that "Get Off Of My Cloud" had reached number one in both America and England. They had driven from the airport to the hotel and had met up with a huge illuminated picture of themselves high atop Times Square.

It was the most fantastic reception that they had ever received in America and quite naturally they were pleased. I suppose through all of their excitement their minds couldn't help wandering back to that first Stateside visit.

That was the trip they were looking forward to so much. Of course, they were worried about how they would be received. After all, they weren't that big in America and as Mick said: "America's so vast."

They were determined to make a go of it in the U.S. They knew that if they could only make it here, there'd be no stopping them.

There is really no use reopening old wounds. You all know that for the most part that first tour went the disaster route. But it did serve a definite purpose. It made the Stones realize that America was a hard place to conquer but that it *was* possible to conquer it.

Because of that first trip they became known to the U.S. teenagers as five distinct individuals with names and personalities of their own. They were no longer just the Rolling Stones. They were people.

When they left the U.S. with the pain of the Hollywood Palace still hot, at least they had the satisfaction of knowing that they had made some fans.

Teenagers who sympathized with the horrible way in which the Stones had been treated rallied to their side. And never forgot.

"The Usual"

Screaming, fainting, crashing through barricades and policemen stopping the shows. "The usual," Bob Bonis told me whan I again caught up with the Stones in Dallas.

There have been some funny moments for the Stones too. They were in New York during the recent power failure. Luckily, it was a day off so they were not forced to cancel any of their shows.

But the five Stones were spread all over the city when the power went out. Charlie was shopping. Keith was out somewhere and made it back to the hotel via the public bus. Which must have been some sight with all the young bus riders blowing their minds because a live Rolling Stone was aboard.

It was their one night off and they had originally planned on throwing a party at one of New York's largest discotheques. With the lights out, the party was can-

...THE ROLLING STONES SAY THEY ARE THE DIVIDING LINE BETWEEN ART AND COMMERCE — BUT THE BEAT SAYS THEY ARE THE GREATEST GROUP AROUND!

KRLA ARCHIVES

ues Triumphantly Along

BEAT Photos: Robert W. Young

... "Think she'd like this pair, Keith?"

... Brian glances through "Peanuts" while Bill just looks.

ceiled and so the Stones spent a swinging night sitting around by candlelight—talking.

Outdrew Beatles

One of their biggest triumphs on this tour to date occurred in Boston where they outdrew the Beatles both in attendance and in money.

They've been making their personal appearances by using various modes of transportation. Probably the funniest was in Fort Worth.

Being Texas, naturally the place where they were appearing was huge in the extreme. There was no feasible way of getting the Stones from the dressing room to the stage without getting them all killed.

So they did the only logical thing. They used an armored truck to drive the Stones out to the stage through the packed auditorium.

During this tour the Stones have seen the release of their newest album, "December's Children," tear up the album charts. Obviously, they are completely knocked out especially because as it is their fastest selling LP yet.

Violins, Mick?

One of the tracks off the album, "As Tears Go By," has stirred up quite a bit of controversy. Without a doubt, it is the most played track on the entire album.

What is causing the controversy is the fact that Mick is backed up by strings. No one ever thought that they would hear Mick singing with violins, even though he does have Keith's expert guitar playing behind him as well.

A few critics are crediting the Stones with pulling a Beatles. Refering, or course, to the string backing on "Yesterday."

But the Stones declare that they are not pulling a Beatles at all. The string backing was the only possible way of doing the song justice. Somehow "As Tears Go By" just wouldn't be the same wailed in the usual Jagger manner with the Stones usual R&B backing.

So, the Stones' tour continues to roll—packing more houses, evoking more screams, causing more officials to turn prematurely grey.

I think hysteria is the word. Stone-style, of course.

... The classic "Charlie Look" — unruffled.

... Bill — Still looking.

KRLA ARCHIVES

...THE ASSOCIATION

Meet The Association Agents Of G.R.O.O.V.E.

By Barri

There's a powerful organization lurking just around the corner, and it isn't undercover anymore. They are out to capture the attention and approval of every single human being in the world, so you'd better watch out. Their name? *The Association!*

They are six in number and bountiful in talent and headed right for success with a capital "S"! If you were to be confronted by them in the corner grocery store, you would find yourself confronted by Jim Yester, Gary Alexander, Ted Bushell, Russ Jeguere, Terry Kirkman and Brian Cole.

If you were able to pin these master-performers—all of them licensed to entertain and delight—down for more than five minutes at a time, you might be able to tack a label of sorts upon them. But beware—they harbor a distinct aversion to tags deep within their souls and about the closest you will come to a difinition of their activities is the following statement from Agent 00Terry: "We have a jazz, folk-rock, Dixieland, several other sound-combination, making a unilateral hexagrallagram type of music singing groovy songs."

Nope—I don't understand it either, but it sounded very impressive!

All of the members of this devious organization retain certain idols within their own field of endeavor—which can be loosely defined as music—including the Beatles, Beachboys, Dylan, Rolling Stones, Fortunes, Elvis, the Motown artists, and the MFQ. And then of course there is ol' Gar—Gary Alexander, by name, who sharply resembles Doctor Zorba when he's at home!—who professes an extreme adoration of the great Ravi Shankar. He also finds Randy Sterling to be quite "groovy."

"Ol' Gar" is actually the brain-machine of the group, strongly resembling a complex computer. Snooping into his background somewhat, *The BEAT* obtained this exclusive confession from Mr. Alexander: "I was a high school drop-out, *however*—I went on to the Service where I was incarcerated in Uncle Sam's Canoe Club (literal translation: the Navy) for three years, four months, 28 days, 17 hours, and 22 minutes, in which time I took several classes in advanced mathematics, calculus, physics, and several mid-Eastern philosophies."

These are clever fellows, and in their scheme to capture the fancy of the entire world, they have come up with some amazing plans of action. In fact, the following plot was overheard in a conversation between Brian and a tall, green Coke bottle: "We have plans to publish books and everything else about some of the things we've done. We've already made up card games, such as *Association* (did you catch that sneaky little plug, there Readers?!) and another one called *Tournequet*, which is *really* crazy!" Yeah Brian—I'll bet!!

All of the boys have written music for the group and will continue to do so in the future. They have also expressed the desire to make a movie which should prove quite a simple task for the six boys, as they are all natural-born hams!!! But if you sneak up behind them in an unguarded moment, you might find them doing any number of odd things. For example, cute Beatle-haired Jim Yester: "I'm sort of an out-of-doors freak and I dig ornothology, and if I ever have the time I'll probably go back into falconry, training hawks and owls like I used to do. I like to fish an awful lot, and I dig sitting around and freaking out on classical music and that sort of thing. I like to paint a lot—not anything in particular—I just dig colors!"

These boys are *all* very colorful, and if you don't watch out for them, they are going to color your imagination with all sorts of groovy (their favorite word) ideas, such as: The Association are conquering the world! The Association are great! The Association are happening!! The Association—are *Associated!!!*

Over and out!

Troubles For Kinks

Those poor Kinks seem to go from one piece of trouble to another. It all started months ago when King split-up rumors ran rampant through the industry.

Of course, there was no truth to the rumors—but then there seldom is.

And now a huge dispute over their records has broken out which might conceivably halt all of their releases.

It seems that a music publishing company claims to have a five year contract to publish all of the Kings' songs, most of which are written by Kink Ray Davies.

However, another publishing firm has gotten a hold of what is to be the next Kink single. So, just about everyone under the sun is being sued by someone.

More Troubles

Unfortunately, the Kinks troubles don't end there, either. Larry Paige (who has some sort of connection with the Kinks but exactly what that connection is no one seems to be sure) has issued a writ against the Kinks' co-managers for alleged breach of contract.

The whole mess probably makes the Kinks wish they were back in the good old days when no one knew or really cared enough about them to issue any kind of writ.

And to put a topping on the already saturated cake, the Kinks' recent U.S. releases have been complete bombs. Guess they are discovering the hard way that the recording business is not so easy after all.

It's In The Bag
By Eden

Well, well—it looks as though the Sonny and Cher fans are up in arms at me these days for panning Sonny's record, "The Revolution Kind." Arrows shot in my direction included such sharpshooters as: "Who are *you* to condemn Sonny's records?" and the complaint: "So you have the right to 'protest' against Sonny Bono, but Sonny can't put on record what he believes in?? Until you have reached the fame these two people have—say *Hi* instead of *WHY!!!*"

Sort of strange when you think about it, isn't it? Here the Sonny and Cher fans are demanding that I allow Mr. Bono to express any and every opinion which his little heart desires, and in the same sentence, *forbidding me* to exercise the same privilege! Now, just *who* did you say is being hypocritical???

I think that Sonny would be the last one to deny the free expression of criticism—both for *and against*—anything. I have on occasion said many nice things about the talented twosome, but may I remind you that no one is perfect and occasionally we *all* make mistakes of some sort.

The important question is can we accept criticism of those mistakes with humor and understanding? Can we learn from those mistakes?

...SONNY BONO

Bad Disc

I criticized Sonny's disc—which I felt to be a bad one—with humor but certainly not with malice. Nothing which might damage the personal reputations of Sonny or Cher was included in those statements, and I think that even devout Sonny and Cher fans will concede that there must have been some element of truth to what I said, as the record has only barely dented the top thirty in some areas, and hasn't even come close to the top ten.

No, I wasn't protesting, and as far as I'm concerned—Mr. Salvatore Bono can make as many protest records as he wishes, and if they are good ones, I will be the first to say so.

But I also maintain my right to knock a "loser" and this one definitely was. By the way — I am anticipating the next good Sonny and Cher hit right along with the rest of you.

Paul's Turn

Beatle Paul has gone on record lately with his views on the protest movement, and now John-John has decided to join him in some caustic commentary. Says the authored Mr. Lennon, MBE: "If there is anything I hate it is labels such as this (protest). The 'Protest' label in particular means absoltely nothing—it's just something that the press has latched on to, and as usual is flogged to death!

"Some of the songs which appear to come under this heading are simply good songs—some are not. But personally I have no time for the 'Eve of Destruction' songs."

Poor Pauly. He just couldn't resist the opportunity to get in a few more words of scorn for the Cult Protestive, and so he took over for John.

"I think Barry McGuire's 'Eve of Destruction' is rubbish. And when I first heard it I thought it was bad. When I saw McGuire in person leaping around in those boots and growling, I just fell about!

"The Manfreds did a protest number on TV which was the end. It was so bad they must have written it themselves. The pay-off was when Paul Jones turned dramatically on the camera and said 'It's all those bad schools'—it was too much!"

Whew!! When you sound-off, you really let the steam go, don'tcha Paul-luv?! Well, so much for protest!!

* * *

Ramblings, here and there . . .

Andrew Loog (Luv that middle name!) Oldham has purchased a new home in Hampstead, England for a reported 40,000 pounds—approximately $112,000 Uncle Sam-style. Meanwhile, he is renting Noel Harrison's diggings in Hurlingham—wherever *that* is!!

Must be that "Yesterday" is the fastest standard in the history of pop music. Already it has been recorded by Tony Bennett, Andy Williams, Sarah Vaughn, Matt Munro, Marianne Faithfull, and an obscure group by the name of The Beatles. That song called "Yesterday" is certainly creating a lot of pretty tomorrows for a few talented vocalizers.

Spearking of the Four Fab Ones, their ex-chauffeur—Bill Corbett—has seen the pop-light and is now managing a group of his own called the Small Faces.

"Treat Her Right" man—Roy Head—appeared on a British telly show recently and when our Foggy Friends caught sight of his wild act, they immediately dubbed him "Rubberlegs".

Aw c'mon now. They're talking about the "good old fog of home"—namely the fog in Los Angeles, California. Dusty Springfield, recently returned to Britain from her American tour, told her British buddies: "It's not at all like the Englsh fog. It's wet and you can't really see it. But it stings the eyes and throat." Well! To think that our fog isn't good enough for her!! Listen, Miss Springfield: fog is *fog!!!*

KRLA ARCHIVES

The Everly's British Tour
A BEAT Exclusive

The Everly Brothers went, they saw and they conquered—England that is.

The two brothers from Brownie, Kentucky recently completed a smash tour of England that coincided neatly with the climb up the British charts by their latest release, "Love Is Strange."

Did the tour go over as well as they had hoped?

"Infinitely better," they both agreed. "It's no use denying that we were just a little worried on our arrival—partly because our last disc hadn't made the charts and also because we'd heard that there had been a recession in the British pop business.

"Of course, we knew that we had a hard core of fans over there and we knew we could count on them—but we wondered how we would be received by the new generation of fans who weren't around when we first came on the scene. As things turned out, we had a great tour."

Other Acts

Appearing on the tour with them were Billy J. Kramer and England's own Cilla Black and the Lionel Blair Dancers. Don and Phil had nothing but praises for the other acts.

"Cilla knocked us out every time," exclaimed Phil. "She's possibly the best girl performer in the world today. And what a character!"

"We enjoyed Billy J.'s work tremendously and the rest of the show—well, it all blended together so effectively, we're confident audiences were really well entertained." And that's what tours are for, fellows.

All in all, it was a great tour, and no one had any complaints. But

THE EVERLY BROTHERS, Don and Phil, wearing happy grins as they complete a smash English tour. It was neatly timed with the British success of their new record, "Love Is Strange." Note Phil's new hair style. It's a U.S. Marine original, but those English lasses loved it.

BILLY J. KRAMER looks a bit tired. Maybe it's cause he had a rough time trying to learn to dance the Kick.

PERT CILLA Black and Phil Everly enjoy one of the few quiet moments during the tour. Phil says Cilla's the best girl performer he's ever seen.

Don and Phil did take time out to explain why they haven't jumped on the protest wagon.

"We have no objection to protest songs—people have a right to say what they want to say. You can't put someone down in a democratic society for practicing freedom of speech.

"But for our personal taste, protest and pop don't mix. That's why we've not written a protest song—and probably never shall."

The night before the tour ended the entire cast celebrated with a swinging party at a Chesterfield hotel. Everyone had a great time but there were some close moments.

Phil caught a case of the 24 hour flu and had to leave. "I spent about 10 minutes at the party and then had to go to bed. Everybody keeps telling me what a great time I missed."

Billy J. got brave and tried the new dance called the Kick which Cilla and Lionel Blair had been demonstrating, but somehow he just couldn't seem to get the hang of it and it finally got him.

"I was doing fine," he says. "Then suddenly my foot just gave under me. I had to go to the hospital and the doctor said it was badly sprained and would take a couple of weeks before it was better."

But Billy couldn't miss the last night of the tour just because of a sprained foot so he bravely went on stage the last night and sang from atop a stool.

The tour ended and the boys came home after promising to go back again next year. But before they left Phil asked all the friends he'd made in England to keep their eyes open for a genuine antique four poster bed for him.

"I must have one of those crazy beds," he laughed. "I'm looking for the Elizabethan style of thing, with curtains all around it."

PHIL EVERLY smiles from the head of the bus they used during the tour. The second girl back on the left is Cilla wearing Audrey Hepburn sun glasses. Wonder what the guy sitting next to her is looking at that perturbs him so much?

DON EVERLY changes clothes for about the millionth time. The boys really had a great time on the British tour.

KRLA ARCHIVES

TIPS TO TEENS

Q: *I have very naturally curly hair and I hate it! Could you please give me the name of a product that will straighten my hair without my having to go to the beauty parlor? During damp weather, my hair gets so frizzy, I can't do anything with it. It won't even stay combed!*

(Mary M.)

A: There are several such products. Take a look at what one of the larger department stores has to offer along these lines and then ask the cosmetic clerk to suggest the best straightener. But, don't forget that naturally curly hair can be very attractive if it isn't too long. Long hair may be in style, but it's a lot better to be pretty than it is to be fasionable if you have to choose between the two.

Q: *I met a member of a certain English group who is my same age. He gave me the number where they would be when they come back in town, and a certain password to say so someone would call him to the phone. And he said not to forget to call. Now I'm getting worried that it'll look too forward if I do call when he comes back. After all, he has my phone number also.*

(Barbara T.)

A: In a case like this, we suggest you go right ahead and call. He asked you to, and besides, if you don't, he might get very busy and forget to telephone you. And you know how phone numbers have a habit of getting lost. By the way, we sure wish you'd have told us what group he's with. We're practically dying of curiousity!

Q: *I really have a problem. Whenever I apply lipstick, it becomes dry in just a few minutes and starts cracking. Is there anything I can do to clear up this embarrassing problem?*

(Joanne Q.)

A: First of all, try buying one of the many lipsticks with a lanolin base. If this doesn't solve your problem, use Blistex under your lipstick for a few days. That will clear up the problem. And an occasional application of same when you don't even need it should help keep this condition from returning.

Q: *This may be a dumb problem, but I have it anyway. My family moved and now I'm about twice as far away from school. A lot of times I have to go out in the evening without having a chance to get home first. For some reason, this makes me feel so grubby I could scream. Can you think of something I could do to get over this feeling?*

(Adrienne P.)

A: You aren't the only one who has this "dumb" problem, and you're about to hear what may seem to outsiders as a "dumb-er" answer. When you don't have time to go home, make sure you take a moment to wash your hands and face and brush your teeth. No, we aren't on a brush after every meal crusade (although it's a good idea), but this last beauty pick-up will work wonders. Try it and you'll see.

Q: *I have a telephone in my room and I pay for it out of my babysitting money. My problem is that my younger sister just can't resist using it when I'm away from home. She always says she'll stop when I catch her (she makes toll calls yet), but then she starts up again. I'd make her pay for the calls, but her allowance is small enough as it is. What can I do?*

(Jennifer D.)

A: Buy a small padlock, then dial one of the last numbers on the dial. When the finger rest (sounds odd, but you know what we mean) is in the middle of two holes in the dial, slap on the padlock. Which just has to be the world's most confusing answer, but will work.

HINT OF THE WEEK

I've found a way to iron hair without damaging it in any way. At least it works well for me.

Just heat the iron a little bit and turn it off. Then place a cloth between your hair and the iron and iron away. Make sure you never touch your hair with the iron though, or else!

My hair is about 22 inches long and I iron every single strand of it, even my bangs.

If your mom complains about this method, assure her it's a lot better than a curling iron, and a lot safer!

(Kathy W.)

DISCUSSION
By Eden

It has been a very long while since we have heard from the Seekers, but they have returned to the Weird World of Wax with a new 45er, entitled "The Carnival is Over." The song was written for them by Tom Springfield, who is the brother of a certain Dusty. It's a good sound, although it is a little slow, and it is already climbing charts in Blightyland. Unfortunately, it shows no signs of doing too much on this side of the Atlantic.

* * *

Yes, I like it—in fact, it's very good. The new platter by the new group, The Association. Six extremely talented guys have gotten together and recorded Bobby Dylan's song, "Too Many Mornings", and it really sounds—in a word—groovy!

* * *

The Beatles have recorded two songs—"Daytripper," and "We Can Work It Out." Rumorizing produced the theory that the "A" side of this single would have Indian scales for it's basis. Hmmmm —getting a little international, are ya now? Oh well—Beatles are great in any language—and *any* scale!!!

* * *

Animal Eric Burdon ferociously attacks their latest hit, "It's My Life." Says he doesn't like it, although "now I'm beginning to get used to it." But that's not all. Eric would like to bring back the music made popular by your hero and mine—Elvis the Pelvis.

Says Mr. Burdon: "We recorded 'Heartbreak Hotel' a few weeks back and it came out with that old exciting Presley sound. Only my vocal sounded different and I tacked a 'Ah've split my jeans' on the end for a giggle." Oh, ha ha Eric, baby!

* * *

Go back a few years and see if you can recall an Everly Brothers hit titled "Bird Dog." Well, believe it or not, that same record is the number seven hit on Norway's top ten this week! Sure took that ole dog a long time to get there, but better late than never!

* * *

Sound effects: This week finds some pleasant sounds hanging 'round our town. Hang an ear lobe on "The Love Theme from the Sandpiper," by Tony Bennett. It's almost as pretty as the movie by the same name.

Chad and Jeremy have rejoined our air waves with still another of their British beauties, "I Have Dreamed." A very "dreamy" record, to be sure.

Another of those blond-and-British types from over the pond is sigh-guy Adam Faith, and he has a hit-disc on its way with "I'm Used To Losing You." I like it.

Gerry and the Pacemakers have also returned from an extended absence on the American pop scene with "Walk Hand In Hand." This one is not only beautiful, but great.

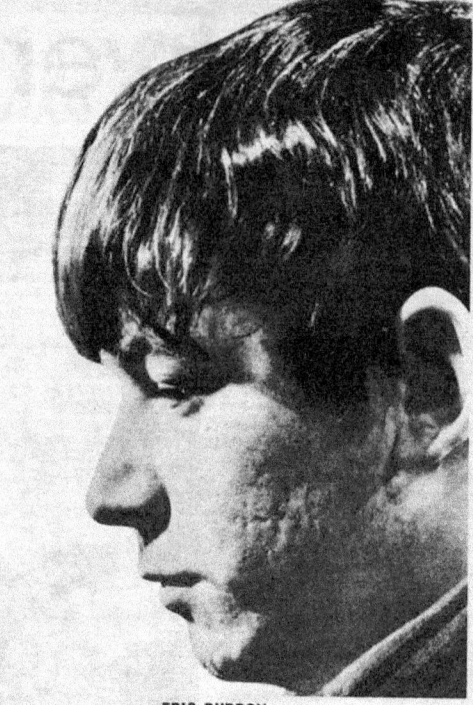

... ERIC BURDON

Eric Describes Real Animal Life

By Barri

Eric Burdon, chief Animal-in-residence, never has been one for conventionality—wherever *that* may be. However, he really seems to have taken a trip off the deep end recently when he was asked to describe his life and the world in which he lives.

The BEAT notes that Eric claims "It's My Life" in his latest hit disc with the Animals, but just what kind of life *is* that, Mr. Burdon?

"It's full of contrasts. One moment it's a kind of Cinemascope, Technicolor World out in Beverly Hills. It's a world where you can't order bacon and eggs without the waiter wanting to know if you like them 'sunny-side up, light-weight, flipped' or the bacon 'streaky, side rasher or ham.'

"It's a wonderful world full of luxury and expensive surrounds, where you meet the Mayor of Mississippi, wo is an ordained minister and swears like a trooper and your recording company representative was once Frank Sinatra's road manager.

"It's a world where you are talking on the phone to your own idol Ray Charles. He's telling me how much he digs the Animals and how he hopes we can meet personally next time we come to the States!

"He tells me about his own recording company, Tangerine, and I tell him that I want to write about him in my book.

"Suddenly everything goes bang and you find yourself flying back to London in a jet at 500 miles an hour. There's a TV set above your plane seat. The whole world is flashing by.

"Suddenly, bang again! You're arriving in a dirty old van with autographed messages scrawled all over it at the TV studios, and you pull up next to a hired Austin Princess, in which the Rolling Stones travel. No one believes that you still ride around in that dirty old wagon.

"Next moment you are changing in a sweaty little room in the back of a club where you're lucky if you can grab a coke and a hamburger. No one waits on you. There's no palatial hotel and if you're lucky you get to bed some place in the early morning.

"It's a great scene for us. It teaches you never to become big-headed. You make the best of both worlds and you can get as big a kick playing in those little clubs as the Hollywood Bowl.

"The pace is the most frightening thing."

Yes, it does seem just a little terrifying, Eric. Well, anybody care to be a pop star?!!

No Truth To P&G Rumors

Peter and Gordon's latest release in England, "Baby I'm Yours," is doing great and Peter thinks that's great because it'll end some of the rumors that the two are splitting.

"There's been some comment that Gordon sings more on this disc than I. I think that is all to the good—it should kill those rumors about him going solo. He's already a star on his own . . ."

"WE'RE ABSOLUTELY DELIGHTED that you liked our record, 'You're Absolutely Right,'" exclaim the Apollos after their recent hit.

KRLA ARCHIVES

Bay Area – Another Liverpool?

San Francisco is a city of bright lights and beatniks and beginnings. Many of America's most popular singing groups have left their hearts in the city by the bay and gone on to fame.

The city that sired such diverse entertainers as Johnny Mathis, the Kingston Trio and Phyllis Diller is also the home grounds of the Beau Brummels, We Five, Vejtables, Grass Roots, Mojo Men and many others.

Beau Brummels

The Beau Brummels not only live in the Bay Area but were discovered by former disc jockies Tom Donahue and Bob Mitchell.

The two clever DJ's recognized the talent of these four guys and signed them to an exclusive management and recording contract. Their first record, "Laugh, Laugh" on the Autumn label was a nation wide best seller and put the boys on the way to the top. They followed that with "Just A Little" and "Don't Talk to Strangers" and people began to think there was more to San Francisco than folk music and demonstrations.

We Five

Another group that really brought an exciting modern pop sound to the scene is the We Five. San Franciscans all the way, these four guys and one cute girl bounded up the charts so fast with their first release that they made "You Were On My Mind" a household term.

But they didn't just "wake up this morning" and find themselves on the top. It took several years of just plain hard work in and around the Bay Area before this group felt they were ready to hit the world with their sound.

They had a bad time at first because they were trying to sell a folk sound to an already folk saturated San Francisco. But with the help of one of the group's brothers, John Stewart of the Kingston Trio, they finally found an entirely new style that made them a hit and added more to the city's reputation for turning out great acts.

... WE FIVE

Grass Roots

Another growing group from Northern California is the Grass Roots. Their first release, "Ballad of a Thin Man" or "Mr. Jones" (it goes by both titles) by Bob Dylan came out at the same time as Dylan's longer version of the same song. But these relative new comers gave the old pro Dylan a run for his money.

These four guys are loyal to their home city too. They've always been great fans of the Beau Brummels since the old days when they used to stand outside the back door of places the Brummels were playing and wait for them to come out.

Mojo Men

The Mojo Men, four college students from Florida and New York, migrated to San Francisco looking for new musical ideas and a place to try out their sound. They found it and cut their first record, "Dance With Me." These guys are getting better every day and will add even more to San Francisco's reputation as the place to be from.

The Vejtables

"I Still Love You" was the record that put another group, the Vejtables, in the national spotlight. The record shot all the way to the top and netted the four guys and one girl several nation-wide television appearances. The Vejtables are currently vying with the Dillards over "The Last Thing On My Mind," which both groups have released. Watch for the Vejtables' version to walk all over the Dillards'.

There are hundreds of groups grooming in San Francisco, and we'll undoubtedly be hearing from many of them. Groups like the Great Society, whose first release is due sometime this month, and many others who are getting their start in the city that not only "knows" but causes "what's happening."

Yep, San Francisco may just become what Liverpool used to be – *the* place to start. There's some magic quality about the city that breeds talent and success.

... MOJO MEN

... GRASS ROOTS

... BEAU BRUMMELS

KRLA ARCHIVES

It's Here! Hollywood's Moulin Rouge Becomes

DAVE HULL'S
HULLABALOO

6230 Sunset
Across from
Palladium

The Showplace of the World Becomes
The <u>Rock & Roll</u> Showplace of the World

The Sensational! PALACE GUARD

Plus

The World's Top Recording Stars

(Follow The BEAT for details on scheduled Guest Appearances)

Plus
★ Continuous entertainment—on three stages—Including one of the world's great revolving center stages!
★ Continuous dancing—Good Food—All the Glamor and Showmanship of Hollywood's Finest.
★ Home of the Rock & Roll Hall of Fame—Footprints, Handprints and Momentos of the great rock stars.

ROCK WITH DAVE HULL AT THE HULLABALOO
NO MINIMUM—NO COVER—ALL FOR $1.50 ADMISSION

Host of 1st Annual Pop Music Awards Dinner Dec. 8

KRLA ARCHIVES

Inside KRLA

Just recently, a 13-year-old boy from La Mirada, Calif., paid a visit to KRLA and a happier young man than Mike Sandoval just couldn't have been found.

Mike was the winner of the "Say KRLA" contest, in which he won $3,150. Along with his parents and his sister and younger brother, he had come to the studio to meet all of the KRLA DJ's and receive his fabulous prize.

Mike's father told *The BEAT* that it was actually Mike's sister—Mary—who had begun answering the phone with "KRLA," but Mike assured us that he had been saying KRLA for two or three weeks before he hit the jackpot.

Mike seems to be a very level-headed young man for his 13 years, and when we asked him what he intended to do with his prize money, he said: "I'm going to use most of it for my education. My Dad is also thinking of putting some of it in stocks and bonds for me."

When Mike first found out that he was the winner, he promptly ran to tell his father: "Dad—I think I just won $3,000." Mr. Sandoval told *The BEAT*—"I was under the car in the garage at the time, and I got up and said, "Mike—let's go inside and have a talk.""

Congratulations to Mike from *The BEAT* and from KRLA—where *all* the winners are!

Big news from the Hullabalooer. He has just moved into a new home in the highlands of Arcadia. It's a beautiful rustic ranch-chalet with a fantastic living room complete with a huge fireplace in the center of the room, which is *twice* the size of the control booth at KRLA! That should make for some kind of marshmallow roasting, Hullabalooer!

During the recent rainstorm, blue-eyed Bob Eubanks had a rather weird experience. He was sitting in his home in Hidden Hills when suddenly he saw his pool talbe fly past the window. Quipped Robert: "The only thing that was so unusual about that is that we live on the *17th floor!!*"

Hey—watch out for flying saucers, everyone! They're coming in for a landing and KRLA's got them!!

Don't be surprised if you cast your orbs heavenward some eve and discover a large, round, red object hovering in the heavens. It will be one of the KRLA flying saucers, piloted by Captain Showbiz or one of the KRLA DJ's.

However, if you are unable to follow their stratospheric sojourns—you will be able to get a glimpse of them at some of the parades and community projects in which KRLA will be participating in the future. So *beware*—the Saucers are coming!

An awfully nice Yule-type project belongs to Bob Eubanks this year. "I'm going to pick an underprivileged family and give them a Christmas this year. I'll make sure that the kids will have nice toys and bicycles and things."

KRLA Tunedex

DAVE HULL

BOB EUBANKS

DICK BIONDI

JOHNNY HAYES

EMPEROR HUDSON

CASEY KASEM

CHARLIE O'DONNELL

BILL SLATER

This Week	Last Week	Title	Artist
1	1	LET'S HANG ON	Four Seasons
2	2	STILL I'M SAD/I'M A MAN	The Yardbirds
3	9	LIES, LIES	The Knickerbockers
4	4	1-2-3	Len Barry
5	3	I HEAR A SYMPHONY	The Supremes
6	6	TASTE OF HONEY/3RD MAN THEME	Herb Alpert
7	11	RISING SUN	The Deep Six
8	24	EBB TIDE	Righteous Brothers
9	17	IT'S MY LIFE	The Animals
10	5	TURN, TURN, TURN	The Byrds
11	13	I CAN NEVER GO HOME ANYMORE	The Shangri-Las
12	31	FLOWERS ON THE WALL	Statler Brothers
13	26	RUN, BABY, RUN	The Newbeats
14	8	I GOT YOU	James Brown
15	7	GET OFF OF MY CLOUD	Rolling Stones
16	30	YOU DIDN'T HAVE TO BE SO NICE	Lovin' Spoonful
17	12	LET ME BE	The Turtles
18	16	HANG ON SLOOPY	Ramsey Lewis Trio
19	18	PIED PIPER	The Changin' Times
20	19	OVER AND OVER	Dave Clark Five
21	32	THE LITTLE GIRL I ONCE KNEW	Beach Boys
22	33	ENGLAND SWINGS	Roger Miller
23	23	MY GIRL HAS GONE	The Miracles
24	—	I WILL	Dean Martin
25	35	I FOUGHT THE LAW	Bobby Fuller Four
26	—	STAND BY ME	Earl Grant
27	40	THE SOUNDS OF SILENCE	Simon & Garfunkel
28	34	HERE IT COMES AGAIN	The Fortunes
29	—	LETS GET TOGETHER	We Five
30	—	YOUNG GIRL	Noel Harrison
31	—	MY BABY	The Temptations
32	—	SHE'S JUST MY STYLE	Gary Lewis & The Playboys
33	39	THE DUCK	Jackie Lee
34	38	THUNDERBALL/KEY TO MY HEART	Tom Jones
35	37	ALL OR NOTHING	Patti LaBelle
36	—	BUCKAROO	Buck Owens
37	—	MY GENERATION	The Who
38	—	I SEE THE LIGHT	Five Americans
39	—	WE CAN WORK IT OUT/DAY TRIPPER	The Beatles
40	—	JENNY TAKE A RIDE	Mitch Ryder & The Detroit Wheels

HELP!

HELP!
I'm collecting pictures and articles on Sonny and Cher to plaster in my room. If anyone has extras please send to Lisa Hurley, 20635 Londelius St., Canoga Park, Calif.

HELP!
Our band is in need of a bass guitar player. Must own guitar and amp, be 13 to 16 and live in Inglewood area. Write Rick Heltebrake, The Castles, 1222 S. Inglewood, Calif.

HELP!
Lost at Aug. 30th Beatle performance in Sec. F., a reply from Louise Harrison. It was a postcard of the Fab Four, their signatures and a note on the back addressed to "Rose." Please return to Rose Perezselsky, 2009 Summerland, San Pedro, Calif.

HELP!
My hobby is collecting pictures of Donovan. Any duplicates would be appreciated. Fay Metze, 2430 Chatsworth Blvd., San Diego, Calif.

HELP!
Anyone having the back issue of *The BEAT* containing the interview with George Harrison please notify Mary Cisniros, 3231 Pasadena Ave., Los Angeles, Calif. I will be glad to pay for it.

OPENING DEC. 7
Hoyt Axton

OPENING DEC. 21
Joe & Eddie

CLOSING SUN., DEC. 5—BUD & TRAVIS

...At Doug Weston's
Troubadour
9083 Santa Monica Blvd. at Doheny, L.A.
STUDENT DISCOUNT—MINORS WELCOME
RESERVATIONS CR 6-6168

TIM MORGON'S
DIRTY FEET
Showing
Dec. 26-30 (8:00 p.m.)
COSMOS FOLK CLUB
Seal Beach, Calif.
Phone: 596-4132 For Reservations

SONGWRITERS

A survey has been made to determine which Publishers will review songs of new writers. A list has been compiled containing 151 names and addresses of those who have indicated they will. List shows who will take leads only; who will take tape, and those wanting demos. Where known, list shows whether ASCAP or BMI, and type songs wanted. Price $1.00. Also available at $1.50 is Folio of 27 songs in popular and contemporary style. Frank D. Grace, 1726 Crest Dr., Los Angeles, Calif. 90035.

KRLA BEAT Subscription

SPECIAL OFFER—Deadline Jan. 1
SAVE 60% Of Regular Price
☐ 1 YEAR—52 ISSUES—$3.00
Enclosed is $3.00 ☐ CASH ☐ CHECK
Send to:..Age..........
Address:...
City..........................State..........Zip................
MAIL YOUR ORDER TO:
KRLA BEAT
6290 Sunset, Suite 504
Hollywood, Calif. 90028
Foreign Rate: $14.00—52 Issues

GIFT SUBSCRIPTION

Please send a one-year gift subscription to:
_____
Who lives at:_____
City:_____ State:_____ Zip:_____
Send a card saying it is from:_____

Enclose $3 for each subscription. Mail to:
KRLA BEAT, Suite 504, 6290 Sunset, Hollywood, Calif 90028

KRLA ARCHIVES

Adventures of Robin Boyd
By Shirley Poston

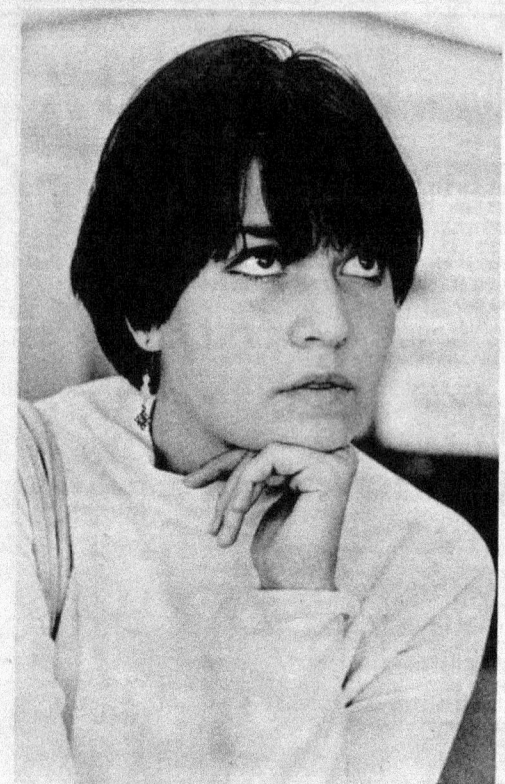

BEAT Photo: Chuck Boyd
WATCHA THINKING so hard about Beverly Bivens? She's probably concentrating on what to wear for the We Five's next stop on the Dick Clark Caravan which the group has been touring with for the past several weeks. Of course, she could also be wondering about how the Five's current release, "Let's Get Together" is doing nationally. Needn't worry, Bev, it's doing just fine.

CHAPTER SIX

Ringo leaped to his feet, breaking one drumstick and both ankles (well, it *felt* like it), and raced into the next room.

He found John staring at a very ordinar-looking window sill. There was not, as his leader had just stated, a bird (*real*) there, wearing *glasses*.

"It's flown off," John explained with a nervous gesture.

Ringo groaned inwardly. Also outwardly. "When did you first start feeling feverish?" he questioned with much genteleness, his eyes roaming the room in search of a thermometer.

John turned to him. "I'm in love with you and I feel fine," he answered without much genetleness. "And *I did* see a real bird at the window wearing *glasses*."

"The bird or the window," Ringo laughed jovially, certain that John would *never* guess that he was attempting to change the subject by passing the whole thing off as a joke.

"You're attempting to change the subject by passing the whole thing off as a joke," John guessed, taking careful aim at Ringo's shin with an ultra-pointed winkle-picker.

"You'd best not kick Ringo in the shin with an ultra-pointed winkle-picker," George adivsed helpfully from the doorway of the adjoining room. "You'd only break it."

"The ultra-pointed winkle-picker, that is," Paul advised helpfully.

"And then what would you wear to pick winkles in?", Ringo advised helpfully.

"Drop dead, the lot of you," John advised helpfully, preparing to kick all *three* in the shins with an ultra-pointed winkle-picker.

But, just then, a knock came at the door. "Five minutes," came the well-known message. And birds-at-the-window and winkle-pickers were forgotten as the familiar rush began.

Forgotten by all except John, that is, who peered at the window on his way out, and left the room fearing for his sanity.

Had he been able to see just *outside* the window, he would have stopped being fearful. He would have become *hysterical*. For, clinging frantically to the stoney exterior of the London Palladium *was* a *real* bird wearing *glasses*. (No one is perfect.)

"Whew," whooshed Robin Boyd as she heard the dressing room doors slam behind the Beatles. That had been a close call!

She hadn't inteded for John to actually *see* her, not in bird form anyway.

As she hopped back to the window sill and flexed her feathers, she vowed never to be so careless again. In fact, she was going to say the magic word and turn herself right back into her sixteen-year-old self this very minute!

And she would have if she hadn't heard a deafening roar of approval.

The *Beatles* were on *stage!* The concert was beginning! Without her! And, completely forgetting who she was (or *what*), Robin flew through the transom and flapped wildly down the deserted halls.

Moments later she was perched high to the left of the stage, cheering with the rest of the audience.

(She'd tried applauding and had nearly landed atop Ringo's bass drum as a result.)

And there they were. The *Beatles!* In *action!*

And she was so *close* to them. She could see George grinning just a little at the corner of his mouth as he concentrated on playing lead. And Paul bouncing tuffly. And Ringo's hair swinging to the beat. And *John*. She was practially right *above* her John, who looked absolutely *marvelous* in spite of a rather glazed gleam in his eyes.

Needless to say, Robin gasped extra noisily when it was John's turn to announce the next song.

"I've had many requests about this coming number, but I'm going to sing it anyway," John quipped, placing his guitar pick between his teeth in a familiar gesture. "Paul usually does it, you know. It's called 'Til There Was You'."
Robin fainted (briefly) (you'd better believe it) and John began.

Everything went smoothly for the first chorus. Then it happened.

It happened when John had just finished warbling the line . . . "there were birds on the sill" . . .

Then he suddenly stopped warbling and turned as white as a sheet.

Oh no, Robin thought in panic. John, it's not birds on the *sill!* It's birds on the *hill!*

Regaining some of his composure, John re-placed the guitar pick between his teeth in a familiar gesture.

"I've forgotten the next line" he drawled, trying to appear relaxed when he looked more like he wanted to throw himself into a corner and sob bitterly.

Fighting off the urge to throw *herself* into a corner and sob bitterly, Robin suddenly realized what she must do.

After a few preliminary flutters, she flew onto the stage at supersonic speeds.

"John," she hissed into his ear as she shot past him. "The next line is 'but I never saw them winging'."

John looked up.

"Thank you," he said politely. Then he turned white as *six* sheets and swallowed the guitar pick in an unfamiliar gesture.

(To Be Continued Next Week)

Len Knocks Out Stones

Our own Len Barry has done it – knocked the Stones out of the number one spot which they have been holding down for the past several weeks.

Len's "1-2-3" has been steadily climbing up the British charts and we knew it would only be a matter of time before this talented South Philadelphian captured the coveted number one.

It's a toss-up over who will be the next number oner. Both the Seekers with "The Carnival Is Over" and The Who with "My Generation" are sure bets to gain the top spot. This week they stand at number two and number three respectively.

Falling down after long chart residencies are the Stones and "Get Off Of My Cloud" and "Yesterday Man" by Chris Andrews. This week finds the Stones at number four and Chris at number five.

Another American group, The Toys, are still climbing the charts with their "Lover's Concerto." In the U.S. it's dropping off but in England it jumped up this week from number ten to number six.

Cliff Richard, England's answer to Elvis Presley, has yet another hit. This time around it's "Wind Me Up" traveling from number 13 to number eight.

Bob Dylan has managed to get his "Positively 4th Street" into the top ten this week at number ten. Dylan has been on the British charts with the song for ages now and it looked like he would eventually drop off without ever having dented the top ten. But being typically Dylan – he surprised us all.

British Top 10

1.	1-2-3	Len Barry
2.	THE CARNIVAL IS OVER	The Seekers
3.	MY GENERATION	The Who
4.	GET OFF OF MY CLOUD	Rolling Stones
5.	YESTERDAY MAN	Chris Andrews
6.	A LOVER'S CONCERTO	The Toys
7.	TEARS	Ken Dodd
8.	WIND ME UP	Cliff Richard
9.	IT'S MY LIFE	The Animals
10.	POSITIVELY 4th STREET	Bob Dylan

Toys Signed For 1st Film

The Toys, who recently soared up the charts with their "Lover's Concerto," have been signed for their first film.

The trio, Barbara Harris, Barbara Parritt and June Monteiro, will join Tommy Kirk, Deborah Walley, the Animals, Castaways and Gentrys in the Paramount release "The Girl in Daddy's Bikini."

The Toys have just completed an engagement with Jackie Wilson and are currently on a two week Christmas tour of the South, including North Carolina, Georgia and Florida.

KRLA ARCHIVES

What Next, Bill Slater?

If Bill Slater ever decides to sprout wings and fly or grow gills like a fish and live underwater, don't take any bets that he won't do it.

KRLA's all-night disc jockey entertainer has done just about everything else in his twenty-odd years and he hasn't let anything stop him yet.

Bill's ambition right now is to make the late-late and early-early hours between midnight and 6 a.m. as cheerful and enjoyable as possible for those who are awake at that strange hour. And judging by the response of KRLA listeners, he has succeeded in that also.

A check with former associates reveals that before moving to Southern California the lean, handsome Texan accomplished such things as:

(1) becoming an expert pilot while still in his teens, gaining national headlines during several search-and-rescue missions;
(2) satisfying his curiosity about the weather by studying it and becoming an accomplished meteorologist;
(3) becoming a top-flight local television director as well as a popular TV personality;
(4) realizing his ambition to become a disc jockey, moving from the all-night program to the afternoon slot and becoming the top-rated deejay in Houston, Texas—all within one year.

Frustration

Bill's only "failure" came when he attempted to set a new world marathon broadcasting record. After being on the air constantly—day and night—for a full week he came within three hours of the record. But fatigue finally took its toll and he fell unconscious at that point—in front of hundreds of spectators—and the doctor in attendance refused to let him continue.

Even that wasn't a failure, for Bill was performing the marathon for the Cystic Fibrosis Foundation and his efforts not only helped public understanding of the cruel disease but also raised a large amount of contributions for research and treatment of its victims.

Bill's wit and good-natured satirical humor make his six-hour nightly show entertaining for himself as well as his listeners. He's agreed to let The BEAT accompany him on one of his famous guided tours of "Bill's Weather Room."

You'll have to provide your own sound effects, unfortunately."

"Let's check the weather in Bill's weather room. Up the elevator, and now I'm going to explain to you just what it looks like. You'll notice the elevator is built with lemonwood and several old pear boxes you'll see on the side. Jarvis the Janitor uses this as a trash can to carry things down from the weather room into the main lobby.

Points of Interest

"Here we are at the second floor of the KRLA building, overlooking the beautiful pool and patio area, which is actually an old bird bath situated right next to the Wesatch tree, which is just below the window here which has been knocked out by a playful ball.

"Over on your left side as we walk into the main hall that leads into the weather room, there are a lot of pictures. There's one of Emperor Hudson—upside down, standing there with his crown just about to go!

"Now here's the smog machine, which I was the very

KRLA'S Bill Slater, Byrds' Gene Clark chat backstage.

first to bring up here, and it has the complete information on the smog: it says 'Yes' or 'No!'

"There are other things like this in here.

Jarvis the Janitor occasionally comes up to clean it out, and it's always a pleasure to have him up here because to tell you the truth—I've always been afraid to go up there alone!!"

Serious Side

Aside from being witty, blue-eyed and adorable, Bill also finds time to be an exceptionally compassionate human being. Recently he began taking calls from listeners to send to our boys in Viet Nam.

"About the Viet Nam thing, I thought it was a nice thing that the kids and adults did. After I'd read the letter from Robert Blattner, who is stationed in Viet Nam, over the air—I had them call and let me know if they would like to send a letter to the Marines stationed in that area.

"We made a tape recording of their calls and bundled up letters I received. I put them in a box and sent them to Viet Nam in the hopes that it would show them that we were interested in how they were feeling, and how they were doing, and that we were supporting them; that we'd like to give them some comfort if we could because we know that it's not comfortable to be in a war zone."

If you would like to join this attempt to cheer up all the guys across the sea, drop a couple of lines to them and send it in care of Bill Slater at KRLA.

In the meantime—try turning your days around a little bit, and enjoy some of the sunshine which Bill is spreading around every night.

KRLA BEAT

America's Largest Teen NEWSpaper
KRLA Edition

Volume 1, Number 41 — LOS ANGELES, CALIFORNIA — 15 Cents — December 25, 1965

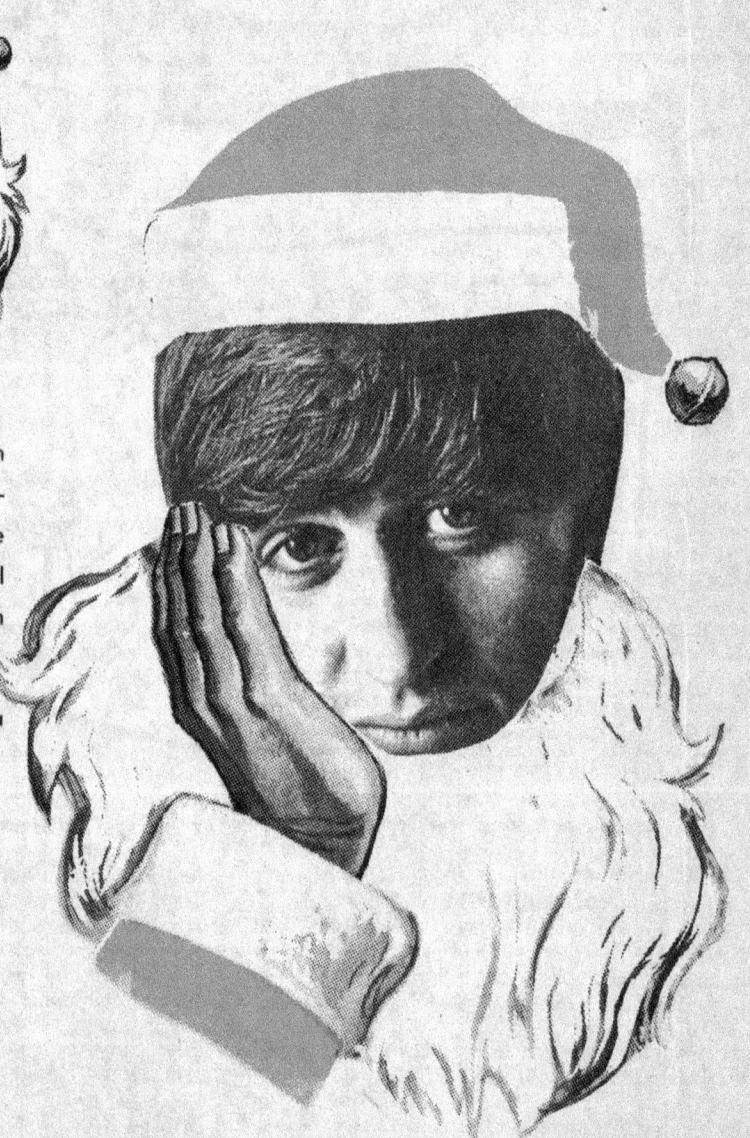

Dear Santa,

Please try to make room on your sleigh for some very special gifts which we would like to send to some very special stars. You'll find our list on pages 3 and 4.

Thanks, Santa
The BEAT

KRLA ARCHIVES

KRLA BEAT

Los Angeles, California — December 25, 1965

Christmas Greetings From the Stars to You

It's been a wonderful year for us at The BEAT—our very first year—and during this holiday season many of our friends have called, written and sent telegrams of Christmas greetings. We'd like to share some of them—a Christmas card from The BEAT to you:

"How can we ever thank all our friends at The BEAT for publishing so many stories and pictures about us this year—and all our wonderful West Coast fans who purchased our records, saw our movies and attended our performances? We're looking forward to seeing everyone at our next concert in August. Merry Christmas from the Land Down Under."
THE BEATLES

"Ever since you did that marvelous story on me in The BEAT I am always being stopped by people who want to say hello. I'd like to thank all of you and wish you all a very Merry Christmas."
ROBERT VAUGHN

"I would like to wish a very merry Christmas to all my friends who read The BEAT. Thank you for a wonderful year."
DAVID McCALLUM

"Happy holidays to all of my friends, wherever they may be ... and thank you for a wonderful year."
GARY LEWIS And The PLAYBOYS

"Holiday greetings to all. This will truly be my happiest holiday." Gratefully, **BILLY JOE ROYAL**

"May Santa bring to The BEAT and all its readers a lot of happy music for the holidays. Kris joins me in sincerely wishing everyone a Merry Christmas and a Happy New Year."
RICK NELSON

"Merry Christmas and a Happy New Year to all the readers of The BEAT. We hope to see you at some of our concerts in the coming year."
BRIAN WILSON

"I'd like to wish everybody a Merry Christmas and a happy and prosperous New Year. And I want to thank everyone for making this such a wonderful year for me."
JOEY PAIGE

"I wish I had enough money to send a Christmas card to everyone but I'll do it through The BEAT instead, especially since I found a little verse which could help the world so much if we could live with these blessings: The Spirit of Christmas—which is Peace ... the Gladness of Christmas—which is Hope ... and the Heart of Christmas—which is Love. Merry Christmas, everyone."
JIMMY O'NEILL

"Berry Mismus and Dapy New Year!!"
JAN AND DEAN

"We would like to extend our wishes for an out-of-sight holiday season to all the readers of The BEAT, and wish it our sincere thanks for all the groovy things The BEAT has said about us."
BOBBY AND BILL, THE RIGHTEOUS BROS.

"Just a plain ol' Merry Christmas and a Happy New Year to all."
JOHNNY RIVERS

(Turn to Page 7)

Inside the BEAT

Gifts for the Stars 3-4
Marvin Gaye 5
On The Beat 6
Stones' World Tour 7
Dave Clark 5 8
Robin Boyd 11
Visit with Elvis 12
T.A.M.I. Show 13-14
Liverpuddles 15
Holiday Hair Styles 16

The BEAT is published weekly by BEAT Publications, Inc., editorial and advertising offices at 6290 Sunset Blvd., Suite 504, Hollywood, California 90028. U.S. bureaus in Hollywood, San Francisco, New York, Chicago and Nashville; overseas correspondents in London, Liverpool and Manchester, England. Sale price, 15 cents. Subscription price: U.S. and possessions, $3 per year. Canada and foreign rates, $9 per year. Application to mail at second class postage rates is pending at Los Angeles, California.

MERRY CHRISTMAS FROM THE BEAT

KRLA ARCHIVES

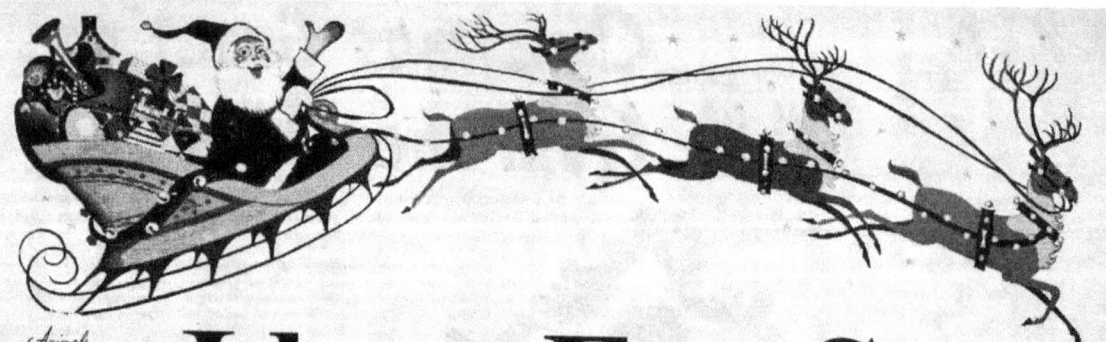

Ideas For Santa

Animals

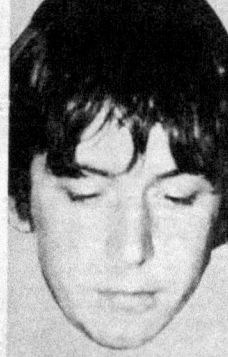

AN ANIMAL record that Eric likes, since he never likes their own music.

Bob Dylan

VOICE LESSONS

Byrds

A REVOLVING stool so they can keep on turning.

Rolling Stones...

A NEW CLOUD for the Rolling Stones, 'cause everyone tromped on their last one

Barry McQuire

THE AMERICANISM AWARD

Gary Lewis

A SKATE board since he's got 13 cars.

Beach Boys

SOME NEW surf boards.

Sonny and Cher

A ZOO so Sonny can grow his own clothes.

KRLA ARCHIVES

From The BEAT

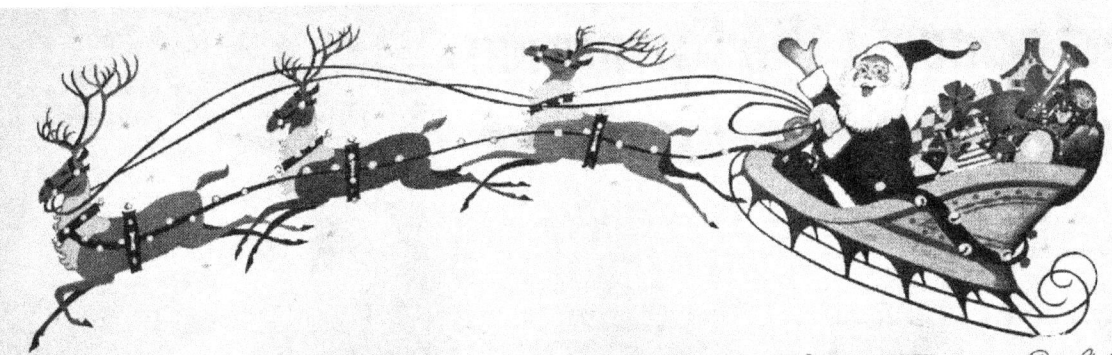

Beatles

SOME GLUE for the Beatles to paste on their "Rubber Soul"

Dave Clark

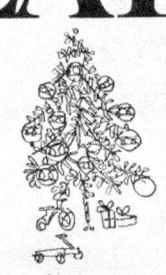

A PANCAKE flipper so they can keep turning over and over.

Herman

A NEW FANG to replace the one he lost.

Noel Harrison

A LIVE GIRL

Tom Jones

THE ENTIRE female portion of **The BEAT** staff.

Shangri-Las

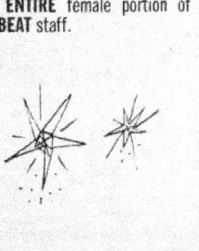

A NEW HOME and a new mother.

Righteous Bros.

A STOOL to make Bobby as tall as Bill.

Chad and Jeremy

A GIRL for Jeremy to stop the rumors that the act's splitting up.

KRLA ARCHIVES

Performer's Performance Equals Mr. Marvin Gaye

By Barri

It was a very quiet evening; it was still early and the crowds had not yet gathered. Inside the elegant hotel a very quiet calm reigned over the plush gold interior.

My knock on the door was the only break in the prevailing silence, and then a very attractive young woman opened the door, and warmly greeted me: "Hello, I'm Mrs. Gaye, won't you come in?"

Sitting comfortably on the elegant golden couch was a young man quietly speaking to someone on the phone. He quickly finished his conversation and we were introduced. Then Marvin Gaye sat quietly back and began to think about the first question which I had asked him.

"What kind of songs do I like to sing? It really doesn't matter; I enjoy singing rhythm and blues, and whatever success I have had has come to me through R 'n' B. I also enjoy singing ballads."

A television set in the corner of the room was tuned to a popular spy-western series, and a sudden series of gunshots attracted Marvin's attention. Turning back to me, he continued discussing the Motown sound. "I definitely feel that there *is* a Motown sound. We might change it a little here and there with each different artist, but there is definitely a distinct Motown sound.

"I change quite a bit, and I feel that an artist like myself can't afford to stay in the shadows of himself for too long. I intend to touch on *every* part of this musical industry. I want to try *every* musical sound."

Marvin noticed my amusement at his great absorption with the TV set in the corner, and he laughingly confessed, "I'm a TV fiend!" But he also went on about some other loves: "I like to play golf, and I love animals. I had a little puppy, but he died after he choked on a chicken bone. I've wanted to get another dog, but somehow I just couldn't. I'm sort of a one-dog man!"

The sound on the TV set died away as the scene became very quiet. Marvin, too, seemed quiet as he reflected on some of the different sounds in the music industry today.

"I like 75% of the British groups today. I think that the Beatles are great. Not because they are *said* to be great, but because of their musicianship, writing ability, and because of their subtle originality.

"Protest songs? I think I like them because I like any artist or any writer who shows an ounce of guts! I think it shows extreme originality and intelligent thought.

"I've written music like *nobody's* written music! I've written symphonies and Broadway production things and play scores. I think that next to singing, I'm closest to music. I like to fool around with different instruments — I can play the guitar, the piano, drums, and an instrument like a flute, called a 'recorder.'

"I wrote all three of my first hit records — 'Pride and Joy', 'Hitchhike', and 'Stubborn Kind of Fellow.' I also wrote 'Dancing in the Street' for Martha and the Vandellas, and the Marvellettes first hit, 'Beachwood 45789.'

Hates Writing

"I've got such a thing with writing — I *hate* to write. I hate the actual physical writing; I'd like to *dictate* — but writing is just agony! I would like to write a book, though."

Marvin had done a lot of thinking and in his own quiet way a great deal of talking. Now, he was silent once again. Watching the TV in the corner as the action came to a climax.

He laughs very easily and communicates with other people very effortlessly. There is no strain to understand what he is saying when he speaks, although his every word is interesting.

He used his gentle sense of humor as he talked about things he would *like* to do: "I'd like to make a movie and use karate. I think I'd make a *great* spy!!

Scientist

"If I had my choice of another career — I would become a research scientist technician and find cures for diseases and things. I love chemistry and science."

Marvin lounged comfortably on the plush golden couch and summed up his whole attitude with a few words of philosophy: "I don't really look forward to a lot of glamorous things — I kind of take life easy. I just like to sit and listen and take whatever comes to me, and accept whatever the good Lord has in store for me."

The hour had grown later now, and the TV program was over. Marvin had finished talking and the only words left unspoken were the farewells. In just a few minutes, Marvin would change clothes and leave for the club where he was currently appearing.

It was quiet now in this pale, golden suite, but in just a few moments, the gentle, quiet young man would pick up a stage microphone and make a lot of noise. For Marvin Gaye is a wild, enthusiastic, noisy entertainer — when he is on stage he makes a lot of great noise!!

...AND WAILIN'

...STRUTTIN'

Dear Susan

By Susan Frisch

Does Marianne Faithfull have any pets? —Denise Sovell

She has a cat named Mirella and a dog named Sara Bingley.

Who are Marianne Faithfull's favorite singers? —Bruce Loventhol

Joan Baez and Maria Callas.

Can you tell me something about Don Murray of the Turtles? —Sandy Demira

He is 19 years old. He is 5'9" and weighs 160. Has brown hair and eyes. Plays drums and harmonica.

Can you please give me the birthdates of the Byrds? —Carolyn Schell

Jim McGuinn; July 13, 1942. Mike Clarke; June 3, 1944. David Crosby; August 14, 1941. Chris Hillman; December 4, 1942. Gene Clark; November 17, 1941.

What is Mike Clark's favorite food? —Helena Gortiaz

Cheeseburgers and coke.

Who wrote Universal Soldier, the song by Donovan? —Harry Lond St.

Buffy St. Marie.

What color ties does Paul McCartney like to wear best? —Katy Tomkiss

Black ties. He thinks they're the smartest.

When was Gerry, of the Pacemakers, married? —Fran Ziegler

On October 11, 1965.

What size shoe and collar does Hilton Valentine take? —Mag Thornsey

14½ collar, and size 8 shoe.

How long has Dave Clark been married? —Rose Switzer

Who ever said he was married?

Who is Marianne Faithfull's favorite Beatle and Rolling Stone? —Cindy Kratz

Beatle Paul, and Rolling Stone Brian.

Is "Hard Days Night" and "Help" going to be released again? —Mary Jane Fletcher

Yes they are. They should be out right now, so check your local theaters.

Will the Beatle Christmas Telecast be broadcast in the States? —Mary Fletcher

No, but we're hoping for next X-mas!

Where can I write to Gene Clark and make sure he gets it personally? —Elise Bussard

Write to Gene in care of 9000 Sunset Blvd., #805, Hollywood, Calif.

Are Donna Loren and Bobby Sherman engaged? —Debbie Cutley

No. They are just good friends.

How long have Sonny and Cher been married? —Paul Ustople

For 2 years.

Is it true that Wayne Fontana and the Mindbenders broke up? —Carol Knapp

Yes.

KRLA ARCHIVES

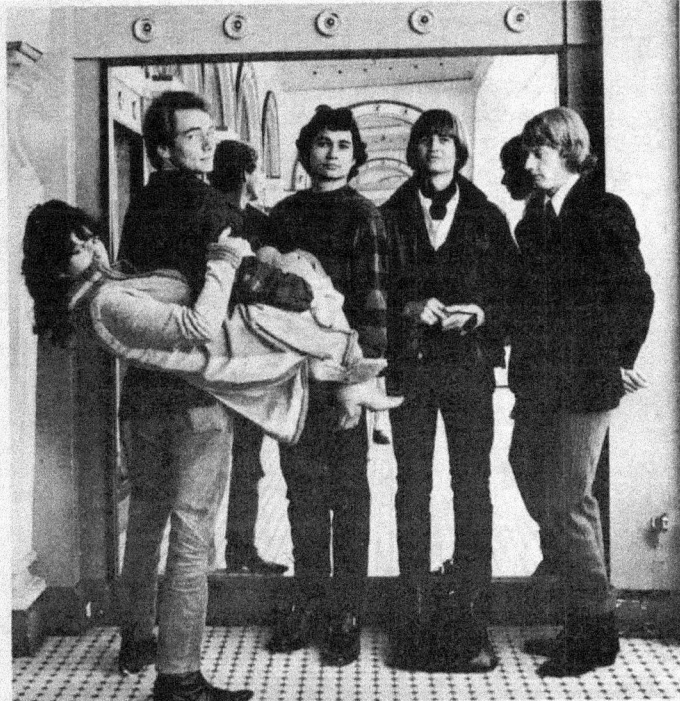

...GRACE, JERRY, DAVID, BARD AND DARBY

A Sloppy Great Society Offers Some Free Advice

By Carol Deck

The Great Society is about to give out with some free advice, musical type free advice.

The Great Society are five young singers from San Francisco who are about to burst on the scene with their first release, "Free Advice."

The group is made up of Jerry Slick, his wife Grace, his brother Darby, Bard Dupont and David Miner. They've only been together three months but they've already got an original sound and have been getting a lot of experience playing in clubs around the Bay area.

Jerry's the drummer and has a thing about wearing wild red shirts. He graduated from San Francisco State College, where as a cinema major, he made films like "Everybody Hit Their Brother Once."

"Clothes Horse"

His wife Grace was a "clothes horse" for I. Magnins before she went into singing. She does a lot of the lead singing and plays a variety of instruments including bass and rhythm guitar, piano, drums and recorder. She has a dry, quick wit and describes the clothes the group wears on stage as "stuff."

Lead guitar player Darby Slick is the youngest of the group (a mere 21) and the author of both "Free Advice" and it's flip side, "Someone to Love." Before joining the group he worked in a chemical laboratory which he refers to as the "glue factory."

Bass and harmonica player of the group is Bard, who's also the oldest (all of 22). He's an expressive young man who used to write short stories and hack fiction and likes blues type music but can't stand folk music.

Wrapped Wire

David Miner, rhythm guitarist and vocalist, is a quiet, solid sort of guy who almost seems out of place in the group. When asked what he did before he started singing professionally, he just says "wrapping wire" and then another member of the group will explain that he was an electrician.

Their first record has a definite Indian sound and they admit that they were influenced by Ravie Shankar and Ali Akbar Khan, two of India's top singers. But David says he writes Country and Western type songs by listening to the two Indians.

They describe their stage appearance as sort of a mess. Grace calls it "sloppy" and Jerry says it looks "like a band of gypsies sort of settled there." Something about their appearance makes people think of Chuck Berry because the one number that they get the most request to play is "Memphis," but they only do original material.

More Good Times

Jerry sums up the group's goals with "we hope to keep having a good time and not make a business out of it."

They stole the name from LBJ but they have a sound all their own, so watch for the Great Society and their first record which is due this month.

A Xmas Wish For My Fave

I realize I'm growing up
There are many ways to tell
But I never knew until today
That I'm growing **out** as well.

This dawned on me unexpectedly
While doing a simple task
When making up my Christmas card list
I compared this year's with last.

There were several names on 64's
But many more in sixty-five
Friends who have also been added to **me**
And that makes me more alive.

I wondered how this had happened
Then, in a moment, I knew
The brand new people in my world
Happened because of you.

I met some through your fan clubs
Some I knew but didn't care
To really get acquainted
Until we had someone to share.

Others will give you diamonds
And a golden Christmas tree
I only send my luv and thanks
For happening to me.

On the BEAT

By Louise Criscione

Since this is our Christmas issue I thought I'd change the format of ON THE BEAT this week and instead of telling you what your favorite people have been up to record-wise I'm going to let you in on what they've been buying themselves for Christmas.

Brian Jones is sporting a new pair of shoes with rubber soles which cost him 50 shillings (however much that is!). Anyway, Brian is so proud of his shoes that he has been wearing them everywhere.

Herman, Englands' best dressed man, is the secretary of the Bowler Hat Brigade (self-appointed I assume) and so has purchased for himself a black bowler trimmed with plastic eyes and mouth. In fact, Herman liked his black bowler so much that he had some more made up in red, pink and green.

The Yardbirds are thinking seriously of buying themselves some of those Vinyl jackets with the leather buttons. The boys have been shopping around for the jackets for ages now but so far no one has seen a live Yardbird actually wearing one.

Dave's New Watch

Dave Clark *is* wearing a new white gold wrist watch with a beautiful Florentine finish. And Dave's also sporting a matching ring with a freedom of youth seal firmly attached to it. Looks great on Dave, too.

...BRIAN JONES

Ringo bought himself as well as his family a Christmas present some time ago when he purchased that huge house in Weybridge. But the Starr family is only now ready to move into the home with its own private grounds and celebrate their first Christmas together.

John Lennon has a fine Christmas present for himself too. He is one of the exhibitors in an art showing in London at St. Martin's Nell Gwynne Club. Bet John's painting is the first one sold!

Donovan has decided to go pop art and so has purchased a shirt with cirles, lines and squares all over the place. It sounds horrible, I know but Don really looks kind of nice in it. I also saw Donovan wearing a pair of those glasses similar to the ones which John of the Lovin' Spoonful wears.

Teddy Bear

John Walker of the Walker Brothers has treated himself to a new Teddy Bear type three-quarter length coat in fawn.

His fellow Walker Brothers have also been busy shopping. Scott has designed himself some leather boots complete with side zippers and knife pockets. However, Scott assures us that the knife pockets are just a joke.

Gary Leeds couldn't be left behind by his "brothers" so he really went all out and bought himself three new suits and some leather pants with matching vests.

I ran into the Byrds yesterday and it didn't look much like they had been shopping. David had on his favorite suede cape which he swears he won't give up.

Jim McGuinn looked sharp in a dark blue sports coat with a white shirt and tie and *no glasses!* He definitely does have eyes, you know.

Bobby's "Disguise"

Bobby Hatfield apparently bought himself a new black hat in which to escape unnoticed (he thinks) in crowds. I saw him wearing it in the record store the other day.

It was really kind of funny. Either no one recognized Bobby in his hat disguise or else they did recognize him but were too embarrassed to talk to him. However, an unusually large number of "Ebb Tide" singles were sold during Bobby's shopping spree. So, you can draw your own conclusions.

Barry McGuire, whom I jokingly call The Leader Of The Pack because of the clothes he wears when he rides his motorcycle over to our offices, has bought himself a couple of Christmas presents.

First off, he is having a cape made by the same person who created David Crosby's. Also, Barry has a new pair of things which I can only describe as cowboy chaps.

And now I'm so broke I'm bringing my own lunches to work in a paper sack!

Oh, well. Have a swingin' Christmas.

...BOBBY HATFIELD

KRLA ARCHIVES

Rolling Stones World Tour Set

The Rolling Stones have just completed their most successful American tour to date. But their work's not nearly finished yet. Waiting for them in the first *eight* months of the New Year is a world-wide tour!

Tito Burns, the Stones' British agent, announced their huge world tour. The boys are now taking a long-needed vacation in various parts of the world and are due to return to England in the early part of January.

Although Mick Jagger let it be known that he is not too jazzed over Christmas he has also let it be known that he is hurrying home in time to celebrate the holiday.

The Stones are due to leave in mid-February for an Australian tour which will be followed by personal appearances in Hawaii and Hong Kong.

Breathing Time

They will then have a chance for a very short breathing spell before again departing in mid-March for their continental tour which is scheduled to begin in France.

The continental tour will be made in two-week spans which will allow the Stones to return to England between their appearances.

In addition to France the Stones will also perform in Belgium, Holland, Germany, Scandinavia, Portugal, Spain, Turkey and Poland.

That's enough work to keep anybody busy, isn't it? Well, as you already know, the Rolling Stones are not just anybody so they have piled some more work on themselves.

In August, they take off for personal appearances in Nice, Cannes, Morocco and possibly Italy.

Album Success

Between all these appearances the Stones have managed to send their newest album, "December's Children," flying up the charts all over the world.

It has been their fastest selling album so far and quite naturally the Stones are extremely pleased over it's great success.

While in Hollywood the Stones spent an entire week recording at their favorite studio, RCA. Their next single as well as several album cuts were hopefully produced at this session. So, you can expect to hear even more great sounds from the Rolling Stones in the very near future.

... PAUL REVERE AND THE RAIDERS

Paul Revere and Raiders Looking For A Number One

Beware! There's a group of raiders around.

They've been stealing shows from top name performers and they cause general chaos at every performance they do.

They are on television more than practically every other American pop group, but they've never had a number one record.

How do Paul Revere and the Raiders persistently draw such huge crowds to their live shows and get so many TV spots without a top selling record? Maybe it's just because they put on one of the wildest shows ever seen. The Raiders' performance can only be described as all-out chaos. All five of them have been known to climb all over a stage and everything on it including themselves and their instruments.

Unlikely Start

And the whole thing had a very unlikely beginning. It started a few years ago when Paul Revere (that's his real name) got expelled from school in Portland, Ore. He hadn't been real interested in that school anyway, so he went out and enrolled in a barber's school.

After graduating, he took some money his grandmother had left him and bought a barber shop. Such a shrewd fellow was he, that he soon had enough money to sell the barber shop and buy a drive-in restaurant and an apartment house. To show how clever he is, for the restaurant he paid $5,000 cash and a boat which the original owner of the restaurant figured was worth $3,000 (Paul had bought it for $350.)

Meanwhile he had formed a group and was playing here and there. A guy named Mark Lindsay was delivering bread to Paul's restaurant and used to ask to sing with the boys, until one day Paul finally realized this was no ordinary bread deliverer and asked him to join the group.

They goofed around for a while, broke up for a year, and then Paul and Mark got back together again. They met Mike Smith at a club in Portland and Paul said Mike was the worst guitar player he'd ever heard, so naturally Mike became the group's drummer.

Later they were joined by Drake Levin and Mike Holladay, but Holladay left the group to settle down somewhere and was replaced by Philip Volk. In 1964 Roger Hart, a Portland disc jockey, heard the boys, realized how great they could be, and finally convinced them to let him manage them.

Many TV Spots

Since then they've been on Tonight, Hullabaloo, Lloyd Thaxton, American Bandstand, Shebang, 9th Street West, Hollywood A Go Go and have had to turn down three spots on the Merv Griffin Show.

But they still haven't had a number one song. Their first release, "Louie Louie" has wandered up and down the charts a number of times but never all the way to the top. Their second one, "Sometimes," went absolutely nowhere but their third, "Steppin' Out," did a lot better. It made the national charts, but still no number one.

Now they are trying again with their latest single, "Just Like Me." Maybe this will be the one. And they have their second album coming out right quick like. It's called "Just Like Us" and includes some of the first vocals by Drake and Philip. Up until now Mark has done most of the lead singing.

The group's just completed a tour with the We Five, the Byrds, and Bo Diddley and are all set for a Christmas jaunt to Viet Nam. Keep raiding boys.

DISCussion
By Eden

It's awful nice to know that there's such a thing as a Tom Jones. In fact, it would be kinda nice to find him under the tree come Christmas morning wouldn't it? Can you imagine being able to prop him up on a candy cane and just have him sing "Thunderball" and all of his other hits all day long?

Yeah, I know—he'd never fit on top of a candy cane! Oh well—there's always the gingerbread-man cookies!!!

* * *

Great Christmas gifts this year have included the Stones' new El-pee–"December's Children" and the long-player by The Silkie–"You've Got To Hide Your Love Away."

And I wonder how many Beatle albums were all dressed-up in their Yule-tide best this year.

Donovan has a new album entitled "Fairy Tale" which happens to have greatly impressed one Mr. Paul McCartney, but it sounds like a put-on to me!

(Good record, though.)

* * *

Keep a vacant ear-lobe ready for some brand-new singles, including "The Knack" by Jordan Christopher, who *definitely* has it. (That's what Sybil tells us, anyway!)

The new 45 RPMer by Billy Joe Royal is "I've Got To Be Somebody" and this sounds like another winner for the good-looking Southerner.

And Len Barry has a brand-new disc, "Hearts Are Trump." Wonder if this one will go as far as the first? Well, we should be finding out, *"one-two-three!"*

The Beach Boys' new album is entitled "Beach Boy's Party!" And they certainly do! Mixed in with all the songs are many happy-party-type sounds, and it makes a very fun-type platter.

Selections include "Tell Me Why" by Lennon-McCartney, and from Dylan's pen–"The Times Are A-Changing." Group leader Brian Wilson also takes the lead and includes his own hit-composition, "I Get Around."

* * *

About a month ago, I had the opportunity of hearing an exclusive, sneak-preview of the Beatles' new single. It hadn't yet been released at the time; and it was being kept well under wraps.

I heard the up-tempo side, "Day Tripper" and I was somewhat destroyed, 'cause I just couldn't believe that they had done it all over again, for the umpteenth time. Then I heard the "A" side—"We Can Work It Out"—and I just sort of fell on the floor in a dead heap!

Somehow, it still seems just a little incomprehensible that these four human beings can continue being so completely *super*-human! Each record is just greater than the last, and there is so much in each one that you could probably spend a lifetime analyzing each new disc.

I think I will have to be content to just enjoy their music, and them. And aren't you glad that there are four Beatles in this old world of ours?

Merry, Merry Christmas to you boys, and may the next two-hundred years be as happy and successful for you as have been the last two years.

* * *

And to all of you in this wide world of Pop – A very Merry Christmas!

Christmas Greetings

(Continued from Page 2)

"Once again the time is here –
To send to all, our Christmas cheer.
Have the greatest holiday ever!"
DICK AND DEEDEE

"A very Merry Christmas to all, and to all a good night. Ho ho ho, mostly ho ho!! Peace to good will to all men. Ho! Ho!"
BARRY McGUIRE

"Have an exotic Christmas and a happy New Year."
P.F. SLOAN

Thank you for making our first year as a publication so very successful, and for making us the fastest-growing publication in America. To our subscribers in all 50 states and 11 foreign countries, Merry Christmas and peace, prosperity and happiness to you all.
THE BEAT STAFF

KRLA ARCHIVES

Dave Clark 5 Meet The Press

By Louise Criscione

DAVE CLARK certainly looks pensive doesn't he? Actually he is pondering the answer to a question put to him by **The BEAT**. After all that thinking, Dave managed to come up with a hilarious answer which sent the entire room into stitches! Dave and the rest of the Five are really great guys and it always makes **The BEAT** happy when the boys visit our town. And it makes us even happier when they visit us!

I still get a kick out of press conferences, especially when they are for someone like the Dave Clark Five.

So as I sat munching a breakfast roll and sipping a cup of coffee I was a little more than anxious for the conference to get underway. It was already past the starting time.

The other reporters didn't seem to mind much. They sat chatting away as though this sort of thing happens every day. And so it does. I suppose in a few years I'll think of it as old hat. But right now it's exciting. So, I kept both eyes glued to the door through which the DC5 were due to enter.

The minutes flew by and still no sight of the Five. Then suddenly the door burst open and the DC5 along with their manager, road manager, lighting technician and the sound technician walked into the crowded room and sat down at the long table which was placed at the front of the room.

It's Underway

They reached for their coffee and cigarettes and the conference was officially underway. It was rather disorganized as the reporters simply fired questions at random. It made it hard to hear which question was being answered and quite often the answer was a simple "yes" or "no" — so those questions were completely lost.

The DC5 did not appear to be much at ease. They shuffled back and forth in their seats and gave the general appearance of being scared to death. I can't say I really blame them – reporters *can* be pretty scary sometimes.

Of course, the most frequently asked question was the perennial favorite — do you have steady girlfriends?

Lenny and Rick, being married, were forced to remain mute on the subject but Mike offered the answer that he does have a steady girlfriend in Sweden and he "can't wait to see her again."

Denny Shy

Denny admitted to being shy but said that he liked "girls with long blonde hair." And Dave? He played coy: "I like all girls in general."

Another favorite topic of the conference was movies — past and present. The boys all declared that they enjoyed movie-making very much but that Lenny, Denny, Rick and Mike were a tiny bit jealous. Of what? Of the fact that in their first movie Dave was the only one with a girlfriend!

So, they intend to get this terrible situation rectified in their next movie which is to be a thriller and which is to begin filming shortly.

The new movie will be shot on location in the south of France and in England. Details of the script are not available yet but it promises to be even better than their last.

As you know, the Dave Clark Five recently appeared before the Queen in the Royal Variety Show accepting the invitation after the Beatles had turned it down.

All five of the boys were thrilled at meeting the Queen and said they hoped to be asked again next year. Well, I guess so — it's one of the highest honors an English entertainer can receive.

The DC5 also expressed their approval of the way we American girls dress. They said that the first time they visited the U.S. they were a little disappointed to find that we dressed like "old ladies." But now all that's changed and they are particularly happy to see us Statesiders dressing more like our English cousins.

With their shorter haircuts and their white shirts and ties, the Dave Clark Five seem to be one group who is out for convention in dress. However, looks are deceiving because all of the boys say they like "weird" clothes on both boys and girls!

The End

So, about twenty minutes after it had begun the press conference was over. The DC5 thanked the press for coming and, of course, we thanked the Five for inviting us.

As Dave left the table he said: "See you in December." But he got away before we could ask him exactly when he was returning and why. Pretty clever on his part, I'd say.

And with that they were gone to catch a plane back to New York for "a visit and some rest." The crowded room finished their coffee and hurried out of the hotel and back to the typewriters to let you all in on the Dave Clark Five press conference.

But who knows, they may be back even before you read this.

DAVE CLARK FIVE caught in various poses by our **BEAT** photographer, Chuck Boyd, during their press conference. Rick Picone, the Five's road manager, watches over the boys while they answer the questions shot at them by the reporters.

KRLA ARCHIVES

KRLA Deejays Send Christmas Greetings

"Jingle bells, jingle bells, jingle all . . . "Oh, excuse me – we were just sitting around the giant KRLA Christmas tree opening up all of our gifts.

Say – here are some gifts for *you*. It looks as though they are from the Disc Jockeys. Well – c'mon over and open up your packages, Beaters.

FROM DAVE HULL: "Happy Holidays from the Ol' Hullabalooer, and thank you all for being so kind to me and to all of the KRLA DJ's in 1965. I hope I'll get to meet all of you in 1966."

FROM BOB EUBANKS: Merry Christmas and a Happy Holiday season to everyone. And thank you for making 1965 such a great year for us."

FROM BILL SLATER: "Maybelline Fink just kissed Jarvis the Janitor on his left cheek, under the Mistletoe hanging from the 60-watt bare light bulb in the weather room. That means it's Christmas time again. Merry Christmas everyone."

FROM CHARLIE O'DONNELL: "Thank you all for a wonderful year, and best wishes to all the KRLA listeners for a very happy holiday season and for the coming New Year."

FROM CASEY KASEM: "God be with you each and every day. Merry Christmas."

FROM DICK BIONDI: "I want to wish everyone a happy, holy, and sane Holiday and thank you all for making this one of the best Christmases ever for me, 'cause I'm really happy here! Merry Christmas."

From everyone here at KRLA – thank you for making 1965 one of the best years ever for us, and may this Holiday season bring to you and yours all the joy and peace on earth.

Merry Christmas everyone!!

Hope Santa Finds These

Christmas Cash To KRLA Homes

Santa's on the prowl again throughout KRLAnd. And if he finds your house, you would win a tidy bundle of Christmas cash.

Cruising with the KRLA disc jockeys, Santa is looking for the homes of KRLA listeners – homes and businesses which have a sign with the letters K-R-L-A posted somewhere on the premises, such as the ones pictured here.

Every time he sees a KRLA sign, Santa will stop and award Christmas cash to the occupant. Starting a couple of weeks before Christmas, he's awarding a total of $100 daily, right through Friday, Dec. 24.

IN SEARCH OF FOLKS
Tim's Golden Rule

By Shannon Leigh

You can find them in a coffee house, or singing on the beach; you see them walking down a boulevard, or stopping in some small cafe. Their music can be heard on popular radio stations and sometimes you can even watch them on TV.

Yes, you can find "folk-people" just about anywhere, and that is exactly what we are going to be doing from now on in this column – going "In Search of Folks." We are going to speak with some of the top folk performers in the field of music, and we'll be talking with them wherever we find them.

This week, we have found a Tim Morgon folk-singer – who says he really *isn't* – right here in the *BEAT* offices. His name – Tim Morgon, and although he has a reputation as a fine folk-singer, this tall, blue-eyed 23-year old Californian claims that he is more of a "folk-*type* singer" than a folk singer.

"I don't consider myself really a 'folk-singer'; I sing a lot of folk-type music, but I also sing songs like "Don't Let the Sun Catch You Crying," and "Somewhere."

One thing causing Tim great concern at the moment is the current trend of protest music. Furrowing his brow, he very seriously explains: "I'm not too much in favor of protest songs, because there is war, and death, and destruction and disease all around us all the time.

"In fact, when you look at a children's show on TV, what are the prizes? What are the things they're trying to sell? Like a 'Johnny-Kill-Everybody Rifle,' or a 'Big Bertha 37-Ways-to-Blow-Up-Your-Neighbor.' To me, we have enough war, and death, and destruction without this, and I don't think a song here and there is going to do anything about it.

Golden Rule

"It's the people themselves; I think that if people would treat everybody else the way *they* want to be treated – the Golden Rule – it seems that the world would be a much nicer place to live, instead of shouting about it, or marching about it, or fighting about it."

Tim found some difficulty in describing his own precise "sound" when singing, but he did adamantly maintain that, "One thing I try to stand by is my own individuality. I try to be *myself* onstage – I don't want to get up there and sing like Trini Lopez, or Sinatra, or Harry Belafonte."

Tim is currently making plans for the bright New Year ahead, and included among them will be a singing engagement right after the first of the year at the Cosmos, a folk club in Seal Beach, for six weeks, and then a 30 to 35 day nation-wide tour.

He has already recorded three albums – the first of which was entitled "Tim Morgon at the Prison of Socrates" – on his own label, Fink Records. Just recently, Tim starred in the picture "Dirty Feet," and now he has hopes of continuing to work in the field of acting as in addition to maintaining his career as a singer – folk or otherwise!

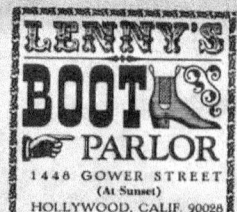

LENNY'S BOOT PARLOR
1448 GOWER STREET
(At Sunset)
HOLLYWOOD, CALIF. 90028
466-7092

TIM MORGON'S DIRTY FEET Showing
Dec. 26-30 (8:00 p.m.)
COSMOS FOLK CLUB
Seal Beach, Calif.
Phone: 596-4132 For Reservations

"COULD GO TO THE TOP" WXRT – CHICAGO
"LIKE THE RECORD" WADM – DECATUR, ILL.

Skyway Records
45-138-A
HOLLYWOOD, CALIF.

NO CHEESE
(On the Xmas tree)

FEATURING BLIMP WHIMP & SKIMP

KRLA ARCHIVES

Inside KRLA

Ever wonder what the ol' Hullabalooer does with his spare time when he's not on the air, or blowing his horn? Well—here's your answer:

"I just had a new set of fencing foils and a fencing mask made up—we're going to hang it over the mantle in our new home. I've spent most of the afternoons this last week working around the yard and painting the house. We're having the yard landscaped."

David was understandably excited about his new house—which he told The BEAT about last week—but he was even *more* excited about the Beatles' new album. In fact, he even explained just exactly who does what on the album for us:

"I've Just Seen A Face"—"Paul takes the lead on this one."
"Norwegian Wood"—"John sings lead with Paul in the background."
"You Won't See Me"—"Paul sings lead and also plays piano on this one, with George and John in the background."
"Think For Yourself"—"George wrote this one and takes the lead on it."
"The Word"—"John, Paul, and George sing on this, with Paul on the piano and George Martin on harmonica."
"Michelle"—"Paul sings this beautiful new ballad, which certainly carries on the tradition of 'Yesterday!'"
"It's Only Love"—"This one is sung by John and Paul."
"Girl"—"John takes the lead with George and Paul behind him."
"I'm Looking Through You"—"Paul sings this with John and Ringo both playing Hammond organ in parts."
"In My Life"—"John and Paul sing this with George Martin on piano."
"Wait"—"Is done by John and Paul."
"Run For Your Life"—"This one is sung for you by John with Paul and George in the background."

At this point, the old Hullabalooer collapsed from sheer excitement, but not before he told us that this is one of the greatest Beatle albums ever. Thank you, kindly Dave.

All of the KRLApes are still excited about their 49 to 39 win over the Los Angeles Times team at the Sports Arena on December 1. After all—it isn't every day (or *year*!) that the Apes win one, you know!

Have you all been watching the skies for a glimpse of one of the KRLA flying saucers? You'd better watch closely or they will pass you by. But if you miss them, you can probably catch them at the drag strip where the DJ's spend their spare time racing with any stray peacocks who happen to fly by.

It's Christmas now, and as all of the DJ's here at KRLA sit around the fireplace in the Emperor's Leopard-skin room waiting for Kris Kringle to drop some new records in their stockings, we'd all like to wish all of you the very merriest of Christmases and a very healthy and happy New Year.

And until next year—Later, baby!

KRLA Tunedex

 DAVE HULL

 BOB EUBANKS

 DICK BIONDI

 JOHNNY HAYES

EMPEROR HUDSON

 CASEY KASEM

 CHARLIE O'DONNELL

 BILL SLATER

This Week	Last Week	Title	Artist
1	1	LET'S HANG ON	Four Seasons
2	3	LIES, LIES	Knickerbockers
3	9	IT'S MY LIFE	The Animals
4	8	EBB TIDE	Righteous Brothers
5	12	FLOWERS ON THE WALL	Statler Brothers
6	2	STILL I'M SAD/I'M A MAN	Yardbirds
7	6	TASTE OF HONEY/3RD MAN THEME	Herb Alpert
8	16	YOU DIDN'T HAVE TO BE SO NICE	Lovin' Spoonful
9	13	RUN, BABY, RUN	The Newbeats
10	11	I CAN NEVER GO HOME ANYMORE	The Shangri-Las
11	27	THE SOUNDS OF SILENCE	Simon & Garfunkel
12	7	RISING SUN	The Deep Six
13	5	I HEAR A SYMPHONY	The Supremes
14	4	1-2-3	Len Barry
15	10	TURN, TURN, TURN	The Byrds
16	21	THE LITTLE GIRL I ONCE KNEW	The Beach Boys
17	20	OVER AND OVER	Dave Clark Five
18	19	PIED PIPER	The Changing Times
19	30	YOUNG GIRL	Noel Harrison
20	24	I WILL	Dean Martin
21	17	LET ME BE	The Turtles
22	25	I FOUGHT THE LAW	Bobby Fuller Four
23	22	ENGLAND SWINGS	Roger Miller
24	18	HANG ON SLOOPY	Ramsey Lewis Trio
25	26	STAND BY ME	Earl Grant
26	—	DON'T THINK TWICE	Wonder Who
27	—	HOLE IN THE WALL	The Packers
28	32	SHE'S JUST MY STYLE	Gary Lewis & The Playboys
29	39	WE CAN WORK IT OUT/DAY TRIPPER	The Beatles
30	40	JENNY TAKE A RIDE	Mitch Ryder & The Detroit Wheels
31	31	MY BABY	The Temptations
32	29	LETS GET TOGETHER	We Five
33	—	FEVER	The McCoys
34	—	MAKE THE WORLD GO AWAY	Eddie Arnold
35	35	ALL OR NOTHING	Patti LaBelle
36	38	I SEE THE LIGHT	Five Americans
37	33	THE DUCK	Jackie Lee
38	37	MY GENERATION	The Who
39	—	FIVE O'CLOCK WORLD	The Vogues
40	34	THUNDERBALL/KEY TO MY HEART	Tom Jones

APPEARING THRU JAN. 2

JOE & EDDIE
with comedian **JOHN MOORE**

MAKE RESERVATIONS NOW FOR A GALA NEW YEARS EVE

Troubadour
RESERVATIONS CR 6-6168

Troubananny's Are HAPPENING Monday

KRLA BEAT Subscription

SPECIAL OFFER—Deadline Jan. 1
SAVE 60% Of Regular Price

☐ 1 YEAR—52 ISSUES—$3.00

Enclosed is $3.00 ☐ CASH ☐ CHECK

Send to:.. Age............
Address:...
City.................... State......... Zip................

MAIL YOUR ORDER TO:
KRLA BEAT
6290 Sunset, Suite 504
Hollywood, Calif. 90028

Foreign Rate: $14.00—52 Issues

WILD SHAPES FOR WILD PEOPLE

THE BENNY $6.00
Lens Colors: Grey, Blue, Pink, Brown, Green, Yellow

THE KOOK $6.00
Lens Colors: Grey, Blue, Pink, Brown, Green, Yellow

THE CELEBRITY $6.00
Lens Colors: Grey, Blue, Pink, Brown, Green, Yellow

THE TEACH $6.00
Lens Colors: Grey, Blue, Pink, Brown, Green, Yellow

THE MARTIAN $9.00
Lens Colors: Grey, Blue, Pink, Brown, Green

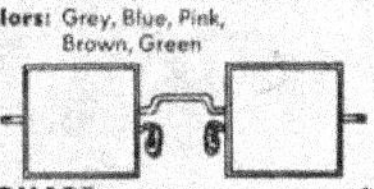

THE SQUARE $9.00
Lens Colors: Grey, Blue, Pink, Brown, Green

THE MOONMAID $9.00
Lens Colors: Grey, Blue, Pink, Brown, Green

THE SWINGER $9.00
Lens Colors: Grey, Blue, Pink, Brown, Green

Dig the latest in QUALITY sunglasses. Styles so far out that they're IN!!! Simulated gold frames with groovy colored lenses. By Tropic-Cal.

WE WILL MAIL TO YOU PREPAID
SEND MONEY ORDER OR CHECK

NAME:_____
ADDRESS:_____
CITY:_____ STATE:_____
LENS COLOR PREFERENCE: (1)_____ (2)_____
NAME OF STYLE:_____

 HOLE IN THE WALL
422 N. La Cienega
Los Angeles 48, Calif.

HOLE IN THE WALL
422 N. La Cienega
Fab Clothes
Groovy
Accessories
For the 'IN' Crowd
Phone: 652-7562

KRLA ARCHIVES

The Adventures of Robin Boyd...
By Shirley Poston

CHAPTER SEVEN

There had never been a Beatle concert quite like the one at the London Palladium that night. And, plodding wordlessly back to their dressing room, the Beatles fervently hoped there would never be *another* one quite like it.

If there ever *was* another one, that was.

Fortunately, most of the friends who were mingling about in the backstage hub-bub took one look at the drawn faces of the foursome and decided to wait until later to congratulate them on another smash performance.

Only one, in fact, dared to penetrate the sudden mask of gloom which had mysteriously fallen over the group.

"Who died?" asked a subtle but curious acquaintance.

"We aren't feeling well," answered George, kindly but firmly locking him out of the dressing room.

Paul flung himself into a chair. "*That*," he said, "was the understatement of the century."

Ringo flung himself into a chair. "We aren't only not feeling well, we're *sick*."

George flung himself into a chair. "Sick, *sick*, sick."

John almost flung himself into a chair. Then he thought better of it. It simply was not wise to go flinging oneself about when one had just swallowed a guitar pick.

"You *saw* it then," he said nervously.

Paul paled. "You mean the bird that flew across the stage?"

George grimaced. "The *real* bird that gave you the line you'd forgotten?"

Ringo reeled. "Wearing *glasses?*"

John jerked, taking mental note to remember the motion the next time he tried to learn the latest dance sensations.

"Then I'm not crazy?" he questioned solemnly.

"No," asnwered the other three solemnly. "We are *all* crazy."

John flung himself into a chair, guitar pick or no guitar pick. "Do you think anyone else saw it?"

The other three shook their heads warily, half afraid the motion would result in a loud rattle.

"It was too fast," Ringo said at last. "And too little."

John smiled smugly. "*See?* I *told* you I saw it at the window before we went on!"

The other three nodded this time, equally as warily.

"Only you thought I'd dropped one, right?"

"Right," they chorused.

John flung himself *out* of the chair.

"Wrong, Johnny, wrong," they re-chorused.

Then they heard it. A sharp noise. Almost like the twang of an invisible guitar string. (An E flat if you care to become technical about it.) (And you *would*.)

"*What was that?*" they shrieked bravely.

Suddenly, John laughed. It was probably only the guitar pick plucking about on his vocal chords.

The he stopped laughing and clutched his throat. What did he mean *only?*

"Let's get out of here," he said, and taking one last fearful glance at the darkened window, they did just that. In a high run.

Had they been able to see what was lurking just *outside*, they would not have glanced fearfully at the window. They would have flung themselves through it. For, again frantically clutching the stoney exterior of the building, *was* a real bird wearing glasses.

It was, of course, none other than Robin Boyd.

And the noise hadn't been plucked from John's vocal chords. It had come from hers.

And it wasn't a twang. It was a *blither*.

"What have I done?" Robin moaned tearfully, which was difficult for a *real* Robin.

Zooming across the stage and whispering the line in John's ear had seemed the very thing to do. After all, wasn't it her fault that he'd forgotten it in the first place?

But her generosity had ended in stark tragedy. Thanks to her, four of the most wonderful people in the world were now going about fearing for their sanity!

Straightening her Byrd glasses and sniffling resolutely, Robin again prepared to say the magic word that would change her back into her sixteen-year-old self. At which time she would rush to the Beatles' side and soothe their ruffled feathers.

What was the blasted word anyway? George (her very own genie) had told it to her over and over... Oh yes, it was Worcestshire.

Opening her mouth – er-beak widely to utter same, she suddenly clapped a hand – er – foot over her mouth – er – beak. Because it simply was not wise to go turning oneself into sixteen-year-olds when one was clinging to the stoney exterior of the London Palladium.

But, as she glared about her in search of a proper landing field, an anguished wail arose from the far-below crowd in the street. And a long, dark limousine pulled hurriedly away from the curb.

Robin began to flap wildly. The *Beatles!* They were getting *away!*

Going out into the night, *fearing for their sanity!*

She flapped wilder. If she lost them now, it was hard telling *how* long it would take to find and convince them that they *hadn't* dropped one (whatever *that* meant.)

But what was she to do? She couldn't say the magic word *now!* She'd *never* catch them on foot! And she couldn't fly high above them because she'd lose them in the snarl of traffic!

And she couldn't fly low because they'd see her again and fling themselves into the streets in an effort to end it all before the men in the white coats arrived!

Then a thought occurred to Robin. And she *knew* what she *must* do.

Moments later, as she clung frantically to the very tip of the limousine's aerial, another thought occurred to her.

There were times, it seemed, when being a bird in both senses of the word was FOR the birds.

(To Be Continued Next Week)

DEADLINE NEAR...
You have until Jan. 1 to take advantage of the introductory subscription offer of $3 for 52 issues.
SUBSCRIBE NOW – SAVE 60%

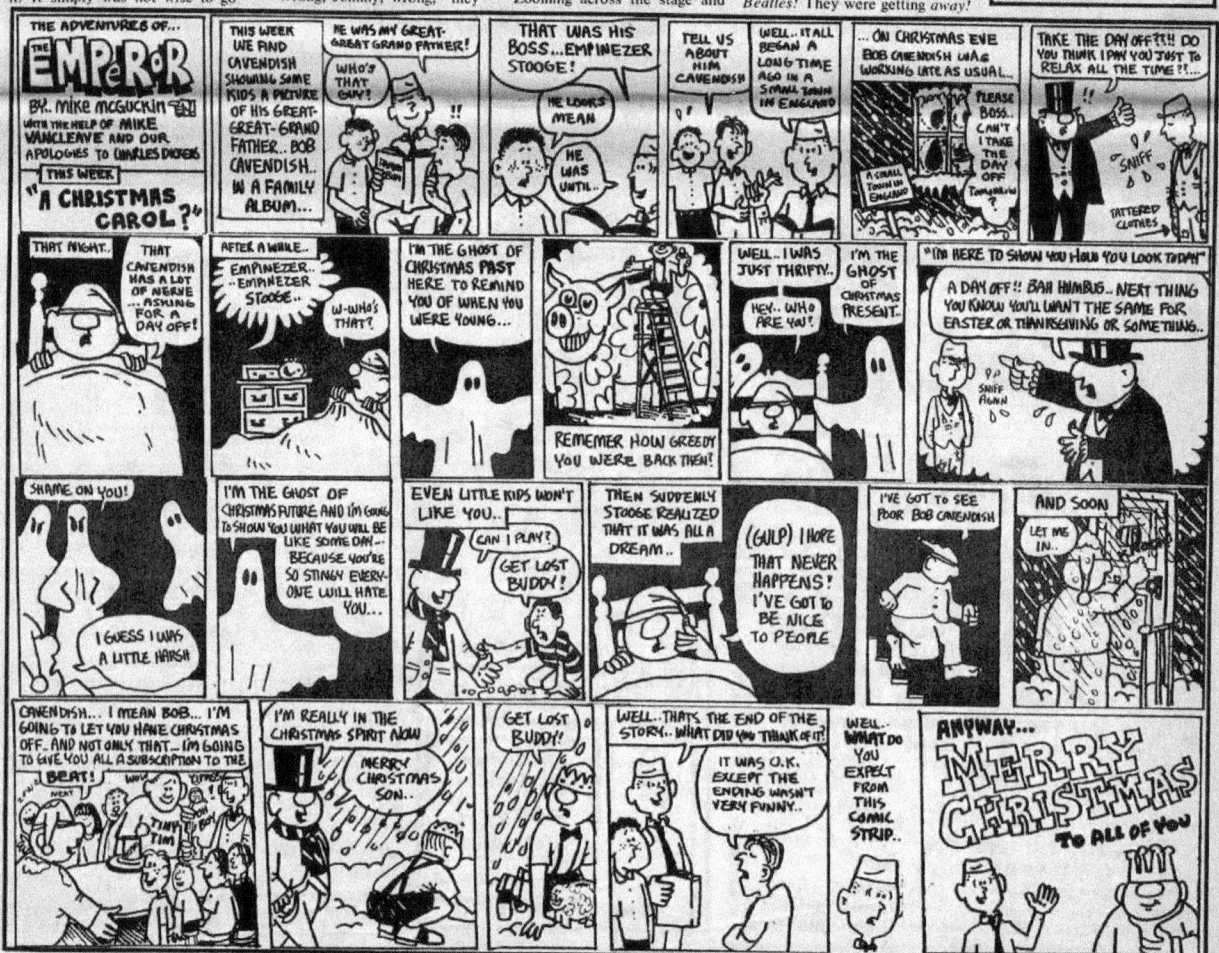

KRLA ARCHIVES

Yeah, Well Elvis
The Boss And I Meet El

By Tammy Hitchcock

Just guess who we have on our "Yeah, Well Hot Seat" this week? The guy who was once the undisputed King of Pop – Elvis Presley.

Of course, it is common knowledge that Elvis would never have gone as far as he did if it hadn't been for the shrewd Colonel Parker.

However, rumor has it that the Colonel will be leaving the Presley camp before too long. "I'm 55," the Col. reveals. "He's 30. I shan't see him retire but he'll see me. Sooner or later, someone else is going to have to take the reins."

Yeah, well I'm really good at taking reins. I always take my horse's reins and tie 'em up to the hitching post. 'Course, everytime I come out of the saloon he's gone!

And I'll tell you one thing – I look pretty ridiculous running down Main Street screaming "Here Oliver." That's my horse's name – Oliver. Which is probably why he runs away!

Anyway, Elvis, I'd love to take your reins. And don't sweat it, boy – I'll have you bankrupt in a week.

You know, everyone is always going on about how hard it is to actually get to see Elvis. Well, don't you believe it.

The boss and I – we met Elvis one time. 'Course, it was only by accident. But still.

You know, how the boss likes to drive her Stingray around, especially in the hills. I don't know why because she always gets lost.

So, she always takes me with her. I don't know why she does that either unless it's to make *sure* we get lost!

Are you ready for this? The boss and I are speeding around and natch we're lost. So, we do the only logical thing – we find the map, which is buried under a pile of James Bond books, last year's calendar, and a half a box of stale popcorn.

Well, we finally uncovered the map (a 1949 edition) and spread it out. Attempting to read a map is always a mistake because it only makes us even more confused (which is really next to impossible!).

Anyway, just picture the boss and I on our hands and knees puzzling over the map when around the bend flies a black Cad. It was going so fast that our map flew right along with it.

So, the boss and I gave the retreating car a really dirty look. And the car began screeching in reverse.

I can tell you right now the boss and I thought we'd *had* it. We ran for the Stingray as fast as our legs would carry us (which isn't too fast, I'm afraid.) The boss made it but I didn't.

First I tripped and fell, then I hit my head getting in (forgot she had the top up again) and when I did get in I got my purse stuck in the door!

But as it turned out I needn't have hurried. The boss couldn't find her keys, anyway. They were in the bottom of her satchel – so, I mean, *forget it!*

There we sat. The boss trying to find her keys and instead coming up with half-eaten candy bars and empty gum wrappers. And there I was trying desperately to get my purse in the door and instead turning it upside down spilling it's contents (which are considerable) all over the street.

When who gets out of the Cad apologizing for sending our map into orbit but ELVIS PRESLEY himself!!!!!

The boss and I we didn't say anything. We just *stared*. I think I stared with my mouth open 'cause something flew into it. But, I mean, who can be bothered with insects when Elvis is standing there – in the flesh yet!

Well, we finally got our wits about us (which isn't too difficult for me since I don't have many wits to begin with). We explained our lost situation to Elvis. And do you know what he did? He personally escorted us back to the main highway.

Nice man, that Elvis.

Yeah, well.

It's In The Bag
By Eden

One of the hottest "bags" in show business today is the one in which Mr. and Mrs. Salvatore Bono reside. We're speaking of course, about Sonny and Cher.

Interesting quote from Cher recently went something like this: "I hate all the protest songs. They're so unnecessary. Is there so much hate in the world that people have to sing about it?" Oh yes she *did* say that; *honest!!*

"I think we sing about the real things that happen. The everyday emotions between boy and girl. But instead of putting it above their heads like so many singers, we bring it into their understanding. That's very important. It means that people can identify themselves with us much more because we are reaching out to them on their level and ours. And there really aren't too many married boy and girl singers around that fit into today's scene."

It wasn't too very long ago that the talented pair ventured forth on a tour of The Mother Country, and they are currently planning on repeating the successful junket. However, they did have some early uncertainties when first they crossed the Pond.

Bad Scene

Sonny explains: "When we first got to England it was a bad scene. They criticized the way we dressed, and wouldn't let us into hotels. Then we found out we weren't unique, and that other singers had had the same problem.

"I still don't think the hotel managements were right, but I suppose people have to follow the rulebook.

"Cher cried. She hated it all. She wanted to get on the next plane and come home. She couldn't understand why everyone was making such a fuss. I guess they don't realize that this is how a lot of people look today, or that on the West Coast, the whole scene is very casual, and when it came to London, we weren't aware that it would be any different.

"But why should we be blamed for dressing how we want?" I'm afraid I don't know, Sonny, I don't make the rules – I just sort of follow that old rulebook.

★ ★ ★

Poor Ringo. Because of problems caused by fans, our favorite blue-eyed wonder has been "removed" from three apartments, and now he is hoping that his problem will be resolved with the new home that he and Maureen have purchased in Surrey. In the meantime, he and Maureen are living in a London flat. "But when the house in Surrey is finished I shall sell this. You see, we couldn't put the baby outside in the pram here.

"Some fan would proably pinch it as a souvenier and paste it in her scrapbook!" Hmmmm – now that you *mention* it, Ringo . . .

Incidentally, the new house is being completely remodeled and redecorated by a company known as the Brickey Building Co., Ltd. This company also just happens to be owned and operated by Mr. Ringo Starr, MBE, in conjunction with his good buddy, Barry J. Patience.

One of the new additions to the house which is especially exciting to Ringo is the built-in pub which is being installed. Really – an honest-to-goodness English Pub.

"My pub will be all in wood," says Mr. Starr, "with swords and old firearms on the walls and a proper bar with stools and those old-fashioned Curiosity Shop windows.

"As for the rest of the house – well Maureen and I sat down for three and a half hours with an interior decorator telling him just what we wanted. He's got good ideas about materials and color schemes and we're having a special hi-fi set-up built-in."

That's going to be some kind of a wild abode for the Starkey family! Well, *The BEAT* sends them all the best wishes in the entire Beatle-crazed world.

★ ★ ★

Speaking of the Beatles, let's clear up a little bit of rumorizing that's been going 'round. Someone started some whispering on the ol' grapevine to the effect that the Fab Foursome had personally contacted Jimmy O'Neill and asked him to do some "Shindig"-type hosting honors on their very next concert in London Town.

Well, I rang Jimmy-O up myself the other morn and he promptly informed me that it just ain't so at all!! Says he, "Oh I wish it were true, but it just isn't. I really don't know where the rumor got started, but it just isn't the truth."

★ ★ ★

Bob Vaughn plans to host a session of "Hullabaloo" and then wing his way across the Atlantic where he will thespianize in Hamlet on the London stage.

Funny – I know there must be a message there some*where*!!

★ ★ ★

At one time, Tommy Steele was the biggest rock 'n' roll star in all of Great Britain. Now he is completely destroying the cool of all Broadwayites with his smash-hit, "Half A Sixpence."

Just think – some day we may even find Ringo emoting Othello. Well, you never know!!!

KRLA ARCHIVES

Fun, Work Behind The Cameras At

By Louise Criscione

A couple of weeks ago *The BEAT* took you behind the scenes of a recording session to show you that it was not so easy to cut a record, after all.

Now we're going behind the scenes of the second T.A.M.I. Show to let you in on what happened during the filming of the fabulous show which you will see previewed on New Year's Eve. You'll find that the show took a lot of work, a lot of planning and a lot of hours to complete.

The BEAT arrived at the filming around four o'clock—the promised starting time. However, it was well after five before the actual filming got underway.

There were hang-ups everywhere. Technical problems, artist problems. Just about everything which could have gone wrong did.

In fact, at 4:30 they were still painting the props!

U.N.C.L.E. Enters

Shortly after five that darling U.N.C.L.E. man himself, David McCallum, came out to the screaming approval of the audience and made his way down the aisle and to the back of the auditorium.

The stage director announced, "McCallum Intro, Take 1," and then David reappeared flanked by four red turbaned escorts. He made his way down the aisle amid reaching hands and screaming girls and onto the stage where he led a 23 piece band in "Satisfaction" (which drew a tremendous response from the audience as soon as the familiar strains of "I can't get no satisfaction" were recognized) and "1-2-3."

Naturally, it didn't go right. David was perfect (of course!) but the band was wrong. At least the musical director, the genius—Phil Spector, *thought* the band was wrong. So, they did it again. And again, and again.

At this point they sort of gave it up and called a break. Coffee cup in hand, David joked around with the audience crossing his fingers and making a face which said: "I hope they make it this time."

The break over they took the shot again. And made it! It was then six o'clock and the show was running a full two hours late. All the officials kept shaking their heads—how were they ever going to catch up?

Petula's Turn

Next out was the lovely Petula Clark. And the takes began again. Petula was to sing out in the audience which was perfectly all right with the audience you may be sure! She sang her biggest smash, "Downtown." And she sang it over and over and over. She sounded great each time but the crew always managed to find something wrong somewhere.

Whenever in doubt call a break. So, yet another break was called. It was now close to eight o'clock and, to be honest, I was getting tired of just sitting. So, I headed backstage to see what was doing there.

David McCallum was there drinking coffee and chatting with everyone. He's really one of the nicest entertainers around and one of the best looking too.

I found Petula (really stunning in a long white gown) stooping over the coffee machine. She had just finished the "Ed Sullivan Show" and had flown in just for the day to tape the T.A.M.I. Show. And immediately after the taping she was heading on home.

And Again

Poor Petula only had time for a sip of her coffee when they called her back out front to sing "Downtown" again.

This time I watched it on the monitor set up backstage. The Byrds were there and the Lovin' Spoonful were there and we all agreed that Petula looked and sounded just great. Apparently, the T.A.M.I. people thought so too because they informed a delighted Petula that they had it and she could go home.

Then another snag developed backstage. Joan Baez, who by the way looks much better in person than she does in her pictures, was standing in the wings all made up and ready to go on. She was ready but T.A.M.I. wasn't.

They had decided to do the Ray Charles spot next so back into her dressing room went Joan.

Along about this time Donovan came wandering through sans his guitar and earring. Don is having all sorts of trouble in England with lawsuits and so is currently banned from working in England until the whole mess is straightened out.

Legal Trouble

It had really nothing to do with Donovan himself. The legal hassle is over his managers and people like that. Anyway, we hope it all gets itself worked out because an entertainer must entertain to stay popular.

The clock had moved around another time and the Electronovision process with its four cameras had only David McCallum, Petula Clark and one Ray Charles number in the can.

That left them with the Byrds, the Spoonful, Roger Miller, Ike and Tina Turner, the Ronnettes, Bo Diddley and Joan Baez left to go.

The audience, many of whom had been in line since noon, were by now famished. And, in fact, mothers were already arriving to pick up their offspring. The entire show was supposed to be over by nine. And it was well past that hour before the great Ray Charles had finished.

Food Coming

The T.A.M.I. people did a nice thing then. They knew their audience was hungry so they sent out for food for everyone. With an audience that size you can bet that it cost *plenty* to get them all fed.

The food finally arrived, everyone ate and the show plodded along. They picked up a little time but they were still hopelessly behind schedule.

Of course, they had tomorrow to finish up.

Bright and early the next day the crew and artists would arrive with crossed fingers that at least *some* of the shots would go right.

Tomorrow's another day, they kept saying. And surely tomorrow will be better.

Tomorrow the show would be finished and by New Year's Eve it would be out in the theaters for a special preview and January 26 it would open its regular run.

They hoped.

And *The BEAT* hopes so too because it's going to be a fabulous show—so don't you dare miss it, you hear? They worked too hard and too long for that.

... LOVIN' SPOONFUL

KRLA ARCHIVES

Filming Of The 2nd T.A.M.I. Show

... THE BYRDS

... JOAN BAEZ

... PETULA CLARK

... DAVID MCCALLUM

KRLA ARCHIVES

THE NEWBEATS run, baby run. And they have to in order to keep up with their busy schedule. They represented the U.S. in the Grand Gala du Disque contest which was shown on Dutch video. They are about to make their movie debut and, of course, they'll be cutting more records to add to their list of hits which have included "Bread & Butter," "Breakaway," "The Birds Are For The Bees" and their current smash, "Run, Baby, Run."

Walker Bros. Coming Back

The Walker Brothers went to England, became a smashing success and said they'd never return to the United States.

But we didn't believe them for a second, did we? And we were right, for the Walkers are returning to America this month, if only for a short three week visit. Most of their time here will be spent in front of television cameras.

This will be the first trip back for all three of them since they left earlier this year.

Scott and John were playing mainly in California night clubs until they got a three week promotion tour in January of this year and left for England.

They were such an immediate hit in England that they brought their drummer, Gary, over in June and what started out as a sort of experimental three week tour turned into a year of success.

Chart-Topper

Along with their success as a live act they put out a record, "Make It Easy On Yourself," which jumped all the way to number one in England and finally began to get a little notice back home here.

After muttering things about never going back to America, the three have finally been convinced that we'll listen too, so, a year after their departure as a little known act, they are returning as stars.

And Smash Records is currently rushing through an album of their material, cut in England, featuring "Make It Easy On Yourself."

Welcome home, boys.

Q: I use mascara on my upper lashes only, but it always rubs off. By the end of the day, I have black circles under my eyes. What am I doing wrong?
(Jane N.)

A: You are probably using a non-waterproof brand of mascara, which could be causing this problem. Just the natural fluid in your eyes will make this type of cosmetic run. Change brands and also remember to brush your lashes after the mascara has had a chance to dry. This should pick up any excess makeup. Also, you may be rubbing your eyes witout realizing it. Make it a point to remember not to.

Q: I really have a problem! My boyfriend works on weekends and I can't go out on school nights! What shall I do?
(Peggy B.)

A: You'd better get together with your parents and arrange a new schedule for your dating. See if you can't talk them into letting you go out at least once during the week, on a night when you have the least omework. You may have to promise to stay home Saturday night in the bargain, but it'll be worth the sacrifice!

Q: I am fourteen years old and only 4'9" tall. People are forever asking if I'm eleven and it's really quite embarrassing. I make some of my clothes to escape the children's clothes route (I wear a size ten in children's), but I can't make my whole wardrobe. What can I do?
(Kathy M.)

A: You may be going to the wrong places to buy what ready-made clothes you do purchase. In larger stores, women's and girl's sizes go all the way to five and even three. However, with the young look being THE look in all of today's fashions, why don't you concentrate on other ways to look your age? Like wearing your hair away from your face and adding a few light touches of makeup (if your parents don't mind.

Q: I am planning to buy an electric air comb. Will the $5 model work as well as the much more expensive one? Also, do you apply the conditioner before or after using the comb, and how long does the conditioning process last?
(Name Withheld by Request)

A: As with any beauty equipment, you get what you pay for, but the inexpensive air comb should do nicely for your at-home needs. As for conditioner, apply it before using the comb, and check the label to see how often it should be applied.

Q: I have the weirdest problem. My skin isn't too oily and my complexion isn't bad at all. But, no matter what I do, my nose always turns red. It has only been this way for about six months, and I hate it! I put makeup on it, but it's red again in ten minutes. Please help!
(Jane S.)

A: You might feel silly going to a doctor or dermatologist with a "red nose," but there doesn't seem to be any other way out. And don't worry, the doctor won't think it's weird at all.

Liverpuddles
By Rob McGrae
Manager, The Cavern

Well here we go again – this time I want to tell you all about two of Liverpool's favorite people, Ken Dodd and John Donaldson of the Hideaways.

Ken Dodd

Ken Dodd, the Liverpool comedian, has done it again. Hot on the heels of his big hit record "Tears," which incidentally was on top of the British Hit Parade for longer than any other record has been, comes his latest release, "The River," which jumped into the British charts at number 15 after only one week.

Ken is one of the two honorary members of the Cavern Club, the other being Liverpool M.P. Mrs. Bessie Braddock. Ken has become very popular with the teenagers through his own special brand of comedy. He has just completed a fantastically successful season at the London Palladium where every English performer hopes to play one day. He broke every attendance record at the Palladium and had the longest running show the theater's ever seen.

He still has one more great ambition – to be a success in America. From the number of American tourists who've seen him at the Palladium, I'm sure it's bound to happen.

Four of Ken's biggest fans, by the way, are the Beatles, who sent him a telegram congratulating him on his number one success. It read "Congratulations Ken, what are you trying to do, put us out of business."

The Hideaways

I was talking to John Donaldson, the dummer with the Hideaways, and he told me that the lads were absolutely knocked out by the mail they received after I wrote about them in *The BEAT*. "We honestly never expected to receive as much mail as we did and we are still desperately trying to answer it all," he told me. "But we hope to be in America early next year and hope to meet as many of these girls as possible."

Before then however, the boys will achieve another of their ambitions by visiting Ireland. John said, "From what we have been told, Ireland is a really raving place so we should really enjoy ourselves over there."

Judd Lander, the group's harmonica player, has been nicknamed Judd "Set the Trend" Lander by the Cavern D.J. Billy Butler after he recently turned up at the Cavern wearing a white fur eskimo coat.

Billy "Spin-a-Disc" Butler

Billy, the Cavern D.J., is quite a comedian and this week I asked him to finish off the column with a number of quips which I am sure you will like. So over to you Billy.

Well, thanks a lot Bob for that build up which did not do me justice, seeing as I have been writing your column for the past 12 weeks I think it's about time you mentioned me.

Readers did you know that the photograph of Bob at the top of this column was taken 44 years ago when he was 22. No, he truthfully is a great guy and if you think I am only saying this because he has 12 tickets to the Beatle concert here this month, you are right.

I would like to close by thanking all the readers for the old records which they did not send me. But seriously, I am very rarely serious, I am usually mad, I would like to thank everyone for the letters I received and say once again if you do have any old records which you no longer want, I would be very grateful if you would send them to me c/o The Cavern, 8/12, Mathew Street, Liverpool 2.

Olé
Seasons Greetings
Herb Alpert

HERB ALPERT & the TIJUANA BRASS

A&M RECORDS

KRLA ARCHIVES

HEADLINERS HAIR BEAT
Holiday Hair Hints

By Robert Esserman and Frank DeSanctis

Holiday parties coming up—Christmas Eve, New Years Eve, two really big dress up evenings.

What should my hair look like? Should it really be different?

These two questions are our assignment to assure all *The BEAT* readers of a looking pretty swinging year end fiesta.

HAIRDO'S FOR THE REALLY BIG NIGHT

If you have been wearing your hair short but smooth be sure you have your hair done with touseled tops, lots of bangs and softness on the sides.

For those that have been wearing the short in the back, long on the sides, its a gassey idea to have your hair done partially up. This can be be achieved by taking the long sides and pinning it on top of your head. By using the top hair you can make curls.

Here it somes—surfers—yes I know you have had your long straight hair all year and you couldn't think of cutting it. But don't you think it would be a wild surprise for all the girls and boys at the party.

Since Christmas and New Years parties are really a big shebang, this year you could secure your social life by cutting in a new medium or short hairdo. Just think a new hair fix will get you lots of dates for "66."

DRESS IDEAS FROM THE HEADLINERS

A line dresses seem to be ala carte this year. Dresses ending just above the knees OOLALA. Certainly cocktail dresses would be the smart buy; black sheaths are always a favorite.

Remember never think it's smart to wear all your fancy jewelry and accessories. Pick the smartest ones and be sure you get a few opinions on your choice. Sometimes four eyes are better than two.

We would now like to take this opportunity to wish all our readers a very merry time for the holidays coming, and thanks for supporting our Headliners Hairbeat column.

THE HEADLINER HEADACHE SECTION

Do you think my boy friend has the right to tell me how to wear my hair?

Answer: Its a touchy situation, so we'll answer this way. He wouldn't be your boy friend if your hair wasn't right from the beginning, dig?

Where do you suggest I should go shopping for the clothes you've suggested?

Answer: Check your daily newspapers and teenage magazines.

How can I go about buying my girl friend a hairdo at your shop?

Answer: The Headliners are now selling gift certificates which are available at any time. Just drop by.

BARBARA EDEN out of her Gennie outfit and into a chic style.

P. J. Proby Flat Broke, May Return

P.J. Proby's got problems, lots of them. Like he's broke, his hand's in plaster and he has to get out of England.

The young American who got so much publicity because of his rather wild public performances and his disagreement with Jack Good, who was then producing *Shindig*, has been living in England for a while now but it looks like he may be coming back to California.

"My work permit expires Dec. 4," he explains. "And I have to get out of this house on the same day. If I haven't got a new manager to straighten out my problems by then I'll probably put on my jeans, borrow the fare home to Hollywood and get out there and then.

"The trouble is that I went out on a limb for my friend Bongo Wolf. I refused to work when the authorities wouldn't let him back into the country and that caused the break up between me and my manager, John Heyman.

Permit Expires

"In any case I have to leave the country in January for at least six months because my visitor's permit runs out then and there's no chance of getting it renewed.

"Right now things couldn't be much worse—I'm flat broke, penniless, destitute, call it what you like. I have a little store of canned food downstairs which I'm living on and I rely on friends to buy me a drink occasionally. It's a horrible position to be in."

And on top of all his legal and financial problems, his dog lit into him too. His giantic Saint Bernard dog, Athesius, mauled his arm badly recently and he's now up to his elbow in plaster.

So he may be packing his bags and coming back to America soon. And he doesn't seem very anxious to leave. "I've become very attached to Britain," he sighs.

Seekers' "Carnival" Tops

British Top 10

#	Title	Artist
1.	The Carnival Is Over	The Seekers
2.	1-2-3	Len Barry
3.	My Generation	The Who
4.	Tears	Ken Dodd
5.	Wind Me Up	Cliff Richard
6.	A Lover's Concerto	The Toys
7.	Yesterday Man	Chris Andrews
8.	Get Off Of My Cloud	Rolling Stones
9.	Princess In Rags	Gene Pitney
10.	The River	Ken Dodd

The Seekers gained the top spot in England this week with their "The Carnival Is Over" by knocking off Len Barry.

Len is in this week at number two with The Who and "My Generation" remaining in the number three spot.

There are only two new members to the top ten this week. Gene Pitney who enjoys tremendous popularity in England and who has just completed a sell-out tour of Britain moved his "Princess In Rags" into the top ten at number nine.

Ken Dodd who kept his "Tears" at the top of the British charts for what seemed like centuries has a new record out, "The River," which moved in this week at number ten.

This makes two in the top ten for Ken. His "Tears" is still hanging in there at number four which is really quite an achievement for Ken. Because, you see, last week "Tears" was number *seven*.

Which means that it is moving up again and what a novelty it will be if "Tears" recaptures the top spot. It just could happen you know.

The Four Seasons jumped up this week with "Let's Hang On" moving from number 15 to number 12. Also jumping is Fontella Bass and her "Rescue Me." It's up this week from number 21 to number 15.

The Walker Brothers have a new one on the charts. "My Ship Is Coming In," which debuted this week at number 23. Looks as if their ship is *really* coming in.

KRLA ARCHIVES

America's Largest Teen NEWSpaper

KRLA BEAT
Edition

Volume 1, Number 42 — LOS ANGELES, CALIFORNIA — 15 Cents — January 1, 1966

1ST ANNUAL POP MUSIC AWARDS

SOUVENIR EDITION

- Outstanding Record Company
- Best New Female Vocalist
- Best Vocal Album
- Best New Group
- Best Female Group
- Outstanding Group
- Best Duo
- Best Composer
- Best Female Vocalist
- Best 45 Instrumental
- Best Male Vocalist
- Outstanding Producer
- Best Instrumental Group
- Best 45 Vocal Record
- Best New Male Vocalist

1965 BEAT POP MUSIC POLL WINNERS

KRLA ARCHIVES

Sonny, Cher, Beatles, Dylan Win

KRLA BEAT

Los Angeles, California — January 1, 1966

Beau Brummels, Stones, Supremes Also Win Awards

Sonny and Cher, the Beatles and Herb Alpert were showered with multiple honors to highlight *The BEAT*'s first annual International Pop Music Awards.

They received a combined total of nine of the 16 awards presented during a glamorous ceremony attended by the world's top stars and almost 1,000 representatives from the music and record industries.

Other major winners included Bob Dylan, The Beau Brummels and the Supremes in the first public selection and recognition of those who have contributed most to pop music during the past year.

The awards were based on ballots mailed in by *BEAT* readers from not only California but all 50 states and 11 foreign countries.

Official results of The BEAT Pop Music Poll:

Male Vocalist .... Bob Dylan
New Male Vocalist .. Sonny Bono
Female Vocalist .... Cher
New Female Vocalist .... Cher
Vocal Group .... The Beatles
New Vocal Group ..... The Beau Brummels
Female Vocal Group ...... The Supremes
Instrumental Group ... Herb Alpert and The Tijuana Brass
Duo .... Sonny and Cher
Vocal (45 RPM) ..."Satisfaction" (Rolling Stones)
Vocal Album .... "Help" (The Beatles)
Instrumental (45 RPM) ... "A Taste of Honey" (Herb Alpert & the Tijuana Brass)
Instrumental Album ... "The In Crowd"

(Turn to Page 16)

BEATLES — SENT WIRE THANKING BEAT, FANS FOR THREE AWARDS.

SONNY & CHER — TOP DUO PLUS SOLO VOCAL HONORS FOR EACH.

MICK JAGGER Accepts Stones' Award

BOB DYLAN Male Vocalist Award

HERB ALPERT Double Award-Winner

MORE ACCLAIM FOR SUPREMES — OUTSTANDING FEMALE GROUP.

BEAU BRUMMELS' JOHN PETERSEN, RON ELLIOTT — GROUP AWARD

More Exciting Awards Photos On Pages 3-10

The BEAT is published weekly by BEAT Publications, Inc., editorial and advertising offices at 6290 Sunset Blvd., Suite 504, Hollywood, California 90028. U.S. bureaus in Hollywood, San Francisco, New York, Chicago and Nashville, overseas correspondents in London, Liverpool and Manchester, England. Sale price, 15 cents. Subscription price, U.S. and possessions, $3 per year; Canada and foreign rates, $9 per year. Application to mail at second class postage rates is pending at Los Angeles, California.

KRLA ARCHIVES

BEAU BRUMMELS — NAMED BEST NEW GROUP — DOING BYRDS' BIG HIT, "MR. TAMBOURINE MAN."

THE DEEP SIX — THEY CAME UP WITH INTERESTING GROUP VERSION OF "EVE OF DESTRUCTION."

THE VOGUES — OUTSTANDING MEDLEY PROVED THEY'RE AS GOOD IN PERSON AS ON RECORDS.

GLEN CAMPBELL
Fabulous "Crying in the Chapel."

BRENDA HOLLOWAY
She's found "That Lovin' Feelin'."

JOEY PAIGE
Singing "Like A Rolling Stone."

JERRY NAYLOR
Roger Miller's: "King of the Road"

KRLA ARCHIVES

BEAT POP MUSIC AWARDS SHOW
Stars Sing Each Other's Hits in Tribute to Top Ten Songs of 1965

THE KNICKERBOCKERS — THEY AMAZED EVERYONE WITH PERFECT MIMICRY OF BEATLES IN "HELP."

APRIL AND NINO — DOING GREAT VERSION OF "BABY DON'T GO."

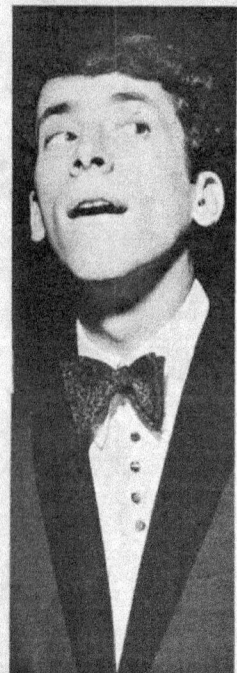

GARY LEWIS
Nominee listens for group awards.

IAN WHITCOMB
Fond memories of "Mrs. Brown."

...thanks

(Best Record Company)

(Best Male Vocalist - Bob Dylan)

COLUMBIA RECORDS

KRLA ARCHIVES

Top Stars View BEAT Pop Music Awards

BEAU BRUMMEL'S RON ELLIOTT, GORGEOUS DONNA LOREN ADD GLAMOR TO BEAT AWARDS SHOW.

MOTOWN'S MARC GORDON WITH SUPREMES' TROPHY. BEHIND HIM: EVIE SANDS, CHAD STUART.

HANDSOME LOU CHRISTIE AND BEAUTIFUL LINDA SCOTT
Another glamorous couple attending BEAT Pop Music Awards.

THE BEES JOIN 1,000 OTHER ARTISTS AND RECORD COMPANY PERSONNEL AT BEAT POP AWARDS.

NO RECORD AWARDS FOR JOSE, BUT BILL DANA WINNER AS M.C.

KRLA ARCHIVES

Phooey on Music Awards—Gary Lewis Wins Photo Award

GARY ARRIVES WITH DATE, TV STAR SALLY FIELDS ("GIDGET")

...SPOTS CAMERAMAN EYING BARRY McGUIRE & SCORES AGAIN!

UNCLE'S ROBERT VAUGHN LEARY... But proves hip to music scene.

BILLY JOE ROYAL WITH MUSIC PUBLISHER STEVE CLARK AND COLUMBIA'S ALLEN STANTON.

...THEN STOPS FOR A QUICKIE POSE WITH APRIL AND NINO

The Big Sound Of

THE ASSOCIATION

On The Charts!!!

"One Too Many Mornings"

VALIANT #730

Valiant records inc.

6290 SUNSET BOULEVARD
HOLLYWOOD, CALIFORNIA
90028

KRLA ARCHIVES

IN SEARCH OF FOLK
He's No Discovery

...MASON WILLIAMS

By Shannon Leigh

The biggest problem with discovering a talented human being is that usually, it is no discovery at all. That is – the person has generally been around for quite some time – just as talented and wonderful as ever-but also quite unrecognized.

So – this week *The BEAT* proudly announces the discovery of an extremely talented young man named Mason Williams, who is really no discovery at all! He is simply unbelievable!!

Mason was born on the twenty-fourth day of August, 1938, in Abilene, Texas. He began his college career at Oklahoma City College as a music major, and soon found it interrupted by a two year hiatus in the Navy!

Mason filled his hours in the Navy with many non-nautical activities, including writing songs for any and all occasions. Songs for food demonstrations, for the anniversary of the destroyer section of the Navy, and in January of 1962 when the attack transport – The Paul Revere – on which Mason was stationed rescued the crew of a helicopter which crashed in the sea – Mason composed a folk song within six minutes commemorating the event, and was singing it by the time they pulled the men on board!

Lectures Too

He also found the time to lecture at San Diego State College, and to sing in many of the top folk houses in the San Diego area in the evenings when he was off-duty.

One of Mason's outstanding features is his unbelievable versatility and only he could even *begin* to describe it to you:

"The kinds of writing I do? I'm concerned with poems, songs – especially in the experimental stage – and I also like to work with words out of context.

"I've gone through all kinds of 'bags' – a Woodie-Guthrie type stage writing warm and human things; an Elizabethan-type thing, where I tried to use the best English I could come up with; and a kind of protest thing, especially when I was in the Service, 'cause I didn't care for it!

"Then I got into a kind of country and western bag. It was my idea to try to write in any form there was. I go in poetic and song cycles; sometimes I'll write nothing but poetry and sometimes I'll concentrate on songs, and the two don't necessarily mean the same. I have found that a good poem will not really make a good song because poetry is more concentrated.

Pop-Art Bag

"I also went into a pop-art song bag. I found that you can borrow ideas from different arts and apply them to yours. I borrowed some of these concepts and applied them to songs."

But they call the young man "folk-singer." Is he?

"As for me being a folksinger: believe it or not, that depends on whether or not you accept it, which is totally contradictory to folk music. There's a clique of ethnics, and a clique of popular folk-singers, and whatever you do with folk music is valid, regardless – because folk music is the music of the people.

"I'd rather think of myself as a *'singer'* – I just happened to learn to write some folk music. I once had a composition teacher who said 'The best way to learn how to write something is to learn 500 of whatever you're trying to write.' So I know 700 or 800 folk songs."

Mason's first book – "Bicyclists Dismount" – is an outstanding example of his amazing versatility and talent. Some of the chapters included are "Them Poems," which he frequently recites in his club act: "Sillies," "Gerpfs," Lovies," and "Other Lovies." And the eighth chapter in the book, entitled "Section Eight," which concerns the Navy! There is also a 60-verse epic poem, which has also been recorded as a 24-minute song, called "Amberwren."

An excellent singer himself, Mason has had his own compositions recorded by such artists as Smothers Brothers, Joe and Eddie, Johnny Desmond, the Kingston Trio, Gale Garnett, and Glenn Yarbrough. Currently, he is acting as the musical director for the new Smothers Brothers album being readied for release.

Mason describes himself as being a "terrible romantic," and confesses to having written reams of poetry for the women in his life. But taking some of his beautiful poetry into consideration – it doesn't seem as though the ladies in question would have objected too much!

Hopefully, the future holds appearances on television as well as radio and record work and a continuation of his concerts.

We mentioned before that very seldom is any true talent ever really "discovered," however Mason retains a certain amount of wry humor to his own long overdue discovery by the public. In a final message to all the people as yet unexposed to his diverse talents, Mason smiles and says: "I would like to thank almost everyone for all their indifference; it keeps me wondering about who's out there."

Adventures of Robin Boyd
By Shirley Poston

CHAPTER EIGHT

When the Beatle limousine ground to a shuddering halt, Robin Boyd (who was still clinging frantically to the aerial) lost her balance and landed in a corner of the garage. Also in a heap.

After the Beatles had hurried through the side door, she struggled to her feet, flapping her wings to make sure nothing was broken.

Nothing was, to her amazement. But her Byrd glasses were missing and she was blind as six bats without them!

Getting down on all fours (which isn't easy for a *real* Robin), she searched for the tiny specs while snickering to herself.

Wow. A few days ago, if someone had told her that she'd be crawling around on the floor in one of the Beatles' garages, in *England* yet, she would have gone off in search of a doctor.

But, there she was. Doing exactly that. And it was her own fault, as usual.

Through a series of gross booboos and un-cool moves, she had allowed all four Beatles to see her. And, although the Beatles had been around and figured they'd seen everything, they had come to this conclusion *before* coming face to face with a *real* bird wearing *glasses*.

As a result, they were now cowering somewhere inside the adjoining house. Fearing for their sanity. A problem Robin was now faced with solving. Or else.

But, there was a second problem. That being just *how* she was going to solve the first one. She'd tried to make plans during the endlessly bumpy ride from the London Palladium, only to discover that thinking sensibly was just one of the *many* things one could not accomplish while clinging frantically to an aerial.

Then, as she found her glasses at last, Robin *knew* what she must do.

She must say the magic word, turn herself back into a sixteen-year-old bird of the *fan* variety, get into the house somehow and explain the peculiar events of this evening to the Beatles.

Then she must take off like a bat out of Stepney, zoom back to California and home and get to work on the English (of all things) theme that was due Monday morning.

Taking a deep breath, Robin uttered the magic word.

But nothing happened. She remained a bird in *both* senses of the word.

"Wor-chester-shire", she said again. "As in sauce," she added hopefully.

Nothing happened again.

"*Wooster-chester-shire?*" she continued, trying to remain calm. "*GEORGE!*" she concluded, failing to remain calm. "*Help me!*"

Seconds later, George Harrison popped his head through the side door of the garage.

"Did someone call me?" he asked nervously.

"Not *you*," Robin blithered helplessly. "I want George the *genie!*"

George the Harrison popped his head back through the side door of the garage and slammed it in stark terror. (The door, not his head.)

"Oh no," Robin further blithered. "I've done it again!"

And she had. In fact, she could still hear the frantic pounding of George's footsteps as he raced through the house in search of a doctor.

If at that terrible moment, she hadn't run smack into a huge, familiar winkle-picker, she would surely have run amuck.

"*George*," she breathed joyously, falling upon the shoe and hugging it. "*You're here!*"

George (the genie) picked her up in the palm of his hand, none too gingerly. His handsome face was stern.

"You," he announced in luvly Liverpudlian, "are some kind of a noot."

Robin nodded shamefully.

"Do you realize that you have the Beatles in a lather? Going about thinking they've dropped one?"

Robin re-nodded shamefully. Then she sniffled. "I'm sorry," she wailed. "I didn't mean for them to see me. And now I can't say Worchester - er - woosterwest – I can't say that *WORD* right so I can turn myself into me and explain things to them!"

"*What?*" thundered George. "Don't ever tell *anyone* about your magic powers! If you do, you'll *lose* them! Just as I'd lose mine if *I* told anyone how I came by them," he further thundered.

"I'm sorry," she repeated meekly. "But what about the poor Beatles? We can't have them going about thinking they've - er - dropped one!"

George gave her a withering glare. Then he turned and snapped his fingers three times. "There," he said not without a touch of pride (George was a doll of a genie, but also an incurable ham). "Now they won't remember ever having seen you." Then he took on a stern look again. "But this is the *last time* I'm getting out of a nice, warm tea pot at the crack of dawn to get you out of some blasted mess!"

Robin smiled rather prettily, for a real bird wearing glasses anyway. She even tried to bat an eyelash or two (providing, of course, that she *had* some) (she'd have to remember to look next time she flew past a mirror), but it failed to improve George's dark mood.

"You don't need a genie," he even further thundered. "You need a *leash!* Now get in my pocket! We are going *home!*"

When Robin was snuggled warmly in the pocket of his jacket (which wasn't easy because his jacket did not *have* a pocket), she called to him.

"Now what?" he snapped.

"What does '*dropped one*' mean?" she asked sleepily.

George said nothing, but he did pat his pocket rather fondly as they disappeared.

(*To be Continued Next Week*)

"COULD GO TO THE TOP" WXRT – CHICAGO
"LIKE THE RECORD" WADM – DECATUR, ILL.

KRLA ARCHIVES

THE ROLLING STONES pose pretty for our **BEAT** photographer, Robert Young, outside of their dressing room before one of their sell-out concerts. Keith and Charlie are carrying on quite a conversation, right?

Yeah, Well Stones...

Stones Tread All Over

By Tammy Hitchcock

I realize that I put the Rolling Stones on our "Yeah, Well Hot Seat" not too many issues ago but I was reading this story in *Newsweek* which was aptly titled "The Rolling Stones — Where The Beatles Fear To Tread." And I just had to share some of their artistic journalism with you.

The article started out by describing the illuminated sign which hung high above Times Square to herald the Stones' arrival in New York.

The paragraph ended by stating that: "The Stones can afford such lavish salutations."

Yeah, well *Newsweek*'s right. The Stones are certainly lavish. I mean, anyone can tell how lavish they are by just looking at the ultra lavish clothes they wear. And how about that lavish shampoo which Mick uses to keep his locks extra clean and shiny?

Gantlet?

Newsweek continued on by bringing up the huge success of the Stones' just-completed American tour. "Their tour has run a gantlet of pubescent fanaticism."

Yeah, well the Stones ran all right. They ran from planes to limousines, from limousines to hotel rooms, from hotels to limousines, from limousines to theatres.

And you know, with all that running the Stones entirely forgot that they ran a gantlet of pubescent fanaticism. Actually, they might not have forgotten. Maybe they just didn't know what a pubescent fanaticism was!

I'd help them out there — except that I don't know either. And to top the whole mess off, I can't even pronounce those big words.

It's a known fact that wherever the Stones go so go their fans. But I guess *Newsweek* didn't quite understand what that means. So, when a few devoted Stone fans attempted to scale the walls of a hotel to reach the Stones (the usual) *Newsweek* thought it was so fantastic that they gave space to the story.

Long Climb

"In New York, five adrenalized striplings climbed 45 flights to the Stones' suite at the New York Hilton before the law stepped in."

Yeah, well for once the Stones were glad the police stepped in. You see, the Stones thought those were *girls* climbing up the walls — they had no idea they were *adrenalized striplings* for heaven's sakes!

The article just couldn't end without some sort of a description of the Stones. "With their jackknife profiles, junior Rasputin coiffures and cockney calls for 'girlie action,' the Stones have been cast as the bad boys of popland."

Yeah, well I can swallow (not very easily though) that whole "description" except for the part about the Rasputin coiffures. That I cannot take.

The Stones' hair styles (I was almost going to say hair *cuts* but I thought better of it at the last moment) are certainly not Rasputin. They're Beethoven.

Keith's Twin

Keith was then quoted as saying: "In London, we looked just exactly the same as the audience."

Yeah, well I don't know about that, Keith. I've been in a lot of audiences in my time and I have *never* sat next to anyone who looked even *remotely* like you. Unfortunately.

Newsweek ended their work of literary art by telling us what we like about the Rolling Stones. "What people see is five hipless moppets dressed like carnival coxcombs, spread across the stage in rock 'n' roll formation."

Yeah, well it's sure nice of them to let us know why we dig the Stones. It's because they're hipless, look like coxcombs and spread themselves across the stage?

Yeah, well what are you going to do?

Noel Harrison Off To A "Dead" Start

"Dead."

That's how he ends his current chart climbing record, "A Young Girl," but Noel Harrison is very much alive.

He first appeared on television in 1951 and hundreds of appearances have followed, most in England where he's from.

Then in 1960 he finally came over to visit America. He did two Ed Sullivan shows and played many of the New York night spots and was off to a great start.

Since then he's toured South Africa, played every last one of London's West End Clubs and appeared on *Hullabaloo* and *Tonight* in America.

And he's spent a good deal of time trying to solve a problem shared by many top singers lately — how to get started in your own career when your father's a star.

You see, Noel Harrison is the son of that most handsome of all Englishmen, Rex Harrison. England scores again.

On the BEAT
By Louise Criscione

The Rolling Stones' day was complete when *Newsweek* called up to apologize for a cutting story which appeared several months ago in the magazine knocking "Satisfaction."

Newsweek explained that the story ran when their music editor was out of town. No matter what the reason, a magazine as big as *Newsweek* rarely apologizes for anything.

So, the Stones should put themselves up for some sort of an award. Like a Magazines Be Kind To Stones Week.

Remember the Animals' film, "Animal Life In Poland?" The short film was supposed to be shot during the Animals' tour of Poland but Dave Rowberry says: "There was absolutely nothing to do and the projected film about a raving group abroad didn't get off the ground.

However, the camera crew is still in Poland hard at work trying to get *something* in the can. Dave says they'll probably film in England too and change the film's format to "Animal Life At Home And Abroad."

"Tripper" Best?

Which side of the new Beatles record do you like best? I kind of go for "We Can Work It Out" but John keeps insisting that "Day Tripper" is the best. Suppose the boy knows, but . . .

Tom Jones thinks that perhaps singing all those ballads has given him "a bit of a square image." You must be joking, Tom. *You* a square? That's like saying the Beatles don't make hit records.

...DAVE ROWBERRY

One of the funniest Beatle stories ever comes from Walter Shenson. "Paul once came to me with a newspaper review from a London paper. 'I don't think it's fair,' he said.

'This chap says we're boorish. That's the one thing we're not — we never bore.'

So, Shenson explained to Paul that boorish doesn't mean boring — it means uncouth. "Oh, uncouth," Paul said. "Well, I think *that's* fair enough."

Ever wonder how much money groups like the Beatles and Stones haul into their bank accounts each year? Well, *they* wonder too! At least, Brian Jones does.

"It's impossible to work out just how much money we have got," says Brian. "But the expenses are always high, especially on hotels. You've got to stay in the best places, otherwise you don't get a good night's sleep.

"You just go on spending but you never know exactly how much money is coming in. People seem to think we could retire tomorrow. Well, we couldn't. Anyway, we wouldn't want to."

Well, that piece of brilliance from Brian ought to make all you Stone fans happy.

The McCoys are sure a cute bunch of guys who just can't believe what's happened to them since they cut "Hang On Sloopy."

Rick Zehringer, McCoy leader, says: "I can't really believe it even now. We've seen a heck of a lot in these couple of months. It's been an education and it's fun."

A lot of groups (entertainers in general, really) start out like that. Full of excitement and grateful to anyone who even offers to help. Then they get a few hit records under their belt and the whole bag changes.

It's no longer exciting to be recognized — it's only a drag. And you don't ever have to thank anyone. Because, you see, they owe it to you now — you're a star.

Anyway, I don't think that we have to worry about the McCoys. They're recording stars but sans the swelled heads.

Yardbird First

The Yardbirds have been invited to enter the competition at the International San Remo Song Festival. It's quite an honor for the boys as they will be the first British group to ever compete at San Remo.

ON THE BEAT says good luck to the Yardbirds. And they'll need it — not because they're not a great group but because they'll be competing against lots of other great groups.

Did George Harrison really write "If I Needed Someone" as a tribute to the Byrds? Byrds' publicist says he did but George never said anything about it.

...KEITH RELF

KRLA ARCHIVES

Inside KRLA

Happy New Year, gang. Can't believe that another year has gone by our window-sills already, but it has. So, may we at KRLA be among the very first to welcome you to 1966 and hope that it will bring you everything you may have missed in 1965.

The last week or so has been one of great activity at the KRLA studios in Pasadena. Christmas was celebrated and preparations made for the New Year, and in the meantime, there were many guests to be entertained.

Dropping by the studio in the last few days to say hello were The Changing Times—two young men well on their way to a second smash hit record—and Andrew Oldham dropped in to have lunch with old Uncle DM. Of course it has been rumored that Andy Loog-Luv brought with him a certain number of rather Stoned—you should excuse the expression!—young men, but of course—you just never know about these rumors!

A new group called The Boys also paid a visit to the hallowed halls of KRLA, but strangely enough, these "Boys" are a group of three singing girls!! Well, I guess it had to happen someday!

Pop Award Talk

All the groovy, groovy, super-cool guys here at KRLA are still talking about the ultra fantastic KRLA *BEAT* Pop Awards ceremony on the eighth of December. It was a night which won't soon be forgotten.

Dick Moreland told *The BEAT* that Roger Miller's mother had tears in her eyes after Dick announced to the star-studded audience in Dave Hull's Hullabaloo that it was Mr. and Mrs. Miller's 50th wedding anniversary.

Then Dick confided that there were almost tears in *his* eyes when Roger told him of his mother's reaction later in the evening.

Johnny Hayes—another of the KRLA DJ's who presented some of the awards—was so enthusiastic about the evening's proceedings that he even called the *BEAT* offices the next day to rave on some more about it!

The ol' Hullabalooer was, of course, in Seventh Heaven. It was *the* night, for the Master Hornblower of KRLA. But he did voice one criticism the next day, and that was in regard to the award presented for the best vocal record of the year.

Dave Unsatisfied

The Stones' record—*Satisfaction*—had walked off with the top honors in this category, but Dave felt that the results should have been otherwise. "I think that this award should have gone to the Beatles for 'Yesterday.' Of course, the kids all voted for 'Satisfaction,' and I bow to their wishes—but I think that 'Yesterday' should have received the award.

"'Satisfaction' was Number One for four weeks and it was on the charts for six weeks. 'Yesterday' was Number One for only three or four weeks, but it was on the charts for *17* weeks.

"I think that not only I, but *anyone* who is at all connected with the Beatles would have liked to see them win this award. But they did walk off with three awards while the Stones received only one.

"Of course I congratulate the Stones and I respect the kids wishes, 'cause they voted for these awards, but I think that the Beatles should have won."

Oh well—maybe next year, Dave. Poor Beatles!!!

Coming up in the future, Dick Biondi will be taking his road shows to Daniel Murray High in Hollywood on Friday, January 14, and to Arcadia High on the 19th of January, so watch out for them.

Before we go, just one more reminder—have you been watching your heavens above for sight of the KRLA Flying Saucers? You'd *better*, 'cause you just never know when they're gonna come in for a landing!!

Happy New Year everyone!

KRLA DJs Present First Pop M

DAVE HULL, HULLABALOO MANAGER

DURING TV SPECIAL ON BEAT MUS

DAVE HULL'S NEW CLUB, THE HULLABALOO, HOSTS AWARDS SHOW.
Dave is interviewed by Charlie O'Donnell during awards presentations.

THE PALACE GUARD, REGULARS AT THE HULLABALOO, LIVEN THINGS UP DURING AWARDS SHOW. HER

APPEARING THRU JAN. 2

JOE & EDDIE

with comedian **JOHN MOORE**

MAKE RESERVATIONS NOW FOR A GALA NEW YEARS EVE

Troubadour

RESERVATIONS
CR 6-6168

Troubananny's Are HAPPENING Monday

KRLA ARCHIVES

Music Awards

ARY BOOKASTA (RIGHT) BRIEF AN USHER.

"THE NEXT AWARD WILL BE..." Charlie "O" assists M.C. Bill Dana

AWARDS, KRLA'S DICK MORELAND INTERVIEWS DICK AND DEEDEE.

ALPERT RECEIVES FIRST OF TWO AWARDS FROM JOHNNY HAYES, BILL DANA

KRLA Tunedex

DAVE HULL • BOB EUBANKS • DICK BIONDI • JOHNNY HAYES
EMPEROR HUDSON • CASEY KASEM • CHARLIE O'DONNELL • BILL SLATER

This Week	Last Week	Title	Artist
1	29	WE CAN WORK IT OUT/DAY TRIPPER	The Beatles
2	1	LET'S HANG ON	The Four Seasons
3	11	THE SOUNDS OF SILENCE	Simon & Garfunkle
4	2	LIES	The Knickerbockers
5	5	FLOWERS ON THE WALL	The Statler Bros.
6	4	EBB TIDE	The Righteous Bros.
7	8	YOU DIDN'T HAVE TO BE SO NICE	Lovin' Spoonful
8	9	RUN, BABY, RUN	The Newbeats
9	—	LIGHTNING STRIKES AGAIN	Lou Christie
10	3	IT'S MY LIFE	The Animals
11	28	SHE'S JUST MY STYLE	Gary Lewis & The Playboys
12	19	YOUNG GIRL	Noel Harrison
13	13	I HEAR A SYMPHONY	The Supremes
14	17	OVER AND OVER	Dave Clark Five
15	12	RISING SUN	The Deep Six
16	10	I CAN NEVER GO HOME ANYMORE	The Shangri-Las
17	22	I FOUGHT THE LAW	Bobby Fuller Four
18	16	THE LITTLE GIRL I ONCE KNEW	The Beach Boys
19	18	PIED PIPER	The Changin' Times
20	20	I WILL	Dean Martin
21	23	ENGLAND SWINGS	Roger Miller
22	27	HOLE IN THE WALL	The Packers
23	30	JENNY TAKE A RIDE	Mitch Ryder & The Detroit Wheels
24	26	DON'T THINK TWICE	Wonder Who
25	25	STAND BY ME	Earl Grant
26	36	I SEE THE LIGHT	Five Americans
27	37	THE DUCK	Jackie Lee
28	39	FIVE O'CLOCK WORLD	The Vogues
29	38	MY GENERATION	The Who
30	34	MAKE THE WORLD GO AWAY	Eddy Arnold
31	40	THUNDERBALL/KEY TO MY HEART	Tom Jones
32	—	ONE HAS MY NAME	Barry Young
33	—	PUPPET ON A STRING	Elvis Presley
34	—	PLEASE DON'T FIGHT IT	Dino, Desi & Billy
35	—	SUNDAY AND ME	Jay and the Americans
36	33	FEVER	The McCoys
37	—	UPTIGHT	Little Stevie Wonder
38	—	A MUST TO AVOID	Herman's Hermits
39	—	ONE TOO MANY MORNINGS	The Association
40	—	HOW IS THE AIR UP THERE?	The Changin' Times

DEADLINE NEAR... You have until Jan. 1 to take advantage of the introductory subscription offer of $3 for 52 issues. SUBSCRIBE NOW – SAVE 60%

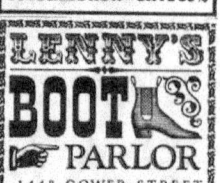

LENNY'S BOOT PARLOR
1448 GOWER STREET
(At Sunset)
HOLLYWOOD, CALIF. 90028
466-7092

KRLA BEAT Subscription

SPECIAL OFFER — Deadline Jan. 1
SAVE 60% Of Regular Price
☐ 1 YEAR — 52 ISSUES — $3.00
Enclosed is $3.00 ☐ CASH ☐ CHECK
Send to: .... Age ....
Address: ....
City .... State .... Zip ....
MAIL YOUR ORDER TO:
KRLA BEAT
6290 Sunset, Suite 504
Hollywood, Calif. 90028
Foreign Rate: $14.00 — 52 Issues

GIFT SUBSCRIPTION

Please send a one-year gift subscription to:
Who lives at: _____
City: _____ State: _____ Zip: _____
Send a card saying it is from: _____

Enclose $3 for each subscription. Mail to:
KRLA BEAT, Suite 504, 6290 Sunset, Hollywood, Calif 90028

KRLA ARCHIVES

FOR JAMES BROWN, commercial success is no stranger. He has long been recognized as one of the top rhythm-and-blues artists. But 1965 will probably go down as his most satisfying year — the year he also became universally acclaimed as a pop artist. Another James Brown record, "I Got You," has made it to the top.

What A Mess The Pop World Is In!!

By Carol Deck

Gad! Such confusion there is in the pop world today.

I mean how can you really expect some poor innocent radio listener to keep the Who, the Guess Who and the Wonder Who straight? Especially when the Wonder Who are identified as the Four Seasons half of the time and the Wonder Who the other half.

And what about the Byrds and the Yardbirds—they sound a lot alike when you're only half listening to the old radio. And those Clarks—Dave, Dick and Petula (sounds like a new group to rival Peter, Paul and Mary.)

And there's a group called the Rising Sons but there's also a song called "The Rising Sun" put out by the Deep Six. Yeah, there's a lot of numbers running around now—is it the Dave Clark Four and the Bobby Fuller Five or the other way around? And don't forget the Four Seasons and the Four Tops.

Look Alikes

And it's not just names that get a little on the confusing side—what about looks? Ever notice how much Tad Diltz of the MFQ resembles John Sebastian of the Lovin' Spoonful? And there's Chris Hillman of the Byrds and Denny Ellis of the Grassroots. And how many of you noticed that the drawing of UNCLE'S David McCallum that *The BEAT* ran on the cover a few weeks ago looked vaguely like Jack Parr? Louise even reported in her column that one of the English pop papers ran a picture of Mick Jagger where he looked like Herman — come on now, Mick and Herman!!?

There are sound-alikes too. Remember when Them released their first record and everyone thought it was the Rolling Stones under another name. And who can deny that the Knickerbockers' "Lies, Lies" sounds an awful lot like early Beatles?

As if this wasn't enough to confuse the poor listener there's the problem of songs recorded by more than one group at the same time.

Too Many "Yesterdays"

Like Paul McCartney's "Yesterday," for instance. Aside from Paul's magnificent original version, it's also been recorded by Matt Monroe, Marianne Faithfull, Barry McGuire and who knows who else. And remember that hot race between Cher and the Byrds over "All I Really Want To Do."

For a while there we even had two versions of the same song on the charts at the same time when the Ramsey Lewis Trio released a jazz version of "Hang On Sloopy" while the McCoys swinging version was still high on the charts.

Who's Tears?

And then there's "As Tears Go By." Mick Jagger and Keith Richards wrote it but Marianne Faithfull made it a hit. Now Mick does it on the Stone's latest album while Marianne does the Beatle's "I'm a Loser" on her album. Who's recording who's material?

Add to all of this mess a couple of groups that can't spell too well — like the Byrds and the Vejtables -and the whole scene is like chaos.

Maybe some day everything will be simple again and everyone will look and sound unique and have totally different names so the listeners will have a little easier time telling what's going on. Until then I guess we'll just have to hang tight and stay sharp.

And, by the way, just what is that line in "Satisfaction?"

Liverpuddles
By Rob McGrae
Manager, The Cavern

Hi there everyone—Liverpool certainly has been busy lately what with the appearance of Wilson Pickett and Georgie Fame and the Blue Flames at the Cavern.

Wilson Pickett appeared before a capacity crowd here towards the end of his tour of England. He told me he was delighted that his tour had been so fantastically successful. He was, however, disappointed that he has to work so hard since he's arrived, thus making it impossible for him to see any of England's tourist centers which he had longed to see. He was however determined to come back again even if it is only for a holiday.

The Cavern audience really enjoyed him from the very moment he went on stage. His act only lasted for about 30 minutes but the amount of work he put into those 30 minutes left him completely exhausted.

During the act he brought members of the audience on stage to dance and sing with him. Some of the high notes he achieved left the audience disbelieving.

Georgie Fame

Yet another person who is always welcome at the Cavern is Georgie Fame. The audience went wild over him during his recent all night session. He was born not very far from Liverpool, in Leigh, and was a member of Billy Fury's backing group before he got his own group together. He had his first big hit last year with "Yeah, Yeah." Since then had many big hits in England and his most recent one on the charts is "Something."

Jackie Lee

Every week the Cavern issues its own top 30 list based on the number of requests we receive for records. I am very happy to say that among the recent batch of records sent over from America was Jackie Lee's version of "The Duck." It's become so popular with Cavern Club members that's it's number five on our charts now.

If any reader wishes us at the Cavern to plug their favorite artist's record here we will be very pleased to do so if they send us a copy of the record. I will be very pleased to keep you informed on the records that are popular at the Cavern now. So send your records and requests to me at either 17, Heydean Road, Liverpool, 18, or c/o The Cavern, 8/12, Mathew Street, Liverpool, 2.

GEORGIE FAME rests up after his stint at The Cavern. He hasn't done much here in the U.S. since his smash, "Yeah, Yeah," but in England he swings.

Chad, Jeremy Not Palefaces

It looks like Chad and Jeremy won't be palefaces after all.

The British duo has been signed to star in their own television TV and it was to have been titled "The Paleface."

"The Paleface" was also the title of a Bob Hope movie for Paramount a while back but it was thought that there would be no conflict.

However they did run into some legal problems and have dropped that title and are searching for another.

Meanwhile, Peter Graves, Marlyn Mason and Arch Johnson have been signed to appear in the pilot of the show which will be a spinoff from the "Laredo" series. The pilot will be titled "What A Way To Go, That A Way."

How about the Chad and Jeremy Show, fellows? That's always a good start.

KRLA ARCHIVES

...THE VEJTABLES

Vejtables Growing In San Francisco

By Carol Deck

The last thing on anybody's mind would be to call themself a vegetable, but five young San Franciscans have gone one step farther and call themselves the Vejtables.

They appeared on the national charts once before with "I Still Love You" and now they're back with "The Last Thing on My Mind."

The Vejtables are Ned Hollis, 21; Jim Sawyers, 20; Frank Smith, 22; Bob Baily, 23, and Jan Ashton, 22. As for their name it seems that a friend of Bob's thought it up as a joke and somehow it stuck after they changed the "g" to a "j".

The forming of the group was no accident. Bob and Ned decided one day that it was about time someone let their hair down and did Beatle songs with a little touch of originality. At that point the only group in the Bay area who had come near it was the Beau Brummels.

Beatles and Byrds

So the two found three more people who were the right age and started off about a year ago. Although most of them do write songs, their act primarily consists of material by the Beatles, Stones, Byrds, Animals and other top groups.

The first thing you notice about this group when you see them is that their drummer is a girl. But Jan doesn't think there's anything peculiar about her being a girl, or a drummer either for that matter. A lot of people in her family, including her father, are drummers and she just beats the skins because it's "fun and different."

There's nothing ordinary about the rest of the group either. Ned, who plays 12 string and rhythm guitar, wanders around in a huge, long haired green coat that looks like it ought to be either fed or mowed.

And Frank goes wild over toys that do absolutely nothing and likes to tell people that his name is Pipe. He describes the group's sound as "indescribably delicious."

The group disagrees on many things — like protest songs. Jim says too many people are cashing in on them, but Jan feels they say something that ought to be said. Frank chirps in that the only thing he protests is "running out of toothpaste."

Before forming the Vejtables, all five of them were in other phases of entertainment. Frank was in a band called the Misfits (that's logical), Jan was with Jean and the Ethics, Jim was in a rhythm and blues group called the Otherside, Ned played organ in a trio and Bob was studying acting.

Likes Girls

What kind of audience do they like to play to? "Girls," says Jim but Jan adds that they like to play to younger audiences because "you feel better when you do something for younger kids."

And so San Francisco sends us another winner. This city may yet replace Liverpool.

And Frank feels that the Bay area has had a definite influence on the group. "We all have more colds."

Bob And Bill Smash Record

The Righteous Brother's latest record is "Ebb Tide" but they sure aren't acting like any ebb tide. They recently smashed the standing show attendance record at the Cave Supper Club in Vancouver, British Columbia.

Brenda Lee had set the old record of 1300 but Bob and Bill practically smashed that on opening night alone.

1265 people showed up for the two performances the first night and after three shows they had moved the record up to 1652.

That's righteous, brother.

Best Wins Opener In Beatle Suit

Few people thought that he would seriously do it, but Pete Best (former Beatle drummer) has won the first round in his libel suit against the Beatles and *Playboy* magazine.

The suit is being brought in a New York court. The Beatles had asked the Court to grant a motion to dismiss the charges and to have the legal action transferred to an English court.

The Beatles tried to base their motion on the grounds that since they do not do business in the United States they are not subject to our jurisdiction.

Best Wins

But the Court wouldn't have it. They liked Best's grounds better. He asserted that since the Beatles work in America, collect royalties here, own several corporations which are based in New York City and, in fact, have themselves used New York courts they are indeed subject to New York jurisdiction. And the court thought so too.

So, Best has won the opener. Round two is about to begin and, who knows, the Beatles just might taste defeat in this round as well.

In the meantime, Pete has released "Boys." Yes, the same "Boys" which the Beatles recently released as a single and as hurriedly withdrew from the market. Rather interesting, isn't it?

PETE BEST stands solemnly contemplating what will happen now that he has won the opener in his libel suit against the Beatles.

KRLA ARCHIVES

For Girls Only
By Shirley Poston

Hmmm. I'm not sure, but I just may be having a change of heart.

Remember when I came up with a brilliant (oh, sure) solution to keep boys from horning in on *our* column? You know, when I suggested that one of them write a "For Boys Only" column!

Well, I've received so many offers from boys who say that although they'll go on reading our column whether we like it or not, they would also like to contribute one of their own!

Sounds like a bit of all right there. Also a smashing idea if I do say so myself (and I just did) (which figures.)

So, boys, since anyone who'd make all those generous offers can't be all bad, I've turned your letters over to *The BEAT* and will see what I can do about nagging the powers-that-be into accepting one of those offers.

Here's hoping they do. I can hardly wait to read the first installment of "For Boys Only," whether they like it or not!

Speaking of George Harrison (well, I was *thinking* about him and that's next best), I'd like to comment on another letter I received recently.

Hate Pattie?

Some time ago I mentioned the fact that several of you seemed to dislike Pattie Boyd with a purple passion. I couldn't quite figure this out because although I luv George with the same purple passion, I've never passed beyond a pastel shade of envy-green where Pattie is concerned. (Is it Pattie, Patty, Patti or what? I always forget. Which also figures.)

Anyway, I got quite a few answers to this question and the best one came from... oh, nuts... I've lost the letter somewhere under one of the ceiling-high piles on this desk.

Well, what whoever-it-was said was this. In her opinion, Pattie seems to "take away" from George. She explained her feeling this way—in photographs, Pattie always seems so serious when everyone else is having a good time, which makes a lot of people wonder if George is really happy with her.

Interesting thought, huh? I don't mean that this is the case with Pattie. I mean that if she does give that impression, that's why many Harrison-maniacs have a different feeling toward her than Lennon-maniacs have for Cyn.

Just by a look or a touch, Cyn always seems to add something to John. And when you really care about someone, it's natural to feel the "mean reds" in the direction of anyone who might be subtracting anything from him.

Purple Dislike

I doubt if this is the way things are between George and Pattie. (Rats! I just HATE to write *George and Pattie!* Down girl!) If they weren't happy together (blast it all!), I don't think they'd be together, which they are (phooey!) But it does explain the purple dislike instead of envy green.

Why don't we all drop Pattie a line and tell her to smile more! (If I didn't have a great deal of self control, I'd also suggest that we all drop her a line and tell her to *get lost*, but would *I* say a thing like *that?*) (I'm only kidding, really!)

Before I get off the subject of George (which may happen in the early spring of 1984), I'd like to thank a certain Beatles' fan club for sending me one of those wild tapes (the kind you make with a punch type machine) (which makes about as much sense as I usually make when I'm trying to explain something) that said: "There Is No Comparison To George Harrison."

Amen.

Since that club also has the world's wildest address, I just have to print it. If you'd like to join, send a letter to 836 HARRISON St., San Francisco 7, Calif.

Speaking of coincidences, before I start raving about something sensible (which may *also* happen in the early spring of 1984), I'd also like to thank Lorelle McCartney of Del Mar, Calif. for the gastric pictures of George.

I ask you. Why couldn't my name be Shirley *Harrison?* Otherwise known as Mrs. George, that is.

Well, it seems as though my chances of getting anything rational accomplished in this column this week are unusually slim. So, while I'm in a ranting mood, another personal question like the ones I keep asking all of you.

Question Time

Still another question. Are you the type of wife who stays home and minds the store (or some such) while hubby is on tour, or do you go right along with him (or else?) And which of the two is the best role for a star's wife to play, do you think? Let me know how you feel on this subject and we'll talk more about it soon.

Uh-oh. You won't believe this, but I feel something sensible coming on. Oh—good! It just went away again. Now, back to George.

Whoops. Here it comes again, so I might as well say it and get it over with.

Remember how we were all going to get together and swap notes about what to buy a boy for Christmas? You know, *months* in advance? Well, I forgot all about it until this very moment!

Well, I'll tell you what. Next year, *months* in advance, we're just going to *have* to get together and swap notes about what to buy a boy for Christmas.

Where "Better late than never" used to be my *motto*, it is now a way of life!

Don't you just love this time of year? Every single relative I have back East always says "how can you have Christmas without *snow?*"

Gee, it's easy. It just sort of happens every December.

Nuts, I'm out of room (also my mind) and here I was going to announce the latest album winner and our new Beatle album contest! Oh well, next week.

Please have a wonderful holiday season, hang up a stocking for George, and if you haven't already sent a card to your favorite star, do it right this minute (better-you-know-what-than-never.) See you next *BEAT!!*

From Student To Stardom

There are definite advantages to success.

A few years ago a University of Minnesota student was performing in small night spots around Minneapolis for as little as $5 a night. And he usually had to beg to get even those little chances to show his stuff before an audience.

Recently, this now former student, Bob Dylan, earned $26,038 for a one night stand in the same city. In a 9,000 seat auditorium there were only 232 seats unsold.

You're coming up in the world Bob.

BRITISH TOP 10

The Beatles score again! They debuted this week at number one with their double-sider, "Day Tripper" and "We Can Work It Out." From nothing to one—that's the fantastic Beatles for you!

P. J. Proby is back in the top ten again—this time with his great vocalizing on "Maria." Yes, the same "Maria" from "West Side Story" and the same P. J. Proby from the hip-wiggling fame.

Chris Andrews, who almost had a number oner with his, "Yesterday Man," is back again with "To Whom It Concerns." This week it jumped up from number 17 to number 14 and if it keeps climbing Chris just might make it to number one this time around.

It's a strange situation in England. Jim Reeves, although he has been dead for sometime now, continues to be very popular in Britain. And everytime his record company releases one of his old records it soars up the British charts.

This time it's Jim's old release of "Is It Really Over," jumping up from number 21 to number 18.

1. Day Tripper/We Can Work It Out		The Beatles
2. The Carnival Is Over		The Seekers
3. 1-2-3		Len Barry
4. Wind Me Up		Cliff Richard
5. My Generation		The Who
6. The River		Ken Dodd
7. A Lover's Concerto		The Toys
8. Tears		Ken Dodd
9. Maria		P. J. Proby
10. Princess In Rags		Gene Pitney

... JOAN BAEZ

The Real Joan Baez

Joan Baez is a woman of mystery—or at least her press releases would have you believe that her life is shrouded in deep, dark mystery.

Of course, everyone knows that she operates a pacifist school in Northern California because she is firmly against war. So, most people have her pegged as some kind of a protestor with a guitar. A person who rarely finds anything to laugh at.

How wrong they are. Joan is one person who always seems to be laughing. "You have to laugh at everything or you'd die," she says. "Humor is very important in my life."

But perhaps the most important thing in her life right now is her school. If you get Joan talking about her pacifist school, she'll go on for hours.

Peace Of Mind

Joan says that her non-violence school is not limited to teaching just non-violence. "I want people to be more aware of themselves. The school is meant to promote peace of mind which brings about peaceful acts," Joan declares.

Joan was not always the non-violent type. "I never realized how much violence there was in me before I took the time to think and discuss it with others," she says.

When Joan did decide that she was all for non-violence and pacifist tactics she went all out. She toted her guitar along to console the Alabama Freedom Marchers. Then when all the demonstrations over our policy in Viet Nam developed she jumped right on the bandwagon and marched along.

With all her protesting Joan is basically a rather lonely person. This is typified in the fact that she lives in a lonely area of California with her two goats, her two dogs and the sea.

Lonely Sea

"I love the sea," says Joan. "It's probably the loneliest sight in the world."

Another place which Joan loves is the desert. She admits that sometimes she feels as if the desert is her only real home. "There is a lot of Indian blood in me and the desert is also lonely and at peace," Joan declares.

Joan was clearly in the mood for sad things so she revealed that to her the saddest sight in the world is "old people who have never had a chance to be anything but tramps."

Protest Songs?

How about protest songs? As a folk singer and as an obvious protestor, what does she think about our current protest songs?

"I think Dylan has got out of hand now," says Joan who once used to be Dylan's closest friend.

"So many of his songs mean nothing because his words can only mean something to him. Barry McGuire was completely out of hand with 'Eve of Destruction' but there will always be something of value in both Dylan and Donovan's songs," continued Joan.

Although we don't fully agree with Joan's opinions, we do believe that she has a right to them. And so should you.

KRLA ARCHIVES

Work Permit And Contract Save Proby

P. J. Proby may not be coming back to America after all.

After a six hour meeting with Proby, agent Tito Burns signed the Liberty recording artist and began plans for a theater tour for this month.

Burns also made arrangements for the extension of Proby's work permit which will allow him to stay until April at least.

The move comes just in time to save Proby from having to come back to America because his work permit was running out and he was evicted from his house in England.

Burns also serves as the British agent for the Rolling Stones, Dusty Springfield and the Searchers. He got help from an unnamed financier to try and rebuild Proby's career.

January Tour

"I am setting up a tour for January," Burns said. "And if we have difficulty in getting some circuit theaters as a result of the fiasco of a year ago, then I shall book independent venues. In February I expect Proby to honor the cabaret engagements he recently cancelled."

Proby's also doing better on the charts now. His release of "Maria" has jumped to number 10 in England in its second week and his third British album is due next month.

Ups and Downs

Proby has had many ups and downs in his career and it looks like he's headed for another up. He started as an American singer, then went to England to become famous. His return to America brought only a riff with Shindig producer Jack Good and trouble with the critics over his wild live performances. So he returned to England, had a couple of hits and then announced recently that he was broke and homeless and might be returning to the United States.

Time for another try Mr. Proby.

... THE CHALLENGERS (l. to r.) Phil Prenden, Art Fishek, Edward Fourdier, Richard Delvy, Randy Naugent.

Challengers Join UNCLE

By Louise Criscione

It seems like just about everyone is getting into the U.N.C.L.E. bag nowadays, doesn't it? The latest to join the U.N.C.L.E. wagon are the five swinging Challengers.

The group is not planning on becoming secret agents or anything like that but they have recorded a pretty exciting single in "The Man From U.N.C.L.E." A rather unique title, don't you think?

The Challengers have certainly come a long way since they first hit the publics' eye during the surfing sound era.

They have played every pop show imagineable and have entertained at teenage clubs all over the country drawing capacity crowds everywhere.

Movies Too

They've already appeared in two movies, "Take Her, She's Mine" and "For Those Who Think Young."

Now the Challengers are branching out and hitting the college circuit. Again, with great success. Their appearances at UCLA, the University of Colorado, the University of Arizona and the University of Santa Barbara (to mention a few) drew raves from everyone—including the faculty members who were brave enough to attend a show with their students.

Besides records, television shows, clubs and colleges the Challengers have also ventured out into the cruel world of commercials.

They filmed one of those "Tony The Tiger" commercials for Kelloggs. Watch for it—release date is sometime in the New Year.

Yes, the Challengers have come a long way since they abandoned their surfboards. And they'll probably go a lot further before they put their instruments down.

Pet Clark Writer Too

The lady's name is Petula Clark and she is the possessor of talent which just won't stop. Her early life was spent as England's most famed child star.

As inevitably happens, Pet grew up and became one of the most charming women around. She and her French husband took up residence in Paris but Petula still clung to her English accent.

For quite sometime she remained relatively quiet and content with being a wife and mother. But then she found Tony Hatch and with Tony she penned "Downtown." That did it—from then on she's been in demand from one end of the world to the other.

You are probably not aware of the fact that it was Petula and Tony who created "You're The One," the record which was such a smash for the Vogues.

"Pet wrote most of the melody line of 'You're The One'" reveals Tony Hatch. "I wrote the lyric and added a little to the tune." And there you have it—an instant hit.

Pet recorded the song and released it in England where it did very well on the charts. But in America the song belonged to the Vogues. Their version of Pet's song climbed the charts until it just couldn't climb any higher.

Tony, being an extremely frank man, admits that composers tend to dry up after awhile. And if this happens he figures that Petula can keep singing and he can continue recording her.

It's always handy to be doubly talented but if Pet's song writing ability ever ceases we'd venture to say that she could make a very substantial living by simply singing.

She's such a bright spot to have on any bill. No matter where she plays—if it's to a teenage audience or to an audience made up of teenagers' parents—she always draws raves.

She's one performer whom The BEAT hopes will never stop performing. We dig her—how about you?

South Rises Again With Statler Brothers

The South has risen again.

Not many country and western or gospel singers ever make it big in the pop world but the Statler Brothers have proved to be the exception.

The four boys from Staunton, Va., are smashing right up the charts with their "Flowers On the Wall," a record that can't be classified as anything but country and western.

The group was formed in 1955 and were an almost immediate hit in the South and Plains region. Their big break came when they were discovered by Johnny Cash and asked to join his touring show. But now they've broken into the pop world and it may never be the same again.

Two Brothers

The group is made up of two brothers, Harold and Don Reid, and two close friends, Lew DeWitt and Phil Balsley.

Don is the youngest member of the group and the only single one. He sings second tenor, acts as master of ceremonies, writes songs and plays baritone ukelele.

His brother Harold is the bassomanager of the group and a talented song writer. He's been known to play banjo every now and then. He and his wife have two children.

Lew Writes

"Flowers on the Wall" was written by Lew, who sings first tenor, is married and the father of two sons and a daughter.

The group's baritone is Phil who was born in Augusta County, Va., and is the father of two sons.

They've been popular regionally for a long time but this record has put them in national prominence.

Looks like the Statler Brothers no longer have time for counting flowers on the wall or playing solitaire 'til dawn.

... THE STATLER BROTHERS

KRLA ARCHIVES

THE RASCALS have one heck of a gimmick, don't they? They appear complete with knickers, Buster Brown collars, short ties and caps. The group recently broke records at New York's Phone Booth Club (which incidentally, has no phones) like they were going out of style. Seen applauding in the audience opening night — the Stones, Bob Dylan, Herman's Hermits, the Lovin' Spoonful, Barry McGuire and Lesley Gore. Looks like the Rascals did themselves proud.

The Lowdown On The British Rubber Soul EP

Beatles here . . . Beatles there . . . Beatles Beatles everywhere . . . So the Fab Foursome has produced another unbelievably sensational album. So what, right? Wrong, 'cause once again they're setting trends in this world of pop.

By now, literally thousands upon thousands of copies of their new "Rubber Soul" album have been received as Christmas gifts by delighted Beatlemanicas everywhere. Unfortunately, in America we are given only twelve of their new tunes, while the British LP has 14.

Therefore, for all the Americans who haven't yet been exposed to the other new Beatle tunes, and for any *BEAT* readers who do not yet have their own copy of the album, we're going to do a little review of the whole Elpee for you right now, and tell you all about each cut on the 14-track British disc.

The first song on the first side is a tune called "Drive My Car," with Paul and John both singing lead. It has a medium sort of tempo and finds Paul cutting up on the piano in the background.

Second cut on the album is "Norwegian Wood," which is also included on the American record. This tune is softer and a little slower, and carries along a feeling of a sort of John Lennon-type folk, with the inimitable John-John lead-vocalizing. Second title for the tune is "This Bird Has Flown." It is possible that the new song is an adaptation. This cut also features George on the Sitar, which is an Indian instrument.

The third cut is also included on the American disc, and is entitled "You Won't See Me." One of the greatest arrangements and blending of melodies by the Beatles on this tune, and it has to be one of the best cuts on the disc. If you listen closely, you will also hear road-manager Mal Evans doing his share on the organ in back.

Fourth tune is only on the British disc, called "Nowhere Man." John, Paul and George all combine their golden tones on this one, and the result is very pretty. A little slower than the other cuts, but melodic and nice to listen to.

Next up is "Think For Yourself," a George Harrison composition, which George lead-vocals for himself. Wonderful sound effect achieved by Pauly on the buzz-bass (that fuzzy bass sound you hear in the background) on this one, and a good, strong, driving beat will keep this one on top.

The next tune is one of the favorites, called "The Word." John, Paul, and George are all singing on this one, and the harmonies and special tune-and-word blendings on this one are absolutely out of sight!! Beatle recording producer, George Martin, joins in the festivities on this one by playing the harmonium — whatever that is! Great song.

The last cut on this side is the beautiful ballad "Michelle" by Paul. Although it doesn't sound at all like his fantastic "Yesterday," it is another tender love song, sung as only Paul could sing it. He even croons the choruses in French — and what better language for a love song?! By the way, if you were wondering what that French means — it is simply a repeat of the first chorus of English lyrics — "these are words which go together so well."

The first cut on the second side of the British Elpee should come as somewhat of a surprise to most Americans. It's called "What Goes On," and features Ringo singing with his favorite Country and Western sort of style. Surprise? Well, Der Ringo helped John and Paul in the penning of this little ditty, and it sounds pretty good — so *there!*

Next, is the sad and wistful ballad, "Girl," sung by John. George and Paul join forces to create an atmospheric background here, and the whole cut is sort of a mood-tune. Try it next time you feel depressed. Only kidding, 'cause there's a good deal of feeling coming through on this record.

Next tune swinging 'round the disc is the really swingin' cut, "I'm Looking Through You." Paul belts this rocker for us, and Ringo leaves his drum kit long enough to raise havoc on a Hammond organ. Wonderful fun, almost-bluesy sound on this one.

"In My Life" is another of the philosophical sounds on the album, and is a down-tempo tune crooned by John and Paul. Good harmony and a strong over-all feeling on this one.

"Wait" is a rough-edged up-tempo tune sung by John and Paul, with some excellent guitar and tambourine work. Good off-and-on beat.

The next cut offers the second surprise for Beatlemaniacs in the Colonies. On the British Elpee, this next track is the second tune penned by G. Harrison, MBE, entitled "If I Need Someone." This has a good sound, and has already been recorded by another British group, the Hollies.

The last tune on the album is "Run For Your Life," with John singing lead, and is one of the most energetic and exciting tracks on the album. This is another typically Beatle fast-paced number. Great.

And that's it. Another Beatle album has been released, so what? SO . . . WOWWWWWWWWWW! Happy New Year, everyone.

Donovan's New Staff

Donovan's got a new manager — his father.

Donald Leach has been appointed the British singer's personal manager in a slight re-arrangement of staff.

Vic Lewis is now Donovan's agent and Ashley Cozack is business manager.

Donovan has just finished a very short American trip and an 18 day tour of Scandinavia. He's also recorded several of his past hits in French, German and Spanish for sale in Europe.

TIPS TO TEENS

Q: *I'm fourteen and I like a certain girl very much. I think she feels the same way, but every time I'm around her I get real nervous and fidgety, and I never know what to say to her. How can I start a conversation?*
(Steve H.)

A: Stop thinking that you have to. If she's shown an interest in you, she probably likes the strong, silent, fidgety type. If you'll stop stifling yourself by trying too hard, conversation will come easily. Also, keep in mind that she's undoubtedly twice as nervous as you are.

Q: *How much is peroxide, how do you use it and how long do you leave it on?*
(Julie R.)

A: Peroxide isn't very expensive, but it can be extremely dangerous if not used according to instructions. Tell the drug store clerk what you intend using it for and she'll take it from there.

Q: *I have a terrible weight problem. I've gained eighteen pounds in the last year and need to lose at least thirty according to the weight chart. People say it's baby fat and that I'll outgrow it, but I'm already thirteen and that isn't exactly a baby. I want to lose the pounds gradually, over a six month period. Is this possible and how should I go about it?*
(Eileen M.)

A: Five pounds a month seems a sensible amount to lose and shouldn't create any health hazards. But, you should definitely get a doctor's advice before you begin a diet. The wrong reducing diet has been known to cause just as much trouble as overweight! But forget about the baby fat and you'll-outgrow-it routine. They're just trying to be nice and make you feel better. If you don't nip this in the bud now, you might grow into it, not out.

Q: *I would like to know if it is considered good manners to exchange a gift. I received a sweater I just don't like, but I don't know how to explain the exchange. It wasn't too big or anything. Please help.*
(Marcia L.)

A: Most gift-givers go all out to encourage you to exchange any presents you don't like, but some of them do get slightly miffed when you take them up on the offer. If the friend who gave you the sweater is this type of person, you'd better come up with a reasonably good reason why you took it back. Like it just wasn't your color, or made you look like a balloon. You know, make it your fault, not the sweater's.

Q: *I got too near the fireplace and parts of my hair have sort of sizzled. What can I do about these frizzy ends? There aren't too many, but they look weird!*
(Judy M.)

A: Brush your hair extra-often for the next week or so. The sizzled hairs will break off and brush out before long.

HINT OF THE WEEK

I think I've just found a way to revolutionize the pen pal game. I have several pen pals, and a long time ago we ran out of stuff to tell each other. We talked about our own activities, but that was pretty boring to people half way across the world. So, we started having discussions, if you know what I mean. In each letter, I write my opinion about something and my pen pals write me his or her opinion on the same subject. It's really cool and a lot more interesting than discussing the weather and your homework.
(Donna K.)

A Shock For Keith

By Jill Richard

SACRAMENTO — It was the second show at the Sacramento Memorial Auditorium for the Rolling Stones. Near the end of their American Tour, and only a week away from going home, after three months of tours.

The audience was live, the Stones were swinging and the show was moving on in style.

Through the first six songs, Mick jumped, shook, got down on his knees, did the splits and, as is normal, drove the girls mad.

Three sentences into the first verse of "The Last Time," girls were screaming, hands were clapping — then it happened. From Keith Richard's microphone sparks flew like cynical fireworks. Keith fell to the floor. For an immeasurably short space of time nothing happened. Music and screaming continued as usual. But as the realization of what happened hit, there was absolute silence.

A second later, heartrending, horrified screams filled the air as Bill, Mick, and Brian rushed to the side of their beloved mate.

The curtains closed.

For several long, long minutes, the stage was bare. From every corner of the auditorium girls like those never heard at a pop concert before were audible. Some girls prayed. Some just sat, too shocked to move.

When the announcer came onto the stage, there was a hush.

"Keith is all right." Words sweeter than any music. And a soft wind blew as the breaths that we had been holding were let out. Keith walked out of the auditorium under his own power, and an ambulance took him to his hotel where he was examined by a doctor. And he was all right.

The performance was short by two numbers and many were disappointed at that. But far greater than their disappointment was their happiness at knowing, "Keith is all right."

KRLA ARCHIVES

THE RISING SONS, recently signed by Columbia Records to an exclusive recording contract, pose here in Columbia's Hollywood sound studios following their initial recording session. Taj Mahal (left), Jesse Lee Kincaid, Gary Marker, Ry Cooder and Kevin Kelley cut the group's first single last week.

BIRD WHO DISLIKES BIRDS

Marianne—Surprise Star

Marianne Faithfull is one of England's nicest little birds but she personally doesn't care for the birds — the feathered variety that is.

"When I was young, say fourteen," she explains, "My pet dog used to sleep with me (now she sleeps in the kitchen when she's at the flat.) Anyway, one day she caught a small bird in the backyard and brought it into the house. While I was sleeping, she dropped it right onto my foot. The pesky little thing was still alive too!"

Unlikely Star

Marianne's only been in this business a short while but she's already had four smash hits. She was born in Hampstead, Eng. and brought up in St. Josephs Convent in Readying, Eng.

With a university lecturer for a father and a former ballet dancer and Baroness for a mother, she doesn't exactly seem like the sort that could be a hit in the pop world, but Marianne fooled them all.

Andrew Loog Oldham, manager of the Rolling Stones, discovered her at a party in June 1964 and sent her on her way to fame.

She's had some impressive people writing songs for her. Her first record, "As Tears Go By," was written by Mick Jagger and Keith Richards and her second was "Blowin' In the Wind" by Bob Dylan. She followed these two with "Come and Stay With Me" by Jackie DeShannon and her plaintive "This Little Bird."

But she recently took a little time off from her busy career to get married. She and John Dunbar were married in a registry office last May 6 and then in a Catholic church on June 24.

John just recently went into a partnership with Peter Asher of Peter and Gordon in a London bookstore but Marianne's pretty busy herself taking care of her son, born last month.

When Marianne looks at the future she sees only happiness. "I see everything on a long term basis," she explains, "I see myself as I am today with my wonderful career as something that will last maybe for two years. I see also, another 60 years looming ahead when I still want to laugh and cry and be comforted. Marrying John is forever, I've absolutely no doubt that it is the right thing to do. He fits into the whole 60 years."

We Disagree

Well, The BEAT disagrees with Marianne on one point there. We think her career will last a lot longer than two years.

She says she changed a little since she became a singer. "Since I became a pop singer, I learned to be organized and calm. I was untidy at school, but now I hang up my clothes because I have to look nice every minute of every day. At first I was very impressed with the pop world and I fell for some pretty super pop stars. But I knew soon that it was just a game. I said to myself, 'This is for the present; for the duration of a tour or for the brief star-studded time you are famous. This isn't for keeps.'"

If she keeps putting out great songs as faithfully as she has, it'll probably last a lot longer than she seems to think. Keep it up Marianne and Happy New Year.

...MARIANNE FAITHFULL

Dylan Sells Out Seven West Coast Concerts

"He'll be America's greatest troubador, if he doesn't explode." That was folk writer and singer Pete Seeger talking about Bob Dylan some time ago. Dylan didn't explode and he certainly has come to be America's greatest troubador.

Dylan is a vague, mysterious character whose songs have been recorded by so many different performers that it's impossible to list them.

But he's also very successful as a performer himself, even though his voice may not be the most pleasing in the world. It has a haunting quality about it that suits the words he writes.

He recently visited the West Coast for several weeks and managed to keep very busy while he was here.

He was signed to do two concerts near the University of California at Berkeley campus. Both concerts were sold out so fast that he was forced to do a third in San Francisco, which was also sold out.

Then he went on to sell-outs in San Diego, Long Beach, Santa Monica and Pasadena. Somehow he also found time to continue work on the album he's currently cutting for Columbia Records.

He also found time to honor an up-and-coming new group called the Rising Sons by dropping in on their recording session.

Taking his road manager and Robbie Robertson, his lead guitarist, with him he spent over an hour watching the Sons record.

The group wasn't exactly strangers to Dylan either. Taj Mahal, leader of the group, used to play the same circuit with Dylan back in the early '60's and the two have always admired each other's work.

The Rising Sons are a folk-blues group who utilize such varied instruments as jugs, mandolin, and banjo as well as the standard electric guitars. They play only original stuff on traditional blues but they do not do any of Dylan's songs.

Gary Marker, bass player for the group, said Dylan "was knocked out" by the session.

BEAT Awards
(Continued from Page 2)
Composer...Lennon-McCartney
Record Producer...Brian Wilson
Outstanding Record Company...
Columbia

Bill Dana was a masterful as well as witty master of ceremonies for the banquet and awards show. He proved he can be as hilarious being himself as when he is Jose Jiminez.

The capacity audience included many top movie and television personalities as well as record stars and executives from all the major record companies. Some of them are pictured in this issue.

Many of the stars contributed their talents in staging a fabulous show to go along with the presentation of awards.

Although facilities were not available for public admission to this year's ceremonies, the event was so successful that negotiations are already underway for showing the second annual BEAT Pop Music Awards on national television.

We are grateful to the record industry, whose enthusiastic response to this year's BEAT awards insured their success as an annual endeavor.

NEW

a great new product to meet the growing market for a young man's hair spray

man spray
a MAN'S hair spray
holds hair all day
always looks natural
adds extra bounce
and body

Regular Price $1.25
SPECIAL BEAT OFFER
$1.00 each
Includes tax, postage and handling.

a MAN'S hair spray
• Created to hold hair perfectly—all day.
• Always looks natural—never sticky or tacky.
• Unique conditioning ingredients add extra body and bounce to today's new hair styles for men.
• Clean, manly aroma.

take advantage of this new trend in spray usage with a product specifically designed to work on a man's hair

L. B. LABS, INC.
P.O. BOX 430
GLENDALE, CALIF. 91209
Please send me _____ cans L.B. Man Spray. I enclose $_____
($1.00 for each can)
NAME:
ADDRESS:
CITY:_____ STATE_____ ZIP_____

KRLA ARCHIVES

America's Largest Teen NEWSpaper

KRLA *Edition* BEAT

Volume 1, Number 43   LOS ANGELES, CALIFORNIA   15 Cents   January 8, 1966

The Rolling Stones—Five Pages of Unbelievable Photos

KRLA BEAT

Los Angeles, California — January 8, 1966

Roger Miller: '65's Pop Surprise Man

With the Old Year now just a part of history, there is one man in this world of pop who must undoubtedly have been quite sorry to say good-bye to 1965.

The man is Roger Miller and 1965 has been his year. Roger suddenly appeared out of nowhere and set the music world literally on its ear by producing hit after hit.

Unbeknown to most, Roger began his career not in 1965 but way back in the late 50's. However, Roger never had a really huge record. And, in fact, everyone scoffed at the very idea of country-boy Roger Miller *ever* getting a hit on the pop charts.

...ROGER MILLER

The whole idea was simply ridiculous. Or so *they* thought, anyway. But Roger showed 'em by sending "Dang Me" soaring up the charts. The knockers do not give up easily so they credited "Dang Me" to beginner's luck or a kind of a freak hit.

Never Make It

They maintained that Roger's richly country flavored music was not the sound of the day. Roger didn't say much. He just followed up "Dang Me" with "Chug-A-Lug." And, of course, he had *two* hits under his belt.

The knockers didn't quite know what to make of this second Miller hit. They scratched their heads, gave the matter considerable thought and finally decided that "Chug-A-Lug" was another freak hit.

But when "King Of The Road" was released and went bounding up the charts the knockers threw up their hands in bewilderment. They didn't know what Roger had but whatever it was the record-buying public was going for it in a big way.

More Hits

Roger was not yet quite through, however. Before 1965 had run its course we were treated to two other Miller smashes, "Engine Engine #9" and his current hit, "England Swings."

The record buyers were the first to spot Roger's considerable musical talents but it didn't take the music industry too awfully long to see the light as well.

And when the Grammy Awards were presented it was Roger who swept the entire show by winning *five* precious Grammies!

Yes, 1965 was a fantastic year for Roger Miller. But *The BEAT* is betting that 1966 will be even better for Roger—if that's possible.

Russians Yell 'U.N.C.L.E.'

Somebody has been criticizing "The Man From U.N.C.L.E." And guess who it is – Russia.

Pravda, the official newspaper of Moscow, has dennounced David "Illya" McCallum as a "certain scoundrel of Russian descent, who like many other U.N.C.L.E. agents, used to work behind the Iron Curtain."

The paper continued with "He, like James Bond, works like a machine, without reasoning, and precisely executes the orders of Mr. Efficiency. In striving to command the attention of reader and viewers, the preachers of the 'right to kill' will stop at nothing.

"They deliberately corrupt young people, using stronger and stronger doses of bloodthirstiness, eroticism and violence..."

How does it feel to be corrupted, fan?

And what do the producers of the series think this criticism means? "We've made it," says Norman Felton, executive producer.

Inside the BEAT

The Rolling Stones	3-7
Four Seasons Are Back	11
Adventures of Robin Boyd	11
Herb Alpert Going Places	11
Bobby Fuller Still Talking	13
On The Beat	13
Meet The Swingin' Who	14
It's In The Bag	14
Vogues Took Seven Years	16
These Sheep For Real	16

The BEAT is published weekly by BEAT Publications, Inc., editorial and advertising offices at 6290 Sunset Blvd., Suite 504, Hollywood, California 90028, U.S. bureaus in Hollywood, San Francisco, New York, Chicago and Nashville, overseas correspondents in London, Liverpool and Manchester, England. Sale price 15 cents. Subscription price: U.S. and possessions, $3 per year; Canada and foreign rates, $9 per year. Application to mail at second class postage rates is pending at Los Angeles, California.

THE BYRDS HAVE "TURN, TURN, TURNED"—right into the number one spot on the national charts for the second time in five months. Their first chart-topper was the Dylan tune, "Mr. Tambourine Man." But this time they've scored with a Pete Seeger composition, "Turn, Turn, Turn (To Everything There Is a Season)." Of the first three singles released by the Byrds, two in the number-one spot is a pretty good beginning—reason enough to fly as high as they wish!

Memories of 1965

Happy New Year everyone—welcome to 1966. This is the time of year when most people begin looking ahead and making skillions of bright, shiny plans for the New Year ahead. It is the time to make resolutions, and now that we are well into the second week of the New Year, it is time to begin *breaking* those resolutions, as well!!

But *The KRLA BEAT* isn't quite ready to say good-bye to our old pal, 1965, just yet. No—we have a little bit of reminiscing to do, first.

Let's take a little trip, then, back along the paths of 1965 via the route of *The KRLA BEAT* and some of the top headlines and stories of the year.

Back in February *The BEAT* first began to be printed in newspaper form, and it has been growing steadily ever since. From a four-page local newspaper, it has grown to 16 full-sized pages of the largest and fastest growing teen newspaper in the United States, even reaching out to 11 foreign countries.

The first few editions of *The BEAT* were four pages containing news about The Beatles, The Stones, and many other British and American groups and artists. There were exclusive on-location interviews with each of the Beatles and play-by-play accounts of the spread of a brand new phenomena known as "Hermania."

And there were fantastic exclusive pictures and stories by and about the unbelievable KRLA DJ's.

On the ninth of June *The BEAT* published the cover of the brand new Beatles album in red and black as a world-wide exclusive.

From there, we went on to the excitement of the summer months as we anxiously awaited the arrival of the Beatles in the U.S. With the beginning of August, we not only had the excitement of the Beatles' arrival to contend with, but Dylan concerts to attend as well.

And then there were the numerous articles on the Rolling Stones as we followed them all through their childhood days, right up to their present-day smash success.

We heard more about the Stones in August, and then the exclusive pictures and stories of the Beatles' new movie, "Help!" appeared in the August 21 *BEAT*.

More talk about the Beatles, Chad and Jeremy, Dick and Dee Dee, Dino, Desi, and Billy, The Stones, and the We Five.

Then—suddenly they were here. The Beatles had arrived at last! *The BEAT* had pictures and stories exclusively for its readers on all of the Beatles activities while they were here and of their fabulous concerts as well.

Barry McGuire made his first appearance in the September 4 issue of *The BEAT* as he hit the top of the national charts with his protest record, the "Eve of Destruction."

The BEAT fell ill to some strange maladies on October 9 as were struck by both Beatlemania and Hermania all at the same time!!

Donovan was interviewed for the first time in *The BEAT*, and Paul and Ringo Beatle smiled at all their *BEAT* friends from the cover.

During the rest of October *The BEAT* welcomed such friends as Elvis, the Byrds, the Lettermen, Tom Jones, Billy Joe Royal, Sonny and Cher, John Lennon, David McCallum, P.F. Sloan, the Yardbirds, Len Barry, Herman, the Righteous Brothers, the Walker Brothers and Herbie Alpert.

The first international *BEAT* Pop Music Awards Poll was begun, and soon the excitement built to a crescendo peak. *The BEAT* was visited by many friends—old and new—during the months of October and November, and then the big evening of the *BEAT* Pop Music Awards Banquet arrived with all the excitement and glamour of any of the biggest Holly-
(Turn to Page 10)

Beatles Need Help on Their Third Movie

What's happening with the Beatle's third movie?

"Hard Day's Night" and "Help" were both huge smashes and the world is waiting for a third. But there's a lot of confusion over what their third movie will be or where it will be filmed.

They were originally set to start filming one called "A Talent For Loving" in Spain as soon as they returned from their last American tour.

That was postponed and the reason given was that the weather in Spain was unreliable at that time of year. But reports from London say that the weather had nothing to do with the postponement and the real problem was that the Beatles didn't like the script as it stood then. It was reported that as soon as some script changes had been made that filming would start.

Then later there were reports that an American movie company had offered the Beatles $50,000 and 50% of the profits to do a movie here. There has been no confirmation or denial on this offer.

And now there's a rumor floating around that Walter Shenson has commissioned Max Wilk to write a picture for them to be filmed here. It's reported to be set in America during the American revolution against England.

So what goes fellows? We loved the first two movies and we're anxiously awaiting the third. So let's get the contracts straightened out, get a good script, decide where to film it and get going. We're waiting.

Mick, Keith, Brian, Bill And

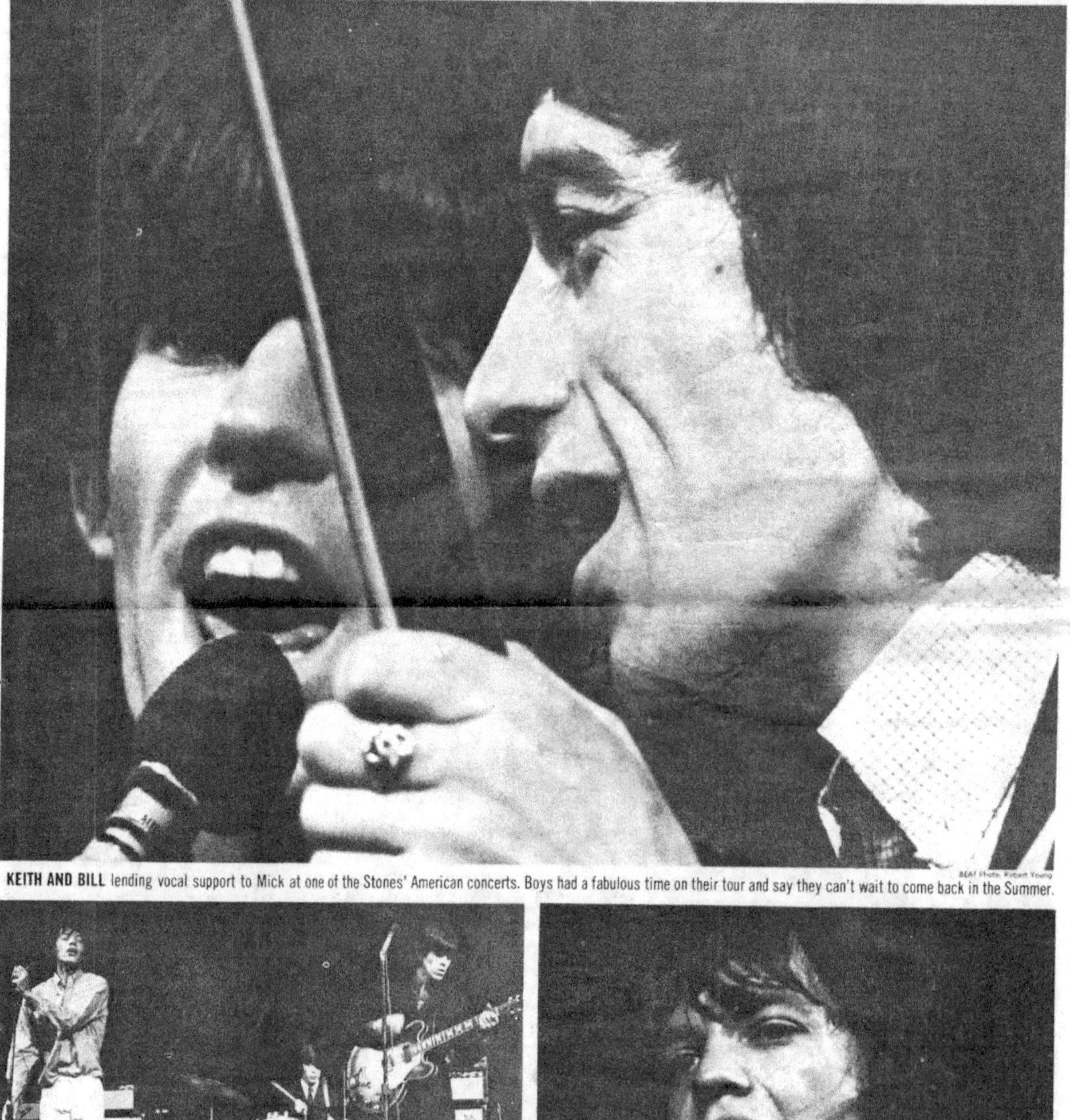

BEAT Photo: Robert Young

KEITH AND BILL lending vocal support to Mick at one of the Stones' American concerts. Boys had a fabulous time on their tour and say they can't wait to come back in the Summer.

BEAT Photo: Chuck Boyd

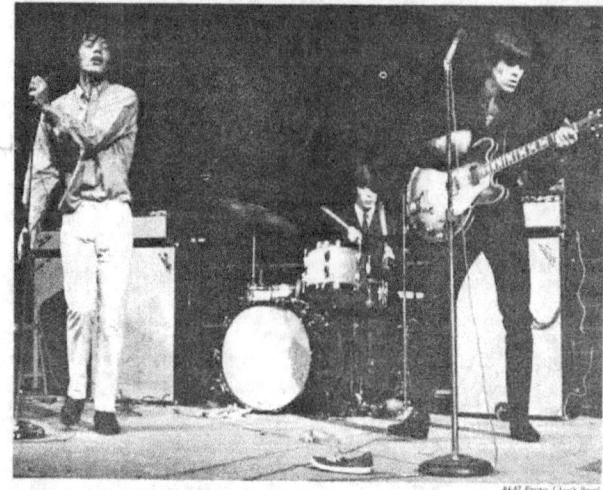

. . . **MICK, CHARLIE AND KEITH** swingin' amid a littered stage.

BEAT Photo: Robert Young

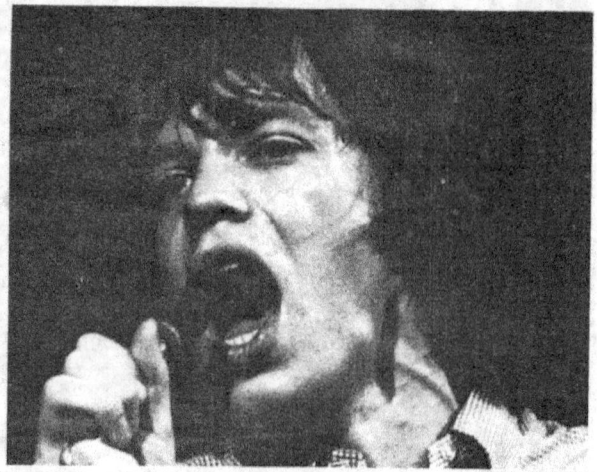

THE JAGGER wails as only he can do, shaking up every female in the audience with his on-stage performance. It's wild — it swings and Mick admits that it's "suggestive."

KRLA ARCHIVES

Charlie—Stones In Action

BRIAN JONES concentrates on his guitar playing while a wall of screaming hysteria falls down on top of him. But Brian doesn't let that bother him — he just keeps playing.

MICK throws around those maraccas as he waits for Keith to finish his guitar solo.

...CHARLIE — about as in action as he'll ever get!

BRIAN JONES AND KEITH RICHARD pose nicely with BEAT reporter, Louise Criscione, at their press conference. And then they hurried out to record some more tracks at RCA.

The Rolling Stones In Repose

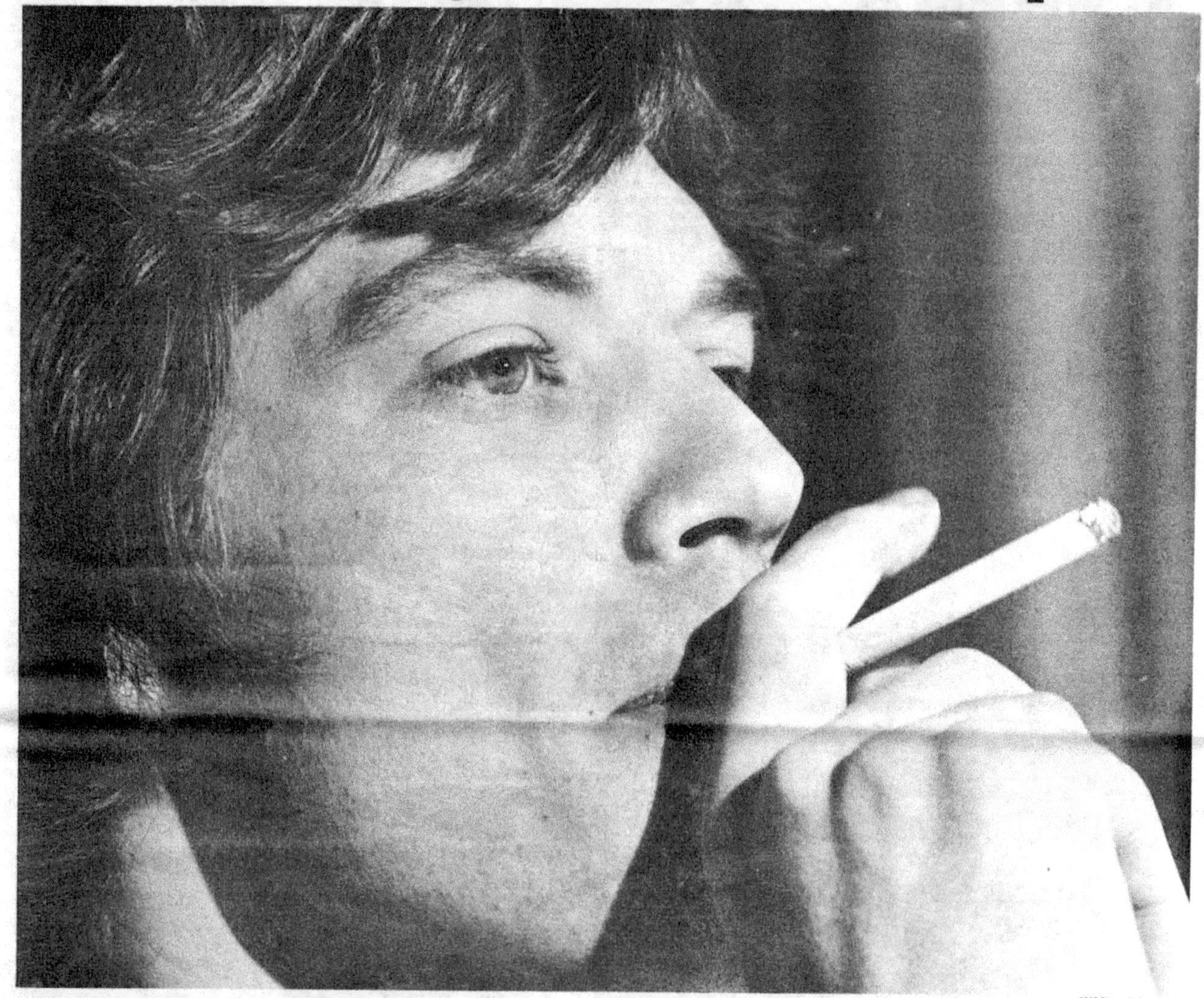

BEAT Photo: Robert Young

BEAT Photo: Robert Young

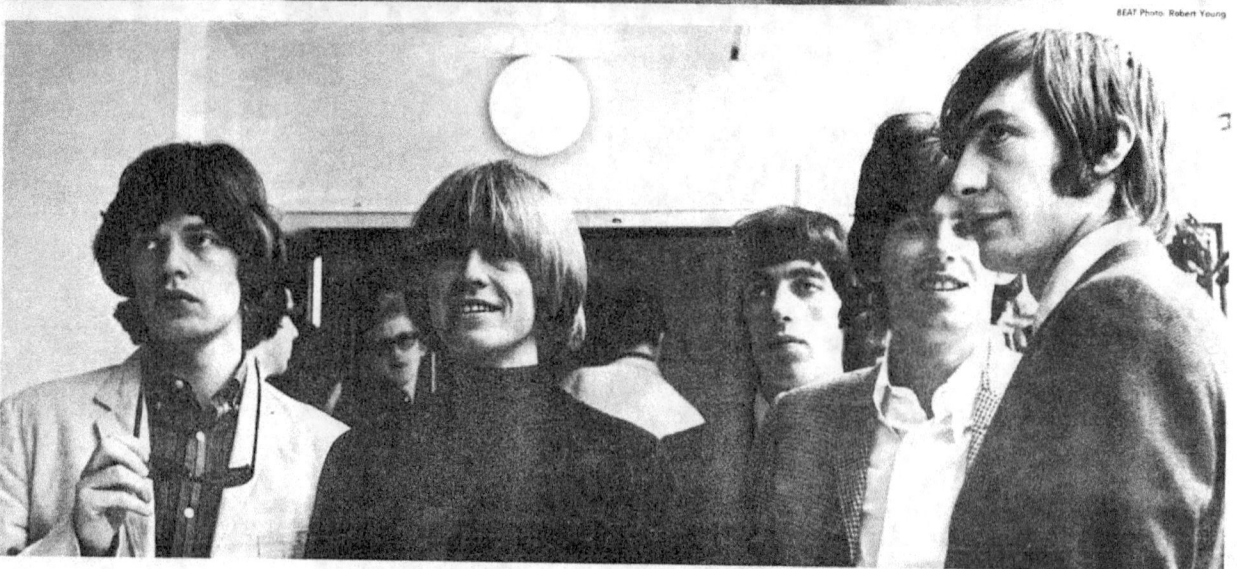

KRLA ARCHIVES

The Many Faces Of Mick Jagger

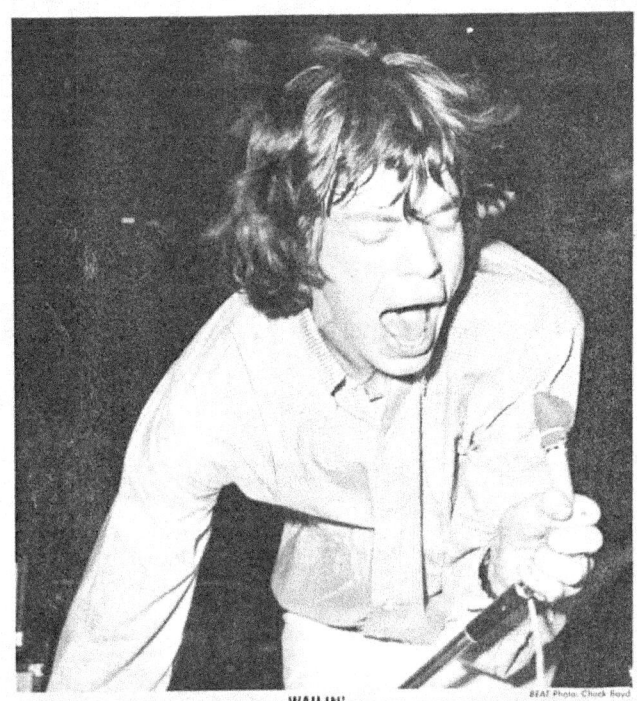

...WAILIN'.

...AND SMILIN'.

...MICK AND FRIEND?

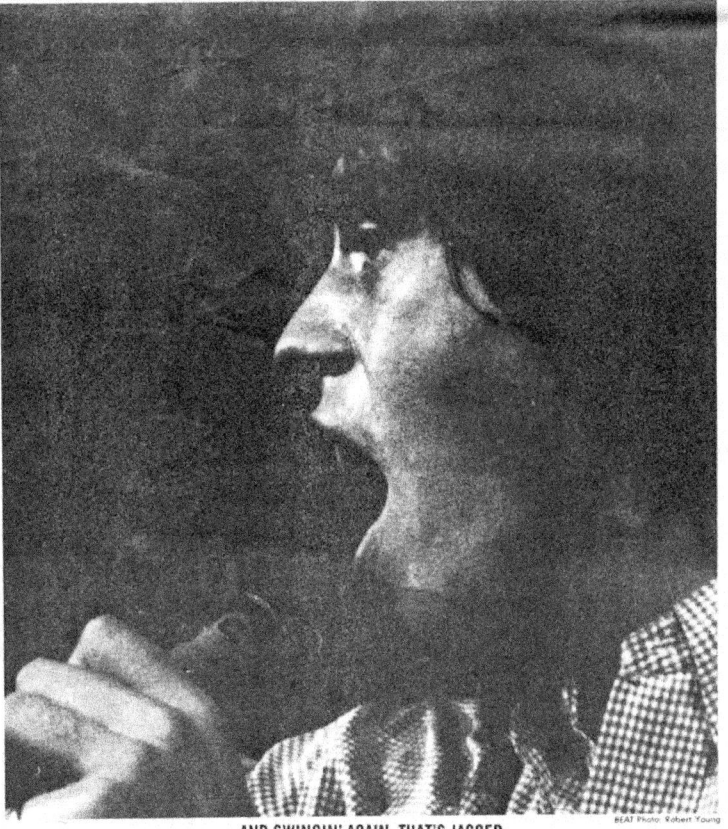

...AND SWINGIN' AGAIN. THAT'S JAGGER.

KRLA ARCHIVES

The Stones Speak To The Press

By Louise Criscione

The Rolling Stones held one of their rare press conferences recently. It was a wild scene, as usual. Although the press conference was extremely small and extra secretive, the ever-present Stone fans were lined up outside the hotel waiting for a glimpse of their favorites (which they never got because the boys came in the back entrance).

After checking in at the door the press was ushered into the Cabana Room to await the arrival of the Stones.

Shortly after three o'clock Charlie, Bill, Keith, Mick and Brian paraded through the door and took their places at the table.

As the flash bulbs went off Keith sat scratching his head, Brian played with his glasses and Charlie merely sat there looking either extremely bored or extremely tired.

Question Time

After ten minutes of picture taking, reporters began throwing questions at the Stones—all of which they answered expertly and with ease and wit.

The first question asked concerned the boys' plans for the next few weeks. Mick answered: "We're going on holiday—you know, vacation. We're going to different parts of the world for a couple of weeks rest."

The Stones' movie plans were finally officially announced at the conference and the Stones had plenty to say about their future films.

Their first movie venture, tentatively titled "Back, Behind And In Front," is scheduled to begin filming in April and should take seven or eight weeks to complete.

The entire movie will be shot in Europe and the Stones were very explicit that it will be a movie with a strong plot.

No Vehicle

"It won't be a vehicle for singing," stated Mick. "We have to sing but we want it to be something with a story."

Keith went on to add that if the Stones merely wanted to make money, "we would have made one of those pop films two years ago."

Although Keith made it clear that the Stones were not in the movie business strictly for some easy money, when asked if they were expecting a fair-sized gross profit Charlie grinned: "Very much so."

The only other question answered by Charlie throughout the whole conference was whether he was going to play himself in their up-coming movie. "Certainly not. I shall be acting," declared the straight-faced Charlie Watts.

A question which I'm sure you girls have been dying to find out was asked Mick. Is he married to Chrissie Shrimpton and if not does he have any altar plans?

"It's not true—no," declared Mick.

Conformists?

A reporter asked Mick if he and the rest of the Stones weren't conforming by wearing long hair, etc.

"What's a conformist?" shot back Mick. "I don't have to change just because everyone copies us."

"We conform to our own standards," added Brian. But when asked just what his standards were, Brian grinned: "I pass."

Oddly enough, "December's Children" is the Stones' fastest selling album so far but the Stones declare that it is actually "a mixture of very old stuff and some new things."

Brian even went so far as to say that it was "an album of rejects."

Another reporter asked Keith why the Stones disliked the older generation and he quipped: "They dislike me."

Mick's Advice

Mick was questioned about any possible advice he might have to young people attempting to break into show business. And he offered: "Be different from everyone else. Look different and write your own songs."

One of the funniest questions asked was what Mick thought of people saying that his actions on stage were suggestive. "They are," he laughed.

"It's like any dancing is suggestive," continued Mick.

Another amusing question concerned where the Stones invested their money. Perhaps in themselves? "No," quipped Mick, "we invest in more solid things."

When asked if the police always protect the Stones from their anxious fans, Mick answered: "Sometimes they don't."

Well, then what do the Stones do, the reporter wanted to know? "We run," laughed Mick.

Have you received any broken bones, persisted the reporter? "No," deadpanned Keith, "they don't break."

Since the Beatles received the MBE awards, a reporter wondered if the Stones thought *they* would be winning them next year.

Obscene?

"No," they chorused together. "We've already been convicted of obscenity charges in England," added Keith, "so we couldn't get any MBEs."

The Stones refused to comment further on the obscenity charges but they did admit that the charges concerned that gas station incident some months ago. But Keith did insist that "we were framed."

Mick admitted that the Stones' music has changed considerably since they first started. "If you don't change you're not getting anywhere," said Mick.

Rumor has it around town that the Stones' next single would be "As Tears Go By," the most popular track off their "December's Children" album.

But the Stones told me that it wasn't true at all and that, in fact, they were right in the middle of cutting their next single. And as soon as the record was cut it would be released.

Not Keith

The Stones have now traveled to every part of the world except the Communist countries. When asked if they were afraid to visit these countries, Keith replied: "*I'm* not afraid of the Commies, sir."

What about when the Stones retire? What will they do—settle on a farm somewhere? "I'll settle somewhere," said Keith, "but I don't know about a farm."

The talk again turned to the Stones' long hair and Keith commented: "We're not forced to wear our hair long. I wear mine long because I have big ears!"

Would he ever cut his hair? "Not unless it falls out," laughed Keith.

A reporter then brought up the fact that it was different for the Stones to be wearing long hair. After all, they were performers—but what about the ordinary kids?

"If they like it, they should wear it," answered Keith, "and, anyway, we're ordinary kids."

Brian's Movie

The last question was directed at Brian. Since the Stones had been rather evasive concerning the details of their first movie, would Brian care to be more specific about the movie which he was supposed to have produced?

"No," said Brian, "I'm going to be evasive about that one too because I haven't done it yet."

And with that the Stones thanked the press for coming, got up and made their way to the door.

But before they left they took time out to pose for some pictures for *The BEAT*. And then they jumped into their limousine and were gone.

However, they did announce that they will be back Stateside around the end of the summer.

THE ROLLING STONES revealed plans for their first movie at their press conference. The film will be shot in England and in four Iron Curtain countries beginning in April.

BEAT Photo: Robert Custer

KRLA ARCHIVES

many thanks.... To all our fans and to
The BEAT for voting us BEAT Pop Awards...

Best New Male Vocalist
Best New Female Vocalist
Best Female Vocalist
Best Duo

SONNY AND CHER

Management:
Greene-Stone
7715 Sunset Blvd.,
Los Angeles, Calif.

KRLA ARCHIVES

Bobby Fuller Great On KRLA 'Wheels' Album

The Bobby Fuller Four have put together a collection of the most exciting sounds of the year on the album pictured above—"KRLA King of the Wheels."

It's on sale at leading record outlets throughout Southern California, and sales figures indicate it's an instant hit. KRLA is donating the proceeds to charity.

It's an unusual album, combining the songs of the track with other original sounds of the Bobby Fuller Four, one of the most popular and dynamic new groups in the world.

One side contains their first big hit, "Let Her Dance," and five other hit songs written by Bobby Fuller.

Side two contains six other new songs Bobby has written for this special album. One of them, "KRLA King of the Wheels," tells the story of the famed KRL"A".

Among the others, "The Lonely Dragster" and "KRLA Top Eliminator" are sure to put you right in the driver's seat roaring down the track at 200 MPH plus. Other selections on side two are "The Phantom Dragster," "Little Annie Lou" and "Saturday Night."

Spend the Holidays with ♪ MIKE ♪ CLIFFORD At The GALLEY WEST

Marineland's Fabulous New Dining Spot
Palos Verdes Peninsula
Phone 377-1547 for Reservations — Free Parking

KRLA BEAT Subscription
SAVE 25% Of Regular Price

☐ 1 YEAR — 52 Issues — $5.00 ☐ 2 YEARS — $8.00

Enclosed is ☐ CASH ☐ CHECK

Send to:..Age............
Address:...
City......................State..........Zip................

MAIL YOUR ORDER TO:
KRLA BEAT
6290 Sunset, Suite 504
Hollywood, Calif. 90028

Foreign Rate: $14.00 – 52 Issues

The Liverpool Five are Coming!!!!

Inside KRLA

Greetings all-groovy group in KRLA-land. It's been a busy week here at KRLA beginning with a visit from the Statler Brothers at the beginning of the week. These four guys are more fun than a candy store and *much* better singers, too!

Other visitors to the studio this week included everybody's favorite person, Joey Paige. In fact, the day Joey visited, it rained quite heavily, and as we went next door to the hotel for lunch, we received quite a good drenching! Oh well – all's fair in times of flood and famine!!!

The KRLA flying saucers are still flying high, and recently they came in for a brief, but very successful landing at Cal State college. But in no time at all, good ol' Captain Showbiz had them airborne again. But then, you know him – groovy, groovy, ultra-cool Captain Showbiz!

If you don't know what the Captain looks like, you can recognize him quite readily by his ever-present side-kick and constant companion – Karen Kabunga Doll!!

Have you fallen by Dave Hull's Hullabaloo yet? If you haven't – you'd better do it soon. Well, yes – it is great and all that – but the old Hullabalooer cries a lot if he's left alone for long periods of time, so we've sort of promised him that all of his Hullabalooers would band together and make sure that he doesn't have the opportunity to become at all lonely.

I mean after all – it really *is* kind of pathetic to watch a grown man cry! Especially a grown *Hullabalooer!!*

Had a great time last week when I visited Bill Slater in his internationally famous weather room. I just happened to be flying around Pasadena in my gold-plated, maroon monogrammed flying saucer (presented to me by the gear KRLA DJ's, of course!) when I decided to drop in on Bill, who just happened to be doing his all-night show at the time.

I made the most beautiful emergency landing you've ever seen – really!! My Splash Down came at exactly 1:17 in the center of the giant bird bath located in the beautiful patio area on the second level of the KRLA studio.

I was really having a great time downstairs in the broadcast booth while Bill was doing his show, until he invited me to ride upstairs to Bill's Weather Room with him and Jarvis the Janitor.

Let me tell you, friends – I never should have gone! Once we got up there, I immediately proceeded to walk through the wrong door – which turned out to be a *window*!

After holding on to the window ledge desperately for 4-1/2-terror-filled minutes, Bill and Jarvis finally managed to retrieve me. Then, we went into the weather room, at last, where I promptly managed to slip and fall on a slip rod which Bill had carefully placed over a hole in the floor, caused by the recent flooding – which had leaked! Needless to say, I completely destroyed my ankle for all time. Well – would you believe a slight *sprain??!!!*

Ah, but it was all in the spirit of fun, so I guess I can't be *too* upset. Besides, the doctor says that I will probably be able to take the cast off in time for next Christmas!!!

The KRLA Deejays

By Jeannine Hubert

EMPEROR HUDSON
'Twixt 6 and 9 in the morning' time
There's a famous man,
With a bright "hello" and a cheery smile –
He sets the world a 'glo!

CHARLIE O'DONNELL
This daddy-o is the King of the show
And hip as hip could be
With his coffeebreakers and doubleplays –
Makes him a real winner with me!

CASEY KASEM
12-3 is his regular spot
With retrospection galore.
His velvety voice and witty charm
Make me wish for more, more, more.

DAVE HULL
A Beatle fan if I ever saw one,
And always full of fun.
He makes me wanna "Jump and Shout" –
But "Clarence" keeps me down!

BOB EUBANKS
Alas ... we come to that sophisticated (?) gent,
His nightly "Teen Toppers" salutes us all.
How sweet it 'tis to listen to him –
Do you not agree?

DICK BIONDI
Now, let me think – what can one say?
I know!! This skinny "Italian"
Is great – marvelous, amorous – and ...
Oh, well, I dig him anyway!

BILL SLATER
'Though I've only heard him once or twice
This fellow is quite nice.
Too bad he's on so terribly late (or is it early?)
'Cuz I think he is just gr-r-reat!

JOHNNY HAYES
With a quiet calm, he performs his job
In a way to please all listeners.
He's a deejay's deejay and tops in his field.
This cat's really making the scene!

DICK MORELAND
This "buddy-boo" of the radio world
Really gets me going.
The truth is – he's a gas
And positively "4th Street" – hmmmmm??

THE END
(of this poem, but never of great entertainment)

KRLA ARCHIVES

More Scenes from BEAT Pop Awards Show

THIS IS PART OF THE CROWD OF 800 STARS AND CELEBRITIES ATTENDING THE FIRST ANNUAL BEAT POP MUSIC AWARDS BANQUET AT DAVE HULL'S HULLABALOO.

KRLA Tunedex

This Week	Last Week	Title	Artist
1	1	WE CAN WORK IT OUT/DAY TRIPPER	The Beatles
2	3	THE SOUNDS OF SILENCE	Simon & Garfunkle
3	2	LET'S HANG ON	The Four Seasons
4	4	LIES	The Knickerbockers
5	9	LIGHTIN' STRIKES	Lou Christie
6	5	FLOWERS ON THE WALL	The Statler Brothers
7	7	YOU DIDN'T HAVE TO BE SO NICE	The Lovin' Spoonful
8	8	RUN, BABY, RUN	The Newbeats
9	11	SHE'S JUST MY STYLE	Gary Lewis & The Playboys
10	10	IT'S MY LIFE	The Animals
11	6	EBB TIDE	The Righteous Brothers
12	12	A YOUNG GIRL	Noel Harrison
13	22	HOLE IN THE WALL	The Packers
14	26	I SEE THE LIGHT	The Five Americans
15	23	JENNY TAKE A RIDE	Mitch Ryder & The Detroit Wheels
16	17	I FOUGHT THE LAW	The Bobby Fuller Four
17	20	I WILL	Dean Martin
18	16	I CAN NEVER GO HOME ANYMORE	The Shangri-Las
19	21	ENGLAND SWINGS	Roger Miller
20	14	OVER AND OVER	The Dave Clark Five
21	27	THE DUCK	Jackie Lee
22	18	THE LITTLE GIRL I ONCE KNEW	The Beach Boys
23	24	DON'T THINK TWICE	The Wonder Who?
24	29	MY GENERATION	The Who
25	30	MAKE THE WORLD GO AWAY	Eddy Arnold
26	28	FIVE O'CLOCK WORLD	The Vogues
27	—	NO MATTER WHAT SHAPE	The T-Bones
28	36	FEVER	The McCoys
29	—	AS TEARS GO BY	The Rolling Stones
30	37	UPTIGHT	Stevie Wonder
31	31	THUNDERBALL	Tom Jones
32	32	ONE HAS MY NAME	Barry Young
33	35	SUNDAY AND ME	Jay & The Americans
34	—	MY LOVE	Petula Clark
35	38	A MUST TO AVOID	Herman's Hermits
36	33	PUPPET ON A STRING	Elvis Presley
37	39	ONE TOO MANY MORNINGS	The Association
38	—	LIKE A BABY	Len Barry
39	—	SLOOP DANCE	The Atlantics
40	—	LOVE BUG	Jack Jones

DAVE HULL

BOB EUBANKS

DICK BIONDI

JOHNNY HAYES

EMPEROR HUDSON

CASEY KASEM

CHARLIE O'DONNELL

BILL SLATER

NINO TEMPO AND EVIE SANDS JOIN AUTOGRAPH LINE AT DOOR.

Memories of 1965

(Continued from Page 2)

wood premiers. It was a total success, thanks to the many wonderful readers of The BEAT who eagerly participated and voted for their favorites.

December 18 at The BEAT had another exclusive with the Beatles' new album right on the cover of the paper, and then on Christmas all of The BEAT's many friends in the industry showed their appreciation to The BEAT and to all of The BEAT's readers by personally stopping by to wish everyone a very Merry Christmas and a Happy New Year.

Yes—it had been quite a year. A year of The Beatles, a year of The Rolling Stones, a year of Sonny and Cher, of protest, of bell-bottoms and long hair, a year of the rise and fall of "Shindig," a year of success and failure in the wide world of pop.

It was a year which *you* made very successful for *us*. We have said it before, but just because we will never stop being grateful to you, we'll say it again—and go *on* saying it—Thank You for all of your support and participation. Because of *you*, The BEAT has become America's largest and greatest teen newspaper, and *with* your continued support—it will become even larger and greater!!

From all of us here at The BEAT—may you have the happiest and most prosperous New Year possible, and may the dreams you wished for at Christmas become reality in this New Year.

KRLA ARCHIVES

The Adventures of Robin Boyd...
By Shirley Poston

CHAPTER NINE

When Robin awakened, she found herself to be wound tightly in a shroud of corduroy.

There are some people in the world who would become *upset* should they find themselves in such a predicament. And Robin Boyd was one of them.

"Help!" she shrieked, clawing the imprisoning bands.

"Ouch," said a disgruntled voice. "Quit yer peckin' at me!"

Then Robin remembered. The voice belonged to George. George the genie, that is, in whose jacket pocket she happened to be residing at the moment.

For an instant, Robin considered pecking him a really *good* one for addressing her in that ungentlemanly tone, but then she thought better of it. After all, hadn't he gone out of his way to rescue her from the Beatles' garage? About ten thousand miles out of his way to be exact?

And hadn't he rescued her Beatles, too, by removing from their troubled minds all memories of having come face to face with a *real* bird wearing *glasses?*

Robin smiled fondly, preparing to re-snuggle, but she didn't have a chance to. Suddenly she wasn't in George's pocket. She was in her own room, back to her sixteen-year-old self! And George was nowhere to be seen.

Then Robin smiled fondly again. Of *course*. He was back in his tea pot (the one on her dresser), taking a well-deserved rest.

At the mere thought of the word *rest*, Robin realized how exhausted she was and flopped down on her bed. Whew! No wonder she was tired after all the things that had happened since . . . since . . .

Robin flopped back up from her bed in a large hurry. "Since *when?*" she breathed in horror. What day was this anyway? So much had taken place, her mind was a complete blank!

After a few panic-stricken laps around the room, she came partially to her senses (no one is perfect) and looked at the clock. The hands pointed to four-thirty.

Dashing to the window, Robin raised the shade and peered out into the darkness.

Four-thirty *a.m.*, she deducted (brilliantly). Then it came back to her. Although it seemed like years since she'd winged off to London to terrorize – er – visit the Beatles, it had been only yesterday morning! That had been Saturday, so today was Sunday. (Another brilliant deduction if she did say so herself.) (And, she did.)

Well, she whooshed inwardly. *That* was certainly a relief. But, almost instantly, she retracted the whoosh.

Had she or had she *not* told her mother that she was going to visit Aunt Zelda in Catalina over the weekend?

She *had*.

And could she or could she *not* explain to her mother why and how she had *returned* from Aunt Zelda's at four-thirty in the morning?

She could *not*. Not without telling the biggest, fattest, un-whitest lie of the century, she couldn't.

Then Robin knew what she must do.

Walking to her dresser, she gently lifted the lid of the tea pot. It was empty, except for her tiny Byrd glasses, but that was perfectly natural since George was invisible most of the time. (There are some people in the world who would *not* find this perfectly natural, but Robin Boyd was no longer one of them.)

"George?" she crooned. The tea pot remained silent.

"George," she repeated, adding a "dear" at the last minute for good measure.

The tea pot gave a low moan, and Robin shook it in desperation. "*George*," she insisted. "Come out of there. I *need* you!"

"And I need you," said a sleepy voice behind her. "Like a hole in me head."

Robin jumped several feet, but regaining her composure, turned to him gratefully. "I have a terrible problem," she began.

"*That's* the God's truth," George groaned, rubbing his eyes.

"No, no, I mean I have to go over to Zelda and visit Aunt Catalina," she babbled. "Or I'll have to tell my mother a whopper and I . . ."

"Cannot tell a lie," George interrupted resignedly.

Robin nodded. "Right! And I still don't know how to pronounce Worchester – wooster – that *word*, you know, to turn me back into me and . . ."

"*Shurrup!*" roared George. "I'll take you meself! I'm so tired I couldn't pronounce the blasted thing either!"

Robin dimpled, which wasn't easy because she didn't have dimples. "You're a luv," she said tenderly. And he was. Him so good to her and all, and looking like George Harrison the way he did, and having that Liverpool accent . . . well, he just *was* a luv.

George almost grinned, then he stopped short. Then he muttered something under his breath. Then he pointed at the dresser.

"Oh, *no*," Robin wailed. "It's gone!" And it was. (The tea pot, not the dresser.)

"Oh, *yes*," George replied. "And the next time you come round naggin' in the wee hours, you'll find me on the living room mantel. And you know what your mum might think if she found you lurking about in the middle of the night, conversin' with a *tea pot!*"

Then he did grin, fiendishly. "Now," he finished. "Let's get this over with!"

Robin couldn't help but grin back. "Should I say Liv...whoops . . . I mean the other word and get in your pocket or what?"

"How could you manage that?" George laughed. "I don't have a pocket." (And he didn't.) (Which figures.) "Just give me your hand, that's enough."

Robin did as she was told, and although she wasn't quite sure, she could have sworn George squeezed that hand a little before they vanished.

But she was definitely sure that the next voice she heard was Mick Jagger's.

(To Be Continued Next Week)

4 Seasons Back Again

The Four Seasons are one group of terrifically talented guys. They are also a group of very shrewd people. They began hitting the charts ages ago and have enjoyed hit after hit.

Then rather suddenly they disappeared. No one knew where they were or what they were doing. They had simply vanished.

Now, of course, they are back on the charts with not one hit but two. "Let's Hang On" is the more successful of the two, topping the charts almost everywhere.

Their second chart number is "Don't Think Twice" cleverly recorded by the Four Seasons under the name of The Wonder Who.

Secret's Out

Okay, so now they've returned. But where have they been? The answer is finally out – they've been working out a really great stage act.

They begin their act by doing 25 full minutes of standard Broadway songs and then go into all sorts of different material including their past hit songs.

The Seasons have just cut a fantastic album which includes one side devoted entirely to Burt Bacharach compositions and the other side devoted to Dylan songs.

With two hit records and one sure-fire album the Four Seasons are very much back on the music scene. And it's nice to have them back, isn't it?

Herb Alpert Going Places in a Hurry

The Beatles have broken just about every record in the entertainment industry and very few people have come along that can break their records.

But when a Beatle record gets broken, it's always by the nicest people. The first person to get a single to number one in America after the Fab Four had pretty well taken over the country two years ago was the one and only Louis Armstrong with his swinging version of "Hello Dolly."

And now another great guy has captured a position that hasn't been held since the Beatles had it. No one group or single artist has managed to have both the number one single and the number one album in the whole nation since the Beatles did it several times.

Chart Toppers

Herb Alpert and the Tijuana Brass put the finishing touch on 1965 by wrapping up the national charts, both singles and albums, putting their names on them and taking them home.

Their "Taste of Honey" single tasted so good you made it number one. And then you turned right around and made their album "Whipped Cream and Other Delights" the number one album.

And this wasn't enough for Herb and the Brass. They added three more of their albums to the charts – "Going Places" went into the top 5 and two of their older albums returned to the charts for an encore – "South of the Border" and "Lonely Bull."

The boys thought this was great fun so they released another single – "Zorba the Greek" and "Tijuana Taxi" – which will, of course, head straight for the top.

Started In Garage

And you'd never guess where all this got its start. In Herb's garage, that's where. Back in 1962 he was fiddeling around with a thing called "Twinkle Star" written by his friend Sol Lake.

Herb re-arranged the number using trumpets, piano, bass drums, mandolin and a few voices, threw in the roar of a crowd and came out with his first smash – "Lonely Bull."

He was on his way now but he was using session musicians for each record and the requests for personal appearances were pouring in. So in the last months of 1963 he hand-picked the 6 members that now join him, and The Tijuana Brass became one of the country's hottest acts.

Herb himself is a slim young man with black hair and dark eyes that make him look like he could be from South of the border.

Played For Moses

He's played trumpet or drums most of his life. He appeared in "The Ten Commandments" as the drummer who played while Moses was coming down the mountain.

And he spent two years in the Army as solo trumpeter with the Sixth Army Band at the Presidio in San Francisco, where he kept in practice by playing taps for as many as 18 funerals in one day.

The practice paid off, as shown by his virtual ownership of the national charts.

And to add to their collection of golden albums and records and the various awards that come with success, the boys also picked up two of *The BEAT's* International Pop Music Awards. You voted the group the best instrumental group and their "Taste of Honey" best instrumental single.

This man knows how to blow that horn!

...HERB ALPERT AND THE TIJUANA BRASS

KRLA ARCHIVES

Our Heartfelt Thanks

for

Brian's Coveted Award

BEST RECORD PRODUCER OF THE YEAR

The Beach Boys

KRLA ARCHIVES

Bobby Fuller Four Are Still Talkin'

By Tammy Hitchcock

Since the last time they talked to *The BEAT*, they've acquired a hit record and a new drummer. But the Bobby Fuller Four still continue to speak their minds on practically every subject which most entertainers avoid.

Their hit record, of course, is "I Fought The Law" and their new drummer is a quiet Texan tabbed D.P. When I say quiet I mean just that. D.P. sat there in our office and never *opened* his mouth—at least, not audibly.

His three cohorts fared a little bit better, speaking up whenever the mood hit them. First thing out of Randy's mouth was the lament that he would like nothing better than to wear his hair long and Beatle-style. However, "our manager, Bob Keene, doesn't like us to have long hair."

So, as soon as one of the Four allows his hair to land below the collar Mr. Keene gets out his shotgun and prods the unwilling member off to the barber.

Help Randy

Randy thinks that if you girls would like him to wear his hair long and combed forward perhaps you could help him convince Mr. Keene by writing a little note suggesting same. It might help, you just never know.

Bobby couldn't be bothered with Randy's hair problems for two reasons. First off, he likes his brother's hair just the way it is. And secondly, he had other things on his mind.

"We put a tarantula in the elevator in our apartment building," he announced proudly.

And then thought better of it. "Maybe you'd better not print that. They might throw us out," Bobby reflected. And then thought better of that. "No, I guess they'd never read about us, anyway. You can go ahead and print it if you want." We want.

The tarantula incident brought something to Jim's mind and he turned to Randy grinning: "Remember the time you got caught by a skunk?"

Randy remembered—how could he forget? He smelled of skunk for three days!

Apparently, a lot of people have the wrong impression about the Bobby Fuller Four's stand on the English groups. From merely reading their quotes on the subject one comes away with the feeling that the Four despise anyone from England. Which is not true at all.

"What we meant," explained Jim, "was that we don't like a group just *because* they're from England. If they're good we like them and if they're bad, we don't."

In fact, Jim says that he, for one, is glad that the English groups came on our scene because it got rid of the "sick stuff and wishwashy records which were out before the Beatles."

Bobby has just had his tonsils out but it certainly didn't keep him quiet during the interview and it won't hinder his vocal ability on stage. It has changed his voice, though. "Yes, it's changed in the way that it's stronger now," said Bobby.

The Four have played in both teenage and adult nightclubs. What's the difference from an artist's standpoint? "No difference," answered Bobby, "they're just grown-up teenagers."

Perhaps you've noticed that many times the Four are billed simply as "Bobby Fuller." Bobby declared that "it's a mistake." "Yeah, it's always a mistake," shot back brother Randy. "Really, my manager is trying to push me as an actor," said Bobby.

Movie Exposure

The Four have already appeared in one movie, an up-coming Beach Party film titled "Bikini Party At A Haunted House." No one in their right mind would ever call any of the Beach Party movies a work of art.

They are simply hastily put together movies which make a mint at the box office. It's no great acting achievement to appear in one.

So, I wondered why the Four had done it. "It puts your name up there in lights," explained Bobby "and we're not big enough yet that we can't use a little help like that."

Well, at least he's honest about it. And I admire that.

If you'll remember back to that last *BEAT* interview with the Four you'll recall that they disliked the clothing taste of female America. They haven't changed much. Jim still thinks our English style boots look like those worn by trout fishermen. He can't help it, girls. Those boots just remind him of a pair his father used to wear trout fishing!

Likes Legs

Jim also doesn't like textured hose and in his Texas drawl he explains why: "You see, I'm an admirer of legs and when they wear those black stockings I can't see their legs." Naturally this frustrates Jim so he wishes you girls would do away with the leg-concealing stockings.

The Four have been on numerous pop shows and they dig being on television except for one thing—they hate lip-syncing. "I'd rather do a live *anything*," revealed Bobby. "If you lip-sync you have no soul," said Randy.

And soul is one thing the Bobby Fuller Four strive for. And achieve. They're out of sight and they are determined to make it. Will they? That all depends on you.

Wayne's Back

Remember Wayne Fontana and the Mindbenders, and "The Game of Love" and the rumors over whether or not he was leaving the group?

Well, he did, and after a flop record, a nervous breakdown and the group's final break-up, he's now back on the scene.

He's singing solo now with just a back up group and he's been touring with Herman's Hermits and Billy Fury.

He feels that the group did the right thing breaking up when they did. "It was best to split when we did, while we were on top," he said. "If we had done it when records weren't selling, people would have said we were just trying to do something different to keep going."

Wayne still has troubles with his nerves but he's getting over it.

"I can never tell when I'm going to get an attack of nerves. I begin to get the shakes and I'm sure the audience can see my trousers quivering—but they probably think it's all part of the act.

On the BEAT
By Louise Criscione

The Beatles' English tour was a smashing success but their fans have definitely changed. They don't seem to scream so much anymore. Instead they listen.

When the Beatles staged their triumphant return to Liverpool they got the shock of their lives. Naturally, their concert was a complete sellout but when they appeared on stage they were *not* greeted with screaming hysteria.

No, even The 'Pool has matured. The overflow audience welcomed the Beatles home with thunderous *applause*. The Beatles didn't quite know what to make of it but after a few songs they came to the conclusion that the fans still loved 'em. Only now they want to hear them as well as see them! Think that will ever happen Stateside?

Speaking of the Beatles, their father-figure Brian Epstein has been confined to bed for three weeks suffering from yellow jaundice. The illness forced Epstein to cancel a visit to the U.S. to negotiate the sale of the taped Beatles' show at Shea Stadium.

"In" Waiters

Ever hear of Animal waiters? Well, there's such a thing now because Eric Burdon and Chas. Chandler (Animals supreme) acted as waiters at the opening of a new London club, tagged London's In Place. Must have been some sight!

At the Stones' press conference there was plenty of news about their first movie but there was absolutely no mention of Marianne Faithfull appearing in "Back, Behind And In Front."

However, the British press has released a story saying that Marianne is set to star with the Stones in the film. Should be interesting to see how this develops. Can't you just imagine Marianne in a duet with Mick?

The Stones continue to do all right record-wise. They've just won a gold record for "December's Children" which is some sort of an achievement since the album contains some rather old material in it.

Mick told me that "As Tears Go By" would *not* be the Stones' next single. I'd like to know how he figured that one considering the fact that it is already on the market as a single! Typically Jagger.

Hang Len?

While on the subject of new singles I think Len Barry (who is a doll of a guy) should be hung at half-mast for his latest release. Or, at least, he should have titled it "1-2-3 Revisited."

Everyone's getting into the act. John Lennon's father, Alfred Lennon, has just been signed to a recording contract! What next? The Senior Lennon's record debut is set to be "That's My Life," a self-penned song.

Rumor has it that Mr. Lennon has been on the down-and-out for a long time now. I suppose he finally decided to swallow his pride and make some money off his famous son. Don't blame him too much—you don't know the full story. And neither do I.

Probably the only two who know are John and his father. And they aren't talking . . . yet.

Watch out for a new English act which will undoubtedly tear up our charts in the not too distant future. They're a set of twins, Paul and Barry Ryan. They're talented, good-looking and funny.

Two Shots

They once looked like identical twins—now they only look very much related. Paul, for one, is very glad because one time "I got two polio injections and Barry didn't get one."

Dick Clark must be regretting his statement that the Stones are dying (popularity-wise). He's been hearing about it ever since. And none of what he is hearing is good.

In fact, word got out that Andrew Oldham was so mad at Clark that he refused to let the Stones perform at the Clark-sponsored Stones' concert in L.A.'s Sports Arena unless he received a public apology from Dick.

No public apology came forth but something must have transpired between Dick and Andrew because the Stones certainly did appear at the Arena!

. . . JOHN LENNON

. . . MICK JAGGER

KRLA ARCHIVES

It's In The Bag
By Eden

Wait just a minute now... What's this about Our Leader – Mr. Dylan – gettin' hitched in New York? First week in December there were all kinds of press reports that Bobby D. had gone off and gotten himself married, but the only thing that his office would say was "No comment," "We don't know anything about it." Much irritation on that end.

Hmmmmmm – I wonder!!

★ ★ ★ ★ ★

Greatest rage in Blightyland during the Yule season was sending John Lennon Christmas cards. Chad Stuart told me 'bout it, but after reading John's book – it's a little difficult to imagine getting a *Christmas* card like that!

★ ★ ★ ★ ★

Speaking of Chad Stuart, *The BEAT* would like to welcome him, his lovely wife Jill, and his "sometimes singing partner," Jeremy back to the US.

Just back from their trip across the Pond, Chad called to say that the bottle of fog he had promised me was on its way. He explained that he had flown over – complete with a horrible cold! – ahead of Jeremy and had been unable to get the fog before he left. But he assured me that he had impressed upon Jeremy the importance of the item, and asked him to bring it over with him.

But Jeremy rushed over, and he too was unable to snatch a bottle of the foggy stuff before he left, as the airport was clean out of it!!

So, Chad is currently in the process of having a jar of the stuff shipped over from Merrie Olde as a belated Christmas present for me. He's quite a guy, that Mr. Stuart! (But just the same – I would have rather found Paul McCartney 'neath my Christmas tree!!)

Chad also mentioned that he and Jeremy will probably be doing a TV series at Universal – more about that in the future – and asked me to convey a message to you from both him and Jeremy:

"May this New Year be as happy as is conceivably possible for everyone, and may you all be free from strife! We wish all the *BEAT* readers a very Happy New Year!"

★ ★ ★ ★ ★

Also received a call from Joey Paige just before Christmas. He was getting ready to fly home to Philadelphia to spend the holidays with his family, and he was trying to entertain the Stones at the same time.

The Rolling Ones were in town for a concert at the time, and Joey said, "We've been having a ball – in fact, I'm having dinner with Brian tonight." It was a week of many dinners and many of the "in" night spots in town, catching all the great acts performing during the holiday season.

Joey also sent along his best wishes to everyone for a wonderful New Year, and promised to call when he gets back.

★ ★ ★ ★ ★

Darlin' Dusty Springfield did a little sounding-off lately, and since *The BEAT* has very big ears – we decided to listen in on some of her ravings:

On singing: "A great joy when everything's going right but it can be hell if you don't feel like it. I certainly don't do it for the money."

On money: "Oh, oh! the sound of music! I love the sound of money, ha ha. I cannot understand people who say they don't know what to do with it. There's so much you can do with money."

On London clubs: "I think they're pretty awful, that's why I don't go to them. There's very little happening."

Ambition: "To be acknowledged as being good at what I do. I like people to come up and say, 'Oh, I liked that,' but it's even more of a pleasure if the person is qualified to say whether something is good or bad. If somebody whose opinion I respect says, 'I enjoyed you,' that's fantastic."

End of raving.

★ ★ ★ ★ ★

Confession and advice from Charlie Watts of the Rolling Stones: "It took me a year to convince my parents that I really wanted to play drums, and eventually they bought me a very cheap secondhand kit, and away I went practicing to records. When they realized that I intended to stick at it, they helped me to improve the kit as I went along, buying it in bits and pieces until I had the right gear.

"Learn to read music, and get yourself a good teacher so that you get the right technique. I never did either – and have always regretted it!!"

★ ★ ★ ★ ★

Tiger Tom Jones and British star Lulu are cutting an ElPee together across the Pond. Should be a winner for The Tiger.

Speaking of winners, Bob Dylan – winner of *The BEAT's* Favorite Male Vocalist of 1965 award in *The BEAT* Pop Music Award Poll – has spent some time in Los Angeles recently, putting on three sell-out concerts, and cutting a brand new album.

Question of the week? Is it really true that P.J. Proby has cut his shoulder-length tresses? Heavens, I just *shudder* at the thought!

By way of a short apology to Laurie Phillips – please forgive my over-unenthusiasm about the probable impending marriage of Paul and Jane. I, too, would be among the first to wish them all of the happiness possible on this earth, but please remember – I only said that they were *probably* going to get married and that it looked very certain considering the fact that they have already purchased a house. But then, I am seldom able to please *everyone*!

... THE WHO

Meet The Swingin' Who

They're young, they're talented, they're British, they wear far-out clothes and they have a hit record in "My Generation."

They're The Who and *The BEAT* felt it was about time you met the boys individually.

Roger Daltrey is probably The Who who stands out most. He's the group's lead singer and he also is the only one who sports rather long blond hair.

Roger is a Negro "quality" man who goes for R&B singers such as Wilson Pickett and Otis Redding. Roger has one of those hard, earthy styles of singing which reflects his own earthy personality.

A strange thing about Roger is his intense dislike for listening to records. "It drives me mad," Roger reveals. "I had an enormous collection once but I gave them all away. They didn't mean anything anymore."

Who's Image

Funny isn't it? A man who earns his living by making records hates listening to them. It's strange but it fits in perfectly with The Who's image.

They wear these way-out pop art clothes and they go strictly for the visual act. They ruin thousands of dollars of equipment each time they perform because they bang their guitars all around simply for the sound they produce by doing it.

The bass guitarist of the group is John Entwistle. You can never miss John because he always appears in shirts completely covered with military medals and military insignia.

In fact, John has gone so far as to have some clothes designed which look like those worn by the Confederate Army in the American Civil War.

The Quiet Who

John is the quiet, moody member of The Who. And he is the one primarily responsible for keeping the group from venturing too far in their flights of musical imagination.

Pete Townsend is The Who's lead guitarist and is the man accountable for the group's love of pop art as well as their unique musical sound.

Pete is a former art student, one who was and still is very interested in modern forms of art. Thus, we have Pete introducing the rest of The Who to pop art.

Pete is also the one who leads in the guitar smashing. He does it by smashing the neck first into his speaker cabinets, which creates a vibrating whining noise otherwise known as "feedback." The feedback effect is the one which Jeff Beck of the Yardbirds is the absolute master of.

Varied Tastes

Pete's musical tastes are as varied as the sounds which he produces on his guitar. He likes music ranging from Purcell and Bach to modern Electobic Music as well as digging the Everly Brothers and Tamala-Motown.

The youngest and newest member of The Who is the 19 year old drummer, Keith Moon. Keith has a unique way of pounding the drums, one which has been unsuccessfully imitated by groups around the London area for quite sometime now.

Keith twirls his sticks around his head, looking somewhat like a drum major, and then slowly spins them down onto the skins.

Keith is the group member who goes in for tee shirts with wild designs such as targets, arrows and even the word "pow" tatooed on them.

Keith's musical tastes differ from the other members of The Who in that he goes for the West Coast surf sound as typified by the Beach Boys and Jan and Dean.

And that's The Who – one of the swingingest and wildest groups around. Keep an eye on them because they are going to be huge someday. And someday soon too.

The Animals Join UNCLE

The Man from U.N.C.L.E. and the Animals are going to get together for a picture.

David McCallum has been signed as special guest star in "This Could Be the Night," a musical to be produced by Henry G. Saperstein for AIP.

Joining McCallum, alias Illya, will be England's own Animals.

KRLA ARCHIVES

Beach Boys In Hassel Over Movie

Capitol Records made a lot of noise a while back by announcing that they were going into film making and were starring the Beach Boys in their first production.

Well, now it seems the whole thing has fallen through and there may not be any Beach Boys film at all, at least not from Capitol.

Steve Broidy, former president of Allied Pictures was hired by Capitol for the film, which Capitol had hoped would be the start of something great.

No Script

The disagreement between the Beach Boys and Broidy, which may mean the death of the whole deal, seems to center around the lack of a working script. The five California boys want script approval before filming and won't agree to anything until they see a script, which Broidy apparently doesn't have yet.

Everyone involved with the film has gotten a little angry over the delay and even the Beach Boys themselves have been reported to be arguing among themselves over it. There have even been reports that Brian Wilson has been offered other picture opportunities if the Capitol deal falls through completely.

But they are still negotiating over the thing. After all, the Beach Boys are Capitol's top selling American teen act, and Alan Livingston, president of the label, has frankly stated, "We want to make a picture."

LOU CHRISTIE — FORTUNE TELLER WAS RIGHT.

Gypsy Helps Lou Make Hit Discs

By Louise Criscione

Lou Christie strolled into *The BEAT* offices today and completely charmed the entire female portion of our staff. He's an absolute gas, a guy you can talk to for hours without ever getting bored.

He hates phoniness and it shows. He appreciates talent and that shows, too, in his choice of performers — Motown and particularly the Supremes.

Lou has one of the strangest stories to tell on how he got into show business. He's a success because of a gypsy. "She lives like 'I Love Lucy.' She even looks like her," grinned Lou. "It's unbelievable.

"We met in church. When she was a little girl her mother told her she'd be writing with a boy with green eyes," he continued.

That boy, of course, was Lou. And write they did. It was only fitting that the first song they wrote together was a nation-wide smash and was, oddly enough, about a gypsy. You remember "The Gypsy Cried?" It was their first attempt at producing a hit sound and with a little luck from upstairs they succeeded.

Another Smash

Lou followed up "Gypsy" with yet another smash, "Two Faces Have I." And then for a long time there was nothing. "I was very depressed," admitted Lou. "I was in the Army and I was unhappy away from the business.

"And then I was unhappy management-wise," said Lou. But he's not the least bit unhappy now. He's joined the Bob Marcucci camp (discoverer of Frankie Avalon and Fabian) and Lou declares that "I've never been happier in my life."

Lou tells a funny story about how he met Bob. "I snuck into his room one time," grinned Lou. "I met Fabian and it seemed that Bob took such a personal interest in his artists. I wanted to be managed by someone like that."

Besides being happy management-wise Lou is also pretty thrilled record-wise because his "Lightnin' Strikes" is bounding up the charts faster than any record around.

Did he think it was going to be such a huge hit when he recorded it? Lou thought long and hard before answering: "I did — but I also thought that I had recorded better things."

Life's Goal

Lou is one of those people who always wanted to be a performer — there was never any other thought in his mind. "I worked in my dad's pizza house and made good money but I still wanted to be a singer.

"So, I made demos and went off to New York with them. I had a lot of determination and I wanted it so badly. It was really funny. I didn't know a soul in New York.

"I'd just bring my demos and go to all these record companies. I'd knock on the door and tell them that I had an appointment with Mr. So and So.

"The secretary would look at her book and tell me she didn't have my name down. Then I'd tell her that, of course, I had an appointment and I'd come all the way from Pittsburgh for it.

"So, they'd say 'all right, all right — he'll see you.' And that's how I got a record contract."

With a recording contract in hand the next logical step, of course, was a recording session. "I love 'em," said Lou. "It's great after you work so hard. I used to do my own arranging but now I only arrange my girls. I do work very closely with my manager, Charlie Calello."

Loves Motown

Lou is one of the staunchest Motown fans around, declaring that their sound "just tears me up." Over and over the question is asked: what does Motown have? Why do they continue to come up with hit after hit?

Lou has a rather interesting answer to that. "I think it's because they don't produce perfect records," said Lou. "And they all have feeling. They believe in what they're singing."

As soon as Lou gets back from the East where he's cutting an album and also appearing on a huge show with the Four Seasons, he is set to take private acting lessons at MGM. Which makes him extremely excited.

Follow-Up?

In fact, he's already turned down several Beach Party movies because "I think an artist has to have some respect for himself."

However, Lou is not at all against making a movie in which he sings. "If the part came up where I could sing as well as act I'd take it," said Lou.

He is a firm believer in the youth of America, probably because he is a member himself. "Kids are the brightest things," Lou said. "They're smart and you can't fool them."

Whenever an artist has a hit record (which Lou definitely has) the talk in the industry immediately turns to the follow-up. You can't enjoy one success without worrying about the next one. And it can be a bad scene for a performer.

How about Lou — is he fretting about his next release? "No," said Lou, shaking his head. "But I'm not going to put out the same record all over again and just change a few notes. I'll try to come up with something different. Otherwise, you're just cheating the public."

And that's something Lou Christie is not about to do — cheat the public. As long as his stars hold out and his gypsy keeps writing Lou will keep swinging and that lightning will just keep striking hits for him.

For Girls Only

By Shirley Poston

I, dear readers, believe in starting the New Year off right, don't you? So, in order to manage that one, I've made up a list of New Year's resolutions! You know, those things you're *positive* you're going to *stick* to. For at least an hour, anyway.

And, in case you're wondering what those revolutionary resolutions are, here is my list!

1. I am going to write a *sensible, rational* column from now on.

2. I am going to stop sounding like I've just escaped from a funny farm!

3. I am not going to write entire columns about *orange popsicles*.

4. I am not going to compose long and dreary paragraphs about *feet*.

5. I am not going to mention George Harrison's name every other word.

6. I am only going to mention George Harrison's name every *two* words.

7. I am going out of my mind.

Now, let's just see how long I can stick to *those*! Except the seventh of course. That won't present any problem because it's already happened.

Now, onward to something sensible. This week's best dream, for instance, which was sent to me by Mimi Martin (who admits this is a "pen name") (what's wrong with you guys — you don't want to be famous?) from Alamo, Calif. And here goes:

One day as I am flying my own personal plane (I'm too young to drive a car), the motor conks out. I jump out, pull the ripcord and my own pink and purple polka-dotted parachute (yes, I dream in color) floats dreamily.

I am gliding through the air when I notice that my parachute is caught in a hurricane (in Cali-fornia?). When the wind subsides, I peer down at the earth.

"Aha," I say brilliantly. "Looks as though I've blown from San Francisco to L.A." Yep, it seems that way all right.

Just then my parachute catches the eye of an innocent bystander. "Look!" he says, and everyone does. The news of ME soon hits the radio. And Dino, Desi & Billy just happen to hear about it during their coke break (?).

"Well," says Dino (sigh) intelligently. "Let's go see about this."

They all jump on their Triumph 350s (which they're too young to drive) and zoom off towards the Hollywood Bowl where I've finally landed.

Exhausted from my trip, I lie panting in the sawdust (?). Millions of reporters cluster around, but all I can say is "Dino . . . Dino." Then I hear a zoom, zoom, zoom. Yep! You guessed it. Dino, Desi & Billy have driven up. They come tearing into the Bowl and trip over me (I fainted).

Finally I wake up to see three adorably worried faces looking down at me. "Oh, Dino . . ." I say, and the others realize that they are needed elsewhere.

After a few days of motorcycling, skateboarding, and recording a song (oh yes, I get discovered), I must go back to family and friends.

Dino and I cry gallons, but realize this is the way it must be. From then on Dino, Desi & Billy sing only sad songs, but earn tons of money and come to the Cow Palace twice a year.

Dino never forgets me and later, when we're eighteen, we get married and become a singing team.
— *The End* —

Wow, that's one of the best ones I've heard yet. Please keep sending me your masterpieces (masterpi?) and I'll keep printing them here in The BEAT.

KRLA ARCHIVES

America's Largest Teen NEWSpaper

KRLA Edition BEAT

Volume 1, Number 44   LOS ANGELES, CALIFORNIA   15 Cents   January 15, 1966

BEAT Photo: Chuck Boyd

Tom Jones—One "Thunderball" Of A Man

KRLA BEAT

Los Angeles, California — January 15, 1966

"Soul" Nets Gold One For Beatles

By Louise Criscione

A surprise to no one we're sure is the fact that the Beatles have won a gold record for their latest album, "Rubber Soul." What *is* a surprise to many of you is how a gold record is certified. So, with the help of Ron Tepper from Capitol Records we have uncovered the mystery. Would you like to be let in on the secret?

"We'll use 'Rubber Soul' as our example of how a gold record is awarded. In the case of "Soul" the album earned a gold record in one day by selling a million dollars worth of albums—not a million albums.

Elvis Rejects British Offer

Elvis Presley has turned down another offer to appear in England. Promoter Don Arden made a bid on behalf of the National Playing Fields Association for Elvis to appear at a West End Theater.

Proceeds from the show would have brought the Association, of which the Duke of Edinburgh is a member, over 10,000 pounds and Elvis was promised 100,000 pounds from the takings at other theaters where the show would be relayed via closed circuit television.

But Arden received a message from Colonel Tom Parker, Elvis' personal manager, thanking him for the offer and saying that Elvis was unable to take time out from his filming schedule.

The Colonel also said that he was suffering from a back ailment which wouldn't have allowed him to accompany Elvis as the star would have wanted.

Inside the BEAT

Everly Brothers Still Giants 3
Evie Sands—A Real Lady 4
Yeah Well, P.J. 5
Deep Six Rising 6
Matt's Many Names 7
Strange New Game 8
Adventures of Robin Boyd 11
Swingin' Mel Carter 12
Look Back at Ringo 13
Kingston Trio—Entertainers 15
Lovin' Spoonful Speak 16

The BEAT is published weekly by BEAT Publications, Inc., editorial and advertising offices at 6290 Sunset Blvd., Suite 504, Hollywood, California 90028. U.S. bureaus in Hollywood, San Francisco, New York, Chicago and Nashville, overseas correspondents in London, Liverpool and Manchester, England. Sale price, 15 cents. Subscription price: U.S. and possessions, $3 per year, Canada and foreign rates, $9 per year. Application to mail at second class postage rates is pending at Los Angeles, California.

It took the Beatles seven sales days to sell a million albums. Actually the sales figures for the first week totaled 1,192,000 albums sold.

Perhaps you think Capitol counts all those records itself. If you do you're wrong. Before 1958 any record company could award a gold record to whomever they wanted to and there was no one around to dispute the sales.

Legit Winners

But now things have changed. Today the R.I.A.A. does the counting. When a label feels that one of their records has sold the necessary million dollars worth it either writes or wires the R.I.A.A. and then the R.I.A.A. takes an independent accountant out to the respective record company's plant to total the sales.

If the sales are off so much as $100 the gold record will not be certified. The record companies must pay a fee to belong to the R.I.A.A. and they must also foot the bill for the certification of the gold record.

Since the R.I.A.A. has been in existence the number of gold records has been fewer but the number of *legitimate* gold records awarded has gone up. In fact, in the entire year of 1965 only 33 gold records were awarded.

Besides winning a gold one for "Rubber Soul" the Beatles are also set to win another gold record for "We Can Work It Out." What about "Day Tripper?" Wasn't it the flip and didn't it therefore sell just as many copies as "We Can Work It Out?"

Most Requests

Right you are. But in the case of a double-sided hit the gold record is awarded to the side which has the most requests. Okay, but how do you find out which side is the more popular?

They do it very simply. Each record store keeps a chart on which they tabulate the number of requests for records which they receive each week. "Cash Box" and "Billboard" in turn call these stores to find out how the records are doing request-wise.

Having a two-sided hit is a definite disadvantage (funny as that may sound). It means that the requests as well as the air play is split, making it twice as hard to get a record high on the charts.

Except, that is, if you're the Beatles. In which case you earn a gold record in one day and sell a million albums in a week. Pardon me, I mean 1,192,000 albums in a week.

Times are sure hard, aren't they?

MORE RECORDS DUE

Sonny & Cher Blitzing

It's been awfully quiet on the Sonny and Cher scene here on the West Coast lately, so The BEAT gave Charlie Greene, half of the Greene-Stone productions that manages the duo, a call and found out what they've been up to.

If you've been wondering why we haven't had any more records or local appearances lately, it's because Sonny and Cher have been a bit on the busy side.

Tour of U.S.

Greene informed us that they've just completed a tour that covered all parts of the U.S. and have been recording quite a bit.

Sometime this month or next be prepared for two full albums from the Bonos, as well as a single from each one of them.

Cher will have another album out by herself. This one's entitled "The Sonny Side of Cher." And there'll be another Sonny and Cher album, which is not yet titled.

Almost all of the material on the two albums will be written by Sonny but he got a little help this time from two young writers who just broke into the singing field themselves—Artie Kornfeld and Steve Duboff, now known as The Changing Times.

There will also be a single by Sonny and one by Cher but Greene couldn't say what the titles would be because "there's just so much good material to choose from."

First Movie

And between tours and recording dates Sonny has been very busy writing and scoring his and Cher's first movie.

It's tentatively titled "I Got You Babe" and is due to begin filming in Hollywood this month.

They hope to have the movie completed in time for an Easter release but the soundtrack from it should be out in February.

Greene couldn't say much about the movie's plot because Sonny's still working on it but he did say that Sonny "wants to gear it to the fans who buy the records."

T.V., Too

And somewhere between a nationwide tour, two albums, two singles, a movie plus soundtrack, this hard working pair also managed to find time to tape their third *Hollywood Palace* which aired earlier this month and a *Danny Thomas Special* which will air sometime in February.

We don't know what the Bono's New Year's resolutions were, but if they had anything to do with keeping busy they're certainly working hard at it.

KRLA ARCHIVES

U. S. Artists To Invade England

You all know how we believe in equal trade between the U.S. and England when it comes to entertainers. So, during the first part of the year brace yourself for an influx of British artists.

The English are *already* preparing themselves for an overflow of American pop people. Leading the parade off will be the talented Fontella Bass. Fontella will sing her "Rescue Me" to the British record buyers via six pop television shows.

Righton Fontella's tail will be Patti Labelle and her Bluebelles. Patti is going to Enland, of course, to promote her U.S. hit, "All Or Nothing." The English are in for a real treat with these girls because they put on a fantastic show complete with dancing and all.

Then in February it looks as though the whole American pop population will visit our cousins across the Pond. Gene Pitney, who is absolutely adored in England, is set to make a major one-night tour. Gene's British tours are always complete sell-outs and this one sould be no exception.

Len Too

The tour will play for 16 days and Gene's co-star on the bill will be that "1-2-3" man himself, Len Barry. Len's record is way up there in the British charts so this double-headed tour is a sure fire winner.

It's been said that 1966 will be the year of the single artist and apparently the English promoters firmly believe it. And so they have booked such American artists as Wilson Pickett, Otis Redding, Roy Head, Clyde McPhatter, Irma Thomas, Marvin Gaye and Kim Weston to appear in England during February and March.

The English teens are especially keen on our R&B singers (even more so than in the U.S.) so watch for Wilson Pickett and Otis Redding to make really big smashes over there.

There is a very good possibility that the great Everly Brothers will visit England during the first months of the new year. Which makes the British record buyers happy as the Everlys are another of their favorite American entertainers.

Everly's Maybe

For certain Don and Phil will tour Ireland in April and there is a chance that they will perform at the San Remo Song Festival. If they do entertain at San Remo, the Everlys will have to sing in Italian before a live audience which is a rather difficult thing to do if you don't speak the language! But *The BEAT* has great faith in the Everlys so we're sure they can do it if they try!

A NEW GROUP? This talented foursome could certainly produce some fantastic sounds if they did get together, couldn't they? The Everly Bros., Adam Faith and Roy Orbison have already produced some fantastic sounds of their own. Can't you just imagine what treats we'd be in for if they decided to join forces?

Q: How long should a boy keep asking a girl for a date if she keeps on refusing?
(Jerry P.)

A: When this sort of thing happens a couple of times, her excuses could be easily for real – previous plans, etc. But, along about the time you become a three time loser, better find out whether she's trying to tell you something.

Q: I would like to know what causes the ends of hair to split. I used to pin my hair up on bobby pins a long time ago, and got lots of split ends. But now I wear it long and don't set it at all and I still get them! Why, and what can I do about it?
(Sue F.)

A: Split ends are mostly caused by dryness. It's almost impossible for the natural oils in your hair to reach all the way to the very ends, especially when your hair is long, unless you do a lot of brushing. Trim off the ends every month or so, and use a conditioner.

Q: My folks are always saying I don't have the world's best manners, so I want to do things just right about my Christmas presents. Am I supposed to send thank you cards to everyone, or what?
(Ellen H.)

A: Sending cards to everyone from whom you received a gift is a nice but unnecessary gesture. A card becomes a necessity only when you can't thank the gift-giver in person. But, like we said, it's a nice gesture, so go ahead and send to everyone if you want to.

Q: I had a beautiful tan this summer, but now it's almost gone. I don't want to wait several months before starting another tan, so please tell me if you recommend those tan without the sun products.
(Arlene G.)

A: These products work fine for some people and not so fine for others. Before you try one, give yourself a patch-test by putting just a little of the lotion on the inside of your arm. Then you'll be able to tell if it might become discolored or irritated. Actually, you'd be better off buying an inexpensive sun lamp. It takes longer, but the tan is much less fake-looking.

Q: I have just bought a guitar and am about to start teaching myself how to play it. I can't spend a lot of money on chord books, so could you tell me the names of two or three that would be helpful?
(Dennis L.)

A: One of the best we know of isn't a book. It's a "wheel," and by revolving it, you can find related chords, etc. The name escapes us, but any music store would know. Also, any Beatle songbook will be very helpful to you. They write in many different keys and use unusual chords.

Everly Brothers Still Giants

By Barri

Let's see – there was Elvis Presley, James Brown, Chuck Berry, Frankie Avalon, and – the Everly Brothers. They were all very big pop stars in the big Rock 'n' Roll years of the 1950's.

But this is 1966 and this year the Beatles, and the Rolling Stones, and the Yardbirds are the glittering stars of pop. But this year is also a brightly star-studded year for the Everly Brothers who have been pop stars all along.

During 1965, the Everly Brothers became one of the hottest, most popular acts to tour Great Britain, and they plan to do a repeat performance across the Pond again in 1966. Their last two singles hit the top spots on the National British charts and their shows were always sell-outs.

Have they changed any since 1958? Certainly not in talent – they are still just as great as ever; maybe even *greater!!* Of course, there have been a *few* changes. Like Phil Everly, for example.

Most of the credit for this change must be given to dear old Uncle Sam, however, who recently insisted that Phil trim his hair before he paid a month long visit to the Marine Reserves.

Haircuts

Good nephew that he is, Phil promptly obeyed and sheared off his then almost-lengthy locks, combing them into a style more acceptable to the Marines.

Once out of the Weekend Warriors (as the Reserves are sometimes *affectionately* called!), Phil let his hair grow out just a little, but kept it combed in pretty much the same style. Result: Phil Beatle!

Phil does admit that "it's easy to take care of this way – I never comb it!" But then he goes on to explain that he had never combed it *before*, either!

In March, Don and Phil will begin another 'round the world tour, starting off in the Orient, and winding up in Ireland. Phil explained that "a lot of our old records are now Number One around the world, like 'Brand New Heartache' in Israel.' Although it didn't do quite as well over here, their latest single – "Price of Love" – hit the Number One position in Beatle Country and that's really *singing* something!

Beatles Influenced?

Many people have expressed the feeling that the Beatles were very strongly influenced in their style by the Everly Brothers, but Phil disagrees with this. "No, I don't think so. Maybe they were – and that's great – but, I don't know. I think they're good – and it's very flattering."

Like the Beatles, the Everly's have also written quite a number of their own hit records, including "Cathy's Clown," and the "Price of Love," and now the boys have hopes of doing a whole album of just their own tunes which should really be something else.

Before their departure in March, Don and Phil are spending the month of January filming TV shows, including "Hullabaloo" and the "Jimmy Dean Show," and then they will fly briefly to the San Remo Music Festival in England.

The boys are both very excited about the current international trend in pop music, and in speaking of England Phil says that "there's a whole new thing going on over there. We get a lot of mail from the English kids, and they have really been great to us."

Don Everly ("I'm the oldest brother – the one with the *crew cut!*") is the proud new papa of a beautiful little eight-week old daughter named Erin Invicta Everly, so every free minute of his time is spent at home with his wife and baby daughter.

Phil is also spending as much time as possible around the house, these days, but this isn't just any old house.

Phil and his lovely wife have recently moved into a large English-Tudor style home – vintage 1926! – in Hollywood, which they are decorating entirely with antiques.

Right now he is anxiously awaiting the arrival of an antique four-poster bed, built in 1600, which he found in England on their last trip over. The bed measures up to a full seven feet and one inch. (Funny – I could have *sworn* that Phil wasn't *that* tall!)

Outside of foreign tours, American TV appearances, night club appearances, and about a million other things – the only thing the Everly Brothers seem to be doing now is simply increasing their greatness!

They still have one of the most astoundingly *great* sounds around, and their harmonies and arrangements are simply fantastic.

But then, that's just a little something called "talent," more affectionately known to all of us *pop fans* as "The Everly Brothers!"

KRLA ARCHIVES

On the BEAT
By Louise Criscione

Remember last week I was telling you that the English papers had printed that Marianne Faithfull was set to appear in the Rolling Stones' first movie, "Back, Behind And In Front?"

It was news to me – and it was to Marianne too! In fact, Marianne's lawyers have issued a rather harsh denial. "Miss Faithfull has no knowledge of the film referred to and no intention of appearing in it. Neither Andrew Oldham or Allen Klein has any authority to represent Miss Faithfull in anyway whatsoever."

Her lawyers went on to say that Marianne's agent is, however, looking for a movie for Marianne. And Marianne herself told me that she would very much like to make a film. But it will definitely not be "Back, Behind And In Front."

The Beatles had an announcement to make this week about their future movie plans too. As I mentioned before, the Beatles were highly dissatisfied with their proposed film, "A Talent For Loving."

Wrong Again

I really thought that the script would be rewritten to suit them but apparently I was wrong. Beatles' producer, Walter Shenson, revealed: "'Talent For Loving' seemed ideal but when we came to script it we found it almost impossible to adapt something which had already been published without making it look as though it had been sewn together for the purpose."

The Beatles new movie is set to role in April but so far they haven't even found a script which they all like. They state very emphatically that they don't want to go the Elvis route and turn out a picture in three weeks.

. . . MARIANNE FAITHFULL

More power to 'em but they'd better hurry up and find a script before April or they'll be in big trouble.

Hope Rick Zehringer of the McCoys is feeling better. On the group's first visit to England Rick was forced to enter the hospital due to a severe reaction to a smallpox shot.

All is now well – Rick has left London's National Temperance Hospital and winged his way home to America last weekend.

The fantastic Yardbirds are Stateside again and are set to make their U.S. club debut at The Hullabaloo in Hollywood.

Your Big Chance

I keep saying how great they are "live." Now all of you within driving (or flying) distance from Hollywood have the opportunity to see for yourselves. Don't you dare miss it because you'll be sorry if you do.

Another terrific stage act which you shouldn't miss is the Everly Brothers. These guys really know how to put on a show so do yourself a favor and drop in if they are ever playing anywhere near you. Too bad they can't come up with a hit here in the U.S., isn't it?

The question of the week seems to be – what happened to Sonny & Cher? They've disappeared from the charts, from the television and from the news. What's happened to them – did they fall off of their own special world?

Anybody want to buy a used Aston Martin or Ferrari? If you do, look up George Harrison for the Aston and John Lennon for the Ferrari. Both Beatles have put their respective cars up for sale. Times must be bad because John and George have their cars listed in the classified part of the *New York Times*.

Bet you didn't know that David and Jonathan, the ones who have recorded "Michelle," are the same duo who wrote the Fortunes big hit of awhile back, "You've Got Your Troubles."

Don't feel bad – I didn't know either. All of this time I thought they were the same David and Jonathan who had a bomb of a record about six months ago. Goes to show.

The cutest quote of the week comes from Mick Jagger's little brother, Chris. "The main difference between Mick and I is that in London I walk and he takes taxis."

Also goes to show.

. . . CHER

Evie Sands - A Sparkling Young Lady From Brooklyn

By Carol Deck

I knocked softly on the door of the swank hotel room and a cheerful woman opened and said, "Hi. Come on in. Evie's getting dressed. I'm her mother."

As I sat down in a bright pink chair, Evie Sands came bobing out dressed in very attractive modified bell bottoms, a sweater and sandals and started talking.

"I was born and live in Brooklyn. When I was about 14 I decided I wanted to sing. I always had sung but just never thought about doing it professionally until then."

She went on to tell me about a contest that's held in Brooklyn every Easter, Christmas and Labor Day. She entered, but the contest turned out to be phony that year. Anyway out of 5,000 contestants, her singing won her a place in the 40 finalists and that gave her the confidence to go on.

Two False Starts

"About a year and a half ago I met Al Gorgoni, one of my current producers. Twice we thought we were ready, but we weren't. Then we got "Take Me For A Little While."

And the public took her for more than a little while as her first release charged up the charts.

After her first hit she got swamped with offers for new songs but she didn't like any of them. So finally her producers, Gorgoni and Chip Taylor, who had joined them by this time, wrote one for her.

It's called "I Can't Let Go" and you'll be seeing her do it on practically all of the pop TV shows pretty soon.

She described the song as rhythm and blues oriented which isn't unusual since r&b is her favorite type of music. She likes Ramsey Lewis, Nancy Wilson, Otis Redding and said Jackie Wilson was the biggest influence on her style.

Likes Small Places

As for audiences she said "I love intimate places where I can walk right up and sing right into your face." And who could complain with that pretty face of hers.

Then she went on to talk about her goals in life. "I hope to have success with records that will allow me to bring my singing to people.

"And I want to get married and be happy. When I get married my marriage will come first. If I give up my career, I give it up."

Then her dark brown eyes sparkled as she bubbled over about her nephew. He's 14 months old and she says he dances better than most teenagers. "He's out of sight," she exclaimed. "I want to bring him on stage some time when I'm performing. He'll probably steal the show."

Not Embarrassed

From her nephew she somehow got on the topic of Bob Dylan. "He's more commercial now. It's not that he changed his lyrics but he's become more melodic. He used to write weird melodies that kids couldn't hum. But I'm not embarrassed to say that I don't understand him a lot of the time."

That's more than a lot of people will even admit but this 18 year old young lady is quite frank and refreshingly attractive.

Asked to describe the type of songs she sings, she just said, "I like to sing songs that mean something to me."

Time To Go

But now Evie had to change clothes again and rush off to film one more TV show, but she took just a minute more to say how much she loves California.

"I would live here if I didn't live in New York. My ideal would be to be able to have a home in California during the winter months and still be in New York for spring."

She added that the best part about her career is meeting and speaking to people. She enjoys being with people so much that she said what she'd really like to do is have a great big home and say "listen everybody, come on over."

And then we both had to rush off so I bid farewell to the sparkling little girl from Brooklyn who just loves to sing.

BEAT Photo: Chuck Boyd

Minstrels – 4 Years, 4 Million Dollars

There are certain signs in the pop world by which you can tell if a group is successful. Among these are a high income and just plain survival year after year.

By these standards the New Christy Minstrels must be one of the most successful groups around for they just celebrated their fourth anniversary together as well as their fourth consecutive year of grossing over $1 million.

The 10 member folk group was formed in 1961 by Randy Sparks who also started the Back Porch Majority (which was originally a farm club for the Minstrels) and the Elementary School Band. Sparks has also done some singing himself. He sold his interest in the Minstrels in 1964 to Greif-Garris Management. The price for the group has been rumored to be anywhere from a mere $100,000 to over $2 million.

The Minstrels have become so popular that they spend the majority of their time traveling and have recently leased a multi-million dollar jet plane to cart them around the world. The plane reportedly seats 100, has sleeping facilities for the entire group and even contains a ping pong table for recreation. That's traveling in style!

The groups have had many personnel changes since they first formed. Sparks himself was once the lead singer and several members of the group have gone out on their own to seek success. The most famous of these are Barry McGuire, who did the lead singing on "Green Green," which he also wrote, before going on to do "The Eve of Destruction," and Jackie and Gayle, the original two female singers with the group.

The group is currently on a whirlwind college tour which will take them to over 100 campuses.

KRLA ARCHIVES

Yeah, Well P.J. How's Your Pants?

By Tammy Hitchcock

Bow down everyone — we have royalty on our "Yeah, Well Hot Seat" this week. It's that great hunk of manhood, Lord Jim. Better known as P.J. Proby. Suppose I really shouldn't say *better* known — I should have said more *widely* known.

Anyway, now that you all know who I mean, let's get on with it. First off, P.J. has one way or another succeeded in capturing a rather fair-sized following of fans in England.

He smiles sort of sinisterly as he explains why: "I have a thing with the fans." Yeah, well I guess you do, P.J. And I've figured out what it is — communication. On stage communication, that is. In fact, you're probably the only performer alive who can make Mick Jagger look like he's on his way to Sunday school.

The thing which I really dig about P.J. is that he is *so* modest. I mean, modesty is his only policy. Naturally, he was most embarrassed and reluctant to admit what he's done for the British music scene since he first graced their shores. But P.J. did manage to pull himself together and modestly proclaim: "I started big band backings and the big voice sound."

Copying P.J.

Yeah, well that's about the truest statement you ever made, P.J. Actually, I feel sorry for him. He started the sound and now everyone is copying him — and succeeding better than he is. Horrible situation.

Take Tom Jones (and if you don't want him — *I'll* gladly take him). Tom is one of the most popular solo artists around and one of his trademarks is his big voice sound. Now, did he or did he not copy P.J.?

"I don't think Tom Jones copies me voice-wise but I don't think he needs to wear his hair in a ribbon and I don't think he needs to wear fluffy clothes," says P.J.

Yeah, well at least Tom's pants don't split on stage. And as for his ribbon — his wife makes him wear it.

P.J. has wanted to be an actor for a long time now and it looks as if his dream just might come true.

"I have to be very careful about my first film, it's on a very touchy subject and I can't tell you too much about it."

A Tough Wait

Yeah, well that's a real shame, P.J. That you can't tell us about it, I mean. Guess we'll just have to wait breathlessly. It'll be really tough on us, I'm sure.

Proby put his vocal eloquence to work again on the subject of good as well as bad fan mail. "What people don't realize," theorized P.J. "is whether they are upset at me or love me, they are emotionally involved and take time out of their life to write to me."

Yeah, well I guess that I'm emotionally involved with you P.J. 'cause I once wrote you a letter. But it came back — all the way from England. You see, it needed two more cents of postage which was apparently two more cents than P.J. had.

Of course, P.J. is forever running into pants problems: "No pants can ever hold me," declared P.J. Therefore, his pants have the most annoying habit of splitting while he is on stage.

The pants-splitting incidents have gotten P.J. banned from most theatres and practically all of the pop television shows. So, why not get bigger pants?

Baggy Pants

"I have to have 'em tight to show off my body line. For me to wear baggy trousers would be like telling the Paris Ballet Company to wear baggy tights," exclaimed P.J.

Yeah, well the Paris Ballet people would probably look kind of funny in baggy pants but not any funnier than P.J. in split pants.

Proby really has a ball on stage. "The more the kids scream, the more I'm laughing at them. There's not one aspect of seriousness about it," said P.J.

Yeah, well your "performances" *are* pretty funny, P.J. I mean, with the kids laughing at you and you laughing at the kids and the guards laughing at the whole bunch of you — it's just one big joke.

... KNEELIN'.
... AND SCREAMIN'.

P. J. PROBY IN ACTION — Proby loves to tease the female portion of the audience with his highly suggestive stage antics which cause the older members of the audience to stare in utter disbelief at the ultra wild motions of P. J. Proby.

Proby—As Seen By His Ex-Best Friend

By Carol Deck

Revolting, sexy, fantastic, ridiculous, great, absurd — these are some of the varied words that have been used to describe P.J. Proby.

But *The BEAT* recently got a phone call from one person who knows Proby — or *knew* him.

Bongo Wolf was Proby's closest friend for a while. He met Proby through a friend and played with him when Proby had a night club in California called Funky's.

In Oct. '64, Proby paid Bongo's passage to go with him to England.

"He took me over for a side kick," Bongo said. "But his version of a sidekick isn't mine. His version is someone who'll stay by his side at all times.

"It was my misfortune to be by his side at all times.

"He used me as an errand boy and scape goat."

So Bongo left him in Nov. '65 and came back home to California.

Read *The BEAT*

Bongo then read in *The BEAT* the article about Proby's problems — that his work permit was running out, he was being evicted from his home, his dog had bitten him and his best friend had left him.

That best friend was Bongo and so he called to explain.

"It's not my fault that his career was wrecked. I just felt it was time to leave. I traveled around the world with him and spent all my time inside hotels, looking out at cities that I never got to see.

"He said since he brought me over he owned me. He tries to play God and ends up playing the devil.

"I think he's great. I enjoy his show on stage. But as a person, I've known him too many years. He's just a little bit too demanding.

Demands Perfection

"He's extremely hard to get along with. He's very militaristic; he's an extremist; he doesn't believe in moderation; he demands perfection."

Bongo also defended the entire pants splitting bit that got Proby banned in many places. "The pants splitting wasn't his fault. It was the material they bought. They got regular velvet that didn't stretch and on stage that stuff can split. And he gets it so skin tight that his gyrations split it.

"He put a silk suit on underneat it after the first time but they still banned him."

When Bonbo came back after leaving Proby in London, he wasn't able to bring all of his belongings with him and now he wants them back.

A Mean Person

"He has stuff in England that he confiscated some books and clothes. He confiscated them just because he's a mean person at times. He's bitter because I put up with too much of his nonsense and decided it was time to leave."

So now Bongo is just loafing around the West Coast, and Proby? Bongo said, "He says he has no friends and doesn't care if he does."

But Proby has one friend, or at least someone is trying to help him. Tito Burns, one of the Rolling Stones' agents has gotten Proby another work permit and a place to stay and is trying to book him for a tour.

We'll just have to wait and see what will happen next in the saga of P.J. Proby. He's never been real big over here, perhaps because of his falling out with *Shindig*, and as Bongo said "not everyone likes Proby in England either."

Walker Bros. Going British

The Walker Brothers went to England, became stars and are returning home again. But not to stay.

Their "Make It Easy On Yourself" is in the Top Twenty in the nation and they're coming over this month to film an Ed Sullivan Show and possibly other TV shows.

"But we shall not be staying there," stated Scott Walker.

"In fact I personally am going to take out papers and become a British citizen. I see my own future in music publishing, and in producing records."

So, it looks like at least one of the Walkers is going completely British.

Donovan's Returning

Donovan returns to America at the end of this month for a three to four week visit.

He is expected to do live appearances in Los Angeles and San Francisco as well as work out negotiations with producer Phil Spector on two films to be made in Hollywood.

He has also set a 28 day European tour to begin March 15. It includes Germany, Austria, Switzerland, France, Belgium and Holland.

The British singer is still trying to work out the legal hassle between his former agent and his current business manager. Meanwhile, an injunction to prevent him from working has been lifted to allow the American visit.

KARL HERMIT thinks that the other Hermits are "A Must To Avoid" so he is all set to do the boys in!!

KRLA ARCHIVES

A Chat With The Changing Times

By Carol Deck

"I was born," he stated very positively as he sprawled across the end of the bed staring curiously at the ceiling like he'd never noticed it was there before.

"Are you sure?" I queried. "Yes, I *was* born," Artie Kornfeld was very sure about that.

Artie's partner in the writing, producing and singing team called The Changing Times, Steve Duboff, seemed to think that it was all right that Artie was born, so he proceeded to explain where the name Changing Times came from.

"Contrary to popular belief, we didn't get it from the magazine and we didn't get it from a Dylan tune. It just came out of our own feeble brains."

"I'm a sex symbol," Steve added logically (he thought it was logical) "One night a girl told me 'You don't smile, you're sexy', so I guess I'm a sex symbol."

Artie the Clown

Artie figured then, that he must be a clown because he smiles.

Steve, who has the kind of blue eyes they shouldn't put on guys, wouldn't talk about himself, but Artie – that was another question. And Artie got back by firing a few words on Steve at me.

Steve on Artie – "He's funky... dumb ("Everything I write?" Artie demanded while redesigning the coat hanger he was playing with) ... clown ... talent ... fink."

Artie on Steve – "Terrible writer, writes the same things I do ... funny (to me) ... talented (I owe him one good one)...double fink."

Then they got tired of gossiping about each other and decided to tell me about their new release, "How's the Air Up There?" It's very simple, they explained that the song is just a plain old "rollicking funky tune, funky folk-rock, beat-up-beat." Any moron can tell exactly what that song is.

On Protest

"Protest," I said. "Protest," they said, and were off on a half hour babbling spree.

"It's a little over done and used up," Steve said. "It's been said and you can't say it anymore," Artie added. "People know what's wrong with the world and they don't want to hear about it anymore."

"Every song is a protest," Artie exclaimed. And Steve grinned, "Yeah, even 'I Got You Babe' is saying we got each other and we don't care."

"I don't think so," Artie said, but before he had a chance to explain they were off again.

Somehow, out of their chattering, I got that "The Star Spangle Banner" is a protest and so is "Swanee River" ("Get that river out of here" they shouted.)

Audiences Next

"Audiences," I tried. "Audiences," they exclaimed.

"It's nice when they're full," offered Steve. "The more people, the more excitement. If there's 30,000 people out there, we know a couple are enjoying it."

"We play to the kids who buy the records," Artie noted. "The older audiences are responsive but we enjoy the kids more."

"Next question, next question," Steve demanded pounding his fist on the table like Nikita Krushchev.

"Your hats," I said feebly noting the hats that seemed to be growing on their heads. They're similar to the ones you've seen on John Lennon.

"We got them in Greenwich Village," Artie explained. "One of the Lovin' Spoonful told us a shop to go to."

"I take mine off," Steve chirped, "when I go to bed, if I sleep on my stomach."

"I was born," Artie said positively. "Are you sure?" I queried. "Yeah, and I lived in North Carolina for six years."

I Surrendered

I figured that must mean something so I crumpled my totally incomprehensible notes into my pocket and left the two of them babbling away at each other.

That's how it goes when you talk with these two young writers who've just burst into the singing field.

They're both very talented writers. Artie has written hits for Dusty Springfield, Jay and the Americans, Johnny Crawford, Jan and Dean ("Dead Man's Curb") and The Shirelles ("Tonight You're Going to Fall In Love With Me").

Steve's a little newer to the field but he's done things for Teresa Brewer and the Exciters and together they have written for Freddie Cannon, Leslie Gore, Jerry Butler and the Hullabaloos, among many others.

Producers Too

On top of all this they also find time to produce several other acts including some of The Lovin' Spoonfuls' stuff. Artie produces for their label, Philips, and Steve produces independently.

Their most recent writing has been for the Turtles and Sonny and Cher. They did four songs for Sonny and Cher's next album.

The two met two years ago in the office of Chardon Music, one of the publishing firms headed by Charley Koppelman and Don Rubin, who produce the Lovin' Spoonful and many other acts.

The two publishers suggested that Steve and Artie try working together and, well, you can see what happened.

The pop world is going to have to be quick to keep up with The Changing Times.

... ARTIE AND STEVE

Deep Six Rising With The Sun

By Marsha Provost

Four fifths of the Deep Six descended on *The BEAT* offices the other day on their way to a recording session.

The four who came by were Dave Gray, Tony McCash, Dan Lottermoser and Dean Cannon. Don Dunn and Mac Elsensohn had late afternoon classes and were going to meet them later at the session. Dean, by the way, is the female singer of the group.

The group's been together a little over a year now. All six of them were playing in different folk groups in San Diego and then somehow got together.

"We blew our own minds when we put our five voices together," Dan explained. And they've been blowing a lot of other people's minds with their first release, "The Rising Sun."

But there's six of them, and only five voices? The one you don't hear is Mac, the drummer. "He sings but we don't give him a mike," Dave explained.

For the last year they've been "starvin'" and "movin' a lot" according to Tony. But they also played a smash engagement at a San Diego club. They were booked for two weeks and held over for 18 weeks.

Their goals are the usual – success, recognition and money – but Dave adds "We're not trying to impress the world with anything." And so they don't do protest songs and like to do Beatle songs although all six of them write.

They prefer playing to dancing audiences, except Dave who'll be perfectly happy with 20,000 hysterical girls.

They sound sharp and look sharp on stage. "We've considered long hair and wild clothes," Dan said. "But we like to keep a kept appearance."

Dean goes along with the kept appearance by wearing classy corduroy and velvet bell bottoms. She loves all sorts of fashions but gets a little static from the group sometimes on what she wears on stage.

"She decides what she's going to wear and then we complain," said Dan.

This group sings folk, folk-rock, hard rock and just about anything else they happen to like – which is just about everything.

Dave explained "I tend to like all kinds of music but not everything," which no one else in the group could quite interpret but they figured he knew what he liked.

Tony likes rhythm and blues and the old funky Negro sound while Dean likes folk and especially Dylan.

Does she understand Dylan? "She doesn't even understand *me*," noted Dan.

And Dan likes "everything from opera to anything."

They describe their sound as "big" and "full." Dan calls "Rising Sun" folk-rock but Dave, who wrote it, says it's "just a good song."

Dave also offered the only explanation for where they got their name. "Well, there's six of us," he said.

After all, Dave, Dan, Don, Dean, Tony and Mac wouldn't fit very well on a record label. Their next release is due any time now. They're not too sure what it is, but it's coming. So keep your ears tuned for the next hit from the Deep Six.

McGuire Set For 5 Pixs

Barry McGuire has passed the eve of destruction and is on to better things.

Those better things include movies. He's been signed by Paramount to a one year, non-exclusive contract that calls for five pictures.

The roles will include both dramatic and musical things for the ex-Christy Minstrel.

Date for first film hasn't been set yet, but we're waiting, Barry.

... THE DEEP SIX

KRLA ARCHIVES

DISCussion
By Eden

There are something like 150 new records released every single week and of those 150 – very few ever make the top ten on the charts; even fewer make it to Number One.

Some of the new contenders for the Top Spot this week include the new 45 by Little Stevie Wonder – "Uptight (Everything's Alright)."

This one has been out for a little while now, and is already making large-style noises on the radio stations. This is one more example of the great Motown music currently pervading our air waves, and it is definitely Soul Sauce Incorporated!

Stevie Wonder shows every sign of becoming the next Ray Charles in his own right and in a somewhat different vein. Not quite as bluesy as The Genius, Stevie has all the rockin' soul necessary to maintain his own in the field of R 'n' B.

★ ★ ★ ★

Another entry in the Disc Derby of the Turntables is "I Gotta Be With You," by Lulu Porter. This is the second or third record to be released by this young, American songstress and unfortunately – it is just about as bad as all the others.

Lulu's records all have one thing in common – they are all outdated. Somehow the sounds which she pours into her singles just don't return the favor of all her hard work, and they just sound sort of out of place in today's pop market.

★ ★ ★ ★

On the Mira label, the Bees have released a new 45 RPMer entitled "Baby Let Me Follow You Down." This one was written by Lead Bee vocalist George Caldwell, and has a good, strong beat and some very interesting phrasing on the lyrics.

★ ★ ★ ★

Unbelievable is the only way to describe the new record by Charles Boyer. Yes, you read right – Charles Boyer. He has released a beautiful new rendition of the standard – "I Believe" – on Valiant, and it seems a great shame that this disc is probably not going to be commercial.

Monsieur Boyer gives an emotional and beautiful vocal performance set to the lovely strains of an orchestra on his new single, but I'm afraid that the Sam-the-Shamset just isn't ready for his eloquence as yet. Too bad!!!

★ ★ ★ ★

Once more from the Tamla-Motown family the Musical Waxworks have produced a soulful winner. A young lady named Chris Clark has taken a composition from Mr. Motown himself – Berry Gordy, Jr., entitled "Do Right Baby Do Right," and added a large dose of soul-plus-super-sound, and with the producing genius of Mr. Gordy – come up with a tremendous R 'n' B sound.

This one is a slow mover, but if it catches on it could cause a lot of commotion. It's a debut disc for Miss Clark, and if it becomes a hit, we can add her name to the already impressive list of Motown pinch-hitters.

Matt Monro's Many Names

The army, several trucks and Frank Sinatra are the stepping stones that put Matt Monro in the spotlight as one of Britain's most talented singers.

He first became interested in singing when he joined the army at the age of 17½. Trained as an instructor on tanks, he first faced the public at a talent contest in Weymouth, Eng.

He only took second place but it gave him a little confidence to try again when he was stationed in Hong Kong.

This time he took first place. In fact he took first place in the next six contests there, and was then barred from entering any more – to give others a chance.

After getting out of the army he returned to his native London and got a job as a long distance truck driver. He cut a demonstration disc in Scotland and left his truck for a London transport bus.

Terence To Matt

At this time he was still known as Terence Parsons. But then he combined the Christian names of a Fleet Street journalist and the father of Winifred Atwell, who helped him get his first recording contract.

Then things began to happen. He signed for a radio series in Luxembourg and Cyril Stapleton's Show Band on BBC.

But it didn't last too long, and his career was beginning to look a little bleak when Matt was contacted by recording manager George Martin and asked to help Peter Sellers perfect a Frank Sinatra impersonation for Sellers' "Songs for Swingin' Sellers" album.

Matt did a demonstration cut called "You Keep Me Swingin'" to show Sellers the style. But Sellers, one of the world's great impersonators himself, said he could never come that close to the Sinatra sound and suggested that Matt's own version be in the album.

Fred Flange

So for one record Matt became "Fred Flange" and fooled many people into thinking it was the real Sinatra under a phony name. When people did find out who it was, they remembered Matt Monro.

In 1960 he came to America for several night club appearances and was invited by President Eisenhower's personal air crew to entertain them at the Pentagon. He was the first pop artist to do so.

A year later he came back again, this time to cut a jingle for the Pepsi Cola Company and do an appearance for the Ed Sullivan show.

By now, Matt has had smash after smash, including "Love Walked In," "I'll Know Her," "Portrait of My Love," "My Kind of Girl" and his classic "Softly, As I Leave You."

With his fantastic voice and style, we may never allow him to leave us, softly or otherwise.

Dear Susan
By Susan Frisch

When was Marianne Faithfull married?
— Stephie Berkskey
She was secretly married on May 6, 1965, then married publicly in a Catholic church on June 24.

What is Cynthia's maiden name?
— Carol Mattenheimer
Powell.

Does Elvis have any brothers or sisters?
— Georgia Stenwick
He had a twin brother, but he died at birth.

Where can I buy a John Lennon hat?
— Sandy Smith
Try your local department stores.

Where can I write to Roy Orbison?
— Jean DeCampwin
In care of MGM Studios, Culver City, Calif.

Why did the Rolling Stones record "As Tears Go By?" It's not their style at all.
— Craig Bendent
For one, they wrote it.

Is Bob Dylan married to Joan Baez?
— Karolyn Hymen
No, they're just friends.

Will the Dave Clark Five ever be back to the states for any more concerts?
— Marcia Kremplen
Depends on their Stateside popularity.

Can you please give me Sandie Shaw's fan club address?
— Vicky Mowe
181 Rainham Road North, Dagenham, Essex, Eng.

What was the name of Elvis's first hit record?
— Susan Soames
"Heartbreak Hotel."

Does Freddie, of the Dreamers, have any pets?
— Chridine Holts
He has two white Pyrenean mountain dogs.

Are Sonny and Cher getting a divorce?
— Mike Clarke
No.

What are Donovan's favorite drinks?
— Susan McHenry
Milk, and vodka and lime.

Is it true that Kathy Young, the girl who sang "A Thousand Stars," is married?
— Chris Brigham
She married one of the Walker Brothers in California, on June 26.

What has happened to P.J. Proby? I haven't heard too much on him lately.
— Michelle Dupoir
His popularity in the states is far from overwhelming or successful. Perhaps this is the answer.

Can you tell me something about Paul's twin, Keith Allison?
— Babs Holby
Born in Texas some 22 years ago, Keith stands at 6'1", weighs 165 lbs., has brown hair and eyes. Can play harmonica, piano, bass, and drums. His favorites include the Beatles, Bob Dylan, and Chuck Berry. He loves the "British" style in clothes, and wants to eventually buy a Volkswagen or a Cadillac. He is married.

Can you tell me anything about the romance with Herman and Twinkle?
— Sara Sterner
The whole thing was dreamed up in a press agent's office. Herman told me that he took her out for 3 days, just for publicity, and now he never sees her, but when he does they say "hi" and that's ALL.!!!

Are the Rolling Stones splitting up?
— Justice Supreme
No, not for a long, long time.

What do the English groups think of girl 'groupies'?
— Debbie Moss
I can't speak for all the groups, but speaking for Herman and the Hermits I know that they dislike them!

How many children do John and Cyn have?
— Mary Sheperd
They have one; John Julian Lennon, Jr.

Where are the Liverpool Five from?
— Kay West
With a name like Liverpool, can't you guess?!

Are the Beau Brummels English?
— Jim Mores
No, they hail from San Francisco.

When will The Hermits come back to the states?
— Gayle Tamkin
Most likely, sometime next year. The exact date is not known.

Where do the Deep Six come from?
— George Thir
San Diego.

Repeat For The Toys?

The Toys know a good thing when they see it.

They recently smashed up the charts with their very first release, "A Lover's Concerto," which was based on a Bach musical pattern.

No one thought they could sell classical style music but they did it and now they're going to try to do it again.

Their second release is going to be titled "Attack" and it is based on musical patterns by Tchaikowsky.

KRLA ARCHIVES

Simon And Garfunkel Sing Happy

One of the fastest rising songs on the nation's charts belongs to two city-bred folk singers who specialize in singing of the trials and life in the big city.

They're Simon and Garfunkel and instead of singing about just sad things these city-type folk singers also sing of the fun and excitement and the joys of life.

Their "Sounds of Silence" stands to be one of the biggest records of the year but the two are anything but overnight successes.

They met in the sixth grade and have been singing together since they were fourteen. Initially they confined their talents to school functions and private affairs.

In case you're wondering (and we're sure you are) Simon and Garfunkel are their real names. They're Paul Simon and Art Garfunkel.

After thoroughly testing their wings at school functions, the boys embarked on their professional careers at Manhattan's center of the folk world, Gerde's Folk City.

Since then they've played the Gaslight and Bitter End clubs in New York City, the Edinburgh Folk Festival, the Troubador and the Enterprise in London and the Streets Of Paris in France.

Their recording career was born in October of 1964 when they strolled into the New York headquarters of Columbia Records.

They made such an instant impact on the company officials that they were recording their first album a short two weeks later.

"Sounds Of Silence" is their first smash but you can bet on one thing – it won't be their last. They're too talented for that.

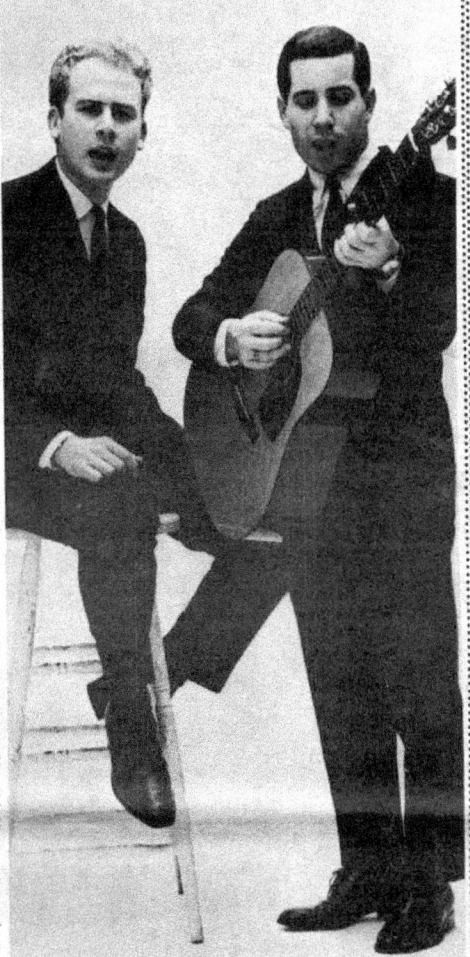

WHO WROTE WHO?
Strange New Game

By Carol Deck

There's a new game going around that has a lot of people muttering some mighty strange things.

The game goes something like this – if you were a book who would have written you, or if you were a play who would have done the music for you? Or maybe you are a painting or a comic strip character.

Anyway, we at *The BEAT* have been knocking around the names of some of our favorites and we'd like to tell you a few.

To start with the obvious, David McCallum just has to be from an Ian Fleming book, writer of the James Bond books.

The Rolling Stones must be a poem by an unknown Greenwich Village beatnik. And P.J. Proby is, of course, one of Shakespeare's tragic heros – the fellow's just plain doomed.

A Frost Poem

Marianne Faithfull is one of those beautiful spring poems by Robert Frost and Herman has to be a creation of Lewis Carroll, who wrote *Alice in Wonderland*.

And some current pop stars could easily be creations of other pop stars. Like Sonny and Cher could be one of John Lennon's short stories (he probably illustrated them too!)

And P.F. Sloan and Eric Burdon of the Animals could be a couple of Bob Dylan's poems (he calls them poems).

Dylan himself is too much for one person to have thought up. He must be a product of the combined efforts of Pete Seeger, Jack Parr and Cassius Clay.

Comic Characters

And then there's the comic strip characters. Ringo is obviously Charlie Brown of "Peanuts" and the Righteous Brothers must be "Mutt and Jeff." And Tom Jones must have been dreamt up by whoever writes "Superman" – he's just too much to be real.

And there's more in our little feeble brains up here! Phil Spector, the unreal producer of the Righteous Brothers, must be either one of those far out Picasso paintings or a piece of pop art.

Gary Lewis is a figment of his father's imagination. Them must have been created by Mick Jagger in one of his weaker moments.

Dick and DeeDee should be the Bobsey Twins and Brenda Lee is Rebecca of Sunnybrook Farm.

Or maybe, on second thought, Tom Jones is Rhett Butler out of "Gone With the Wind."

John Lennon

And John Lennon could only have been created by Andy Wartol, the king of New York's ultra, super-in crowd who makes 8 hour movies of people sleeping and then takes 8 hour movies of people watching his 8 hour movies.

And the King himself, Elvis, would have to be a character in a book by Irving Stone, the guy who writes books like *The Agony and the Ecstasy* about people that are bigger than life (can't you just see Elvis' life in a movie starring Charlton Heston!).

And there are many many more. This silly game has kept *The BEAT* staff babbling for weeks. How about you? If you get some real brain storms send them to us and maybe we can print some of them.

Have Fun!

TV Series For Freddie

Freddie and the Dreamers have had their dream come true. They've been signed for their own American television series.

The five Manchester lads will star in a situation comedy musical show which will be shown on ABC-TV starting next September.

They start filming the 26 episodes in April. Eighteen will be filmed in Britain, two in Paris, two in Rome and four in America.

British actor Terry Thomas is being sought to play Freddie's father.

Dusty Recalls American Fog

Dusty Springfield recently completed an American tour and returned to England to show her stuff at the Royal Command Performance.

As with anyone who's been in both America and England, she found many things very different in the two countries. Among the differences she found was the American fog.

"It's not at all like English fog," she noted. "It's wet and you can't really see it. But it stings the eyes and throat."

So what kind of fog do you have over there, Dusty?

From Elvis To UNCLE

Mary Ann Mobley gets them all. First she played opposite Elvis in "Harum Scarum" and now she's about to go after the men from U.N.C.L.E.

MGM-TV has just signed the former Miss America for the title role in "The Girl from U.N.-C.L.E.," a television series for the 1966-67 season.

She was among nearly 100 of Hollywood's top young starlets who were interviewed for the part, but she won out over them all.

She'll join the men from U.N.C.L.E., Robert Vaughn and David McCallum, this week for the filming of an episode titled "The Moonglow Affair" which will be the pilot episode of "The Girl from U.N.C.L.E."

After completing "Harum Scarum" with Elvis, she also co-starred with Jerry Lewis in "Three On a Couch" for Columbia.

This girl really keeps busy and she gets the best leading men! "The Girl From U.N.C.L.E." is being produced by the same people that produce "Man From U.N.C.L.E." so it can't be anything but a smash.

We're waiting Mary Ann.

SLOOPY'S BACK AGAIN — this time with The Atlantics. Their new record, "Sloop Dance" is rapidly climbing the charts just about everywhere. Which proves that Sloopy is one very popular girl!

KRLA ARCHIVES

SOME WINNING MODELS in the KRL"A" contest are pictured above with their trophies. From left, Robert Judy's winner in junior replica division, Chuck McGehee's first place entry in senior replica division, William Borjes' second place entry in junior open division.

THE EVERLY BROTHERS, sporting new-style haircuts, were a holiday hit at Dave Hull's Hullabaloo.

NEW — a great new product to meet the growing market for a young man's hair spray

man spray — a MAN'S hair spray
holds hair all day
always looks natural
adds extra bounce and body

Regular Price $1.25
SPECIAL BEAT OFFER $1.00 each
Includes tax, postage and handling.

a MAN'S hair spray
- Created to hold hair perfectly—all day.
- Always looks natural—never sticky or tacky.
- Unique conditioning ingredients add extra body and bounce to today's new hair styles for men.
- Clean, manly aroma.

take advantage of this new trend in spray usage with a product specifically designed to work on a man's hair

L. B. LABS, INC.
P.O. BOX 430
GLENDALE, CALIF. 91209

Please send me _____ cans L.B. Man Spray. I enclose $_____
($1.00 for each can)
NAME:
ADDRESS:
CITY: _____ STATE _____ ZIP _____

KRLA BEAT Subscription
SAVE 25% Of Regular Price
☐ 1 YEAR — 52 Issues — $5.00   ☐ 2 YEARS — $8.00
Enclosed is _____   ☐ CASH   ☐ CHECK
Send to: _____ Age _____
Address: _____
City _____ State _____ Zip _____
MAIL YOUR ORDER TO: KRLA BEAT
6290 Sunset, Suite 504
Hollywood, Calif. 90028
Foreign Rate: $14.00 — 52 Issues

THE FOUR SEASONS, in Hollywood for a series of TV appearances, catch up on what's happening.

THE LIVERPOOL FIVE are HAPPENING !!!

THE CHANGING TIMES read the BEAT in their dressing room.

KRLA ARCHIVES

Inside KRLA

Tour-time at KRLA everyone. Yep, today is the big day when we take you on a super-duper extra-special guided tour of the fabulous studios of KRLA located in picturesque Pasadena.

We start our little trip in the lobby of the station, where you can all see the broadcast booth. Right now, the old Hullabalooer is on the air, so why don't we go over and say hello to him.

Here – I'll knock on the window of his "cage" and get his attention. H'lo Hullabalooer, yoo hoo – hello!

Honk, honk – "Hi'ya Hullabalooers. How're ya doing?"

Just fine, Dave. Will you play a couple Beatle records for us? Thank you.

We'll walk through this door over here to our left, around the potted yucca-plant, and up the gold-plated winding staircase. (puff, puff!)

Whew! Well, right down the hall of fame – you will notice the 42 x 93 color photos of all the KRLA DJ's on the walls here – through the first door to your right, you will find Emperor Hudson's Leopard Skin Room.

Careful for that funny-looking leopard by the door as you enter. He is one of the Emp's favorite pets and he has been known to get a little mean when he hasn't eaten for – oh, ten or twelve minutes.

Notice the lovely lavendar-colored, silk-covered walls with the matching royal purple satin cushions on the floor. If you push this little button over here to your left, the walls – all seven of them – will turn themselves completely around and they will be entirely covered with real honest-to-goodness leopard skins.

The only reason His Royal Highness doesn't leave the walls turned 'round to that side all the time is 'cause it seems to have a rather strange affect on people who come in. They begin to growl, and claw, and prowl around the room. Never did understand that!

The Emp's Crown Jewels are in the room right next to this one, but it is locked and so we can't get in. Well, maybe next time.

But we can go right down the hall to the elevator and take a ride upstairs to Bill's weather room. You've all been up here with me before, so we'll just stop in for a minute to say hello.

Well, well – look who we've found in the elevator! It's Jarvis the Janitor. Howdy Jarvis, what's up? We were just about to go upstairs to the weather room.

"Oh, I'm sorry, but you won't be able to get in, 'cause it's being fixed. There were an awful lot of holes in the celing and stuff, and it got sort of moist in there whenever it rained, and then the weather machines would get all haywire. I'm sorry."

Oh, that's okay Jarvis. I just noticed the time and we really have to be going.

Listen everyone – maybe we can finish our tour next week, 'cause it's almost six o'clock now, and they close the studios at six. And if we don't get out of here, we might have to stay all night, and I never really *did* trust that old leopard of The Emp's, anyways!!

So I'll see you all right back here again next week. Till then, later babe!

KRLA Tunedex

This Week	Last Week	Title	Artist
1	1	WE CAN WORK IT OUT/DAY TRIPPER	The Beatles
2	5	LIGHTNIN' STRIKES	Lou Christie
3	2	SOUNDS OF SILENCE	Simon and Garfunkle
4	6	FLOWERS ON THE WALL	Statler Brothers
5	3	LET'S HANG ON	Four Seasons
6	7	YOU DIDN'T HAVE TO BE SO NICE	The Lovin' Spoonful
7	8	RUN, BABY, RUN	The Newbeats
8	4	LIES	The Knickerbockers
9	10	IT'S MY LIFE	The Animals
10	9	SHE'S JUST MY STYLE	Gary Lewis & The Playboys
11	12	A YOUNG GIRL	Noel Harrison
12	11	EBB TIDE	The Righteous Bros.
13	17	I WILL	Dean Martin
14	13	HOLE IN THE WALL	The Packers
15	16	I FOUGHT THE LAW	Bobby Fuller Four
16	19	ENGLAND SWINGS	Roger Miller
17	14	I SEE THE LIGHT	The Five Americans
18	27	NO MATTER WHAT SHAPE	The T-Bones
19	15	JENNY TAKE A RIDE	Mitch Ryder & Detroit Wheels
20	20	OVER AND OVER	The Dave Clark Five
21	29	AS TEARS GO BY	The Rolling Stones
22	34	MY LOVE	Petula Clark
23	21	THE DUCK	Jackie Lee
24	23	DON'T THINK TWICE	The Wonder Who?
25	24	MY GENERATION	The Who
26	26	FIVE O'CLOCK WORLD	The Vogues
27	25	MAKE THE WORLD GO AWAY	Eddy Arnold
28	31	THUNDERBALL	Tom Jones
29	35	A MUST TO AVOID	Herman's Hermits
30	30	UPTIGHT	Stevie Wonder
31	32	ONE HAS MY NAME	Barry Young
32	28	FEVER	The McCoys
33	37	ONE TOO MANY MORNINGS	The Association
34	38	LIKE A BABY	Len Barry
35	33	SUNDAY AND ME	Jay & The Americans
36	39	SLOOP DANCE	The Atlantics
37	36	PUPPET ON A STRING	Elvis Presley
38	40	LOVE BUG	Jack Jones
39	—	I AIN'T GONNA EAT OUT MY HEART	The Young Rascals
40	—	HOW'S THE AIR UP THERE?	The Changing Times

 DAVE HULL

 BOB EUBANKS

 DICK BIONDI

 JOHNNY HAYES

 EMPEROR HUDSON

 CASEY KASEM

 CHARLIE O'DONNELL

 BILL SLATER

WHERE THE ACTION IS — Holiday crowds jam Dave Hull's Hullabaloo, Hollywood's newest, plushest teen night spot. More details on back cover.

BEAT BACK ISSUES

DON'T MISS OUT on any great pictures, fab interviews or newsy items appearing in any of the BEATS which you might have missed. For a limited time only, these BEATS are still available.

4/14 — INTERVIEW WITH JOHN
4/21 — INTERVIEW WITH PAUL
5/5 — HERMANIA SPREADS
6/9 — BEATLES
6/30 — PROBY FIRED
8/7 — DYLAN
8/14 — HERMAN
8/21 — STONES TESTIFY
9/4 — BEATLES ... IN PERSON
9/11 — THREE FACES OF BOB DYLAN
9/18 — PROTESTOR BARRY McGUIRE
9/25 — SONNY & CHER — 5 HITS
10/2 — YARDBIRDS' ORDEAL IN VAIN?
10/9 — PAUL & RINGO NOW SOLO
10/16 — ELVIS — KING OF POP?
10/23 — BEVERLY BIVINS OF WE FIVE
10/30 — RIGHTEOUS BROS. NEW IMAGE
11/6 — DAVID McCALLUM — HERO
11/13 — MICK JAGGER — XMAS RUINED
11/20 — LEN BARRY — EASY AS 1-2-3
11/27 — ROLLING STONES
12/4 — BYRDS
12/11 — CHER
12/18 — BEATLES
12/25 — XMAS ISSUE
1/1 — BEAT AWARDS

To order a back issue send 25¢ (15¢ plus 10¢ postage and handling charge) to: The BEAT, Suite 504, 6290 Sunset Blvd., Hollywood, Calif. 90028. IT IS NO LONGER NECESSARY TO SEND STAMPS OR SELF-ADDRESSED ENVELOPES.

KRLA ARCHIVES

Adventures of Robin Boyd
By Shirley Poston

CHAPTER TEN

The next voice Robin Boyd heard was unmistakably Mick Jagger's.

Listing a bit to the right, she clutched George for support.

"That's Mick singing," she swooned.

George shook her off impatiently. "It's Mick all right," he hissed. "But would you mind telling me what *that* is?"

Robin stared obligingly in the direction of his pointing finger and her mouth fell open in amazement. What *indeed* was *that? That* being a strangely-clad figure visible through the battered doorway of the battered beach cottage, wearing purple bell bottoms, a pink poor-boy and a red wing (the figure, not the cottage).

"Who are you?" Robin cried, rushing through the doorway. "And what have you done with my Aunt Zelda?"

Redecorated

Aunt Zelda grinned widely, raising the red wig in a hearty salute. "I've had her redecorated," she announced, turning the record player up higher. "How do I look?"

"Wonderful!" Robin lied eagerly. (Well, she did look *better*.) Then she stepped firmly on George's winkle-picker.

"Wonderful!" echoed George, listing slightly to the left and clutching Robin for support.

Robin shook him off impatiently, giving a sigh of relief. Aunt Zelda had obviously flipped her wig (no pun intended). In her present condition, she would be the *last* person on earth to ask why Robin and friend were wandering around Catalina at 4:30 a.m.

"Why are you and your friend wandering around Catalina at 4:30 a.m.?" asked Aunt Zelda.

Robin retracted the sigh of relief and thought fast. "Hunting for grunion!" she answered.

"Baloney," chortled Aunt Zelda, thinking faster.

Robin paused. "Training to swim the channel?"

Aunt Zelda shook her head in disbelief and the red wig flew into a corner. "I want the truth," she ordered, smiling fondly as her nineteen cats pounced on the wig and killed it.

Then Robin knew what she must do.

"It's this way," she began, realizing that she could not tell her Aunt Zelda a big fat one. "I said I was coming to see you this weekend, but I went to London instead. Then I had to come here on my way back so I wouldn't be telling mom a big fat one."

George took aim with his ultra-pointed winkle picker and fired. Robin grabbed her shin and glowered at him. What was his problem anyway? She wasn't revealing any magic powers!

"Oh," said Aunt Zelda, perfectly satisfied with this most recent explanation. Then she jumped four feet into the air. "London, England?" she screeched.

"London, England," Robin said proudly, in spite of the fact that George was pinching her arm so hard it felt as though the world was ending.

"Cool," breathed Aunt Zelda. (And Robin had once thought of her as an old creep who lived out in the middle of nowhere without a telephone.) (No one is perfect.)

Fab, Gear, Boss

"Also fab, gear and boss," Aunt Zelda added, taking another red wig out of a battered drawer. Then she went to the stove and poured boiling water into a battered tea pot, causing George to wince visably.

"Now," said Aunt Zelda, placing herself and twenty-two cups on the floor. "Introduce me to your friend and tell me about your trip!"

Robin sank to the floor, pulling a horrified George with her. She pinched him back when he didn't even look at Aunt Zelda during the introduction, but instead gaped incredulously as the cats joined them and began slurping happily.

"Rave on," Aunt Zelda further encouraged, slapping at Tom the Siamese who was trying to spear a second lump of sugar with his left paw.

Visited Stones

Robin took a deep breath and a draught of tea (after having removed Tom's right paw from her cup) (Tom did not give up easily). "Well," she began, wishing she didn't have to do this but knowing she had no choice, "the first thing I did in London was visit the Rolling Stones!"

That, of course, did the trick. Just as Robin had hoped, her story of London, England was forever silenced by Aunt Zelda's monologue about her latest crusade. Which was, of course, a campaign to convince the Rolling Stones to make a personal appearance in Catalina.

Robin listened patiently as dawn broke over the Pacific, pausing only to shoot George an occasional look that said "stay awake or I'll break something over your head."

Recent Hang-Up

"Aunt Zelda, dear," Robin interrupted along about nine a.m. "I think it's wonderful what you're trying to do for the Rolling Stones." Which was certainly no big fat one for she recalled all too well that her Aunt's most recent hang-up had been a crusdae to convince all English groups to make a personal appearance several miles *off the coast of* Catalina. And before that, she'd been down on red wigs.

Curious to know what had changed her Aunt's mind (alleged) about both subjects, she decided to wait and ask sometime when she had a week.

"We've got to be going," Robin said, dragging the semi-conscious George with her as she got to her feet. "But I'll be back to see you again."

"Bring him," Aunt Zelda commanded, taking one last stare at George's dark good looks.

After an endless farewell during which they were forced to shake hands with eighteen of the nineteen cats. (Tom had vanished into the sugar bowl at approximately seven a.m.), Robin and George found themselves walking down the beach.

"I suppose you know what this means," Robin said, squinting at the sun.

"Yes, yes," he sighed, pulling two pairs of sunglasses out of his non-existent pocket. "Next weekend you'll be going to London to visit the Stones to make up for the big fat one you just told Aunt Zelda."

"I won't be getting you out of a warm tea pot in the middle of the night to rescue me this time," she promised as they lost sight of Aunt Zelda's battered cottage.

"You can bet on that," George muttered firmly. "Because I'm going *with* you."

"Huh? I mean pardon?" Robin gasped, not believing her ears.

George said nothing, but when he took her hand in preparation for their journey back to the mainland, Robin could have *sworn* he *squeezed* it.

(To Be Continued Next Week)

RADIO LONDON, a former U.S. minesweeper, broadcasts from outside of England's three mile limit as a commercial radio station.

The Successful British Pirate

As with so many things which we have always had, we tend to take our commercial radio stations for granted. But it's not so with the English. They haven't had it long enough to take it for granted. In fact, it's a whole new bag for them.

Only recently have the "pirate" stations appeared on their scene and the most widely heard pirate is Radio London. And she has quite a story to tell.

During the Second World War the U.S. Minesweeper Density cruised the ocean saving over 500 men from death. Then when the war ended she took up life as a cargo ship.

And now, 19 years later, she has started her life anew broadcasting over 250 miles as Radio London. Besides England she is heard over Sweden, Norway, Holland, Ireland, Denmark, Germany, France and Italy.

Three Miles Out

Commercial radio is banned in England so Radio London is forced to operate from outside the three mile limit. However, Philip Birch, the company's managing director insists: "We are not, and have no intention of becoming, law breakers and we are not assisted in our cause by the 'pirate' tag."

Radio London has a long-range objective — to become a land based station. "Our commercial relations, our program content, and our station behavior proves we are responsible, reliable business people supplying something the public likes and wants," continued Birch.

Wants Top 40

And what the British public wants is a top forty station. They're getting it from the pirate stations but it's not the same as having a land-based station similar to our U.S. stations.

These pirate stations are powerful. They can make or break a record. Barry McGuire is a perfect example of that. His "Eve Of Destruction" was banned on the government owned BBC but was played on the pirate stations. Thus, making it a huge hit.

Rumor has it that a law will soon be passed outlawing the pirate stations. Radio London doesn't seem to be too worried about this turn of events. "If a law is passed which prevents us supplying Radio London from the U.K.," says Birch, "we will supply it from abroad."

One way or another England is bound to get commercial radio — a situation which makes the British teens very happy indeed.

Even if it does come from an old U.S. minesweeper.

WATCH NEXT WEEK'S BEAT for the complete story and exclusive pictures of Bob Dylan's press conference and concert.

KRLA ARCHIVES

It's In The Bag
By Eden

Column time again, everyone. How 'bout if you tell *me* all the news this week? No? Well, would you believe *no* news this week?!!

Only joshing you, folks. Must start off with an apology to Marvin Gaye. I recently mentioned that the soulful singer made "a lot of great *noise*." Seems as how the word *noise* upset Mr. Gaye so may I publicly say that I just simply love all of the wonderfully melodic "sounds" which Marvin produces from deep within his song-box!

Every once in a while, Herman (of the Fang Fame) gets into a mood of candid comment, and *The BEAT* found him in just such a mood recently. Off-the-cuff remarks from Herman went something like this:

"Nowadays I spend a lot of time travelling—and don't really enjoy it that much at all.

"It's true, we see lots of exciting new places and all that sort of thing, but it's the travelling in between that gets me down. While we're airborne, or car-borne, or train-borne, I sleep. Or read. I'm a James Bond fan, and I've read every one of the Bond books.

"I suppose it's only natural that I miss some of the comforts of home during all this travelling. Probably one of the biggest 'misses' as far as I'm concerned is Mum's cooking.

"I've tried cooking myself, but maybe it's better not to go into that one too closely!

"Girl friend? No, there's no particular girl friend. Just girl *friends*. So far!"

No *one* girl friend, just girl *friends*, huh Herman? Hmmmm—would you believe a *harem*?

* * *

Must take out a moment here to mention the dissolution of one of the greatest singing duos ever. Joe and Eddie have now officially split, due to an unfortunate illness for Joe.

Eddie Brown will continue as a solo artist, but I doubt whether anyone who ever had the pleasure of watching these two fine performers entertain can ever forget the fantastic blend of talents which they possessed.

I would like to extend all of my very best wishes for a successful career as a solo artist to Eddie now, but I must also wish Joe a very speedy and thorough recovery, and hope that one day we will see both Eddie and Joe back together again.

* * *

David McCallum has been a very busy little spy lately. Like for example—he will be doing a little snooping around January 19 when he guest-stars on Roger Miller's special.

Last month David snooped right into the Capitol recording studio and cut his second record. One side is entitled "Communication," which he penned himself, and the flip side is "Carousel." Both records feature a McCallum narration set to music.

* * *

Sonny and Cher have a motion picture—their first—coming up, and it will be called "I've Got You Babe." I mentioned this a few columns back, but now the production date has been moved up to January 24.

* * *

It's gonna be a big month for the Supremes, beginning January 31 when they open at El San Juan Hotel in Puerto Rico. On February 9, the sensational trio will begin their first European tour, wrapping it up about the 15th, then they wing their way homeward in time for their February 17 opening at the Copacabana in New York, where they will stay-put briefly until March 2.

Wow—hope those girls are taking their vitamins this month!!!

* * *

Someone asked me recently what my views on the protest movement are. This seems to have been the Topic of the Year last year, and now that we have begun a brand new year, I think that we ought to get the subject out of the way once and for all.

I think that the popular, commercial protest movement—such as it was—started *and* ended with the "Eve of Destruction." That record was a one-time, "freak" sort of a hit, Unfortunately, it was also one of the most misunderstood songs of our time.

Intended to be a sort of "alarm clock" to wake people up to the current world-wide situation, many people understood it to be a dismal forecast of something which was certain to come—at any minute.

However, I do not believe that most people enjoy listening to the sort of negativism which is necessary to construct a really good protest song, and therefore the movement—of necessity—had to die right where it was born, with the "Destruction."

One important effect of the protest movement did emerge, however. That was to improve the quality of the majority of the songs which are being recorded now. Instead of being flooded with innumerable nonsense songs, we are being entertained by songs with good lyric and melodic content.

I think the fact that the "protest songs" had good lyrics which had something definite to say, greatly contributed to this current trend. Along these same lines, I think the music industry can owe a debt of gratitude to Bob Dylan who has greatly expanded the use of good lyrics in a song.

Rather than a continuation of the protest movement, then, I think that the new trends will veer towards "opinion" or "thought" songs; songs which have something to say, regardless of what it is. I don't think that we are going to hear too much more of the old "Bop Bop Shoo Bopp" things anymore.

And while we are about it—we'd better not forget to include a very large thank-you note to the fabulous Beatles, who have so greatly contributed to popular music in too many ways to even begin to enumerate.

Swingin' Mel Carter Setting New Goals

By Louise Criscione

When his heart sings it really sings. His name is Mel Carter and he is one of the few remaining ballad singers who continues to have hit after hit on the pop charts.

As so many Negro singers do, Mel began his career by singing with a gospel group. It was a big break for Mel because this is how he met the man who wrote his very first hit, the late Sam Cooke.

Mel was singing with the Robert Anderson gospel singers when he met Sam, who was also singing with a gospel group. The two became friends and a few years later Sam wrote "When a Boy Falls In Love." Mel recorded the song and it was released on Sam's label, Derby Records.

"Sam and I worked pretty closely together for two years," said Mel. Then Sam began concentrating more on his own career. "Sam was moving into a different bag. The new clubs took just about all of his time," recalled Mel.

Option Time

"We (his manager Zelda Sands and himself) realized that we had to do something ourselves. We had many offers plus they forgot to renew my option.

"I knew it so we decided to go through the waiting period. Legally, Sam could have kept us there but we had a talk with him and he agreed to let me go," said Mel.

So, Mel headed over to Imperial Records where he is very happy because "there is such a family atmosphere."

All of Mel's big hits have been slow songs, "The Richest Man Alive," "Hold Me, Thrill Me, Kiss Me" and "My Heart Sings." "My sound is a ballad singer but I think I have a definite sound," said Mel.

"Nina Simone has made a very big impression on me. We both recorded 'The Twelfth Of Never' and the first twelve bars are exactly the same," revealed Mel.

Mel is accomplishing the impossible in the wide world of pop. "I'd like to be a night club performer who sells records to the teenage market as well as to the adult market.

Mel is never really scared on stage. "I feel at home, very much at ease on stage." Speaking of the stage brought something to Mel's mind and he continued enthusiastically: "I'm going to drama school."

"In other words, I'm trying a different thing—class and commercialism," said Mel.

And is he succeeding? "So far, yes," he smiles.

Oh, so he's an aspiring actor? "Well," Mel grinned, "I'm aspiring to something. A year ago it never entered my mind. You know, I'd go to the movies and come out thinking I'd like to be an actor but I never did anything about it. I wasn't serious.

"I had my first dramatic role in 'Never Too Young,'" Mel continued more than enthusiastic now. "I wasn't scared at first because I thought I was just going to sing, but when I got to the studio they handed me seven minutes of lines."

Mel got through the ordeal with flying colors and liked acting so much that he is concentrating even more on professionalizing his acting ability.

"I'm reading for the part of the brother in 'Raisin In The Sun' in my drama class," said Mel. And he is also going to play the part of a white man while a white man plays the part of a Negro. "We felt like this is the only way we could get into the part."

Mel feels that there is a combination of reasons for the lack of Negro actors. "There is just as much Negro talent as white talent but there aren't enough Negroes trying.

"There is an underlying amount of prejudice in the business. For instance, Lena Horn knows that she is a dramatic act ess but is always type cast as a Negro.

"So, the Negro doesn't have a chance to display his talent," said Mel. But he is not the least bit discouraged. Mel sort of feels that if Sidney Portier can do it so can he.

Pop Films?

Of course, Mel is taking the chance of never being able to display his dramatic ability either. He might just be thrown into a pop film with plenty of singing but no real plot. Would he take it?

"It all depends on whether they were making a movie in which they would give me special staging," said Mel. "I think it has it's advantages. The publicity it gets and the people who see it in the theaters. You get a chance to do something and do it well. The public likes to see an artist," Mel said.

He's "really excited" about going to England in February. In fact, he is currently rehearsing a new act. "We start out the first of the year with a whole new act.

"It usually takes three to six months to get a new act but we've already done three months work in three weeks," said Mel.

"Eventually we'll be taking a musical director and a trio with us." However, Mel declares now that he will never take a full review 'ala James Brown, because "I'm not going that route."

Even Keel

Mel says that he doesn't get too discouraged if one of his records is not a top ten hit: "I try to keep on an even keel but I would really like a gold record."

And there are three other things Mel would like very much to do. "I want to record a song in Japanese and I'd like to visit Japan. I think I'd like it there."

And the last wish? "I'd like to be a household name," said Mel softly.

Think he'll make it? Probably—if he keeps turning out those hits. There's really no reason why he shouldn't—he hasn't missed yet.

KRLA ARCHIVES

A Look Back At Ringo

By Jamie McCluskey III

Time once again to open up our BEAT scrapbook and take a look at the childhood memories in picture form, of your Beatle and mine — Ringo Starr.

By now, just about everyone is aware of the fact that Der Ringo had a great deal of illness to contend with during his childhood. As these are not the happiest of memories, there aren't any pictures of those days of Ringo in our book, but there is one which sort of looks back to Ringo's days in school.

Mr. Dawson — who was Ringo's physical training instructor at Dingle Vale Secondary Modern School in Liverpool — provides us with this snapshot:

"He was always wanting to do the same things as the other boys, and I remember one incident which typifies this. It was during the middle of a physical training lesson. All the class was jumping over the vaulting-horse in the center of the gym.

"When it came to Ringo's turn, he was obviously pretty doubtful whether he would get over the obstacle because he had never done it before. He ran up to it, jumped, and just managed to clear it. When he found that he had succeeded and not fallen flat, his face burst into a really broad, satisfied grin."

Ringo's Desk

Mr. Dawson continues his reflections by recounting incidents in the present: "Recently the school put an old desk of Ringo's up for sale. We had thousands of girls queueing up to try and buy it. He has certainly helped to make Dingle Vale School famous."

The next snap in our collection comes to us from Ringo's wonderful Mum — Mrs. Starkey, and she tells us about Ringo's first interest in the fine art of drumming:

"It was in 1957. He was working in Hunt's Sport's Equipment store in Speke at the time, and he started a group, which they called the Ed Clayton Skiffle Group with his only really close friend at that time, Roy Trafford.

"Later on Ringo joined Rory Storm and the Hurricanes. He was playing with the Dark-Town Skiffle group at the time, and met Rory at a 6.5 Special Talent Contest. They got talking and Ringo found that Rory was short of a drummer. He gave Ringo a try, and shortly afterwards, the future Beatle became a permanent member of the group. The Hurricanes had just changed their name at the time. They used to call themselves the Roving Texans, and altered it because they started to play Rock instead of Skiffle."

Nix On Muck

Ringo is a movie star now, and of course he must wear theatrical make-up when he appears on the screen. But he wasn't quite resigned to the whole idea back in "the good old days!" An old friend — Iris Fenton — who also knew George and Paul in the time of the Rory Storm days, provides us with this candid glimpse into Ringo's past:

"The boys were appearing at Butlin's Camp at Pwllheli and it was mutually decided that they would all look more professional if they wore make-up. Mutually, that is, except for Ringo. Ringo flatly refused, saying that he absolutely would not "put that muck on my face!"

He was finally forced to smear on at least a thin layer, which he did — somewhat begrudgingly! Iris continues, saying:

"I remember that he was very popular with the girls staying at the camp. They all loved the grey streaks in his hair, even though Ringo hated them."

Starr Time

"Rory thought a lot of Ringo and gave him his own spot in the act calling it 'Ringo Starr Time.' Ringo sang 'Matchbox' and 'Boys.'

"He did not grow his beard until their second session at the camp. I think it was to try and draw attention away from the streaks in his hair."

Iris' mother joins in here to share a snapshot of Ringo's very first swimming lesson with The BEAT: "Rory found out that Ringo could not swim a stroke so he decided to try and teach him. It was fine at first, but then they became more ambitious and decided to go underwater swimming which almost caused a tragedy. Rory told me that suddenly a pair of hands appeared from beneath the waves, desperately searching for something to grab onto. Ringo's swimming obviously wasn't good enough for under-water yet. Luckily Rory saw what was happening and pulled him out."

We have lots more pictures in our book of Ringo, but I'm afraid that you're gonna have to wait till next week to see those. See ya then.

IN SEARCH OF FOLK
Glen — Real Folk
By Shannon Leigh

Just who exactly are the "folk" of this world? Who are the people behind the "folk music" we listen to? In fact, just what exactly is "folk music?"

The current concensus of opinion is that folk music is simply the "music of the people." Theoretically, then, we'll assume that this takes in all people, of all ethnic origins and cultural environments.

Taking all of the foregoing as a basis for this week's "search," then, we have found a "folk singer" right here in The BEAT offices. His name is Glen Campbell, and he is definitely real folk!!

Glen was born in Delight, Arkansas, on April 22, 1940. He had a 15-minute radio show with his uncle when he was six years old, on which he played rhythm guitar and sang. From there, he went to Texas, and at the tender age of 13 he was playing night clubs, six nights a week.

Glen never had any formal music training, but as he says (drawl and y'all!): "When you play clubs six nights a week, that's like rehearsing five hours a day!!"

Glen is probably one of the most talented guitarists in the field of pop music today, and aside from his own record career, he has played on sessions with Elvis Presley, Sonny and Cher, the Knickerbockers, Ricky Nelson, and Phil Spector.

No Label

As for himself, Glen avoids being tagged with any one label. He will admit to having country and western origins, but then he will go on to explain hat:

"I don't label anybody like — 'Well, he's a country and western singer, you lay him on the shelf there; he's a Rock 'n' Roll singer, you lay him on the shelf there.' Music isn't like that to me.

"You take some of these artists who have had a gimmick record — they're here today and gone tomorrow. But the talent stays!

"The reason, I think, most of the pop artists jump on the country and western tunes is because the country and western songs have so much more meaning, so much more feeling than a typical R 'n' R record like 'Shout.'"

So we have found a "folk" who likes to sing in all different sorts of "bags!" "I'm kind of a funny guy — one day I'll be on a country and western-sounding kick, the next day I'm on a Rock 'n' Roll kick, the next day I'm on a pop kick. It's good to know all of these different things."

Talent

Yes, it is good. But it is also something called "talent," an X ingredient which Glen possesses in very large quantities.

Glen is a tall, good-looking, easy-going young man, with a marvelous Southern drawl in his voice, and a warm, sunny smile on his face. He has a wild sense of humor, and very straight-facedly he informed me of a slight difficulty he has been having lately:

"I've got an Indian fan over in Arizona who keeps sending me smoke signals . . . COLLECT!!"

Glen is also the proud father of a brand new baby boy, named William Travis Campbell. Born December 12, little William weighed nine pounds at birth, and as his Daddy tells it, he was "born standing up and walking!!"

This New Year holds many TV appearances for Glen, as well as many more recording sessions. "I'd like to make good, hit records. But mainly, I'd like to make good, clean records — I won't do anything 'dirty.'" On his latest record session, Glen cut an old standard tune entitled "Satisfied Mind," all done up in a brand new way.

The disc will be released some time this month and it's a record to listen for.

And Glen? Oh well, he's just an average, everyday, all-American good-looking, talented, fun-loving fellow. Come to think of it — ah reckon that he's jest "folk!!"

RECORD QUIZ

It's happening again. Old songs are coming back! Several of today's chart-busters are past tunes with a new twist. Below, you'll find seven such hits. Some are recent revivals, others may take some remembering. The column on the left lists the names of the songs and their present artists. The column on the right is a jumbled collection of the original artists. See how many you can match!

1. "You've Got To Hide Your Love Away" — Silkie   a. Paul Anka
2. "Over And Over" — Dave Clark Five   b. Little Willie John
3. "Hong On Sloopy" — Ramsey Lewis Trio   c. Kingston Trio
4. "Don't Think Twice" — Wonder Who?   d. Thurston Harris
5. "Fever" — The McCoys   e. John Lennon
6. "All Of A Sudden My Heart Sings" — Mel Carter   f. The McCoys
7. "Where Have All The Flowers Gone" — J. Rivers   g. Peter Paul & Mary

ANSWERS (AND STOP THAT TRYING TO READ THEM UPSIDE DOWN, IT'S BAD FOR YOUR EYES!) 1 — e, 2 — d, 3 — f, 4 — g, 5 — b, 6 — a, 7 — c.

KRLA ARCHIVES

For Girls Only

By Shirley Poston

I do hope that I'll be able to stop stuffing myself with holiday goodies long enough to write this column. I also hope I'm the only one who gains approximately forty tons every Christmas season. I sure wouldn't wish this predicament off on anyone else.

Guess it's time to get out my Beatle albums and start doing some deep knee bends. Really, their discs are great to do exercises by, especially the "Hard Day's Night" album. It has lots of jumpy songs that set the old flab to bouncing.

Good grief. The way I express myself has *got* to go! Allow me to rephrase that last sentence. It has lots of jumpy songs that jiggles your jowls maybe? No, that one was even worse.

Sometimes I think I'm in the wrong business. I should be writing for a medical journal with my nauseating touch. No, come to think of it, I should be writing *to* medical journals. For help!

Speaking of George (enough of this rational stuff—it's getting on my nerves), I have a wonderful idea about what all of we (us?) (oh, well) G. Pant Harrison fans can do next New Year's Eve. We can all meet at International Airport, storm the runway and "borrow" a fleet of planes and go visit George! Of course, between now and then, a few of us are going to have to learn to fly DC5's (of the winged variety), but it's a sacrifice worth making.

I dreamed that one up because I just never have any fun on New Year's Eve. I think it's because I try too hard, thinking I'm-going-to-have-a-good-time-or-else. So, I like to conjure up things that I *know* would be fun. And, I must say, that suggestion was the most ridiculous I've *ever* managed to dredge up.

Oh, well, just bear with me. It must have been something I ate. Like those three rum cakes, for instance.

But, does that ever happen to you? Not having fun when you're supposed to, I mean? That happens to me a lot. I usually have a better time when things aren't all planned and you end up doing some kicky spur-of-the-moment thing.

Now, back to the Beatles. I received a great letter from *BEAT* reader April Orcutt who lives in Tustin, California. Inside (where else, pray tell?) she'd enclosed several copies of a Beatle survey she'd made up, and asked me to pass them out to my friends.

I started to do just that and then realized that all of you might like to get in on this. So, I'm going to print a list of the questions April asked, and I know she'll flip if you'll each send her a letter with your own opinions and answers.

Before I forget, her address is 16596 Townhouse Drive.

Now, onward. My own answers appear in parenthesis (so I can't spel) after each question.

1. *Who is your favorite Beatle and why?* (George Harrison because he is George Harrison.)
2. *What is your favorite Beatle song?* (Tie between "Don't Bother Me" and "Day Tripper.")
3. *What is your least favorite Beatle song?* ("Mr. Moonlight.")
4. *Why do you like the Beatles?* (I don't like them. I love them. There aren't any words warm enough for why.)
5. *What other groups do you like?* (The Stones.)
6. *What is your opinion of the movie "Hard Day's Night?"* (It was sheer magic.)
7. *What is your opinion of the movie "Help?"* (I loved it just as much, but in a different way.)
8. *Which Beatle do you think is the best actor?* (Paul McCartney.)
9. *Which Beatle do you think has the best singing voice?* (George Harrison!!)
10. *Do you think you will still like the Beatles if and when Paul and George get married?* (Yes, definitely!!)
11. *Why or why not?* (If there's anything that *could* make me stop liking them, it hasn't been invented yet. However, George, I do expect you to be *very* upset when *I* get married.)
12. *Do you think the Beatles will last?* (Forever.)
13. *Why or why not?* (Because they are totally unique and widely talented. There's never been anything like them before and there never will be again.)
14. *What do your parents think of the Beatles?* (They didn't much care for them until I nagged them into seeing "Hard Day's Night." After that, they could hardly wait to see "Help.")

There you have it. Hope you'll be able to find time to send your answers off to April. In a month or so, I'll write and ask her how the survey came out and then print the news here in my column.

Hmmm. I do wish April had asked which Beatle was the you-know-whatiest. The answer to which would have to be John Lennon, of course. (Sorry about that, George.)

Well, I'm out of room (and my mind) as usual, and I still haven't given you the name of the Rolling Stones album winner. Who just happens to be Laurie Riedinger of Los Alamitos!

I also have a confession to make. You already know how disorganized I am and all. Well, I've done it again. We've had three album winners so far, and I haven't sent out the albums yet! I promise I'll do it tomorrow, so help me! Let's face it. I mean well, but I'm not.

If there are any Donovan fans (besides me) (slurp), you'll be glad to hear that he's the object of our next little for-girl's-only-or-else contest.

"I'll send a copy of his "Catch The Wind" album to the first person who can tell me what his last name is! Hint—it starts with an L.

Keep your letters coming and I'll see you next Beat!

Sincere Thanks
for voting

'The In Crowd'

BEAT Pop Awards

Best Instrumental Album of the Year

Ramsey Lewis Trio

KRLA ARCHIVES

THE BEATLES were unable to attend our Pop Awards Banquet, as you all know. They were kind enough to send us a telegram explaining that they were on their British tour at that time. But this morning the postman delivered a real surprise to us—actual proof of where the Beatles were on December 8. They were getting off the plane in Sheffield, England. So **The BEAT** forgives them.

Lurch Looks At Protests

Protest, protest, protest—that seems to be the main topic of discussion ever since "Eve of Destruction" took over the charts.

But at least one person has looked at the whole scene objectively. Ted Williams, better known as Lurch of The Addams Family, says he's for protest and he seems to have some pretty good reasons.

"I can't help but think that it's all a part of the fear of finality," he explained during a break in the taping of a television show.

"It's kind of like you're saying 'somebody help us. The world got away from us and we don't know what to do about it.'

"You can't ignore protest. I'm for it, for only through protest can we get both sides of the question.

"You've got to have people on the fringe. If you've only got middle of the roaders, you just don't ever make progress."

Ian Hosts Show

That British bundle of energy known as Ian Whitcomb is returning to America the 18th of this month and has just been signed to a new venture.

He's signed as the host emcee on a new half hour musical game show called "Pop-Opoly."

The show is produced by Al Burton, Frank Danzig and Bart Ross from Teen-Age Fair Productions.

Kingston Trio— Folk Entertainers

By Shannon Leigh

Searching, searching—yes, we're still searching; searching for folks in a very folky world. This week, we have discovered three very nice folks on the grounds of a large, plush hotel.

Oddly enough, almost any "folk singer" with whom you speak these days claims *not* to be a folk singer! We posed the question of identity to the Kingston Trio, and John Stuart replied:

"We never claimed to be folk *singers*—we're folk *entertainers*. I think if you have to put labels on something—a folk singer is someone who presents folk-songs because they're folk songs and the entertainment is within the songs, and not within the presentation.

All Types

"We sing many types of songs and we sing them with folk instruments and with folky harmonies, rather than modern harmonies and folky instrumentation. But we sing popular songs, and Broadway show tunes, and parodies, but we sing them in a folky manner."

John continued along this line of thought and extended it even further into the field of pop music:

"When folk music was really popular, then 'Shindig' and the Beatles came along and the pop music fans didn't want to drop their folk root, so the performers adopted both the electricity of 'Shindig' and the Beatles and the folk idiom, and then combined them.

"It seems that all popular music is combined into one now—country and western has a big influence on groups like the Lovin' Spoonful, who are in no way country and western.

Next Fad?

"So, with this amalgamation of music, I think that this will continue and become even more prevalent. I wish I could tell you what would be the next fad, but I don't know."

Many people have suggested that the modern popular folk movement actually had its beginning when the Kingston Trio made a chart success of their first disc—"Tom Dooley."

Theorizing on this idea, Nick Reynolds explains: "I think the pop trend of groups, quartets, trios, folk choirs—I think we started that particular part of it.

"I'm not going to say that there would have been no Bobby Dylan without the Kingston Trio! But, maybe his interest got started back then with some folk group or singer, but I don't know."

British Sound

Bob Shank seemed to express the feelings of the group as he spoke about the British sound and influence which has been so prevalent in the last year and a half.

"I think it's had a great influence on American style. They have had a lot of great new groups come out *because* of it. I think the surfing bit is a combination of the British *sound* and the American *health!*"

The Kingston Trio—as folk singers, pop singers, or just plain *great* singers!—have been making hit records consistently for nine years now. In that time they have produced 26 best-selling albums, and a number of successful singles.

Their latest album is entitled "Something Else"—in which the boys experiment for the first time with electrified instruments, somewhat more in the pop vein, and their new single from that LP is "Parchment Farm," which is already doing very well on the charts.

Race Driver

The boys also find time in their hectic schedules for hobbies. Bob Shank builds and races sports cars, and he finished second on the West Coast last year on the whole Pacific division in his class, which is a formula class for the Lotus 22.

John Stuart writes songs, both for the Trio and for other groups as well. But currently he is involved in a much larger project, which he explained to *The BEAT* very briefly:

"I'm doing a project for the Kennedy library. It's collecting the contemporary folk songs from the three years President Kennedy was in office.

"Any music—especially folk songs—gives an element of emotion that biographers and historians *won't* be able to capture. But 100 years from now, we'll get an indication of how the younger people were reacting to the events of the years.

"There are about 500 songs collected so far."

Well, *they* claim that they aren't folk *singers* but folk *entertainers*. Alright—would you believe three great entertainers singing some folk songs just about as well as they're gonna get sung?!!

PAUL REVERE AND HIS RAIDERS are pictured here with Dick Clark minus the rest of the "Action" gang. The trouble with this on location filming is quite simple and most obvious—it's cold on the beach! But the show must go on and so the Raiders bravely play their instruments despite rain, sleet, etc.

KRLA ARCHIVES

Spoonful Of Lovin' Words

By Eden

...JOHN SPOONFUL

...JOE SPOONFUL

It isn't everyday that one meets John Sebastian of the Lovin' Spoonful and has the opportunity to sit and talk with him. *The BEAT* had that opportunity the other day, when we found John sitting alone in a darkened nightclub.

It was the middle of the afternoon, and the nitery was very silent and abandoned. John and I sat down at one of the little tables near the stage and began to talk about things—all kinds of things, like the way the group was formed:

"I met Zolly about two years ago and then about ten months ago I met Stephen and Joe Butler. Joe became the drummer a short time after Stephen had joined the band.

"The whole thing germinated in the fact that Zolly and I wanted to work together just because we liked the music that we could play together. I guess that all of us involved were interested in making music and working with a band and I think that none of us had really found the right combination of people yet."

Sounds

We spoke of other things as well; we spoke of sounds, and the particular sounds made by the "Spoonful." "We're the group that cries out *not* to be labeled." I think that if you've heard our album, you know that we make a lot of *different* sounds, so that no one *specific* sound could really be characterized as what we 'sound like.'

"Because, with different combinations of instruments, different styles of playing—the sound of the group is not *singular* but *multiple*."

As John was speaking, the topic of protest music came into the conversation, and John has some very definite feelings about these songs; we mentioned the possibility of Dylan being the father of the protest movement, and John tinued from there:

"If Dylan fathered it, then it's certainly his illegitimate son, because the protest music is certainly not the direction of Dylan right now, on the same terms.

"The protest music is a phenomena and we don't do it. Probably because we're very ill-acquainted with politics, which is what it mostly is—most of the source material for writing protest songs is newspaper data which most of us aren't well acquainted with in the first place."

Have A Ball

The evening had grown later and it was time for John to rejoin the other members of his group, and as he bid farewell to *The BEAT*, we asked him one final question: what would he do with the future, what hopes does he hold for the group? "We'd like to carry on—have a good time—more than anything else. We want to have fun!"

He was gone then, suddenly, but at least we had been treated to a small taste of The Lovin' Spoonful.

...STEVE SPOONFUL

...AND ZOLLY LOVIN'

KRLA ARCHIVES

The Rock & Roll Showplace of the World
Dave Hull's
Hullabaloo
starring
THE WORLD'S TOP RECORDING ARTISTS

NEW YEARS WEEK
Dec. 27 - Jan. 2
Mitch Ryder and The Detroit Wheels
plus
The Girls and The Palace Guard

COMING IN CONCERT

JANUARY 5, 6, 7, 9
THE YARDBIRDS
First and Only Time in Los Angeles
Get Your Tickets Early

– Coming January 9 –
THE LIVERPOOL FIVE
Direct From England

Hullabaloo's OWN
PALACE GUARD

SPECIAL GIANT JAM SESSION — January 2, from 2 p.m. – 7 p.m. – All Your Favorite Groups on Stage –

THIS COUPON WORTH 50¢
OFF Regular Admission When Presented at the Door
DAVE HULL'S HULLABALOO
6230 SUNSET (AT VINE)   Phone: HO 6-8281
Hollywood, Calif.   For Reservations

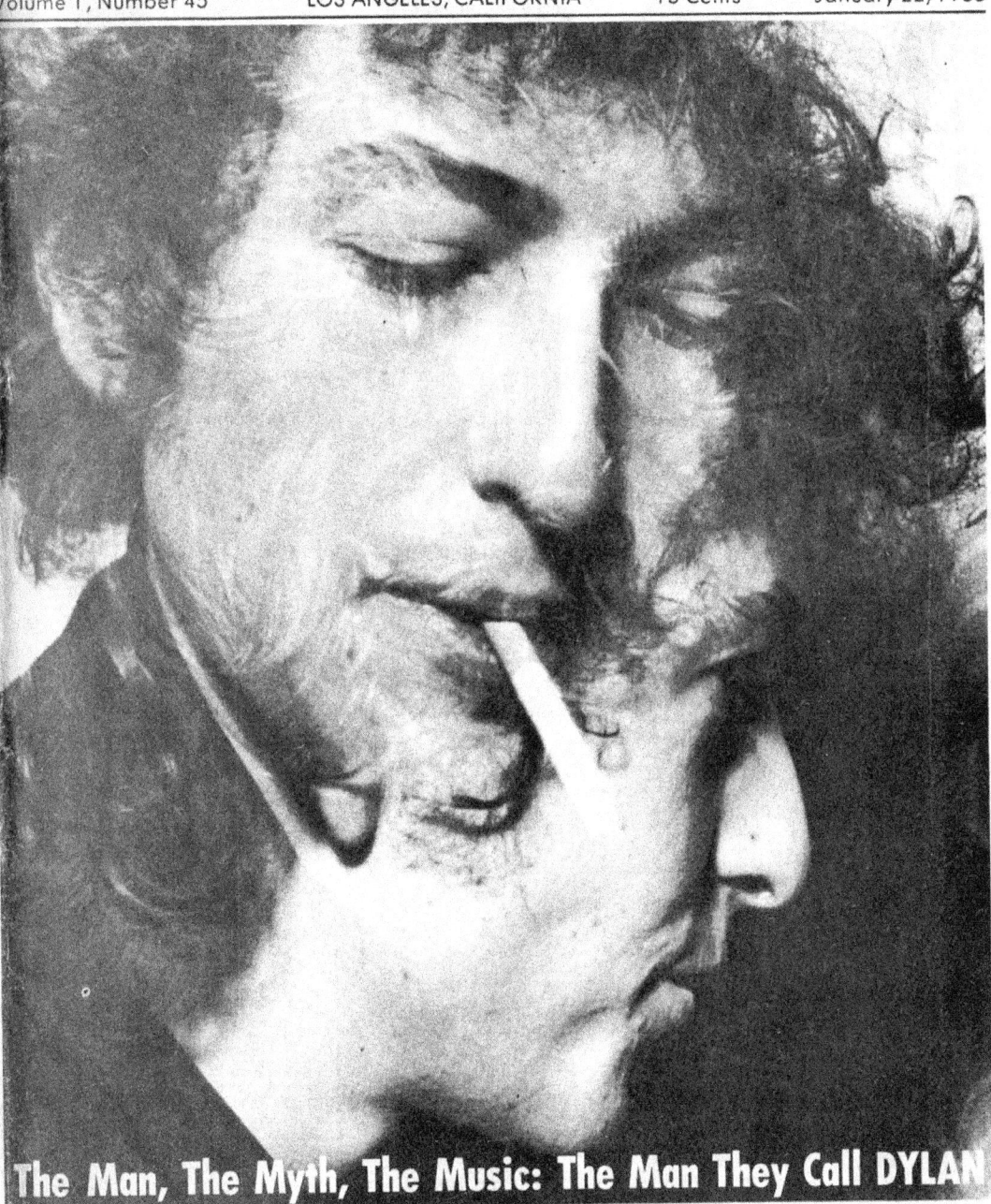

KRLA BEAT

Los Angeles, California — January 22, 1966

Rolling Stones Up To Plenty

By Tammy Hitchcock

The Rolling Stones are still vacationing and the five of them are spread all over the world. Since their American tour they've been up to nothing but rest and relaxation. Something which they deserve but don't get much of.

However, before they took the vacation route they were up to plenty. Charlie (who, by the way, can and does talk) has been very busy the past several months getting his second book ready for publication. His first, "Ode To A Highflying Bird," was quite a success in both England and the U.S.

This time around Charlie is working on a children's book. It should be appearing in your book shops in the not too distant future and will go under the name of "Zoo Of Flags."

Bill, the other quiet Stone who also talks when the mood strikes him, has been occupied with fixing anything which happens to go wrong with the Stones' amplifiers. Except in the U.S. if any union men are within eyesight. In which case, Bill touches nothing (unless their backs are turned, of course!).

Keith's Dog

Keith has kept himself busy by looking after a little puppy given to him by a Stateside friend. Keith thought around for quite awhile searching for a different name for the dog, finally gave the situation up as hopeless and simply calls the pup "Dog." That's different?

Keith's habit of sticking pencils and papers and that sort of thing into his mouth has got to be stopped. Riding a London bus recently Keith folded up his bus ticket and stuck it into his mouth, which really didn't hurt anything but the ticket—until later, that is.

Keith can sometimes be a bit absentminded. So, when Stones' road manager, Ian Stewart, lit a cigarette Keith leaned over and got a light from Stu.

One small problem—Keith lit the bus ticket! The burning ticket almost turned Keith's precious bangs into ashes (still precious, though). Maybe now he'll learn not to stick *everything* into his mouth, or at least not to set them on fire!

Brian has been busy phoning girls who throw stuffed animals at him with their phone numbers attached conveniently thereupon. He phoned a girl in L.A. who had hurled a stuffed toy at Brian on the stage in Long Beach when the Stones appeared there last May.

'Cause Of A Seal

Latest girl to receive a call from Mr. Jones was a lucky New York fan who took aim at the Stones' speeding Cadillac and tossed a toy seal at Brian. Again with phone number written on it. When Brian returned to the hotel he sat down, phoned the girl and talked to her for nearly *two* hours. Some people have all the luck, don't they?

When Brian was in California he wanted desperately to go horseback riding, so he called up his friend, Joey Paige, to invite Joey to go along. Which was all very fine except that the two of them never made it—they couldn't find a horseback riding stable which was open! Maybe next time, Brian.

And Mick? What's he been up to? Well, he's been talking to the press about a lot of things. But mostly about the Stones' first movie venture which is set to roll in April. Mick's really very excited about it and most anxious that it turn out just right.

He refuses to have it become a pop film, declaring that if the Stones wanted to appear in one of those they would have done it two years ago. Mick very seriously wants to act and not just be a decoration.

He'd like it very much if the whole world didn't know the plot beforehand, so he and the other Stones are keeping it top secret. He does hope his fans will like the movie but he couldn't care less what the Stones' critics think about it.

Mick's like that, you know.

Inside the BEAT

Dylan	3-6
Jones Boy Makes Good	7
The Shindigger Returns	7
Four Seasons on TV	8
For Girls Only	11
Adventures of Robin Boyd	12
Tips To Teens	13
British Top 10	13
Sam The Who and The What?	14
Notes From the U.K.	15
Winning Recipe For Jay	15
Beat Goes To The Movies	16

The BEAT is published weekly by BEAT Publications, Inc. editorial and advertising offices at 6290 Sunset Blvd., Suite 504, Hollywood, California 90028. U.S. bureaus in Hollywood, San Francisco, New York, Chicago and Nashville; overseas correspondents in London, Liverpool and Manchester, England. Sale price, 15 cents. Subscription price: U.S. and possessions, $5 per year; Canada and foreign rates, $9 per year. Application to mail at second class postage rates is pending at Los Angeles, California.

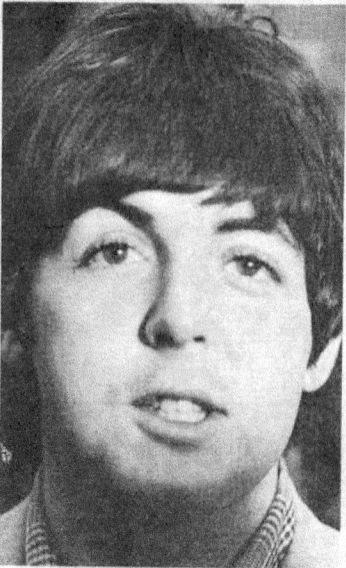
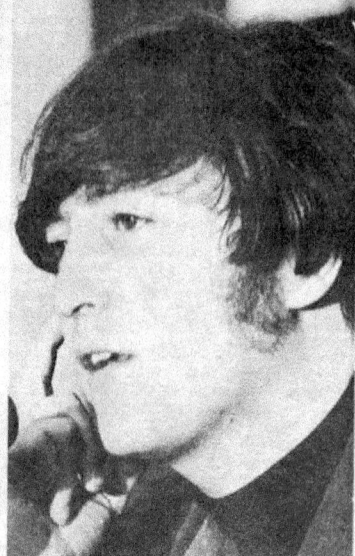
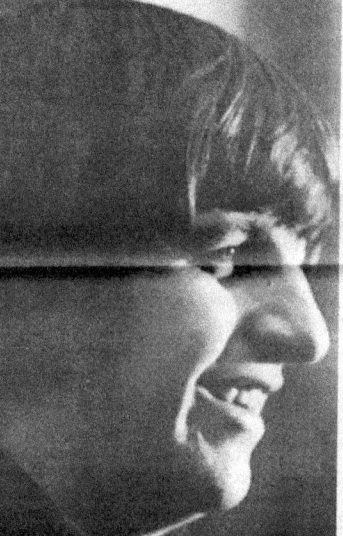
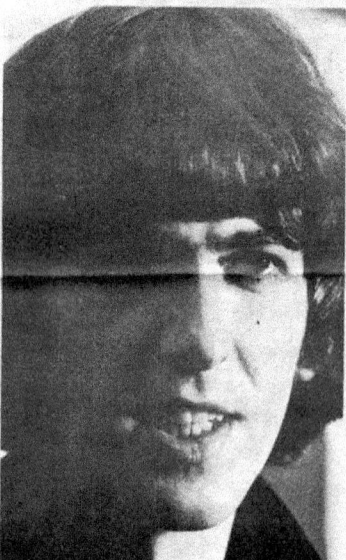

THAT ELUSIVE MOVIE SCRIPT

Beatles Still Looking

By Louise Criscione

As of today the Beatles are still in hot water over their next movie. They have a bit of a problem as you know—they're minus a script!

All four of the Beatles, and especially Paul, seem to know exactly what they *don't* want. They don't want "A Talent For Loving" because they'd look like four long-haired Roy Rogers singing to their horses.

If they can possibly avoid it they don't want another script like "Help." Although Paul declared that he liked "Help" and enjoyed watching it he did not feel that he and his buddies were necessary characters in the story. He considered them merely incidental to the plot and not a real part of it.

They don't want to do another "Hard Day's Night." Not because they didn't like the movie—they did very much. But after all, it was a sort of documentary type film and how many of those can you make? Especially if you are creative, and the Beatles are.

They don't want to pull an Elvis. They don't want to rush a movie out in three weeks and they don't want to make a movie which is merely a vehicle for music. That would be too much like a pop film —all songs and no plot.

Write Their Own?

Okay, then why don't the Beatles write their own movie— they've done everything else. Well, as a matter of fact, they have attempted to write a script. But they just couldn't complete it to their satisfaction.

Paul reveals that he and John tried to write one but ran into all kinds of snags along the way. The plot revolved around a man named Pilchard, who was really supposed to be Jesus Christ.

However, there were all sorts of holes in the story and so to fill them up John and Paul continued to add more characters. And by the time they had finished the story they had about a hundred characters involved in the plot! So they chucked it.

The Beatles are all a little tired of playing the good guys. They figure that a piece of good goes a long way. They wanta be bad guys for a change. You don't think the four Beatles could be bad guys? Well, then stretch your imagination! Of course, they'd probably be *good* bad guys.

Another problem facing the
(Turn to Page 7)

DYLAN

At first there were just the four of us—just four people alone in a room. Quiet—then we spoke some words to one another, but there was really nothing to say. We were strangers all alone.

It was a small room and there were no windows; only doors which opened from the outside. It was a recording studio, and now it was filling up with television cameras and radio microphones—and people.

There were many people in the room then talking all at once. No one was really saying anything, but everyone was just sort of waiting—there was going to be a press conference for a man named Bob Dylan.

And suddenly he was there ... Dylan.

It became somehow like a giant Alice-in-Wonderland zoo, grotesque, with all of the animals peering out from behind their fiberglass bars at all of the odd-looking people on the outside.

Reporters and journalists and TV cameras all had come to see a freak in a sideshow, all had come to be entertained. Instead, they found a human being. Instead, they found a man—*Dylan*.

Some people were nosey, and asked questions which were out of place: *How much money do you make Bob?*

"I don't know how much money I make and I don't ever want to find out. When I want some money, I just go and ask for it, and then I use it. When I want some more I go and ask for some more."

Some round-looking people tried to squeeze their questions into little square pegholes, and hoped that Dylan would follow after. They tried to pin him down: *How exactly do you write your songs and poems?*

"I just sit down and all of a sudden it's there. I just sit down and write and the next thing I know it's there."

Bob Dylan just won't fit into little square cubby-holes—he's much too big for that.

Some questions were quite foolish, like those who tried to ask them: *How do your parents feel about your success?*

"Well, I hope they can handle it!"

Sometimes words were spoken, and their speaker was Bob Dylan:

"I'm a mathematical singer—I use words like most people use numbers."

"I'm just an entertainer, that's all. I'm addressed to everyone."

"I sing mostly love songs—I like to sing and play."

"I'm gonna write a symphony with words—I don't know if it's gonna be vague or not. There will be one song in one key, and another song in another key. Everything will be happening all at once."

Sometimes people threw their verbal harpoons at him, only to find him throwing them right back—with deadly aim! "I bet you couldn't name *one* thing I participate in—go ahead, I *dare* you!!!"

And there was no one there to accept the challenge.

People asking foolish and irrelevant questions found that they received their answers in direct accordance. *Why did you come to California, Bob?*

"I came to find some donkeys for a film I'm making!"

Are you gonna play yourself in the film?

"No, I'm gonna play my *mother*, and we're gonna call it 'Mother Revisited!"

There was a slight, fragile young man sitting at the table in the front of the brightly-lighted room. It was like an operating room with a hundred amateur physicians all trying to dissect one human form.

But they couldn't make the crucial incision, and the anaesthetic worked on *them*, instead.

And then the man named Dylan rose and slowly left the room. The TV cameras turned off their blinding klieg lights, and the radio men turned off their prying microphones. Slowly all the reporters and the journalists disappeared through the one-way door, returning to their one-way lives.

And then the room was quiet—there was no one left inside.

DYLAN ... DYLAN ... DYLAN ...... listen to his words:

"the town i was born in holds
no memories
but for the honkin foghorns
the rainy mist
an the rocky cliffs."

He was born in the ageing mining town of Duluth, Minnesota. When just a child, his family moved further downstate to Hibbing.

"it was not a rich town
my parents were not rich
it was not a poor town
my parents were not poor
it was a dyin town."

He was a restless child, always moving ... running ...

"i end up then
in the early evenin
blindly punchin at the blind
breathin heavy
stutterin
an blowin up
where t go?
what is it that's exactly wrong?
who t picket?
who t fight?
behind what windows
will I at least
hear someone from the supper table
get up t ask
'did I hear someone outside
just now?'
an there was no sound except
for the wind
blowin thru the high grass
and the bricks that fell back
to the dirt from a slight stab
of the breeze ... it was as tho
the rains of wartime had
left the land bombed out an
shattered.

south Hibbing
is where everybody came t
start their
town again. but the winds of
the
north came followin and grew
fiercer
as the years went by
but i was young
an so i ran
an kept running ..."

In his own explanation of his early experiences—"My Life in a Stolen Minute"—Bob has written: "Hibbing's a good ol' town. I ran away from it when I was 10, 12, 13, 15, 15½, an' 18. I been caught an' brought back all but once."

In 1961, Bob Dylan was 20 years old—he had sung his way half-way through the States, and he was in New York.

"Winter time in New York town,
The wind blowin', snow around,
Walk around with no where to go
Somebody could freeze right to the bone.
I froze right to the bone."

Where Is He Now?

He is 24 years old now, and he has travelled half-way round the world.

I don't know where Bob Dylan is now, although I have a vague idea of where he has been. It seems quite certain that his future direction is only up, but his path veers off to obscurity.

He involves himself with the human condition—with love, and hate, and fear, and bitterness, and poignant feelings of everything. He feels them, he writes them, he

CONFERENCE

*Silenced, darkened room of space ...
Patternless walls of white
One-way doors and no-way windows ...
People blotting out the light.*

*Cameras like giant scalpel-claws, and Microphones of lead—no plugs;
Fifty carniverous carnival freaks, earless—
Who came to hear.*

*Deafened pens and blinded eyes ...
Laughter horrifying fear—
Jungle-hunters ... two-by-four
Waiting for their prey, and springing on a friend.*

*A human being in a cage,
Of flesh and blood entrapment, kept—
Detained for one brief moment's nausea, the answer to his unasked question—
Answered far beyond those doors—
An eternal-seeming captivity.*

—By Eden

sings them. There are a lot of people who try to listen. There are some people who hear what he is saying.

Dylan seems to be the hereditary genius of the immortals speaking with the tongue of here and now. He is a highly emotional, passionate observer of the world around and within him, expressing his many moods in a manner uniquely his own—Dylan, powerful, ever-changing, *Dylan*.

He seems at once to be coming, to exist, to be in the process of self-evolution, and to be infinite. He is the translation of words and music and cultures into the most profound aesthetic experiences.

He has said: "*Open up your eyes and ears an yer influenced—an there's nothing you can do about it ... I just seem to draw into myself whatever comes my way and it comes out me.*"

Dylan's Influence

I find myself influenced by Bob Dylan and I am not alone. There are many who have felt the touch of Dylan on their thoughts. Many try to copy, some endeavor to understand. He can be the most absorbing thought ever to fill a mental space, or he can be the incomprehensible dreams of far-off childhood.

There is no definition of Bob Dylan, no simple explanation of his being. There is only his existence, and his talent, and his art, and the opportunity which he offers to us to share this world with him.

There is only Bob Dylan—somewhere.

KRLA ARCHIVES

"love minus zero/no limit"

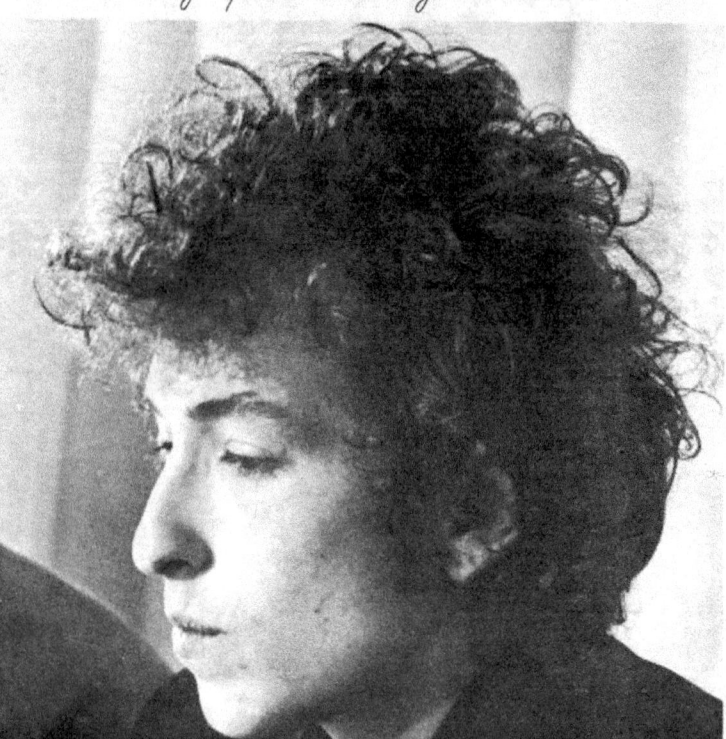

"can you please crawl out your window?"

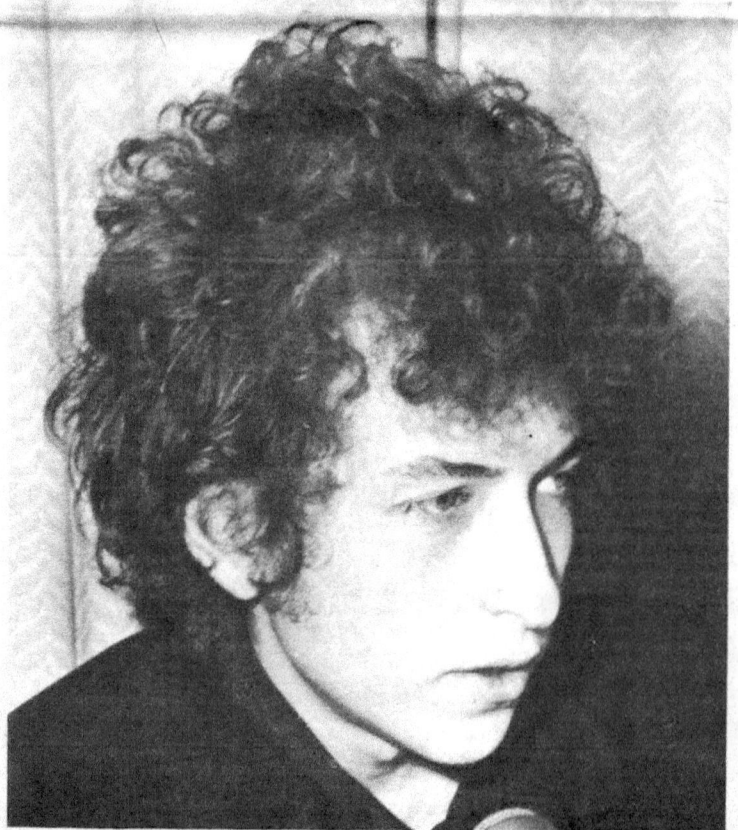

"it's alright ma, i'm only bleeding"

"subterranean homesick blues"

KRLA ARCHIVES

"the times they are a changing"

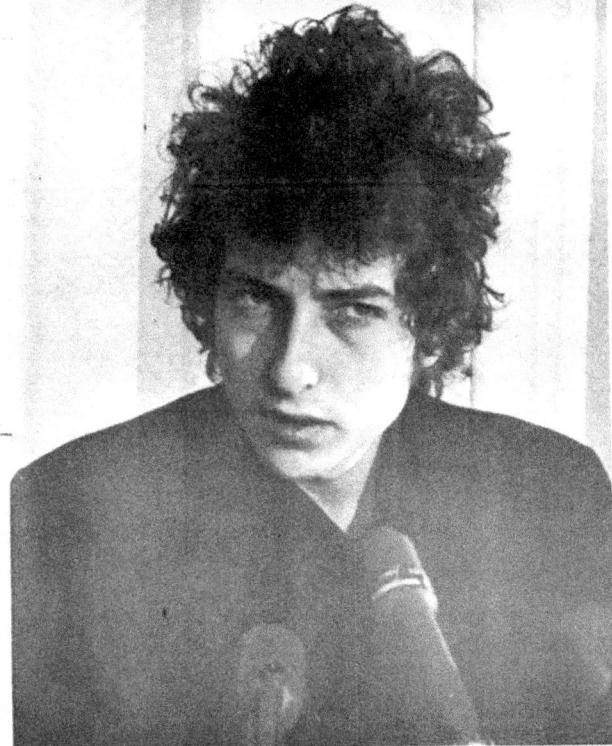

"only a pawn in their game"

KRLA ARCHIVES

DYLAN

By Eden

You're searching—you're looking everywhere—you're trying desperately to find the man they call *Dylan*. You ask everyone—maybe even *him*—and you struggle to discover just exactly "where he's at."

And you fail—as you *must* fail—because Bob Dylan can be in no one place. He never stands in yesterday, and he hasn't yet arrived at tomorrow. And today? Well, that's almost gone.

He isn't what *I* say he is, nor is he all the things which *you* might want him to be. He might be the composite of all the observations made of him, but mostly he is—Dylan.

Possibly the only honest representation of the man they call Dylan which I can offer you, then, is just the one composed of all those observations.

One man who has had the vantage point of closer observation is Billy James, Manager of Talent Acquisition and Development for Columbia Records.

Billy immediately shrugs off the robes of the "Cream judge:" "I cannot take the position that I am a *friend* of his—I have been a business associate of his for the length of time he has been signed with Columbia records. As a business associate, I prefer never to discuss artists' personal lives, particularly when they are extremely well-known."

Tries To Like

So often Dylan is plagued by the useless, irrelevant questions of nagging reporters attempting to tie him down. Having watched this, Billy comments: "I think he will make attempts to like people even when it's obvious to him that they *dislike* him. *His* evaluation of silly questions and a *questioner's* evaluation of a silly question may be different."

At a recent press conference which Bob held at Columbia Records in Los Angeles, someone asked him if he had any feelings. Annoyed with this sort of inane question, Billy continues: "I think it's ludicrous for one human being to ask another human being—'Don't you have any feelings?'

"Nevertheless, someone *did* ask that question. So, the question *deserved* a silly answer, and he said 'No!'"

Dylan has written—"She Belongs to Me,"—in which he says, "She's got everything she needs—she's an artist, she don't look back."

Bob Dylan is an artist, and perhaps in *this* context, he belongs to *us*. Considering Dylan, for a moment, as an artist attempting to communicate with people, Billy theorized:

"I think whatever process goes on within the mind of an artist concerning communication, goes on in Dylan's mind. I don't think he directs his work *toward* anyone—I think he *works*. People respond to this work or they don't. Any 'act' is communication, so of course—what he does *communicates*.

"If everything could be explained in words, art wouldn't exist in the first place, and it's grossly unfair to expect an artist to explain his work *in other words*. You know—'what does that painting *mean*?'—it means what it *means* and that's it!

"The function of the artist is that which *he* attaches to *himself*."

Dylan Cult

In speaking of the so-called "Dylan-cult" which recently declared itself so upset over Dylan's electrification in concert, Billy explained: "They accepted him when they could identify with him easily. When they could buy a corduroy cap and a harmonica holder just like his. When he sang songs of social protest—songs that *seem to them* to be songs of social protest, when he was communicating on a level that was understood quite readily by a certain segment of his audience—then he was accepted.

"When he moved out—he picked up people *and* lost people—every step of the way. It hasn't moved smoothly."

But what of Dylan's influence on contemporary thought, and music, and literature? *He* will deny its existence.

Billy is somewhat more positive in his own personal analysis of Dylan's influence: "Sure, he has become the most significant creator in the field of literature and popular music in the United States. His influence is quite, quite far-reaching—musically and verbally.

"That influence manifests itself in his ability to make people think and also to help them enjoy themselves. I think we get kind of pompous in evaluating Dylan. Hey!—he's a lot of fun, his work is *fun*!!"

Dylan? No, that was Billy James' observations *on*, and *around* Bob Dylan. If you really want to find Bob Dylan, you're going to have to find him for yourself.

BEAT Photo: Chuck Boyd

It may be a very long search for you—but undoubtedly, one well-worth the journey.

"I'll never finish saying everything I feel, but I'll be doing my part to make some sense out of the way we're living . . . or not living."

"Whatever else you say about me, everything I do and sing and write comes out of ME."

These words belong to Bob Dylan, and Dylan belongs—to no one. He only sort of *shares* himself—briefly—with anyone who might be interested. He shares himself, too, with time—with all the ages, for Dylan seems to be infinite—a universal entity.

But most of all—Bob Dylan is a human being. Someone pretty much like you and me—only different.

Barry McGuire spent several evenings talking with Bob, sharing with him a moment or two in time. "I was really *gassed* to meet Bobby—the words he has written gave me the impression that he was some sort of prophet. I was very anxious to meet him—and when I did, I was speechless!"

Barry found Bob for just a few brief moments, but when he did, he "found a very searching, hungry person. He chooses his words very carefully and hesitates between each one—so he sometimes appears to be stumbling. When he's just with two or three people, he becomes very focused and intent on what he's saying."

Digs R&B

Barry remembers how Bob laughed and said, "People ask me how come I'm using a R 'n' R band—ain't that weird? Other than the fact that I *dig* it—if I told people why, it would be all over! So I won't tell 'em!!"

Then Barry softly recalls attending one of Bobby's performances: "The concert was really like going to church. There were thousands of kids there, and they just sat and listened!!"

Then, his voice caught by emotion, Barry says: "He's so fragile—so frail—he looks like they could really hurt him. He's so very delicate, that I just sort of want to be his bodyguard to make sure that no one hurts him."

Dylan shares with his fans, an admiration of other artists and performers. So, in turn, other performers are fans of his. John Lennon of the Beatles said: "We were in Paris, back in January '64. Paul knew of Dylan. We cadged an LP

I am still runnin I guess
but my road has seen many
 changes
for I've served my time as a
 refugee
in mental terms an in physical
 terms
an many a fear has vanished
an many an attitude has fallen
an many a dream has faded
an I know I shall meet the snowy
 North
again – but with changed eyes nex
 time round
t walk lazily down it's streets
an linger by the edge of town
find old friends if they're still
 around
talk t the old people
an the young people
running yes . . .
but stoppin for a while
embracin what I left
an lovin it – for I learned by now
never t expect
what it can not give me
 —DYLAN

of his—'Freewheelin'—went potty over it. In America we met him. He was great, once you got to know him. He has a Beatle sense of humor."

Bob has subsequently said that John is one of the few people whom he has been able to like every time he has met him.

Self-Taught

Bob is a talented, sensitive musician and he has taught himself to play the piano, guitar, organ, autoharp, and the harmonica. His former record producer, Tom Wilson, has said of him: "He is a fine piano player, you know. People don't know that. And hearing his songs for the first time is like a big emotional experience. You just know it's something beautiful whatever the subject. He's a poet."

In contrast, Bob has said that the only instrument which he really has fun with is the harmonica, because it's the only instrument he feels really comfortable with.

A reporter once told Dylan that he looked like a young Charlie Chaplin, to which Bob replied: "Chaplin *did* influence me, believe it or not. I watched all his silent movies, copied some of his movements." The reporter then went on to exclaim his great surprise.

Joan Baez has said of Bob's writing: "Bobby's songs are powerful as poetry, powerful as music. Bobby is expressing what I—and many other young people—feel, what we want to say."

Many people—both young and not so young—have adopted Bob Dylan as their spokesman, their leader, the man who represents the ultimate and final truth in the universe for them.

Find Your Own

But Bob will take no credit for this, will disengage himself from this position entirely. He writes for himself, and offers it to any who will listen and can find a meaning for themselves within his work.

"I listen all the time. Not to the radio. But out there in the street where it's all going on." This is Dylan.

"You ask 'How does it feel to be an idol?' It'd be silly of me to answer, wouldn't it?" And this is Dylan.

Dylan—a man of words, and songs, and feelings. A man of love and hate and fear. A man like every other in the world—a man who stands alone, surrounded. A man—named DYLAN.

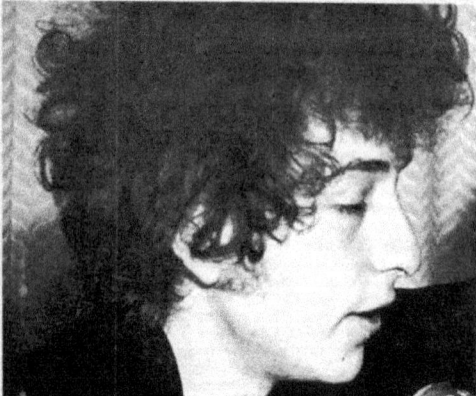
"like a rolling stone"   BEAT Photo: Chuck Boyd

KRLA ARCHIVES

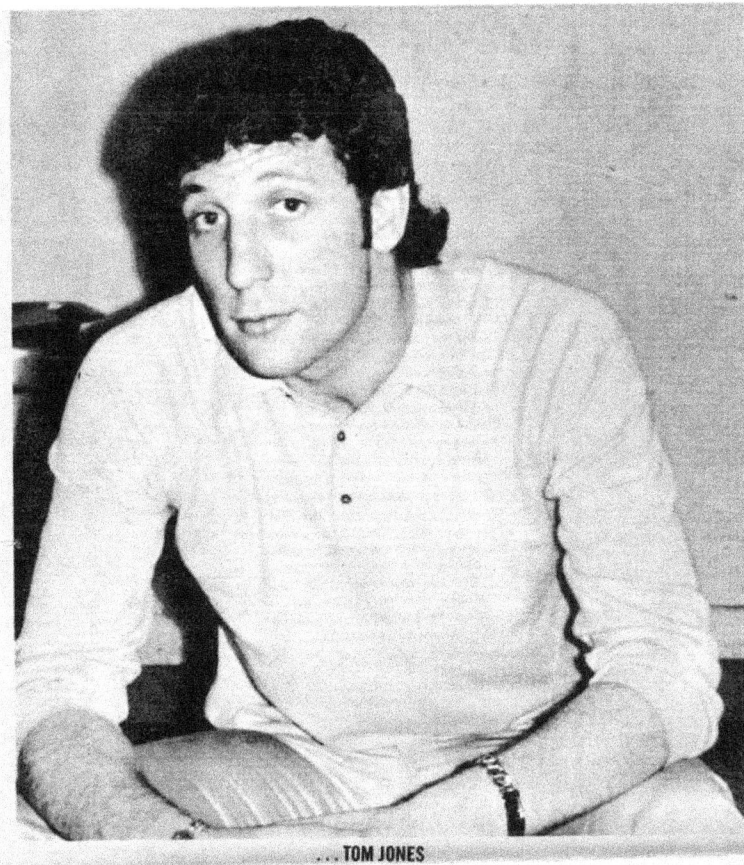

...TOM JONES

Yeah, Well Tom...
A Jones Boy Makes Good

By Tammy Hitchcock

Well, I finally did it—got Tom Jones on our "Yeah, Well Hot Seat." Of course, I was unduly pressured into it. Every female in *The BEAT* office is mad for the guy (myself included only I don't admit it). So, whenever we need a story or a picture of just about anything else someone always pops up with: "How about Tom Jones?"

Yeah, well how about Tom Jones? First off, you all know that Tom is from Pontypridd, Wales. The Pontypridd citizenship considers Tom a real hometown boy made good. But Tom just considers himself Tommy Jones Woodward.

So, it was a complete shock to Tom when he paid a visit to his home and was actually mobbed. "You just don't expect people that you've known all your life to suddenly chase you down the street!"

Yeah, well why not, Tom? I mean, people I've known all of my life chase me down the street. Bill collectors, dog catchers, neighbors I've borrowed a car from and forgotten to return (well, I'm not perfect you know. *Almost* perfect, though). Anyway, all those kind of people chase me *all* the time so I don't know why you should be any exception even if you are Tom Jones.

Love?

Now, of course, Tom is a big star all over the world. But it wasn't always such easy going. "For a long time we were just getting by, had a lot of let-downs. I talked it over with Melinda and I said, 'What do you think, love?'"

Yeah, well my name is *not* Melinda, Tom. It's Tammy. And Tammy doesn't sound even *remotely* like Melinda. So, naturally I'm crushed.

But you did tag a love onto the end of it so I guess that makes up for it a little bit. Only how come you didn't spell it "luv?" Maybe you didn't know that everyone from the British Isles spells love "luv." They'd *better* spell it "luv" 'cause that's where we copied it from and we're bound to get our Yankee tempers up if we find out we've been cheated!!!

Tom has a fantastic voice and everyone knows it—even Tom. "If I didn't have the voice I would never have had the nerve to be a singer," says he.

Yeah, well with your looks, Tom, who cares what you sound like? I mean, you could just stand there and read the stock market reports out loud and I'd dig you (and so would the boss.)

Proby Vs. Tom

P. J. Proby has been constantly bringing up the subject of how much Tom tries to sound like P.J. (or so P.J. *thinks* anyway). But Tom declares: "I'm sure we are different enough for this not to matter much."

Yeah, well you bet your life you're different, Tom. Your pants don't split!

Tom's manager, Gordon Mills, was explaining how they cut "It's Not Unusual." "We tried different instrumentations. We tried vibes and glockenspiel and all sorts of different combinations..."

Use Tom's Voice

Yeah, well all that's fine but why didn't you guys forget the glockenspiel and just use Tom's voice backed up with an orchestra in the first place instead of fooling around with the glockenspiel and nockelfogal and all that other.

You may think that the minute a record is a hit the money begins rolling in. Tom says it just ain't so. "It'll be months before the money from the record comes in."

Yeah, well you think *you've* got it bad. It'll be at least *centuries* before any money from a record of mine comes in!

When Tom left Pontypridd to conquer the world of pop he was especially determined to make it because "I don't think I could face the boys back home if I didn't make it."

Yeah, well never mind the boys back home. You could face me any time, Tom. Which reminds me, I haven't seen you around me in quite sometime. Fact of the matter is—I haven't seen you around me at all! Now, I wonder why that is.

The Beatles' Movie Script

(Continued From Page 2)

Beatles is simply that there are *four* of them. What difference does that make, you say? It makes a big difference. It means that whatever script they finally decide upon must have *four* equally important roles. Because the Beatles insist on sharing equally.

It also means that before they make that final decision all four of them must agree on it. If only one of the Beatles is against the proposed movie—it's off.

Paul states this emphatically when he says that they must have "complete" agreement among themselves before they will even begin a movie.

So, there you have it. The Beatles know what they *don't* want for their next film and they know what they *do* want. But they can't find it. Want to help?

At this point with only three months left before they are scheduled to begin filming they are open to any suggestions. Piles of scripts are being read everyday in the hopes of uncovering the one they want. If you are a budding script writer or know of someone who is, by all means submit the scripts to the Beatles.

You never know, you may be lucky this time.

The Shindigger Returns
Wellingtons Entertain Our Troops

By The Shindigger

Howdy Hi, Shindiggers. Bet you thought you'd heard the last from me. Well, just between the two-million of us—so did I! But I have something very special to tell you about, and so they have allowed me these few lines to talk to you.

I'm sure that you all remember the Wellingtons—the wonderful group of boys who sang regularly on "Shindig." Well, during the last two weeks in December of last year, I spoke to George Patterson of the group, and he told me something which I just have to pass along to you.

People seem to be very quick these days to put down the younger generation. But there are some members of that younger generation who ignore "some people" and go right on being great anyway.

We all know that there is a war going on in Viet Nam, and some of us are trying to do something about it. Some of us are just sitting back and pretending that it isn't there. Some of us are trying to help the others who are over there fighting in any way we can.

Ease The Pain

People like Bob Hope, and other fine performers give of their time and energies to entertain our fighting forces in Viet Nam, so that we can try to ease the pain of war at least a little bit.

But we forget sometimes that Viet Nam isn't the only troubled spot on earth, and that we are sending our young men in uniform to other places on the globe, to protect our freedom and defend our way of life.

Our story starts back about three months ago when "Shindig" was filming two special shows on location in Hawaii. It was there that George ran into an old high school friend who had been flighting in Viet Nam for a year and a half, and was on a short leave.

He explained to George that his regiment hadn't had *any* entertainment of *any* sort in all that time, so George and the other two Wellingtons—Eddie and Kirby—decided that they should do something about that.

So, the three decided that they would form their own little show, and began talking to the appropriate people in Washington for a clearance to complete their plans.

Enough, Thanks

But they were told that they were already more than enough volunteers to entertain the fighting men in Viet Nam, and that actually entertainers were more badly needed in places like Korea, Japan, and the Phillipines. At first it seemed kind of odd, because people had all but forgotten these places, but it didn't take the Wellingtons long to agree to go. They wanted to help out—no matter *where* they were needed—even if it wouldn't mean quite as much glory.

So, together with some of the "Shindig" dancers, and Dolan Ellis, who used to be with the Christy Minstrels, they put together a show, took their shots, and headed for the Orient.

All three of the Wellingtons have already served their active duty, and they are well acquainted with the loneliness which one can experience on a Christmas away from home. So they sang no Christmas songs on their show—only tunes which could boost the morale of the men in their audience.

No Medals

There won't be any grand State Department medals awarded to these boys. They didn't go to Viet Nam to entertain our boys while under fire. They didn't put in any comical appearance on the battle front.

But they *did* remember that we have young men and boys in uniform in places all around the globe, and those boys will be very grateful that someone remembered them during this last Christmas time.

Christmas is the time of giving, and the Wellingtons saw to it that many men, far away from their native land, received their gifts during the Yuletide season—they gave to them the gift of love. And, isn't that what Christmas is all about?

KRLA ARCHIVES

Taping A TV Show With The Four Seasons

By Carol Deck

The stage was cold and there were very few people around. This wasn't the usual chaotic taping session, for although they were in America, what they were taping would be shown in England.

The few technicians present were slowly and silently getting ready for the act they were about to film.

Bob Gaudio was the first of The 4 Seasons to come up from the even colder dressing room. He was quickly joined by Tommy DeVito, Joe Long and the "Sound of the 4 Seasons" Frankie Valli.

All four were dressed in slacks, boots and velour shirts. Frankie's velour was a brilliant blue, while the others' were brown.

Bob took time to answer a few questions for a young reporter, then all four gathered quickly on stage.

Camera Set

"Let's Hang On" burst from the sound speakers and The Seasons lip-synced it once while the technicians set up camera angles and everyone got ready.

Then the director said "let's take it" and they ran through the entire number. The director said "I like it, do it again." Frankie asked if they had done anything wrong and the director told them no, just to do whatever they had done the first time one more time!

So they ran it through again. Even though they were supposed to be lip-synced all four of the boys were singing their hearts out. Their music means too much to them to fake it, they have to do it real.

They did the entire number several more times. Between takes they would answer more questions for the reporter and smoke a few cigarettes.

One question which they have been asked by everyone who interviews them is "Why the Wonder Who?" They had a fast rising "Let's Hang On" on the charts then they put out "Don't Think Twice" under the name The Wonder Who and everyone has been wondering why.

Bob explained simply, "We had 'Let's Hang On' out and we felt that another record under the name 4 Seasons at the same time would hurt us." They didn't seriously expect to fool anyone, for after five years together Frankie's high true voice is recognizable to practically everyone, but Bob said: "People caught on a little sooner than we expected."

Then they went back for another take of the number for England's "Tops in Pops" television show. The show was only one of numerous ones they were filming during their week's stay on the West Coast.

Busy Week

In four days they filmed this same song for "Lloyd Thaxton," "9th Street West," "Hollywood Discotheque," "Never Too Young," and "Where The Action Is."

Bob admitted that it does get a little tiring to keep singing the same song over and over but they've found a way to relieve the monotony.

"We sing out of tune." When a group is lip-syncing for TV, the audience can't hear anything they actually sing anyway so these boys come up with some really weird sounds on taping sessions sometimes. "It helps you to smile in the morning," Bob added.

He also tried to explain or describe the Season's sound, which ideas on which of today's acts will last as long as they have. They all

has been selling hits for over five years now. "It's a little more thought out than a lot of things nowadays. We don't sing in thirds, we do more four part things with our voicing."

Having been around for five years, they have some definite agree that of today's top acts, the Beatles and Supremes are sure to last for many years.

Nineteen Hits

Since their first big hit, "Sherrie," they have had 19 single hits and have the distinction of having had two of those at the peak of the Beatle's virtual ownership of the American charts. Both "Dawn" and "Rag Doll" came during that national epidemic known as Beatlemania.

After the taping was finally finished the boys rushed off to tape three more shows. And as soon as they finish this series they'll probably start another with their next release – a single and an album titled "Working My Way Back to You."

They certainly live up to their name – year around, every year the 4 Seasons are great.

On the BEAT

By Louise Criscione

An English reporter got brave and asked Paul McCartney if the Stones weren't more popular Stateside than the Beatles. Paul grinned: "Are they? I don't think so. I wouldn't like to say who's more popular. The Stones have got their publicity agent and we've got ours. It's up to you who you believe."

Paul then went on to say that the Stones were "good lads" and "I don't want people to think that it'll come to us sticking our tongues out at each other like school kids."

Case you girls are interested, Paul declares that he and Jane are not married but that he will probably marry her eventually because they have been going together for three years now. Least he's honest, I think.

Herman was talking to Georgie Fame recently and he had quite a bit to say about our West Coast. "Los Angeles is one of the worst cities in America. It's not surprising they have so much racial trouble."

Thanks, Herman

"It's like a million worlds rolled into one. All around Beverly Hills are some real drag slums and dirty filthy shack towns. The contrasts are so violent that racial bitterness is really bad."

However, Herman did go on to say that San Francisco is a great place but "you must never call it 'Frisco' – they get a bit upset about that!"

... PAUL McCARTNEY

Leave it to Herman. He really is a nice guy but he seems to be forever opening his mouth and saying the wrong thing. Suppose he'll learn one of these days.

Another mouth-opener is P.J. Proby. Last week he mentioned to the press that Gary Leeds of the Walker Brothers wears a wig because he thinks his hair is getting thin in front. Well, you can just imagine Gary's absolute fury when he read P.J.'s remarks!

Although Dylan continues to deny that he is married it has been confirmed that Dylan was indeed married on Nov. 22 in New York. The bride is reportedly from Bearsville, New York but is as yet unnamed.

Brian Epstein thinks that Ringo is the best thing that ever happened to the Beatles despite the fact that Pete Best is in the process of suing them over that very thing. "It was something they wanted and that I carried out," said Epstein. "It was for so many reasons a quite brilliant move." Agreed.

DC5 — Maybe Not

Dave Clark, as you know, has been offered an American TV series but he says that he might decline because "it could be overexposure." Time will tell but personally I think it would be good for the Five and even better for their fans.

Think the Remains are gonna be big? I guess Ed Sullivan does because he put them on his show. Time will tell about this one too.

Motown thinks that Len Barry's "Like A Baby" is an awful lot like the Supremes' "Baby Love." They're joking, right? "Like A Baby" is a carbon copy of "1-2-3."

Funny caption in "Fabulous" under a picture of Brian Jones. Said: "I know I'm naughty but I'm nice."

Charlie Watts says that the Stones' latest recording session at RCA was their best yet. "They were all originals written by Keith and Mick and although I don't say they are the best songs the Stones have ever written I think that musically they are the best thing we've ever done."

Charlie went on to reveal that they did one 12 minute track which will undoubtedly be featured in one of their up-coming albums.

Charlie said that when the Stones played a few dates on our college circuit they couldn't understand why there were no screams. But when the college kids began giving them standing ovations at the end of each song they figured they were doing all right!

QUICK ONES: Supremes honored again. They will be featured in a layout in *Look* as the nation's number one female group and will also appear on the cover of the U.S. official publication, *Africa* ...

... CHARLIE WATTS

Win two weeks in the Swingingest cities in America plus $5,000 spending money and a part in a Hollywood movie!

HOLLYWOOD! **SAN FRANCISCO!**

IT'S PROCTER & GAMBLE'S SWING DING SWEEPSTAKES!

A SWINGING DISCOVERY OF AMERICA ON AN AMERICAN AIRLINES ASTROJET

NEW ORLEANS!

NEW YORK!

Win the swingingest trip of your life! Grand Prize is two weeks in four of America's greatest cities: New York! New Orleans! San Francisco! Hollywood! American Airlines will take you there—Procter & Gamble will give you $5,000 to make sure you have fun!

Plus—when you're in Hollywood you'll have a part in an American International movie like "Robinhood Jones." Dine with American International's stars. Meet other stars, too—like David Janssen and Chuck Connors. And you can bring two people with you!

**50 Special Local Winners!
One in your area!
Win a trip to Hollywood
and a part in a movie!**

50 2nd-prize winners get a trip to Hollywood and will appear in an American International movie...and nobody makes Bikini pictures like 'em! It's an expense-paid trip for you and two other people! There'll be a winner in your area so your chances are great!

MORE THAN 10,000 OTHER PRIZES!
3rd 50 swinging Honda motorbikes
4th 50 $100 shopping sprees at your favorite store
5th 100 General Electric stereo Mustangs—portable phonographs
6th 1,250 G.E. transistor radios
7th 10,000 swinging Long Play record albums

You can't win unless you enter—so send in the coupon now. Enter as often as you like. You'll find extra entry blanks at the Swing Ding Sweepstakes Display where you shop.

Great products that keep you looking, acting, and feeling—swinging!

RULES: Send entry blank with proof-of-purchase from any two of these products—Lilt, Head & Shoulders, Gleem, Secret, Hidden Magic, Liquid Prell (both end flaps from carton, or label from bottle or can); or with plain paper (approx. 3" x 5") on which two of these product names are written in plain block letters. Entries from Missouri must be on plain paper and not accompanied by proof of purchase. Submit as many entries as you wish, provided each is in accordance with the rules and mailed separately. Prizes as listed will be awarded from a random drawing to be conducted by the D. L. Blair Corporation, an independent judging organization. Decision of judges final. Only one prize awarded to any person or household. Rules and extra blanks available at your store or by sending stamped, self-addressed envelope to Swing Ding Sweepstakes, P. O. Box 432, Cincinnati, Ohio 45299. Sweepstakes open to residents of the U. S. except employees of Procter & Gamble, D. L. Blair Corporation, their advertising agencies and families. Government regulations apply. **No purchase required.**

Win two weeks in the swingingest cities in America!
Mail to: Swing Ding Sweepstakes, Box 671, New York, N.Y. 10046

Name

Address

City   State   Zip Code

Please place the call letters of your favorite radio station on the outside lower right-hand corner of your envelope.

Entries must be postmarked by March 15, 1966, and received by March 25, 1966. Extra entry blanks are at your local store.

KRLA ARCHIVES

Inside KRLA
By Eden

Hi gang! Promised that we would continue our little tour of the fab studios of KRLA this week, so if you're ready—here we go again!!!

This week we are beginning in rather an unusual sort of a spot. If you look around you and find that you don't recognize anything —that's 'cause we're standing in the KRLA DJ Redecoration Center.

You might be interested to learn that the ol' Emp has decided to completely *redecorate* himself. Yep—that's what he said on his program a few weeks back.

Now, I don't really know quite what the old Royal One has in mind, but it must be something really super fantastic, or something. Anyways, you'll notice all the hubbub and total chaos in the room. That's to be expected, of course—after all, it's not every day that an emperor remodels himself.

But since he hasn't finished quite yet, I guess we'll just have to wait for the results.

In the mean time, The BEAT would like to congratulate Mel Hall—our program director—on being selected Program Director of The Year, by Bill Gavin.

More congratulations going out this week to all of the lucky listeners in KRLA-Land who won some of the over $20,000 in cash and over 600 records which were given away during the first week and a half of January in the Music and Cash contest.

Yep—ya gotta hand it to Captain Showbiz—he really *is* some kind of contest-thinker upper!!! Now, just wait till you see what he's got *thunk-up* for February!!!

While I'm thinking about it, did all of you catch Dick Biondi's fantastic show on New Year's Eve? That was probably about the greatest thing ever! There were nearly eighty different artists and entertainers who fell by to say hello and to drop in a little New Year's greeting to everyone at KRLA.

People on the show included The Beatles, The Rolling Stones, The Dave Clark Five, The Supremes, Smokey Robinson of the Miracles, Jonathan Winters, Shelley Berman, Stan Freburg, Andy Williams, Brian Wilson, Frank Sinatra, Sonny and Cher, the Byrds, and nearly everyone else in the entertainment industry.

Yep—it's *always* KRLA. First in music, first in fun—*first* in the hearts of Los Angeles!!!

Four New Records For Dave's Fans

Hey gang—big news for all of you Hullabalooers out there. In keeping with the spirit of the New Year, Dave Hull has done a little up-dating on his fan club, and now there are a whole new set of officers.

The outgoing officers were: Colleen Ludwick and Rhio—both girls are graduating this year and going back East in June.

The incoming officers are Linda Thor, Kim Sudoll, Anne Cummings, Ellen Campbell, and Jan Jackson. Oddly enough, all of these new girls go to the old Hullabalooer's cross-town high school rival—Mark Keppel High.

But both the Hullabalooer and The BEAT welcome these new officers and wish them a lot of luck in the New Year—and with the old Hullabalooer around . . . they'll probably *need* it!!

More big news about the club is the new membership campaign now in progress. To join, just send $1.00 with your name, address, zip code, and your birthdate to: the Dave Hull International Fan Club, 634 Sefton Ave., Monterey Park.

Members will receive tickets to premiers, bulletins and pictures each month, and will have a chance to be in on all the zany fun and activities of the Hullabalooer.

And right now, each person who recruits 25 new members for the club will receive four new records from the Fab KRLA Tunedex.

So hurry up and join everyone, 'cause there's a whole year of fun 'n' stuff waiting for you with the Hullabalooer and all his friends.

NOW! Thru Jan. 30
THE DEEP SIX
With Their Hit
"The Rising Sun"
The ICE HOUSE GLENDALE
folk music in concert
Reservations: 245-5043
also on the show
Fred Thompson

KRLA BEAT Subscription
SAVE 33% Of Regular Price

☐ 1 YEAR — 52 Issues — $5.00   ☐ 2 YEARS — $8.00
☐ 6 MONTHS — $3.00

Enclosed is _____   ☐ CASH   ☐ CHECK
Send to: ....
Address: ....
City: .... State: .... Zip ....

MAIL YOUR ORDER TO: KRLA BEAT
6290 Sunset, Suite 504
Hollywood, Calif. 90028
Foreign Rate: $9.00—52 Issues

KRLA PROGRAM DIRECTOR MEL HALL, selected as one of the nation's "Radio Men of the Year," is shown here with a special trophy presented to him in honor of his selection—the "pidgeon of the year" award.

KRLA Tunedex

DAVE HULL

BOB EUBANKS

DICK BIONDI

JOHNNY HAYES

EMPEROR HUDSON

CASEY KASEM

CHARLIE O'DONNELL

BILL SLATER

This Week	Last Week	Title	Artist
1	1	WE CAN WORK IT OUT/DAY TRIPPER	The Beatles
2	2	LIGHTNIN' STRIKES	Lou Christie
3	3	SOUNDS OF SILENCE	Simon & Garfunkel
4	4	FLOWERS ON THE WALL	Statler Brothers
5	6	YOU DIDN'T HAVE TO BE SO NICE	The Lovin' Spoonful
6	5	LET'S HANG ON	Four Seasons
7	18	NO MATTER WHAT SHAPE	T-Bones
8	15	I FOUGHT THE LAW	Bobby Fuller Four
9	17	I SEE THE LIGHT	Five Americans
10	9	IT'S MY LIFE	The Animals
11	22	MY LOVE	Petula Clark
12	7	RUN, BABY, RUN	The Newbeats
13	8	LIES	The Knickerbockers
14	10	SHE'S JUST MY STYLE	Gary Lewis & The Playboys
15	11	A YOUNG GIRL	Noel Harrison
16	14	HOLE IN THE WALL	The Packers
17	13	I WILL	Dean Martin
18	12	EBB TIDE	Righteous Brothers
19	21	AS TEARS GO BY	The Rolling Stones
20	16	ENGLAND SWINGS	Roger Miller
21	30	UPTIGHT	Stevie Wonder
22	29	A MUST TO AVOID	Herman's Hermits
23	19	JENNY TAKE A RIDE	Mitch Ryder & The Detroit Wheels
24	—	JUST LIKE ME	Paul Revere & The Raiders
25	26	FIVE O'CLOCK WORLD	The Vogues
26	23	THE DUCK	Jackie Lee
27	25	MY GENERATION	The Who
28	31	ONE HAS MY NAME	Barry Young
29	33	ONE TOO MANY MORNINGS	The Association
30	28	THUNDERBALL	Tom Jones
31	34	LIKE A BABY	Len Barry
32	—	SANDY	Ronnie & The Daytonas
33	—	ILLUSIVE BUTTERFLY	Bob Lind
34	39	I AIN'T GONNA EAT MY HEART OUT	The Young Rascals
35	—	A WELL RESPECTED MAN	The Kinks
36	36	SLOOP DANCE	The Atlantics
37	—	SET YOU FREE THIS TIME	The Byrds
38	—	CRYIN' TIME	Ray Charles
39	—	MY WORLD IS EMPTY WITHOUT YOU	The Supremes
40	35	SUNDAY AND ME	Jay and The Americans

KRLA ARCHIVES

For Girls Only

By Shirley Poston

I have a feeling this is going to be one of my shorter columns (only nine million words instead of ten million). Why this sudden change? Well, it's this way. At the moment, my mind happens to be a complete blank. Like always. Only this time, it's worse.

You see, there's this boy. He's a good friend of mine, and although he doesn't know it, I'm an even *better* friend of his. If you get the picture.

And my mind is a complete blank because he just stopped by the office.

I fear that by the time he left, he *also* got the picture. You know, I said hello very casually while I was fainting.

Talk Trouble

I've never exactly had a lot of trouble talking, as all of you know all too well. But honestly, when he walks into a room, I can't even *think*, much less *talk*.

And when I do talk, I say things backwards or make really moronic remarks. Isn't that a ghastly feeling? I wonder what causes it.

Come to think of it, I *know* what causes it. I only hope that *he* doesn't. Maybe he just thinks I'm the nervous type or something. He probably also thinks I've just robbed a bank the way I couldn't look him in the eye.

The only good thing about that feeling is the fact that it's a universal problem. It even happens to boys when they're around someone they have a thing about.

Yes, yes, I know, it's about time for me to stop talking about rational stuff and say "speaking of George." Okay, you asked for it.

Harrison Fan

Speaking of George, I've received a letter from another Harrison fan, containing the greatest "dream" yet! Naturally, I lost the letter immediately (what is my problem?) (never answer that question), but I do remember the general gist of her masterpiece.

It seems that for some reason she is walking along a ledge outside a hotel. Well, the ledge is on the hotel, and she's on the ledge. Oh, nuts. Why can't I ever explain ANYTHING?

Anyway, I hope you get the idea because I can't think of any sensible way to express it.

So, she's walking along this ledge (Oh, I remember, she was locked in her room and couldn't get out so she decided to pull a Robin Boyd) and whose room should she pass but George (Yum) Harrison's. At which time she conveniently becomes very dizzy. George, of course, races to the rescue and climbs out on the ledge after her. Then they both get dizzy and have to hang on to each other for dear life. (Now, isn't that a *shame*.)

That's where her "dream" ends, because that's as far as she's gotten. Incidentally, they've been up there on that ledge for three weeks now.

Speaking of Robin Boyd (and, for a change, I was), I want to say thanks for all the comments you've made about our rare bird. I just luv to write about her (and turn green with envy), and it's nice to know that you like to read about her nutty adventures.

One question though. I could go on writing about her for the next jillion years, but I would like to ask your advice. Like, should I? I mean, if you ever get tired of her, let me know!

Now I'd like to ask you another question. Have you ever shut your ear in a car door?

Broken Ear

Well, were you ready for that? No, I didn't figure you would be. But I'd really like to know. If you haven't, or don't know of anyone who has, that means I am the only living human being (using the term loosely) in this world who has ever broken an ear! In a car door, that is.

Could this have happened to me because I am also the *clumsiest* living human in this world? Could be.

Seriously, it really did happen, and if you've ever done anything this utterly ridiculous, will you please write immediately and tell me all about it so I can stop feeling like such a dolt.

Oh, a bit of news. The latest expression in Jolly Olde England is "dolly," which means a pretty bird. Oh, you've already heard about it? Well, it was news to *me*.

Writhing "Girl"

More news. If John Lennon could see me and two of my friends writhing in front of the hi-fi, playing his "Girl" track over and over, he would call the men with the nets. And it's all his fault. No one, and I repeat, *no one* has the right to make a record that great.

No kidding, every time he takes that deep, long breath, I absolutely *panic*. Comments, anyone?

Say, boys (I mean *come on*, you surely don't think I don't *know* you're still reading this column whether I like it or not), I have good news for you.

I just heard from one of my spies that the fashions for the new year will feature even shorter skirts, if such a thing is possible.

I'm not too upset about it all. After the 1965 styles, everyone already knows I have creepy-looking knees, so what the heck.

But think about *this* for a moment. No one gets all bent about shorter skirts on girls, but just let some poor boy let his hair grow a little long and wham, off to the detention ward.

I think that is the most unfair thing I've ever heard of. It is really *mean*. Because it's so snivley (if that's the way you spell it) (it's the way *I* spell it) and petty and dumb to judge a person by his hair style.

If I were a boy, I'd grow a pony tail, just for spite. And tie it up with a red ribbon! After all, do people go around telling girls how to wear their hair? Course, a couple of people *have* mentioned that it would be nice if I'd *comb* mine once in a while, but that's beside the point.

Really, you would think the older generation would have better things to do besides getting all shook up over *hair*, of all things.

Oh, there I go raving. And this was going to be one of my shorter columns. Sure, Shirl, tell us another.

Well, I'd better get going. There'll be another of my strange little record contests next week, so if you're a Herman fan, stay tuned. And if you aren't, stay tuned away and I'll see you next *BEAT*.

Bob and Bill to Produce

Shindig regulars the Wellingtons have been signed by United Artists Records for their first record.

The single will be titled "Go Ahead and Cry" and was written by Bill Medley of the Righteous Brothers.

It will be the first record produced by the Righteous Brothers, whose own releases are produced by Phil Spector.

KRLA ARCHIVES

This Mr. Jones Knows What's Up

The record business has been dominated by hard rock, folk rock, folk, protest, r&b, and other assorted pop music for quite a while now, but Jack Jones still consistently comes through with some smooth ballads that sell just as well.

From his first hit, "Lollipops and Roses," Jack has had nothing but success and even picked up two of the highly-prized Grammy awards along the way.

He won the Grammy for "best vocal performance, male" in 1961 for "Lollipops and Roses" and again in 1963 for "Wives and Lovers."

Jack is unique in that he appeals to practically everyone – adults and teenagers. His records are played on top 40 radio stations as well as middle-of-the-road and so-called 'good music' stations.

He attracts Broadway and Hollywood producers too, and has become one of the leading singers for movie and show songs.

Introduced "Livin'"

He introduced on records "Got A Lot of Livin' to Do" from "Bye Bye Birdie" and "Real Live Girl" from "Little Me."

He sang the winning song at the Academy Awards presentations in 1963 – "Call Me Irresponsible." And three of the five songs nominated in 1964 were also recorded by Jack – "Dear Heart," "My Kind of Town" and "Where Love Has Gone."

He has had great success with movie titles too. He sang "Where Love Has Gone" behind the actual picture credits and both his "Love With the Proper Stranger" and "Wives and Lovers" did very well on the charts.

Brief Recess

Then he took a brief recess from ballads and did "The Race Is On," a cheery country tune, before returning to ballads with "Just Yesterday."

This tremendous hunk of talent was discovered in San Francisco by Pete King, one of the industry's top arrangers.

Pete was visiting a small club in the Bay Area called Facks II when he heard this then 22-year-old baritone who was just starting out on his own after working a while with his actor-singer father, Alan Jones, in a night club act.

Pete was so impressed with the young singer that he placed a long distance call to the president of Kapp Records in New York and ranted and raved until he got the OK to sign him that very night.

5 Years Later

That was five years ago and neither Kapp Records nor Pete King have ever regretted the move. Jack just can't seem to miss at anything.

He's come through with a dozen best-selling albums, most of which bear the titles of his best selling singles.

His latest album is entitled, "There's Love and There's Love and There's Love." And that's about all you can say about this magnificent collection of love ballads so beautifully arranged by Nelson Riddle – there's love and there's love and there's Jack Jones, forever and ever.

Adventures of Robin Boyd

By Shirley Poston

CHAPTER ELEVEN

Robin Boyd went to bed very early Friday night and didn't sleep one single wink.

For the first half of the night, she stayed awake thinking up ways to get out of the house the next day without passing the tea pot on the living room mantle.

The second half of the night she stayed awake fearing for the sanity of people who stayed awake the first half of the night worrying about tea pots.

Well, that's not quite true.

There was nothing that odd about her wanting to elude said tea pot. Because George happened to be in it. (George, of course, happened to be her genie from Liverpool, who looked remarkably like another Liverpudlian of the same first name.) (Three guesses who.)

Fears For George

Actually, she had really stayed awake the second half of the night fearing for *George's* sanity. Because there was suddenly something *very* odd about *him*.

At first, George was forever grumbling at her. For giggling while he was trying to give her bird lessons. For nagging at him to tell her how he became a genie and how he was able to bestow upon her the magic power of turning herself into a *real* robin. For the way she dragged him out of a nice warm tea pot in the wee hours to come rescue her from the Beatles' garage. That sort of thing.

However, the last time she'd seen George, things had changed.

Oh, he still grouched at her and all, just like old times. *But*, he had, of *all* things, *squeezed* her hand. Not just *once*, either. *Twice!*

And this bit about the Rolling Stones. That *really* had Robin floored.

George was simply not the sort of genie who liked to go wandering about the four corners of the earth. *But*, what had he said when she'd told him she was going to England this weekend to find the Stones???

He said *"I'm going with you."* And what's more, he gave her a *look*.

Hmmmm, thought Robin, strangling her alarm clock before it had a chance to go off and awaken the entire household (to say nothing of the dead.)

George's Problem

What was George's problem anyroad? Could it possibly be that he was *interested?* (If you know what I mean.) (If you don't, get help.)

Pshaw, thought Robin, wondering what in the world a pshaw was. George *interested?* How ridiculous. Now what would a tall, dark, handsome, scrumptious, English genie see in *her?*

No, that wasn't his problem (blast it all) (as you may have gathered, Robin considered George to be somewhat of a luv) (if you *haven't* so gathered, get more help.)

Then it dawned on her.

"Ahah!" she cried, having seen too many old movies on the telly. Underneath her calm exterior, old George was a bit of a raver! And he wanted to get in on all the fun she was going to have terrorizing – visiting the Stones.

Well, George, good luck on *that* one! When Robin Boyd flew Stone-ward, Robin Boyd flew *alone*. She'd already promised herself that she wouldn't do anything silly, like kidnapping Mick Jagger for instance.

Three A Crowd

But, should she just happen to decide to break that promise, three would be a crowd. And not exactly what she had in mind.

(Robin was not a partial bird, but should she ever be forced to choose between her many faves, Mick Jagger's chances were excellent.) (So were John Lennon's.) (Guitar pick and all.)

Crawling wearily out of bed, Robin staggered to the closet and began plowing through it.

Things were going to be different this time. This time she was not going to spend her entire visit in real-robin form. In fact, she was going to change back into her sixteen-year-old self the moment she located the Stones. And she was going to look sharp!

In view of this happy prospect, Robin fainted repeatedly in her closet. During her moments of consciousness, she resumed her plowing.

By noon, Robin had found just the right thing to wear and had finally arrived at a plan. Which hadn't been easy because she not only had to escape from George, she also had to give her mother a rational explanation (which would be a nice change), as to why she would be away from home during the afternoon and evening.

The George part was a snap. After she'd dressed and washed and ironed her hair, Robin simply crawled out her bedroom window and entered the kitchen through the back door. Bypassing living room and tea pot entirely.

However, although she had conceived the aforementioned rational explanation (in other words, another big fat one), Robin feared the Mum part would be less of a snap.

But, when she found the kitchen empty, and a note on the table, she stopped being fearful. And became panic-stricken.

"Dear Robin," read the note. "We have gone over to Catalina to visit Aunt Zelda. Since you were there only last weekend, I felt you would rather remain at home. Besides, when I went into your room to discuss the matter, you were asleep in the closet. When we return home late this evening, I would like to discuss the matter of why you were asleep in the closet."

Robin dropped the note in horror. Oh, no! What if Aunt Zelda told them that although her beloved niece *had* been in Catalina last weekend, she had arrived at four-thirty in the *morning*, accompanied by a *genie*.

Then, as Robin struggled to regain her composure, she *knew* what she must do.

Kidnap Mick

When one was on one's way to kidnap Mick Jagger, one worried about tomorrow, tomorrow. And what she must do right now was *get cracking!*

And she did. After whispering the magic word ("Liverpool") so George wouldn't hear her, she took off so fast she all but left tire marks on the kitchen table.

Moments later, had anyone been scanning the stratosphere with a mighty telescope, they would have gone off to the nearest closet and fainted.

Not necessarily because of the small bird streaking through the skies.

Because of the object following that bird at the distance of approximately one mile.

For, you see, Robin was being tailed by a tea pot.

(To Be Continued Next Week)

Would You Believe...

By Susan

That the Animals plan on going into service to try and *put an end to war* ... when Mick Jagger was a boy he hated people kissing him... the Walker Brothers are American, but want to be British citizens ... Cher sometimes puts all her makeup on while driving a car ... Twinkle's real name is Lynn Annette Ripley ... Herman misses his mother's cooking when he's away ... George sent the Byrds a copy of "Help" from England ... Brian Epstein's father is the manager of John Lennon's father ... when Brian Jones quits the Stones, he wants very much to move to California because he considers it his second home ... two of the Animals opened up a bar in England and it really swings ... Roy Orbison is going to star in M.-G.M.'s "The Fastest Gun In The West" ... Marianne Faithfull has all her clothes made at Patrick Kerr's boutique ... Billy J. Kramer loses weight by drinking 3 glasses of water a day and eats nothing ... Jay of Jay and the Americans, was once a shoe salesman ... Elvis' first film, "The Pied Piper of Cleveland" was never released ... Twinkle got an idea for one of her songs from a girl whose boyfriend was in prison ... Andrew Oldham has cut a record entitled, "A Run In The Green and Tangerine Flaked Forest ... Sonny and Cher are number one in Switzerland ... Bob Dylan wrote "She Belongs To Me" about Joan Baez ... Eric Burdon's car bears a plate saying, "Florida, The Sunshine State" ... "Hard Day's Night" was banned in Mexico because of its "spicy-sexy" dialogue. It was thought unsuitable for children ... The Beach Boys have sold over 10 million records ... John Lennon is really Phil Spector in disguise??

KRLA ARCHIVES

Q: *My girlfriend and I have both liked the same boy for about two months, but he didn't pay any attention to either of us. Now all of a sudden he's starting to talk to me and has asked me to go out with him. I accepted, and this made my friend furious. How can I handle this situation without losing her as a friend? I really like this boy.*
(Jennifer T.)

A: Ask your girlfriend point-blank if she thinks you should break the date. If she says yes, she really isn't worth keeping as a friend because she's only thinking of herself. No matter what she says, don't break the date unless you really want to, and it doesn't sound like you do.

Q: *I tried your suggestion about fastening my hair with masking tape instead of a rubber band, but my hair is heavy and the tape won't hold it. I wear an up-do, and have to find something to hold it in place. Any more suggestions?*
(Pam K.)

A: Try using a shoe lace instead of tape. It can be tied tight enough to hold and won't break the hair like a rubber band.

Q: *I had a pair of white boots dyed black and now I want them white again. I can't afford to have it done at a shoe shop. Could you tell me if the dye you can buy would work, white over black I mean?*
(Simmie D.)

A: If the boots are leather, the new shoe coloring should work fine. If they're made from synthetic materials, we don't advise trying to dye them yourself.

Q: *This is a dumb question, I know, but I'm sixteen and I can't figure out why my eyes crinkle when I laugh. I thought this only happened to older people. Another thing, in movies and on TV, when stars smile, their eyes don't crinkle. Not even if they're about fifty years old. What can I do about this problem? (if it is one)?*
(Donna M.)

A: Some people "crinkle" around the eyes at sixteen, and some never do. It all depends on your skin and facial structure. About stars, watch closely next time and you'll see that many of them smile sideways instead of up-at-the-corners style (sounds odd, but you'll see what we mean). It's just one of many on-camera tricks. About your problem, it isn't one!

Q: *I would like to know how to end a telephone conversation politely. I know it's okay for you to say you have to go when you made the call, but what if someone calls you and talks for hours and you don't really want to talk? I have four close friends, and they all call me everyday. This is great, but I spend so much time on the phone, I can't even get my homework done. What can I do?*
(Georgeann P.)

A: This is a rather touch-type problem, but there is one way you can get around it without hurting anyone's feelings. If your folks haven't gotten after you about being on the phone so much, why not "encourage" them a little? Like saying "don't you think I spend too much time on the phone?" When they shout "YES!" there's your out, and your polite way of ending this endless conversation.

HINT OF THE WEEK

I think I've found a good way to soothe parents. My folks have been against the Beatles ever since I started liking them, and this caused a lot of family arguments. What I finally did was buy tickets to "Help" (I didn't know you could buy movie tickets in advance, but you can at some places) and that made it impossible for them to refuse to see the movie. When they did, they were really amazed. They actually thought the Beatles got up on stage and twitched or wiggled or something. They were pleasantly surprised, and things are a lot more pleasant at home now. Try this if your folks have doubts about your favorite!
(Ellen W.)

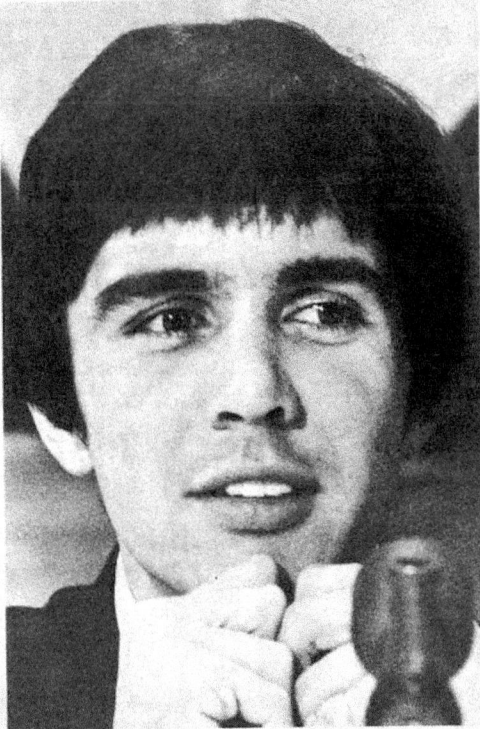

Look Before You Declare Dave Dying

Everyone (well, maybe not everyone. Maybe just the skeptics) continues to herald the death of the Dave Clark Five, popularity-wise. If they would only stop to think about it they would see how foolish and premature their predictions are.

For the Five are very much alive and kicking. Their latest single, "Over And Over," reached the number one spot on the nation's charts during Christmas week.

"Each of our 12 singles has sold a million," declared a delighted Dave Clark. "In under two years we have sold 12½ million records – that is not counting the current one.

"I'm really delighted to get a number one in the States in Christmas week," continues Dave, "the toughest week of the year when all the big artists have singles out."

Just off their "Having A Wild Weekend" success the Dave Clark Five are currently looking around for a follow-up movie. Dave says that both Warner Brothers and Paramount have offered the group a movie with both companies agreeing to put up a minimum half a million dollars for the respective movies.

Vacationing

However, Dave has yet to decide if he will accept either one of the offers. The Five are currently on a six week vacation and during his vacation Dave is busily reading the scripts.

Dave says that the Five's next movie will *not* be a musical but *will* have a sound track. Also Dave is demanding the choice of script, director and just about everything else. In this way, Dave feels that he will get exactly what he wants. And if what he wants is not what the fans want, Dave feels that he will have only himself to blame.

One thing for sure – the Dave Clark Five will not be turning out movies every few months. Dave plans to do only one film a year because "if you do too much of one thing you get bored."

Too many promoters have been burned recently when their shows failed to come out in the black. They talked of cutting their big tours down to only one a year, such as the Beatles do.

However, Dave Clark does not plan to cut his U.S. visits at all. "We shall still do two tours a year. What is happening in the U.S. is what has already happened in England," says Dave.

"All the promoters have got to do is make sure they don't have three or four shows playing the same town in one week," Dave continued.

Dave had just one last thing to say about America – as much as he likes it he says there is no place like England. Which is understandable. It's his home.

DISCussion
By Eden

If you have com this far already, than you must have noticed the *few* little words about Mr. Dylan printed here and there in this week's publication.

Okay – so we know that he's a genius, and all that – but I'd like to know, how come we aren't hearing more of Bobby's latest single?

It's a cut off his latest album – the title tune, in fact – "Highway 61 Revisited," b/w "Can *You* Please Crawl Out Your Window?" Both sides are quite good, but the "A" side ("Highway") should be doing much better.

Hmmm – do you suppose The Poet is just a little *too* deep for the record buying public?

They're ready for *us*, but the question is: are *we* ready for *them*?? They call themselves The Mamas and Papas, and their first record, currently in release, is "California Dreamin'," written by John Phillips of the group – *theoretically* one of the *Papas*.

It's true, they may not look like you or me – but they do have an absolutely fantastic sound. Great harmony and powerful vocal combinations, backed up by some fine musicianship and sharp producing make this a group to keep your ears on.

I'm really amazed that we haven't heard P.J. Proby's latest single – "Maria" – in this country yet. It has been a smash hit in Great Britain for the past few weeks, and certainly lives up to the great success of one of P.J.'s earlier discs – "Somewhere" – also from West Side Story.

Now, I *know* that we are all deep enough for P.J.!!! I suppose the question here would be: Is P.J. deep enough for *us*??!

There are now at least six different recorded versions of the beautiful Lennon-McCartney composition, "Michelle." Bud Schenk's instrumental rendition seems to be heading the pack, but I'm still partial to Pauly's warbling of the song. Love that Beatle!!

You all watch the telly-tube from time to time, right? And you're all more than familiar with every commercial ever shown on the boob tube, right? So naturally, you have all been singing – and laughing – right along with the T-Bones' hit discing of "No Matter What Shape Your Stomach Is In," from the commersh of the same name, right?

Well, the word is that this group, until recently, was actually just a group of musicians used primarily to create hot rod, surfing, and motorcycle tunes.

But not anymore. Oh no – bright young record producer, Joe Saracino, has organized the group and will now produce an album of songs, which will include such all-time "standards" as, the TV themes for Chiquita Banana and Nabisco.

Small snag, though – the members of the original group were all studio musicians, members of other groups who were just brought in to play on various sessions. Now a whole new group of permanent T-Bones must be formed. Even so, there are some people in these musical circles who are predicting big things for this group – *whoever* they may turn out to be!!

British Top 10

1. DAY TRIPPER / WE CAN WORK IT OUT ...... The Beatles
2. THE CARNIVAL IS OVER .... The Seekers
3. THE RIVER .... Ken Dodd
4. WIND ME UP .... Cliff Richard
5. 1-2-3 .... Len Barry
6. TEARS .... Ken Dodd
7. MY SHIP IS COMING IN ...... Walker Brothers
8. KEEP ON RUNNING ...... Spencer Davis Group
9. MARIA .... P. J. Proby
10. RESCUE ME .... Fontella Bass

KRLA ARCHIVES

Sam the Who and the What?

Sam the Sham and the Pharaohs seem to have taken a few New Year's Resolutions to heart.

The wild Wooly Bully group have gone and shaved off their beards and traded in their gold sparkling coats for brilliant velours.

Sam's been through a lot of change — like when he cleverly decided that Domingo Samudio was a little hard to remember and became Sam the Sham, which you have to admit slides off the tongue a little easier.

And then too, he used to wear a turban as part of his regular act, but that hasn't been seen in a while. He says he "got so jazzed with it" during a New Orleans concert that he ripped it off and threw it in the audience. Whoever the lucky fan was that got it never returned it, and he wouldn't wear any other, so Sam's hair joined the act.

Two of the other members of the group have now taken up wearing hats, but they are more of the John Lennon variety than of the Pharaohs variety.

In fact the entire group looks more like a group of Dutchmen than Pharaohs, don't you think?

Maybe they didn't really cut their hair at all, maybe they just moved their beards around on top of their heads.

MEET THE NEW Sam the Sham and the Pharaohs. They now have longer hair, velour shirts and are without beards. Like Dutchmen, maybe?

THE OLD Sam the Sham, complete with turban and beard.

THE NEW Sam looks a little like actor Ricardo Montalban.

THE ORIGINAL "image" of Sam the Sham and the Pharaohs when they favored bright jackets and ties. They looked older then, didn't they?

KRLA ARCHIVES

A Winning Recipe For Jay and The Americans

Take three college students who like to sing. Add a shoe salesman (you wear out a lot of shoes on the road to success). Toss in a mortician (in case they don't make it?) Blend in a day of the week.

And what do you have?—Jay and The Americans and "Sunday and Me." (The Me is a bonus.)

Jay Black is the leader of the group and the shoe salesman. He was born Nov. 2, 1941, in Brooklyn, N.Y., and worked with several groups during his teen years.

Sold Shoes

But he couldn't seem to find any sense of satisfaction so he gave up show business for a year to sell shoes. Then The Americans came along and convinced him to join them as lead singer.

At first the decision to give up the steady income of shoe selling was a little difficult but after the group's very first record, "She Cried," became number one in the nation, it was obvious where he was headed.

His philosophy about the group's success is "When you think you're on top, you must always look higher, otherwise there's nowhere to go but down."

The mortician in the group is Howie Kane. The fact that he actually is a licensed mortician as well as the self-proclaimed "lover" of the group puts him in for a lot of teasing, but he's gotten used to it and has also been dubbed a good sport by his mates.

He was born June 6, 1942, in Brooklyn, where he now lives and is a talented song writer as well as vocalist.

The three students are Kenny Vance, Sandy Deane and Marty Sanders.

"Quiet American"

The other four have nicknamed Kenny "The Quiet American" and he wears the title well. While the other four clown around between shows, you can always find Kenny off somewhere buried in a book, working crossword puzzles or discussing Wall Street and stock investments with anyone who'll listen.

He was born Dec. 9, 1943, and lives in Rockaway Beach, New York. He also collects odd little things from antique shops around the country while the group is touring.

Sandy joined the group after graduating in Business Administration from New York University. He calls himself a "very dirty blond" and talks about going into the business end of recording, if he ever finds the time.

Marty is one of the busier members of the Americans. He plays guitar, writes prolifically and produces records as well.

No Sense of $

His parents bought him an expensive piano when he was nine years old, but it didn't impress him much so he just sort of glanced at it once in a while. Then when he was 15 he bought his own $20 guitar and was off on a very successful career. For all we know that expensive piano may still be sitting in a basement in New York collecting dust.

Marty's the shy and moody one of the group and is sometimes called "Mutty." He can't figure out if it's because of his name or his appearance.

In his spare time he actually likes to garden and has grown many exotic plants in his home. He was born Feb. 28, 1941, in Brooklyn.

The group was officially formed in September of 1961 and they followed "She Cried" with hit after hit—"Only in America," "Come a Little Bit Closer," "Let's Lock the Door and Throw Away the Key" and "Think of the Good Times."

And now they're back again with another chart climber—"Sunday and Me"—and like all the others this one will undoubtedly be a great hit. That's gotten to be a habit with these five, who have stood out as definite Americans with a definite American sound all during this British invasion.

Keep it up, fellows.

Mystery T-Bones

No matter what shape your stomach's in, you may have been wondering who in the world the T-Bones are.

Well, so have a lot of other people but Liberty Records has been holding off on revealing this little tidbit of information.

The BEAT, however, has learned that the T-Bones are actually a group of session musicians, A&R men and heaven knows who else.

By Gil

The most authoritative popular music poll in Britain, conducted by the "New Musical Express," credits John Lennon as the U.K.'s most popular musical personality. The same poll gives Elvis the title of most popular male singer with Cliff Richard coming in second. Dusty Springfield was voted most popular female vocalist with the former champ, Brenda Lee, in the follow-up spot. The Beatles received the award for most popular group and the Rolling Stones were voted most popular R&B group. According to the poll, Jimmy Saville is the most popular British disc jockey.

★ ★ ★

Prediction: Paul and Barry Ryan, seventeen year old twins, will soon acquire a huge following. Their mum, Marion Ryan, has long been an established singer in the swinging U.K. . . . What's the matter with the Rolling Stones? Maybe they should change their names to the Insolent Tones . . . British Beatle fans are becoming impatient with the lack of personal appearances by their idols. Many claim that the Beatles tour the U.S. more than they do the U.K. The truth is that the boys really don't need to promote their discs with personal appearances any more as their records are certain hits anyway. But to placate the fans, the Beatles have filmed a short for television. The film consists of the Beatles singing "We Can Work It Out" and "Day Tripper."

★ ★ ★

The Guiness book of records claims that the Beatles have sold 115 million discs, compared to Elvis' 110 million. Both have a long way to go before they beat Sinatra's 300 million . . . Gene Pitney reported to an English columnist that sensational news regarding Sonny & Cher was about to break. Whatever it is, it will have to be anti-climatic.

★ ★ ★

The wife of the leader of the Beatles is a fan of British singer/comedian Ken Dodd. No I don't mean Cyn. I mean Mrs. Harold Wilson, wife of the Prime Minister of Britain. Ken Dodd recently sold a million copies of a song called "Tears." So far the song is just not hacking it in the States. The song, a romantic ballad, has been subjected to violent tirades from some of the beat groups. The Stones and Manfred Mann have both condemned it as rubbish. Don't ask me why—it's a pleasant enough ballad.

★ ★ ★

Tom Jones was very uncomplimentary to the Beatles in a recent interview by the British paper, "News Of The World." He even sounded a little bit conceited . . . Herman has revealed a great admiration for Col. Tom Parker . . . I am an old fan of Dean Martin but isn't he working his image to death . . . Peter Sellers has recorded "Help" coupled with "A Hard Day's Night." He speaks both lyrics.

KRLA ARCHIVES

THE BEAT GOES TO THE MOVIES
'WHEN THE BOYS MEET THE GIRLS'

By Jim Hamblin
(The BEAT Movie Editor)

A long time ago, about 30 years in fact, the huge high buildings in Culver City housed some of the greatest talent in history. The place, located on Washington Boulevard, was called METRO-GOLDWYN-MAYER. There were other film studios in business, but not so you'd notice...

For MGM had the greatest stable of stars ever collected. In one sound stage, Wallace Beery would be pulling his beefy hand across his face, perhaps in a scene with Jackie Coogan. Next door, Marie Dressler would be working, and not far away, Marjorie Main. And Shirley Temple. And Edward G. Robinson. And dozens more of the greatest names in show business.

Ginger Rogers and Fred Astaire would glide across polished marble studio floors, in a musical extravaganza. *That* was the MGM of 1935.

Then somebody panicked. Television, they thought, would wipe out everyone. But that we'll never know because the studios gave up first. The mighty titans of the Silver Screen just folded up and left town. Dust moved in, and lonely bits of paper floated across the backlots of the major film studios as idle winds drifted across the once-busy workshops of make-believe. Everyone was gone.

Today happily that is all changing for the better. MGM now makes more money producing TELEVISION shows than it did in its heyday. And the list of film features they are releasing should make even the most frightened stockholder smile.

One of the first of these will be WHEN THE BOYS MEET THE GIRLS. The stars are Connie Francis (who sings great) and Harve Presnell (who sings great, too) in what passes for an "almost-return to the good old days."

Based on "GIRL CRAZY" by Gershwin, the film features a production number ballet scene that suddenly gives back some of the old spark to an MGM musical.

Harve Presnell looks and talks like a young Howard Keel. And that's good.

But the action in the film comes from the guest stars, headlined by England's HERMITS. The pictures to the right tell the story.

TEENAGERS, MOSTLY GIRLS, mob one of HERMAN'S HERMITS as he starts for the gate at MGM. The Culver City studio was the scene of mass pilgrimages by screaming fans when word leaked out that the HERMITS were working on a film there. The studio had to add extra police guards to hold back the enthusiastic crowds. By the way, the front of the MGM studio is seen in the movie — doubling for Brookley College in the story of a rich playboy who goes out West to get away from a certain young lady dancer friend.

SINGING STAR HARVE PRESNELL in a relaxed moment between takes on the set. Harve sang for many years in a popular choral group before his starring role in the MGM color feature.

That one and only **LOUIS (Satchmo) ARMSTRONG**, as he appears in WHEN THE BOYS MEET THE GIRLS. There are other surprises, too, for the audience in this fast moving musical.

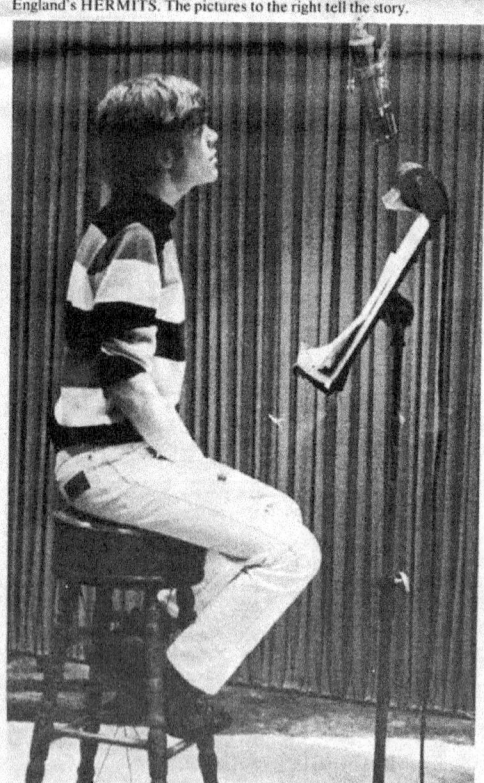 

HERMAN (of the HERMITS) gets ready for cue to pre-record one of the songs he delivers in the film. Because of technical requirements, what you see on the screen in the finished movie is actually HERMAN "mouthing" to his own voice, recorded before they film him singing it.

STRICT SECURITY IS MAINTAINED AT MGM at all times. Except when the crowds broke through to get at the HERMITS. Here we see the PHARAOHS checking in for work. Pictured are (l-r) Jerry Patterson, Butch Gibson, Sam, David Martin, and Ray Stinnett. And, believe it or not, the guard's name — KEN HOLLYWOOD!

KRLA ARCHIVES

America's Largest Teen NEWSpaper

KRLA Edition BEAT

Volume 1, Number 46 — LOS ANGELES, CALIFORNIA — 15 Cents — January 29, 1966

"WHAT NOW MY LOVE?" ASK SONNY AND CHER — Pg. 2

BEAT Photo: Robert W. Young

KRLA ARCHIVES

KRLA BEAT

Los Angeles, California　　January 29, 1966

Some Don't Forget

Show business is a funny world — a world where, if you're a star, you tend to easily forget all the little nice things that people do for you, but the little hurts stand out. You remember how rude people can be.

But Sonny and Cher remember the little things and they repay them every chance they can.

Last September they were appearing at a West Coast club and packing it every night when they received a very special invitation.

They were invited to perform for a private party being thrown in New York for Jacqueline Kennedy. It was a great honor to be asked but they were wary of not fulfilling their engagement at the club.

Owner Said Go

However, the owner of the club told them to go, in fact, he went with them, and he never deducted any pay for the night they took off to appear in New York. He refunded or exchanged all the tickets that had been sold for that night.

So the Bonos appeared one night at the club, flew to New York for the next night, and then rushed back to the club for the following night to put on their usual fantastic show even though both were exhausted from lack of sleep.

But Sonny and Cher didn't forget the generosity of the club owner.

They recently went back to the club and did a highly successful one night stand to make up for the night they took off to go to New York.

Once again Cher wasn't feeling very well but against Sonny's wishes they stayed on stage for almost an hour.

Packed House

The wall-to-wall mass of fans heard their favorite duo go through "Walkin' the Dog" into "Bad Boy Pete" and "Talk Like Love." They sat spell bound through Sonny soloing on "Laugh At Me," "Ebb Tide" and "Revolution Kind" and Cher alone on "Where Do You Go?" and "Unchained Melody."

And that night Sonny and Cher introduced their latest single release, "What Now My Love?" which is backed with "I Looked For You," another original by Sonny.

The duo ended the performance with their top selling hit, "I Got You Babe" but were called back to encore with "Just You."

But even then the fans wouldn't let them leave and after waiting around for the fans to leave so he could get Cher home, Sonny asked to have the police help them get out of the club.

Some people do remember favors.

Inside the BEAT

The Yardbirds 3-4
Beatles on Hullabaloo 6
Stevie's Back 13
The Elusive Butterfly 15
Movie Review 16

... REMEMBERING

... AND REPAYING

KRLA ARCHIVES

Havin' A Wild Rave-Up

By Eden

The term is "Rave-up"—the sound is *great*—the group is THE YARDBIRDS!!

If you have heard their fabulous Number One hits—"For Your Love," "Heart Full of Soul," "I'm A Man," and "Still I'm Sad"—you *still* haven't heard *anything!* But you might have some idea of just how great they really are.

The Yardbirds have developed a new sound—they call it a "Rave-up" and as each new record climbs steadily to the top of all the charts they are rapidly becoming one of the most popular and most successful groups in the world. Also, one of the most respected.

These five boys—Keith Relf, Jim McCarty, Jeff Beck, Chris Dreja, and Paul "Sam" Samwell-Smith—have taken the now ordinary instruments such as the guitar, the harmonica, the drums, and their own voices and created their own highly unique sound with them.

These boys aren't just another long-haired British group—they are musicians . . . *good* ones . . . and fine entertainers.

This has been the second visit the Yardbirds have made to the shores of the U.S. Happily, this one was a far sight better than the first. You may remember that back in October when they first came to California they were shown every discourtesy possible.

Insults Everywhere

They were, without valid reason, refused their hotel reservations, prevented from fulfilling obligations to perform on television and in night clubs because of some rather selfish, narrow-minded labor officials, and repeatedly insulted to their faces without due reason or just cause.

It would have been very understandable if they had simply left our country and sworn never to return. Inhospitality of such large proportions doesn't usually make for the greatest love affairs between a group of entertainers and a foreign "host" country.

But the Yardbirds were gentlemen throughout their entire unwarranted ordeal. They simply pulled their coat collars up to their ears, pasted broad smiles 'pon their lips, and displayed a little something which certain Americans were without—*class*.

Fortunately, this latest trip to America was far more successful and enjoyable for the Yardbirds. The boys received their official welcome at a press party. *The BEAT*, along with many other top publications and radio and television representatives, joined the fab group for an informal gab session set to the background of red lights and loud music.

Swingin' Party

From there, *The BEAT* travelled along with the Yardbird five to a party being given in their honor at the ultra-in home of record producer-promoter Kim Fowley.

Kim is the gentleman who entertained the boys in his home last year on the first visit they made to America, but this year he found himself playing host to about seven and a half times as many guests.

The house could probably hold—*uncomfortably*—about, oh . . . 75 or 80 people. Well, there were about *five hundred* and seventy five people present. It was rumored that nearly everyone who was "anyone" in Hollywood was at the party—including Sonny and Cher, the Byrds, Bob Dylan, Peter, Paul, and Mary, David McCallum and many others—but that was only rumor. Mainly 'cause there were so many people there that you couldn't see the face of the person standing next to you!!

Ah, but that didn't stop the Yardbirds from treating everyone to a special performance of their great music. They simply plugged in their equipment, crawled over the heads of about 31 people to the balcony area—and from their little alcove in the corner let out with some of the wildest sounding music heard in a long, long while.

Rave, Baby

We mentioned the word "rave-up" before. It's an English expression, coined expressly for use in speaking about the Yardbirds and their kind of music. The thing is—it's just about as hard to explain the word as it is to describe their music!

To "rave" is to be really excited about something, to really pour your heart and soul—mostly *soul*—into something, to really break it up and have a great time.

Well, to have a "rave-up" is to have a really great time; to blow your cool and just . . . well, just *rave!!* And that's just about exactly what this fantastic group does, and does to their audiences as well!

They have worked painstakingly with their instruments and equipment until they have perfected their sound to the very peak of perfection. They are able to come up with any variety of new and original sound combinations and new expressions in the field of pop music.

Jeff's Great

Their music seems to be a combination of R & B, hard rock, soul music and just plain *great* music. They have even perfected the usage of the reverb. Jeff Beck, lead guitarist for the group, has a way of backing his guitar up to his amplifier and in harmony and counterpoint and things for which there aren't even *names* yet—he contributes along with the other four members of the group a sound which just defies description.

I can say this much, however—when several members of *The BEAT* staff fell by the Hullabaloo night club in Hollywood where the Yardbirds were appearing in concert they found the plaster from the exceptionally high ceiling raining down upon them during one of the numbers. No, the building wasn't falling apart—the Yardbirds were just *tearing* it apart!

Theirs is the music which you will feel in every muscle of your body, not only during the performance, but for hours afterward. It is an emotional experience in which you become completely involved, and it's for certain that you won't soon afterwards be able to uninvolve yourself. Nor will you want to.

It's often been said that you must see a group in person to be able to truly appreciate them. This must be true of the Yardbirds. The only problem is that you might find yourself a little more confused *after* you have seen them perform in person. They are so phenomenal that it almost seems incomprehensible! Except for the great communication the boys have with their audiences. They are funny, they are serious, they are five musicians working together as one to come up with one of the most fantastic sounds ever.

With any luck on our part, the Yardbirds will decide not to do too much flying in the future and hang around the pop scene for a long while to come.

And with any intelligence on our part—maybe we can find a pair of shears and clip their wings so they'll *have* to stay around. They're just too good to lose.

THE CAMERA CATCHES BEAT reporter, Louise Criscione, and Yardbird drummer, Jim McCarty, backstage trying to snatch a few minutes of quiet conversation. But we sure fooled them, didn't we?

KEITH RELF, lead singer for the fantastic Yardbirds, demonstrates the way to have a "rave-up." He simply works his harmonica, shakes his tambourine and wails like no one you have **ever** seen or heard.

KRLA ARCHIVES

With Five Yardbirds

THE YARDBIRDS (l. to r. Jeff Beck, Jim McCarty, "Sam" Samwell-Smith Chris Dreja and Keith Relf) arrived Stateside at the cold and ridiculous hour of 4:30 in the morning. Of course, we awakened our sleepy-eyed photographers to greet the equally sleepy-eyed Yardbirds.

...CHRIS DREJA

...SIMPLY "SAM."

...JIM McCARTY

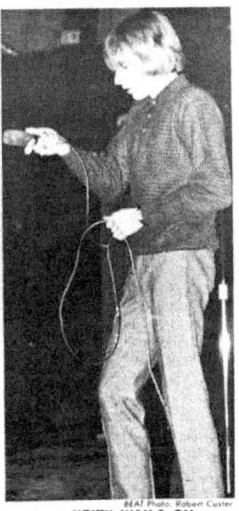

...KEITH WAILS ON.

THE YARDBIRD SOUND is aided and abetted by the very able lead guitar of Jeff Beck. The music which Jeff can produce defies description but is used effectively to "rave-up" and blow your minds.

KRLA ARCHIVES

It's In The Bag
By Eden

Dear Column Readers; It's nothing personal, of course, but would you please excuse me for a few moments while I take care of a little note I've been meaning to jot off to a friend of mine? Oh – I really don't mind at all if you'd like to read along with me.

Dear Elvis,

Hi luv, How've you been? I was just wondering – not having seen you, for so long, and all. Just sort of wondered what you've been up to lately.

I mean, you obviously haven't been making records – *new* ones – the last few years, so I sort of figured you must have found some new passtime with which to occupy yourself.

Most of us have always kind of felt that you were more or less responsible for popularizing rock 'n' roll and initiating the beginnings of the real pop music trend. And yet, you haven't made a new disc in ages.

Your last hit single – "Crying in the Chapel" – was a huge success on both sides of the Great Pond, and yet even that was recorded several years ago – as were most of your last few singles.

What gives, El? We'd all kind of like to hear what you sound like *this* century. You *are* still singing, these days . . . aren't you?

But – perhaps I should have addressed this letter to Colonel Parker. He seems to be the man who has always guided – and/or *pushed* – your career along, so maybe he would know where you've been and what you've been doing.

Or maybe I should have addressed this little note to the lost and found! I know that *we* seem to have lost you some years back, but I'm just beginning to wonder if you are ever going to be *found* – or if you even *want* to be.

Well, if it means anything to you – anytime you're ready, El, we'll all be more than happy to welcome you back to the pop scene with open arms. Honest El – even if your hair *isn't* as long as Mick Jagger's – I'm sure that we can all love you just as much as ever.

At any rate – you could at least drop us a line or two on a post card to let us know that you are still alive and well.

Thanks for listening, El – I know you must be busy – playing touch football, and such. But if you think that you can spare a minute or two from your hectic schedule – well, we'd love to hear from you.

Just ring us up here at *The BEAT* anytime – and if the girl who answers the phone doesn't recognize your name, just ask for me – *I* remember you.

You know El – I bet I'm not the only one.

Love,
Eden

Thanks for your indulgence, pop fans. Now on to other things.

Quips 'n' Quotes from Beatle-Brain Brian E.:

"Eppy" recently tossed off some quotes on various little items, like "love," for example: "A good word in pop songs."

Alright. What about the whole idea of *not* being loved? (You know really sort of *disliked*.) "I suppose I'm conscious of it. It can't be helped."

Ohhhh? Well, what are your views on money? "Still scarce." On dogs? "Terrified of dogs. Almost put me off people." On liars: "Almost everyone."

Aw, c'mon now, Eppy! Hey, what about your nickname – *Eppy?* "I quite like it but I don't like it being used to my face. I don't mind the Beatles using it. I know they do."

And what about success, Eppy? "I'm told I'm successful but I really don't believe it." Oh no? Well, would you believe utterly wealthy?!!!

Now then, how 'bout some capsule reviews on the Beatled ones?

John: "Lennon. Great mind, great person. One of the best people I've ever met. He's an interesting character to watch develop."

Paul: "Probably the most changed Beatle. He's mellowed in character and thought. A fascinating character and a very loyal person. Doesn't like changes very much. He, probably more than the others, finds it more difficult to accept that he is playing to a cross section of the public and not just to teenagers, or sub-teenagers, whom he feels are the Beatles' audience."

George: "Harrison. I always think of George as a friend. Somewhat inconsistent person. Can be difficult. Never has been with me. Great personal charm, but this goes for any Beatle. Any faults the Beatles are supposed to have are never apparent individually. Any faults they have probably only come when they are together as a group. When there is too much talent in one room."

And what about a chap named PJ. Proby, Brian? "I should have managed him."

* * *

I don't know how your televiewing is coming along these days, but if you saw Sonny and Cher two or three weeks ago on the Hollywood Palace – I'm sure that you will agree that the talented twosome looked and sounded unusually good.

I was especially fond of Cher's little conversation with host Bing Crosby. When Der Bingle queried 'How did you find Sonny?' the long-tressed thrush replied: "I just parted his hair and there he was!!"

* * *

I know the Beatles haven't yet found a script for the movie which they are to begin filming in April of this year, but since I'm such a good guy about things of this sort – I've decided to volunteer my services for the part of female lead in the picture – whatever it may turn out to be! In fact, I'll even help them write the plot!!

Hmmmmm – do you think we might be able to interest Paul McCartney in the role of male lead??!!!

BEAT Photo: Mike Conroy

Lunch With Gary Lewis

By Jamie McCluskey III

I think I would have rather had the "Diamond Ring." Yeah – I really think I would. Well, I mean – there was nothing *wrong* with the food, don't get me wrong. It's just that . . . well, I really *am* supposed to be on a diet!

But look – when Gary Lewis and the Playboys have a fancy cocktail luncheon to commemorate their first year together as a group, in which time they have enjoyed five consecutive hit records, well – you just don't go and *watch*!! (Besides – I've always been sort of partial to steak!)

So, like I was saying – there I was, eating all of that delicious food which I shouldn't have been eating, when a tall, monocled gentleman sat down next to me and asked me my name.

So, I told him. Then I asked him *his* name and what he did.

You guessed it, loves – Mistake Number One! – and I hadn't even finished my salad yet!!

He was only the President of the Foreign Press Association, representing 91 foreign publications around the world. Oh well, what's in a salad anyway?

Slurpin'

It seemed as though everyone who was anyone at all in the world of Hollywood Press circles was at this luncheon. In fact, Gary Lewis and his four playful Playboys even showed up, and as soon as everyone finished slurping coffee, crunching garlic bread, and wrapping up pieces of steak for all the starving mutts they left behind at home – the press conference began.

Gary seems to have become very international all of a sudden. For example, he began talking about the way English girls dress. He explained that their dress was "about five inches shorter and the *tightest* you ever saw! It looks pretty good!!!"

From there, ol' Gar hopped across the ol' channel and declared that he had no use for France. At which point a lady from a French publication introduced herself. Then he proceeded to spend the next thirty minutes explaining why it was his very favorite country ever!

Well, you see – it's really just this one cab driver that Gary hates, and that's only 'cause he doesn't speak English!

Someone from the more prehistoric sort of days asked Gary why he had let his hair grow long (which it isn't) and if it helped his music any. Gary answered that it didn't and that he never really would let his hair get as long as, for example, "hers." He was pointing at me. My hair isn't really long – *for a girl that is*.

It's sort of shoulder-length, kind of, and it features matching shoulder-length bangs, too – kind of.

Gary On Guitar

Well, anyway – he said his hair would never be that long, and then he went on to tell us that he was now playing guitar (although he sometimes goes back to drums) and that the group has a new member who does most of the drumming.

Well, you know what *I* always say – what's another Playboy here or there? Among friends, of course!!

All of the Playboys and Gary received Gold Records for all five of their hit records, each of which has sold at least one million copies.

Gary also did a lot of Jerry Lewis kind of things, and then he introduced one of his younger brothers, who is also a Jerry Lewis kind of thing.

I asked Gary if he planned on seriously studying drama, but he jokingly replied that he never was the type for Hamlet. No, it's strictly comedy for ol' Gar.

He clarified this further by explaining that "there's already a pretty funny guy living in our house, and that's enough for now."

Well, after Gary thanked us all, and told us that his main ambition now is just to go on making a whole lot of hit records for always and always, we all gathered up our expensive furs and stuff (including the two ladies with napkin-wrapped steak in their purses) and fell out to the parking lot to wait for about forty-five minutes until we could collect our Rolls Royces and Mercedes Benz's.

Except me. I just waited for about an hour and a half to gather up the remnants of my vintage 1900 Roadster, Model Q.

You know – I *still* think I woulda rather had that *Diamond Ring* that ol' Gar is always singing 'bout!!

Supremes – Busy Girls

The ever-great Supremes have announced their plans for the coming year, and if you're trying to get a hold of them, don't bother until after June. They're booked solid until then.

After finishing up at the Eden Roc in Miami, their schedule for 1966 looks like this: Jan. 9, Ed Sullivan Show; Jan. 17-30, Roostertail, Detroit; Jan. 31-Feb. 8, El Juan Hotel, Puerto Rico; Feb. 9-16, Concert tour in Germany and France; Feb. 17-March 3, Copacabana, New York; March 4-20, Eastern U.S. Concert tour; March 23-April 3, Blinstrub's, Boston; April 8-17, Deauville Hotel, Miami; April 19-26, Caribbean Islands Conert tour; May 19-June 8, Fairmont Hotel, San Francisco.

KRLA ARCHIVES

Beatles Good Even When They're Not

BEAT Photo: Robert W. Young

If you're a Beatle fan, there's a good chance that you almost left home on January 3, 1966.

Why? Because the following is a good example of what happened on that particular date. In homes all across the nation, and especially in California, the number one Beatle stronghold in America.

The time was 7:30 p.m. The scene, your living room. The cast of characters, your family.

Mum and Dad looking bored on the sofa. Little Brother draped over a chair. You sitting cross-legged in front of the telly.

The event? Something you'd been waiting for all day, all month, practically forever.

The Beatles' debut on "Hullabaloo".

When you heard the familiar theme song, you started holding your breath. But host Roger Smith was first on the bill.

You like Roger Smith. He's a nice guy. Cute, too. But you seriously wondered if he would *ever* finish the opening number.

Finally, he finished. And finally, the Beatles began.

George and Ringo came on the screen first. Kidding around before the start of their first song. Then they were joined by Paul and John and "Day Tripper" filled the room.

But, after a line or two, a new sound was added. Somewhere behind you, Little Brother was *talking*.

You turned around, aghast. "*Shhhhh*," you hissed.

But Little Brother does not give up easily.

No Color

"Why aren't they in color?" he hissed back.

"They just *told* you why," you snapped in a stage whisper, trying to speak and concentrate on the Beatles at the same time. "This is a *film* clip from *London*!"

That shut him down for the moment, but just as you turned your rapt attention back to the foursome, Mum piped up.

"Ringo isn't really playing the drums," she announced.

You sighed wearily. "I know. They aren't really singing either."

Dad snorted. "That's for sure," he announced.

"*Dad*," you wailed. "I mean they're lip-syncing their record!"

Then you returned to George, who was flirting into the camera and flexing his long fingers as they flew about the neck of the guitar.

"Wow," you breathed. "Look at *that*."

"He isn't really playing," Mum reminded patiently.

"Amen," amended Dad.

"He is *so*," you quivered. "You do play and sing when you lip-sync. What I meant was that no one *hears* you."

"We should be so lucky," offered your little brother, but before you had a chance to throw something at him, the song was over.

Unfortunately, the conversation was not.

"Why didn't they wiggle?" inquired Mum.

"They *never* wiggle," you answered, shocked.

"I suppose they never stomp or scream either," remarked Dad.

"*No, they don't*!"

"That hair is terrible," continued Little Brother. "John looks like a camel."

Well, that did it. That's when you decided to leave home. Right *after* the Beatles' second number.

All was silent in the living room until Paul was two bars into their encore.

Then, Mum spoke. "What's a day tripper?"

"*Mother!*"

Then, Dad spoke. "Do not address your mother in that tone of voice."

"*Please!* I'm *trying* to watch the *Beatles!*"

Then, Little Brother spoke. "You're trying all right. *Very*."

Then, when you were about to burst into tears, Mum, Dad and Little Brother burst into laughter. And you joined them.

No one talked during the rest of the song, and you made a swift and solemn promise to luv John Lennon for the rest of your life.

"They aren't *too* bad," Dad admitted when you snapped off the telly. "And that what's-his-name, the guy at the piano. He's funny."

You smiled fondly and decided not to start packing after all.

Those Beatles were really something, you thought to yourself. In the short time it had taken to sing "We Can Work It Out," they had done exactly that.

You were right.

Close To Bad

The Beatles had once again proven why they are the most powerful and popular stars in history. Because they are the best even when they're at their worst.

If they weren't at their worst on "Hullabaloo," they came close. For several reasons.

Being live performers, they aren't used to the lip-sync process, and this caused a few mistakes. The process was used only because the production of a sound tape would have been too expensive and too time consuming. But, after a goof, the Beatles just forged ahead and most viewers didn't even notice the errors.

During "Day Tripper", the photography left a lot to be desired. They appeared to be on two separate spliced-together films, with George and Ringo on one and Paul and John on the other. This may not have been the case, but whatever was, in order to get all four Beatles on the screen at once, the camera had to pull back so far, it was difficult to see any of them clearly.

However, this mattered little, thanks to a series of breath-taking closeups. The two-part clip contained some of the finest footage ever shot of Paul McCartney. He looked so adorable, he probably heard the screams all the way to London.

And George Harrison fans surely must have come apart at the seams. He looked more handsome than ever before.

The perfect balance of the appearance was supplied by Ringo and John.

Frosted Cake

Ringo's dead-panning and kooky antics were jolly good fun. John's mugging into the camera was the frosting on the cake, and the ice-breaker.

In some living rooms, the scene was more hectic than in the one we "visited." A Beatle fan's reaction to the foursome depends upon her degree of involvement.

If you just *luv* the Beatles, you watched in fascination. But, if you really *love* Paul or George or John or Ringo, there's panic intermingled with your fascination. A panic that stems from caring about someone who's so close and so far away.

A lot of tears were shed in front of TV sets that night. And a lot of worried parents looked on with a mixture of amazement and concern.

John dried many of those tears and quelled a lot of fears. His wry humor changed the mood by saying "Surely you don't think we take ourselves *seriously*." It also helped many parents realize that Beatlemania is not an unnatural or unhealthy thing.

That it is, instead, a perfectly natural reaction to four totally irresistable individuals.

For a group which had none of the technical elements on their side that night, the Beatles accomplished a lot.

But the most important thing they did was agree to appear. Accepting what payment the show could afford to give us a mid-term boost, and making it a little easier for us to wait until summer for the real thing.

Yeah, yeah, yeah.

KRLA ARCHIVES

For Girls Only

By Shirley Poston

I'll never be the same (which will certainly be an improvement)

Yesterday I was as sensible and rational a person as you'd ever hope to see (providing that you kept your eyes clamped tightly shut at all times).

And what am I today? A screaming meemie (whatever that is).

And when I tell you what *happened* to me, you won't blame me a bit for going off my nut.

Call Me Granny

I was sitting in a rocking chair (just call me granny) (gown, that is) minding my own business, reading my mail when all of a sudden I notice this newspaper in my lap.

Naturally, I unfolded it. And, when I did, you could hear the shrieks (shreiks?) (nobody's perfect) for *miles*!

Because that newspaper *said*, in giant black *headlines*: SHIRLEY POSTON WEDS GEORGE HARRISON!

No, this isn't one of my "dreams." It really happened! And after my folks finally got me down off the door sill, I found out *how* it happened.

You see, I open a whole bunch of letters and then I read them (which sounds logical). What I mean is, I open them all first.

Nuts!!! I am getting nowhere fast. What I am trying (very) to say is this. If I have ten letters, I open all ten before I read any of them.

Oh, crumbs. That still isn't right, but you know what I mean.

Anyway, I figured the paper must have fallen out of one of the letters (either that or I've been living a double life), so I plowed through them and finally found the right one.

Then I *really* had a nervous breakdown, because the letter read: "I just wanted to be the first to congratulate you on your marriage to George."

Fortunately, I noticed the P.S. before dashing off to England to join my husband (however, I was half-way to the airport *before* I saw it). (The P.S., not the airport.)

It turned out that it was one of those fake newspapers you can have printed, and even if I did fall out of my tree, I'll be forever grateful to *BEAT* reader Paula Schulte of Woodland Hills, Calif., for sending it to me.

Bit of Melodrama

I now have the newspaper on the wall in my room, and there it shall remain until death do us part (nothing like a bit of melodrama, I always say). And every time I look at it, I get about eleven million chills, shivers, shudders and fits. Because I immediately start thinking, *what if it were really true?*

All I can say is this . . . George, when you come back to America, and you see me coming, you'd better run for your life, little boy (sorry about that line I swiped, John and Paul).

Say, I just thought of something. Do you realize that I used up several paragraphs of this column telling you how I *open letters*? I do hope that you will clip out this column and keep it forever. You certainly wouldn't want to part with *valuable* information like *that*, now would you?

Do you ever have the feeling they're coming for you? Well, relax. They aren't. They're coming for *me*.

Oh, *George*, just *think* . . .

Greatest Dream

Sorry about that. Got carried off there for a sec. Now, back to something even more rational and sensible. Like the greatest dream I've ever heard in me entire life (still going through that English phase, I'm).

I'm not going to print just the dream either. I have to print every *word* of that letter. Starting right now.

"Dear Shirley:

"My pen-name is Narcissa Nash (my real name's too ridiculous). Anyway, I've got a daydream to tell you about. So, without wasting time, here goes.

"I'm taking a friendly walk down by the river, walking my pet tiger and whistling Beethoven's Ninth Symphony. Suddenly, a Mr. Whippee ice cream truck whizzes by with John Lennon inside yelling 'Help'. Which is quite an appropriate thing to yell since he is being kidnapped at the time.

Strawberry Ice Cream

"After chasing the truck on my skis, I finally catch up with it and I throw a curling stone at the driver. But he throws a fiendish thingy at me, which happens to be a strawberry ice cream cone. This makes me furious because I absolutely hate strawberry.

"Meanwhile, John has seen me and he is pleading for me to help him. Noticing that there is more here than meets the eye, I dash into the nearest phone booth and put on my rubber Ringo mask.

"When I catch up with the truck again, the driver kidnaps me, thinking I am the famous Ringo. Next thing I know, I'm in the back of the truck with John and three other Oriental thugs.

"John, who is quite surprised to see me, says: 'Ringo, what are you doing here?'

"A bit confused, I answer 'Posting a letter', which seems to satisfy John.

"Finally, the thugs (with their filthy Eastern ways) abandon us at the nearest abandoned island in the Bahamas, and they go off to collect the ransom money. But they never get it, because while John has been gone from England, another group has topped the Beatles and nobody wants John back now anyway.

"So we are abandoned on the island forever, and after I reveal to John that I am not really Ringo, we have a gay old time playing 'Beep-Beep' all over the island.

"That's the end of the daydream. At least that's as far as I can tell you.

Cyn Who?

"Now that you know that I'm a real twit and off my equilibrium and all, I spose you're thinking—where does Cyn come in? Well, all I have to say is *Cyn who?*"

Is that not the masterpiece of all time? Luv-a-duck, that last line FLIPS me. Next time someone brings up a certain Miss Boyd (not Robin), I'm going to say *Patti who?*

Ratzafratz. I've used up my whole column raving, and now all the *really* sensible and rational things will have to wait until next week.

Which is just as well. I'm not myself. How could I be? I'm Mrs. George Harrison (don't I *wish, wish, wish*).

Please write and see if you can't calm me down, and I'll see you next *BEAT*.

KRLA ARCHIVES

Yeah, Well Byrds...

Perched Atop A Fence

By Tammy Hitchcock

The Byrds are back swinging again with a new record, "Set You Free This Time," so I thought it would be nice if we stuck them on our "Yeah, Well Hot Seat" this week.

But I'll tell you right now it was plenty hard getting those five Byrds to stop flying around this town long enough to perch on our "Hot Seat."

I almost caught a couple of them at the Yardbirds' party the other night but they escaped over the fence. Of course, I followed right after them but I got stuck just as I was about to go over the top and one of the Yardbirds had to climb up and rescue me!

Yeah, well you don't know how embarrassing that was. I mean, just picture me (bell-bottoms and all) with my hair blowing around in about 65 different directions and my boot heel captured securely in the fence.

And if that wasn't bad enough (and, believe me, it *was*) I had to explain to everyone how a lady-like little thing like me happened to be hanging from the top of a fence at 2:30 in the morning!

Snake Eggs?

Naturally, I didn't want to tell anyone the horrible truth. And, anyway, who would believe that I was chasing Byrds? So, I explained quite simply that I was looking for rattlesnake eggs. *That* they believed!

I guess I got a little carried away with my fence adventures. Sorry about that. So, speaking of the Byrds which I *was* doing back in the first paragraph, as you all know they paid their first visit to England several months ago.

On the whole their British tour could be classified as a success but they did meet with many problems along the way and some vicious attacks from the British press.

Still, the Byrds dug England and the English audiences. "With a few exceptions we've found British audiences very similar to those in the States," said Byrd leader, Jim McGuinn.

"In some cases our reception has been a little ahead of what we've been used to. I think that's because the lyrics of our numbers are poetry and appeal to those who have a cultural heritage a little in advance of some of the isolated agricultural communities we've played to in America."

Yeah, well what's the matter, Jim? You don't like farmers?

Trick 'Em

The Byrds are really fun type guys who make it a policy to never give a straight answer to a question unless they're tricked into it.

So, when someone asked Gene Clark what his biggest break was he replied deadpan: "To my left leg." Yeah, well that must have been exciting. The only breaks I ever get are to my fingernails!

Most people who enter show business do it because they have been influenced by someone or something. And that something is usually money or fame. But then the Byrds are not most people. So logically they went into the business because of hair.

Mike says his career was most definitely influenced "the day I saw R&B bands growing their hair long."

Yeah, well I'm glad you followed suit, Mike, and grew your hair long too. I dig long hair, you know. Even wear mine long—about the same length as yours.

Everyone has favorites, right? Well, on this one point the Byrds *are* the same as everone else. They too have their favorites and Gene's favorite drink is "wet water."

Yeah, well wet water is all right but you should try *dry* water—it's out of sight, Gene.

Chris Hillman (who has really gotten quite cute since he had his hair straightened) says he likes to gather with his friends.

Yeah, well I used to gather with my friends too, Chris. But this one time we were gathering wild berries and after I had gathered a fourth of a bucketful I sat myself down to eat them. One slight problem—I sat in a patch of poison ivy! So, you see, my gathering days are over. And my itching days are finally over too!

David Crosby (who still hasn't parted with that beloved cape of his) says his most thrilling experience was "standing watch at night by myself."

Yeah, well what did you watch all that time, Dave?

Mike's Kick

Mike Clarke declares (when there aren't any policemen around) that he gets his biggest kick out of going 180 miles an hour in a Ferrari.

Yeah, well I know a guy who owns a Ferrari and once he went 180 miles an hour and then his motor fell out. Which wouldn't have been so bad, really, except that after that he got a ticket for going too *slow*.

Naturally, he was going slow—he was *pushing* the car with one hand and holding the motor with the other. And he was still doing 30 miles an hour, which I thought was pretty good considering. Guess the policeman didn't agree, though.

Yeah, well.

On the BEAT
By Louise Criscione

Paul McCartney was stopped a little short when a reporter asked him what the Beatles hoped for in the New Year. "All I know," declared Paul, "is that 1965 has been another really terrific year for us, so much that it seems a bit of cheek to hope things will be even better in the year to come."

But it wasn't so hard for Paul to answer what he personally hopes for in 1966—some peace and quiet every so often. He knows that he won't get it but he can still hope, can't he?

Isn't the Kinks' "A Well Respected Man" a gas of a record? The Kinks also have a New Year's wish—they want to be taken seriously and not as just a group full of nothing but gimmicks.

The Who have shot a half hour film for American television. In the film The Who sing four songs and the whole thing was directed by the group's co-manager, Chris Stamp.

It seems as if everyone in the pop world is either busy making a movie, planning to make a movie, currently on tour or mapping a forthcoming tour.

Thinkin' Big

Dave Clark and his Five are mapping out their next Stateside tour which will probably take place from June 10 to July 24. The tour's opener will be in New York's Yankee Stadium with none other than Bob Hope as the show's headliner.

The rest of the Five's dates are not even tentatively set as yet but when they are we'll let you know.

Meanwhile Dave is still puzzling over the group's next movie. He's been reading scripts until they're coming out of his ears. Apparently, Dave was not satisfied with any of them and so is writing the story himself (but not the script). Dave really wants to do a thriller so that *may* be what he is writing.

...DAVE DAVIES

Tom Jones and Herman's Hermits are currently touring Australia and New Zealand together. When the tour ends on February 7, Herman heads on to Japan for personal appearances from February 10 to February 20. This makes two firsts for Herman—his first visit to Australia and his first glimpse of the Orient.

Sonny & Cher have wanted to open their own boutique for a long time now. They never made it but they've done the next best thing. They've just signed a deal with Gordon & Marx and Lucky Girl clothing manufacturers for the exclusive rights to manufacture and distribute Sonny & Cher originals.

The clothes will be designed by Sonny & Cher themselves and will be sold all over the country.

Yardbirds Swing Now

What a difference a few months make! When the Yardbirds first hit our shores in September they were rather down and out because of work permit trouble.

Hardly anyone knew they were here and those that did didn't really care. Now the Yardbirds are back, minus work permit difficulty (I think) and the parties that have been thrown for them are out of sight!

Epic Records threw a cocktail meet-the-press type affair at one of the local clubs but the swingingest one of them all was held high up in the hills with security men checking names at the door. But more about that elsewhere.

QUICK ONES: The Supremes started the New Year off right by performing at the Inaugural Ball for Detroit's Mayor Jerome P. Cavanaugh... By the way, the "Motown Sound" can now be heard on car tapes... Brian Jones spent his Christmas in the Virgin Islands with a virus infection! All Stones, including Brian, are now back in England... The Kinks are tentatively set to tour Scandinavia during the early part of '66... February 11 is the date set for the release of the Animals follow-up to "It's My Life"... Stones knocked off the Beatles as the most popular group in England's "New Musical Express" poll.

...DIANA ROSS
BEAT Photo: Chuck Boyd

KRLA ARCHIVES

Inside KRLA

Greetings people in KRLA land. Thought that I might answer a few of the questions you've been asking in your letters.

Many of you have wanted to know some of the "behind-the-scenes-stuff" of KRLA, so I spoke to a very "behind-the-scenes" sort of gentleman named Bill McMillan. You have probably heard Bill at one time or another, as he is the former news director for KRLA. Currently, he is the Director of Station Relations.

The radio station first went on the air in September of 1959, and the only original member of that staff still with the station is Richard Beebee of the news department. None of the original disc jockeys are still at KRLA. Here, Bill takes up our "Saga of a Radio Station:"

"I joined the station in November of 1959 as head of the news department. Shortly after that, Dick Moreland joined the staff and then Bob Eubanks.

"Before the station was KRLA, it was well-established as a country-and-western radio station and had the call letters of KXLA. The two live studios of KXLA which KRLA took over had been the home of such people as Tennessee Ernie Ford, who started out here; Polly Bergen got her start here, and Brenda Lee and many of the hillbilly and country and western stars were frequent live performers on the air.

"There have been an awful lot of people in the studios of KRLA who have gone on to bigger and better things.

"When KRLA took over the station and changed the format to Top 40 programming and music, there were still many of the artifacts from the 'hillbilly reign' still left over here at the station. Namely, one of the largest country and western libraries in the entire United States. And all of those records were donated to whichever group of charities put in a bid for them.

"When KRLA went on the air, it was officially listed in the ratings as 26th. By the end of five months with this kind of programming, we were Number 3, and have never been lower than Number 3. This is due, in large part, to the personalities that have always been featured on KRLA. We've made it a point to find the best and bring them out.

"KRLA has won a number of awards in the news and public service areas. In five year's time, we've won close to 200 special plaques and awards, certificates of merit for jobs we have done for people in the public service agencies. We have always been a competitor in the top news awards with our news department, and we've won our share of those, including the Golden Mikes from the Radio and Television Association, and special awards for extra-special news programs we've done.

"We have won awards from school groups, for working with youth in a particular program, and trying to involve them a little bit in their city government and their school government."

Anyone who listens regularly to KRLA is aware of the many fantastic and fun contests always going on, and Bill took a moment to remember some of the most fun ones:

"The first one of note was the Secret Word Contest which drew about 30,000 entries and that was when we had been on the air for only four or five months. We gave away cars, and trips to Hawaii, and television sets, and things like that.

"I think the most exciting contest we had — which really started out as a kind of a joke — was the Find The Black Cat That Can Say KRLA for a Halloween contest. We tried to find a black cat that could actually say KRLA, and we imagined that the contest would be something to listen to because we sent one of the newsmen out to record all these people who called in and said they had black cats that could talk.

"The funny part of it was hearing the lady or the man say, 'Okay cat — say KRLA!' and at least hearing a squeak or a growl or a scratch.

"But one day our man came running back very excited, because he had — on tape — a cat that actually did say KRLA. We put that on the air for everyone to hear.

"But something we didn't know until we did the contest was that it has been scientifically proven that of all the animals in the world, the cat comes the closest to being able to speak a language, and a cat can actually make 17 sounds of the alphabet."

There's really lots more to the KRLA story, but not too much space to put it in this week. So c'mon back next week for the exciting conclusion to the Bill McMillan Thriller-Chiller Radio Story of the Month.

KRLA BEAT Subscription

SAVE 33% Of Regular Price

☐ 1 YEAR — 52 Issues — $5.00   ☐ 2 YEARS — $8.00
☐ 6 MONTHS — $3.00

Enclosed is .... ☐ CASH   ☐ CHECK
Send to: .... Age ....
Address: ....
City .... State .... Zip ....

MAIL YOUR ORDER TO: KRLA BEAT
6290 Sunset, Suite 504
Hollywood, Calif. 90028

Foreign Rate: $9.00 — 52 Issues

SEEING DOUBLE? No, it's Dave Hull with Chad Stuart and Jeremy Clyde standing beside larger-than-life murals of themselves — part of the fabulous collection Dave has hanging in his new Hullabaloo Club.

KRLA Tunedex

DAVE HULL

BOB EUBANKS

DICK BIONDI

JOHNNY HAYES

EMPEROR HUDSON

CASEY KASEM

CHARLIE O'DONNELL

BILL SLATER

This Week	Last Week	Title	Artist
1	1	WE CAN WORK IT OUT/DAY TRIPPER	The Beatles
2	2	LIGHTNIN' STRIKES	Lou Christie
3	3	SOUNDS OF SILENCE	Simon & Garfunkel
4	7	NO MATTER WHAT SHAPE	T-Bones
5	4	FLOWERS ON THE WALL	Statler Brothers
6	11	MY LOVE	Petula Clark
7	9	I SEE THE LIGHT	Five Americans
8	5	YOU DIDN'T HAVE TO BE SO NICE	The Lovin' Spoonful
9	8	I FOUGHT THE LAW	Bobby Fuller Four
10	6	LET'S HANG ON	Four Seasons
11	10	IT'S MY LIFE	The Animals
12	19	AS TEARS GO BY	The Rolling Stones
13	16	HOLE IN THE WALL	The Packers
14	21	UPTIGHT	Stevie Wonder
15	12	RUN, BABY, RUN	The Newbeats
16	24	JUST LIKE ME	Paul Revere & The Raiders
17	14	SHE'S JUST MY STYLE	Gary Lewis & The Playboys
18	Ret.	THE MEN IN MY LITTLE GIRL'S LIFE	Mike Douglas
19	23	JENNY TAKE A RIDE	Mitch Ryder & The Detroit Wheels
20	15	A YOUNG GIRL	Noel Harrison
21	38	CRYIN' TIME	Ray Charles
22	22	A MUST TO AVOID	Herman's Hermits
23	25	FIVE O'CLOCK WORLD	The Vogues
24	27	MY GENERATION	The Who
25	28	ONE HAS MY NAME	Barry Young
26	—	ARE YOU THERE?	Dionne Warwick
27	40	SUNDAY AND ME	Jay & The Americans
28	—	GOING TO A-GO-GO	The Miracles
29	39	MY WORLD IS EMPTY WITHOUT YOU	The Supremes
30	30	THUNDERBALL	Tom Jones
31	31	LIKE A BABY	Len Barry
32	33	ELUSIVE BUTTERFLY	Bob Lind
33	32	SANDY	Ronnie & The Daytonas
34	—	SPANISH EYES	Al Martino
35	37	SET YOU FREE THIS TIME	The Byrds
36	34	I AIN'T GONNA EAT MY HEART OUT	The Young Rascals
37	35	A WELL RESPECTED MAN	The Kinks
38	—	A SWEET WOMAN LIKE YOU	Joe Tex
39	—	BELINDA	Vito and The Elegants
40	—	UNDER YOUR SPELL AGAIN	Johnny Rivers

KRLA ARCHIVES

KRLA'S CASEY KASEM, host of "Shebang" on Channel 5, talks to Steve Scott of Northridge about his novel hot rod creation, the "Uncertain T." Scott spent three years and $10,000 on his award-winning custom.

IAN WHITCOMB can hardly believe that this is really sunny Southern California. This snowy scene is taking place on the set of "Shebang" — and the snowflakes looked so real that Ian almost caught cold from the white drifts of snow which formed on his long brown British locks.

MIKE BANDUCEA of Pasadena wins an album for this humorous cartoon depicting a KRLA News mobile unit.

Liverpool 5 Going North

The Liverpool Five, one of England's new sensational groups who have recorded "Heart" — written and recorded by Pet Clark — just finished a week's stay at Hollywood's newest teen night club, The Hullabaloo.

After finishing a successful engagement here, the five — Steve Laine, Dave Burgess, Ken Cox, Ron Henley, and Jimmy May — are now headed back up North for more personal appearance tours.

Before coming down to L.A. they spent about two months in the cold North, and topped all charts with their new record.

There are rumors spreading that the boys may go home to England after their tour is finished.

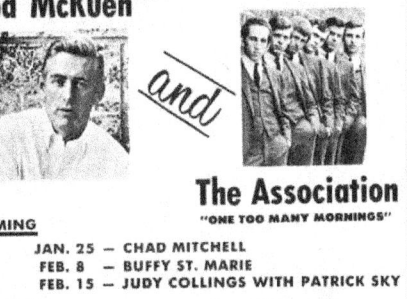

OPENING ONE WEEK ONLY JAN. 18

Rod McKuen and **The Association**
"ONE TOO MANY MORNINGS"

COMING
JAN. 25 — CHAD MITCHELL
FEB. 8 — BUFFY ST. MARIE
FEB. 15 — JUDY COLLINGS WITH PATRICK SKY

AT DOUG WESTON'S
Troubadour
RESERVATIONS: CR. 6-6168
9083 SANTA MONICA BL. L.A.

KRLA ARCHIVES

Intellectuals On The Rise?

Why is it that absolutely *nobody* wants to be a folksinger anymore —'specially *folksingers?!!!*

Not too very long ago, I found two young men (whom I had previously considered to be folksingers) in a restaurant in a large hotel. Along with about ten other people then, we dawdled over breakfast, talking to and about these two young men who say they *aren't* folksingers—they are just Simon and Garfunkel.

Respectively, they are Paul Simon and Art Garfunkel, both originally from New York. As a team, they are currently enjoying all the niceties associated with a Top Ten hit record all across the nation.

But, oddly enough—the boys never really planned this hit. In fact, they never even planned to release the record. Paul had been spending some time in England with Art—who later returned alone to New York—when suddenly, Columbia Records informed them that they had taken this cut off their first album, recorded about a year and a half ago, and released it as a single.

By the time they learned of the record's release—it was already well on its way to becoming one of the larger hits of 1965. Nothing like a pleasant surprise!

Originally, the song had been recorded with a sort of "folk background," but when it was released on a single, a rock backing was added. Still, there is some distinctive quality about the sound and the voice combinations on the record, even though both boys claim "That's just what happened—people tell *us* we have a distinctive sound!"

Art and Paul have known one another since they were children together in The Great City, and have been singing together professionally for several years, off and on.

During the occasional intervals, Art attended Columbia University, where he was studying to be an architect, and Paul majored in literature at Queen's College in New York.

Both Art and Paul have a distinct aversion to being labelled or tagged in any way—and that seems quite reasonable. They refuse to be called "folksingers" or even entertainers who sing in the folk field.

Paul had some very definite ideas about this which he enthusiastically elaborated upon over an elaborate piece of pastry:

"I come from a folk background—not pop. I think that folk songs are songs which reflect people and times—so I guess that means that I'm a folk singer!

"My idea of a good song is one which gives a good emotional wallop. I like almost all music, but in general I don't think that pop music is creative."

Art joined the conversation to say that "The whole rock-folk thing is a good, healthy sign," and both boys agreed with me when I suggested that folk music seems to become "folk" music primarily in retrospect. Paul added

... SIMON AND GARFUNKEL

to this, "I think that time is the important factor in folk songs."

Paul was responsible for the penning of the boys first hit disc, and he is also the author of the second record about to be released. In his spare time, he also writes short stories and possibly someday will combine them in a book.

Paul did admit that "the only thing I want to do in my whole life is write. When I've finished with *this*—that's what I'll do.

I guess he noticed my somewhat puzzled expression which appeared quite suddenly over my coffee cup at that moment, so he continued:

"I couldn't stand to be doing the same thing year after year. It's only a big game we're playing.

"Big sums of money mean nothing to me. I have nowhere to spend it—everything that I want—I can afford to buy now."

They were popular as—shhh ... "folksingers" (or *something*) ... a few years back in Greenwich Village, and they were popular as performers in England. Now they are becoming more popular and successful than ever in their own native country.

On the new album which they are preparing for release, they will be including a jazz instrumental, two solos each, about three quiet vocals—"pretty much straight *folk*"—and all but one track on the LP was written by Paul. Some of his other songs have been recorded by people like Chad and Jeremy, the Seekers, and the Bachelors.

Perhaps they aren't folksingers, or folk artists, or even folk entertainers—but it seems certain at this point, that the public is now willing to accept them on *their* terms—whatever they may be. But that's mostly 'cause—like it or not—they still fall very definitely under one label—talent.

And that's about enough.

Congratulations Beatles—their latest LP, "Rubber Soul," sold 1,200,000 copies during the first nine days of its release. It has been estimated that it has been selling approximately 140,000 copies *a day* since its release last December 6.

Capitol Records originally ordered 2,000,000 copies to be distributed and sold in this country—the largest initial order ever—and by the middle of December at least 60% of that number were already sold.

* * *

Just wonderin'—will Sonny and Cher release "And Now" which they duoed so beautifully on the Hollywood Palace at the beginning of this month? Could be another hit for the two if it is.

* * *

The new single by newcomer Bob Lind—"Elusive Butterfly"—has been making a few motions on various record charts here and there, but frankly I think the sound is much too "elusive" to become a big nation-wide hit.

* * *

Be sure and check out the first fantastic album by the Knickerbockers, entitled "Lies," after their smash-hit single of the same tag. If you had any doubts about the talent and versatility of these four boys, just lay an earlobe on this new piece of wax—really super sensational!

* * *

Watch out for British singing duo Paul and Barry Ryan to become a big hit on this side of the foam as well. They will be releasing the boy's smash British hit-discing, "Have Pity On The Boy" over here soon, which should send them singing up the charts here in the Colonies.

* * *

There is a beautiful French girl named Francoise Hardy who is a singing star in her own country as well as most of the United Kingdom. Now she has released a record Stateside, entitled "Just Call and I'll Be There." It's a longshot, but this one might just reach for the stars in our country pretty soon.

Anyways, Mmle. Hardy is a pleasant change-of-face *and voice!*

* * *

Where are they now? Gerry and the Pacemakers—one of the best groups to come out of the British invasion of 1964; Freddie and the Dreamers—one of the most *energetic* of the British groups; the Zombies, Billy J. Kramer and the Dakotas, Wayne Fontana and the Mind Benders—and all of the other British groups who had such big records during 1964 and part of 1965. Where are all of these artists from way over the Big Pond now?

You don't suppose they all got lost in the fog, do you??

THE BEAU BRUMMELS have finally returned home to California after a tour of the East coast and a guest shot in the movie "Wild, Wild Winter." But fellows, wasn't it a bit cold out there on that train all the way from the East? You could have asked for seats inside.

Lesley Gore On Funny Vacation

Lesley Gore sure has a funny idea about what vacations are for!

While everyone else took a couple of weeks off from school and saw all the good movies that came out, ate too much and exchanged all the lovely gifts they got for Christmas, Lesley took a couple of weeks off from school too, but for a different purpose.

She jumped at the opportunity to do a little more work! Vacationing from her studies at Sarah Lawrence College, Lesley completed her first dramatic role on ABC-TV's Donna Reed Show.

Then she flew Off to New York as one of the lucky stars selected to participate in Hullabaloo's year-end show on The Song Hits of 1965 for NBC-TV.

All this and straight A's too!

So that's your idea of a vacation, Lesley?

Managers Outdo Sonny and Cher

By Carol Deck

Sonny and Cher may be two of the wildest dressers in show business, but when it comes to wild parties, their managers showed them up last New Year's.

While Sonny and Cher were attending what Charlie Greene termed "a nice quiet private party," Charlie and his co-managing partner, Brian Stone, were taking a little ride.

All the way to Great Running River, Wyo., which Charlie assured me actually does exist.

Great Running River, Wyo., consists of "a bar, and that's about it," Charlie said, but it is exactly 24 hours away which Charlie and Brian thought was a good enough excuse to visit it.

So these two chartered a train, invited about 20 friends and took off the Thursday before New Years.

They rode all the way to Great Running River and then they rode all the way back. Now what better way can you think of to spend New Year's Eve than on a train with 20 friends on the way to Great Running River, Wyo.?

When they returned they went merrily off to see a James Brown performance but Charlie admitted that "after the first three hours of the party I remember very little, I fell asleep."

Charlie called it "the first rolling New Year's party" and the "great train ride." "It's the greatest

... GREENE AND STONE

innovation in parties," he stated.

In fact they thought it was such great fun that they're planning to do it again for the New Orleans Mardi Gras. They want to charter another train and ride all the way to New Orleans and back with a bunch of friends, including their latest talent discovery, Ronnie Danon.

Charlie sees the idea as something that could become a national pastime. He's predicting the day when "you'll pull into a train station and have four parties to choose from."

The BEAT thinks this is a great idea—at least it would solve some of the gargantuan traffic jams that occur with every holiday—but Great Running River, Wyo.?

KRLA ARCHIVES

How To Get Song Recorded
After Writing A Hit, Here's The Next Step

If you look at the labels on the Beatles' latest album "Rubber Soul," you will discover that every single one of the tracks was written by the Beatles. On previous albums, they have recorded mostly their own material, and added just a few of their favorite songs by other entertainers.

But it is becoming increasingly popular to write and record your own material. It seems somehow to lend a sort of distinctive sound to the end product.

Therefore, you find the Beatles writing and recording their own songs, and the same goes for Sonny and Cher, The Rolling Stones, Bob Dylan, and many other artists and groups.

But these people also write material for other artists to record, and The BEAT thought it might be sort of interesting to find out just how a writer goes about getting his material recorded by an artist.

I spoke with several of the top writers in the pop field today, including Brian Wilson, of the Beachboys.

Brian not only writes the songs which his group records, but he also arranges them and produces the sessions. He explained that, "Sometimes artists *ask* writers to write for them. I've had a few songs recorded by other people. I've written for Jan and Dean, and the Hondells and a few others. But mostly I just write for our group."

Tin Pan Row

In the East Coast area, there is Tin Pan Alley – the half-real, half-fictitious place where songwriters can grow and develop. It is a place where song writers will labor eight and ten hours a day on a song and work with it till they have it perfected.

Not so in the West Coast way of writing. In the West Coast area – without the benefit of a Tin Pan Alley – most of the songwriters want to do everything by themselves. They want to produce and arrange as well as write. Unfortunately, there are not enough good, straight song writers in this area.

But the field of music is not all that geographical, and is not necessarily strictly dictated by physical location. Much of the success of a pop song today depends on the basic material, and this in itself is something of a new phenomenon in the area of popular music.

Until very recently, a hot artist – accustomed to having chart successes with each single – could release almost any Bob Bop shoo bop bop type of record and expect it to sell.

Now, thanks to people like Bob Dylan, the listening public seems to be demanding a higher quality of song. Therefore, we have talented writers such as Burt Bacharach coming to the fore; the fantastic team of composers known as Lennon-McCartney; the young and talented writer-composer-singer P.F. Sloan, and several others.

Sloan Now Singing

In California, a young man named P.F. Sloan has been consistently turning out top notch material for other artists for some time now, and only recently has he turned to performing it himself.

The BEAT went to speak to Lou Adler, who is a publisher, producer, friend, and guide to P.F. – and a man who is well-acquainted with all of the technical aspects of producing a record.

We asked Lou just how an artist goes about getting his material recorded by various artists, and he explained that it all has a great deal to do with the way in which a song is serviced to the different artists.

"It's very diversified. Writers like Brian Wilson, for example, aren't really generally serviced. His songs are usually picked off an album which the Beachboys have already recorded. But then, he writes mostly for himself.

Songs Are Serviced

"Now with a writer like Flip (P.F. Sloan) – songs of his which we're very excited about are serviced to the various artists or individual A and R men whom we really respect.

"This happens when a writer – like Flip – is exclusive to a publisher, as Flip is to me. Then of course, a writer might get to the stature where the songs on his albums are picked off and recorded by other artists."

This has happened frequently with Flip, as well as Bob Dylan and other top composers of today.

Lou stressed the importance of the relationship between the publisher and the various A and R men. The A and R men, by the way, are the men who will send demos – demonstration tapes – of the songs written by their artists to various record companies or record producers for their artists to record.

A successful record producer will receive many such demos each week, therefore he quite frequently will listen first to the ones sent to him by the A and R men whose judgment he values and respects.

Writing Records

The whole area of demos is important too. Contemporary writers of today are not writing songs, as such – they are writing *records*. The fact is, that most of the successful singing artists today can't read music, therefore sheet music is of no great use to them.

Because of this, a writer will have his material recorded for him on what is known as a demo – a demonstration recording, which many times is as good or better than the finished product, or the master, as it is called. The sound achieved on this demo is, then, very important because it must accurately and flatteringly represent the writer's work.

Lou feels that the most important thing is "to have humility and patience in the people who represent you. You have to have faith. Amatuer writers should read the trades, etc., to find out which publishers are successful in the area of writing in which they are interested, and then take their work to them."

Keep Trying

He went on to explain that this work might not necessarily be accepted immediately by the first publisher on your list, but it is important not to give up after that first try. A good publisher can be of great value to a young writer in helping him to develop his talents.

We will continue this article in next week's *BEAT*, when we will be talking to P.F. Sloan, as a writer and a recording artist himself. Also, we will speak with Mason Williams, who is an extremely talented writer in the folk area, having written material for nearly all of the top entertainers in the folk field.

We will also interview several top producers and A and R men for some more exclusive behind-the-scenes information about the wide world of recording.

Three More For The Beach Boys

By Lynne Rosenthal

The place – a cocktail party – held in a large reception room in the Capitol tower in Hollywood. And the occasion? The presentation of three gold records – totaling fifteen gold records when presented to each individual Beachboy – by the RIAA (Record Industry Association of America).

The gold records were presented to the boys for more than one million dollars in sales on each of the three albums, which were "Surfin' USA," "Surfer Girl," and "Beachboys Today."

The Beachboys actually earned gold records for all five of the albums which they released during the year 1965, the other two being "Beachboy's Concert," and "All Summer Long," and in so doing, they topped the list of winners. There were only 28 other gold records awarded by the Association, and the Beachboys walked off with more than any other artist or group of artists.

There was, of course, speculation that possibly another group recording on the Capitol label – The Beatles – might have walked off with their share of the honors, but they received only two gold records for album sales in 1965 from the Association.

The reason for this being, primarily, that they had released only two *new* albums during the year which went immediately over the one-million dollar sales mark. All other albums released previously had already reached – and surpassed – the million dollar mark and had received awards for those sales.

Although not all of the five albums by the Beachboys were *released* in 1965, they all reached the million dollar sales plateau in that year.

Since the first Beachboys album – "Surfin' Safari" – released in November of 1962 – the group has become the largest selling American recording group in the world, and have sold over 15,000,000 records in that three-year period.

Brian Wilson, who is the leader, producer, arranger, and songwriter for the group, has won seven BMI songwriting awards during this three year period which is the largest number of awards yet presented to any American songwriter associated with this performing rights firm.

The Beachboys are currently concluding a month-long tour of the Far East which began on January 6, and are preparing their next single release for Capitol. Their latest LP was a live production, entitled "Beachboy's Party."

Dress Trouble Again For S&C

Sonny and Cher recently attended the ultra-high society premier of Richard Burton's latest movie, "The Spy Who Came In From the Cold," and apparently caused a little commotion due to their dress.

Burton and his wife, Elizabeth Taylor, showed up in their finest attire and Sonny and Cher showed up in *their* finest too.

But someone seemed to think that their dress wasn't up to par and the duo was seated a ways from ringside.

But Burton's ex-wife, Sybil, and her husband, Jordan Christopher, apparently think a little more of the Bonos. Sybil and Jordan are reported to have attended a costume party in New York dressed as Sonny and Cher.

And for those of you who have been wondering – Sonny and wife gave their managers, Charlie Greene and Brian Stone, a Cadillac convertible for Christmas, and Greene and Stone slipped them a ski boat.

British Top 10

1. DAY TRIPPER/ WE CAN WORK IT OUT......The Beatles
2. THE RIVER..............................Ken Dodd
3. THE CARNIVAL IS OVER..........The Seekers
4. KEEP ON RUNNING..........Spencer Davis
5. TEARS..................................Ken Dodd
6. WIND ME UP....................Cliff Richard
7. RESCUE ME....................Fontella Bass
8. MY SHIP IS COMING IN...Walker Brothers
9. 1-2-3...................................Len Barry
10. MERRY GENTLE POPS......Baron Knights

KRLA ARCHIVES

"Uptight" Brings Stevie Back In The Spotlight

"Little" Stevie Wonder is no more—now he's just Stevie Wonder. It seems the young blind harmonica player from Michigan is growing up.

"Little" Stevie joined the professional world of music at the young age of 12 and by the time he was 14 he was already a seasoned veteran.

His hit "Fingertips" stayed number one in the nation for over a month and brought in a series of tour and appearances including *The Ed Sullivan Show* and *American Bandstand* here and *Ready, Steady, Go* and *Thank Your Lucky Stars* in England.

Stevie was born in Saginaw, Mich., the third child of six. He's spent most of his life in Detroit, where his family moved shortly after he was born.

Studies Braille

Despite the handicap of being born blind he has mastered the piano, organ, drums and harmonica and sings as well. He has attended the Michigan School for the Blind, has a special education teacher when he's on the road and studies Braille music after hours.

His determination shows in the way this young boy has successfully joined that select circle of blind entertainers including the late Alec Templeton, George Shearing and the greatest of them all, Ray Charles.

Stevie was first attracted to show business when he visited the home of a friend, Gerald White. Gerald's brother, Ronnie White of

the Miracles, heard Stevie sing and brought him to the attention of Berry Gordy Jr., head of the highly successful Tamla-Motown Records.

His first release for Tamla was "I Call It Pretty Music" and sold quite well. He followed that with "Contract On Love," "Fingertips," "Workout, Stevie, Workout," "Harmonica Man" and "High Heel Sneakers."

He toured the country with he Motor Town Revue, which featured Motown's top artists such as Marvin Gaye, Martha and the Vandellas, Smokey Robinson and the Miracles and The Supremes, but he held his own among such impressive company.

Along the way he managed to cut six albums and film two of the Beach Party movies for American International Pictures.

It's been a little while since we've heard from Stevie, but now he's back with another smash—"Uptight."

He's no longer little, but he's as great as ever.

It's good to have you back Stevie.

Pop In Space

Good pop music is not only being played all over the world—it's being played in outer space too.

Paul Haney, the voice of Gemini, has said that pop recordings are a "tremendous morale booster" to the astronauts during their long flights in outer space.

The astronauts who made history with America's latest space venture, Gemini 6 and 7, were treated to recordings by Herb Alpert and the Tijuana Brass, Ramsey Lewis, Frank Sinatra and Dean Martin during their flights.

All recordings heard by the astronauts during their flights are donated by the recording companies.

The BEAT wonders how this will effect the charts—like outer space isn't a country, so on who's charts do the astronauts' listening habits show up?

Dear Susan

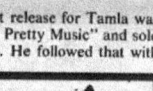

By Susan Frisch

Is there a "Help" album out in the U.S. with just the songs, and no instrumentals? —Blake Loutensock.

No.

How many children does David McCallum have? —Joanne Rutzig.

He has 3 boys.

Who is the girl who dances on Where The Action Is, and has long blonde pig tails? —Mike Stork

Joy Ciro.

Are the Beatles coming back for sure this year? —Sally Jo Kooper

Yes!

Does James Brown and the Flames plan on doing a tour of England in the near future? —Frank.

There has been no confirmation of a tour.

Do you know what month, and what places the Stones will go to in their next tour of the States? And where I could get tickets? —Donna Braddock

The exact date and locations are not yet known.

How much is a John Lennon hat? —Tommy K.

They run from 2 to 4 dollars.

Is John Lennon writing another book? —Beatle Fan

He has made no confirmation.

What is the translation of the French words that Paul sings in Michelle? —Kathie Hancock

They are the same words as sung in English.

Will the television special honoring John and Paul be shown soon?

This year, no.

How old is Phil Spector? —N.R.

In his twenties.

Where can I write to Elvis Presley and be sure of him getting it personally? —Wanting to Know

In care of R.C.A. Victor, 6363 Sunset Blvd., Hollywood, Calif.

Is it true that Gene Pitney is going to sue Sonny and Cher? —A Fan

For what!!!!!!

Do you know when the Rolling Stones will be back to Calif? And where can I write them a very personal letter and be sure of them getting it? —Lydia Perez

They won't be back till next year, probably around summer. Write to them at London Records, 539 W. 25th St., New York, N.Y.

Can you please give me the address where I can write to Ian Whitcomb, besides Tower Records? —Barbara Sirchia

Sorry, but Tower is the best I can give you.

ALBUMS GO 'ROUND
LP's Are Happenin'

The BEAT keeps it's readers well informed about what single discs are popular where, but many of you have written, asking how your faves rate on the LP charts.

Well, here's how! They don't just rate. They dominate!

A few years back, albums sold mostly to adults, and sales were low and slow. Then teenagers got into the act and now business is booming!

Each week, the 150 best-selling albums in the country are tabulated. During the last week in December, 90 of those LP's were by teenage favorites, and that's a pretty good average of how many of "our people" register on the charts every week.

During the week just mentioned, four of the albums were by the chart-toppers of all time, the Beatles. To date, the Beatles have recorded eight albums, and every one but "Rubber Soul" reached the number one slot.

'Rubber Soul'

"Rubber Soul" hasn't as yet because it hasn't had time. It appeared on the charts for the first time during the week just mentioned, coming in at #106.

It generally takes from six to twelve weeks for an album to hit the top (if that's the direction it's headed in). The Beatles usually manage it in two or three. So it's only a matter of time for "Rubber Soul."

Since albums remain on sale much longer than single records, they also remain on the charts longer (providing that they're selling, of course.)

The other three Beatle albums which are still best-sellers are "Help" (#11 after 18 weeks on the chart), "Beatles VI" (#54 after 27 weeks), and "Beatles '65" (#113 after 52 weeks).

As these albums travel back down the best-seller lists on a return voyage from the number one slot, they'll meet "Rubber Soul" on its way up!

Single record sales are a good indication of what will happen on the album charts. When an artist or group has a hit or two, their next venture is usually an album. And if their hits were hot enough, that album will register on the LP charts.

Newcomers

Newcomers like the Gentrys are a good example. After a smash single, their album of the same name ("Keep On Dancing") is on its way up, holding down the #121 spot its second week on charts.

The Turtles' LP ("It Ain't Me Babe"), now at #134, also shows promise of going much higher.

There are also a number of artists whose albums are *guaranteed* to hit the charts hard. When the Rolling Stones cut an LP, everyone knows it will head right for the top.

Groups and artists who are surefire bets often have more than one best-seller on the charts at a time.

The Stones have two others at present, besides their new "December's Children," which is #8 in the nation.

"Out Of Our Heads" is #19 after 21 weeks, and "The Rolling Stones Now" is #53 after 41 weeks.

Best Bets

Other best bets are the Supremes, the Beach Boys, Roger Miller, Elvis, Joan Baez, Bob Dylan, the DC 5, the Tijuana Brass, Herman's Hermits, Sonny and Cher, the Righteous Brothers and James Brown, just to mention a few.

All have one or more albums on the charts now, as always.

Coming up fast in the album world, with several LP winners to their credit so far, are Jay & The Americans, Gary Lewis & The Playboys, Donovan, the Four Seasons, the Animals, the Ramsey Lewis Trio and the Byrds.

Some artists prefer to concentrate largely on albums. The Ventures, for instance, have had many more top LP's than they've had singles. The Kingsmen have also had more success at 33-1/3 than at 45 rpm. In fact, their "Louie Louie" album has been on the charts longer than any other teen-oriented LP (as of this writing). After 102 weeks on the charts, it's still staying in there at #111.

The two albums which have stayed on the charts the longest in history are "Johnny's Greatest Hits" (Johnny Mathis), which is #91 after 377 weeks and "My Fair Lady" (Original Broadway Cast), now #148 after 477 (honest!) weeks.

Other Highlighters

Other highlighters on that week's charts were "You Were On My Mind" (We Five—#32), "The Miracles Going A Go-Go" (#59), "Hang On Sloopy" (McCoys—#78), "Having a Rave Up With The Yardbirds" (#121), "The Baroque Beatles Book" (The Merseyside Kammermusikgisillschaft?—#122), and "Go Away From My World" (Marianne Faithfull—#138).

That's about all the album news and notes we have room for this issue, but we promise more of the same soon.

Gary Lewis Busy

Gary Lewis and the Playboys, currently on the charts with "She's Just My Style," are going to be a little busy next month.

The group has been booked solid for the entire month of February on a concert tour that will include Iowa, Nebraska, Michigan, New York, Pennsylvania, Maryland, Maine and Massachusetts.

And somewhere along the way they're slated to film their third Ed Sullivan Show which will air Feb. 20.

KRLA ARCHIVES

Adventures of Robin Boyd
By Shirley Poston

CHAPTER TWELVE

The last thing Robin Boyd remembered was being just off the coast of England, happily winging her way toward the Rolling Stones.

The next thing she knew, she was peering groggily up at a blue jay wearing a silver helmet.

There are some people in this world who would have been disturbed by a situation of this nature.

And, being one of those people, Robin broke into noisy sobs.

"Hush," the blue jay said sternly. "You'll be all right. Maybe this will teach you to watch where you're going."

"Huh?" Robin blithered.

"You ran smack into me," the blue jay explained, looking sterner. "At a speed of *6,000 miles per hour*."

6,000 M.P.H.

Robin broke into noisier sobs, noticing the badge on his helmet. This was no ordinary blue jay who got his kicks flying about in silver helmets. This was a member of the dread Bird Patrol, and since Robin had been exceeding the speed limit by no less than *1,000* m.p.h., she was in a pickle less than pretty.

But, Robin Boyd was a rare bird in both senses of the word, and well accustomed to getting herself out of various jams (not to mention several jellies.)

"Officer," she purred charmingly, using the same tone which had worked on the policeman who had recently undertaken to inform her that one does not make a left turn while on a freeway.

"I had no *idea* I was going that fast. And my glasses were fogged," she added, pointing to her tiny Byrd specs and giving him a myopic but not unattractive bat of the old eyelash.

The blue jay tried not to smile and Robin leaped at the chance to firmly cement her defense.

"Besides," she hurried. "I've been looking all *over* for you."

The bluejay perked up his ears (which ain't easy and you'd better believe it). "For me?" he echoed.

Robin nodded warmly. "I came all the way from America to see the Rolling Stones and now I'm *hopelessly* lost." (Just another in a long line of big fat ones.)

"I'll take you to the Stones myself," the blue jay said proudly. "On two conditions."

"Anything," Robin promised rashly.

"You will never again exceed the speed limit," said the officer of the law.

Robin crossed her heart.

"And you will meet me after the concert," said the officer of the law.

Robin crossed her eyes. Inwardly, of course.

"I'd love to," she simpered, this being the biggest and fattest one thus far.

Seconds later, the twosome were winging away from the Bird Patrol outpost (atop the mast of Radio Caroline) and in only moments they came to rest on a marquee.

"You'll find the Stones here," said the blue jay. "And I'll find *you* here later."

"Definitely," Robin promised, her knees almost knocking at the nearness of Mick Jagger.

The blue jay leered openly.

Teapot Ticketed

"Good," he said. "That way I won't have to give you a ticket. I had to give one earlier, you know. To a tea pot," he added confidentially.

Robin's knees stopped almost knocking and rapped loudly.

"Did you say a *tea pot*?" she quaked.

When the blue jay nodded, Robin rose six feet into the air and flew hysterically through a nearby window.

Fortunately, the window was open at the time and Robin landed in a deserted but cluttered room. Whereupon she immediately threw herself into the nearest corner and had a tantrum.

And, who *wouldn't* have? It wasn't bad *enough* that she had a late date with a *blue jay*. She was also being followed by a *tea pot*. A tea pot containing the one person she didn't want around when she had come all this way to kidnap Mick - er - see the Stones. A sneaky genie named George, who else?

Suddenly, Robin's tantrum was interrupted.

A light was snapped on, and the room was quickly filled with, from Robin's vantage point, feet.

Oh, no, she shrieked inwardly. What if they *see* me? Before I change back into my sixteen-year-old self, that is?

Terrified

And she had good reason to be terrified. There was nothing like the sight of a *real* robin wearing *glasses* to make one feel like one had surely dropped one. (If you don't believe it, just ask the Beatles.)

Looking wildly around, Robin searched for a hiding place. Then she saw it. Just above her. A jacket hanging on a clothes rack.

Quickly, in one silent (she hoped) flutter, Robin leaped for the jacket and sank her claws into it. Seconds later, she was huddled safely in the pocket.

At least she *thought* so for about three seconds. Then she changed her mind. Because someone suddenly removed the jacket from its hanger and put it on (the jacket, not the hanger).

The Last Time

Then that same someone began to hum a familiar tune in a familiar voice. "This could be the last time," hummed said someone, and Robin promptly fainted.

Not only because she was in the pocket of *Mick Jagger's* jacket. Also because it could well *be* the last time she was in *anything* with the possible exception of a very small grave.

For, before this night was over, Robin Boyd was going to be folded.

(To Be Continued Next Week)

Cannibal's No Longer Hungry

From the "Forgotten Village" to the "Land of 1000 Dances" Cannibal and the Headhunters have come out as the leaders of the "blood sound."

Joe and Robert Jaramillo started singing together as part of an occupations therapy program in the "Forgotten Village," a Federal Housing Project known as Ramona Gardens.

They were members of an organized teen age club called The Headhunters, sponsored by the Los Angeles juvenile probation department and encouraged by the Federated Youth Council. The club's purpose was to keep underprivileged youth out of trouble by providing organized recreation.

In another organized teen club called the Romanos, part of a similar program, was a young boy with no given name, known only as Cannibal Garcia. He was singing with a rock and roll band in the club.

Yo Yo and Rabbit

Joe, who's called Yo Yo, and Robert, known as Rabbit, met Cannibal at a party after a talent show for all the FYC groups. The three just started singing together and discovered they had something.

That night they spontaneously became Cannibal and The Headhunters and have been together since.

During the year they worked and worked on their sound and their music and were finally asked to leave their clubs to make room for other needy youth. They were no longer considered needy – they were too good, too popular, making money and considered professionals.

They were spotted at a California teen night club by the head of Faro Productions, who arranged for them to return to the same club for another appearance and set up a "live" recording session there.

From that session came "Land of 1000 Dances" and the three boys danced right into the hearts of thousands.

The record stayed near the top of the national charts for 27 weeks and has been making spasmodic returns across the country ever since. It was number one in Cincinnati just before Christmas and is back in the top 10 in Philadelphia now.

In April, 1965, they were part of a show that broke all attendance records with a ten consecutive day stay at the Fox Theater in Brooklyn, N.Y.

Then in August, 1965, we all got to see them when they were honored by being asked to join the Beatles' second American tour.

A Big Year

In one year they've had three hit singles and have put out their first album and appeared in concert at more than 200 cities in 45 states and three foreign countries. They've also been seen on practically every American television show that features pop singers.

There's just too much talent in this group for them to be anything but great.

In addition to singing, Cannibal plays the piano and saxaphone, arranges the group's harmony, writes songs and is an outstanding Mexican folk dancer.

Rabbit and Yo Yo both excel in gymnastics, tinker with automobiles and confess a certain fondness for girls.

The group has just finished another appearance at the Fox Theater in Brooklyn with the Murray the K Show, and they're on the prowl again.

Watch for Cannibal and the Headhunters.

THE FIVE AMERICANS were formed in mid-1964 while most of the boys were attending Southwestern State College. They soon became well-known throughout the states of Oklahoma, Texas and Louisiana. Then along came "I See The Light" and now the Five Americans are known all over the U.S. You see, music lovers have finally seen the light of the Five Americans.

KRLA ARCHIVES

Elusive Butterfly Brings Bob Lind

An elusive butterfly has brought us a brand new and refreshingly original talent by the name of Bob Lind who should be around for quite a while.

Bob was born in Baltimore, Maryland, Nov. 25, 1942 and raised in Chicago. He's had very little formal musical training, mainly because he can't stop writing songs long enough to *learn* how to write them.

He picked up a guitar when he was 11 and started taking lessons. But his teacher moved after four lessons and Bob decided he could do better on his own.

When he couldn't remember lyrics to songs he'd fill in his own, becoming more and more interested in writing songs himself.

First Break

His first break came when he was in college. He won a Hootennanny contest with two of his own songs. The $10 prize money wasn't much but the encouragement was.

It was enough to make him drop out during his last year at college and move to Denver to try his luck. For a while it seemed that nobody was interested in his originality until he met Al Chapman. Chapman owned The Analyst coffee house where he gave Bob his first professional proving ground. Bob proved himself so solidly that he stayed at The Analyst for a year and a half.

Then Chapman came through again by mailing a tape that he had produced by Bob to World Pacific Records. Dick Bock, head of WPR, liked it so much that one week later Bob found himself in Hollywood signing an exclusive contract with Bock as a recording artist and with Metric Music Publishing as a songwriter.

Dylan Fan

Bob's favorite composer is Bob Dylan and people often ask him if he writes about the same things Dylan does.

"Not at all," he replies. "Most of the time Bob sings about people who HATE each other and can't get along, while I stress the problems of those who LOVE each other and can't seem to make it."

But Bob recognizes that Dylan has opened the door for people like himself to break into the writing field.

Bob Lind is in love with living and the world is in love with his first release, "Elusive Butterfly."

We'll be hearing more from this boy.

... BARRY GORDON

Barry Gordon An Old Timer At 17

By Louise Criscione

The young man has been praised by most of the big stars in Hollywood, he's been on Broadway, appeared in Vegas and has guested on practically every one of the top television shows. His name is Barry Gordon and at 17 he is already an old-timer in the entertainment business.

Currently, Barry is starring in "A Thousand Clowns" alongside Jason Robards Jr. and Barbara Harris. It was Barry's performance in "Clowns" which prompted Jack Lemmon to say as he was leaving the theater, "Gordon gave as exciting a performance by a new actor as I have ever seen.

"Certainly deserving of an Academy Award nomination for Best Supporting Actor."

Everything Lemmon said is true except the part about Barry being "new." He isn't. "I started singing when I was about four," Barry told me.

A neighbor heard Barry singing around the house, recognized his talent and arranged for Barry to appear on "Ted Mack's Amateur Hour." Barry's parents knew nothing about it until they received a phone call from the television station advising them when to bring Barry down for the show.

A Winner

Barry won first prize in the regional Amateur Hour and with Mack returned to New York for the National Finals. NBC-TV's "Startime" spotted Barry and quickly signed him as a two-year regular on the show.

And others spotted Barry too. He appeared on "The Jackie Gleason Show," "The Milton Berle Show," "The Perry Como Show," etc., etc.

Vegas beckoned to Barry along about this time so he hurried off to the gambling capitol with Ken Murray and his famous "Blackouts."

It was during this period that Barry released a record which has become a Christmas classic, "Nutting For Christmas," a record which sold one and a half million the first year.

"People saw me in Vegas and asked me to come to New York to act," revealed Barry. So the Gordons moved back to New York and Barry took up acting on such shows as "Danny Thomas" and "Ann Southern."

Hollywood next called the talented Barry and so the Gordon family made another move—this time to the West Coast. And again there were more television shows for Barry.

Broadway Calls

"Then in 1962 we got a call from New York," explained Barry, "saying there was a major role on Broadway in 'A Thousand Clowns'."

You guessed it—the Gordons moved back to New York and Barry embarked upon a very successful run of "Clown."

He's 17 now and all of his school life has been spent as a professional entertainer. How does he manage? "When I was on the West Coast I went to public schools and then whenever a role came up I had a tutor," Barry said.

"When I was in New York I went to a professional school and on the road I did my schoolwork by correspondence."

Barry is now a senior at University High School in Los Angeles. I wondered if his fellow students treated him differently because he is an entertainer.

"No, not my real friends," declared Barry. "I never talk about show business with them. But I love it—it's not a grind for me. It's a lot of fun."

What about after he graduates? "I plan to go to UCLA and major in Theatre Arts, directing more than anything else," said Barry.

Ambitious

He's intense and ambitious. "I don't want to limit myself too much," he says. And he's kept his word so far. He's been on Broadway, in the movies, on television and in the clubs.

But that's not all. He has a record which will soon be released entitled "Let Me Try." "And when I go to college I'll be concentrating on screen writing."

Barry's very interested in politics and has been since he helped in the Kennedy campaign. If he had his way about it he'd lower the voting age to at least 18. "I think there is a great interest in politics among the teenagers who can't vote.

"Adults have so many things on their minds whereas teenagers don't have that much on their minds. A lot of people just don't care about the big world around them."

Barry has an opinion about most of the problems facing us today. What about these anti-Vietnam demonstrations so popular among our college students?

"It's hard for me to say because I don't agree with them. I could say that I believe in free speech and being able to voice an opinion. I don't have to agree with them but they can say it.

Stop The Marches

"I don't think they should make such a big issue out of it by marching down streets and blocking traffic. Just talk about it."

Along the lines of today's pop scene Barry says: "I don't think the English groups have had it yet. I don't feel that music should be a national trend. I see nothing wrong in importing English groups and singers if they have merit.

"I love the Beatles. I enjoy the Rolling Stones. The Beatles are so versatile and always stay one jump ahead of everyone else.

"I think protest songs will always be around. They're slacking off now a little bit. I think things will even out and there will be the same number of English groups as American groups."

Since he's sampled them all, what facet of the entertainment business does Barry enjoy the most? "I don't really know. Each one has its good points and its bad points. I like movies because it's much more creative to be a movie director. I like films because they're more relaxing."

A many talented person is Barry Gordon. And who knows. Maybe twenty years from now he'll be one of our Senators or Governors. I wouldn't put it past him.

... BOB LIND

KRLA ARCHIVES

THE BEAT GOES TO THE MOVIES
"PATCH OF BLUE"

By Jim Hamblin
(The BEAT Movie Editor)

STRINGING BEADS IN THE PARK, the blind girl for the first time in her life has left the scroungy apartment, where she lives with her frumpy mother and drunk grandfather.

A friendly voice greets her in the black sightless world of which she knows nothing. The voice is Gordon. He helps her. And comes back again and again to help her.

Sound like a simple story? It is. Simple, and beautiful. Watch for this movie to make a big impression on all those who see it. The Ku Klux Klan "ain't gonna' like it," but any person who has a soul at all will enjoy this touching photoplay, that brings together great talent.

Negro film star SIGNEY POITIER, (whose name, by the way, is pronounced PWAH-tee-ay), is Gordon. The girl is played by Elizabeth Hartman. It is her first movie, but we can assure you that it will *not* be her last. Her name is the favorite topic of Hollywood now as the new "find" in movie-making.

Metro-Goldwyn-Mayer producer Pandro Berman, who made this film, assumes that it will not even be shown in some Southern states. For the first time, a white girl kisses a Negro on the screen. How and why you can see for yourself, but Mr. Berman doesn't care. He knows he has a fine film, and that is satisfaction enough for him.

Berman has left many punches un-pulled in this dramatic film, and the enjoyment is all the better for it.

Our only argument is that the picture was made in the same primitive black and white that Charlie Chaplin used to use. What happened to color, and wide-screen movies? We're supposed to be in an age of technological advance, but insistance that "drama" must always be on little teeny screens and in grainy black and white is an old wives' tale.

Quite by coincidence, Poitier has also made another film that is somewhat similar in content, called "THE SLENDER THREAD." It has been released at almost the same time as "PATCH OF BLUE," but Producer Berman says he welcomes the two films.

"If the public sees one good movie," he noted, "then they want to come back again soon, and see another. It's the bad movies that drive everyone away for weeks."

Unfortunately, SLENDER THREAD is also *another* little tiny movie in black and white. If for no other reason, you'd think they'd make the movies in color to suit the demand of TV, when it gets old enough to be purchased by a network.

With the special symbolism of a black and white movie, there is still tremendous impact to PATCH OF BLUE. It has a moral to the story each of us should learn very carefully.

It's not all "drama," either. The funny moments come often, and PATCH will be one of 1966's most entertaining films.

MEETING IN THE PARK, the two central characters begin to get acquainted It is her first outing in the park, after 13 years of living in a crummy apartment, not even going to school. Gordon, who works for a newspaper, finds the girl in need of help, and finds something else as well. The story, which stars Elizabeth Hartman in her first film, is one of the best made films of the year.

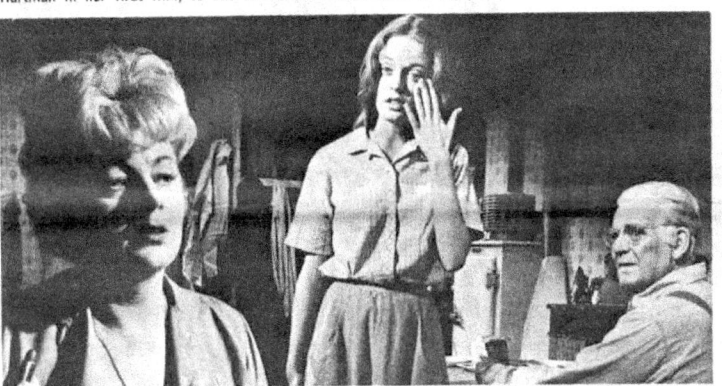
"ARE MY EYES UGLY, MOM?" The girl, who has never been outside this tenement dwelling, wonders if she is pretty. Her eyes are scarred, and she is blind, because of a fight her mother had with a lover, many years before. The girl has been locked up in a box, virtually, ever since. Academy Award winner Shelley Winters plays one of the most forceful and effective roles in her career. The grandfather, who can only offer alcohol for himself as a solution to the problems of life, is played by Wallace Ford, one of the great stars of the early days of film making in Hollywood.

A TENDER MOMENT as the blind girl explores the face of her new friend. Explosive suspense is built in the story as the girl's mother, a streetwalker, soon learns of her friendship with the man. Pulling no punches, the film reveals that the mother hates all Negroes, and she takes out that hatred in violence against the girl. The heart of this picture is the fact that the film portrays these things in an open and frank manner, and leaves you chilled by the reality that such hatred can destroy as surely as a rifle bullet.

IF YOU THINK IT'S EASY TO ACT in movies, try this scene on for size: You are Elizabeth Hartman, you have worked in New York and here and there, many times as a helper on the set of a play, but suddenly you are jetted to Hollywood, and must sit in front of a crowd of technicians, and act both dramatically and convincingly. What you see is film director Guy Green talking over the next scene What will appear on the screen is an intimate moment, of two people sitting by a tree. The film was shot in Douglas MacArthur Park, in Los Angeles, outdoor crowd scenes are in the Westlake District. The result of Miss Hartman's fine work may be a gold statue named Oscar.

KRLA ARCHIVES

FANTASTIC NEW POLICIES AT
The Rock & Roll Showplace of the World

Dave Hull's HULLABALOO

**NOW OPEN ON FRI., SAT., AND SUN., ONLY
PLUS SAT. AND SUN. MATINEES**

Held Over By Popular Demand

THE LIVERPOOL FIVE
Jan. 14, 15 & 16

2:00 P.M. SAT. & SUN. AFTERNOONS   JAN. 15 & 16

THE FORTUNES

Plus

THE LIVERPOOL FIVE

Plus

THE HUMAN BEINGS

Please Get Your Tickets In Advance

APPEARING ON EVERY SHOW
Hullabaloo Regulars
The PALACE GUARD

Take Advantage of our New Box Seat Policy

THIS COUPON WORTH 50¢
OFF Regular Admission When Presented at the Door
DAVE HULL'S HULLABALOO
6230 SUNSET (AT VINE)   Phone: HO 6-8281
Hollywood, Calif.   For Reservations

KRLA ARCHIVES

America's Largest Teen NEWSpaper

KRLA *Edition* **BEAT**

Volume 1, Number 47 LOS ANGELES, CALIFORNIA 15 Cents February 5, 1966

Batman: 'I'm the World's Greatest Put-On' . . . Page 2

KRLA ARCHIVES

KRLA BEAT

Los Angeles, California — February 5, 1966

FOR MOVIE SOUNDTRACK
Stones To Visit Coast In March

Andrew Oldham has announced that the Rolling Stones will make a surprise visit to Los Angeles sometime in March to record the soundtrack for their first movie, "Back, Behind And In Front."

All the songs for the movie were written by Mick Jagger and Keith Richard. There has to date been no confirmation on the type of songs which will be featured in the film nor has there been any hint of the movie's plot.

The Stones are keeping it top secret and are only revealing that the starting date is scheduled for April 10 and that the movie will be shot in England and in four Iron Curtain countries.

Although we'd all like to know what the movie will be about, it's actually better that we don't. Think back to "Help." Before the movie was even released we all knew the entire plot. And not only did we know the plot but we had seen all kinds of stills from the movie.

So, when we finally did arrive at the theater to view "Help" for ourselves it was as if we had seen the whole movie before. There was no surprise.

The Stones don't want that to happen to their movie. Instead, they want their audience to sit on the edge of their seat wondering what will happen next.

Following a guest appearance on "The Ed Sullivan Show" the Stones fly to Hawaii and then on to Australia where their tour opens on February 18 in Sydney.

In addition to Australia the Stones will appear in New Zealand at Wellington and Auckland, ending up their tour on March 3.

Japan is the next stop for the Stones. It is to be a very short visit to appear on a major television show but the boys are very excited about it as it is their first visit to Japan.

Winding up their business in Japan the Stones head Stateside for the RCA Recording Studios in Hollywood. They will barely have time to cut the soundtrack before flying off to England to actually begin filming.

It's a good thing that the Stones took a nice long breathing spell after their last American tour because it doesn't look like they'll have much time to rest until "Back, Behind And In Front" is filmed, scored and heading for your local theaters.

Beau Brummels' Ron Elliott Marries College Sweetheart

The BEAT has learned in an exclusive that Ron Elliott of the Beau Brummels is to be married on January 29 to Evelyn Kay Dane.

The ceremony will be held in San Francisco with only members of the family and a few close friends in attendance. Those close friends will, of course, include the other three Brummels—Sal, John and Ron.

Evelyn (or Danish as Ron calls her) is a 20 year old co-ed at San Francisco State College where she is majoring in Psychology. Danish was born and raised in Oakland and after their marriage the couple plan to live in San Francisco.

Ron met Danish when he was a student at State. They began dating off and on about two years ago and then Ron took to the road when the Brummels began making it big.

However, the two got together again when Ron was forced to stop touring about two months ago because of ill health. Don Irving, a friend of Ron's, has been taking Ron's place with the Brummels on the road but Ron does make all of the important dates.

Following their wedding Ron and Danish will take off on an extended honeymoon. Danish plans to take a leave from school but will return and finish her last year at State.

The BEAT would like to take this opportunity to wish Danish and Ron the very best of luck and just all kinds of happiness. We know that the rest of you Beau Brummel fans do too.

...HAPPY BRIDEGROOM

Batman Confesses!

"I don't know who it is behind that mask—but we need him, and we need him now."
—The Commissioner

By Homer Grouse

GOTHAM—In answer to that desperate plea, Batman has made his entrance on the American scene with a *Pow* and *Zap* and a *Bop* unequalled in television history.

And, golly whiz, gang, he's brought his young friend Robin and the Batmobile and the batcave with him. It's all there on Wednesday and Thursday nights on ABC.

Some cynics have declared that it's all a put-on—and they're absolutely right. Batman is putting on the whole world, and judging from initial response to the show, the world loves to be put-on.

Adam West, who now occupies the innermost position with the "in" group, explained it all to *The BEAT* as he sat between shows dressed in his Batman outfit, replete with a black bat emblem on his chest.

Square Hippy

"Batman is so square he's the greatest hippy in the world," West explained. And the tall, well-muscled man with blond hair and a clean-cut face readily confirmed our suspicions when he admitted, "Actually he's putting on the whole world.

"This whole thing is an insane, mad fantasy," laughed West, "and my goal is to become America's biggest put-on."

West, who used to be on the Detectives series with Robert Taylor, seems to be the perfect choice for the role. He can't talk about the show without breaking up.

Part of Batman's charm is that he's a human hero. Superman can go out on a job confident that bullets will bounce off his superchest. But unlike Superman, Batman isn't super strong. He can't fly through the air like a plane or a bird. Thus, he has to rely on his own skill, plus a pure and fearless heart and an assortment of bat-gear.

According to the Batman legend, Bruce Wayne is a young millionaire whose parents were killed by bandits when he was a child. He lives in a mansion, and to most people he is just a philanthropist. But we know better, and so does Dick Grayson, his young ward, who goes out on the prowl with Batman as his young sidekick Robin and helps him Zok crooks and decode mysterious riddles.

Pure Motives

West says that Batman is the only hero on the air motivated by pure do-goodism. All the rest are paid detectives, spies, military men or just plain sadists. Assisted by Robin, Batman is a one-man poverty-peace corpsman.

As for his personal life, West admits that he enjoys his off-duty hours on Saturday nights. Then he can just be himself.

"I get to use the Batmobile on Saturday nights," West explained. "I can ride around town with my two pets, Squeak and Squawk."

"Squeak and Squawk? What are they?"

"Bats," said West.

"...PUTTING ON THE WHOLE WORLD"

Beatles Loafing Through First Six Months of Year

LONDON—The Beatles are in such a high tax bracket they will practically loaf the first half of this year, according to BEAT informants.

George Harrison disclosed part of the story behind the relaxed schedule, stating that the famous foursome has not a single date fixed for all of 1966.

But friends explain that this is only because some details, now being negotiated, have not been completed. Manager Brian Epstein is now abroad arranging an American tour for late summer, although all details are not yet known.

However, The BEAT has learned that the Beatles are tentatively scheduled for concert dates in Los Angeles and San Francisco in August—approximately the same dates as last year's concerts.

RINGO STARR sports a movie-type beard as he leaves London Airport for a vacation in the Caribbean. "It's just that I haven't been working and I haven't had to shave," he explained. "I hate shaving anyway." His wife, Maureen, and Mr. and Mrs. John Lennon were also on the trip.

Inside the BEAT

Fortunes—Funny Guys	3-4
Teddy Bear and Lurch	5
Sonny and Cher At Home	6
Adventures of Robin Boyd	7
McCallum Records Lennon	8
Lennon's Legend	8
Visit With Yardbirds	11
Yardbirds At Ease	12
How Hits Are Written	13
Kingsmen Need Perry	14
Change For Billy Joe	15
Kinks Take Big Splash	16

The BEAT is published weekly by BEAT Publications, Inc., editorial and advertising offices at 6290 Sunset Blvd., Suite 504, Hollywood, California 90028. U. S. bureaus in Hollywood, San Francisco, New York, Chicago and Nashville, overseas correspondents in London, Liverpool and Manchester, England. Sale price, 15 cents. Subscription price: U.S. and possessions, $5 per year, Canada and foreign rates, $9 per year. Application to mail at second class postage rates is pending at Los Angeles, California.

KRLA ARCHIVES

A Fortunate Day For The Beat

By Carol Deck

The word fortune is used to describe good luck, bad luck and five fantastically funny guys from England.

The Fortunes – Rod Allen, Andy Brown, Dave Carr, Glen Dale and Barry Pritchard – dropped by *The BEAT* office during their recent American visit and left the place in a state of even more than usual chaos.

It went something like this – there I sat peacefully behind the desk, not doing anyone any harm, not doing anything as a matter of fact, when in walks this perfectly adorable young man, shakes my hand and says "Hi, I'm Glen" flashing the world's greatest smile.

He was followed in quick succession by four more hand shaking smiling fellows and their manager.

Babbling all at the same time, they proceeded to tell me about their act.

"It's great," Rod said modestly.
"It's nothing really," added Barry helpfully.
"We're the same now as we'll always be – great."

Hand Springs?

And what is this fantastic act? Well, according to these five, Barry does hand springs while playing a solo on the guitar, and Andy hangs from the chandelier while playing the drums.

"He got the idea from Perry Como," added Barry.

The secret to their success with such hits as "You've Got Your Troubles" and "Here It Comes Again"?

"We sing good," offered Glen.
"We have a fantastic drummer," added Andy (guess what instrument he plays.)

"Our drummer has one more tom tom than anyone else," said Barry, "that he plays with his nose."

How long has he been playing tom toms with his nose? "About

...GLEN

seven inches," he chirped, gazing down his nose.

Then they proceeded to try and convince me that Mick Jagger just got a Yul Bryner hair cut (you know, like bald) and the rest of the Stones now have Pat Boone style hair cuts. Sure, fellows.

From Stones to Beatles they went. Glen had it all figured out.

"They'll never dwindle, they'll pack up and get out."

When they do pack up and get out he figures John will become a producer, George will form an orchestra, Paul will continue singing and writing and Ringo will become a "personality, opening stores and things."

The Fortunes generously said that when they get their own show that the Beatles can guest on it individually or as a group. This group is just full of modesty and generosity.

Then things somehow got a little out of hand and I found myself being interviewed by their manager while they interviewed each other. Now, that's no way to conduct an interview, so I yelled "Stop" and they did – sixty seconds of dead silence. That's no way to conduct an interview either, so we went on to talk about America.

Before coming over here they thought the country would be cold and unfriendly, mainly because of some of the American servicemen they had met in Germany. Glen expected America to be "loud and fast moving."

Well, then they arrived in New York and formed some more definite ideas about America.

Rude

"I hate New York policemen," said Glen. "They're downright rude." He added that pizza is also on his hate list and Rod tossed in that *he* hates black olives and white olives.

"Your hotels are useless," said Glen.

...ANDY

"The rooms are great, but the service is terrible," said Rod.

"And you can't get Yorkshire pudding anywhere," complained Glen.

Barry added that he really likes America but "there are too many bloomin' Americans here." He then continued on to say that he thinks polar bears make great couches and asked me to pass on a request to all American girls. "Tell all the girls not to cut their hair," he pleaded (and with Barry's magnificent sparkling blue eyes, you listen when he pleads) "they're all cutting their hair in England."

Glen tossed in another point for American girls – he thinks they're more "genuine" than British girls.

Actually it's amazing that they have any good impressions of America at all. They've run into trouble everwhere they go here.

They arrived in New York with visas in hand and were refused work permits. They finally received permission to film a Murray the K special but were stopped from doing a Hullabaloo episode, and the Moody Blues, who came over around the same time, couldn't get any kind of work permit and returned sadly to England.

More Trouble

The Fortunes then came on to the West Coast to film some television shows and do several live performances but ran into more troubles getting work permits and hotel accommodations.

"They didn't believe we were a group because we weren't dressed in tatty jeans," explained Glen.

For a while they were even afraid they were about to be deported, but they finally worked out their problems with immigration and the musicians union and were able to complete everything they were booked for.

The conversation then went on to music and cowboys.

GLEN DISCUSSES Yorkshire pudding with **BEAT** reporter Carol Deck, and what is Louise Criscione gazing at? The other 4 Fortunes, of course.

KRLA ARCHIVES

WAR GAMES — Dave deplores droughts, Glen studies mushroom clouds, Barry hides things behind his back, Andy threatens poor little Rod with a chocolate covered marshmallow.

...BARRY

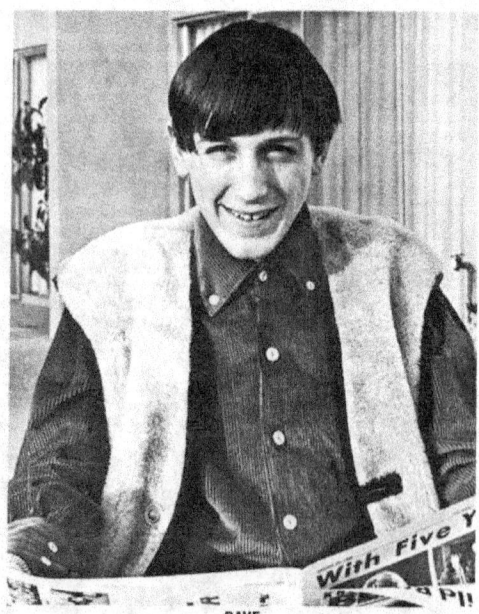

...DAVE

Glen prefers to listen to Andy Williams, opera, jazz and the "Bootles." Andy likes "Twitt Conway and Allen Sherbet." Barry likes Tommy Sands and Brain Wilson. Rod likes Timi Yuro, the Drifters and anything that's good and Dave said he likes Dionne Warwick, Jackie DeShannon and the Four Seasons (and added with a smile "who else do we want to like *us*?)

And all five think Sammy Davis Jr., is the greatest since they got to see "Golden Boy" during their New York stay.

And cowboys? Don't ask me why, but they think Roy Rogers is a much better cowboy than Gene Autry. Barry proudly proclaimed that he had touched Trigger when he (Barry) was eight and Glen announced that he's the fastest draw in Ashford, Eng. OK fellows, if you say so.

The boys spent a good deal of time watching television while they were here. What did they watch? "Commercials," they all shouted at once. They particularly go for the Doublemint gum commercial.

Movie Wishes

They saw a few movies in between commercials and decided *they* wanted to do a movie. Barry would like to do a horror movie while Glen would prefer a western. Dave would like to do a James Bond sort of thing and Rob wants to play Pinnochio.

At this point Barry tossed in a very helpful definition. He said, "A song is a song with words that was written by somebody" Bet ya didn't know *that*.

Then Glen, while slowly dismantling the desk set, said, "We're quite proud of our ability to hear a record and predict if it's going to be a hit." And what do they predict is going to be the next big hit? "This Golden Ring" by the Fortunes," they shouted in unison.

Then time ran out, and after all five of them and their manager had kissed my hand, they departed, leaving me utterly destroyed.

KRLA ARCHIVES

...TOM POOLE, TOM FUNK, NOONEY RICKETT, KENT DUNBAR

The Nooney Rickett Four – A Teddy Bear and Lurch

By Carol Deck

When some people hear the name Nooney Rickett Four they respond with 'what's that, some kind of disease?' But once you've seen the group perform you know exactly what they are.

They're four very talented fellows who are slowly working their way straight to the top.

Nooney Rickett, and that really is his name, is a solid down-to-earth guy who goes on stage like a smooth guy but comes off like a large ruffled teddy bear.

He's a quiet sort who drinks hot tea and honey 'cause he likes it and because he can cream his way through "Shout" longer since the honey keeps his throat in good shape.

But when he gets on stage and gets going, he gets all worked up, his hair gets a bit messed and he looks just like a large ruffled teddy bear.

Lurch?

The group's drummer, Kent Dunbar, is something else. He'll sit on stage looking very much like Lurch of the Addams Family, with little or no motion or expression. Then after a while, he gets warmed up to a number and he'll slowly break into a smile that's actually more like a leer and then rock out with some of the wildest drummin' you'll ever hear. He's just too much to believe.

Then there's the two Toms. Tom Funk is the saxophone player who claims the group is the laziest group around. Asked about the group's plans for the future he said, "I thought we might try some rehearsals." You see they never rehearse except maybe once a gig. They just sort of work things out on stage. They sometimes even try to learn the words in the middle of a performance.

Those Eyes

Tom Poole has got a set of eyes that look right through everything – walls, people, everything. He possesses a tremendous ability to concentrate on one matter. The rest of the group claim that Poole can start a conversation with someone, get rudely interrupted, and three days later he'll start off exactly where he left off. He just sits there, solid as a rock, and waits. It's like impossible to get him off a track once he gets on it.

His power of concentration comes through on stage too, as he stands there calmly playing the trumpet and bass guitar at the same time. He holds the trumpet with his right hand while playing the guitar with his left.

Health Nuts

And all four of the group are health fiends. Their favorite foods are avocados, carrots, celery and such. All four once lived on nothing but berries for two weeks. Asked if this inspired them at all, Nooney replied "Yeah, it inspired us to eat more berries."

They feel that the way you eat reflects the kind of person you are. "The better you eat, the better you are," explained Funk, "so why just eat traditional?"

And traditional is one thing this group isn't. They're fast moving up-to-date guys who can play just about everything from rhythm and blues to hard rock to gospel.

They're a tremendous dance group and a group of really great guys. And they've just released their very first single "Bye Bye Baby," which they also wrote.

Soon the whole world will know exactly what the Nooney Rickett Four is, so watch for them.

On the BEAT
By Louise Criscione

The Rolling Stones are coming Stateside again to pay their third visit to the "Ed Sullivan Show" on February 13. They will stop off in New York for the show and then fly on to Hawaii for two concerts before jetting to Australia for their last tour before beginning "Back, Behind And In Front."

During the Beatles' last U.S. visit Brian Epstein let it be known to all promoters that the Beatles were on their last American tour.

However, Epstein has now changed his mind and has announced that it is highly likely that the Beatles *will* tour America again at the end of this summer. But it all depends on how their third movie goes.

And as of right now, it's not going too well. So, it looks as if the starting date will be pushed back from April. Naturally, if this happens the Beatles will be tied up longer than originally expected, thus forcing their U.S. tour to be either delayed or cancelled.

Herman's Coming

While the Beatles and Stones are busy making movies in April, Herman will be visiting his Stateside fans again. Herman is still lamenting the fact that he is not too terribly big in Britain. "Although it's great to be big in America I wish even more that we could get another number one record in Britain."

Herman admits that he has changed considerably in the last year and credits his changed self to the many people whom he has met and who have advised and helped him along the way.

...JOHN LENNON

Herman then added with a grin: "I now take a lot more interest in the welfare of the group and I've learned a lot about profits and percentages."

We haven't heard from Donovan for quite some time now but he is just about ready to hit us in the ears with his next single, one side of which is scheduled to be "For John And Paul."

You guessed it. "For John And Paul" is Donovan's tribute to the Lennon-McCartney songwriting team. Don says: "I have tried to create something new and I hope the record buying public will like it."

Do We Care?

Poor Tom Jones is all bent out of shape because so many U.S. teens have never even *heard* of the great American soul singers. He says: "I wonder sometimes if they care about something that's really good or whether it means more if it's just up there on the hit parade."

Think it over. Is Tom right? Do we really not care who's good and who is bad but has somehow managed to get a record high on the charts? Personally, I think Tom is about half right. A perfect example is the Yardbirds.

The BEAT has been telling you how fantastic they are for months and months now. But I wonder how many of you actually believed us until you saw The Yardbirds for yourselves.

We do know for a fact that those of you who did see them "live" absolutely blew your minds over them. We know because our phones have been ringing off the hook ever since the boys hit town!

And the letters have been driving our poor mailman crazy – he says his back just won't take much more of it! Anyway, it looks as if all kinds of people are switching their allegiance from the Beatles and Stones to the Yardbirds. So watch for Keith, Jim, Jeff, Chris and Sam to be the next really big group Stateside.

Well Respected Ray

How do you think Ray Davies got the inspiration to write "A Well Respected Man?" He says it came to him while he was staying in a "snobbish" hotel. "I felt a bit sick – even though I was paying the same money as all the business men who were also there.

"But I was wearing old jeans and so on. So the way I felt, the way I wanted there and then to be respected, which has nothing to do with money, I wrote a song. It was 'Well Respected Man.'"

...RAY DAVIES

QUICK ONES: The Spencer Davis group receive quite an honor when they play two 30 minute spots at Yale University on February 25, the biggest night of the year at Yale... The Beatles all have new Mini cars..

KRLA ARCHIVES

Exclusive BEAT Tour
Sonny and Cher - At Home

BEAT Photos: Bob Feigel

By Bob Feigel and Jeanne Castle

Sonny and Cher cordially invite BEAT readers on the first tour of their new house.

As we drive through beautiful Encino and approach the top of one of the highest hills, we pull into the circular drive of the spacious Spanish Rustic-style home of two of our favorite stars, Sonny and Cher.

Our anxiety reaches its peak as we approach the front door, wondering if we should remove our shoes. We knock—No!—a butler doesn't answer—it's Sonny with a dust cloth in one hand and a vacuum cleaner in the other.

Sonny says "Come on in kids" and off he goes to put away the vacuum (until later). Cher waves as she runs from one room to the other and says "Hi, be right with you; come on in."

Take A Peek

While we wait for Sonny and Cher to escort us on our visit, we can take a peek around the corner to the right and see the beautiful powder room with flowers cascading from a huge wrought iron bird cage.

Oh! Our host and hostess are here now, and we proceed down the hall beyond and to the right of the powder room and we enter the master bedroom. On the right is a king size bed with a massive Spanish headboard made of antiqued off-white and gold wood. The bed is covered with an off-white brushed velvet bedspread. Cher shows us her beautiful new white negligee with ostrich feather sleeves. Wow!

While Sonny shows Bob the intricate design in the rest of the Spanish-style antique furniture and the sculptured wrought iron candelabra bedside lamps, we can stray over to another room off the bedroom.

No, it's not an indoor Grecian swimming pool; it's the master bath with sunken tub and flowers growing everywhere. The color scheme here is light and dark greens and brown, to enhance the marble top dressing table.

Across the Hall

We now go across the hall to the formal dining room. This room is one such as you would see in an old Spanish castle. The first thing that we notice is the unusual wrought iron light fixture that hangs low over the massive round dining table. The table is surrounded by high back wrought iron chairs with seats covered in a rich green plush. The drapes are deep green with a white fringe.

Against one wall is a large Spanish-style chest of drawers with two wrought iron candelabras. On another wall are two intricately designed iron candle holders, each with two large gold candles. The other wall has a large mirror set in an antiqued wood frame. The wall paper is contemporary Spanish Baroque in gold and white.

Across the hall and through the two wrought iron doors into the den, where we can sit a while and relax. We can look out into the patio area, beyond the crystal blue water in the pool and see the entire valley—it's almost breathtaking.

Strange Chess

We are sitting on a white and gold couch and in front of us is a huge round coffee table; across the room is another round table somewhat taller, on which they have a most unusual chess set.

The kitchen is just across and

SONNY AND CHER pause and clown a bit in front of the mirror in the formal dining room of their new home.

THE BONOS — in love again, this time with their new California home.

down the hall from the den. Come in, it's a bright, cheerful room. The table and chairs are wrought iron, the light fixture above the table is another unusual wrought iron design. There are several potted plants with yellow and orange flowers on a shelf along the wall.

The wall paper is light and has a border of yellow and orange flowers, and the appliances are brown. (Can't you just see Sonny cooking spaghetti in here?!!)

Baby Room?

Cher has just invited us to follow her to the blue room and the baby room (Boy, we'll have to find out about this!). The blue room is a guest room with twin corner beds; the rug is beige and the wallpaper is light blue, with light blue, dark blue, and light green huge flowers. The furniture is white.

We are about to trip over each other going down the hall to see the "Baby Room"—we don't see any play pen or baby crib, so Cher explains: "It's called the baby room because it is done in pale yellows and beige and gold tones."

This room has a beige rug and beige and gold furniture. There are two twin corner beds covered with beige spreads. This room can be converted into a nursery at some later date.

That Garage

Well, we have been through the whole house and agree that it is really a storybook showplace. 'Scuse me for a minute—there is a door off the kitchen and we weren't invited to see, so I want to find out what it is. Oh!! it's the garage (Pardon me!)—Sonny's music room.

We are back in the den again and have been invited to sit around the table and have pizza pie with Sonny and Cher, who are sitting on the floor around the table. We are discussing Sonny and Cher's new movie and their new records and albums for the near future. They will keep us informed as to what will transpire and when.

While eating pizza the subject gets around to cooking and we find out that Sonny likes to cook but the kitchen isn't big enough (he has to use the den and other rooms in the house)—perhaps it's the overflow of pots, pans, and dishes he uses.

Cher is content doing (what she calls) menial chores such as picking up and cleaning after Sonny.

Wilson Type

Cher is so proud to tell us that her interior decorator is the famed Ronnie Wilson who did the house in contemporary Spanish motif.

As we look out into the patio area the sky is getting slightly dim towards late afternoon and we must get ready to leave. We go across the room to look at the beautiful view of the valley once more as we bid good-night to our gracious hostess Cher.

But! We can't find Sonny. Here he comes walking towards us carrying the vacuum cleaner. He hands Cher the dust cloth and away they go back to work.

Many thanks to you both, Sonny and Cher Bono, for inviting all the *BEAT* readers to take this exclusive tour through your beautiful home. We wish you many years of happiness.

KRLA ARCHIVES

The Adventures of Robin Boyd...
By Shirley Poston

CHAPTER THIRTEEN

Robin Boyd had always been under the impression that the process of seeing one's life passing before one's very eyes was reserved only for those who would go to any length to attract the attention of a handsome lifeguard.

She remained under this impression until shortly after she began seeing her entire life passing before her very eyes. At which time she realized that similar private screenings are available to one when one is about to meet one's maker in Mick Jagger's pocket.

And, not being so blase that she didn't long for a box of popcorn (buttered), she sat back to watch.

As her early years sped rapidly by, Robin felt reasonably sure that this portion of the program would never go into re-runs. There was simply nothing that interesting about watching a red-headed budding kook maturing into a red-headed full-fledged kook.

Not until, that is, the aforementioned kook passed her sixteenth birthday and also passed an abandoned tea pot on the way home from school (on the kook's way home from school, not the tea pot's).

(At this point in the story, Robin became so fascinated, she began biting her nails.) (Which is not only difficult for a *real* Robin, but also smarts.)

Respectable Nut

And her fascination was understandable. For although the tea pot bore no resemblance to a magic lamp, Robin took the tea pot home and did as any respectable nut would have done.

Rubbed it mercilessly.

The genie who appeared shortly thereafter bore no resemblance to Aladdin or any of his turned-up-at-the-toes cohorts, but he did look so much like George Harrison it was unbelievable.

(And if you think *that's* unbelievable, stick around.)

After the genie (who, by some strange coincidence, not only looked like George but was *named* George) (and, by some even stranger coincidence, came from Liverpool) had revived Robin from a graceful (she hoped) faint, he then told her he was there to grant her fondest wish.

This, he explained, was to be her reward for being such a good bird in the fan sense of the word, always running fan clubs and sneaking off to the airport in the dead of night to welcome arriving faves, and that sort of thing.

Robin was then faced with the difficult decision of which of her fondest wishes to wish (all of us should be faced with such difficult decisions.)

A Dreamin' Nut

So, she thought for a moment. Then, partly because she was sure she was only dreaming, and mostly because she was some kind of a nut, Robin told George of her secret wish to be a bird in both senses of the word, so that she might fly about the world in search of the aforementioned faves.

The next thing Robin Boyd knew, her wish had been granted, and shortly thereafter, she wang (or is it winged?) (wung?) off to England.

The next thing the Beatles knew, they were trying to explain to themselves just how four rational, sensible people could possibly have come face to face with a *real* robin who not only *talked* but wore *Byrd glasses*. (No one is perfect.)

Fortunately, George arrived on the scene just in time to rescue Robin from the Beatles' garage, and rescue the Beatles from the nearest bin (as in loony). At which time he threw an absolute *snit* about nuts who forced him to crawl out of a nice warm tea pot in the wee hours.

Changed Tune

George, however, soon began to change his tune. And, after squeezing her hand not *once*, but *twice*, announced that on the following weekend, when she intended to fly off in search of the Stones, he was going *along*.

Robin, however, would have none of that. Although she had secretly considered squeezing back (not once, but twice) (George you understand, was what is commonly known as a little bit of all right), when one was about to meet the Stones, six was company and seven a crowd.

Therefore, she had gone well out of her way to elude the tea pot (which resided on the living room mantle) when she took off for a visit to Jolly Olde.

Her scheme, however, was a dismal failure. Just off the coast of England, she was stopped by the dread Bird Patrol (for exceeding the 5,000 mph speed limit). Whereupon she learned that she was being tailed by the aforementioned tea pot.

Fortunately, in return for the promise of a late date after the concert, the arresting officer (a blue jay with a tendency to leer) took Robin to where the Stones were appearing.

Unfortunately, once inside the Stones' dressing room, there wasn't time to change back into her sixteen-year-old self, and Robin was forced to take refuge in the pocket of a nearby jacket.

Safety?

But her feeling of safety was short lived. Because she soon discovered who the jacket belonged to.

At this point in the story, Robin's private screening faded from view. That was all there was to her past. And it was now high time to start worrying about the present.

Sniffling slightly, Robin burroughed deeper into Mick's pocket, in an effort not to bounce about as he walked onto the stage. But as the screams grew deafening and the first strains of "Satisfaction" were heard, Robin couldn't help smiling with same.

When one was in Mick Jagger's pocket, one was surely living. And there were moments when the fact that one would surely not continue living much longer scarcely mattered.

But, as the concert progressed, and the shrieks grew even greater in volume, Robin stopped smiling. There wasn't time to be going around grinning when one was lurching about in a swaying pocket.

And, when Mick *really* went into action, Robin's very teeth almost vibrated out of her very head.

Then it happened. A noisy kind of breathlessness fell over the crowd. An anticipation Robin knew well, having sat in the front row at several Stones' concerts.

It is time, she thought bravely, wishing at least for a blindfold.

And it was.

Slowly but surely, the combustible Michael P. Jagger began to remove his jacket.

Roarin' Robin

The crowd roared. Then he folded his jacket. Then Robin roared.

But suddenly, at the sound of a voice that rose above the others, Robin forgot that she was being suffocated.

For the voice said "Throw it, Mick!" And the voice belonged to *George!*

Robin clawed frantically. George was in the front row! And he knew where she was! But was he trying to save her? No!

Instead of letting her suffocate in peace, he was trying to coax Mick into tossing her into the crowd, where she would surely be ripped into six pieces. (A conservative estimate.)

And Mick would do it, too! George would see to that (him and his blasted magic powers!)

It was then that Robin knew what she must do.

For an instant, Mick Jagger stood motionless, fearing for his sanity. He had never thrown his jacket before, but he suddenly knew he was about to, whether he liked it or not.

An instant later, four more Rolling Stones and five thousand fans were fearing for *their* sanity, too.

For, when Mick Jagger hurled his coat into the waiting mob, it did not land among the sea of waving hands.

Instead, it flapped wildly out of the auditorium.

(To Be Continued Next Week)

Jackie Lee Is Really Double

While "The Duck" is storming up the nation's charts and everyone is busily learning how to "Duck" not many know who the song's singer, Jackie Lee, is.

Well, he's really two people! One of them, of course, is Jackie Lee but the other one is Earl Cosby, the other half of Bob and Earl. You remember them, don't you? They're the ones who have had such previous hits as "Don't Ever Leave Me," "Deep Down Inside," and "Harlem Shuffle."

Jackie, or Earl if you wish, was born in Oakland, California but attended Jefferson High School in Los Angeles where he played football and ran track and contributed his voice to the school's Men Chorus and A Capella.

As so many artists before him have done, Jackie began his singing lessons in church harmonizing and soloing in the First Baptist Church.

Accidental Career

Jackie actually began his professional career quite by accident. He dropped into the Cotton Club in Los Angeles to see a friend of his, Bobby Day, who was at that time singing with the Hollywood Flames.

Bobby invited Jackie to join the Flames which Jackie readily did. It was while Jackie was singing with the group that they had their smash, "Buzz, Buzz, Buzz."

In 1961 Jackie decided to leave the Flames to team up with Bobby Garrett as Bob and Earl.

And now he's simply Jackie Lee and the proud possessor of another hit. It seems as if hit records just follow Jackie wherever he goes.

Jackie is currently on the one-nighter circuit thanks to "The Duck." He is quite a prolific song writer, specializing in ballads, some of which he will be waxing as a possible follow up to "The Duck."

Dusty Is Coming

Dusty Springfield is coming back to us towards the end of this month.

After completing a ten day tour of Ireland which starts Feb. 1, she will fly to New York for several television appearances and then on to the West Coast, where she'll guest on the Red Skelton Show.

She'll be accompanied on the tour by the Echoes.

It'll be good to have her back among us, don't you think?

DIXIE RAIDERS? — The Dixie Cups are surrounded — by Paul Revere and the Raiders (left and right), a group of fans and the Action Dancers (Hawaiian costumes) on the set of "Where The Action Is."

KRLA ARCHIVES

McCallum to Record Lennon's Poems

Hey, it's finally happened—The Beatles have joined U.N.C.L.E.! Now, don't go getting excited—no, John, Paul, George and Ringo aren't coming over here to film an episode of our favorite television show.

In fact, one of the men from U.N.C.L.E. is going over there to pull off a deal with John Lennon. David "Illya" McCallum is going to England to cut an album for Capitol of, are you ready for this, John Lennon's poetry.

The album was originally set to be cut here in America but it was switched to London so McCallum can do it at the same time he's filming "Three Bites of the Apple."

Done By June

The filming starts March 23 and has to be completed by June, when he returns to film more U.N.C.L.E.

This really shows the impact of John's writing on the world. Everyone's been talking lately about Bob Dylan but no one has ever made an album reading Dylan's poetry, unless that's what you consider Dylan's own albums.

And as for whether or not John's writings are any easier to comprehend than Dylan's, well that's up to you.

David McCallum reading John Lennon's poems—this could be better than Charlton Heston reading the Bible.

What more could we ask for, fans?

Lennon's Legend

By Gil McDougall

Such is the impact of John Lennon upon people who come into contact with him that the Lennon attitude is fast becoming a cult. That aggressive humour that we link so easily with the Beatles is an integral part of John's character. His acid wit has withered many a stuffed shirt you may be sure.

When Lennon was the guest of honor at a rather pompous luncheon, held as a tribute to the success of his first book, he rose to answer a toast with: "Thank you very much, you've got a lucky face."

John was criticized severely for this, as many thought that he should have given a speech. He later answered the criticism with: "Give me another fifteen years and I might make a speech, not yet."

None of the Beatles suffer fools easily but John refuses to suffer them at all. His remarks have often been described as cruel. But undeserving sources will rarely feel the acidity of his tongue. He delights in deflating officials who are full of their own self-importance.

At a Chicago press conference, a rather somber looking gentleman stood up and said: "I am the acting British Consul General (at which point all the Beatles stood up and saluted). Are you doing a good job for your country?"

"Yes," answered John, "Are you?"

The original Beatle Fan Club President, Roberta Brown, had this to say of John: "His humour is very intelligent, half of the time I couldn't understand his jokes. He's very comical but a serious person really. I think he's very shy and to cover up this shyness he has this way of being funny." This is not an opinion that many would agree with—but then few have been as close to John as Roberta has.

When Lennon does make a friend he seems to stick with them. Witness his long-standing friendship with McCartney. Most people credit John as having the dominant voice in the group. It has been suggested by many that Paul relies heavily on his mate's judgment and friendship.

Even so, McCartney is no robot. He has very strong opinions and ideas of his own. Sometimes it takes Paul to get John and the others out of touchy situations. As Lennon has said many times, Paul has the Mary-Sunshine approach to life and usually soothes over any upheavals that Beatle talk sometimes arouses.

In his book, "A Cellar Full Of Noise," Epstein has this to say of Lennon: "John Lennon is, in my opinion, a most exceptional man. Had there been no Beatles and no Epstein participation John would have emerged from the mass of the population as a man to reckon with.

"He may not have been a singer or a guitarist, a writer or an artist but he would most certainly have been a something. You cannot control a talent like this. There is in the set of his head a controlled aggression that demands respect."

Instant FUN!

"THE WORLD'S MOST EXCITING DANCE GAME"

Get your party going QUICK-LIKE —and keep it ROLLING!

You'll have a "swingin' affair" with DANCE-MATE—the really "in" game!! **Different!**

As easy to play as writing your own name.

Up to 12 couples can **all** play at the exact same time with no one ever left out! You just SIGN — SPIN — and when one couple gets "a-GO-GO"-ing......... ....EVERYONE does!!!

Be the **first** in **your** set to have the most FABULOUS party-time **ever**.

Even the most bashful girl and shyest guy will "turn on" when you play this exciting new party game.

Sold only by mail. Just fill out the order coupon below, enclose only $1.50 and mail to: DANCE-MATE, 6290 Sunset, Suite 504, Hollywood, Calif. 90028

IMMEDIATE DELIVERY — MAIL COUPON TODAY!

Only $1.50 for each game
We pay postage

MAIL COUPON TO:
Dance-Mate
6290 Sunset, Suite 504
Hollywood, Calif. 90028

Send cash, check or money order
Sorry no C.O.D.

YOUR NAME _____ (PRINT CLEARLY)
ADDRESS _____ (NUMBER) _____ (STREET)
CITY _____
STATE _____ ZIP _____

KRLA ARCHIVES

Inside KRLA

Welcome back, everyone. We're just about ready now to pick up where we left off in last week's column. When we were so rudely interrupted by Father Time last time, we were speaking with Bill McMillan – Director of Station Relations at KRLA – who was telling us about some of the contests which have been held.

This week, we rejoin Bill as he tells us about some of the promotional campaigns which the radio station has conducted. "Probably the most notable was the Freedom From Hunger promotion which we did, in which we got the club leaders from some 400 clubs in the Los Angeles area to a meeting at the Hollywood Palladium, and explained to them what Freedom From Hunger was and why we needed their help. Then they went out and raised funds for the Freedom From Hunger organization.

"That was a pattern that was looked upon favorably by the United Nations group that sponsors Freedom From Hunger and it is a pattern that they will soon be putting into use in other cities in the United States.

"The campaign was very effective and the whole thing culminated in a big show at the Shrine Auditorium with a tremendous array of talent, which was produced by Jack Good.

"We have recently gone into the car business – we have a Model A that is really very eye-catching, and we have a 200 mile an hour dragster which appeals to a lot of people.

"Recently we acquired some flying saucers – these are air cars – and we fly those at parades and at car shows and drag strips."

One In The Nation

KRLA has been the Number One rated radio station in the Southland for quite some time now, and at one time it was even the Number One station in the *entire nation!!* I asked Bill what went into the making of KRLA's success story, and after thinking about it for a moment, he replied:

"There are a lot of things that listeners probably won't realize that contribute to the over-all importance of KRLA. Number One – and I think they'd realize it if they stopped to think about it – we have never over-commercialized our programming. We feel that people like to hear commercials, but they don't like to hear them three at a time! So our commercial policy calls for only 12 commercial minutes an hour, and this, we feel, is ample; it services the advertiser as well as the listener very well.

"We've always done a tremendous amount of public service on the air, and I think that our record of public service is probably a lot higher than some of the other stations in town. I know that the frequency, and the number of people that we do public service for and do special campaigns for is very well accepted all around the country by the public service agencies.

Station Callers

And what about visitors to the Hallowed Halls of KRLA? Well, you read about them here every week, and Bill also explains:

"KRLA is a frequently visited spot by people like the Rolling Stones, the Lovin' Spoonful, and the Dave Clark Five. If a top recording star is in town, he wants to make it a point to come out to KRLA and let some of our audience see him, because we have a tremendous number of visitors to the radio station.

"It would be hard to go through the list and mention all of our visitors over the last five years, but they have been just about all the top ones."

The radio station has had a star-studded, successful past, and KRLA is looking forward eagerly to the future. Now into the second month of this new year, Bill tells us: "The future plans for the radio station are merely to perform the job that we're now doing in a better way, and we feel as though if we do it in the best possible way – then *every*body will listen to us. The constant goal, of course, is to have a radio station that serves everybody's needs and one that everybody is satisfied to listen to. Of course, that's a goal that is impossible to attain – but we're going to try it!!"

Many of you have asked about KRLA – about its past, its present, and its future. I hope that we have been able to answer many of your questions the last two weeks, and maybe even a few more!

And to Bill McMillan – a very large thank you for telling us all about KRLA – The Station That's Won The West!!!

KRLA BEAT Subscription
SAVE 33% Of Regular Price

☐ 1 YEAR – 52 Issues – $5.00   ☐ 2 YEARS – $8.00
☐ 6 MONTHS – $3.00

Enclosed is _____   ☐ CASH   ☐ CHECK
                        PLEASE PRINT

Send to: .... Age ....
Address: ....
City .... State .... Zip ....

MAIL YOUR ORDER TO: KRLA BEAT
                      6290 Sunset, Suite 504
                      Hollywood, Calif. 90028
Foreign Rate: $9.00 – 52 Issues

KRLA Tunedex

DAVE HULL

BOB EUBANKS

DICK BIONDI

JOHNNY HAYES

EMPEROR HUDSON

CASEY KASEM

CHARLIE O'DONNELL

BILL SLATER

This Week	Last Week	Title	Artist
1	1	WE CAN WORK IT OUT/DAY TRIPPER	The Beatles
2	2	LIGHTNIN' STRIKES	Lou Christie
3	3	SOUNDS OF SILENCE	Simon & Garfunkel
4	16	JUST LIKE ME	Paul Revere & The Raiders
5	4	NO MATTER WHAT SHAPE	T-Bones
6	6	MY LOVE	Petula Clark
7	21	CRYIN' TIME	Ray Charles
8	14	UP TIGHT	Stevie Wonder
9	7	I SEE THE LIGHT	Five Americans
10	27	SUNDAY AND ME	Jay & The Americans
11	9	I FOUGHT THE LAW	Bobby Fuller Four
12	26	ARE YOU THERE?	Dionne Warwick
13	8	YOU DIDN'T HAVE TO BE SO NICE	The Lovin' Spoonful
14	29	MY WORLD IS EMPTY WITHOUT YOU	The Supremes
15	5	FLOWERS ON THE WALL	Statler Brothers
16	13	HOLE IN THE WALL	The Packers
17	12	AS TEARS GO BY	The Rolling Stones
18	18	THE MEN IN MY LITTLE GIRL'S LIFE	Mike Douglas
19	28	GOING TO A-GO-GO	The Miracles
20	22	A MUST TO AVOID	Herman's Hermits
	23	FIVE O'CLOCK WORLD	The Vogues
21	37	A WELL RESPECTED MAN	The Kinks
22	24	MY GENERATION	The Who
23	32	ELUSIVE BUTTERFLY	Bob Lind
24	31	LIKE A BABY	Len Barry
25	30	THUNDERBALL	Tom Jones
26	—	ATTACK	The Toys
27	—	IT WAS A VERY GOOD YEAR	Frank Sinatra
28	36	I AIN'T GONNA EAT MY HEART OUT	Young Rascals
29	33	SANDY	Ronnie & The Daytonas
30	—	BARBARA ANN	The Beach Boys
31	35	SET YOU FREE THIS TIME	The Byrds
32	34	SPANISH EYES	Al Martino
33	38	A SWEET WOMAN LIKE YOU	Joe Tex
34	—	YOU BABY	The Turtles
35	—	TIME	The Pozo-Seco Singers
36	40	UNDER YOUR SPELL AGAIN	Johnny Rivers
37	—	GEORGIA	The Righteous Bros.
38	—	I'M SO LONELY I COULD CRY	V.J. Thomas & The Triumphs
39	—	THE CHEATERS	Bob Kuban & The In Men
40	—	GOING NOWHERE	Friday Night and Saturday Night

HALL OF FAME — Dave Hull and the Vogues look over their life-size, newly-completed mural. It's part of the Rock and Roll Hall of Fame collection now hanging in Dave's Hullabaloo Club on Sunset Blvd. in Hollywood.

KRLA ARCHIVES

Home Of Folk — The Troubador

By Shannon Leigh

For many years, the Troubador has been the home of folk music — of *fine* folk entertainment — in Hollywood, and this is where our search for folks has brought us this week.

The founder and owner of the club is a young man named Doug Weston. Tall, slender, bespectacled and be-Beatled — Doug is the perfect host and gentleman, and over a steaming bowl of soup we discussed his role — and the role of his club — in the folk world.

The Troubador was first begun about nine years ago at a time when the coffee houses were the vogue of the day. It began as a small coffee house itself, seating just about 70 people, and specializing in entertainment and nearly gourmet-style food.

Of the name itself, Doug explains: "I chose the name 'Troubador' because troubadors were — historically — men who travelled from town to town during the period when the Church completely blackened out all communication during the Middle Ages.

"There were no newspapers and there was no way for people of one town to know what was happening in another town. So these men travelled from place to place and did a chant-like song which was a living newspaper. They were the only body of people disseminating ideas at that time."

Expanded

Within about two years after the original Troubador had been established, Doug found himself frustrated by its small size and began looking for a larger place. He found a building which was then a combination art-gallery and coffee house, and it became the present club site.

Currently the club is undergoing extensive redecoration — Doug has decided to "posh it up slightly" — which should be completed within the next three or four months.

There have been many internationally famous entertainers who have appeared on the stage of the Troubador, and many more who have sort of received their start with Doug at the club. Among them, were the New Christy Minstrels.

Randy Sparks had come to Doug with his idea for a large folk group and Doug suggested several of his own performers. The group was assembled and then did all of their rehearsing at the club and eventually played a 12-week engagement there.

Byrds Began Here

Although it may come as a bit of a surprise to you, the Byrds actually received their start at the Troubador. Doug related the story to *The BEAT* with a smile: "Jim McGuinn was an accompanist for the Chad

Mitchell Trio, and it was through me and the club that he made his first contacts in the folk field.

"During a Hoyt Axton engagement, I used Jim as a single act. It was then that he came bringing Beatles' music and playing that in a folk surrounding on an accoustical 12-string guitar. After that, he got the other boys around him and started teaching them Beatle music and that's how the Byrds were actually formed at the Troubador in the summer of 1964."

They subsequently played a three-day engagement there, and still remain, in Doug's estimation, "a very good example of a fine, folk-rock group."

There have been many performers who have lived at the Troubador for some length of time, and it has become truly the "home of Folk" in Southern California.

Father Of Folk

And Doug? "I picked up the name of 'West Coast Father of Folk Music' because folk singers would tell one another and usually they could depend on a hand-out or a free cup of coffee or a place to stay if they showed up at the Troubador and said they were in need. People were showing up at my door all the time and it became sort of a Stray Boys' Camp for Folk Singers!"

A close observer of music, Doug made a few predictions for *BEAT* readers: "New trends I'm aware of in music — Number One is the electronic music of the Yardbirds. I think there's going to be more and more of this far-out, electronic, weird music — with and without lyrics.

"The second trend is in music that sort of springs off of 'Yesterday.' It's almost a kind of chamber music with a rock feeling. I think there's going to be more and more of these combinations of different kinds of music."

Doug Weston is a very warm person. He has helped a lot of people to get their start in one of the roughest professions in the world. He has been father, mother, and older brother to a good part of the contemporary folk music culture in Southern California.

His own ambitions include "staying 19 years old for the rest of my life," and "I want to provide as wide a range of entertainment as possible." He is now working in the publishing business, and will shortly go back into management, and hopes to enter the field of acting and establish himself as an entertainer and a personality on his own.

With his talent, and warmth, his sincerity and depth — it seems unlikely that his future will hold anything but success.

KRL'A' and Dragster At 1966 Auto Show

KRLA's famed Horsepower Engineering Dragster and the KRL"A" will be among the world-renowned exhibits on display at the 1966 Winternational Motorama Auto Show Feb. 3-6 at Pan Pacific Auditorium.

KRLA disc jockeys will kick off the show opening night with personal appearances. Visitors will be given free Polaroid pictures of themselves with their favorite deejays.

The nation's most novel and spectacular car show, Winternational Motorama will be the premier showcase for a host of American and foreign experimental models, one-only prototypes, limited production cars, revived classic replicas and show cars never exhibited before.

DeVincis and Michaelangelos of the custom car world will exhibit fabulous machines tailored to order for movies, television, Hollywood stars, wealthy eccentrics and exacting customers.

Also shown will be championship drag racers, prize winning customs, antiques of the past and dream cars of the future, unusual hot rods and exciting attractions of all the automotive sports.

One of the most weird and beautiful custom coupes in the nation will be brought from Illinois for its first West Coast showing. This is the "Illusion," a Ford-based creation built and entered by Dave Puhl of Palatine, Ill. Built for one who travels along, the sleek and versatile coupe provides space only for the driver, none for the passengers.

Among others participating will be racing personalities, including top-name drivers and accessory manufacturers, who will feature the latest in performance needs and mechanical gadgetry.

Entertainment geared to automotive-minded audiences will include top singing groups and recording personalities.

"THE ILLUSION," a beautiful and fantastic custom automobile built in Illinois, is one of the spectacular American and foreign experimental machines, antiques, racing cars and boats on display at the Winternational Motorama Auto Show at Pan Pacific Auditorium.

Fan Clubs

SONNY & CHER
Diane Hochman
20940 Lull Street
Canoga Park, Calif.

JAMES BROWN
Eileen Pedraza
603 Brightwood Street
Monterey Park, Calif.

BEATLES
1936 E. 75th St.
Los Angeles, Calif.

HERMAN'S HERMITS
16537 Sunset Blvd.
Pacific Palisades, Calif.

ROLLING STONES
11360 Howard Drive
Norwalk, Calif.

JAN & DEAN
2669 Ovile St.
Huntington Park, Calif.

BEAU BRUMMELS
2052 Mallory Street
San Bernardino, Calif.

LESLIE GORE
1925 E. Glenoaks
Glenoaks, Calif.

Preview Records
"MEN FROM MARS"
Weird Sounds!!
by the **FUGITIVES**
Ask your DJ to play it!

Charlie-'O' Now On TV

Once upon a time there was a television program called "Hollywood Discotheque" — and now that program has moved. The show can now be seen from 5:00 to 6:00 P.M. every Saturday, hosted by KRLA's own Charlie O'Donnell.

The BEAT spoke to Charlie shortly after the show had moved and changed its name to "Top 40 Discotheque," and he told us a little bit about his ideas and plans for the show:

"We've tried to incorporate this concept of Top 40 with format television, almost the same as the Top 40 format radio.

"We play one record after another, and we usually average about nine guests a week.

Not All Tops

"What I'm very proud about is that they're not all top acts. A lot of the acts from California — groups and single artists who would never have a chance to appear on TV — are showcased on our show. We do this, and also book the top stars. It gives the smaller groups a chance to work with the big names of the business, and at the same time gain experience in TV appearances.

"Occasionally I'll interview some of the guests, and I hope I'm asking questions that the young people would ask themselves if they were there in person.

"I'm glad we have moved to the 5:00 to 6:00 time slot because it gives a lot more people a chance to see the show and to see a lot of the newcomers from the Los Angeles area."

And that's the latest word from Charlie. And the latest word from *The BEAT*? Well, watch the show, of course!!!

WANTED
Young Rock and Roll Musicians
Age 12 to 15 Only
Write Instrument Played, Age and Experience
To: ROCKER
415 S. El Molino, Pasadena, Calif.

Tell your friends about
Dial-A-Phone
HO 1-2220

KRLA ARCHIVES

"AH, THIS CALIFORNIA SUNSHINE," says Jim McCarty.

"YEAH, IT'S A BIT OF ALL RIGHT," agrees Chris Dreja.

The Yardbirds At Ease

...THE ORIGINAL THINKER — KEITH RELF.

"WHAT I WOULDN'T GIVE FOR STRAIGHT HAIR," sighs Sam.

KRLA ARCHIVES

Here We Are In All Our Glory

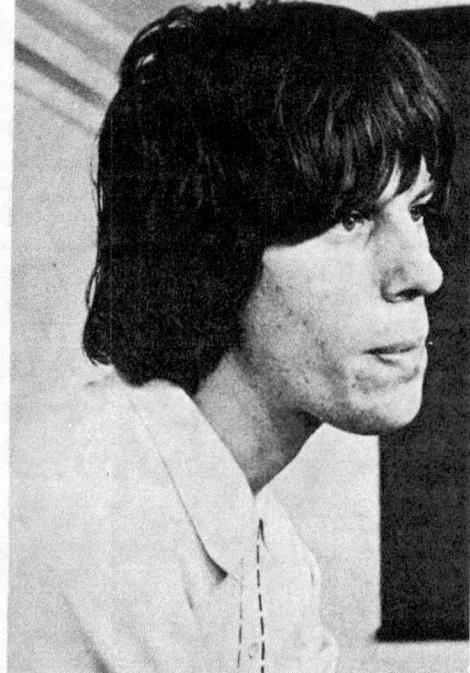

... JEFF BECK CAPTURED WITHOUT HIS GUITAR.

HOLLYWOOD — Dressing rooms in the backstage area of night clubs are often this way, and tonight was no exception. It was an important evening — the closing night of a four-day engagement at the Hullabaloo club in Hollywood for the Yardbirds. Fans, press, girls, and friends all gathered 'round them now to wish them well — or simply to be near them. People like to be near those who are great.

In the far corner, lead guitarist Jeff Beck was quietly talking to a very beautiful blonde girl. He looked tired — almost sad, but he's frequently like that. Like his four mates, Jeff is emotional . . . perhaps a little more so than the others. But it is *because* of this sensitivity that he is capable of creating the unique and beautiful sounds which he does.

More people milling about, and then — in the middle of the room, perched on the dressing table — was Yardbird Keith Relf. Keith of the deep blue eyes, and the deep thoughts of many things.

Keith, the introspective one, who spoke to us of freedom: "Freedom very rarely occurs. My freedom? I dream about the freedom I will get one day — to be in the wide-open spaces and away from cities. I get claustrophobia in cities. I like wide-open spaces and fields and woods — just to be alone, generally."

He lit a cigarette and smiled slightly, then contemplated the question I had just asked him. What about the labor unions which had caused the Yardbirds so much trouble.

Not Very Much

"I don't like them much, but they're probably worried that too many English groups are coming over."

Keith — onstage — has called the Yardbirds' music "pop art." Off stage, he clarifies that statement: "It's abstract expressionism."

Moving further along towards the door, we could see Chris Dreja sitting in a corner resting and watching all of the people in the room. Many people would speak to him, and he would answer them each politely — fairly quietly. He isn't very talkative, but it's obvious that he has a good sense of humor. He has a lot of fun onstage, and though he raves it up along with the others — he does it in his own quiet way.

An empty chair by the dressing table — oh, marvelous! I sat down and almost immediately Jim McCarty appeared, as if from nowhere. He found one more chair, and pulled it over close to mine so that we could talk.

He's a rare bird, this Yardbird — someone very nice to find. He is an outgoing sort of person, but in his own rather quiet way. He might sit and talk for hours, but you'd never feel as though you had been presumed upon.

We spoke again of the labor unions, and Jim explained: "It seems silly, really. I would have thought that anyone who's going to be popular — anyone who's going to entertain someone — should be let into the country, and be allowed to play for the people and be paid for it. We always give people their money's worth.

"It was *terrible* coming over the first time, and this time has been much better. It's just been through experience that we've known about the whole scene over here; we didn't know too much about it before we came."

A very good drummer, to watch Jim playing on stage is to see someone completely immerse himself within his music. He tried to explain just how the Yardbirds' sound had developed to the present:

"A lot of sound just came about on stage. It came through us playing as we *felt*. The numbers have gradually developed from basically very simple numbers — sort of fairly way-out ones. It's just the way we felt."

Then I asked him to describe the sound as it is now. He wrinkled his forehead in thought, then began: "I don't really know — it's a very *atmospheric* type of thing. Futuristic rock 'n' roll, if you like. It *could* be termed 'pop art' — I never thought of that. It depends what a person *wants* to call it."

Feedback

Sam frequently acts as musical director on the Yardbirds' albums, and he had a few ideas of his own about their particular sound:

"We started developing the sound about two years ago by using feedback techniques and counter rhythm techniques.

"The thing evolves: We start with a number and we play it on stage — say, 100 times — and everytime we play it, it might get a bit better or we might learn something from it. Somebody might start playing something different; we remember it, and the next time we play the number we take that thing he did and expand on it. It sort of builds up.

"It's *not* pop art; it's futuristic sort of music. It's experimental futuristic — essentially electronic music."

Not unlike the other members of his group, Sam had formed his own very definite ideas about the American labor union situation.

"They've been nice and nasty — sort of hot and cold. I'm sure they're right but there's a lack of understanding between us. *We* don't know what they want us to do, and *they* don't know what we're trying to do. That's the trouble."

Star Audience

It was time to leave the crowded, noisy room then. The boys had to change quickly and go downstairs for their last performance. Outside in the audience they were eagerly awaited by nearly 2,000 people — including some of the Byrds, Jackie deShannon, the Grass Roots, the Fortunes, Chad and Jeremy, and as many more pop personalities as the huge club could accomodate.

They had brought to us some music — music that was new and exciting. They had added a little thing called *life* to our existences, and soon they would fly away. Back to England, back to their world, back to — perhaps — some other crowded dressing room in a night club somewhere.

They were saying good-night, saying good-bye, saying thank you for coming along. And then the door closed behind us and we stood for a moment in the dark-ended hallway outside their room.

There were still a lot of people, but it wasn't noisy anymore. Somehow worlds of thought had overtaken empty words, and everyone headed quietly downstairs to watch the final performance.

Good-night Yardbirds — and thank you.

KRLA ARCHIVES

Part 2, Writer's Hints

How The Hits Are Written

Last week we began our exploration of the pop song-writer's world and the way in which he goes about having his songs recorded by other artists. We spoke with Lou Adler, who is both a record producer and publisher.

This week we are going to speak with two of the top writers of today, both of whom are capable of writing in several different mediums.

If you have heard "The Eve Of Destruction," by Barry McGuire; "Let Me Be," by the Turtles; "A Must to Avoid," by Herman's Hermits; "I Found A Girl," by Jan and Dean; and countless others included on albums by many of today's popular recording stars—then you are somewhat acquainted with a young man named P.F. Sloan.

Flip—as he is known to his friends—is one of the brightest, most talented young writers in the music business today.

Contacts

How does Flip get his material to an artist for it to be recorded? "With some particular artists—such as the Turtles—their producer happens to know me, and asked if I had anything for them.

"With the Hermits—I met their manager, Mickie Most, and went to a club in London with Peter (Herman). Then I played a song for him—and he liked it."

At times, Flip will write a song specifically for an artist, or group of artists. Then, he says, "I figure out what I'd like to say—and what I'd like to hear them say—and write the song."

The BEAT asked Flip for any advice he might give to aspiring writers, and after thinking it over carefully for a few moments, he replied:

"I think that they should make a demo tape of as many of their songs as possible. Then, submit them to a publisher who has the kind of writers they personally dig. If possible, get the songs sung by someone with a good voice."

"Also, you should never abuse personal relationships. Have your publisher, or even your friends solicit your material for you. And be sure to have a good artist, or group, record your demo for you."

All Sound Now

This idea of putting songs onto demos—demonstration recordings or tapes—is all important now, as sheet music is no longer being used as a means of communication or sale in the pop field. Success is entirely dependent upon the "sound" of a product, and the better the sound you present as a sample of your work, the better your chances are of being accepted.

Mason Williams is a young man of phenomenal talent—writing not only songs, but poetry and literature of all sorts as well.

Quite frequently, Mason will establish himself with one particular artist or group of artists and write specifically for them. For example, the Smothers Brothers have recorded 15 of Mason's songs to date; the Kingston Trio has recorded nine; and Glen Yarbrough has recorded four of Mason's tunes.

Trying to discover just how a writer *begins* to have his songs published and recorded, we spoke to Mason, who explained: "You start very slowly. At first you can't get your songs to *anybody*. And that's the purpose of a publisher—he is supposed to have contacts with the A & R men.

"After a while, you get to be better known to the artists and the A & R men and people begin to come to you. After a while, you will write specifically *for* people; you'll write with someone in mind.

"It all boils down to being professional about it. There are some things you write just to express something. If you're professional, you can also come up with things that people want to hear."

Good Publisher

Drawing on his own experiences, Mason also had some very valuable advice to contribute: "The first thing to do is get with a publisher—someone who is good for *you*, and who handles *your* kind of material.

"Most songwriters, and publishers want to hear a finished product. The more it sounds like a record the better it is. You should make

Mason also explained just briefly the relationship between the song writer and his publisher: "Nobody's working for anybody—you work for each other. You give him a product, and he sells it. It is a partnership—you don't write *for* a publisher."

First Rights

Mason writes exclusively with Dave Hubert's Davon Music Publishing Company, which means that Dave has the first and exclusive rights to all of Mason's material.

Just briefly, then, we have taken a quick look at the way a contemporary song writer gets his material published, to the artists, and recorded. It is frequently more complicated than this, but for the most part—much of a composer's success will rely upon his talent, his reputation, and on the salesmanship of his publishing representative.

Next week, The BEAT will explore the area of record production and go behind the scenes in an exclusive report to find out just how a record comes out sounding the way it does. We will trace it from the rough demonstration stage, to the finished product ready for commercial release.

Win a free trip to LONDON With all expenses paid! or 1,200 Other Prizes! NO PURCHASES NEEDED

Official London Look Sweeperoo Rules

1. Print name and address on entry form below or on plain paper, and also print the name and address of your cosmetician or local druggist. No purchase is necessary.

2. Mail your entry to Yardley Sweeperoo. Enter as often as you wish, but each entry must be mailed separately. Entries must be postmarked on or before March 31, 1966, and received no later than April 11, 1966.

3. Winners will be chosen by random drawing conducted by an independent judging organization. Drawing will be held April 15, 1966, and winners will be notified by April 29, 1966. No substitutions will be made for any prize offered. Judges' decisions on all phases of Sweepstakes will be final.

4. Entrants must be residents of the United States. Employees and their families of Yardley of London, Inc. and its advertising agencies and judging organization are not eligible.

5. Teenage winners or winners under legal age must be accompanied by parent or guardian. Trips may be taken any time during 1966.

6. For list of winners, send stamped, self-addressed envelope to Yardley Winners, P.O. Box 32F, Mount Vernon, N.Y., 10559.

7. This Sweepstakes is void in Florida and wherever taxed, prohibited or restricted by law. This sweepstakes is subject to all Federal, State and local laws and regulations. Taxes on prizes are the sole responsibility of the winners.

8. Entrants who don't win, mustn't cry.

Fill in and return to: SWEEPEROO SWEEPSTAKES, 6290 Sunset Blvd., Suite 504, Hollywood 90028, Calif.

NAME _____ (PLEASE PRINT)

ADDRESS _____

CITY _____ STATE _____

NAME OF COSMETICIAN OR DRUGGIST _____

ADDRESS OF STORE _____

CITY _____ STATE _____

YOUR CHANCE TO WIN AN ABSOLUTELY FREE EXPENSE-PAID TRIP TO LONDONTOWN ITSELF IN YARDLEY'S Sweeperoo Sweepstakes!

Yeah! Yeah! Yeah!

8 FREE TRIPS TO LONDON FOR 4 LUCKY PRIZEWINNERS AND THEIR COMPANIONS! FLY ABOARD A B.O.A.C. VC10 JET! HAVE A WHOLE EXPENSE-PAID WEEK IN LONDON (ROOM AND BOARD) AND 4 WINNERS EACH GET £100($280.00) TO SPEND WHILE THERE!

OTHER SWINGING PRIZES, TOO! 200 SCRUMPTIOUS BERNHARD ALTMANN CASHMERE SWEATERS!

1,000 BOTTLES OF OH! DE LONDON. YARDLEY'S FRISKY NEW SCENT.

HAS THERE EVER BEEN A CONTEST LIKE IT? NO. NEVER!

What's the catch? Not a one. Nothing to write. Nothing to buy. Nothing to guess at. All you need to win the London Look Super Sweeperoo is luck.

The two lucky first prize winners jet to London with a friend (with a parent or guardian, if a teenager or under legal age.) And the cosmeticians or druggists whose names appear on these winning entries also get a free trip to London with a companion. For the lucky runners-up there are 200 Bernhard Altmann cashmere sweaters. And that Oh! de London? 1,000 of you will get a bottle each as a sweet wild consolation. Oh! Isn't it all exciting? Oh! Can you hardly wait to enter?

KRLA ARCHIVES

Kingsmen Need Perry Mason

By Louise Criscione

Whenever the Kingsmen are mentioned, one automatically thinks of "Louie, Louie"—right? Well, The BEAT staff used to think that way too but as of yesterday things have changed.

Now, whenever we think of the Kingsmen, we think of five extremely nice and equally funny young men with fabulous personalities. You see, they visited us yesterday and I'm sure our office will never be the same.

The five Kingsmen with road manager and manager in tow, trouped en masse into our office and plopped themselves down in hastily dragged in chairs.

The first thing on their minds was a pending lawsuit. "There is a fellow who used to be with our group and quit because he was going to school," explained Len. "He was out of it for a year or a year and a half and then he started using the name 'Kingsmen'," said Len.

Mistaken Identity

It would have been all right with the original Kingsmen if their ex-group member had billed himself as once having been with the Kingsmen but the way in which he publicizes his group has led only to confusion.

People who have heard of the Kingsmen but have never seen them simply accept these second "Kingsmen" as being the one and only "Louie, Louie" guys.

Naturally, the Kingsmen are suing for damages but they really don't care if they get any or not. They just want the other group to stop using their name.

Kingsmen Push

On the happier side of things, the Kingsmen are about to embark on a tour which will hit the remainder of the college circuit through New England and the South.

The Kingsmen like to give all they've got on personal appearances because as Lenny so aptly puts it: "We're playing to intelligent people—not slobs."

Since the Kingsmen are on the road roughly 80% of the year they have acquired a bus which is not any ordinary bus. No, the Kingsmen have a full sized Greyhound bus which they have kingly titled, Herkimer. Actually, they are not quite sure how to spell it and after a quick consultation they decided it was spelled H-e-r-k-i-m-e-r. However, you can beg to differ on that point if you wish!

Dick reveals that: "It's a very nice bus. In fact, it's been so nice to us that we gave it new carpeting for Christmas!"

Of course, Herkimer can be very temperamental at times and simply refuses to start, leaving the five Kingsmen to *push* their beloved bus until it decides to move under its own power.

Another small problem which the Kingsmen have encountered with their bus is that the fans write all over it with lipstick. Oh well, it's just one of those occupational hazards, so what are they going to do?

It pays to have a little bit of extra talent in the group, as the Kingsmen found out when one of their members, Norm Gunn, had all of their amplifiers made by his company.

They are very particular about their on stage sound—so the Kingsmen carry along their own sound system. Len says: "If you're going to do it, then do it right."

They purchase thousands of dollars worth of equipment each year. Partly because it has a habit of being stolen and partly because they just *like* to buy new equipment.

Hit One

Mike, who is the Kingsmen's lead guitarist, recently went to Mexico and purchased three new guitars. Dick declares that he now has 137 drums—*but* there is a definite method to his madness.

You see, the way Dick figures it if you set up 137 drums you can throw your sticks around anywhere and still hit at least one of the drums!

The Kingsmen all have their on stage clothes made by Pendleton. All except Kerry, that is. "I have tents made for me by Omar," he grinned.

The Kingsmen have continued to survive the British invasion without bending to long hair. They say that they are very un-British and proud of it. And Mike even goes so far as to say: "I like to look like a boy."

But they all hasten to add that they like the English groups very much—it's just the American groups who imitate the English that the Kingsmen can't abide.

Anything To Help

The Kingsmen have ridden the pop film route. They did the soundtrack from "How To Stuff A Wild Bikini." They thought that it was a good career move because they would like very much to go into movies and they felt that "Bikini" at least put their foot in the door.

But Mike had a slightly different reason for liking the group's film debut. "You know, the kids in the Midwest have never seen the ocean," Mike patiently explained, "so by making the movie we helped them to see what it looks like."

Public Service

"Sure, we're doing a public service," grinned Len.

In addition to being the Kingsmen, Mike, Dick, Len, Kerry and Norm are all individuals. They each have their own likes and dislikes and they each have their own outside interests.

Len has an acting background; Norm, of course, has his amplification company; Mike is building a resort hotel; Dick won a scholarship to the Julliard School Of Music; and Kerry was a drama major at the University of Washington.

"Louie, Louie" is somewhat of a phenomenon in the record business. It has never been re-released and yet it continues to pop up in charts all over the country. In fact, as they sat in The BEAT office they learned that it was once again climbing the charts in Boston where it has already been number one three times!

Guess it just goes to show that you can't keep a good record off the charts—or a good group either.

KRLA ARCHIVES

For Girls Only

By Shirley Poston

Prepare yourselves.

I have a feeling this is going to be one of *those* columns. You know, where I write about really fascinating things. Like *feet*, and *orange popsicles*, for instance.

My mind is still a complete blank because I still haven't recovered from the newspaper I told you about last week. Every time I even *think* about those headlines (SHIRLEY POSTON WEDS GEORGE HARRISON) I have a relapse.

Sigh, pant and/or slurp.

In case you didn't read last week's column and haven't the foggiest notion what I'm raving about, let it suffice to say that I didn't really marry George Harrison. But that I am sure as heck going to try harder from now on.

I once read that if you *really* want something, and are willing to make a lot of sacrifices to get what you want, you do get it. (Which has to be the strangest sentence ever composed).

I wonder if that's true. It just could be. Just in case it is, why don't we form a Mrs. George Harrison Club, and all work together to make sure that at least one of us ends up marching him off to the nearest altar.

Anyone interested in joining such a club, please let me know. 'Course, I'll have to have my padded cell enlarged, but it's worth it.

Robin Boyd

Not to change the subject or anything, I got a letter asking about Robin Boyd. I mean, asking a question about one of her weird adventures. Naturally, I've already lost the letter, so I can't address my answer personally, but here it is.

The writer wanted to know if the audience ever forgave John (of Beatle fame) for forgetting the line of the song he was singing, and for swallowing his guitar pick when Robin Boyd flew across the stage and told him the line.

Well, the audience was doing so much screaming, most of them didn't really notice what happened. Those who were aware of the missing line did forgive John, because no one is perfect (Lennon, however, sure comes close). And, when he swallowed the pick and had a very noisy coughing fit, his fans just clucked sympathetically, thinking he'd been smoking too much.

Hope that answers your question, and also proves that I am not a well girl. I don't know why I make up things that don't even happen in the stories I write, but I always do.

Even when I'm staring at the ceiling in the middle of the night, making up wild dreams about George, I always have to have every little detail just perfect.

Red Sweaters

Like the time I happened to meet him walking down a lonely beach (ahem). We were both wearing red sweaters, and things were working out just fine when I all of a sudden remembered I don't have a red sweater.

I then decided I must have borrowed it, but that didn't jell because no one I know has a red sweater.

Then I tried to tell myself I'd just bought it that morning, and that failed, too. Because I didn't have a cent to my name at the time (as usual).

Honestly, I spent about three nights figuring out how I did get the sweater. (It turned out that George's mum knitted it for me.) (Never dream anything small, I always say.)

Oh, that reminds me of something. Do you remember the column in *The BEAT* that told about the Who Wrote Who game? You know, things like John Lennon wrote Sonny & Cher, and probably illustrated them, too.

Well, that has prompted a whole series of goofy games, like Unlikely Album Titles, for instance. Such as "Jack Gilardi Sings Annette Singing Anka," "George Harrison Meets Segovia," and wouldn't you just know that I can't think of one single title that's funny now that I've brought up the subject? Anyway, it's a fun game to play. Let me know if you come up with any good ones, and I'll try to remember some of the goodies I've forgotten.

There's another name game where you make up unlikely guest stars for television shows. Like Bob Dylan on the "King Family," Leonard Bernstein on "Hullabaloo," P.J. Proby on "Meet The Press."

Boy, were *those* hilarious. This certainly isn't my day, is it? Well, anyway, you get the idea.

Now, back to George.

No, really, I wouldn't dream of saying another *word* about him in this column. After all, there are other things in this world to talk about (no there aren't, but don't go blabbing it around.)

On Donovan

I know, let's talk about Donovan (pant). Remember the contest where I was giving away his "Catch The Wind" album? Well, me and my brilliant ideas. I asked all of you to enter the contest by telling me what Donovan's last name is, and then the fun began.

I never in my wildest dreams imagined that one short little name could have so many spellings. Really, no two entries were alike! (Well, it wasn't quite that bad, but you did manage to come up with over ten ways of spelling Licht, Leach, Light, Leich, or whatever the blame thing is.) (Sorry about that, Donovan.)

Anyway, I looked up the spelling in *The BEAT*. Then I found it spelled another way somewhere else, so I'm so thoroughly confused, I guess I'll just have to wait until he gets into town and ask him.

And won't that be just *terrible*? Whenever I do find out, and can stop fainting long enough to write it on paper, I'll announce the winner.

Oh, that reminds me, one of the entries had the cutest word on it. The girl said she was a *Donofan*. If anyone can dream up any more of those, let me know and I'll print same!

Now, about that Herman contest. If you don't have their "Introducing Herman's Hermits" album, please drop me a postcard c/o *The BEAT* and tell me what the group's first American hit was. The album will go to the 99th person who gives me the right answer, so race off to the post office.

Speaking of racing off, I'd better. Please keep your letters coming and I'll see you next *BEAT*.

Pace Change For Billy Joe Royal

By Carol Deck

Still lamenting the fact that he'd missed "Batman" the night before because of a filming, Billy Joe Royal took a little time out from his busy schedule for a short talk over lunch.

Billy Joe's a Georgia gentleman who thinks that Atlanta is about to come into its own as a record producing city.

"Nashville has been *the* place to record in the South," he said, "but Atlanta's really coming into its own."

He says he can hear ten records and tell excactly which ones are from Nashville. "They use the same musicians over and over and a musician can just have so many new ideas."

So he thinks Atlanta's coming up. He calls the Atlanta sound "a touch of Nashville but not so much country and western."

Billy Joe's got a new record coming out pretty quick and it's a change of pace piece for him. It's more of the R & B type than his previous records.

Happy Song

"It's not really saying much. It's just a happy song, a sort of non-offensive song." The world can always use happy songs.

As for the reasons behind his success with such hits as "Down In The Boondocks," he thinks it's because his songs tell a story. "They're not just a lot of words, the words tell a story."

He describes the sound of his newest single as more like Phil Spector. Billy Joe greatly admires Spector and the works he's produced for such artists as the Righteous Brothers. In fact he calls "You've Lost That Loving Feeling" a "work of art."

Billy Joe feels his next record is like Spector's sound in that it's more of a production number. It's sort of tastefully off-beat.

Between roast beef and coffee he also chatted about band wagons and how music comes in trends. He feels that when something good comes along everyone jumps on the band wagon.

"But when the band wagon goes everyone on it goes," he said. He agrees there are exceptions though, like Elvis and the Beatles.

He confessed a couple of secret yearnings too.

One, he liked to act. But he feels he'd be best at supporting roles. "I just don't look the part for a leading man." One thing he knows for sure is that he doesn't want to do a Beach Party movie.

"I'd rather do a walk-on in a John Wayne movie than have the lead in a Beach Party movie," he stated.

His other secret desire is to live in Cincinnati, Ohio. As a performer he prefers the West Coast because of it's numerous opportunities, but his private life is something else.

A Normal Life

"If I were to settle down and lead a normal life I'd probably move to Cincinnati," he said. The reason he's so fond of the city is because of an incident a while back.

He was at a very low point in his career and very disillusioned about his own talent when a local disc jockey asked him to do a bit for the John F. Kennedy memorial library.

At the performance, the kids responded so enthusiastically and formed fan clubs for him that it was a real shot in the arm and gave him the confidence to go on.

So keep forming those fan clubs, fans, the performers really do appreciate them.

Billy Joe chatted a little more about the groups he really likes. He thinks the Beatles and Hollies are about the best and admires anything produced by Phil Spector.

And then he had to rush off and get a few last minute details out of the way so he could be sure not to miss "Batman" the next night.

...BILLY JOE ROYAL

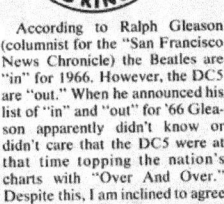
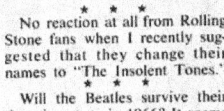

According to Ralph Gleason (columnist for the "San Francisco News Chronicle) the Beatles are "in" for 1966. However, the DC5 are "out." When he announced his list of "in" and "out" for '66 Gleason apparently didn't know or didn't care that the DC5 were at that time topping the nation's charts with "Over And Over." Despite this, I am inclined to agree with the summation.

* * *

No reaction at all from Rolling Stone fans when I recently suggested that they change their names to "The Insolent Tones."

* * *

Will the Beatles survive their American tour in 1966? It seems that the fans are out to get them. During a Beatle concert everything is thrown on stage, from autograph books to underwear. Paul was once almost blinded by a hat pin. George was hit in the ear by a silver dollar. And at the last concert in San Francisco John was hit in the eye by a jelly bean. If fans of the Beatles want them to give up tours then they are certainly heading in the right direction. After all, why should the Beatles risk injury in this fashion. John Lennon still remembers the time that fans ripped off the door of his car after a performance and threw themselves into it. So please give the boys a break and leave your jelly beans at home in '66.

KRLA ARCHIVES

Yeah, Well Kinks...

Kinks Take Big Splash

By Tammy Hitchcock

The Kinks have been favorites of mine for ages now (at least, 3 months!) but I haven't put them on the "Hot Seat" 'cause, you see, they haven't had a smash record for awhile and so I really didn't have any excuse to give the boss.

But now all that's changed. The Kinks have a fantastic disc in the form of "Well Respected Man." So, I went bravely to the boss and asked her if I couldn't write about the Kinks. And do you know what she said? Quote: "*Of course*, you can write about them! In fact, why haven't you written about them before?"

Stuck On Kinks

I guess I should have figured out that the boss was rather stuck on the Kinks and being so stuck I wouldn't *need* an excuse to write about them.

Anyway, the reason the boss is so hung up on the Kinks is because *they* are quite hung up on her! Which figures. The last time they were in town they invited the boss and I over. Naturally, we went. What do you think we are—crazy or something?

We were sitting around the pool and the boss was making one huge impression on the Kinks. But I want you to know that I did the boss one better—I made a huge *splash* on them. I, being my usual graceful self, gracefully fell into the pool!

Wet Or Dry

Well, I just thought I'd let you know why the boss likes the Kinks and why the Kinks think I'm a wet blanket. And now that I've done it I might as well get on to the Kinks themselves, who are really a group of very talented performers—wet or not.

Ray Davies is, of course, the chief Kink and writer of all their hits. "I'm a collection of loose ends," says Ray. "I don't want to be a pop star. I think that this is just a part of my life which will come to an end."

Yeah, well don't feel too badly, Ray. I'm a collection of very loose ends myself. Fact is, I'm not even collected at all! I probably wouldn't mind being a pop star except that my voice doesn't even sound good when it's all drowned out. And I'm hoping that that part of my life will come to an end—and soon.

Ray A Fighter

Ray really started out to be a fighter, believe it or not. "I did quite well in the school championships," Ray recalled, "until I came up against the Schools Champion of Great Britain. I hit him three times and hurt my hands. He knocked me out in the first round."

Yeah, well don't feel too badly about that either, Ray. *You* knocked *me* out the first time I saw you singing "You Really Got Me." And that was only on television!

Dave Davies is Ray's younger brother and the one who shakes up all the girls in he audience. Dave is the cut-up of the group, the one with the wild ideas and the equally wild personality.

Who's Last First?

He admits that he gets along best with Mick Avory, Kink drummer. In fact, they share an apartment in London. "The only thing about Mick is that he insists on being last," grinned Dave. And what a grin he has!

"We have a great competition in the morning to see who is last dressed. It's generally afternoon before I give up," announced Dave.

Yeah, well I think you and I would get along very well, Dave. Of course, I'd win everytime because it's generally night before I get up.

Dave has been blowing his mind over model cars. It all began when he was still living at home with his parents. It was there that he began building a huge racing circuit in his bedroom, causing his mother to become a bit undone because she couldn't even get in the door to make the bed.

"I had 12 model cars and a network of rails and track. Then I began building paper mache mountains and scenery. Everything's so big now that I can't get it out of the room!"

Yeah, well that's a real shame, Dave. I mean, just imagine those poor mountains gathering all that dust and dirt and spiders and things. I think we ought to all take up a collection and get Dave's racing circuit out of his bedroom and into *The BEAT* office.

We'd all have a great old time, I'm sure. In fact, to show just how sure I am—*I* will donate a dime to the cause.

Mick Avory is really a highly intelligent person but he disguises it. You see, Mick is fed up to here with "out of it" people who come up to him and make snide remarks.

Looks Like Idiot

So, he has worked out a perfect system whereby he sits there looking like an absolute idiot until the ignorant people are gone. Then he smiles happily and declares: How can you argue with an idiot?"

Yeah, well I hate to disillusion you, Mick. But it can be done. I mean, people argue with *me* all the time.

Everything seems to happen to poor Mick. "When we go through Customs it's always me they pick on to turn inside out. I buy a new car with a radio because the one in the old van is not working and when I get the car home the radio in that one doesn't work!"

All Solved

Yeah, well I can solve your car problem for you, Mick. You see, your trouble is that you bought a new car and so naturally the radio didn't work because everything else was working.

What you should hae done was to buy an old car in which *nothing* worked *except* the radio. And I have just the car for you—mine!

The last and probably the friendliest Kink is Pete Quaife. He's the one who delights in talking to fans and who is never too tired to sign an autograph.

Pete is basically a happy person and has only one slight problem—money. "I used to go through the week quite happily on one pound," revealed Pete, "but when you start earning hundreds a week it seems to vanish into thin air."

Yeah, well I wouldn't know about making *hundreds* a week, Pete, but I sure would be interested in knowing how you got "happily" through the week on roughly $3.00. Maybe you didn't eat?

Thinking the whole thing over, Pete decided that he did have one other slight problem—his kid brother, Dave. "Last week I arrived home to find he'd been selling my shirts to fans as souvenirs!"

Yeah, well that wouldn't have been so bad except that Pete says: "He'll end up just like me—only richer!"

In which case, I heroically offered to sell Pete's shirts myself. I'm not proud. I don't care if I become just like him—only richer, or course!

... THE KINKS

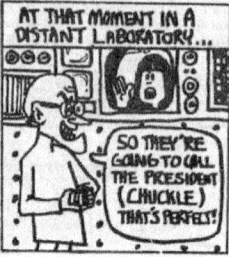

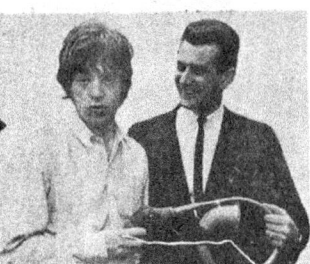

KRLA ARCHIVES

America's Largest Teen NEWSpaper

KRLA Edition BEAT

Volume 1, Number 48 — LOS ANGELES, CALIFORNIA — 15 Cents — February 12, 1966

Exclusive: George And Patti — Rumors Now Fact

KRLA BEAT

Los Angeles, California — February 12, 1966

Harrisons In Seclusion After Surprise Wedding

HOTLINE LONDON:
Eyewitness Report On Beatle Wedding

(Editor's Note: This is the first of what will be a weekly report written exclusively for The BEAT by Tony Barrow, a widely-known British journalist who made many friends in America while accompanying the Beatles on tour. As friend and press officer, he was one of the few persons attending George Harrison's wedding.)

By Tony Barrow

LONDON—In the suburban town of Epsom, ten miles south of London in the heart of Surrey's well-known stockbrokers' belt, a third Beatle took his bride.

The occasion had been a closely guarded secret and there was no crowd of fans outside Epsom Registry Office to see the couple arrive. Inside Ashley House were best man Brian Epstein, Beatle Paul McCartney, Mrs. D. Gaymer-Jones (Patti's mother), Mr. and Mrs. George Harrison (George's parents) plus some of Patti's other close relatives including her sister Jenny and brother Colin.

Few people were told about the wedding in advance but George and Patti shared their secret with the Lennons and the Starkeys. Cynthia and John, Maureen and Ringo were told before they left for their vacation in the West Indies. Patti and George received a lengthy telephone call from the West Indies shortly after the ceremony today.

Wedding gifts include a magnificent antique dining table, the present selected for Patti and George by Brian Epstein.

For the wedding ceremony George wore a black Victorian suit. Nobody can remember when they last saw this Beatle wearing a formal suit; he does so only upon the most special of special occasions. Petite and pretty Patti wore a dark red shot-silk dress with a red fox fur coat. I don't know why they call it red fox fur because it looked a sort of ginger color to me.

Patti's very beautiful ring is of white and pink gold. George claims it is about half an inch thick and it certainly looks more bulky than the average wedding ring.

Dave's Cool On Marriage

By Sue Greene

I spoke to the Hullabalooer shortly after the third Beatle marriage, and he gave me a few of his own ideas on the events just past. Said he, "It was all done in secret; nobody knew it was coming. But then, this is the way they have led their lives—in secret. Of course it took us all by surprise, and it was a shock for all of George's fans who love him—but now they can just love him in a different way.

"George is the one who is a little fed up with being a Beatle now—in fact, he always has been. And now he wants to settle down, and invest his money, and raise a family. I think that if any of the Beatles were going to leave the group, he would be the first one to do so.

"I think now it will be only a matter of time until Paul gets married—he has no reason not to now. I think that it will probably happen within a year's time. Between now and the first of next year, I am sure that Paul will probably marry Jane.

"I think that it's time that George and Patti were married—all of the boys are going to marry the girls that they have been going with anyways. And I think that alone should say something for them. They are more mature now, and I'm glad it happened."

Jones, McCartney Hurt

Paul Jones, singing favourite with the Manfred Mann unit, will undertake concert engagements next week with his shoulder in plaster. He's just spent almost a week in the hospital after smashing a collar bone in an automobile accident.

Less severely hurt in a recent road crash was Paul McCartney. The Beatle was visiting his father and step-mother at their Cheshire home, just south of Liverpool.

He was out riding around the Cheshire countryside on one of his two Moped motorized bicycles when the machine skidded on an icy road and threw him to the ground. Paul collected a deep cut to the side of his mouth and five stitches had to be put into the wound.

Now it's healing nicely and Paul feels fine again. The injury is not leaving a scar and Paul says it hasn't turned him against his fave pastime of Moped cycle riding.

News Briefs

Tom Jones, currently touring Australia with Herman's Hermits, will fly direct from down-under to New York for his latest "Ed Sullivan Show" appearance on February 13. His next single in the U.K. is to be "Big Man Cry," out early next month...

Paul Simon—half of your highly successful "Sounds Of Silence" duo—has penned a new number called "Some Day One Day" for the Australian folk unit The Seek-

(Turn to Page 15)

PATTI'S PROFILE

What's the new Mrs. Harrison like?
Patti is a doll. Her vital statistics:
She's 21 years old, has blue eyes and is five feet seven inches tall. Educated in a convent, she comes from a family of six, was born in Somerset in Southwestern England and spent most of her childhood in Kenya, where her father had a farm.

Patti started work as a hairdresser, like Ringo's wife, Maureen, but soon became bored with it and turned to modeling. Her "Dolly Girl" looks made her a favorite among leading fashion photographers and led to her part in "A Hard Day's Night."

They met during the movie and started dating.

GEORGE AND BRIDE LEAVE REGISTRY OFFICE AFTER WEDDING.

BAT-TLE FATIGUE
Batman Collapses!

Krunch! Bamm! Zot! Crash! Holy Popcorn, the worst has happened!!!

Stop the world, our fearless leader, crime stopper of all times, half of the dynamic duo, BAT-MAN is ill!

In an exclusive interview with a bat, The BEAT has learned that Adam West, also known as Bruce Wayne, better known as Batman, recently worked himself to the point of collapse and was given three days off from his exhaustive schedule to recuperate.

The bat revealed that the entire Batman crew has been working from 6 a.m. until almost midnight every day and even a Batman

(Turn to Page 5)

Another Beatle Gone; Now Paul Is Only Survivor

By Elden Chance

ESHER, ENGLAND—Surrounded by a 14-foot-high wall, England's most famous newlyweds remain in seclusion after a long-rumored surprise marriage that left only one unmarried Beatle.

George Harrison and his bride, baby-faced fashion model Patti Boyd, are staying at George's $56,000 five-bedroom bungalow in Esher, a wealthy residential estate in southern England.

It is only a few miles from Epsom, where George married his girlfriend of the past two years in a seven-minute ceremony on Jan. 21.

"It's the happiest day of my life," said blue-eyed Patti, who met George when she made her one attempt to act—a two-minute appearance in the 1964 Beatles' movie "A Hard Day's Night."

Said George, "Of course I am very happy, but we shall not have a honeymoon yet. We would just be hounded and wouldn't get any privacy."

Only immediate relatives and a few close friends knew about the late-morning wedding in the little blue and white registry office in Epsom. Paul McCartney, now the only bachelor of the group, was the only other Beatle present.

"Both George and Patti decided they wanted the quietest wedding without any fuss," a spokesman for the couple told The BEAT.

News of the closely-guarded wedding was announced half an hour after the ceremony, and word quickly flashed to fans around the world that another of the Beatles had taken a wife.

After the ceremony Paul said with a sigh, "Now the rumors can start about me, I suppose."

Actually rumors of Paul's impending marriage to actress Jane Asher started long ago, but nothing has been announced.

Rumors about George and Patti also started in 1964 when they went on vacation together to Ireland and then to the Bahamas. But George denied there were any wedding plans—right up until the day of the marriage.

Inside the BEAT

Paul and Barry In 3
Walker Brother Speaks 4
George and John Look Ahead 5
Mitch Ryder Takes A Ride 7
Marvelletes And Miracles 8
Wild Affair At The BEAT 11
Adventures of Robin Boyd 13
Success Of T-Bones 15
Beat Goes To The Movies 16

The BEAT is published weekly by BEAT Publications, Inc., editorial and advertising offices at 6290 Sunset Blvd., Suite 504, Hollywood, California 90028. U.S. bureaus in Hollywood, San Francisco, New York, Chicago and Nashville; overseas correspondents in London, Liverpool and Manchester, England. Sale price, 15 cents. Subscription price: U.S. and possessions, $3 per year; Canada and foreign rates, $9 per year. Application to mail at second class postage rates is pending at Los Angeles, California.

KRLA ARCHIVES

Paul & Barry Out Yet In

By Tammy Hitchcock

They're good looking, rather clean-cut, sort of on the wealthy side, sharp dressers and talented. They are 17 year old twins, Paul and Barry Ryan. And with all that going for them you wonder how they'll *ever* make it.

Three years ago they would have made it easily but today being clean-cut, wearing tailored suits and being rich to begin with counts them out, right? The rule of today is hip-hugging Mick Jagger pants—not white shirts and ties.

Making It Big

But despite all these handicaps, Paul and Barry *are* making it and making it big. They've already had a smash record, "Don't Bring Me Your Heartaches," in their native England and now they're crossing the Pond to appear on non other than "The Ed Sullivan Show."

Show business fell into Paul and Barry's laps quite by accident, if you discount the fact that their mom, Marian Ryan, is a very well known star in England.

The twins were born and raised in Leeds, England. Which doesn't matter much except that it meant the boys were out of the pop world, about as far out as they could be. When they had finished school in Leeds, Paul and Barry decided to go to London. Not to become famous but to enter art school.

However, upon their arrival in London they discovered that one had to be 17 to enter art school. That presented a small problem to Paul and Barry because they were then only 16.

So, they could do either one of two things. They could return to Leeds or they could remain in London. It wasn't too tough a decision to make—London won hands down.

Although they had definitely decided to be London-based for a year, they were not completely happy. Like most other young people they were anxious to get moving, a year of waiting seemed like an eternity to them.

With nothing but time on their hands, Paul and Barry became frequent visitors to the "in" spot of a year ago, The Ad Lib. It's lucky they chose the Ad Lib, things would have most certainly turned out differently if they hadn't.

Beatle Help

Because it was on one of their visits to the club that they ran into the Beatles. Paul and Barry had brought their famous mom along with them and when this beautiful, charming and very famous lady walked into the Ad Lib, naturally, the four Beatles found their way to her table.

It marked the first time that the Beatles had ever met her twin sons and they just *assumed* that since their mother was a singer, Paul and Barry were following in her footsteps.

That meeting planted a thought in the twins' minds. They weren't singers yet but they *would* like to give it a try. It might be fun.

They didn't have to wait long to find out because the very next day an enterprising young A&R man phoned Paul and Barry. Would they like to make a demonstration record?

Of course, they would! A quick check with Mrs. Ryan and the session was set up. Their mother thought it would be great because she knew her boys considered making a record a breeze. She wanted them to find out that it wasn't so easy, after all.

Instant Hit

You can guess what happened next. Paul and Barry made "Heartaches," Decca Records picked it up and the next thing they knew it was racing up the charts. And within three very short weeks the twins were on 16 television shows, which is rather difficult in England since they don't *have* very many TV shows to begin with!

Now, we are about to get our first glimpse of Paul and Barry Ryan. Now, *we* have the chance to make or break them Stateside. I think we'll love 'em—even though they *are* rather clean-cut, good-looking, wealthy, sharp dressers etc., etc.

What do you think?

On the BEAT

By Louise Criscione

Did you ever think that there would be a day when the Beatles weren't working? Well, neither did they! But just such a day has come and it has now multiplied into months.

George says that it doesn't bother him much because he putters around the house and goes to the movies and clubs and things. And since Ringo and John now live fairly close to George the three Beatles spend a lot of time visiting each other.

Still, it seems funny, doesn't it? All four Beatles just lazing around. 'Course, if I had their money and prestige I'd just laze around too!

If The Who (and particularly Pete Townsend) don't watch out they're going to lose every fan they ever had. Pete recently admitted that The Who don't mind keeping the audience waiting, or playing badly. Which figures since Pete also feels that a vast number of his fans are stupid morons and idiots. I guess he feels they have to be to like The Who. Which is a shame really.

Best Anywhere

Fontella Bass is very impressed with the English groups, declaring them the best in the world. And American groups? "Very few of them are original or exciting. Probably the best are the McCoys, the Byrds and the Gentrys. The rest of them either copy these three or try to get the English sound."

Donovan or his record company or somebody chickened out at the last minute and changed the title of his scheduled single from "For John and Paul" to "Superlove."

No wonder Dave Clark isn't more popular in his homeland. He

... PETE TOWNSEND

has an answer for every bit of constructive criticism which his fans give him. Which I think is a mistake on his part.

The fans tell him he isn't on TV enough and Dave says that he doesn't want to be over-exposed. They say that he is featured too predominately in the group and he answers that they've been the *Dave Clark* Five for three years now. And *that* has something to do with Dave being featured too much?

And so it goes. No matter what *anyone* says Dave manages to come up with some kind of an excuse. Which is fine except that Dave can't figure out why he is so unpopular in Britain.

Turtles Feelin' Good

Ran into Howard and Don of The Turtles today. The boys were feeling so good over the way their new record, "My Baby," is bounding up the charts that they were busily buying up all the trades.

Rumor had it that The Turtles had changed some of their members but Howard and Don assured me that they haven't and aren't even *considering* doing so.

QUICK ONES: Walter Shenson reveals that there will be romances for the Beatles in their next movie... Word out now is that starting date for Beatles' movie number three will be June. What about their August tour of the U.S.?... Sat through a good 45 minutes of the Human Beings thinking that they didn't know the words to any of the songs they were singing. But I found out later that they *deliberately* changed the words, which is okay but they should have informed the audience first... Mick Jagger digs Patti LaBelle and her Bluebelles. And no wonder—they're fabulous.

I have another great group to make you aware of—the Liverpool Five. They really put on a fantastic show, utilizing the voices of all five members. They're very versatile on stage switching from a beautiful "I Believe" to a swinging "Talkin' 'Bout My Babe."

Anyway, be on the look-out for

... KEN COX

them because with just a little bit of luck, Steve, Ken, Dave, Ron and Jimmy are going to go a long way in this business. One other little note—besides being talented they're also five extremely nice guys, which is a pleasant change from big-headed artists. Case you're interested they're current single is "Heart."

KRLA ARCHIVES

BEAT Exclusive
A Walker Brother Speakin' His Mind

By Mary Ellen Criscione

Have you ever been just sitting there wondering what to do next (if anything) when through your door walks John Maus of the Walker Brothers? Well, that's exactly what happened to me.

Totally unannounced but certainly not unwelcome, John appeared at the door with a smile on his face about as wide as he is tall. Which is quite a smile, believe me!

As you undoubtedly know, John and his other two Walker Brothers, Scott and Gary, have been in England for some time now. In fact, Scott and Gary are still there but John decided to take a short vacation and return Stateside.

John couldn't get over the changed scene here in the U.S. Especially "all the American cats with long hair," grinned John whose own hair is practically shoulder length.

The Walker Brothers were not making much noise over here so they decided to go to England. "We really weren't doing badly," said John. "We had just made one record and we were doing television shows but it just seemed like it would be nice to go to England."

Cheese And Crackers

However, they were not an instant success in England either. Actually, they almost starved! "Our land-lady paid our rent for awhile and sometimes she even fed us," revealed John. But mostly the three Walker Brothers existed on cheese and crackers.

They had a tough time deciding what to drink, too. "Their water you can pick up with a magnet," said John. "But, you know, they deliver the milk on the doorstep." And you can interpret that last statement any way you want to!

"At first we did nothing, then we did a television show," John recalled. "But we didn't work until the Kinks got into a fight on stage. Then they called us to finish up their tour for them."

And all of a sudden they were a sensation in England. Why? "I don't know. To start off with, before we even had a record out we were being mobbed. It must have been from the Kinks' tour," John concluded.

The mobbing bit got so out of hand that the Walker Brothers finally cut out ballroom appearances altogether. Rumor had it that the reason the Walkers were getting mobbed so badly was because they walked right out into the audience and really asked for it. But John looked both surprised and crestfallen when I mentioned it. "No, man, that's not safe," he said with a shake of his long hair.

To Get Inside

But speaking of mobbing brought all kinds of memories flooding back to John. Like how much they have to go through to even get *inside* the place where they are scheduled to appear.

"First, you park the car down the road about a mile. Then you hide down inside and the road manager goes running up to the theater and says we're here and what door do we use. There are always fans waiting around outside, so you pull the car up to the door, jump out, run inside as fast as you can, lock the door and pray! It's that hairy," John admitted.

He believes that the Beatles have the greatest security plans yet invented. "We saw the Beatles at Finsberry Park," said John. "Of course, the place was packed. They say the Beatles are losing their popularity – Ha! Ha!

"The Beatles are very cool people. We went into their dressing room and out comes a TV. So, we sat there watching television. It was a gas.

"Anyway, when their show was finished they were out of there so fast, *we* had more trouble getting out than they did!

"It's weird how they get so excited. Our fans are really wild. I like fans – fans are cool. They send us cakes and things. In my whole life I've never had so many birthday cards," John said.

And they send those "things" right to the Walkers' homes. They find out where they live and then take up permanent residence on their front steps.

"When I first got there I lived in this one-room thing," laughed John. "The living conditions were terrible. Then Gary and Scott moved to Chelsea. Big mistake. You're not there five minutes before the phone starts ringing. You pick it up and there's a little giggle on the other end. I guess they're afraid to talk to us."

Fans and England brought back a hilarious memory to John. "We were going to meet in the office one day," he recalled. "There were about 50 fans outside and if you stop to sign autographs for that many you're there three hours. So, Gary and Scott decided to run through the fans to a taxi.

... MORE DRESSED UP, The Walker Bros. (l. to r. Scott, Gary & John) accept award for "Brightest Hope."

"Well, one of them grabbed Scott so he and Gary started running. And they *all* started chasing after them down Kings Way, which is like the main street in Chelsea.

"They were running along and some man pulled up in a little car like the one everyone in England drives. He rolled down the window and said, 'Get in, man.' So, they got in and it turned out to be Lennon and Harrison," John laughed.

Dual Citizens

Word out of England was that the Walker Brothers were going to take out English citizenship. "We're going to have dual-citizenship," explained John. "It's odd that we had to go to England to make it. We're going to stay there. It's almost a moral issue. I mean, it's the English fans who made us."

All of the Walker Brothers dig England and the English people. They're cool, as John would say.

"If you go to a good restaurant which is full of moms and dads, you walk into the place and they don't say anything. Then just as you're ready to leave the waiter comes up with 15 napkins and a pen!" grinned John. "And, you know, this is the Rolls Royce crowd."

John reveals that it's not at all easy for an American to live in England. "Most people over there don't make a week what my apartment costs. So, the standard of living can't be too high."

Besides the long hair on American males, John was also surprised at the U.S. record scene. He thinks it's terrible. "I turned on the radio and I couldn't believe it," John said. "There's so much garbage on the air!"

One song which John did like was the Byrds' latest release. Naturally, speaking of the Byrds caused John to remember the fiasco which occurred when the Byrds paid their first visit to Britain.

"They came with the wrong attitude. I think they thought they were the American answer to the Beatles. Their attitude was 'don't bug me, I'm cool.' I seriously don't think they'll ever get work over there again," said John quite frankly.

"Everybody over here is trying to be like somebody else. The Knickerbockers are trying to be like the Beatles, Paul Revere is trying to be like the Kinks. One thing you can't do in England is copy the groups. I don't understand the point. It's all right to be a group but try to do something which is your own."

Grabbing

John admitted that the scene in England was also bad for awhile. "They were grabbing at things. First it was folk with the Seekers. Tom Jones doesn't make it over there now. And they're not crazy over Herman. The Stones always do well and, of course, the Beatles."

Before John left he expressed sympathy for *The BEAT* girls who wear their hair long. He knows what we have to go through because with his hair the length it is he has the same problems as we do!

"I gotta use creme shampoo, then I have to put on a conditioner, then I take that off and put on a creme rinse," John lamented. So, why doesn't he put his hair up? "I tried that once – failed."

And with that John Maus was gone. "Cool" surprises like John should come my way more often!

... THE NEW STYLE WALKER BROTHERS POSE IN AN ENGLISH ALLEY.

KRLA ARCHIVES

BEAT Scrapbook
George And John Look Ahead

By Jamie McCluskey III

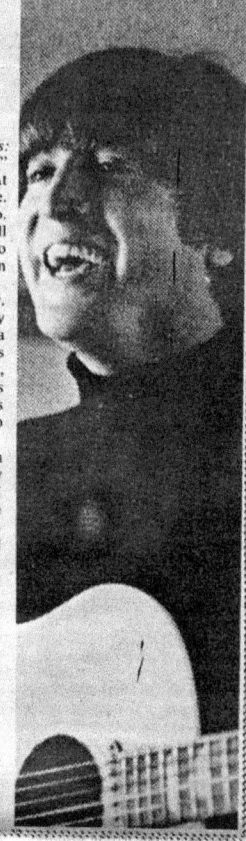

If you have been reading *The BEAT* regularly—as you *undoubtedly* have!—you know that we have been taking weekly peeks into our *BEAT* scrapbook and peering backwards into the Beatles' early lives.

This week, however, we are going to view a few snaps from the present. And presently, we, will be viewing George Harrison and John Lennon of the MBE set. Okay, Ready—Steady—Goooo!!!!

Now we all know how hectic a Beatles' schedule can get, and how hectic the Beatles' schedules have been for the last couple of years. But suddenly George informs us that the fab foursome has found itself with some time on its hands.

"It may seem funny to some people that we Beatles haven't got a single date in our 1966 diary. Not one job of work is fixed! It's about the first time I can remember since we first started that we haven't been able to say 'we've got to play at such-and-such a place on that date.'

Another Film

"Mind you we *know* that in about two months we've got to make another record and we *know* that some time this year there's another film to do. But that's quite a way off."

Gee fellers—if times are really all that hard, we could always use a couple of extra copy boys up here in *The BEAT* offices!

As we turn the page in our *BEAT* scrapbook now, we can see a few snaps of George's home. In fact, if you look real closely—you may even see George telling us all about the things he's *going* to do with his Humble Hearth.

"I'm getting tape recorders—like Johnny and Paul have—fixed up into a sort of home studio. They can over-dub vocal and instrumental tracks so that when they get an idea for a song they can make a demo record by themselves. I want to do the same."

Of course, George is now living in Weybridge, England—which is quite a considerable distance from the familiar old Liverpudlian homestead of yesteryear—but never say that George isn't loyal:

Goes Home

"I go home to Liverpool about once a month now to see relatives and friends. We're still getting things for the house I bought my parents, so that takes up some of the time.

Alright Beatle fans—now that we have seen a few little candid glimpses of George, how 'bout turning the page and joining John-John?

Just for fun, we decided to let Johnny have some words to play around with—being that he's a famous author in his own writ and all!—and in these pictures you will see his very own reactions.

Money: "Nice. Great." *Guitars:* "Guitars are great. Part of life." *Airplanes:* "I don't like them. At first they were a nice adventure. I like flying less the more we do. We can get to most places well enough by road. We've flown so much, something could happen the more we do."

Eppy: "He's great, you know. When people talk about him, they say he's harsh and hard. He's a businessman, so he has to be. He's never a businessman with us, though. We only talk business about twice a year. He sometimes has a go at us, then we have a go back and it's forgotten."

Liverpool: "It's still home. Even though my aunt has moved away and I have to stay with Paul if I go there. If I'm in London, home is Weybridge, but if I say I'm going home, I mean Liverpool. It'd be the same if I was from Paris and lived in Marseilles. Paris would always be home."

Sketching: "I don't sketch. I occasionally draw things but I don't sketch."

Sure John

Okay John, luv—if you say so. But you lost me!!

Anyway—hope you've all enjoyed going through *The BEAT's* scrapbook with me today—I know *I* have. But then, what can you expect from an incurable Beatlemaniac??!!!

For Girls Only

By Shirley Poston

Linda Jackson, I luv you!

You may think that's a strange way to start a column, but I don't (which figures.) And neither will you when I tell you *why* I luv Linda Jackson (who happens to be a *BEAT* reader from Torrance, Calif.)!

Because she made me a George Harrison doll with her own two hands! It's sooo adorable, and it's over a foot high! Besides that, the card she sent with it really got to me.

Harrison Fan

It said "From a giant great McCartney fan to *the* giant great Harrison fan." Honestly, I get *shivers* every time I read it.

Speaking of George (which I hardly ever do, you know), you all remember the "Bev" incident where I asked all of you to write a certain girl who felt she had nothing to live for because she would never be able to meet Paul?

Well, I promised not to open the letters, but I opened one by mistake. And if *anyone* is *the* giant great Harrison fan, it's the girl who wrote it. I won't give her full name because she might be embarrassed, but the first part of it is Mary Ann.

I don't think I'll ever forget that letter if I live to be two hundred. Mary Ann is desperately in love with George, but she's found a way to live with it by doing everything she can to become the kind of person he would *want* to meet. And I'll just bet she will meet him someday! With an attitude like hers, she can't fail. George is one lucky boy to have someone like her care that much for him.

Mystery Singer

Attention all Northern California readers. Something good is coming your way! Make that *someone* good. A certain pop singer from Liverpool, who was just getting his career going in this country when he was drafted, has been stationed at Fort Ord.

As soon as I have his address, I'll tell you all about him! But, another word of warning. Don't forget to put in a good word for me with him, too! He's a doll!!

Back to George. Okay, okay, I won't spend this entire column raving about him. Just two more things. Did you know that George's mum had an accident and broke her hip? And did you know that our boy Harrison sent her off to Spain to recuperate? I think that's really wonderful.

So is she. Mrs. Harrison has done more to help the Beatle cause than any one person I know of. Just by being so thoughtful and answering so many thousands of letters.

If you'd like to send her a get well card (please do, she'd love it), and if you don't already have an address for her, send them in care of me and I'll forward them on to her.

Oh, just one more thing (sorry about that.) I do want to thank *BEAT* readers, Phyllis and Judy Mancz of Centerville, Ohio for their hand-made Christmas card. It showed George dressed up in a Santa suit with Paul, John and Ringo snickering at him.

He got back at them (on the inside of the card) by filling their stockings up with coal. The ones they had hanging by the fireplace, that is. Which somehow figures.

Speaking of—no, I'm NOT going to say *George!* See, I fooled you! I was going to say speaking of *Elvis!* Which I wasn't, of course, but that's beside the point because I am now.

Presley Fan

I also got a Christmas card from El and the Colonel, and although I hate to part with it, I will (for a price) (stop that snarling, I'm only kidding). Seriously, I am a Presley fan, but I know there are many others who are more devoted to E.P. than I am.

I think one of *those* giant great fans should have this card, so if you'd like it, please send me a postcard. I'll put them all in a hat or vat or something and draw one out. But hurry. You know me. If you wait too long, I'll lose the card and we'll have to wait until next year.

Now, what was it I was going to write about next? (No, it wasn't George! What do you think I have, a one track mind or something?) (Never answer that question.)

Oh, I know what it was. A certain California teen is in sort of a pickle because her family moved from Palo Alto to Carbondale, Ill. Not that there's anything wrong with Illinois, but she's homesick like she can't believe and would like to hear from all of you. Her only connection with California now is *The BEAT*, which helps a lot, but a lot of letters would help even more!

Homesick Reader

You can write to her c/o 2012 Woodriver Dr., Willowbrook Apts. No. 3, in Carbondale. Hope you will.

Just thought of something. If I have two "contests" going at once, I'll get so mixed up I won't be able to find my way home from the office (I'm having enough trouble managing that one now.) So, guess our Herman album will have to wait until next week.

If you're getting tired of having or going to the same old kind of parties, here's a way to liven things up.

Have a party in honor of your favorite star (George, for instance). Send out invitations saying who the guest of honor will be (although he won't really be there). Then serve his favorite foods, play his records, make your decorations in his favorite colors, dress like him if you want. You know, just let him be the theme of the whole party.

Well, I'd better shush so someone else can get in a word edgewise. Dont' forget to let me know about the Elvis card and I'll see you next *BEAT*.

Batman Collapses

(Continued From Page 2)

can get tired after a few weeks like that.

The bat also revealed that this is not the first case of exhaustion on the set. It seems Boy Wonder, Robin, in the person of Burt Ward, being a younger man, also suffered from overwork some time ago and was also given some time out.

However, Batman had managed to work on in his never ending fight against crime until he reached the point of exhaustion. He was then ordered to bed for three days and all the insiders who knew, including of course *The BEAT* staff, by way of the bat, waited anxiously, hoping the Penquin or the Riddler would not choose this particular time to strike.

Never fear though, peace loving citizens of the world, the bat assured us that Batman is being well cared for by his faithful butler, Alfred, Robin, his aunt, and a fleet of bats.

Nothing can stop a Batman.

KRLA ARCHIVES

The Man Behind The Talent

By Shirley Poston

Have you ever met Bobby Vinton? Well, if you haven't you're about to. And I think you're in for a surprise.

I sure was.

Being a graceful sort of person with a tendency to fall down manholes and up stairs, I am always unnerved by the thought of "interviewing" a star.

Everything about Bobby runs into millions. His number of fans. The amount of records he sells every year. Not to mention his bank account.

Number One

Also, he has broken attendance records at all of America's plush nightspots, where the audiences are mostly adults. And been voted the nation's number one vocalist time after time.

I thought about all these accomplishments on my way to meet Bobby. I also thought about gnawing off a nail or two.

I'm going to be very frank about why I felt that way. It wasn't just because he is an extremely famous and successful personality. It was partly because I didn't know him from Adam as a person.

I'd heard all about his talent, but I couldn't help but wonder why I hadn't heard more about the man behind it.

By the time I arrived at the chosen place, I was really off and running. A jumble of questions were racing through my alleged mind.

Was something *wrong* with Bobby? Too sophisticated maybe? Sort of stuck-up? Ultra-conservative? Maybe even *square*?

Well, my mental interrogation soon came to an abrupt halt. And so did I. Because I ran into someone. Literally, I mean. And all of my questions were answered the second I saw who the someone was.

It was—you guessed it. And there was nothing, and I do mean *nothing*, wrong with Bobby Vinton.

He looked great in a light blue denim shirt-and-slacks set (I was expecting maybe white tie and tails?), and the first thing he did was laugh.

When I tried to apologize for practically mowing him down, he just kept laughing and sort of patted me.

After we'd found a table and Bobby had ordered a sandwich for him and coffee for me (who could eat a a moment like that?), I asked for a large helping of Vinton's vital statistics, wanting to get the "interview" over so we'd have time to just talk.

Bobby started at the beginning. He was born in Canonsburg, Pa. (a suburb of Pittsburgh) and inherited a love of music from his bandleader father.

At the age of 15, Bobby organized his first band. Besides being the leader of the group, he also leanred to play every single one of the instruments.

Star Quarterback

The band played on through high school and college (during which time Bobby was also the star quarterback on the football team.) Then Bobby changed his tune to a rousing march tempo and hut-two-three-foured his way through two years in the Army.

After his discharge, he struck up the band again, traveling all over the country to back the pop idols of the day. Such as Bobby Rydell, Fabian and Frankie Avalon.

In 1961, Bobby's band recorded their first two albums. But it wasn't until Bobby put down the baton and picked up a microphone that he had his first number one record. The sweet smell of success came in the form of "Roses Are Red." Since then, Bobby's had hit after hit ("Blue Velvet," "Mr. Lonely," "Blue On Blue," and I could go on forever), appeared on too many TV shows to even count (he was in town at the moment to film a guest spot for "Danny Kaye"), and more.

His future plans include the San Remo Song Festival (where he'll have to sing in Italian) (as he put it, "I'm Polish, but I'll manage"), movies (he has a five picture contract with Paramount), more TV, and, of course, more and more records.

San Remo Festival

And not all of them will be the love ballad type tunes he's famous for. Bobby digs all kinds of music and would like to branch out a bit. In fact, his very next record may be a song-with-a-beat. One he wrote himself.

When Bobby told me this bit of good news, I sighed happily and said, "I've always wanted to hear you sing a real *mover*."

Boy, did that *break* him. And it really wasn't that funny. (Or was it?) (What does that word *mean* anyway?)

We talked about England, and the big blow-up that occurred when Bobby visited Jolly Olde. After going over to promote a Vinton disc that was recorded *in* England, with English musicians, he was forced to cancel all his TV and personal appearance commitments. The British refused, at the last minute (at customs, actually) to issue a work permit, or whatever you call it.

The permit was finally granted on the day Bobby had to leave, but the trip wasn't a total waste. He spent his unexpected "vacation" with the Stones and other U.K. friends.

Likes New York

We talked about Hollywood ("I like California, but I'd rather live in New York") ... about teenagers ("I dig them—I think the world's getting better") ... about the Beatles ("their music will outlive all of us") ... about hairstyles ("long hair is no big problem, it's just a trend.")

Mostly, we just raved on, about everything and nothing, for two hours instead of one.

And, when I finally did get back to work (or else), I had the answer to another question. I knew why I had, until that day, known of Bobby as a star instead of a person.

The Vinton subject has been thoroughly covered, but that was a long time ago. Since then, Bobby's old following has grown up, and his new fans don't really know much about him.

As a result, his records sell like hot cakes, but no one screams when he walks out on a stage. Because no one screams at strangers.

Bobby Vinton, who has a habit of being painfully honest about himself, told me he'd *love* to be screamed at. And I'd like to tell you why I think he's worth screaming about.

I'm not going to bore you with any of those great-guy-with-a-wonderful-personality routines. He is exactly that, but he's more.

In a word, he's a gas. And you'd flip if you knew him. So get acquainted.

We fell in love with the English stars because they were so down to earth. And so different from some of our American idols who were perfect, polished, and just too goodie-goodie to be true.

Well, Bobby has that same quality. That naturalness. A lack of pretense and an obvious lack of interest in anything that isn't for real.

And he has the well-sharpened sense of humor that's such an important part of being a non-phony. I don't mean one of those highly-trained-toss-the-good-doggie-a-funny-bone sense of humor. I mean the unguarded, unconscious kind that makes it impossible for you to laugh just because you know you're supposed to. And makes it impossible not to laugh when you know you're not supposed to.

Like at lunch that day. We were deep in conversation when a young woman walked up to the table and started talking about the dress she was wearing.

Bobby and I immediately looked at each other, realizing this was one of those luncheon fashion shows, but for some reason, we started cracking up.

And once we got started, we couldn't stop. But don't feel sorry for the poor model. About half way through her "speech," she started cracking up too.

There you have him. The star I thought would be unapproachable. Because I didn't know any better. Well, I do now, and I hope you do too.

... BOBBY VINTON

British Top 10

1. DAY TRIPPER/
1. KEEP ON RUNNING ... Spencer Davis Group
2. DAY TRIPPER/
   WE CAN WORK IT OUT ...... The Beatles
3. SPANISH FLEA .... Herb Alpert
4. LET'S HANG ON .... The Four Seasons
5. MY SHIP IS COMING IN ... Walker Brothers
6. MICHELLE .... The Overlanders
7. A MUST TO AVOID ...... Herman's Hermits
8. THE RIVER .... Ken Dodd
9. THE CARNIVAL IS OVER ...... The Seekers
10. TILL THE END OF DAY .... The Kinks

KRLA ARCHIVES

NOTED IN THE UNITED KINGDOM
By Gil

Unlike JOHN and GEORGE, PAUL has elected to live right in BIG L. Even so he is forty mintes from JOHN'S Tudor Mansion, depending on the amount of traffic about. London traffic can turn a fifteen minute drive into an hour's frustration. PAUL and JANE ASHER are giving such close attention to PAUL'S house hat there is only one conclusion to be drawn.

* * *

The credits' for the movie, "Having A Wild Weekend," which was pretty much of a drag anyway, should have read co-starring the Dave Clark Five. Mr. Clark himself seemed to have a much larger part than any of the other four. This is pretty surprising, when you consider that MIKE SMITH does most of the singing for the group.

* * *

GEORGE HARRISON has surprised a great many people with the quality of his compositions to date. In particular, his contribution to "Rubber Soul" was very melodic. When you consider how much the interests of the four BEATLES vary, it is pleasnt to hear that they are still very good friends. Despite all reports to the contrary, JOHN LENNON has no intention of giving up music and concentrating on a literary career. LENNON will complete his third book in the spring if the movie schedule permits. The movie schedule itself is very much behind and it will have to be completed much later than anticipated. The delay on the BEATLES third movie is also a threat to their 1966 American tour. Many arrangements have been finalized for the tour, but if the movie is not completed in the time, the dates for the tour will have to be set for later in the year.

When JERRY LEE LEWIS married a girl very much his junior his popularity seemed to suffer. Now that BRIAN JONES has been ordered by a London court, to pay for the suport of his four-r year old child, will his popularity suffer too? Yours truly certainly hopes not. The private life of any performer should not influence the public's support of his professional status.

* * *

When in the U.K., BOB DYLAN usually visits MR. & MRS. LENNON at their home in Weybridge. Contrary to popular belief Weybridge is not a suburb of London, but is in fact a small village some twenty miles from BIG L, as the swingers call the big city.

* * *

Take a letter: Dear Peter, While I realize that you are feeling pretty despondent about all the money that you don't have, I wonder would you mind belting up for a couple of weeks. Frankly, me old mate, these continuous articles poppping up on your rather drab financial status are getting to be pretty much of a drag. If you could stifle the sobs for just a fortnight, it would be greatly appreciated.

Mitch Ryder Takes A Ride With Jenny

By Anna Maria Alonzo

Detroit has long been known as the Motor City, and now there is a pop group on the scene racing up the charts at higher than high speeds, and they're called Mitch Ryder and the Detroit Wheels.

There are five members in the group, but not a Fifth Wheel among them! Individually, they are Mitch, Jim, Earl, John, and Joey.

They originally formed their group after a chance meeting in a club in Detroit where Mitch was performing with another group. After a short time, they all rolled into a recording studio to cut their first record together. But that was the record that was!

Recorded 'Help'

"We had a record out before "Jenny Take A Ride," called "Help"—but unfortunately it was released the same time as the Beatles' "Help!" so it didn't have a big chance!"

Not about to just roll around town feeling sorry for themselves, Mitch and his Wheels turned right around and released a second record, which has now hit the Top Ten in charts all across the nation.

Theirs is a somewhat unique sound, and Jim McCarty tried to describe it to The BEAT: "Our sound is definitely Rhythm and Blues. We try to stay away from the English trends because we feel there's too much of it going on. We like to stay in our own bag—which is the colored sound."

Jim has called it the "colored sound;" others have described it as "soul music." Whatever it is, though, it is distinctly theirs.

Alan Stroh, who manages the five boys, tried to further explain their music for us: "I think that the most important thing about this group which sets them apart from any other group in this country—is that these are young boys who grew up in the city of Detroit, in the environment of R 'n' B. What they do is what comes from their environment and it's a n ural thing. It's what they really know, not something which they have imitated or copied, which many groups do.

"They are the most soulful white group in the country."

At that point, the boys were all laughing and joking around together, and I asked them what kind of humor they have together as a group. Their reply in unison—"Warped!!"

"Seagull" And Cake

All of the boys are individually talented in their own right. John has written a collection of poems entitled, "Poor Seagull." Earl studied commercial cooking and baking for a year, and "he sort of takes care of the group." He's also chief Birthday Cake Baker!

Jim thought about the years ahead of him for a moment, than very earnestly explained to The BEAT: "I enjoy playing rock 'n' roll from the excitement stand-point of it—it's a lot of fun playing to a large audience.

"But when I 'm about 25 or 26, what I would like to do is to slide from the rock field into legitimate jazz. The most important factor involved right now is that I'm gaining experience, and this is the most important thing to me."

Mitch likes to dabble in art and has sold some of his paintings already. But he insists, "I like *real* art, I don't go for the modern art. I'd like to get back into art eventually and record production. Something that doesn't involve a lot of travelling.

The future is full of bright expectations for these boys, and soon they will be seen on the Ed Sullivan show, as well as several other TV shows and possibly even a movie.

Other than that? Well, Mitch has a few ideas for the future of the group: "I'd like to see everybody's talent—their *real* talent—brought to the peak of what they can do. If they have a talent for something, I'd like to see them bring it out in the group."

There is a whole lot of talent in this group and they are all headed straight for the top. So you'd better watch out for them 'cause they could roll right over you when your ears are turned the other way. And this is one sound not to be missed!

...MITCH RYDER AND THE DETROIT WHEELS

Ray Peterson Communicates

...RAY PETERSON

By Carol Deck

Communication is the profession that Ray Peterson is engaged in.

Whether it be on stage, in front of television cameras, on the golf course or over a cup of coffee in a small restaurant — Ray communicates.

The slender, six foot Texan, well tanned from daily golf games, talks easily and expressively about himself, his career, clothes, audiences and golf. In fact, if allowed, he'll talk your ear off about golf.

He started playing just four years ago. His first attempts were awkward, due to a weak leg from a bout with polio some years ago. But Ray was a champion athlete in high school and a couple of years with a brace on his leg doesn't slow him down any.

His determination to learn the game has payed off in tournaments and courses across the nation and last summer he was awarded the "Best Sportsmanship" trophy at the annual musicians tournament in Palm Springs.

Likes Blue

Ray is very interested in clothes and likes to dress sharp but not flashy. One of his favorite golf attires is all blue—blue pants, shirt, sweater and even blue shoes!

He says, "I like to be seen and not heard, on the golf course." He doesn't sing on the golf course or play golf on the stage and feels that one ought to dress appropriately.

On stage he wears suits he designs himself, mostly mohair with just a touch of braid or velvet, just enough to give it that sharp look.

But on girls he likes styles that are relaxed and up-to-date. He likes tight fitting bell bottoms but says "I don't think they look good on men." And he goes for sharp sweaters and boots.

Since 'Corinna'

And when it comes to audiences, Ray has probably played every kind and size of audience possible in the years he's been topping charts since the days of "Corinna-Corinna."

He says if he could hand pick his own audience, he would like one that "is interested in what you're trying to do and one that is relaxed."

Of all the audiences he's performed before, one that sticks out in his mind was a mob in Cleveland, Ohio, back when Bobby Rydell, Fabian and Frankie Avalon were the biggest things around.

The show was free except for a small parking fee and 70,000 cars were parked that day. The stage was constructed of four by fours and sat in front of a lake.

Ray recalls it this way, "People were being carried out. The audience actually started to riot. The four by fours were breaking and the stage was being pushed into the lake."

But Ray took the whole thing as a sort of challenge and asked if he could go on. He walked on stage and sang "You'll Never Walk Alone" giving his all and there was dead silence. The audience was stunned by the power and feeling that Ray put into that song.

"But don't think I wasn't scared," Ray says. Of all the audiences he's played he seems to like the really huge ones best, better than intimate clubs or studios. "You give your all for 80,000 people," he explains.

And now the tall slender Texan is giving his all again with his latest release, "Love Hurts." Could be another in his long line of hits.

you love to feel a fluffy fur
SNUGGLE BALL
ONLY
$1.98 EACH
BUY TWO GET ONE FREE

Genuine mouton fur ball with key ring... a beautiful decorative pom-pom fashion accessory for keys, clothes, purse, car and 1000 fun uses. Everyone will want Snuggle Balls!

10 WILD COLORS!!!
☐ Azure Boy Blue   ☐ Dark Mood Blue
☐ Crybaby Yellow   ☐ Tickled Pink   ☐ Rock 'n Roll Red
☐ Livid Lavender   ☐ Bitter Black   ☐ Outrage Orange
                   ☐ Always Olive   ☐ Tough Turquoise

HOLLYWOOD HOUSE
Box 869, Dept. B-25
Hollywood, Calif. 90028

Rush me _____ Snuggle Balls marked above @ 1.98 each SAVE 1.98 — buy 2, get 1 FREE (enclose only 3.96 for 3 balls).

name _____
street _____
city _____
state _____ zip _____

KRLA ARCHIVES

DISCussion
By Eden

Instrumental sounds are coming on bigger and bigger all the time, and Ramsey Lewis and his trio have succeeded in capturing the instrumental-jazz sound on the pop scene.

Their first two records—"The In Crowd," and "Hang On Sloopy,"—were both smash hits, and now this throbbin' threesome has come up with one of their greatest records yet. They have recorded the Beatles' "Hard Day's Night" in jazz and the disc is racing right up to the top of all the charts. I'd like to hear the Trio do an entire LP of Beatle tunes in jazz. That's really some kinda soul.

* * *

And speaking of *soul*, have you heard Billy Medley (one-half of the Righteous Brothers dual-cool) singing his latest release, "Georgia?"

No? Well, I'll bet that you're wrong! You have probably heard it and thought that it was the Genius of Soul himself—Ray Charles, but it's not. It's just Bill wailing a few notes of soulful song, and it's a great record.

Just out of curiosity though—wonder when the Righteous Brothers are gonna start singing as a *team* again?!!

* * *

Whewwwwww!! Probably the best record they have ever made together. Talkin' 'bout the new 45er from Sonny and Cher called "What Now My Love." The tune was penned by the great French singer-composer Charles Aznavour and comes across like gangbusters with the inimitable song-stylings of Mr. and Mrs. Bono. Congratulations kids—this should put you right back up on the top side of the charts.

* * *

P.F. Sloan has been keeping himself occupied lately by writing a few million hit records for some of the top pop artists. Latest to join the singers-of-Sloan-songs is Glenn Yarbrough who has recorded "Ain't No Way." Good record, but what did you expect? These guys can do no wrong. It's something they've started calling *talent*.

* * *

Once again we find Mr. Sloan falling into a winning combination, but this time with the fast-moving Turtles, and their new entry into the 45 RPM race—"You Baby." They had a Number One disc together before, and it looks like a repeat success story this time around.

* * *

Once again you read it first in *The BEAT* as we take the wraps off of the brand new disc by the Yardbirds. This group has invented the exciting new sound they call "rave up," and their new record certainly runs true to form.

Entitled "The Shape of Things," it was written by Keith Relf—lead singer for the Yardbirds—while the group was in Los Angeles recently to perform at the Hullabaloo club in Hollywood.

This group deserves to go straight to the top and *stay* there and its up to you to give them a "ticket to ride!"

...THE MARVELETTES

Marvelettes Back Again

The Marvelettes first appeared on the recording scene in 1961 with "Please Mr. Postman" and the postman hasn't stopped bringing in the response yet.

These attractive girls first began singing together in high school in Detroit and were persuaded to enter a school talent show.

The show went over so well that one of their teachers arranged an audition for the group with Berry Gordy Jr., the man who's made Motown Records Inc. one of the most successful and respected labels in the recording industry.

Gordy, now world famous as a star finder, signed them immediately and the group went on to fame with numbers like "Beechwood 4-5789."

Their live appearances have included the Apollo Theater in New York, the Cow Palace in San Francisco, the 40 Thieves Club in Bermuda and the Macambo Club in Montreal.

There were originally four members of the group but Georgianna Gordon retired recently leaving lead singer Gladys Horton, Katherine Anderson and Wanda Rogers. Wanda, by the way, is married to Bobby Rogers of the Miracles, another smash Motown group.

And now the Marvelettes are back with what looks like another hit to add to their collection. They are climbing charts everywhere with "Don't Mess With Bill."

THE MIRACLES at a Go-Go doing "Going to A-Go-Go" in their typical show stopping fashion. That's Smokey Robinson a go-going on the right, assisted by Warren "Pete" Moore, Bobby Rogers and Ronnie White. They seem to have stunned that guitar player seated between them.

KRLA ARCHIVES

Around Came The Guard

By Annette & Renee' Schenely

We were on our way to a new teenage night club which has opened recently in the very heart of Hollywood. It was Dave Hull's Hullabaloo and we had seen the premiere of the club on television the night that *The BEAT* Pop Music Awards were given out.

So, we decided to take a look at it ourselves. It was just a normal, sunny day but little did we know that our "normal" day was going to turn into a day we'd never forget.

When we finally arrived at the door we were met with a giant picture of the resident band, the Palace Guard. Being teenagers, we naturally get all stoked over long-hair so we gave the picture a second, third, fourth, fifth, sixth, seventh, and eighth look.

But we didn't need another look to tell us that the Palace Guard were going to be quite popular with the female part of our race. And we must say, we were looking forward to hearing what kind of a sound they were going to produce on stage.

We sat ourselves down in the front row along with a couple of our girlfriends and took a long look around us. The room had a great atmosphere and we got the feeling that something was going to happen but we just couldn't figure out what it was.

Around They Came

As the room filled rapidly, the show was about to begin. The curtain opened and around came the Palace Guard. The reason we say "around" is because the Hullabaloo's stage is not just any ordinary stage—it revolves!

One look and one song was enough to make us want the Palace Guard to answer all of our questions. So, after the show we got down to serious business. It took us two full weeks to get permission from the management but at last we had a date set for the interview.

The time was 4:30, the day was Saturday. And what a Saturday it was! We were very nervous but our jitters vanished as soon as the six Guards marched into the room.

Don, the group's leader, began teaching himself the guitar in mid-1964 and soon thereafter decided to form a group of his own. As luck would have it, Don ran into Emitt Rhodes. Emitt was already a rather proficient drummer and he, like Don, had an ambition to join a group.

Just drums and a guitar would never do so Don drafted his two brothers, Dave and John. And shortly Rick joined in with his bass guitar and Chuck with his lead guitar and the Palace Guard were then complete.

Little In Common

All three of the Beaudoin brothers were born in Montreal, Canada. Dave, John and Don differ in just about everything else, though. Don is quite easy-going, John is rather easy-going and Dave is a little on the temperamental, moody side.

Chuck McClung is the businesslike member of the group. He's got a fantastic sense of humor—he'd have to in order to raise that menagerie he keeps around his house! And Chuck has only one ambition—to be rich. *Filthy* rich, if possible.

Rick is the quiet Guard, standing on stage playing his guitar but never smiling. He honestly looks like a Palace Guard, only with long hair, of course!

Emitt is the friendly, out-going Guard—sort of the Paul McCartney of the Palace Guard. He's the happy-go-lucky type who always has a smile ready for anyone who happens to be looking.

Singin' Lead

He enjoys leaving his drums to stand in the spotlight and sing lead for a change. He especially loves singing Beatle songs such as "Michelle," "Norwegian Wood" and "It's Only Love."

So, there are the Palace Guard. And what a group they turned out to be! They got their first big break when KRLA disc jockey, Casey Kasem, asked them to play on his television show, "Shebang."

Hullabaloo Sets Dance Contest

Dave Hull is going to provide some nimble footed person a chance to have his own personalized music wherever he goes.

On Feb. 11, Dave will draw the names of 10 couples to compete in a swingin' dance contest Feb. 19 at Dave Hull's Hullabaloo in Hollywood, accompanied by the Palace Guard.

To enter, just put your name and partner's name on a card and drop it in the box in the lobby of the club. Be sure you get it there before the 11th.

First prize will be the fabulous B & N "Musicar," the only 4-speed automatic portable record changer on the market.

The "Musicar" plays as many as 8 albums or 9 singles and plays through existing car radio speakers so installation is no problem.

It's all chrome plated with a rich stained walnut door, that'll make any rod's interior look like a Rolls.

This is the same unit that George Barris is featuring in all his latest custom creations. It's so technically perfected that it's guaranteed for one full year with a 10-year guarantee on the special diamond needle.

Check the B & N "Musicar" display in the lobby of the club and don't forget to put in your entry for the dance contest.

KRLA must not feed Bob Eubanks enough. The poor dee-jay has to chew on ropes while trying to rope some beef for his dinner.

PLAYING THRU FEBRUARY 6th
CHAD MITCHELL
HIMSELF

OPENING FEB. 8   BUFFY SAINTE MARIE

FEB. 15   JUDY COLLINS & PATRICK SKY

AT DOUG WESTON'S
Troubadour

RESERVATIONS: CR. 6-6168

9083 SANTA MONICA BLVD. NEAR DOHENY IN LOS ANGELES

KRLA ARCHIVES

Inside KRLA

Colyumside once again everyone, and this week we have a special message to deliver to everyone. I just got through speaking with the old Scuzz himself, Dave Hull, and David has asked me to please convey his most sincere thanks to all those who came through to really help him celebrate his 28th birthday in a big way.

On the 20th day of January, Dave welcomed in his 28th year, and there to help him on such an auspicious occasion were all sorts of greetings and gifts from his many loyal Hullabalooers out in KRLA-land.

The Hullabalooer told me that, "I've gotten *tons* of wires. The kids have been so very nice to me. So please thank everyone for me."

Along with the tons of wires, Dave also received countless cards and letters all wishing him well. And gifts? Well, the Scuzz informs us that he received every possible gifts imaginable, including poems, ties, cuff-links, and even balloons!!

Well, from everyone here at The BEAT—a very happy birthday to you, Hullabalooer.

Hey—I've got a great new dance for everyone to try. It was suggested to me by one of the greatest dancers in all of KRLA Kountry (whose name I am sworn not to mention) and it should be taking the country by storm any day now.

The dance is called The Kami Kaze. Everyone lines up on opposite sides of the room, and then you just make like a plane and crash into the opposite wall.

Now, if you happen to be just a little creative, you can form two lines of people, and crash into one another. But then, we'll leave that to your own discretion.

Have you noticed that the Beatles—fabulous be their name!—have held the Number One spot on the KRLA tunedex for over seven weeks with their latest single, "Daytripper," b/w "We Can Work It Out." Now just who says our boys are slipping?

HELP!

HELP!
My name was in a mag in England and I'm getting hundreds of letters which I can't possible answer. If you would like an English pen-pal, drop me a note and state your age, favorite singers and interests so that I may match you with someone similar. Rick Kozy, 1743 West 261 St., Lomita, Calif.

HELP!
Girls needed who play any kind of guitar, drums or piano for an all girl band. Experience isn't necessary but you must be willing to work hard and have fun at the same time. Must be at least 15 and either live in or have transportation to the Long Beach area. Write Marsha Parmelee, 1326 Lee Ave., Long Beach, Calif.

One Week Only!
FEBRUARY 1-6
THE GREENWOOD COUNTRY SINGERS
with their hit
"Frankie & Johnny"
with
George McKelvey
The ICE HOUSE GLENDALE
folk music in concert
phone 245-5043 for reservations

VALUABLE COUPON
THIS COUPON WORTH 50¢ OFF REGULAR ADMISSION
WHEN PRESENTED AT THE DOOR
Dave Hull's Hullabaloo
6230 SUNSET (AT VINE) HOLLYWOOD, CALIFORNIA
PHONE: HO. 6-8281 FOR RESERVATIONS

KRLA BEAT Subscription
SAVE 33% Of Regular Price
☐ 1 YEAR — 52 Issues — $5.00   ☐ 2 YEARS — $8.00
☐ 6 MONTHS — $3.00
Enclosed is _____ ☐ CASH ☐ CHECK
PLEASE PRINT
Send to: .... Age ....
Address: ....
City .... State .... Zip ....
MAIL YOUR ORDER TO: KRLA BEAT
6290 Sunset, Suite 504
Hollywood, Calif. 90028
Foreign Rate: $9.00 — 52 Issues

KRLA Tunedex

DAVE HULL

BOB EUBANKS

DICK BIONDI

JOHNNY HAYES

EMPEROR HUDSON

CASEY KASEM

CHARLIE O'DONNELL

BILL SLATER

This Week	Last Week	Title	Artist
1	1	WE CAN WORK IT OUT/DAY TRIPPER	The Beatles
2	4	JUST LIKE ME	Paul Revere & The Raiders
3	—	LIGHTNIN' STRIKES	Lou Christie
4	10	SUNDAY AND ME	Jay and The Americans
5	7	CRYIN' TIME	Ray Charles
6	5	NO MATTER WHAT SHAPE	T-Bones
7	3	SOUNDS OF SILENCE	Simon & Garfunkel
8	6	MY LOVE	Petula Clark
9	8	UP TIGHT	Stevie Wonder
10	12	ARE YOU THERE?	Dionne Warwick
11	14	MY WORLD IS EMPTY WITHOUT YOU	The Supremes
12	21	A WELL RESPECTED MAN	The Kinks
13	18	THE MEN IN MY LITTLE GIRL'S LIFE	Mike Douglas
14	23	ELUSIVE BUTTERFLY	Bob Lind
15	19	GOING TO A-GO-GO	The Miracles
16	9	I SEE THE LIGHT	Five Americans
17	20	A MUST TO AVOID	Herman's Hermits
18	15	FLOWERS ON THE WALL	Statler Brothers
19	20	FIVE O'CLOCK WORLD	The Vogues
20	—	LOVE MAKES ME DO FOOLISH THINGS	Martha & The Vandellas
21	22	MY GENERATION	The Who
22	27	IT WAS A VERY GOOD YEAR	Frank Sinatra
23	34	YOU BABY	The Turtles
24	32	SPANISH EYES	Al Martino
25	29	SANDY	Ronnie & The Daytonas
26	25	THUNDERBALL	Tom Jones
27	28	I AIN'T GONNA EAT MY HEART OUT ANYMORE	Young Rascals
28	31	SET YOU FREE THIS TIME	The Byrds
29	—	MY BABY LOVES ME	Martha & The Vandellas
30	24	LIKE A BABY	Len Barry
31	30	BARBARA ANN	Beach Boys
32	26	ATTACK	The Toys
33	35	TIME	Pozo-Seco Singers
34	—	WHAT NOW MY LOVE	Sonny & Cher
35	—	A HARD DAY'S NIGHT	Ramsey Lewis Trio
36	33	A SWEET WOMAN LIKE YOU	Joe Tex
37	37	GEORGIA	Righteous Brothers
38	—	WORKING MY WAY BACK TO YOU	Four Seasons
39	36	UNDER YOUR SPELL AGAIN	Johnny Rivers
40	38	I'M SO LONELY I COULD CRY	V.J. Thomas & The Triumphs

SOME WELL RESPECTED MEN — That's Johnny Hayes, Dick Moreland and the Kinks during their L.A. visit.

KRLA ARCHIVES

L.P. Corner

By Tracey Albert

The small but swinging Bantams have released their first album, titled appropriately enough, "Beware: The Bantams!" The three young Bantams—Jeff, Mike and Fritz—are great fans of the Beatles and it is very evident in the selection of cuts on their debut LP.

The boys have included such Beatle greats as "Twist And Shout," "Please, Please Me," "I Should Have Known Better," "Please Mr. Postman," "Ticket To Ride" and "From Me To You."

But they don't stop there. No, instead the Bantams have also recorded a couple of Beatle-penned hits which were recorded by other artists. The Bantams do a fantastic version of Peter & Gordon's smash, "World Without Love" as well as Billy J. Kramer's "From A Window."

The Bantams have used the simplest of backings with only bongoes, maraccas and guitar supplementing their three very young and very fresh voices. If you buy "Beware: The Bantams" you won't be sorry.

Dino, Desi And Billy

Dino, Desi and Billy have finally come out with their long-awaited second album. Their first, as I'm sure you remember, was dubbed "I'm A Fool" after their first smash single. In their second effort, "Our Time's Coming," Dino, Desi and Billy have chosen 12 cuts featuring practically every single one of the top groups.

Side one opens up with a version of "Get off My Cloud" in which you can actually *understand* all of the lyrics. Desi next gets his chance to go solo and he picked the Beatles' "Act Naturally" for his break away from the drums.

Brian Wilson's songwriting talent is used on the first side when Dino and Billy team up for one of the Beach Boys oldies, "Fun, Fun, Fun."

Side one closes with an all instrumental version of the Byrds' "Turn, Turn, Turn." Other hits included on "Our Time's Coming" are "Yesterday," "Hang On Sloopy," "Sheila" and "Let Me Be." If you have already purchased these hits by their original singers, you might as well save your money and forget buying "Our Time's Coming."

Although Dino, Desi and Billy do a great job on them they haven't bothered to re-arrange the songs at all. Which is somewhat of a shame. However, if you like the oldies but haven't bought them before you will probably enjoy Dino, Desi and Billy's versions very much.

Freddy's Back

But some of that old talent shouldn't be forgotten either. And one of the "old-timers" who should *never* be forgotten at all is the fabulous Freddy Cannon.

Warner Brothers has just released an album which will tear you up—it's "Freddy Cannon's Greatest Hits" and one of the wildest LPs to hit your record stores in a long time.

To those of you who are at least 18 it will bring all kinds of memories flooding back and to those of you under 18 it will bring a half an hour of dancing music or sing-along music—whichever you feel like doing.

The album includes all of Freddy's hits such as "Way Down Yonder In New Orleans," "Palisades Park," "Muskrat Ramble," "Tallahassee Lassie," "Okefenokee," "Transister Sister," "Abigail Beecher," etc. etc.

All of the cuts are done in that driving, pounding Cannon-style. It's one of those albums where you can't possibly just sit still and *listen*—you've got to *move*.

THE WILD AFFAIR: left to right, Bill Wild, Chuck Morgan, and Rod Birmingham.

Wild Affair At The BEAT

By Sue Greene

Oh, they're a Wild Affair all right! Like, they really are way out, huh? As a matter of fact, would you believe a group of boys with *normal* haircuts, *good* voices, and a *great* stage presence? Yes, I know it seems a little unbelievable in this day and age,—however force yourselves!!!

Knows Kazoo

There are three members of the Wild Affair — Rod Birmingham, Bill Wild and Chuck Morgan and between them they play a wide assortment of musical instruments, including the drums, guitar, bass, harmonica, and Chuck boasts tha he is "the world's foremost authority on kazoo!" Rod claims that he can get along on the guitar, drums, bass, and "about two inches of piano."

The boys have been together for about a year now, and of those early days, Chuck fondly reminisces: "It was the beginning of 1965 and I was contemplating becoming a Fuller Brush Man. I'd been out of work for six months and I wanted to play in a group very badly, so a mutual friend of ours called Bill up and we decided to form a group. We rehearsed about three hours then we went to work that night — and we haven't stopped working since."

Although they are a group of three integral parts, the boys still manage to maintain their individual personalities. As Bill explains: "There are three completely different personalities working here and it comes out in the music. Everybody contributes their own style or way. We're just coming into a whole new thing now where we're beginning to *feel* the music. Some of our songs now last, oh— an hour and 43 minutes, where before they used to be the usual 2:20!"

Rod is the songwriter for the group, and has written one side of the boys' first record which will be released this month. The "A" side is titled "So In Love," and features the excellent harmonies for which the boys are noted.

Beatles At Top

Rod has his own favorites in the music world, but ranks the Beatles at the very top of his list. "As far as the Beatles are concerned, I think that they are some of the most talented guys in the world. I think the songs they write are great—they're original, they're different—no one has ever written anything like they have. I respect them for their ability."

All three boys are very much down-to-earth, level-headed fellows. Bill is an excellent example of this as he philosophizes: "As long as every day that goes by— you do something that's constructive towards your goal—no matter how little or how big it is, or if you learn something every day—you can't help but get better. If you let one day go by where you don't do anything but sleep—it's one day completely lost.

"I think that society is ready for a semi rock 'n' roll type of music, mixed in with popular music and maybe a little classical music. I think our group is capable of it, and we're sure gonna give it a heck of a try."

KRLA ARCHIVES

Young Rascals Pick Appropriate Name

By Louise Criscione

Because they were over three hours late for the interview and because they hadn't even bothered to phone and explain that they would be late, I had it set in my mind not to like the Young Rascals much at all.

But I have to confess that I was charmed out of my bad mood when the four Young Rascals finally did appear in The BEAT offices, apologizing profusely and blaming their tardiness on their publicity man. Which is as good an excuse as any, I suppose.

It was the Rascals' first visit to the West Coast and they admit that they were a bit dismayed when they opened at a local club packing the night spot but not drawing much of a reaction from their audience.

"You see, in New York they applaud when they like you," commented Gene. "But here they don't applaud much—they just keep coming back to see you. So, the first few nights we were worried thinking that they weren't digging us."

New York is home-base for the Young Rascals, they hit it big on the East Coast when they played a most successful summer season in Southhampton in 1965.

From All Over

That one summer engagement brought teens from New York, Connecticut and New Jersey to witness the Rascals for themselves. And they liked what they saw.

So, by the time the Young Rascals moved into the Phone Booth in New York they had a following as large as any well-established recording artist. In fact, they caused such a sensation that people like the Rolling Stones, Bob Dylan and Barry McGuire came around the Phone Booth to see the Rascals for themselves.

I wondered if having such big-name recording artists in their audience bothered the Rascals at all. "No," answered Gene, "it makes us feel proud." "It's out of sight," agreed Eddie, "especially when they keep coming back to see us."

The Young Rascals have on stage outfits which set them apart from everyone else in the world. They appear in knickers, Lord Fauntleroy shirts and peaked caps. Why? They feel that they have to have a gimmick to make it?

"We don't want to wear suits," replied Gene. "And besides suits are very conventional."

A Put-On

"We do it just to be different," said Eddie, "it's really a put-on but we think our sound is much more important than the way we dress."

"And it's easy to play in," added Dino Danelli, the Rascals' drummer.

They all express a disliking for groups who copy other entertainers. "It's bad," said Dino, "because they're not accomplishing anything. You have to be original."

And the Young Rascals feel that they are original because they re-arrange all the material which they use in their act. "And some-

... THE YOUNG RASCALS (l. to r. Gene, Dino, Eddie, Felix).

times we even change the words to the songs," said Eddie, "especially when I forget them!"

"Really, the only reason that we don't copy other groups is because we're not good enough," laughed Eddie.

The Rascals have spent their lives on the East Coast, they found the audiences different in California but how about the pop scene itself?

"It's different too," replied Eddie. "New York is, first of all, older. The talent has been in New York longer than on the West Coast. It's sort of a melting pot.

"Until recently, groups would come to New York from all over the country because all the big recording companies were there. You find that when a group does come to New York they gain from the groups already there and they lose a little too."

"Phil Spector should get the credit for the West Coast sound," finished Eddie.

It appears that the day of the stand on stage and do little else groups has come to an end. The wild, rave-up acts have now taken over. What about the Rascals' stage act?

"It's terrible," grinned Eddie.

"It's sort of a free feeling," answered Gene seriously. "There is very little routine. It's all expression and it's very visual."

"Sensual is the word for it," Eddie added helpfully.

As in any other business, jealousy runs high between those groups who have made it and those who haven't.

Aren't Making It

"It really depends on the groups," said Felix (who had just appeared in the door after a small shopping spree across the street). "The groups who aren't making it are the ones who knock everyone else. But the big groups have their way and we have ours."

"The big groups are all in the same boat," added Eddie, "and I don't think you should even have time to knock another group."

"R&B will be the next big thing," commented Gene. "Most of the English groups are using it but they're just copying. I mean, it all comes from the Southern U.S. The English groups are more conservative and they don't know how to scream."

Not Beatles Only

"They're not conservative at all," argued Felix. "Look at the Yardbirds and Stones. When you are talking about the English groups you're not just talking about the Beatles."

If they can possibly help it, and they can, the Rascals next single will be completely different from "I Ain't Gonna Eat My Heart Out Anymore."

"If you put out a second record which sounds exactly like the first, why should the kids buy it?" asked Gene.

Too Much Talent

"I think there is too much talent in this group to do something like that," said Eddie. "Too many ideas to fall into that bag."

"Our music has changed so much already," added Dino. "You have to change to progress musically."

Because three of the Rascals wear their hair on the long side they've run into all kinds of thick-headed people who insist upon judging people by the length of their hair.

"I just turn the other cheek," laughed Felix, "only now I'm running out of cheeks!"

"I take out my wallet and thumb through the bills," said Eddie.

"But what gets me is that these people come into the club and heckle us but they forget that they paid to see us. So, while they're making fun we're making money from them."

Following their West Coast club date the Young Rascals will return to the scene of one of their biggest triumphs, The Phone Booth in New York. And while they're there they will also appear on "The Ed Sullivan Show."

They're a funny bunch, those Young Rascals. No wonder they chose that name for themselves! It fits.

KRLA ARCHIVES

Adventures of Robin Boyd
By Shirley Poston

CHAPTER FOURTEEN

When George finally found Robin two hours later, she was cowering under a park bench in London's Berkeley Square, still in the pocket of Mick Jagger's jacket.

Spying the quivering coat, George resisted the urge to stomp it into the ground with an ultra-pointed winkle picker. Instead, he snatched Robin out of the pocket and shook her until her teeth rattled.

"You bloomin' *nit!*" he bellowed, shaking her twice as hard when she tried to gnaw his thumb off with an ultra-pointed beak.

"Help, murder and/or police," Robin bellowed back, taking a large bite of his palm.

George gasped. From pain, and also from the possibility of being arrested for beating up on a bird (a *real* bird wearing *glasses* yet.) Snapping one of his remaining fingers in disgust, he turned Robin back into her sixteen-year-old self.

"You *rat fink*" Robin further bellowed when she pushed the long, red hair out of her eyes and came face to face with her attacker. "This is the *second* time you've tried to *murder* me tonight!"

Repair Damages

Sinking to the park bench, George moaned in exasperation. But, when Robin kicked him right square in the left shin, he shushed. He also yanked her down beside him with a bone-shattering thump.

"Don't do that again," he warned in calm but deadly Liverpudlian, giving her arm an extra yank for good measure.

Robin gulped. George was obviously not like American boys, and had no *intention* of doing the gentlemanly thing and hobbling off into the sunset.

"And don't you say a *word* 'till I finish," he further warned, rubbing his wounded shin with his remaining hand.

Robin shook her head, fully expecting it to rattle.

"All right," George began. "In the first place, I told you not to come here alone, because I knew you would do something moronic."

Robin started to protest that remark, but decided against it when George gave her another yank. (The next time she watched "A Yank In The R.A.F." on the telly, it would have a deeper, more personal meaning.) (If she lived.)

"And," continued George," you did exactly that. You, in fact, *outdid* yourself!"

"You did it, not me," Robin cried, unable to contain herself.

George narrowed his eyes.

Right Square

Robin gulped another mouthful of Londonderry air. A habit she was going to have to kick immediately because it was giving her gas.

"When I realized that you were being folded in Mick's coat," George went on, "I told him to throw it! So I could catch it, you *twit!* But what do you do? You go flapping out of the concert, jacket and all. And now the entire U.K. is in an uproar!"

"Really?" Robin breathed happily, prompting the yank of a lifetime.

"Quite." George hissed. "And there's nothing I can do about it this time."

Robin turned as white as six sheets. "Nothing?" she echoed. "You mean you can't just wipe out everyone's memory like you did for the Beatles when I . . ."

"I *cannot*," George interrupted thunderously. "There's little I *can* do at the moment, and you're in the same pickle. *We* are on *probation!*"

Robin turned as white as sixteen sheets. "*Both* of us?"

"*Both* of us."

"Because of me??"

"Because of *you!!*"

"For how long?"

Kick The Gulp

George snarled. "For two weeks. If, by the end of that time, you have managed to, as *they* put it, *prove your good intentions by using your own iniative to repair some of the damages incurred tonight*, your powers will be returned."

Robin quaked. "You mean I have to solve this mess *without* my powers."

George nodded. "And they've taken mine away temporarily so I can't help you."

"Who do *they* think *they* are anyway?" Robin said savagely, stamping her foot.

"*Quiet!*" George whispered, yanking her arm clean out of the socket (well, it *felt* like it.) "You're in enough trouble as it is."

Because that was certainly the understatement of the century, Robin remained silent for a moment. But suddenly, she leaped to her feet.

"What if I *can't* repair some of the damages?" she cried helplessly. "Won't I ever get to be a bird again . . . and . . . and won't I ever get to see you again?"

George stood up slowly, and for the first time that evening, he grinned. And he looked so much like George Harrison that Robin had to allow herself one final gulp before quitting forever.

"You'll think of something," he soothed. "With an imagination like yours, you'll think of something."

"But what if I don't?" Robin persisted. "Won't you at least drop by and say *jeweler, you've failed*, or tell me goodbye, or something?"

(Robin immediately wanted to kick *herself* right in the left shin. Why on earth was she worrying about George when she *should* be worrying about losing her powers??)

"No," said George, trying to sound gruff. "We'd better say goodbye now, just in case. So . . . goodbye."

A Kiss?

"George," she wailed, wanting to kick herself in *both* shins for what she was about to say. "Is that *all* you have to say after what we've been *through* together? Just *goodbye?*"

George laughed. "Girl," he said, leaning toward her. "You're a silly clot. Now shurrup and give us a kiss before they send you home."

But, just as Robin shurrup (in one *large* hurry) (you better believe it), she vanished.

The next thing she knew, she was walking through the front door of her home in California.

Hopefully, Robin raced to the mantle, but the tea pot wasn't there.

"He's gone," she blithered sadly, "he's really *gone*."

Then suddenly, she blithered joyously. Because the jacket she was hugging had just, for one quick second, hugged her back.

(To Be Continued Next Week)

DAVE CLARK is smilin' happily over his latest smash, "At The Scene."
BEAT Photo: Robert Custer

KEITH ALLISON stares out at the city wondering what tomorrow will bring him. Naturally, he'd like his career to keep progressing the way that it has been these past few months but if it doesn't, he'll be just as content to tote his guitar around to the small clubs. But **The BEAT** just doesn't think that will **ever** happen to him again.

Keith Allison To Aid Corps

Keith Allison just happens to be nice, that's all. It's taken him a long time to make it and now that he has, he refuses to fall in love with himself.

He still doesn't consider himself a star, only a guy from Texas. When the Rolling Stones appeared in Southern California, Keith sat in the audience munching a cold hot dog the same as everybody else. And would you like to hear thing even funnier? No one even bothered to ask him for an autograph. Instead, they just stared at him, shook their heads and decided that *it just couldn't* be.

After all, if he *was* Keith Allison, he'd be sitting *backstage* with the other stars, or at least way up in the front row. He'd never be sitting in the back with the people who had actually *paid* to see the show. But then, they didn't know Keith.

His newly-found success has not traveled to his head. So, while the rest of the "Action" show continues to film at various locations Keith has taken off for Santo Domingo. Not to play at some posh night club but to work for the U.S. Job Corps.

Keith Allison just happens to be nice, that's all.

KRLA ARCHIVES

TIPS TO TEENS

Q: *I like this boy but I doubt if he likes me. The only thing he ever says to me is "Stones Rule, Beatles Hang" and I say back the same thing in reverse. By the time I want to say something else, he's gone. What should I do?*
(Darlene V.)

A: Since he doesn't give you much time to come up with something, why not think of a new retort to his "greeting." Instead of saying the same thing in reverse, answer with something new. If that doesn't start a conversation, do the same thing next time, only with another new reply. Pretty soon, he'll be coming back again and again just to see what you're going to answer. Hopefully, one of those times he'll stay awhile.

Q: *I have long hair and my parents don't like it. They say it's stringy and all of that noise. I want a pair of those knee boots very much and my dad said I can have them if I'll cut my hair. That's blackmail! How can I keep my hair and get my boots too?*
(Cathy J.)

A: Does sound a bit like blackmail, but it also sounds like your dad is trying to tell you something. It's possible that the longer styles just aren't flattering to you, or that you don't have the kind of hair which can be worn long and straight without becoming stringy. Why don't you compromise? At least have your hair shaped and trimmed. That does wonders without chopping it off. Also, you can wear your hair up while you're at home. Your dad probably wouldn't object to an updo or pony tail, and if you want both the boots and the hair, this plan might do the trick.

Q: *I have a problem. I write songs which I think are fairly good. However, I haven't the faintest idea as to how to go about getting them published. How could I go about finding a reliable publisher?*
(John F.)

A: That's a question and a half, and one we can't answer here in just a few words. What we will do is compile the information you need and print it in The BEAT just as soon as we finish researching the subject. There must be many others reading this who would also like to know how to go about selling their songs, so stay tuned to The BEAT.

Q: *Last year my hair was 18½ inches long and I started ironing it. I finally had to stop because I burnt it all up! Now my hair is kinky, full of split ends and a big mess. And it hasn't grown an inch. I'm ironing it again now because my girlfriend says it looks a little better when I do. I can't afford a wig. What can I do?*
(Robin W.)

A: Stop ironing your hair immediately, no matter what anyone says. Ironing doesn't seem to damage some hair, but others have had problems even worse than yours. Buy a conditioner that has to be applied through the heat method. (Use hot towels, or whatever the instructions suggest.) Do this at least once a week for a month and if the condition doesn't start to get better, see a beautician.

Q: *I have a naturally fair complexion to begin with. I belong to a swim club, and during our daily work-outs, the chlorine in the pool beaches my skin even whiter. I don't want to wear a darker shade of makeup, and I've tried those instant suntan products (I turned yellow). I've thought about a sun lamp, but would it work? And isn't it very expensive?*
(Sue W.)

A: A small sun lamp costs about $10 and you can buy just a bulb (which fits in most any lamp) for even less. But, have you thought about leaving your skin color the way it is? A lot of people flip over very white complexions. Jill Hayworth, the actress, was discovered because she had just about the palest skin ever. Think that over before you decide what to do.

Q: *What does a boy who is 14 and goes to an all boys school do for dates when he doesn't know how to get acquainted and is, truthfully, a little scared?*
(J.G.)

A: You must know a lot of boys at school who have sisters they're just dying to palm off on someone. Pass the word that you're available for sister-sitting. You might not end up with the world's greatest dates, but you will get over your feeling of being "scared." Also, try going to some of the popular teen spots in your area. You'll probably feel uncomfortable and alone at first (take a friend along if you can), but if you keep going back, you'll get to know others without even trying. And some of those others are bound to be girls.

Q: *I have been writing to a member of an English group, but the letters keep coming back. It really bugs me to take the time to write nice long letters and then have them returned a month later. He lives in England, so I can't hitchhike to his house and yell my head off, but I'd like to. Can you think of a solution?*
(M.S.)

A: Tell your blood to stop boiling. There's only one possible reason for this problem — you have the wrong address! Either that or the star has moved and left no forwarding address. If you will write to this column and tell us who the star is, we'll try to give you the address of a record company where he can be reached.

HINT OF THE WEEK

I have a hint for your readers. Many of us are using those new shoe colorings and it gets quite expensive to buy that clear cleaner which you are supposed to use. I've found that plain rubbing alcohol is just as effective and certainly less expensive. Alcohol is also very good for cleaning purposes.
(Charlotte P.)

If you have a question you'd like answered or a tip for teens, send same to this column c/o The BEAT.

Sam's Beard Rejoins Act

Sam The Sham And The Pharaohs were in an awful uproar when they took off for Germany. As you know, Sam had done away with his beard and the Pharaohs had thrown away their robes. They hated those robes anyway so it was with great pleasure that they finally decided to get rid of them.

But before embarking for Germany, France and England they ran into one slight problem. Their Continental audiences were looking for beards and robes! "Wooly Bully" was a giant, huge hit all over the world and the accompanying photos of Sam and the Pharaohs had them all decked out in their finery.

So, a quick consultation was held and it was reluctantly decided that they would just have to go back to their original beard and robe routine.

Actually, it was a compromise decision. They would land in Europe with beards etc. but before they left for home they vowed to shave the beards and discard the robes for good. In this way, when they land Stateside they will be back to smooth skin and regular clothes.

Apparently, it was a wise decision because when the group arrived in Germany for their first appearance at the Star Club (yes, the same Star Club in Hamburg, Germany, where the Beatles got their start) they were an immediate sensation. Opening night caused the management a little concern because the Star Club holds only 900 people yet the line stretched outside numbered 2,000! Which figures since Sam and the Pharaohs are now the number one group in Germany.

Sam made a rather startling announcement to *The BEAT* just before the group took off for Germany. He has studied music very seriously and has a very real dream to be a Metropolitan Opera star!

Sam also informed us that his group really loves to play blues and that they will be incorporating more and more R&B numbers into their stage act.

Following stops in France and England, Sam and the Pharaohs will jet directly to the West Coast where they will appear at a popular night club on Hollywood's Sunset Strip. Minus beards and robes, of course!

...SAM THE SHAM & THE PHARAOHS

KRLA ARCHIVES

Dear Susan

What is Ray Davies wife's name? —Sharon Slavert
Rasa.

What are Herman's favorite television shows? —Cookie Williams
None. But he loves the commercials.

Why does Donovan wear a hat? —Mary Nannini
Because he likes it, and it's the only protection he has from wind and rain to keep his hair dry, which is very important to him.

What label does Gene Pitney record for? —Chris Mattenheimer
Stateside.

Has anyone ever recorded "Smokestack Lightnin'" by the Yardbirds? —Toni Allen
Yes, Manfred Mann

Where can I write to join a Manfred Mann fan club? —Kathy Rose
35 Curzon Street, Londong W. 1., England.

Who are the Stones' favorite group? —Sue Gordon
The Who.

When is Gene Pitney's birthday? —Gayle Axelrod
February 17, 1941.

Who does Donovan consider to be his best friend? —Mike Roberts
I don't know about friend, but Joan Baez is the most important person to him.

What kind of guitar does Donovan have? —Carolyn Tanzinni
A Gibson

Where can I join Elvis's fan club? —Debbie Wexler
Write him in care of 1853 Balmoral Ave., Westchester, Ill. 60156.

What 'bugs' George the most? —Ruth Dunn
People who put down pop music as something daft or dirty.

Where can I write to the singing group, The Palace Guard? —Joan Beaudoin
In care of the Hullabaloo Club, Sunset Blvd., Hollywood, Calif.

When will the Liverpool Five be back in California? —Eva Goodich
As plans have it, sometime in late March or early April.

Where was Keith Allison born, and does he have a girlfriend? —Donna Dalo
In Texas, and he is married.

Will ('Act Naturally,' 'Yesterday,' 'We Can Work It Out,' and 'Day Tripper' ever be released on albums in the U.S.? —Armi Santa Cruz
Eventually, yes.

Are the Sangrai-la's sisters? —Sherry Serrano
Yes, two sets of sisters.

When will John's new book be released? —Cathy Evers
In April.

Is it true that the U.S. as well as England will be seeing films of the Beatles Shea Stadium appearance? —Becky Young
Yet to be confirmed.

When is Marianne Faithfull going to make another album? —Mike Pearce
She just finished one in England. It should be out soon.

What language does Paul sing in 'Michelle?' —Janet Kanfer
French.

Where can I send a present to Donovan and be sure he gets it? Please, not a fan club —Debbie McMillen
C/O Southern Music, 8 Denmark Street, London W, 1, Eng.

What is a 'day-tripper' and what does it mean? —Donna
'Haven't the foggiest!'

What type of Breck shampoo does Brian use, and what kind does Keith use? —Jessie
Brian uses 'normal,' and Keith uses whatever he can find.

How does Ian Whitcomb like to see girls dressed? —Carol Seibert
He likes his girls to wear pants. Courderoy or just the jean levi type.

When will the Beatles be back? —Jane Henderson
August

...THE T-BONES?

From Commercials to T-Bones to Success

There was this guy, see, and he was watching television. And what do you see most of on TV?—Commercials, right?

Well, this guy, named Joe Saraceno, who's a record producer for Liberty records, is watching this Alka Seltzer commercial, you know the one with all the stomachs, and he likes the background music.

So what does he do? He does what any smart record producer would do. He turns the background music of this commercial into a hit single.

And that's how the T-Bones and "No Matter What Shape" (Your Stomach's In) came about.

Saraceno got permission from the commercial people to turn the music into a single and then he went out looking for the right musicians to do it.

The first people to come to his mind were two brothers, Danny and Judd Hamilton, who as members of the Marketts had had such hits as "Out of Limits," and "Surfer' Stomp."

Youngest

Danny, the youngest brother, has worked with recording groups like Ronnie and the Daytonas, toured with Chad and Jeremy and written for many groups including the Ventures.

His brother Judd was formerly a solo singer before teaming up with Danny as the Hamilton Brothers. Both boys toured with the "Shindig" road tour and were members of the Marketts.

The two brothers brought in Gene Pello, a 24 year old Californian to play drums with the group. Gene's been playing drums since he was three and has worked on television shows and recording sessions with people such as Bobby Darin, Wayne Newton, and the late Spike Jones.

George Dee was brought in as bass guitar player. Another Californian, he started studying accordian when he was seven but switched to guitar two years ago. He played with the Stepsons and the Billy Watkins Band before forming his own group called Georgie Dee and the Exceptionals.

Organ Player

Last to join the group was Richard Torres, a versatile all-around musician. Officially he's the group's organ player, but he's just as good on clarinet, sax or voice.

He was named "Most Oustanding Soloist of the Year" in 1963 at a California Intercollegiate Jazz Festival. Just a year before he had been named "Most Outstanding Soloist" in the Hollywood Bowl Battle of the Bands.

He's played sax with the Norman Brown and Billy Watkins bands and was a sideman for Nooney Rickett, before becoming a T-Bone.

After getting the group together and naming them the T-Bones merely because he was fond of that particular cut of meat, Saraceno and the boys produced that first record and started for the top.

They had such fantastic success with "No Matter What Shape" that they've recorded their first album, featuring their original hit plus several other things based on unusual TV commercials.

So listen carefully to those commercials from now on. They just may turn out to be more hits for the T-Bones.

Hotline London

(Continued From Page 2)

ers who have had several U.K. chart toppers during the past year. All previous Seeker hits have been composed by Dusty Springfield's brother, Tom...The Kinks plan to start making satirical discs composed by their Ray Davies at regular intervals...

Ringo left for the West Indies with a beard he started to grow just before the Christmas holidays. He's assured everyone he'll shave again as soon as The Beatles are back to work... Rushed three-day March visit to Britain for Herb Alpert and his highly successful sixsome. They'll squeeze in three major TV shows plus a single concert at London's enormous Hammersmith Odeon theater...

Simultaneous release of singles by Dusty Springfield ("Little By Little") and Sandie Shaw ("Tomorrow") promise interesting chart battle between these two top girls... "Sunshine Superman" is the title of the next single penned and recorded by folkster Donovan. Subtitle of the song is "Dedicated to John and Paul."

Mike Douglas Scores A Hit

It's not too often that an established television personality makes a dent on the pop charts but Mike Douglas (star of his own show, "The Mike Douglas Show,") has done it.

His "The Men In My Little Girl's Life" is rapidly bounding up the charts all over the nation. In fact, it has been selling so fast that Mike has hastily put together an album which will be titled after his hit.

Mike's singing career began when he was eleven and on a children's show in Chicago. He continued singing while attending high school and after graduation landed a job as a singing emcee on a Great Lakes cruise ship.

After working at a television station in Chicago, Mike joined a station in Cleveland as the host of his now-famous live 90 minute daily variety show. The program serves as an excellent showcase for Mike's unusual talents as interviewer, comedian and vocalist.

It's rather ironic that Mike should come up with a hit single because before "The Men In My Little Girl's Life" Mike had only released one other album titled "It's Time For Mike Douglas."

Mike sort of believes that you should stick with a good thing so his new album includes several selections dealing with parental love. But he also adds some standards like "While We're Young" And "'A' You're Adorable."

It makes for a well-rounded album which is only logical since Mike is a well-rounded performer.

KRLA ARCHIVES

THE BEAT GOES TO THE MOVIES
"THE BIG T.N.T. SHOW"

By Jim Hamblin
(The BEAT Movie Editor)

THE BIG T-N-T SHOW is one of those rare adventures into black and white film for American International Pictures, a studio widely noted for it's fine color process. The reason for the hue-less show is the fact that it is first a television show, produced with several cameras, then later edited into a film show, using the originally produced TV production as a guide, making improvements wherever necessary, as they go along. One of these days perhaps, all movies will be made this way.

It's called *Electro-Rama*, but let's get on to the music!

Music there is, for an hour and a half some of the greatest sounds ever recorded come booming out, accompanied by a steady volume of screaming teenagers in the audience, who watched the show being made.

The first thing the 1,200 teens saw was that man from UNCLE, David McCallum, as he directed the orchestra in the opening number. He does it *with his elbows*, a fascinating technique.

Then RAY CHARLES, with his own orchestra and singers. CHARLES is as good as anybody in the business, and is a great entertainer. He returns later in the show.

PETULA CLARK, wearing what looks like a house coat, belted out "Downtown" got an excellent reaction from the kids in the audience. Pet, too, does another number later.

THE LOVIN' SPOONFUL perform next, John Sebastian hugging onto that weird thing he plays, and all sounding great.

Next, out in the audience, with whom she seems to communicate so well, is mysterious JOAN BAEZ (BUY-ezz) whose long black hair and clear perfect voice makes her America's foremost troubador. She comes back for an encore, later.

This would be a great show to drag your Mom and Dad to see, if you can get them to go. There is more supreme talent here than any other show we know of, and is an excellent opportunity for any adult who wants to find out what there is about rock and roll music that teenagers dig so much.

After RAY CHARLES pounds out "Georgia On My Mind," and "Let the Good Times Roll," we hear from JOAN BAEZ again, proving she can sing *regular* songs as well, not just folk. Her rendition of "You've Lost That Lovin' Feeling" is the best yet.

Sound like it's too much already? There's more . . . and more. All this without a word of dialogue, too. Just music.

The RONETTES next, wearing *uniforms* rather than costumes. The kind of uniforms that the workers of the "People's Republic" in China wear. But maybe that's camp these days.

Then ROGER MILLER, that amazing man who was featured in the January 8th issue of *The BEAT*. Miller is a natural born entertainer who wowed the kids.

DONOVAN sang "Universal Soldier," and some more songs. It was a credit to a fine group of kids in the audience that during both DONOVAN and JOAN BAEZ, there was not a sound in the room. They were *listening*.

The best, if anybody could be any better than anyone else, was saved for last, as IKE and TINA TURNER bounced on stage and took over. What a night – what a show.

This "All Star Folk Festival" was produced by Phil Spector, the man with the Midas touch.

There is one funny thing about the show. When it comes time to end, it just stops, and that's all there is to it. Kind of a shock.

But I think we can truthfully say the T-N-T show is dynamite!!!

Television star DAVID McCALLUM chats with Joan between "takes" at the T.N.T. movie filming.

The BYRDS belt out another hit. Watch a funny shot of a girl in the audience, during this number.

. . . ROGER MILLER

. . . DONOVAN

. . . PETULA CLARK

KRLA ARCHIVES

Dave Hull's HULLABALOO

The Rock & Roll Showplace of the World

STARRING THE WORLD'S TOP RECORDING ARTISTS

OPEN EVERY FRIDAY & SATURDAY NIGHT PLUS SUNDAY MATINEE

JANUARY 28, 29 & 30
THE HONDELL'S
PLUS
THE PALACE GUARD

FEBRUARY 4, 5 & 6
THE ASSOCIATION
"ONE TOO MANY MORNINGS"
PLUS
THE PALACE GUARD

FEBRUARY 13 — ONE DAY ONLY
THE BYRDS
IN CONCERT
TWO SHOWS ONLY — 4 P.M. & 8 P.M.
— GET TICKETS IN ADVANCE —

COMING ATTRACTIONS
- TOM JONES
- ANIMALS
- ASTRONAUTS
- NEWBEATS
- PAUL & BARRY BRYAN
- KNICKERBOCKERS
- SEARCHERS

THIS COUPON WORTH 50¢ OFF REGULAR ADMISSION WHEN PRESENTED AT THE DOOR
DAVE HULL'S HULLABALOO
6230 SUNSET (AT VINE) HOLLYWOOD, CALIF.
PHONE: HO 6-8281 FOR RESERVATIONS

COMING ATTRACTIONS
- SAM THE SHAM & THE PHARAOHS
- PETER & GORDON
- FIVE AMERICANS
- SHANGRI-LAS
- TOYS
- SIR DOUGLAS QUINTET

www.ingramcontent.com/pod-product-compliance
Lightning Source LLC
Chambersburg PA
CBHW080054200426
43197CB00052B/2791